WHAT IS
a MAN?

WHAT IS A MAN?

3,000 YEARS OF WISDOM ON THE ART OF MANLY VIRTUE

EDITED WITH COMMENTARY BY WALLER R. NEWELL

ReganBooks
An Imprint of HarperCollinsPublishers

Frontispiece: *Tristan und Isolde (1865) by Richard Wagner.* From *Fantastic Opera: The Great Operas Illuminated* by John Martinez, text by F. Paul Driscoll. Copyright © 1997 by Harry N. Abrams, Inc., New York, NY. Used by permission of the artist.

HarperCollins books may be purchased for educational, business, or sales promotional use. For information please write: Special Markets Department, HarperCollins Publishers Inc., 10 East 53rd Street, New York, NY 10022.

FIRST EDITION

Printed on acid-free paper

Library of Congress Cataloging-in-Publication Data

What is a man? : 3,000 years of wisdom on the art of manly virtue / [edited by] Waller R. Newell.—1st ed.
    p.   cm.
  ISBN 0-06-039296-7
  1. Men—Conduct of life Literary collections. 2. Nobility of character Literary collections. 3. Virtues Literary collections.
I. Newell, Waller Randy.
PN6071.M387B66   1999
808.8'0353—dc21   99-36304

00 01 02 03 04 ❖/RRD10 9 8 7 6 5 4 3 2 1

TABLE OF CONTENTS

4. THE FAMILY MAN   287

Boys into Men   290

5. THE STATESMAN   417

The Kingly Man   422

ACKNOWLEDGMENTS

I am grateful to Judith Regan for her early and unflagging enthusiasm for this project, and to my editor, Cal Morgan, for an enjoyable and fruitful partnership. I am also indebted to the friends and colleagues who offered me encouragement and advice about this anthology and its theme. They include Peter Ahrensdorf, David Blankenhorn, Amitai Etzioni, Norman Doidge, Charles Fairbanks, Joan Fairbanks, Bryan-Paul Frost, Francis Fukuyama, Barbara Garner, Barbara Laine Kagedan, William Kristol, Harvey C. Mansfield, Jr., Kenneth Minogue, D. Gregory MacIsaac, Patrick Malcolmson, Arthur M. Meltzer, Rick Meyers, Linda Rabieh, Michael Rabieh, Farhang Rajaee, Robert Sibley, Nathan Tarcov, Micheline White, and Claudia Winkler.

I owe a special word of thanks to my principal researcher, Timothy Voronoff, my erstwhile student. Tim's energy and imagination sustained me at every stage of a sometimes grueling creative marathon. I am grateful as well to my other researchers, Geoffrey Kellow, David Tabachnick, Jarrett Carty, and John Colman, for their hard work and sound instincts.

I cannot end without mentioning Allan Bloom, beloved teacher and friend of my wife's and mine during many years and the greatest man I have known. This book is dedicated to his memory.

Finally and above all, I am profoundly grateful to my wife, Jacqueline Etherington Newell. Without her wealth of insight, learning, discriminating judgment, and prodigious labor on every aspect of this anthology, this book would not exist. She is my true partner in this as in everything.

Introduction

As America heads into the twenty-first century, there is an increasingly widespread feeling that we have forgotten the meaning of manliness. On first reflection, this might seem like an absurd proposition. Across the nation, millions of men do their daily best to meet their responsibilities as husbands, fathers, partners, friends, and citizens. We expect men to behave decently and honorably in those capacities and to pull their weight in families and relationships. But at the same time, we are curiously adrift as a society when it comes to knowing precisely what we mean by manliness—how to describe it, encourage it, and discourage its opposite. Especially in our public discourse, in the worlds of academia, government, the social welfare bureaucracy, the educational establishment, and the learned professions, an open discussion of manliness as a positive form of behavior is almost taboo. In many of these circles, to suggest without a sneer of irony that one should "be a man" would produce ripples of cringing embarrassment over the after-dinner decaf. There is a huge vacuum in our moral vocabulary about the whole subject of the manly virtues, a feeling that even to raise such a matter is retrograde or at least a faux pas, like ordering Chardonnay with beef. We feel manly passions and impulses, but we don't know how to articulate them. This is especially noticeable among young men in their teens and twenties, or even older. They have the same strong passions, the same need for love, that youths their age have always experienced. But, much more so than with previous generations, their passions are sometimes baffled and stifling because they lack the means to express them in a refined yet heartfelt way.

The aim of this anthology is to help fill this vacuum, and to restore a sense of the positive meaning of manliness that we have somewhat mysteriously forgotten. I say mysteriously because, as the reader will see, there is an extraordinary continuity in the understanding of the manly virtues from their earliest origins in the

ancient world until, so to speak, just yesterday. Despite considerable differences in content, style, and intrinsic quality among
ancient and modern artists, thinkers, historians, poets, and statesmen from the classical era to the twentieth century, there is also an
unbroken pedigree in the Western conception of what it means to
be a man. Honor tempered by prudence, ambition tempered by
compassion for the suffering and the oppressed, love restrained by
delicacy and honor toward the beloved—from Plato to the twentieth century, there is a common store of richly textured observations, maxims, illustrations, and confirmations of this enduringly
noble standard of conduct. Thus, although that tradition can be
easily parodied and ridiculed today as something hopelessly outmoded and far away, in fact it is very close. Depending on our ages,
many of us have parents and grandparents still living who embody
the aspiration to those manly virtues; the rest of us, as adults, still
carry their letters, their diaries, and their childhood influence on
us. We don't need to reinvent manliness. We only need to will ourselves to wake up from the bad dream of the last few generations
and reclaim it, in order to extend and enrich that tradition under
the formidable demands of the present.

What are the tenets of manly pride and honor that we need to
impart to young men? How might we recover an understanding of
what it means to be a man in the positive sense—brave, self-
restrained, dignified, zealous on behalf of a good cause, imbued
with sentiments of delicacy and respect for one's loved ones? These
are the questions explored by *What Is a Man?* In its pages, the reader
will find a panoply of examples of manhood at its best. And among
the cases made consistently throughout its pages is that the surest
way of convincing men to treat women with respect is to expose
them to those traditional virtues of manly character that make it a
disgrace to treat anyone basely. Reclaiming the positive tradition of
manly refinement and civility is the surest antidote to the much-
decried balkanization of the sexes that has characterized the last
thirty years. As *What Is a Man?* illustrates through a wide variety of
sources, reverting to the blond beast of either sex is no answer to
our present romantic ills. With all due respect to the proponents of
"men's rights," such adversarial visions of our culture simply mirror
the distortions of the most extreme, exclusionary versions of academic feminism. The answer is not to return to the worship of a pri-
mordial Mother Goddess, or to primeval fantasies of male shaman-
ism and campfire dances, in order to breathe some life back into
contemporary eros. Real and responsible friendships between men

and women can only be lost in the pursuit of a sectarian and rejectionist "gender identity." Instead, we need a return to the highest fulfillment of which all people are capable—moral and intellectual virtues that are the same for men and women at their peaks—while recognizing the diverse qualities that men and women contribute to this common endeavor for excellence. We need a sympathetic reengagement with traditional teachings that stress that men and women share what is highest, while accepting that their passions, temperaments, and sentiments can differ, resulting in different paths to those high standards shared in common. This anthology is meant to be a contribution to genuine friendship between men and women, through a recognition that each makes a distinct contribution to this common feast of excellence.

The original idea for this book grew out of my eighteen years' experience as an educator. During this period, and especially in the last decade, the young men in my university classes have seemed especially lost—shy, confused, lonely, afraid to assert themselves, their trepidation broken only by occasional bursts of pointless cockiness and attitudinizing. At the same time, I was always struck (although officially forbidden by my university to say or even think as much) that my male and female students were very different, although they did equally well or poorly in my courses. Young men are still openly competitive, attention-grabbing, and eager to impress, looking for someone with whom to lock horns but also someone to praise them for doing well, like a brave soldier getting a battlefield promotion. They view a class as both a comradely collective enterprise and a contest in which they need to outshine the other young men. By contrast, female students still seem more self-sufficient, less prone to grab the spotlight, more quietly competent, less in need of hand-holding. They don't need to lock horns or to be constantly assured that they're doing fine. These observations are limited to my experiences as a professor, but similar observations could doubtless be made in many occupations and vocations. Maleness still exists, but in a baffled, confused kind of way. This is especially noticeable when students open up about their erotic relationships. Young men and women today face all the traditional quandaries of love that you will sample in these pages— jealousy, possessiveness, wounded pride, shame, competition for female attention and affection. But they lack the vocabulary even to express these feelings, let alone grapple with them constructively. This culture of romantic bafflement is compounded by the dramatic rise in kids from broken homes, almost the norm now among my students rather than the exception. It is both appalling and deeply touching to see how many young men, even into their thirties, are still so badly hurt by the childhood horror of watching their families disintegrate. It doesn't incline them to trust that love can last. They fear that by saying "I love you," they're making themselves vulnerable to another betrayal like the one inflicted upon them by their parents.

It was musing on these observations that made me wonder what past ages had to say about manliness. What might we learn from history? Would it offer any consistent lessons? What I found can only be described as buried treasure. As I burrowed into the annals of our Western literary heritage, I found hundreds of readings from every period on the theme of manliness—ancient, medieval, Renaissance, early modern and Romantic, down almost to today. Throughout this treasure hunt, I selected the readings for inclusion here by relying on a few fundamental questions: What is a real man like? How does he act and feel? On this basis, the readings sorted out into the eight main sections that comprise this book.

The book is arranged thematically rather than chronologically, allowing readers, if they so choose, to explore the eight chapters out of sequence and browse within each chapter in any order they find appealing. Whenever an author appears for the first time, I provide some essential biographical information for the reader. There is a degree of overlap among some of the eight themes and certain historical periods—chivalry, for instance, is closely associated with medieval knighthood, while gentlemanliness is a favorite theme of both Renaissance- and Enlightenment-era writers. But the primary aim isn't chronological, and the reader will find a wide range of historical eras covered in each of the eight sections. My purpose is to present a conjunction of timeless virtues that can still inspire us today with a series of vividly contrasting portraits of manliness and an appreciation for the enticing variety of manly types. The one exception to this approach is the final section, "The Invisible Man," which appropriately brings us full circle by looking at the confused but in some ways promising signals being sent about manliness in the late 1990s. My aim has been to explore the manly virtues as the key to understanding the male psychology and character, and to refresh our acquaintance with the vibrant, fully rounded knights, lovers, gentlemen, thinkers, artists, statesmen, spouses, and warriors who people our history.

Before letting that chorus of suppressed voices take over, however, let's think a little more about the crisis of manliness in the present, beginning with fatherhood.

• • •

Fatherhood and manliness have always been closely connected, not only because fathering a child is a palpable proof of manhood, but because fathers are supposed to provide their sons with a model of how to live. And yet, as a culture, we have never been more unsure or conflicted about what we mean by manhood.

In a recent novel by Chuck Palahniuk, *Fight Club*, a group of young men in their twenties, stuck in typical Gen-X jobs as office temps and couriers, relieve their boredom by meeting after hours in the basement of a bar and beating each other senseless. Sometimes they show up for work with black eyes and stitches as a warrior's badge of honor. Aside from their jobs—white collar, but holding out no clear career prospects—what these young men have in common is that they are underfathered, the product of divorce and of fathers who had no time for them. "I'm a thirty-year-old boy," says the novel's protagonist. "I knew my dad for about six years, but I don't remember anything. . . What you see at fight club is a generation of men raised by women."

In the absence of a clear idea from their distant, distracted fathers of what it means to be a man, these bored and frustrated youths react against their antiseptic jobs by reverting to the crudest stereotype of "macho" violence. The club's founder, Tyler, progresses from consenting violence among buddies to random murder—a slacker Raskolnikov. The novel is chillingly insightful about the unmapped psyche of young males in the nineties.

Given these signals from the culture, confirmed every day by real acts of mayhem, some hold that we should try to abolish ideals of manliness altogether and make more rigorous efforts to create a genderless personality free of male violence. The recent horrific shootings in American schools from Arkansas to Colorado, with little-boy killers waiting in army fatigues to ambush their classmates and teachers, might suggest that this view is right. Add to this the fact that the majority of violent crimes are committed by young men between the ages of fifteen and twenty-five, and there seems further good reason for discouraging male children from embracing any notion of manly pride.

But it is not so simple. The last thirty years have in fact witnessed a prolonged effort at social engineering throughout our public and educational institutions. Its purpose is to eradicate any psychological and emotional differences between men and women, on the grounds that any concept of manliness inevitably leads to arrogance and violence toward women, and to rigid hierarchies that exclude the marginalized and powerless. This experiment was meant to reduce violence and tensions between the sexes. And yet, during this same period, "macho" violence and stress between men and women may well have increased. Recent crime statistics suggest as much in the United States, Canada, and the United Kingdom—the countries where the feminist social experiment stigmatizing manliness has had the greatest latitude to prove itself.

As a recent book by Barbara Dafoe Whitehead confirmed, the absence of a father is one of the strongest predictors of violence among young men in the United States, at least as important as poverty, lack of education, or minority status. The ease with which men of my baby boomer generation have abdicated their roles as fathers is undoubtedly connected with feminism and with the sexual revolution of the 1960s. Boomers were told not to be hung up about providing masculine role models for children, reassured that we should do whatever made us happiest, including escaping an unsatisfying marriage. After all, to hold things together for the sake of the children would restrict both men and women to old-fashioned "patriarchal" responsibilities. The casualties of this hard, bright credo of selfishness are today's underfathered young men, many of them from broken homes, prone to identify their maleness with aggression because they have no better model to imitate.

This generation's experience is summed up in a brilliant, pathetic scene from a film by Atom Egoyan called *Family Viewing.* The central character, a teenage boy, drifts in and out of his divorced father's house. The father is totally preoccupied with his relationship with a younger woman. The boy's only solid human contact is with his dying grandmother, shunted to a nursing home lest she spoil the father's swinging lifestyle. One day the boy digs out some family videos. At first, he sees a backyard barbecue with happy children and his parents when they were still together. Suddenly, the film jumps to the father and his new girlfriend having sex. The father simply taped over the family movies, literally erasing his son's connection with the only secure part of his childhood.

It seems plain enough that we are missing the boat about manliness. A strong case can be made that manly honor, and shame at failing to live up to it, are the surest means of promoting respect for women. Moreover, manly anger and combativeness can provide energy for a just cause. Horrified as we are by the cult of warrior violence in the Balkans or Rwanda, we may have gone too far toward the opposite extreme in the Western democracies. As Michael Kelly recently observed, "There are fewer and fewer people, and they are older and older people, who accept what every twelve-year-old in Bihac knows: that there are some things worth dying for and killing for." Abolitionism in the antebellum United States, the Allies' defeat of Nazi Germany, or the civil rights movement of the sixties, would never have succeeded without the legitimate expression of anger against injustice. The point is not to eradicate honor and pride from the male character, but to rechannel those energies from the nihilistic violence of *Fight Club* or the Arkansas schoolyard to some constructive moral purpose.

To do this, we must recover a positive sense of manhood. For, if young men are cut off from this positive tradition of manly pride, their manliness will reemerge in crude and retrograde forms. Some thirty years ago, the Rolling Stones recorded a misogynist rant called "Under My Thumb." Today, it is one of the songs that fans most request of these aging shamans of adolescent attitudinizing. In three decades, tension between men and women not only has not disappeared but may actually have intensified, and we must wonder whether the experiment in social engineering itself is one reason why.

For hostility toward women is an aberration of male behavior. If, as the prevailing orthodoxy contends, the male gender were intrinsically aggressive, hegemonic, and intolerant, then by definition male behavior could never improve. The message young males receive from feminist reasoning is not *You should be ashamed of liking "Under My Thumb,"* but *That's the way your gender thinks about women.*

So the first step toward a sensible debate about manly pride is to rescue the positive tradition of manliness from three decades of stereotyping that conflates masculinity with violence, hegemony, and aggression. We have to recognize that men and women are moral and intellectual equals, that decent and worthy men have always known this, and that, while men and women share the most important human virtues, vices, and aptitudes, they also have different psychological traits that incline them toward different activities.

According to the reigning orthodoxy, men and women should have exactly the same kinds of capacities and ambitions. They should be equally interested in becoming tycoons, winning battles, driving tractors, and nurturing children. But this is not the reality.

In general, men don't want to work in day-care centers or teach kindergarten, and women don't want to be truck drivers or join the military. Moreover, women are far more likely than men to leave successful jobs to devote time to families; in fact, women under thirty are more eager for lasting marriages and numerous children than women of their parents' generation (in what may be a yearning for what their parents denied them). We should recognize at last that, as long as women are guaranteed an equal opportunity to pursue whatever occupation they want, it does not matter that men and women on the whole still choose different vocations. We must stop trying to reengineer the human soul to prevent boys from being boyish, while encouraging all forms of self-expression in girls.

All that thirty years of behavioral conditioning has done is drive manliness underground and distort it by severing it from traditional sources of masculine restraint and civility. The gurus of sensitivity have tried to convince men to become open, fluid, genderless beings who are unafraid to cry. But little boys still want to play war and shoot up the living room with plastic howitzers, and we can't give them all Ritalin. Psychologists have begun to express concern about our educational institutions' readiness to pathologize what once would have been regarded as boyish high spirits—roughhousing, "hating" girls, locker-room language—and the use of powerful drugs to extirpate their perfectly ordinary immaturity.

Again, the point is to channel these energies into the development of character. Boys and young men still want to be heroes, and the way to teach them to treat girls and women with respect is to appeal to their heroism, not try to blot it out. Look at those kids performing daring flips on their skateboards, or sailing on their Rollerblades into downtown traffic like warriors contemptuous of fear or danger. Look at that squeegee kid with his shaved head and horsehair plume, decked out like some road-warrior Achilles. Walk into one of those high-voltage computer emporiums, selling our century's most potent icon for the extension of human mastery over the cosmos. Who are the salespeople? Almost always cocky young men, celebrities-in-waiting in dark suits and moussed hair, hooked on the sheer power of it all.

Channel surf on your television late at night and sample the rock videos. Nearly all the bands in rock videos are male, snarling or plaintive over the world's confusions and their erotic frustrations, oozing male belligerence alternating with Byronic alienation and a puppyish longing for attention. Their names (Goo Goo

Dolls) and attitudes (the lead singer of Radiohead is wheeled around a supermarket in a giant shopping cart curled up like an overgrown five-year-old) combine an infantile longing to return to childhood with an in-your-face attitude of distrust and suspicion.

And what else would one expect, since so many of the families into which they were born ended in divorce? By denying and repressing their natural inclination to manliness, we run the risk of abandoning them to such infantile posturing. When they pierce their bodies, it is because they want to experience moral and erotic constraint. Having failed to find an authority they can respect, someone to guide them from boyish impetuosity to a mature and manly vigor of judgment, they confuse authority with oppression. Still, cast adrift in a world without any limitations, they long to pay a price for their hedonism. Since no one is leading them back to the great ethical and religious traditions that set these limits on the highest intellectual and spiritual level, they pierce their bodies in a crude simulacrum of traditional restraint. In that very gesture, they reveal not only the wondrous capacity of spirited young people to see through the aridity of the establishment, but also the potential for an ennobling transformation.

It is precisely in traditional understandings of manly pride and honor that we will find the only sure basis for respect between men and women. The best way of convincing young men to treat women with respect is to educate them in those traditional virtues of character that make it a disgrace to treat anyone basely, dishonestly, or exploitively. Moreover, the surest way of raising young men to treat young women as friends rather than as objects for sexual exploitation is to appeal to their natural longing to be honored and esteemed by the young women to whom they are attracted. When our erotic attraction to another is properly directed, it leads us to cultivate the virtues of moderation, honesty, gratitude, and compassion, all of which make us worthy of love in the eyes of the beloved. We try to be virtuous because we want to be worthy of being loved.

One thing is sure: Given our current confusion over the value and meaning of manliness, we have nothing to lose by reopening the issue. If academic feminism is correct that violence toward women stems from traditional patriarchal attitudes, our grandparents' lives must have been a hell of aggression and fear. Yet, if anything impresses us about our forebears, judging from their lives, letters, and diaries, it is the refinement of their affections for one another, and of men's esteem for women in particular. Perhaps we cannot return to that world. But boys and young men today need to be reintroduced to the tradition of manly civility, to supplement our contemporary insistence that all romantic stress between men and women can be solved by the adjudication of rights and the stigmatization of exclusively male traits of character

Despite recent caricatures of the Western tradition as one long justification for the oppression of women, poets and thinkers from Homer to Rousseau have explored the delicate interplay of love and self-perfection. In Homer's *Odyssey*, Telemachus, son of the great war hero Odysseus, embarks on a search to find his missing father and thereby save his mother from the oppressive noblemen who want her to give up her husband for dead and marry one of them. As he searches for his father, in an adventure parallel to Odysseus's own search for a way home to his long-lost wife and child, Telemachus is educated by his adventures and grows from a boy into a man, guided by the wise goddess Athena who is also his father's best friend among the gods. Telemachus's search for his missing father, guided by the goddess, in effect provides him with the upbringing Odysseus was unable to give him. Even so, Odysseus still inspires his son from afar, because Telemachus learns during his travels of his father's exploits and wants to prove himself the hero's worthy son.

Whenever I describe Telemachus, this boy from a broken home, forced at a too-early age to be his mother's protector from oppressive men, compelled to bring himself up in a way that he hopes his absent father will be proud of, the young men in my undergraduate classes tend to become very quiet and reflective. They are Telemachus.

1

THE CHIVALROUS MAN

WE OFTEN HEAR THAT CHIVALRY IS DEAD. BUT THE VERY FACT that we can lament its passing suggests we still have some recollection of it. What does it mean for a man to be chivalrous? Refined manners, courtesy toward others, respect for women, and a character bred to the virtues of honor, courage, and self-restraint—these would all be part of what we have in mind when the concept of chivalry is invoked. Chivalry is often associated with the ideals of medieval knighthood, as portrayed in the legends of King Arthur and his knights. The perfect knight was thought to embody a distinct array of ideals: piety, valor, gentleness, compassion for the suffering; knights were expected, moreover, to lead a sublime and spiritual inner life. In matters of love, the perfect knight always acted with moderation, composure, and patience in wooing his fair damsel. The chivalrous man wanted his lady to love him for his worthy character and his courage in defending justice, faith, and duty.

Chivalry, then, means much more than simply good manners—opening doors for ladies, for instance, or spreading one's trench coat over a puddle. These are the outward signs of a deeper experience—the process by which a man's love for a woman helps to perfect his own character. A common theme throughout the readings in this section is that love gives a man the strongest motive to overcome and avoid bad behavior, so as to make himself admirable and worthy of affection in the eyes of his beloved. They demonstrate, again and again, one of the paradoxes of the chivalric ideal: that an overwhelming romantic passion can furnish the surest inducement to moral decency. Readers will find in this section guidance from all ages on how a man can make himself worthy of a woman's love, how to avoid the temptations of lust and other excesses of erotic passion, and how to conduct himself toward his beloved in a gracious and admirable fashion.

The Manly Lover

Orpheus and Eurydice

From Thomas Bulfinch,
Bulfinch's Mythology

A man's love for a woman can conquer even death. From the influential Victorian-era collection of ancient and medieval myths.

Orpheus was the son of Apollo and the Muse Calliope. He was presented by his father with a lyre and taught to play upon it, which he did to such perfection that nothing could withstand the charm of his music. Not only his fellow-mortals, but wild beasts were softened by his strains, and gathering round him laid by their fierceness, and stood entranced with his lay. Nay, the very trees and rocks were sensible to the charm. The former crowded round him and the latter relaxed somewhat of their hardness, softened by his notes.

Hymen had been called to bless with his presence the nuptials of Orpheus with Eurydice; but though he attended, he brought no happy omens with him. His very torch smoked and brought tears into their eyes. In coincidence with such prognostics, Eurydice, shortly after her marriage, while wandering with the nymphs, her companions, was seen by the shepherd Aristaeus, who was struck by her beauty and made advances to her. She fled, and in flying trod upon a snake in the grass, was bitten in the foot, and died. Orpheus sang his grief to all who breathed the upper air, both gods and men, and finding it all unavailing resolved to seek his wife in the regions of the dead. He descended by a cave situated on the side of the promontory of Taenarus and arrived at the Stygian realm. He passed through crowds of ghosts and presented himself before the throne of Pluto and Proserpine. Accompanying the words with the lyre, he sung, "O deities of the underworld, to whom all we who live must come, hear my words, for they are true. I come not to spy out the secrets of Tartarus, nor to try my strength against the three-headed dog with snaky hair who guards the entrance. I come to seek my wife, whose opening years the poisonous viper's fang has brought to an untimely end. Love has led me here, Love, a god all powerful with us who dwell on the earth, and, if old traditions say true, not less so here. I implore you by these abodes full of terror, these realms of silence and uncreated things, unite again the thread of Eurydice's life. We all are destined to you, and sooner or later must pass to your domain. She too, when she shall have filled her term of life, will rightly be yours. But till then grant her to me, I beseech you. If you deny me, I cannot return alone; you shall triumph in the death of us both."

As he sang these tender strains, the very ghosts shed tears. Tantalus, in spite of his thirst, stopped for a moment his efforts for water, Ixion's wheel stood still, the vulture ceased to tear the giant's liver, the daughters of Danaus rested from their task of drawing water in a sieve, and Sisyphus sat on his rock to listen. Then for the first time, it is said, the cheeks of the Furies were wet with tears. Proserpine could not resist, and Pluto himself gave way. Eurydice was called. She came from among the new-arrived ghosts, limping with her wounded foot. Orpheus was permitted to take her away with him on one condition, that he should not turn around to look at her till they should have reached the upper air. Under this condition they proceeded on their way, he leading, she following, through passages dark and steep, in total silence, till they had nearly reached the outlet into the cheerful upper world, when Orpheus, in a moment of forgetfulness, to assure himself that she was still following, cast a glance behind him, when instantly she was borne away. Stretching out their arms to embrace each other, they grasped only the air! Dying now a second time, she yet cannot reproach her husband, for how can she blame his impatience to behold her? "Farewell," she said, "a last farewell"—and was hurried away, so fast that the sound hardly reached his ears.

Orpheus endeavored to follow her, and besought permission to return and try once more for her release; but the stern ferryman repulsed him and refused passage. Seven days he lingered about the brink, without food or sleep; then bitterly accusing of cruelty the powers of Erebus, he sang his complaints to the rocks and mountains, melting the hearts of tigers and moving the oaks from their stations. He held himself aloof from womankind, dwelling constantly on the recollection of his sad mischance. The Thracian maidens tried their best to captivate him, but he repulsed their advances. They bore with him as long as they could; but finding him insensible one day, excited by the rites of Bacchus, one of them exclaimed, "See yonder our despiser!" and threw at him her javelin. The weapon, as soon as it came within the sound of his lyre, fell harmless at his feet. So did also the stones that they threw at him. But the women raised a scream and drowned the voice of the music, and then the missiles reached him and soon were stained with his blood. The maniacs tore him limb from limb, and threw his head and his lyre into the river Hebrus, down which they floated, murmuring sad music, to which the shores responded a plaintive symphony. The Muses gathered up the fragments of his body and buried them at Libethra, where the nightingale is said to sing over his grave more sweetly than in any other part of Greece. His lyre was placed by Jupiter among the stars. His shade passed a second time to Tartarus, where he sought out his Eurydice and embraced her with eager arms. They roam the happy fields together now, sometimes he leading, sometimes she; and Orpheus gazes as much as he will upon her, no longer incurring a penalty for a thoughtless glance.

The Art of Courtly Love

Andreas Capellanus

In this thirteenth-century classic from the High Age of Chivalry, The Art of Courtly Love, *Andreas Capellanus diagnoses the sweet suffering of love. A man's love makes him conscious of his imperfections in his beloved's eyes, and gives him the strongest motive to overcome them.*

Love is a certain inborn suffering derived from the sight of and excessive meditation upon the beauty of the opposite sex, which causes each one to wish above all things the embraces of the other and by common desire to carry out all of love's precepts in the other's embrace.

That love is suffering is easy to see, for before the love becomes equally balanced on both sides there is no torment greater, since the lover is always in fear that his love may not gain its desire and that he is wasting his efforts. He fears, too, that rumors of it may get abroad, and he fears everything that might harm it in any way, for before things are perfected a slight disturbance often spoils them. If he is a poor man, he also fears that the woman may scorn his poverty; if he is ugly, he fears that she may despise his lack of beauty or may give her love to a more handsome man; if he is rich, he fears that his parsimony in the past may stand in his way. To tell the truth, no one can number the fears of one single lover. This kind of love, then, is a suffering which is felt by only one of the persons and may be called "single love." But even after both are in love the fears that arise are just as great, for each of the lovers fears that what he has acquired with so much effort may be lost through the effort of someone else, which is certainly much worse for a man than if, having no hope, he sees that his efforts are accomplishing nothing, for it is worse to lose the things you are seeking than to be deprived of a gain you merely hope for. The lover fears, too, that he may offend his loved one in some way; indeed he fears so many things that it would be difficult to tell them.

Now it is the effect of love that a true lover cannot be degraded with any avarice. Love causes a rough and uncouth man to be distinguished for his handsomeness; it can endow a man even of the humblest birth with nobility of character; it blesses the proud with humility; and the man in love becomes accustomed to performing many services gracefully for everyone. O what a wonderful thing is love, which makes a man shine with so many virtues and teaches everyone, no matter who he is, so many good traits of character! There is another thing about love that we should not praise in few words: it adorns a man, so to speak, with the virtue of chastity, because he who shines with the light of one love can hardly think of embracing another woman, even a beautiful one. For when he thinks deeply of his beloved, the sight of any other woman seems to his mind rough and rude.

We must now see what persons are fit to bear the arms of love. You should know that everyone of sound mind who is capable of doing the work of Venus may be wounded by one of Love's arrows unless prevented by age, or blindness, or excess of passion.

An excess of passion is a bar to love, because there are men who are slaves to such passionate desire that they cannot be held in the bonds of love—men who, after they have thought long about some woman, straightway desire her embraces, and they forget about the services they have received from their first love and they feel no gratitude for them. Men of this kind lust after every woman they see; their love is like that of a shameless dog. They should rather, I believe, be compared to asses, for they are moved only by that low nature which shows that men are on the level of the other animals rather than by that true nature which sets us apart from all the other animals by the difference of reason.

Love and Self-Perfection

From Baldesar Castiglione,
The Book of the Courtier

Perhaps nowhere is the ideal of manliness as courtliness better explored than in Castiglione's sixteenth-century Renaissance classic The Book of the Courtier. *According to Cesare, one of the characters in the dialogue, a man will perfect all the virtues in himself in order to prove himself worthy to the lady he loves. Hence, there is no better inducement to goodness than romantic passion.*

Then messer Cesare said:

"The things that my lord Magnifico and I have said in praise of women, and many others too, were very well known and hence superfluous.

"Who does not know that without women we can feel no contentment or satisfaction throughout this life of ours, which but for them would be rude and devoid of all sweetness and more savage than that of wild beasts? Who does not know that women alone banish from our hearts all vile and base thoughts, vexations, miseries, and those turbid melancholies that so often are their fellows? And if you will consider well the truth, we shall also see that in our understanding of great matters women do not hamper our wits but rather quicken them, and in war make men fearless and brave beyond measure. And certainly it is impossible for vileness ever again to rule in a man's heart where once the flame of love has entered; for whoever loves desires always to make himself as lovable as he can, and always fears lest some disgrace befall him that may make him be esteemed lightly with her by whom he desires to be esteemed highly. Nor does he stop at risking his life a thousand times a day to show himself worthy of her love: hence whoever could form an army of lovers and have them fight in the presence of the ladies of their love, would conquer all the world, unless there were opposed to it another army similarly in love. And be well assured that Troy's ten years' resistance against all Greece proceeded from naught else but a few lovers, who on sallying forth to battle, armed themselves in the presence of their women; and often these women helped them and spoke some word to them at leaving, which inflamed them and made them more than men. Then in battle they knew that they were watched by their women from the walls and towers; wherefore it seemed to them that every act of hardihood they performed, every proof they gave, won them their women's praise, which was the greatest reward they could have in the world.

"Do you not know that the origin of all the graceful exercises that give pleasure in the world is to be ascribed to none other than to women? Who learns to dance and caper gallantly for aught else than to please women? Who studies the sweetness of music for other cause than this? Who tries to compose verses, in the vernacular at least, unless to express those feelings that are inspired by women? Think how many very noble poems we should be deprived of, both in the Greek tongue and in the Latin, if women had been lightly esteemed by the poets. But to pass all the others by, would it not have been a very great loss if messer Francesco Petrarch, who so divinely wrote his loves in this language of ours, had turned his mind solely to things Latin, as he would have done if the love of madonna Laura had not sometimes drawn him from them? I do not name you the bright geniuses now on earth and present here, who every day put forth some noble fruit and yet choose their subject only from the beauties and virtues of women.

"You see that Solomon, wishing to write mystically of things lofty and divine, to cover them with a graceful veil composed a fervent and tender dialogue between a lover and his sweetheart, deeming that he could not here below find any similitude more apt and befitting things divine than love for women; and in this way he tried to give us a little of the savour of that divinity which he both by knowledge and by grace knew better than the rest.

"Hence there was no need, my lord Gaspar, to dispute about this, or at least so wordily: but by gainsaying the truth you have prevented us from hearing a thousand other fine and weighty matters concerning the perfection of the Court Lady."

My lord Gaspar replied:

"I believe nothing more is left to say; yet if you think that my lord Magnifico has not adorned her with enough good qualities, the fault lay not with him, but with the one who arranged that there are not more virtues in the world; for the Magnifico gave her all there are."

My lady Duchess said, laughing:

"You shall now see that my lord Magnifico will find still others."

Isis and Osiris

From Thomas Bulfinch,
Bulfinch's Mythology

In ancient mythology, the love of a man and woman had the power to regenerate the cycles of nature.

Osiris and Isis were at one time induced to descend to the earth to bestow gifts and blessings on its inhabitants. Isis showed them first the use of wheat and barley, and Osiris made the instruments of agriculture and taught men the use of them, as well as how to harness the ox to the plough. He then gave men laws, the institution of marriage, a civil organization, and taught them how to worship the gods. After he had thus made the valley of the Nile a happy country, he assembled a host with which he went to bestow his blessings upon the rest of the world. He conquered the nations everywhere, but not with weapons, only with music and eloquence. His brother, Typhon saw this, and filled with envy and malice sought during his absence to usurp his throne. But Isis, who held the reins of government, frustrated his plans. Still more embittered, he now resolved to kill his brother. This he did in the following manner: having organized a conspiracy of seventy-two members, he went with them to the feast that was celebrated in honor of the king's return. He then caused a box or chest to be brought in, which had been made to fit exactly the size of Osiris, and declared that he would give that chest of precious wood to whomsoever could get into it. The rest tried in vain, but no sooner was Osiris in it than Typhon and his companions closed the lid and flung the chest into the Nile. When Isis heard of the cruel murder, she wept and mourned, and then with her hair shorn, clothed in black and beating her breast, she sought diligently for the body of her husband. In this search she was materially assisted by Anubis, the son of Osiris and Nephthys. They sought in vain for some time; for when the chest, carried by the waves to the shores of Byblos, had become entangled in the reeds that grew at the edge of the water, the divine power that dwelt in the body of Osiris imparted such strength to the shrub that it grew into a mighty tree, enclosing in its trunk the coffin of the god. This tree with its sacred deposit was shortly after felled, and erected as a column in the palace of the king of Phoenicia. But at length by the aid of Anubis and the sacred birds, Isis ascertained these facts, and then went to the royal city. There she offered herself at the palace as a servant, and being admitted, threw off her disguise and appeared as the goddess, surrounded with thunder and lightning. Striking the column with her wand she caused it to split open and give up the sacred coffin. This she seized and returned with it, and concealed it in the depth of a forest, but Typhon discovered it, and cutting the body into fourteen pieces scattered them hither and thither. After a tedious search, Isis found thirteen pieces, the fishes of the Nile having eaten the other. This she replaced by an imitation of sycamore wood, and buried the body at Philoe, which became ever after the great burying place of the nation, and the spot to which pilgrimages were made from all parts of the country. A temple of surpassing magnificence was also erected there in honor of the god, and at every place where one of his limbs had been found minor temples and tombs were built to commemorate the event. Osiris became after that the tutelar deity of the Egyptians. His soul was supposed always to inhabit the body of the bull Apis, and at his death to transfer itself to his successor.

Apis, the Bull of Memphis, was worshiped with the greatest reverence by the Egyptians. The individual animal who was held to be Apis was recognized by certain signs. It was requisite that he should be quite black, have a white square mark on the forehead, another, in the form of an eagle, on his back, and under his tongue a lump somewhat in the shape of a scarabaeus or beetle. As soon as a bull thus marked was found by those sent in search of him, he was placed in a building facing the east and was fed with milk for four months. At the expiration of this term the priests repaired at new moon, with great pomp, to his habitation and saluted him Apis. He was placed in a vessel magnificently decorated and conveyed down the Nile to Memphis, where a temple, with two chapels and a court for exercise, was assigned to him. Sacrifices were made to him, and once every year, about the time when the Nile began to rise, a golden cup was thrown into the river, and a grand festival was held to celebrate his birthday. The people believed that during this festival the crocodiles forgot their natural ferocity and became harmless. There was, however, one drawback to his happy lot: he was not permitted to live beyond a certain period, and if, when he had attained the age of twenty-five years, he still survived, the priests drowned him in the sacred cistern and then buried him in the temple of Serapis. On the death of this bull, whether it occurred in the course of nature or by violence, the whole land was filled with sorrow and lamentations, which lasted until his successor was found.

The Rules of Love

From Andreas Capellanus,
The Art of Courtly Love

During the High Middle Ages, people began to write more openly about the purely sensual side of love. Knightly chivalry gave way to the peace-time refinement, luxury, and etiquette of court life. Ladies were won now not so much by fighting in battle or winning a jousting match, as by an elaborate courtship involving exquisite manners, wit, and conversation. Even so, love was not reduced to carnal self-indulgence: the longing for an unattainable love was thought to stimulate finer and nobler passions than easy success. Romantic fidelity was hailed as a superior way of life to the indulgence of every passing carnal whim—although one could have more than one such romance! In The Art of Courtly Love, *Capellanus provides us with thirty-one simple rules for sublime longing and torment.*

    I.   Marriage is no real excuse for not loving.
   II.   He who is not jealous cannot love.
  III.   No one can be bound by a double love.
  IV.   It is well known that love is always increasing or decreasing.
   V.   That which a lover takes against his will of his beloved has no relish.
  VI.   Boys do not love until they arrive at the age of maturity.
 VII.   When one lover dies, a widowhood of two years is required of the survivor.
VIII.   No one should be deprived of love without the very best of reasons.
  IX.   No one can love unless he is impelled by the persuasion of love.

  X. Love is always a stranger in the home of avarice.

  XI. It is not proper to love any woman whom one should be ashamed to seek to marry.

  XII. A true lover does not desire to embrace in love anyone except his beloved.

  XIII. When made public, love rarely endures.

  XIV. The easy attainment of love makes it of little value; difficulty of attainment makes it prized.

  XV. Every lover regularly turns pale in the presence of his beloved.

  XVI. When a lover suddenly catches sight of his beloved, his heart palpitates.

  XVII. A new love puts to flight an old one.

  XVIII. Good character alone makes any man worthy of love.

  XIX. If love diminishes, it quickly fails and rarely revives.

  XX. A man in love is always apprehensive.

  XXI. Real jealousy always increases the feeling of love.

  XXII. Jealousy, and therefore love, are increased when one suspects his beloved.

  XXIII. He whom the thought of love vexes, eats and sleeps very little.

  XXIV. Every act of a lover ends in the thought of his beloved.

  XXV. A true lover considers nothing good except what he thinks will please his beloved.

  XXVI. Love can deny nothing to love.

  XXVII. A lover can never have enough of the solaces of his beloved.

  XXVIII. A slight presumption causes a lover to suspect his beloved.

  XXIX. A man who is vexed by too much passion usually does not love.

  XXX. A true lover is constantly and without intermission possessed by the thought of his beloved.

  XXXI. Nothing forbids one woman being loved by two men or one man by two women.

Love and Valor

From Thomas Bulfinch,
Bulfinch's Mythology

Love inspired Sir Lancelot to great deeds.

Sir Lancelot of the Lake, in all tournaments and jousts and deeds of arms, both for life and death, passed all other knights, and was never overcome, except it were by treason or enchantment; and he increased marvelously in worship, wherefore Queen Guenever had him in great favor, above all other knights. And for certain he loved the queen again above all other ladies; and for her he did many deeds of arms, and saved her from peril through his noble chivalry.

Why Lancelot Doesn't Marry

From Sir Thomas Malory,
Le Morte D'Arthur

Malory's fifteenth-century tale is another great source for the legends of King Arthur and the Knights of the Round Table. In a notable example of not practicing what he preaches, Sir Lancelot claims he avoids love because it conflicts with knightly valor. He does this to protect his paramour Queen Guenever's reputation, but perhaps there is more truth than he would care to acknowledge in what he says.

"Now, damosel," said Sir Lancelot, "wish ye any more service from me?"

"Nay, sir, " she said, "not at this time; but almighty Jesus preserve you wheresoever ye ride or go; for thou art the most courteous knight and meekest who now liveth unto all ladies and gentlewomen. But one thing, sir knight, methinketh ye lack, ye who are a knight wifeless: ye will not love some maiden or gentlewoman. I could never hear that ye ever loved a lady of any manner of degree, and that is a great pity. But it is noised that ye love Queen Guenever, that she hath ordained by enchantment that ye shall never love any other but her, and that no other damosel or lady shall ever rejoice you. Wherefore many in this land, of high estate and low, make great sorrow."

"Fair damosel," said Sir Lancelot, "I may not stop people from speaking of me what pleaseth them. But to be a wedded man, I think not; for then I must couch with her and leave arms and tournaments, battles and adventures. As for taking my pleasure with paramours, that I will refuse in principle for dread of God. For knights who are adventurous should not be adulterers or lecherous, for then they shall not be fortunate in the wars; either they shall be overcome by simpler knights than they are themselves, or else they shall by mischance and their cursedness slay better men than they are themselves. And whoso useth paramours shall be unlucky, and all things about them unlucky."

Older Men Make Better Lovers

From Baldesar Castiglione,
The Book of the Courtier

Whereupon messer Pietro, having first remained silent awhile, then settled himself a little as if about to speak of something important, and spoke thus:

"My Lords, in order to prove that old men can love not only without blame but sometimes more happily than young men, it will be needful for me to make a little discourse to explain what love is, and in what consists the happiness that lovers may enjoy. So I pray you hear me with attention, for I hope to make you see that there is no man for whom it is not becoming to be in love, even though he were fifteen or twenty years older than my lord Morello."

And then after some laughter, messer Pietro continued:

"Seized with desire to enjoy beauty as something good, if the soul allows herself to be guided by the judgment of sense, she runs into very grievous errors, and judges that the body wherein the beauty is seen is the chief cause of it; and hence, in order to enjoy that beauty, she deems it necessary to join herself as closely to that body as she can; which is false: and accordingly, whoever thinks to enjoy the beauty by possessing the body deceives himself, and is moved, not by true perception through reasonable choice, but by false opinion through sensual appetite: wherefore the pleasure also that results therefrom is necessarily false and vicious.

"Hence all those lovers who satisfy their unchaste desires with the women whom they love, run into one of two errors: for as soon as they have attained the end desired, they either feel satiety and tedium, or hate the beloved object as if appetite repented its error and perceived the deceit practised upon it by the false judgment of sense, which made it believe evil to be good.

"Such lovers as these, therefore, love most unhappily; for either they never attain their desires (which is great unhappiness), or if they do attain thereto, they find they have attained their woe, and finish their miseries with other miseries still greater; because even in the beginning and midst of their love naught else is ever felt but anguish, torments, sorrows, sufferings, toils. So that to be pale, melancholy, in continual tears and sighs, to be sad, to be ever silent or lamenting, to long for death, in short, to be most unhappy, are the conditions that are said to befit lovers.

"Hence it nearly always happens that young men are wrapped in this love which is sensual and wholly rebellious to reason, and thus they become unworthy to enjoy the graces and benefits which love bestows upon its true subjects; nor do they feel any pleasures in love beyond those which the unreasoning animals feel, but anguish far more grievous.

"This premise being admitted then,—and it is most true,—I say that the contrary happens to those who are of maturer age. For if such as these (when the soul is already less weighed down by bodily heaviness and when the natural heat begins to become tepid) are inflamed by beauty and turn thereto a desire guided by rational choice,—they are not deceived, and possess beauty perfectly. Therefore their possession of it always brings them good; because beauty is good, and hence true love of beauty is most good and holy, and always works for good in the mind of those who restrain the perversity of sense with the bridle of reason; which the old can do much more easily than the young.

"Hence it is not beyond reason to say further that the old can love without blame and more happily than the young; taking this word old, however, not in the sense of decrepit, nor when the bodily organs have already become so weak that the soul cannot perform its functions through them, but when our knowledge is at its true prime.

"I will not refrain from saying also this: which is, that I think that although sensual love is evil at every age, yet in the young it deserves excuse, and is perhaps in a measure permitted. For although it gives them anguish, dangers, toils, and those woes that have been told, still there are many who, to win the favour of the ladies of their love, do worthy acts, which (although not directed to a good end) are intrinsically good; and thus from that mass of bitterness they extract a little sweet, and through the adversities which they endure they at last perceive their error. Hence, just as I deem those youths divine who control their appetites and love in reason, so I excuse those who allow themselves to be overcome by sensual love, to which they are so strongly inclined by human frailty: provided they show therein gentleness, courtesy and worth, and the other noble qualities of which these gentlemen have told; and provided that when they are no longer of youthful age, they abandon it altogether, shunning this sensual desire as it were the lowest rung of the ladder by which true love can be attained. But if, even after they are old, they preserve the fire of appetite in their chill heart and subject stout reason to frail sense, it is not possible to say how much they are to be blamed. For like fools they deserve to be numbered with perpetual infamy among the unreasoning animals, since the thoughts and ways of sensual love are too unbecoming to mature age.

"I say, then, that as in youth human nature is so greatly prone to sensual desire, the Courtier may be allowed to love sensually while he is young. But if afterwards in maturer years he chances still to be kindled with this amorous desire, he must be very wary and take care not to deceive himself by allowing himself to be led into those calamities which in the young merit more compassion than blame, and, on the contrary, in the old more blame than compassion.

"Therefore when the gracious aspect of some fair woman meets his view, accompanied with such sweet behaviour and gentle manners that he, as an adept in love, feels that his spirit accords with hers: as soon as he finds that his eyes lay hold upon her image and carry it to his heart; and that his soul begins to contemplate her with pleasure and to feel that influence within which stirs and warms it little by little; and that those quick spirits which shine out through the eyes continually add fresh tinder to the fire;—he ought at this first stage to provide a speedy cure, and arouse his reason, and therewith arm the fortress of his heart, and so shut the way to sense and appetite that they cannot enter there by force or trickery. Thus, if the flame is extinguished, the danger is extinguished also; but if it survives or grows, then the Courtier, feeling himself caught, must resolve on shunning wholly every stain of vulgar love, and thus enter on the path of divine love, with reason for guide. And first he must consider that the body wherein this beauty shines is not the fountain whence it springs, but rather that beauty (being an incorporeal thing and, as we have said, a heavenly beam) loses much of its dignity when it finds itself joined to vile and corruptible matter; for the more perfect it is the less it partakes thereof, and is most perfect when wholly separate therefrom. And he must consider that just as one cannot hear with the palate or smell with the ears, so too can beauty in no way be enjoyed, nor can the desire which it excites in our minds be satisfied, by means of touch, but by that sense of which this beauty is the very object, namely, the power of vision.

"Therefore let him shun the blind judgment of sense, and with his eyes enjoy the splendour of his lady, her grace, her amourous sparkle, the laughs, the ways and all the other pleasant ornaments of her beauty. Likewise with his hearing let him enjoy the sweetness of her voice, the concord of her words, the harmony of her music (if his beloved be a musician). Thus will he feed his soul on sweetest food by means of these two senses—which have little of the corporeal and are ministers of reason—without passing in his desire for the body to any appetite less than seemly.

"Next let him obey, please and honour his lady with all reverence, and hold her dearer than himself, and prefer her convenience and pleasures to his own, and love in her not less the beauty of mind than that of body. Therefore let him take care not to leave her to fall into any kind of error, but by admonition and good advice let him always seek to lead her on to modesty, to temperance, to true chastity, and see to it that no thoughts find place in her except those that are pure and free from every stain of vice; and by thus sowing virtue in the garden of her fair mind, he will gather fruits of fairest behaviour too, and will taste them with wonderful delight. And this will be the true engendering and manifesting of beauty in beauty, which by some is said to be the aim of love.

"In such fashion will our Courtier be most acceptable to his lady, and she will always show herself obedient, sweet and affable to him, and as desirous of pleasing him as of being loved by him; and the wishes of both will be most virtuous and harmonious, and they themselves will thus be very happy.

"Therefore the lover who considers beauty in the body only, loses this blessing and felicity as soon as his beloved lady by her absence leaves his eyes without their splendour, and his soul consequently widowed of its blessing. Because, her beauty being far away, that amourous influence does not warm his heart as it did in her presence; wherefore his pores become arid and dry, and still the memory of her beauty stirs a little those forces of his soul, so that they seek to scatter abroad the spirits; and these, finding the ways shut, have no exit, and yet seek to issue forth; and thus hemmed in by those goads, they sting the soul and give it keenest suffering, as in the case of children when the teeth begin to come through the tender gums. And from this proceed the tears, the sighs, the anguish and the torments of lovers, because the soul is ever in affliction and travail, and becomes almost raging until her dear beauty appears to it again; and then it suddenly is calmed and breathes, and all intent upon that beauty it feeds on sweetest food, nor would ever part from so delightful a spectacle.

"Hence, to escape the torment of this absence and to enjoy beauty without suffering, the Courtier should, with the aid of reason, wholly turn his desire from the body to the beauty alone, and contemplate it in itself simple and pure, as far as he can, and fashion it in his imagination apart from all matter; and thus make it lovely and dear to his soul, and enjoy it there, and have it with him day and night, in every time and place, without fear of ever losing it; bearing always in mind that the body is something very different from beauty, and not only does not enhance it, but diminishes its perfection.

"In this way will our unyouthful Courtier be beyond all the bitterness and calamities that the young nearly always feel: such as jealousies, suspicions, disdainings, angers, despairings, and certain furies full of madness whereby they are often led into such error that some of them not only beat the women whom they love, but deprive themselves of life. He will do no injury to the husband, father, brothers or kinsfolk of his beloved lady; he will put no infamy upon her; he will never be forced to bridle his eyes and tongue with such difficulty in order not to disclose his desires to others, or to endure suffering at partings or absences;—because he will always carry his precious treasure with him shut up in his heart, and also by force of his imagination he will inwardly fashion her beauty much more beautiful than in fact it is.

"But besides these blessings the lover will find another much greater still, if he will employ this love as a step to mount to one much higher; which he will succeed in doing if he continually considers within himself how narrow a restraint it is to be always occupied in contemplating the beauty of one body only; and therefore, in order to escape such close bounds as these, in his thought he will little by little add so many ornaments, that by heaping all beauties together he will form a universal concept, and will reduce the multitude of these beauties to the unity of that single beauty which is spread over human nature at large. In this way he will no longer contemplate the particular beauty of one woman, but that universal beauty which adorns all bodies; and thus, bewildered by this greater light, he will not heed the lesser, and glowing with a purer flame, he will esteem lightly that which at first he so greatly prized.

"Therefore when our Courtier shall have reached this goal, although he may be called a very happy lover by comparison with those who are plunged in the misery of sensual love, still I would have him not rest content, but press boldly on following along the lofty path after the guide who leads him to the goal of true felicity. And thus, instead of going outside himself in thought (as all must needs do who choose to contemplate bodily beauty only), let him have recourse to himself, in order to contemplate that beauty which is seen by the eyes of the mind, which begin to be sharp and clear when those of the body lose the flower of their loveliness. Then the soul,—freed from vice, purged by studies of true philosophy, versed in spiritual life, and practised in matters of the intellect, devoted to the contemplation of her own substance,—as if awakened from deepest sleep, opens those eyes which all possess but few use, and sees in herself a ray of that light which is the true image of the angelic beauty communicated to her, and of which she then communicates a faint shadow to the body.

"Deign, then, O Lord, to hear our prayers, pour thyself upon our hearts, and with the splendour of thy most holy fire illumine our darkness and, like a trusted guide, in this blind labyrinth show us the true path. Correct the falseness of our senses, and after our long pursuit of vanities give us true and solid good; make us to inhale those spiritual odours that quicken the powers of the intellect, and to hear the celestial harmony with such accord that there may no longer be room in us for any discord of passion.

"Accept our souls, which are offered thee in sacrifice; burn them in that living flame which consumes all mortal dross, to the end that, being wholly separated from the body, they may unite with divine beauty by a perpetual and very sweet bond, and that we, being severed from ourselves, may, like true lovers, be able to transform ourselves into the beloved, and rising above the earth may be admitted to the angels' feast, where, fed on ambrosia and immortal nectar, we may at last die a most happy and living death, as died of old those ancient fathers whose souls thou, by the most glowing power of contemplation, didst ravish from the body and unite with God."

Having thus far spoken, with such vehemence that he almost seemed transported and beside himself, Bembo remained silent and motionless, keeping his eyes towards heaven, as if wrapped in ecstasy; when my lady Emilia, who with the others had been listening most attentively to his discourse, took him by the border of his robe, and shaking him a little, said:

"Have a care, messer Pietro, that with these thoughts your soul, also, does not forsake your body."

"My Lady," replied messer Pietro, "that would not be the first miracle that love has wrought upon me."

Love or Wisdom?

Francis Bacon

A twist on the formula: It is impossible to love and be wise, says Bacon in his essay Of Love, *because such excess drains our energies from life's serious business.*

The stage is more beholding to love than the life of man. For as to the stage, love is ever a matter of comedies, and now and then of tragedies, but in life it doth much mischief, sometimes like a syren, sometimes like a fury. You may observe that amongst all the great and worthy persons (whereof the memory remaineth, either ancient or recent) there is not one that hath been transported to the mad degree of love, which shews that great spirits and great business do keep out this weak passion. You must except nevertheless Marcus Antonius, the half partner of the empire of Rome, and Appius Claudius, the decemvir and lawgiver; whereof the former was indeed a voluptuous man, and inordinate, but the latter was an austere and wise man; and therefore it seems (though rarely) that love can find entrance not only into an open heart, but also into a heart well fortified, if watch be not well kept. It is a poor saying of Epicurus, "Each of us is to the other a sufficiently large theater," as if man, made for the contemplation of heaven and all noble objects, should do nothing but kneel before a little idol, and make himself a subject, though not of the mouth (as beasts are), yet of the eyes, which was given him for higher purposes. It is a strange thing to note the excess of this passion, and how it braves the nature and value of things, by this; that the speaking in a perpetual hyperbole is comely in nothing but in love. Neither is it merely in the phrase, for whereas it hath been well said that the archflatterer, with whom all the petty flatterers have intelligence, is a man's self, certainly the lover is more. For there was never proud man thought so absurdly well of himself as the lover doth of the person loved; and therefore it was well said, "That it is impossible to love and to be wise." Neither doth this weakness appear to others only, and not to the party loved, but to the loved most of all, except the love be reciproque. For it is a true rule that love is ever rewarded either with the reciproque or with an inward and secret contempt. By how much the more men ought to beware of this passion, which loseth not only other things but itself. As for the other losses, the poet's relation doth well figure them; that he that preferred Helena, quitted the gifts of Juno and Pallas. For whosoever esteemeth too much of amorous affection quitteth both riches and wisdom. This passion hath his floods in the very times of weakness, which are great prosperity and great adversity, though this latter hath been less observed, both which times kindle love, and make it more fervent, and therefore shew it to be the child of folly. They do best, who if they cannot but admit love yet make it keep quarter, and sever it wholly from their serious affairs and actions of life, for if it check once with business, it troubleth men's fortunes, and maketh men that they can no ways be true to their own ends. I know not how, but martial men are given to love; I think it is but as they are given to wine, for perils commonly ask to be paid in pleasures. There is in man's nature a secret inclination and motion toward love of others, which if it be not spent upon some one or a few, doth naturally spread itself toward many, and maketh men become humane and charitable, as it is seen sometime in friars. Nuptial love maketh mankind; friendly love perfecteth it; but wanton love corrupteth and embaseth it.

Love or Duty?

From Xenophon, The Education of Cyrus

Is it possible for a man to do his duty if he is distracted by erotic passion? Cyrus the Great's young lieutenant Araspas contends that a man can fall madly in love but compartmentalize his feelings so as to carry out his duties efficiently. The older Cyrus is not so sure. Eros enslaves a man and makes him lovesick so that he can't get anything useful accomplished. Better to avoid such entanglements! From a work by Xenophon, the celebrated Athenian general and student of Socrates.

And when he received this commission, Araspas asked: "And have you seen the lady, Cyrus, whom you give into my keeping?"

"No, by Zeus," said Cyrus; "not I."

"But I have," said the other. "And let me tell you, Cyrus," said he, "it seemed to me, as it did to all the rest who saw her, that there never was so beautiful a woman of mortal birth in Asia. But," he added, "you must by all means see her for yourself."

"No by Zeus," said Cyrus; "and all the less, if she is as beautiful as you say."

"Why so?" asked the young man.

"Because," said he, "if now I have heard from you that she is beautiful and am inclined just by your account of her to go and gaze on her, when I have no leisure, I am afraid that she will herself much more readily persuade me to come again to gaze on her. And in consequence of that I might sit there, in neglect of my duties, idly gazing upon her."

"Why Cyrus," said the young man breaking into a laugh, "you do not think, do you, that human beauty is able to compel a man against his will to act contrary to his own best interest? Why," said he, "if that were natural, it would compel us all alike. Do you see," said he, "how fire burns all alike. That is its nature. But of beautiful things we love some and some we do not; and one loves one, another another; for it is a matter of will and each one loves what he wishes."

"How then, pray," said Cyrus, "if falling in love is a matter of will is it not possible for any one to stop whenever he wishes? But I

have seen people in tears of sorrow because of love and in slavery to
the objects of their love, even though they believed before they fell
in love that slavery is a great evil; I have seen them give those
objects of their love many things that they could ill afford to part
with; and I have seen people praying to be delivered from love just
as from any other disease, and, for all that, unable to be delivered
from it, but fettered by a stronger necessity than if they had been
fettered with shackles of iron. At any rate, they surrender themselves to those they love to perform for them many services blindly.
And yet, in spite of all their misery, they do not attempt to run away,
but even guard their darlings to keep them from running away."

"Yes," the young man answered, "there are some who do so;
but such are wretched weaklings, the beautiful do not compel
humans to fall in love with them nor to desire that which they
should not, but there are some miserable apologies for men who
are slaves to all sorts of passions, I think, and then they blame love.
But the good, though they also have a desire for money and good
horses and beautiful women, have the power to let all that alone so
as not to touch anything beyond the limit of what is just. At any
rate," he added, "I have seen this lady and though she seemed to
me surpassingly beautiful, still I am here with you, I practice horsemanship, and I do everything else that it is my duty to do."

"Aye, by Zeus," said Cyrus; "for you came away perhaps in less
time than love takes, as its nature is, to get a man ensnared. For,
you know, it is possible for a man to put his finger in the fire and
not be burned at once, and wood does not burst at once into flame;
still, for my part, I neither put my hand into the fire nor look upon
the beautiful, if I can help it. And I advise you, too, Araspas," said
he, "not to let your eyes linger upon the fair; for fire, to be sure,
burns only those who touch it, but beauty insidiously kindles a fire
even in those who gaze upon it from afar, so that they are inflamed
with eros."

"Never fear, Cyrus," said he, "even if I never cease to look
upon her, I shall never be so overcome as to do anything that I
ought not."

"Your proposals," said he, "are most excellent. Keep her then,
as I bid you, and take good care of her."

Now, he wished to send someone as a spy into Lydia to find
out what the Assyrian was doing, and it seemed to him that Araspas,
the guardian of the beautiful woman, was the proper person to go
on this mission. Now Araspas's case had taken a turn like this: he
had fallen in love with the lady and could not resist the impulse to

approach her with amorous proposals. But she repulsed his
advances and was true to her husband, although he was far away,
for she loved him devotedly. Still, she did not accuse Araspas to
Cyrus, for she shrank from making trouble between friends. But
when Araspas, thinking that he should thus further the attainment
of his desires, threatened the woman that he would use force if she
would not submit willingly, then in fear of outrage the lady no
longer kept it secret but sent her eunuch to Cyrus with instructions
to tell him the whole story.

When Cyrus heard it, he laughed outright at the man who had
claimed to be superior to the passion of love; and he sent Artabazus
back with the eunuch and bade him warn Araspas not to lay violent
hands upon such a woman; but if he could win her consent, he
himself would interpose no objection.

So, when Artabazus came to Araspas, he rebuked him severely,
saying that the woman had been given to him in trust; and he dwelt
upon his ungodliness, sinfulness, and sensuality, until Araspas shed
bitter tears of contrition and was overwhelmed with shame and
frightened to death lest Cyrus should punish him.

So, when Cyrus learned of this, he sent for him and had a talk
with him in private. "I see, Araspas," said he, "that you are afraid of
me and terribly overcome with shame. Do not feel that way, pray;
for I have heard say that even gods are victims of love; and as for
mortals, I know that even some who are considered very discreet
have suffered from love. And I had too poor an opinion of myself
to suppose that I should have the strength of will to be thrown in
contact with beauty and be indifferent to it. Besides, I am myself
responsible for your condition, for it was I that shut you up with
this irresistible creature."

"Aye, Cyrus," said Araspas, interrupting him, "you are in this,
just as in everything else, gentle and forgiving of human errors.
Other men make me ready to sink with my shame; for ever since
the report of my fall got out, my enemies have been exulting over
me, while my friends come to me and advise me to keep out of the
way, for fear that you punish me for committing so great a wrong."

"Let me tell you then, Araspas," said Cyrus, "that by reason of
this very report which people have heard in regard to you, you are
in a position to do me a very great favor and to be of great assistance to our allies."

"Would that some occasion might arise," answered Araspas,
"in which I could be of service to you."

"If, then," said the other, "under pretense that you were fleeing from me you would go over into the enemy's country, I believe they would trust you."

"Aye, by Zeus," said Araspas, "and I know that even with my friends I could start the story that I was running away from you."

"Then you would return to us," said he, " with full information about the enemy's condition and plans. And I suppose that because of their trusting you they would make you a participant in their discussions and counsels, so that not a single thing that we wish to know would be hidden from you."

"Depend upon it," said he, "I will start at once; and one of the circumstances that will gain my story credence will be the appearance that I have run away because I was likely to be punished by you."

"And will you be able to give up the beautiful Panthea?" asked Cyrus.

"Yes, Cyrus," said he; "for I evidently have two souls. I have now worked out this doctrine of philosophy in the school of that crooked sophist, Eros. For if the soul is one, it is not both good and bad at the same time, neither can it at the same time desire the right and the wrong, nor at the same time both will and not will to do the same things; but it is obvious that there are two souls, and when the good one prevails, what is noble is done; but when the bad one gains the ascendency, what is shameful is attempted. And now, since she has taken you to be her ally, it is the good soul that has gained the mastery, and that completely."

Lancelot and Guenever

From Thomas Bulfinch,
Bulfinch's Mythology

The conflict between the love of Sir Lancelot and Queen Guenever and their duty to their king leads to tragedy for them and for the kingdom.

So after the quest of the Holy Grail was fulfilled, and all the knights who were left alive were come again to the Table Round, there was great joy in the court, and especially King Arthur and Queen Guenever made great joy of the remnant that were come home, and passing glad were the king and the queen of Sir Lancelot and of Sir Bohort, for they had been passing long away in the quest of the Holy Grail.

Then Sir Lancelot began to resort unto Queen Guenever again, and forgot the promise that he made in the quest; so that many in the court spoke of it, and in especial Sir Agrivain, Sir Gawain's brother, for he was ever open-mouthed. So it happened Sir Gawain and all his brothers were in King Arthur's chamber, and then Sir Agrivain said thus openly, "I marvel that we all are not ashamed to see and to know so noble a knight as King Arthur so to be shamed by the conduct of Sir Lancelot and the queen." Then spoke Sir Gawain, and said, "Brother, Sir Agrivain, I pray for you and charge you move not such matters any more before me for be ye assured I will not be of your counsel." "Neither will we," said Sir Gaheris and Sir Gareth. "Then will I," said Sir Modred. "I doubt you not, " said Sir Gawain, "for to all mischief ever were ye prone; yet I would that ye left all this, for I know what will come of it." "Fall of it what may fall," said Sir Agrivain, "I will disclose it to the king." With that King Arthur came to them. "Now, brothers, hold your peace," said Sir Gawain.

"We will not," said Sir Agrivain. Then said Sir Gawain, "I will not hear your tales, nor be of your counsel." "No more will I," said Sir Gareth and Sir Gaheris, and they departed, making great sorrow.

Then Sir Agrivain told the king all that was said in the court of the conduct of Sir Lancelot and the queen, and it grieved the king very much. But he would not believe it to be true without proof. So Sir Agrivain laid a plot to entrap Sir Lancelot and the queen, intending to take them together unawares. Sir Agrivain and Sir Modred led a party for this purpose, but Sir Lancelot escaped from them having slain Sir Agrivain and wounded Sir Modred. Then Sir Lancelot hastened to his friends, and told them what had happened, and withdrew with them to the forest; but he left spies to bring him tidings of whatever might be done.

So Sir Lancelot escaped, but the queen remained in the king's power, and Arthur could no longer doubt of her guilt. And the law was such in those days that they who committed such crimes, of whatever estate or condition they were, must be burned to death, and so it was ordained for Queen Guenever. Then said King Arthur to Sir Gawain, "I pray you make you ready, in your best armor, with your brethren, Sir Gaheris and Sir Gareth, to bring my queen to the fire, there to receive her death." "Nay, my most noble lord," said Sir Gawain, "that will I never do; for know thou well, my heart will never serve me to see her die, and it shall never be said that I was of your counsel in her death." Then the king commanded Sir Gaheris and Sir Gareth to be there, and they said, "We will be there, as ye command us, sire, but in peaceable wise, and bear no armor upon us."

So the queen was led forth, and her priest was brought to her to shrive her, and there was weeping and wailing of many lords and ladies. And one went and told Sir Lancelot that the queen was led forth to her death. Then Sir Lancelot and the knights that were with him fell upon the troop that guarded the queen, and dispersed them, and slew all who withstood them. And in the confusion Sir Gareth and Sir Gaheris were slain, for they were unarmed and defenseless. And Sir Lancelot carried away the queen to his castle of La Joyeuse Garde.

Then there came one to Sir Gawain and told him how that Sir Lancelot had slain the knights and carried away the queen. "O Lord, defend my brethren!" said Sir Gawain. "Truly," said the man, "Sir Gareth and Sir Gaheris are slain." "Alas!" said Sir Gawain, "now is my joy gone." And then he fell down and swooned, and long he lay there as if he were dead.

When he arose out of his swoon Sir Gawain ran to the king, crying, "O King Arthur, mine uncle, my brothers are slain." Then the king and he both wept. "My king, my lord, and mine uncle," said Sir Gawain, "bear witness now that I make you a promise that I shall hold by my knighthood, that from this day I will never fail Sir Lancelot until the one of us have slain the other. I will seek Sir Lancelot throughout seven kings' realms, but I shall slay him or he shall slay me." "Ye shall not need to seek him," said the king, "for, as I hear, Sir Lancelot will abide me and you in the Joyeuse Garde; and draws many people to him, as I hear say." "That may I believe," said Gawain, "but, my lord, summon your friends, and I will summon mine." "It shall be done," said the king. So then the king sent letters and writs throughout all England, both in the length and breadth, to summon all his knights. And to Arthur drew many knights, dukes, and earls, so that he had a great host. Thereof Sir Lancelot heard, and collected all whom he could; and many good knights held with him, both for his sake and for the queen's sake. But King Arthur's host was too great for Sir Lancelot to abide him in the field; and he was full loath to do battle against the king. So Sir Lancelot drew him to his strong castle, with all manner of provisions. Then came King Arthur and Sir Gawain, and laid siege all about La Joyeuse Garde, both the town and the castle; but in no wise would Sir Lancelot ride out of his castle, neither suffer any of his knights to issue out, until many weeks were past.

Then it befell upon a day in harvesttime Sir Lancelot looked over the wall, and spake aloud to King Arthur and Sir Gawain, "My lords, both, all is vain that ye do at this siege, for here ye shall win no honor, but only dishonor; for if I come out, and my good knights, I shall soon make an end of this war." "Come forth," said Arthur, "if you dare and I promise you I shall meet you in the midst of the field." "God forbid me," said Sir Lancelot, "that I should encounter with the most noble king that made me knight." "Fie upon thy fair language," said the king, "for know well that I am your mortal foe, and ever will be to my dying day." And Sir Gawain said, "What cause had you to slay my brother, Sir Gaheris, who bore no arms against you, and Sir Gareth, whom you made knight, and who loved you more than all my kin? Therefore know you well I shall make war on you all the while that I may live."

When Sir Bohort, Sir Hector de Marys, and Sir Lionel heard this outcry, they called to them Sir Palamedes, and Sir Saffire his brother, and Sir Lawayn, with many more, and all went to Sir Lancelot. And they said, "My lord, Sir Lancelot, we pray you, if you will have our service, keep us no longer within these walls, for know well all your fair speech and forbearance will not avail you." "Alas!" said Sir Lancelot, "to ride forth and to do battle I am full loath." Then he spoke again to the king and Sir Gawain, and willed them to keep out of the battle; but they despised his words. So then Sir Lancelot's fellowship came out of the castle in full good array. And always Sir Lancelot charged all his knights, in any wise, to save King Arthur and Sir Gawain.

Then came forth Sir Gawain from the king's host, and offered combat, and Sir Lionel encountered with him, and there Sir Gawain smote Sir Lionel through the body, that he fell to the earth as if dead. Then there began a great conflict, and much people were slain; but ever Sir Lancelot did what he might to save the people on King Arthur's party, and ever King Arthur followed Sir Lancelot to slay him; but Sir Lancelot suffered him, and would not strike again. Then Sir Bohort encountered with King Arthur, and smote him down; and he alighted and drew his sword, and said to Sir Lancelot, "Shall I make an end of this war?" for he meant to have slain King Arthur. "Not so," said Sir Lancelot, "touch him no more, for I will never see that most noble king that made me knight either slain or shamed;" and therewith Sir Lancelot alighted off his horse and took up the king, and horsed him again, and said thus:

"My lord Arthur, for God's love, cease this strife." And King Arthur looked upon Sir Lancelot, and his tears burst from his eyes, thinking on the great courtesy that was in Sir Lancelot more than in any other man; and therewith the king rode his way. Then anon both parties withdrew to repose them, and buried the dead.

But the war continued, and it was noised abroad through all Christendom, and at last it was told before the Pope; and he, considering the great goodness of King Arthur, and of Sir Lancelot, called to him a noble clerk, which was the Bishop of Rochester, who was then in his dominions, and sent him to King Arthur, charging him that he take his queen, dame Guenever, unto him again, and make peace with Sir Lancelot.

So, by means of this bishop, peace was made for the space of one year, and King Arthur received back the queen, and Sir Lancelot departed from the kingdom with all his knights and went to his own country. So they shipped at Cardiff, and sailed unto Benwick, which some men call Bayonne. And all the people of those lands came to Sir Lancelot, and received him home right joyfully. And Sir Lancelot established and garnished all his towns and castles, and he greatly advanced all his noble knights, Sir Lionel and Sir Bohort, and Sir Hector de Marys, Sir Blamor, Sir Lawayne, and many others, and made them lords of lands and castles; till he left himself no more than any one of them.

But when the year was passed, King Arthur and Sir Gawain came with a great host, and landed upon Sir Lancelot's lands, and burned and wasted all that they might overrun. Then spoke Sir Bohort and said, "My lord, Sir Lancelot, give us leave to meet them in the field, and we shall make them rue the time that ever they came to this country." Then said Sir Lancelot, "I am full loath to ride out with my knights for shedding of Christian blood; so we will yet awhile keep our walls, and I will send a messenger unto my lord Arthur, to propose a treaty; for better is peace than always war." So Sir Lancelot sent forth a damsel, and a dwarf with her, requiring King Arthur to leave his warring upon his lands; and so she started on a palfrey, and the dwarf ran by her side. And when she came to the pavilion of King Arthur she alighted, and there met her a gentle knight, Sir Lucan the butler, and said, "Fair damsel, come ye from Sir Lancelot du Lac?" "Yea, sir," she said, "I come hither to speak with the king." "Alas!" said Sir Lucan, "my lord Arthur would be reconciled to Sir Lancelot, but Sir Gawain will not suffer him." And with this Sir Lucan led the damsel to the king, where he sat with Sir Gawain, to hear what she would say. So when she had told her tale, the tears ran out of the king's eyes; and all the lords were forward to advise the king to be accorded with Sir Lancelot, save only Sir Gawain; and he said, "My lord, mine uncle, what will ye do? Will you now turn back, now you are so far advanced upon your journey? If ye do, all the world will speak shame of you." "Nay," said King Arthur, "I will do as ye advise me; but do thou give the damsel her answer, for I may not speak to her for pity."

Then said Sir Gawain, "Damsel, say ye to Sir Lancelot, that it is wasted labor to sue to mine uncle for peace, and say that I, Sir Gawain, send him word that I promise him, by the faith I owe unto God and to knighthood, I shall never leave him till he have slain me or I him." So the damsel returned; and when Sir Lancelot had heard this answer, the tears ran down his cheeks.

Then it befell on a day Sir Gawain came before the gates, armed at all points, and cried with a loud voice, "Where art thou now, thou false traitor, Sir Lancelot? Why hidest thou thyself within holes and walls like a coward? Look out now, thou traitor knight, and I will avenge upon thy body the death of my three brethren." All this language Sir Lancelot heard, and the knights which were about him; and they said to him, "Sir Lancelot, now must ye defend you like a knight, or else be shamed forever, for you have slept overlong and suffered overmuch." Then Sir Lancelot spoke on high unto King Arthur, and said, "My lord Arthur, now I have forborne long, and suffered you and Sir Gawain to do what ye would, and now I needs must defend myself, inasmuch as Sir Gawain has accused me of treason." Then Sir Lancelot armed himself and mounted upon his horse, and the noble knights came out of the city, and the host without stood all apart; and so the covenant was made that no man should come near the two knights, nor deal with them, till one were dead or yielded.

Dido and Aeneas

From Thomas Bulfinch,
Bulfinch's Mythology

The exiled Trojan hero Aeneas must renounce his love in order to fulfill his destiny.

Carthage, where the exiles had now arrived, was a spot on the coast of Africa opposite Sicily, where at that time a Tyrian colony under Dido, their queen, were laying the foundations of a state destined in later ages to be the rival of Rome itself. Dido was the daughter of Belus, king of Tyre, and sister of Pygmalion, who succeeded his father on the throne. Her husband was Sichaeus, a man of immense wealth, but Pygmalion, who coveted his treasures, caused him to be put to death. Dido, with a numerous body of friends and followers, both men and women, succeeded in effecting their escape from Tyre, in several vessels, carrying with them the treasures of Sichaeus. On arriving at the spot which they selected as the seat of their future home, they asked of the natives only so much land as they could enclose with a bull's hide. When this was readily granted, she caused the hide to be cut into strips, and with them enclosed a spot on which she built a citadel, and called it *Byrsa* (a hide). Around this fort the city of Carthage rose, and soon became a powerful and flourishing place.

Such was the state of affairs when Aeneas with his Trojans arrived there. Dido received the illustrious exiles with friendliness and hospitality. "Not unacquainted with distress," she said, "I have learned to succor the unfortunate." The queen's hospitality displayed itself in festivities at which games of strength and skill were exhibited. The strangers contended for the palm with her own subjects, on equal terms, the queen declaring that whether the victor were "Trojan or Tyrian should make no difference to her." At the feast which followed the games, Aeneas gave at her request a recital of the closing events of the Trojan history and his own adventures after the fall of the city. Dido was charmed with his discourse and filled with admiration of his exploits. She conceived an ardent passion for him, and he for his part seemed well content to accept the fortunate chance which appeared to offer him at once a happy termination of his wanderings, a home, a kingdom, and a bride. Months rolled away in the enjoyment of pleasant intercourse, and it seemed as if Italy and the empire destined to be founded on its shores were alike forgotten. Seeing which, Jupiter despatched Mercury with a message to Aeneas recalling him to a sense of his high destiny and commanding him to resume his voyage.

Aeneas parted from Dido, though she tried every allurement and persuasion to detain him. The blow to her affection and her pride was too much for her to endure, and when she found that he was gone, she mounted a funeral pile which she had caused to be erected, and having stabbed herself was consumed with the pile. The flames rising over the city were seen by the departing Trojans, and, though the cause was unknown, gave to Aeneas some intimation of the fatal event.

Breaking Up Is Hard to Do

From Plato, Symposium

According to the comic poet Aristophanes, as he appears in the Symposium, *men and women were once single beings, rolling around like Cheerios and perfectly happy; the gods split us into male and female halves to punish us for our arrogance. Today, when a man and woman fall in love, each is yearning for that missing half.*

Love is, of all the gods the best friend of men, the helper and the healer of the ills which are the great impediment to the happiness of the race. I will try to describe his power to you, and you shall teach the rest of the world what I am teaching you. In the first place, let me treat of the nature of man and what has happened to it; for the original human nature was not like the present, but different. The sexes were not two as they are now, but originally three in number; there was man, woman, and the union of the two, having a name corresponding to this double nature, which had once a real existence, but is now lost, and the word "Androgynous" is only preserved as a term of reproach. In the second place, the primeval man was round, his back and sides forming a circle; and he had four hands and four feet, one head with two faces, looking opposite ways, set on a round neck and precisely alike; also four ears, two privy members, and the remainder to correspond. He could walk upright as men now do, backwards or forwards as he pleased and he could also roll over and over at a great pace, turning on his four hands and four feet, eight in all, like tumblers going over and over with their legs in the air; this was when he wanted to run fast. Now the sexes were three, and such as I have described them; because the sun, moon, and earth are three; and the man was originally the child of the sun, the woman of the earth, and the man-woman of the moon, which is made up of sun and earth, and they were all round and moved round and round like their parents. Terrible was their might and strength, and the thoughts of their hearts were great, and they made an attack upon the gods; of them is told the tale of Otys and Ephialtes who, as Homer says, dared to scale heaven, and would have laid hands upon the gods. Doubt reigned in the celestial councils. Should they kill them and annihilate the race with thunderbolts, as they had done the giants, then there would be an end of the sacrifices and worship which men offered to them; but, on the other hand, the gods could not suffer their insolence to be unrestrained. At last, after a good deal of reflection, Zeus discovered a way. He said: "Methinks I have a plan which will humble their pride and improve their manners; men shall continue to exist, but I will cut them in two and then they will be diminished in strength and increased in numbers; this will have the advantage of making them more profitable to us. They shall walk upright on two legs, and if they continue insolent and will not be quiet, I will split them again and they shall hop about on a single leg." He spoke and cut men in two, like a sorb-apple which is halved for pickling, or as you might divide an egg with a hair; and as he cut them one after another, he bade Apollo give the face and the half of the neck a turn in order that the man might contemplate the section of himself: he would thus learn a lesson of humility. Apollo was also bidden to heal their wounds and compose their forms. So he gave a turn to the face and pulled the skin from the sides all over that which in our language is called the belly, like the purses which draw in, and he made one mouth at the centre, which he fastened in a knot (the same as which is called the navel); he also moulded the breast and took out most of the wrinkles, much as a shoemaker might smooth leather upon a last; he left a few, however, in the region of the belly and navel, as a memorial of the primeval state.

After the division the two parts of man, each desiring his other half, came together, and throwing their arms about one another, entwined in mutual embraces, longing to grow into one, they were on the point of dying from hunger and self-neglect, because they did not like to do anything apart; and when one of the halves died and the other survived, the survivor sought another mate, man or woman as we call them,—being the sections of entire men or women,—and clung to that. They were being destroyed, when Zeus in pity of them invented a new plan: he turned the parts of genera-tion round to the front, for this had not been always their position, and they sowed the seed no longer as hitherto like grasshoppers in the ground, but in one another; and after the transposition the male generated in the female in order that by the mutual embraces of man and woman they might breed, and the race might continue; or if man came to man they might be satisfied, and rest, and go their ways to the business of life: so ancient is the desire of one another which is implanted in us, reuniting our original nature, making one of two, and healing the state of man. Each of us when separated, having one side only, like a flat fish, is but the indenture of a man, and he is always looking for his other half. Men who are a section of that double nature which was once called Androgynous are lovers of women; adulterers are generally of this breed, and also adulterous women who lust after men: the women who are a section of the woman do not care for men, but have female attach-ments; the female companions are of this sort. But they who are a section of the male follow the male, and while they are young, being slices of the original man, they hang about men and embrace them, and they are themselves the best of boys and youths, because they have the most manly nature. Some indeed assert that they are shameless, but this is not true; for they do not act thus from any want of shame, but because they are valiant and manly, and have a manly countenance, and they embrace that which is like them. And these when they grow up become our statesmen, and these only, which is a great proof of the truth of what I am saying. When they reach manhood they are lovers of youth, and are not naturally inclined to marry or beget children,—if at all, they do so only in obedience to the law; but they are satisfied if they may be allowed to live with one another unwedded; and such a nature is prone to love and ready to return love, always embracing that which is akin to him.

And when one of them meets with his other half, the actual half of himself, whether he be a lover of youth or a lover of anoth-er sort, the pair are lost in an amazement of love and friendship and intimacy, and will not be out of the other's sight, as I may say, even for a moment: these are the people who pass their whole lives together; yet they could not explain what they desire of one another. For the intense yearning which each of them has towards the other does not appear to be the desire of a lover's intercourse, but of something else which the soul of either evidently desires and cannot tell, and of which she has only a dark and doubtful presentiment. Suppose Hephaestus, with his instruments, were to come to the pair who are lying side by side and to say to them, "What do you people want of one another?" they would be unable to explain. And suppose further, that when he saw their perplexity he said: "Do you desire to be wholly one; always day and night to be in one another's company? For if this is what you desire, I am ready to melt you into one and let you grow together, so that being two you shall become one, and while you live a common life as if you were a single man, and after your death in the world below still be one departed soul instead of two—I ask whether this is what you lovingly desire, and whether you are satisfied to attain this?"—there is not a man of them who when he heard the proposal would deny or would not acknowledge that this meeting and melting into one another, this becoming one instead of two, was the very expression of his ancient need. And the reason is that human nature was originally one and we were a whole, and the desire and pursuit of the whole is called love.

UNMANLY TEMPTATIONS

Diana and Actaeon

From Thomas Bulfinch,
Bulfinch's Mythology

Among the lessons a man must learn: if you can't control your passions, they may devour you.

There was a valley thick enclosed with cypresses and pines, sacred to the huntress queen, Diana. In the extremity of the valley was a cave, not adorned with art, but nature had counterfeited art in its construction, for she had turned the arch of its roof with stones, as delicately fitted as if by the hand of man. A fountain burst out from one side, whose open basin was bounded by a grassy rim. Here the goddess of the woods used to come when weary with hunting and bathe her virgin limbs in the sparkling water.

One day, having repaired thither with her nymphs, she handed her javelin, her quiver, and her bow to one, her robe to another, while a third unbound the sandals from her feet. Then Crocale, the most skillful of them, arranged her hair, and Nephele, Hyale, and the rest drew water in capacious urns. While the goddess was thus employed in the labors of the toilet, behold Actaeon, having quitted his companions, and rambling without any especial object, came to the place, led thither by his destiny. As he presented himself at the entrance of the cave, the nymphs, seeing a man, screamed and rushed toward the goddess to hide her with their bodies. But she was taller than the rest and overtopped them all by a head. Such a color as tinges the clouds at sunset or at dawn came over the countenance of Diana thus taken by surprise. Surrounded as she was by her nymphs, she yet turned half away, and sought with a sudden impulse for her arrows. As they were not at hand, she dashed the water into the face of the intruder, adding these words: "Now go and tell, if you can, that you have seen Diana unappareled." Immediately a pair of branching stag's horns grew out of his head, his neck gained in length, his ears grew sharp-pointed, his hands became feet, his arms long legs, his body was covered with a hairy, spotted hide. Fear took the place of his former boldness, and the hero fled. He could not but admire his own speed; but when he saw his horns in the water, "Ah, wretched me!" he would have said, but no sound followed the effort. He groaned, and tears flowed down the face which had taken the place of his own. Yet his consciousness remained. What shall he do? Go home to seek the palace, or lie hid in the woods? The latter he was afraid, the former he was ashamed, to do. While he hesitated the dogs saw him. First Melampus, a Spartan dog, gave the signal with his bark, then Pamphagus, Dorceus, Lelaps, Theron, Nape, Tigris, and all the rest, rushed after him swifter than the wind. Over rocks and cliffs, through mountain gorges that seemed impracticable, he fled and they followed. Where he had often chased the stag and cheered on his pack, his pack now chased him, cheered on by his huntsmen.

He longed to cry out, "I am Actaeon; recognize your master!" but the words came not at his will. The air resounded with the bark of the dogs. Presently one fastened on his back, another seized his shoulder. While they held their master, the rest of the pack came up and buried their teeth in his flesh. He groaned, not in a human voice, yet certainly not in a stag's, and falling on his knees, raised his eyes, and would have raised his arms in supplication, if he had had them. His friends and fellow-huntsmen cheered on the dogs, and looked everywhere for Actaeon, calling on him to join the sport. At the sound of his name he turned his head, and heard them regret that he should be away. He earnestly wished he was. He would have been well pleased to see the exploits of his dogs, but to feel them was too much. They were all around him, rending and tearing; and it was not till they had torn his life out that the anger of Diana was satisfied.

Seduction by the Devil

From Thomas Bulfinch, Bulfinch's Mythology, *and Sir Thomas Malory,* Le Morte D'Arthur

Sir Percival is tempted by the Devil in the form of a woman.

Sir Percival looked forth over the sea, and saw a ship come sailing toward him; and it came and stood still under the rock. And when Sir Percival saw this, he went thither, and found the ship covered with silk; and within was a lady of great beauty, and clothed so richly that none might be better.

And when she saw Sir Percival, she saluted him, and Sir Percival returned her salutation. Then he asked her of her country and her lineage. And she said, "I am a gentlewoman that am disinherited, and was once the richest woman of the world." "Damsel," said Sir Percival, "who disinherited you? For I have great pity for you." "Sir," said she, "my enemy is a great and powerful lord, and once he made much of me, so that of his favor and of my beauty I had a little more pride than I ought to have had. Also I said a word that pleased him not. So he drove me from his company and from mine heritage. Therefore I know no good knight nor good man but I get him on my side if I may.

And, because I know that you are a good knight, I beseech you to help me."

Then Sir Percival promised her all the help that he might, and she thanked him.

And at that time the weather was hot and she called to her a gentlewoman, and bade her bring forth a pavilion. And she did so, and pitched it upon the gravel. "Sir," said she, "now may ye rest in this heat of the day." Then he thanked her, and she put off his helm and his shield, and there he slept a great while. Then he awoke, and asked her if she had any meat, and she said yea, and so there was set upon the table all manner of meats that he could think on. Also he drank there the strongest wine that ever he drank, and therewith he was a little inebriated more than he ought to be. With that he beheld the lady, and he thought she was the fairest creature that he ever saw. And then Sir Percival offered her love, and prayed that she would be his. Then she refused him in such a manner that he should be the more ardent on her, and he ceased not to pray her of love. And when she saw him well enchafed, then she said, "Sir Percival, know well I shall not give ye my love unless you swear from henceforth you will be my true servant, and do nothing but that I shall command you. Will you ensure me this, as ye be a true knight?" "Yea," said he, "fair lady, by the faith of my body." And as he said this, by adventure and grace, he saw his sword lie on the ground naked, in whose pommel was a red cross, and the sign of the crucifix thereon. Then he made the sign of the cross upon his forehead, and therewith the pavilion shriveled up, and changed into a smoke and black cloud. And the damsel cried aloud, and hastened to the ship, and so she went with the wind roaring and yelling so that it seemed as if all the water burned after her. Then Sir Percival made great sorrow, and called himself a wretch, saying, "How nigh was I lost!"

"How nigh I was to have lost that which I should never have gotten again! That was my virginity, for that may never be recovered after it is once lost." Then he stopped his bleeding wound with a piece of his shirt.

Thus as he made his moan he saw the same ship which the good man was in the day before come from the east. He was sorely ashamed of himself, and therewith he fell in a swoon. When he awoke he went unto the good man humbly, and there he greeted him.

He asked Sir Percival, "How hast thou done since I departed?"

"Sir," said he, "here was a gentlewoman who led me into deadly sin." And then he told him all.

"Knew ye not that maiden?" said the good man.

"Sir," said he, "nay. But well I know the fiend sent her hither to shame me."

"Ah, good knight," said he, "thou art a fool, for that gentlewoman was the master fiend of hell, which has power above all devils."

Love, Honor and Chastity

From Sir Thomas Malory,
Le Morte D'Arthur

Premarital sex can be more dangerous than you think.

They then plighted troth, each to love the other and never to fail while their lives lasted.

They both so burned with hot love that they agreed to abate their lusts secretly, and Dame Lyones counseled Sir Gareth to sleep in no other place but in the hall; she promised to come there to his bed a little before midnight. This counsel was not so privily kept; rather, it was overheard, for they were both young and tender of age and had not used such crafts before. The Damosel Lynet was a little displeased, and she thought her sister Dame Lyones was a little overhasty in that she could not await the time of her marriage. To save their worship, she thought to abate their hot lusts. She arranged by her subtle crafts that they would not have their intent—neither with the other in their pleasure—until they were married.

So time passed on. After supper came a full disbanding, so that every lord and lady could go unto their rest. But Sir Gareth said plainly he would go no farther than the hall, for in such places—he said—it was convenient for a knight-errant to take his rest. So great couches were brought and thereon feather beds were placed and there he lay down to sleep. Within a while Dame Lyones came, wrapped in a mantle furred with ermine, and lay down beside Sir Gareth; and therewith he began to kiss her.

Then he looked before him and he saw an armed knight with many lights about him; this knight had a long battle-ax in his hand and made grim countenance as if to smite him. When Sir Gareth saw him come in that wise, he leapt out of his bed, got his sword in his hand, and went straight toward that knight. When the knight saw Sir Gareth come so fiercely upon him, he smote him with a thrust through the thick of the thigh, so that the wound was a handbreadth abroad and many veins and sinews were cut in two. Therewith Sir Gareth smote him upon the helmet such a buffet that he fell groveling; then Gareth leapt over him, unlaced his helmet, and smote off his head from the body. But Gareth bled so fast that he could not stand; so he lay down upon his bed and swooned and looked as if he were dead.

Then Dame Lyones cried aloud so that her brother Sir Gryngamore heard and came down; when he saw Sir Gareth so shamefully wounded he was sore displeased and said, "I am shamed that this noble knight is thus dishonored. Sister, how may this be that ye are here and this noble knight is thus wounded?"

"Brother," she said, "I cannot tell you, for it was not done by me or with my assent. Since he is my lord, and I am his—and he must be my husband—therefore, my brother, I wish that ye know that I am not ashamed to be with him, or to do him all the pleasure that I can."

"Sister," said Sir Gryngamore, "I wish you to know it and Sir Gareth also: it was never done by me. Nor was it with my assent that this unfortunate deed was done."

They staunched his bleeding as well they could, and Sir Gryngamore and Dame Lyones made great sorrow. Forthwith the Damosel Lynet came and took up the head in the sight of them all and anointed it with an ointment where it was smitten off; and she did in the same wise to the other part where the head should rest. Then she set them together; they stuck as fast as ever they did, and the knight easily arose. The Damosel Lynet then put him in her chamber.

All this Sir Gryngamore and Dame Lyones saw, and so did Sir Gareth; he spied well that it was the Damosel Lynet who had ridden with him through the perilous passages.

"Ah, well, damosel," he said, "I thought ye would not have done as ye have done."

"My lord Gareth," said Lynet, "all that I have done I will avow. And all that I have done was for your honor and worship, and that of us all."

Within a while Sir Gareth was nearly recovered and he waxed gay and jocund; he sang, danced, and gamed. He and Dame Lyones were so hot with burning love that they made their covenant for the tenth night following that she should come to his bed. Because he was wounded before, he laid his armor and his sword near his bedside.

Right as she promised, she came; and she was no sooner in his bed but she spied an armed knight coming toward the bed. Therewith she warned Sir Gareth, and quickly through the good help of Dame Lyones he was armed. Then the two knights hurtled together all about the hall with great ire and malice. There was a great light, as if there had been the number of twenty torches both before and behind. Sir Gareth so strained himself that his old wound burst again into bleeding, but he was hot and courageous and took no heed; with great force he struck down that knight, pushed off his helmet, and struck off his head. Then he hewed the head into a hundred pieces, and when he had done so he took up all those pieces and threw them out of a window into the ditches of the castle. When this was done he was so faint that he could scarcely stand for bleeding; and by then he was almost unarmed.

He fell in a deadly swoon to the floor. Then Dame Lyones cried so that Sir Gryngamore heard, and when he came and found Sir Gareth in that plight he made great sorrow. He awakened Sir Gareth and gave him a drink that relieved him wonderfully well. But the sorrow that Dame Lyones made there no tongue may tell, for she so fared with herself as if she would have died.

Right so the Damosel Lynet came before them all. And she had all the gobbets fetched of the head that Sir Gareth had thrown out of the window. Then she anointed them as she had done before and set them together again.

"Well, Damosel Lynet," said Sir Gareth, "I have not deserved all this spite that ye do unto me."

"Sir knight," she said, "I have done nothing but that which I will avow. And all that I have done shall be to your worship and to that of us all."

Then Sir Gareth was staunched of his bleeding. But the leeches said that there was no man who bore life who could heal him thoroughly of his wound except the person who caused that stroke by enchantment.

On Adultery

From Ovid, The Art of Love

Not much has changed on this score since the Roman love poet Ovid (43 B.C.–17 A.D.).

So, that husband of yours is going to be at the party—
Well, I hope he chokes; let him drop dead, who cares?
How am I going to act?—just stare at the girl I'm in love with,
Be just one more guest, let someone else feel your breast,
Let someone else put his arms around you whenever he wants to.
Sit at your side, rub knees, lean on your shoulder a bit?
I can believe what they say of the brawls of the Lapiths and
    Centaurs
Over the fair-haired girl, after the wine went round.
I do not live in the woods, and my members are not like a horse's,
Still I'll be having a time keeping my hands to myself.
Learn what you have to do, and please pay careful attention:
Get there before he does—not that that does any good.
Anyway, get there before him, and when he reclines, you beside
    him,
Modestly on the couch, give my foot just a touch,
Watch me for every nod, for every facial expression,
Catch my signs and return them, never saying a word.
I can talk with my eyebrows and spell out words with my fingers,
I can make you a sign, dipping my finger in wine.
When you think of the tumbles we've had in the hay together,
Touch your cheek with your hand; then I will understand.
If you're a little bit cross with the way I may be behaving,
Let your fingertip rest light on the lobe of an ear.
If, on the other hand, what I am saying should please you,
Darling, keep turning your ring; symbol enough that will be.
Fold your hands on the table, as people do when they're
    praying—
That means you wish him bad luck, yes, and a lot of it, too.
When he mixes your wine, let him drink it himself; so inform him:

Quietly speak to the boy, ask for the kind you enjoy.
When you pass him the cup, let me have a sip as it goes by;
Where you drank I will touch that part first with my lips.
Don't accept any food from a dish that he has first tasted;
Keep his arms from your neck; don't lay your head on his chest;
Don't let his fingers grope in the neck of your dress or your
    bosom;
More than everything else, don't let him kiss you at all.
Don't you kiss him either; you do, and you'll have me announcing
"Hands off there! She's mine"—and then I'll reach out for my
    claim.

I would not dare to defend my absolute absence of morals;
I would not smother my faults under a blanket of lies.
No: I own up; I confess, if any confession can help me;
Wailing *My grievous fault,* how I lash out at my sins!
I hate what I am, and yet, for all my desiring,
Cannot be anything else—what a misfortune to bear!
Borne along like a ship tossed on tempestuous waters,
Out of control, I lack willpower to keep me aright.
There is no definite One whose beauty drives me to frenzy;
No: there are hundreds, almost, keeping me always in love.

Tristram and Isoude

From Thomas Bulfinch,
Bulfinch's Mythology

This tragic love story shows how a man struggles to overcome jealousy and temptation, as his love comes into conflict with honor and friendship. Tristram's manly conduct stands in marked contrast with the unmanly behavior of his king faced with the same conflicts.

    Moraunt, a celebrated champion, brother to the queen of Ireland, arrived at the court, to demand tribute from King Mark. The knights of Cornwall are in ill repute, in romance, for their cowardice, and they exhibited it on this occasion. King Mark could find no champion who dared to encounter the Irish knight, till his nephew Tristram, who had not yet received the honors of knighthood, craved to be admitted to the order, offering at the same time to fight the battle of Cornwall against the Irish champion. King Mark assented with reluctance; Tristram received the accolade, which conferred knighthood upon him; and the place and time were assigned for the encounter.

Without attempting to give the details of this famous combat, the first and one of the most glorious of Tristram's exploits, we shall say only that the young knight, though severely wounded, cleft the head of Moraunt, leaving a portion of his sword in the wound. Moraunt, half dead with his wound and the disgrace of his defeat, hastened to hide himself in his ship, sailed away with all speed for Ireland, and died soon after arriving in his own country.

The kingdom of Cornwall was thus delivered from its tribute. Tristram, weakened by loss of blood, fell senseless. His friends flew to his assistance. They dressed his wounds, which in general healed readily, but the lance of Moraunt was poisoned, and one wound which it made yielded to no remedies, but grew worse day by day. The surgeons could do no more. Tristram asked permission of his uncle to depart, and seek aid in the kingdom of England. With his consent he embarked, and, after tossing for many days on the sea, was driven by the winds to the coast of Ireland. He landed, full of joy and gratitude that he had escaped the peril of the sea, took his rote, and began to play. It was a summer evening, and the king of Ireland and his daughter, the beautiful Isoude, were at a window which overlooked the sea. The strange harper was sent for, and conveyed to the palace, where, finding that he was in Ireland, whose champion he had lately slain, he concealed his name, and called himself Tramtris. The queen undertook his care, and by a medicated bath gradually restored him to health. His skill in music and in games occasioned his being frequently called to court, and he became instructor of the Princess Isoude in minstrelsy and poetry, who profited so well under his care, that she soon had no equal in the kingdom, except her instructor.

At this time a tournament was held, at which many knights of the Round Table, and others, were present. On the first day a Seracen prince, named Palamedes, obtained the advantage over all. They brought him to the court, and gave him a feast, at which Tristram, just recovering from his wound, was present. The fair Isoude appeared on this occasion in all her charms. Palamedes could not behold them without emotion, and made no effort to conceal his love. Tristram perceived it, and the pain he felt from jealousy taught him how dear the fair Isoude had already become to him.

Next day the tournament was renewed. Tristram, still feeble from his wound, rose during the night, took his arms, and concealed them in a forest near the place of the contest, and, after it had begun, mingled with the combatants. He overthrew all that encountered him, in particular Palamedes, whom he brought to the ground with a stroke of his lance, and then fought him hand to hand, bearing off the prize of the tourney. But his exertions caused his wound to reopen; he bled fast, and in this sad state, yet in triumph, they bore him to the palace. The fair Isoude devoted herself to his relief with an interest which grew more vivid day by day; and her skillful care soon restored him to health.

It happened one day that a damsel of the court, entering the closet where Tristram's arms were deposited, perceived that a part of the sword had been broken off. It occurred to her that the missing portion was like that which was left in the skull of Moraunt, the Irish champion. She imparted her thought to the queen, who compared the fragment taken from her brother's wound with the sword of Tristram, and was satisfied that it was part of the same, and that the weapon of Tristram was that which reft her brother's life. She laid her griefs and resentment before the king, who satisfied himself with his own eyes of the truth of her suspicions. Tristram was cited before the whole court, and reproached with having dared to present himself before them after having slain their kinsman. He acknowledged that he had fought with Moraunt to settle the claim for tribute, and said that it was by force of winds and waves alone that he was thrown on their coast. The queen demanded vengeance for the death of her brother; the fair Isoude trembled and grew pale, but a murmur rose from all the assembly that the life of one so handsome and so brave should not be taken for such a cause, and generosity finally triumphed over resentment in the mind of the king. Tristram was dismissed in safety, but commanded to leave the kingdom without delay, and never to return thither under pain of death. Tristram went back, with restored health, to Cornwall.

King Mark made his nephew give him a minute recital of his adventures. Tristram told him all minutely; but when he came to speak of the fair Isoude, he described her charms with a warmth and energy such as none but a lover could display. King Mark was fascinated with the description, and, choosing a favorable time, demanded a boon of his nephew, who readily granted it. The king made him swear upon the holy relics that he would fulfill his commands. Then Mark directed him to go to Ireland and obtain for him the fair Isoude to be queen of Cornwall.

Tristram believed it was certain death for him to return to Ireland; and how could he act as ambassador for his uncle in such a cause? Yet, bound by his oath, he hesitated not for an instant. He only took the precaution to change his armor. He embarked for Ireland; but a tempest drove him to the coast of England, near Camelot, where King Arthur was holding his court, attended by the knights of the Round Table, and many others, the most illustrious in the world.

Tristram kept himself unknown. He took part in many jousts; he fought many combats, in which he covered himself with glory. One day he saw among those recently arrived the king of Ireland, father of the fair Isoude. This prince, accused of treason against his liege sovereign, Arthur, came to Camelot to free himself of the charge. Blaanor, one of the most redoubtable warriors of the Round Table, was his accuser, and Argius, the king, had neither youthful vigor nor strength to encounter him. He must therefore seek a champion to sustain his innocence. But the knights of the Round Table were not at liberty to fight against one another, unless in a quarrel of their own. Argius heard of the great renown of the unknown knight; he also was witness of his exploits. He sought him, and conjured him to adopt his defense, and on his oath declared that he was innocent of the crime of which he was accused. Tristram readily consented, and made himself known to the king, who on his part promised to reward his exertions, if successful, with whatever gift he might ask.

Tristram fought with Blaanor, and overthrew him, and held his life in his power. The fallen warrior called on him to use his right of conquest and strike the fatal blow. "God forbid," said Tristram, "that I should take the life of so brave a knight!" He raised him up and restored him to his friends. The judges of the field decided that the king of Ireland was acquitted of the charge against him, and they led Tristram in triumph to his tent. King Argius, full of gratitude, conjured Tristram to accompany him to his kingdom. They departed together, and arrived in Ireland; and the queen, forgetting her resentment for her brother's death, exhibited to the preserver of her husband's life nothing but gratitude and goodwill.

How happy a moment for Isoude, who knew that her father had promised his deliverer whatever boon he might ask. But the unhappy Tristram gazed on her with despair at the thought of the cruel oath which bound him. His magnanimous soul subdued the force of his love. He revealed the oath which he had taken, and with trembling voice demanded the fair Isoude for his uncle.

Argius consented, and soon all was prepared for the departure of Isoude. Brengwain, her favorite maid-of-honor, was to accompany her. On the day of departure the queen took aside this devoted attendant, and told her that she had observed that her daughter and Tristram were attached to one another, and that to avert the bad effects of this inclination she had procured from a powerful fairy a potent philter (love-draught), which she directed Brengwain to administer to Isoude and to King Mark on the evening of their marriage.

Isoude and Tristram embarked together. A favorable wind filled the sails and promised them a fortunate voyage. The lovers gazed upon one another and could not repress their sighs. Love seemed to light up all his fires on their lips, as in their hearts. The day was warm; they suffered from thirst. Isoude first complained. Tristram descried the bottle containing the love-draught, which Brengwain had been so imprudent as to leave in sight. He took it, gave some of it to the charming Isoude, and drank the remainder himself. The dog Houdain licked the cup. The ship arrived in Cornwall, and Isoude was married to King Mark. The old monarch was delighted with his bride, and his gratitude to Tristram was unbounded. He loaded him with honors and made him chamberlain of his palace, thus giving him access to the queen at all times.

In the midst of the festivities of the court which followed the royal marriage, an unknown minstrel one day presented himself, bearing a harp of peculiar construction. He excited the curiosity of King Mark by refusing to play upon it till he should grant him a boon. The king having promised to grant his request, the minstrel, who was none other than the Saracen knight, Sir Palamedes, the lover of the fair Isoude, sung to the harp a lay, in which he demanded Isoude as the promised gift. King Mark could not by the laws of knighthood withhold the boon. The lady was mounted on her horse and led away by her triumphant lover. Tristram, it is needless to say, was absent at the time and did not return until after their departure. When he heard what had taken place, he seized his rote and hastened to the shore, where Isoude and her new master had already embarked. Tristram played upon his rote, and the sound reached the ears of Isoude, who became so deeply affected that Sir Palamedes was induced to return with her to land, that they might see the unknown musician. Tristram watched his opportunity, seized the lady's horse by the bridle, and plunged with her into the forest, tauntingly informing his rival that "what he had got by the harp he had lost by the rote." Palamedes pursued, and a combat was about to commence, the result of which must have been fatal to one or other of these gallant knights but Isoude stepped between them, and, addressing Palamedes, said, "You tell me that you love me; you will not then deny me the request I am about to make?" "Lady," he replied, "I will perform your bidding." "Leave, then," said she, "this contest, and repair to King Arthur's court, and salute Queen Guenever for me; tell her that there are in the world but two ladies, herself and I, and two lovers, hers and mine; and come thou not in future in any place where I am." Palamedes burst into tears. "Ah, lady," said he, "I will obey you; but I beseech you that you will not forever steel your heart against me." "Palamedes," she replied, "may I never taste of joy again if I ever quit my first love." Palamedes then went his way. The lovers remained a week in concealment, after which Tristram restored Isoude to her husband, advising him in future to reward minstrels in some other way.

The king showed much gratitude to Tristram, but in the bottom of his heart he cherished bitter jealousy of him. One day Tristram and Isoude were alone together in her private chamber. A base and cowardly knight of the court, named Andret, spied them through a keyhole. They sat at a table of chess, but were not attending to the game. Andret brought the king, having first raised his suspicions, and placed him so as to watch their motions. The king saw enough to confirm his suspicions, and he burst into the apartment with his sword drawn, and had nearly slain Tristram before he was put on his guard. But Tristram avoided the blow, drew his sword, and drove before him the cowardly monarch, chasing him through all the apartments of the palace, giving him frequent blows with the flat of his sword, while he cried in vain to his knights to save him. They were not inclined, or did not dare interpose on his behalf.

After this affair Tristram was banished from the kingdom, and Isoude shut up in a tower which stood on the bank of a river. Tristram could not resolve to depart without some further communication with his beloved, so he concealed himself in the forest till at last he contrived to attract her attention by means of twigs, which he curiously peeled and sent down the stream under her window. By this means many secret interviews were obtained. Tristram dwelt in the forest, sustaining himself by game, which the dog Houdain ran down for him; for this faithful animal was unequaled in the chase, and knew so well his master's wish for concealment that in the pursuit of his game he never barked. At length Tristram departed, but left Houdain with Isoude, as a remembrancer of him.

Sir Tristram wandered through various countries, achieving the most perilous enterprises and covering himself with glory, yet unhappy at the separation from his beloved Isoude. At length King Mark's territory was invaded by a neighboring chieftain, and he was forced to summon his nephew to his aid. Tristram obeyed the call, put himself at the head of his uncle's vassals, and drove the enemy out of the country. Mark was full of gratitude, and Tristram, restored to favor and to the society of his beloved Isoude, seemed at the summit of happiness. But a sad reverse was at hand.

Tristram had brought with him a friend named Pheredin, son of the king of Brittany. This young knight saw Queen Isoude, and could not resist her charms. Knowing the love of his friend for the queen, and that that love was returned, Pheredin concealed his own, until his health failed, and he feared he was drawing near his end. He then wrote to the beautiful queen that he was dying for love of her.

The gentle Isoude, in a moment of pity for the friend of Tristram, returned him an answer so kind and compassionate that it restored him to life. A few days afterward Tristram found this letter. The most terrible jealousy took possession of his soul; he would have slain Pheredin, who with difficulty made his escape. Then Tristram mounted his horse, and rode to the forest, where for ten days he took no rest nor food. At length he was found by a damsel lying almost dead by the brink of a fountain. She recognized him, and tried in vain to rouse his attention. At last, recollecting his love for music, she went and got her harp, and played thereon. Tristram was roused from his reverie; tears flowed; he breathed more freely; he took the harp from the maiden, and sung this lay, with a voice broken with sobs:

"Sweet I sang in former days,
Kind love perfected my lays:
Now my art alone displays
The woe that on my being preys.

"Charming love, delicious power,
Worshiped from my earliest hour,
Thou who life on all dost shower,
Love! my life thou dost devour.

"In death's hour I beg of thee,
Isoude, dearest enemy,
Thou who erst couldst kinder be,
When I'm gone, forget not me.

"On my gravestone passers by
Oft will read, as low I lie,
'Never wight in love could vie
With Tristram, yet she let him die.'"

Tristram, having finished his lay, wrote it off and gave it to the damsel, conjuring her to present it to the queen.

Meanwhile Queen Isoude was inconsolable at the absence of Tristram. She discovered that it was caused by the fatal letter which she had written to Pheredin. Innocent, but in despair at the sad effects of her letter, she wrote another to Pheredin, charging him never to see her again. The unhappy lover obeyed this cruel decree. He plunged into the forest and died of grief and love in a hermit's cell.

Isoude passed her days in lamenting the absence and unknown fate of Tristram. One day her jealous husband, having entered her chamber unperceived, overheard her singing the following lay:

"My voice to piteous wail is bent,
My harp to notes of languishment;
Ah, love! delightsome days be meant
For happier wights, with hearts content.

"Ah, Tristram! far away from me,
Art thou from restless anguish free?
Ah! couldst thou so one moment be,
From her who so much loveth thee?"

The king, hearing these words, burst forth in a rage; but Isoude was too wretched to fear his violence. "You have heard me," she said; "I confess it all. I love Tristram, and always shall love him. Without doubt he is dead, and died for me. I no longer wish to live. The blow that shall finish my misery will be most welcome."

The king was moved at the distress of the fair Isoude, and perhaps the idea of Tristram's death tended to allay his wrath. He left the queen in charge of her women, commanding them to take especial care lest her despair should lead her to do harm to herself.

Tristram, meanwhile, distracted as he was, rendered a most important service to the shepherds by slaying a gigantic robber named Taullas, who was in the habit of plundering their flocks and rifling their cottages. The shepherds, in their gratitude to Tristram, bore him in triumph to King Mark to have him bestow on him a suitable reward. No wonder Mark failed to recognise in the half-clad wild man before him his nephew Tristram; but grateful for the service the unknown had rendered, he ordered him to be well taken care of, and gave him in charge to the queen and her women. Under such care Tristram rapidly recovered his serenity and his health, so that the romancer tells us he became handsomer than ever. King Mark's jealousy revived with Tristram's health and good looks, and, in spite of his debt of gratitude so greatly increased, he again banished him from the court.

Sir Lancelot Disgraced

From Thomas Bulfinch,
Bulfinch's Mythology

Sir Lancelot fails for the first time in his quest for the Holy Grail because of his sinful love.

But Sir Lancelot rode overthwart and endlong in a wild forest and kept to no path, but as wild adventure led him. And at last he came to a stony crossroads, which departed two ways in wasteland, and by the crossroads was a stone that was made of marble, but it was so dark that Sir Lancelot might not see what it was. Then Sir Lancelot looked by him, and saw an old chapel, and there he thought he would find people. And Sir Lancelot tied his horse to a tree, and there he took off his shield, and hung it upon a tree. And then he went to the chapel door, and found it waste and broken. And within he found a fair altar full richly arrayed with cloth of clean silk, and there stood a fair, clean candlestick which bore six great candles, and the candlestick was of silver. And when Sir

Lancelot saw this light, he had great will to enter into the chapel, but he could find no place where he might enter: then was he passing heavy and dismayed. And he returned and came again to his horse, and took off his saddle and his bridle, and let him pasture; and unlaced his helm, and ungirded his sword, and laid him down to sleep upon his shield before the cross.

And as he lay, half waking and half sleeping, he saw come by him two palfreys, both fair and white, which bare a litter, on which lay a sick knight. And when he was nigh the cross, he there abode still. And Sir Lancelot heard him say, "O sweet Lord, when shall this sorrow leave me, and when shall the holy vessel come by me whereby I shall be healed?" And thus a great while complained the knight, and Sir Lancelot heard it. Then Sir Lancelot saw the candlestick, with the lighted tapers, come before the cross, but he could see nobody that brought it. Also here came a salver of silver and the holy vessel of the Holy Grail; and therewith the sick knight sat him upright, and held up both his hands, and said, "Fair, sweet Lord, which is here within the holy vessel, take heed to me, that I may be whole of this great malady." And therewith, upon his hands and upon his knees, he went so nigh that he touched the holy vessel and kissed it. And anon he was whole. Then the holy vessel went into the chapel again, with the candlestick and the light, so that Sir Lancelot wist not what became of it.

Then the sick knight rose up and kissed the cross; and anon his squire brought him his arms and asked his lord how he did. "I thank God right heartily," said he, "for, through the holy vessel, I am healed. But I have great marvel of this sleeping knight, who had neither grace nor power to awake during the time that the holy vessel had been here present." "I dare it right well say," said the squire, "that this same knight is stained with some manner of deadly sin, whereof he was never confessed." So they departed.

Then Sir Lancelot woke up, and set himself upright, and thought about of what he had seen, and whether it were dreams or not. And he was passing heavy, and knew not what to do. And he said: "My sin and my wretchedness hath brought me into great dishonor. For when I sought worldly adventures and worldly desires, I always achieved them, and had the better in every place, and never was I discomfited in any quarrel, were it right or wrong. And now I take upon me the adventure of holy things, I see and understand that my old sin hinders me, so that I had no power to stir nor to speak when the holy blood appeared before me." So thus he sorrowed till it was day, and heard the fowls of the air sing. Then was he somewhat comforted.

Then he departed from the cross into the forest. And there he found a hermitage, and a hermit therein, who was going to mass. So when mass was done, Sir Lancelot called the hermit to him, and prayed him out of charity to hear his confession. "With a goodwill," said the good man.

And then he told that good man all his life, and how he had loved a queen unmeasurably many years. "And all my great deeds of arms that I have done, I did the most part for the queen's sake, and for her sake would I do battle, were it right or wrong, and never did I battle all only for God's sake, but for to win honor, and to cause me to be better beloved; and little or nothing did I thank God for it. I pray you counsel me."

"I will counsel you," said the hermit, "if ye will insure me that ye will never come in that queen's fellowship as much as ye may forbear." And then Sir Lancelot promised the hermit, by his faith, that he would no more come in her company. "Look that your heart and your mouth accord," said the good man, "and I shall ensure ye that ye shall have more worship than ever ye had."

Apollo and Daphne

From Thomas Bulfinch,
Bulfinch's Mythology

A god lusts for what he cannot have, but ends up doing a good deed.

Daphne was Apollo's first love. It was not brought about by accident, but by the malice of Cupid. Apollo saw the boy playing with his bow and arrows; and being himself elated with his recent victory over Python, he said to him, "What have you to do with warlike weapons, saucy boy? Leave them for hands worthy of them. Behold the conquest I have won by means of them over the vast serpent who stretched his poisonous body over acres of the plain! Be content with your torch, child, and kindle up your flames, as you call them, where you will, but presume not to meddle with my weapons." Venus's boy heard these words, and rejoined, "Your arrows may strike all things else, Apollo, but mine shall strike you." So saying, he took his stand on a rock of Parnassus, and drew from his quiver two arrows of different workmanship, one to excite love, the other to repel it. The former was of gold and sharp pointed, the latter blunt and tipped with lead. With the leaden shaft he struck the nymph Daphne, the daughter of the river god Peneus, and with the golden one Apollo, through the heart. Forthwith the god was seized with love for the maiden, and she abhorred the thought of loving. Her delight was in woodland sports and in the spoils of the chase. Many lovers sought her, but she spurned them all, ranging the woods, and taking no thought of Cupid nor of Hymen. Her father often said to her, "Daughter, you owe me a son-in-law; you owe me grandchildren." She, hating the thought of marriage as a crime, with her beautiful face tinged all over with blushes, threw her arms around her father's neck, and said, "Dearest father, grant me this favor, that I may always remain unmarried, like Diana." He consented, but at the same time said, "Your own face will forbid it."

Apollo loved her, and longed to obtain her; and he who gives oracles to all the world was not wise enough to look into his own fortunes. He saw her hair flung loose over her shoulders, and said, "If so charming is disorder, what would it be if arranged?" He saw her eyes bright as stars; he saw her lips, and was not satisfied with only seeing them. He admired her hands and arms, naked to the shoulder, and whatever was hidden from view he imagined more beautiful still. He followed her; she fled, swifter than the wind, and delayed not a moment at his entreaties. "Stay," said he, "daughter of Peneus; I am not a foe. Do not fly me as a lamb flies the wolf, or a dove the hawk. It is for love I pursue you. You make me miserable, for fear you should fall and hurt yourself on these stones, and I should be the cause. Pray run slower, and I will follow slower. I am no clown, no rude peasant. Jupiter is my father, and I am lord of Delphos and Tenedos, and know all things, present and future. I am the god of song and the lyre. My arrows fly true to the mark; but, alas! An arrow more fatal than mine has pierced my heart! I am the god of medicine, and know the virtues of all healing plants. Alas! I suffer a malady that no balm can cure!"

And the nymph continued her flight and left his plea half uttered. And even as she fled she charmed him. The wind blew her garments, and her unbound hair streamed loose behind her. The god grew impatient to find his wooings thrown away, and, sped by Cupid, gained upon her in the race. It was like a hound pursuing a hare, with open jaws ready to seize, while the feebler animal darts forward, slipping from the very grasp. So flew the god and the virgin—he on the wings of love, and she on those of fear. The pursuer is the more rapid, however, and gains upon her, and his panting breath blows upon her hair. Her strength begins to fail, and, ready to sink, she calls upon her father, the river god: "Help me, Peneus! Open the earth to enclose me, or change my form, which has brought me into this danger!" Scarcely had she spoken when a stiffness seized all her limbs; her bosom began to be enclosed in a tender bark; her hair became leaves; her arms became branches; her foot stuck fast in the ground, as a root; her face became a treetop, retaining nothing of its former self but its beauty. Apollo stood amazed. He touched the stem, and felt the flesh tremble under the new bark. He embraced the branches, and lavished kisses on the wood. The branches shrank from his lips. "Since you cannot be my wife," said he, "thou shall assuredly be my tree. I will wear you for my crown; I will decorate with you my harp and my quiver; and when the great Roman conquerors lead up the triumphal pomp to the Capitol, you shall be woven into wreaths for their brows. And, as eternal youth is mine, you also shall be always green, and your leaf know no decay." The nymph, now changed into a Laurel tree, bowed its head in grateful acknowledgment.

The Narcissist

From Thomas Bulfinch,
Bulfinch's Mythology

What happens when a beautiful young man falls in love with himself? The lady he spurns gives him a taste of his own medicine. He ends up jilting himself!

Echo was a beautiful nymph, fond of the woods and hills, where she devoted herself to woodland sports. She was a favorite of Diana, and attended her in the chase. But Echo had one failing; she was fond of talking, and whether in chat or argument, would have the last word. One day Juno was seeking her husband, who, she had reason to fear, was amusing himself among the nymphs. Echo by her talk contrived to detain the goddess till the nymphs made their escape. When Juno discovered it, she passed sentence upon Echo in these words: "You shall forfeit the use of that tongue with which you have cheated me, except for that one purpose you are so fond of—*reply*. You shall still have the last word, but no power to speak first."

This nymph saw Narcissus, a beautiful youth, as he pursued the chase upon the mountains. She loved him and followed his footsteps. O how she longed to address him in the softest accents, and win him to converse! But it was not in her power. She waited with impatience for him to speak first, and had her answer ready. One day the youth, being separated from his companions, shouted aloud, "Who's here?" Echo replied, "Here." Narcissus looked around, but seeing no one, called out, "Come." Echo answered, "Come." As no one came, Narcissus called again, "Why do you shun me?" Echo asked the same question. "Let us join one another," said the youth. The maid answered with all her heart in the same words, and hastened to the spot, ready to throw her arms about his neck. He started back, exclaiming, "Hands off! I would rather die than you should have me!" "Have me," said she; but it was all in vain. He left her, and she went to hide her blushes in the recesses of the woods. From that time forth she lived in caves and among mountain cliffs. Her form faded with grief, till at last all her flesh shrank away. Her bones were changed into rocks and there was nothing left of her but her voice. With that she is still ready to reply to anyone who calls her, and keeps up her old habit of having the last word.

Narcissus's cruelty in this case was not the only instance. He shunned all the rest of the nymphs, as he had done poor Echo. One day a maiden who had in vain endeavored to attract him uttered a prayer that he might some time or other feel what it was to love and meet no return of affection. The avenging goddess heard and granted the prayer.

There was a clear fountain, with water like silver, to which the shepherds never drove their flocks, nor the mountain goats resorted, nor any of the beasts of the forests; neither was it defaced with fallen leaves or branches; but the grass grew fresh around it, and the rocks sheltered it from the sun. Hither came one day the youth, fatigued with hunting, heated and thirsty. He stooped down to drink, and saw his own image in the water; he thought it was some beautiful water-spirit living in the fountain. He stood gazing with admiration at those bright eyes, those locks curled like the locks of Bacchus or Apollo, the rounded cheeks, the ivory neck, the parted lips, and the glow of health and exercise over all. He fell in love with himself. He brought his lips near to take a kiss; he plunged his arms in to embrace the beloved object. It fled at the touch, but returned again after a moment and renewed the fascination. He could not tear himself away; he lost all thought of food or rest, while he hovered over the brink of the fountain gazing upon his own image. He talked with the supposed spirit: "Why, beautiful being, do you shun me? Surely my face is not one to repel you. The nymphs love me, and you yourself look not indifferent upon me. When I stretch forth my arms you do the same; and you smile upon me and answer my beckonings with the like." His tears fell into the water and disturbed the image. As he saw it depart, he exclaimed, "Stay, I entreat you! Let me at least gaze upon you, if I may not touch you." With this, and much more of the same kind, he cherished the flame that consumed him, so that by degrees he lost his color, his vigor, and the beauty which formerly had so charmed the nymph Echo. She kept near him, however, and when he exclaimed, "Alas! Alas!" she answered him with the same words. He pined away and died; and when his shade passed the Stygian River, it leaned over the boat to catch a look of itself in the waters. The nymphs mourned for him, especially the water-nymphs; and when they smote their breasts Echo smote hers also. They prepared a funeral pile and would have burned the body, but it was nowhere to be found; but in its place a flower, purple within and surrounded with white leaves, which bears the name and preserves the memory of Narcissus.

The Temptation of Sir Gawain

From Anonymous,
Sir Gawain and the Green Knight

Sir Gawain's honor is tested when his host's wife tries to seduce him twice. From the twelfth-century romance of chivalry.

"But that you are Gawain is hard to believe." "Why so?" said the knight, and he asked anxiously, afraid lest he had been at fault in the way he had spoken. But the lady gave him her blessing, and said: "For this reason: anyone so perfect as Gawain is rightly held to be, and in whom courtliness is so completely embodied, could not have remained so long with a lady, without begging a kiss out of his courtesy, by a hint of some trifling kind at the end of a speech." Then Gawain said, "Certainly, be it as you please; I shall kiss at your command, and more, as befits a knight to do, lest he displease you, so urge it no further." At that she comes closer, and takes him in her arms, lovingly bends down and kisses the knight. Graciously they commend each other to Christ; she goes out of the door without another sound, and he prepares at once to rise, hastening himself, calls to his body-servant, selects his clothes, and, when ready, goes out with an easy mind to mass. And afterward he went to his meal which, as was proper, awaited him, and made merry all day, diverting himself, till the moon rose.

"I have wanted to learn from you, sir," the noble lady then said, "if it would not annoy you, what might be the reason that one so young and so valiant as you now are, so courteous, so chivalrous, as you are acknowledged far and wide to be—and in all the records of chivalric conduct, the thing most praised is the faithful practice of love, the gospel of the knightly profession; for, in describing the deeds of true knights, the inscribed title and text of these works is how men have ventured their lives for their true love, and for their love's sake endured grievous times, and have later vindicated themselves by their valor and put an end to their suffering, and brought happiness to their lady's bower by their own good qualities—and you are reputed the noblest knight of your generation, your fame and your honor are spread abroad everywhere, and I have sat beside you here on two separate occasions, yet I have never heard pass your lips any words that had anything to do with love, not one. And you, who are so courteous and polite in your assurances of knightly service, ought to offer readily to teach a young person some lessons in the arts of true love. What! Are you, who enjoy such a reputation, so ignorant, or is it that you consider me too stupid to appreciate your courtly conversation? Shame on you! I have come here all alone and am sitting here to learn from you some amorous accomplishment; do teach me some of your love-lore, while my husband is away from home."

"Upon my faith," said Gawain, "may God reward you! It is a great joy, an immense pleasure to me, that someone so noble as you should come here and trouble yourself with such a humble person, diverting yourself with your knight by showing him every kind of favor; it affords me delight. But to take upon myself the difficult task of expounding true love, and discoursing on the themes of romance and tales of chivalry to you, who, I know well, have more skill in that art, by far, than a hundred such as I am, or ever shall be, as long as I live on this earth, that would be a manifold folly, my noble lady, upon my word it would. I would wist to do what you desire as far as I can, since I am, and always will be, deeply bound to be your faithful servant, so help me God!" In this way that noble lady tested him and tempted him repeatedly, in order to bring him to grief, whatever else she may have intended; but he defended himself so skillfully that no offense was apparent, nor any impropriety on either side, nor were they conscious of anything but contentment.

They spoke fair words, and had much pleasure in so doing; there was great peril between them, should Mary not be mindful of her knight. For that noble princess pressed him so hard, urged him so near to the limit, that he must needs either accept her love there and then, or refuse offensively. He was concerned for his courtesy, lest he should behave like a boor, and even more for his plight if he should commit a sin and be a traitor to the man who owned that castle. "God forbid," said the knight. "That shall not happen!" With some good-natured laughter he parried all the words of fond affection which fell from her lips. Said the lady to the knight, "You deserve to be blamed, if you do not love the person who is here close to you, of all human kind the most sorely stricken at heart, unless you have a sweetheart, someone dearer to you, who pleases you better, and have plighted your troth to that noble lady, pledged it so firmly that you do not wish to break it—and that is what I now believe. And I beg you now to tell me so frankly; for the love of God and all the saints do not conceal the truth deceitfully." The knight said, "By Saint John," and he smiled gently, "I have none whatsoever, upon my honor, nor do I intend to have one at present."

The husband's reaction:

I know all about your kisses and your conduct too, and my wife's wooing of you; I myself brought it about. I sent her to put you to the proof, and truly you seem to me the most faultless knight who ever lived; as a pearl in comparison with a dried pea is of greater value, so, truthfully, is Gawain beside other gallant knights.

MANLINESS TOWARD WOMEN

In what amounts to a medieval version of Emily Post, the following tales and legends of knights and heroes provide a model for how men should— and should not—behave toward women.

Ladies First

From Thomas Bulfinch,
Bulfinch's Mythology

Sir Bohort, who unlike Sir Lancelot succeeds in his quest for the Holy Grail, is forced to choose between rescuing a woman from rape, and saving his brother's life.

On the morrow, as soon as the day appeared, Sir Bohort departed thence, and rode into a forest until the hour of midday. And there befell him a marvelous adventure. For he met, at the parting of two ways, two knights that led Sir Lionel, his brother, all naked, bound upon a strong hackney, and his hands bound before his breast; and each of them held in his hand thorns with which they went beating him, so that he was all bloody before and behind; but he said never a word, but, as he was great of heart, he suffered all that they did to him as though he had felt none anguish. Sir Bohort prepared to rescue his brother. But he looked on the other side of him, and saw a knight dragging along a fair gentlewoman, who cried out, "Saint Mary! Succor your maid!" And when she saw Sir Bohort, she called to him and said, "By the faith that ye owe to knighthood, help me!" When Sir Bohort heard her say thus, he had such sorrow that he knew not what to do. "For if I let my brother be he must be slain, and that would I not for all the earth; and if I help not the maid I am shamed forever." Then he lifted up his eyes and said, weeping, "Fair Lord, whose liegeman I am, keep Sir Lionel, my brother, that none of these knights slay him, and for pity of you, and our Lady's sake, I shall help this maid."

Then he cried out to the knight, "Sir knight, lay your hand off that maid, or else ye be but dead." Then the knight set down the maid, and took his shield, and drew out his sword. And Sir Bohort smote him so hard that it went through his shield and habergeon, on the left shoulder, and he fell down to the earth. Then came Sir Bohort to the maid, "Ye be delivered of this knight this time." "Now," said she, "I pray you lead me where this knight took me." "I shall gladly do it," said Sir Bohort. So he took the horse of the wounded knight and set the gentlewoman upon it, and brought her there where she desired to be. And there he found twelve knights seeking after her; and when she told them how Sir Bohort had delivered her, they made great joy, and besought him to come to her father, a great lord, and he should be right welcome. "Truly," said Sir Bohort, "that may not be; for I have a great adventure to do." So he commended them to God and departed.

Then Sir Bohort rode after Sir Lionel, his brother, by the trace of their horses. Thus he rode, seeking, a great while. Then he overtook a man clothed in a religious clothing, who said, "Sir knight, what seek ye?" "Sir," said Sir Bohort, "I seek my brother, that I saw within a little space beaten by two knights." "Ah, Sir Bohort, trouble not to seek for him, for truly he is dead." Then he showed him a new-slain body, lying in a thick bush; and it seemed to him that it was the body of Sir Lionel. And then he made such sorrow that he fell to the ground in a swoon, and lay there long. And when he came to himself again he said, "Fair brother, since the fellowship of you and me is sundered, shall I never have joy again; and now He that I have taken for my master He be my help!" And when he had said thus, he took up the body in his arms, and put it upon the horse. And then he said to the man, "Canst thou tell me the way to some chapel, where I may bury this body?" "Come on," said the man, "here is one fast by." And so they rode till they saw a fair tower, and beside it a chapel. Then they both alighted, and put the body into a tomb of marble.

Then Sir Bohort commended the good man unto God, and departed. And he rode all that day, and harbored with an old lady. And on the morrow he rode unto the castle in a valley, and there he met with a yeoman. "Tell me," said Sir Bohort, "knowest thou of any adventure?" "Sir," said he, "here shall be under this castle, a great and marvelous tournament." Then Sir Bohort thought to be there, if he might meet with any of the fellowship that were in quest of the Holy Grail; so he turned to a hermitage that was on the border of the forest. And when he was come thither, he found there Sir Lionel his brother, who sat all armed at the entry of the chapel door. And when Sir Bohort saw him, he had great joy, and he alighted off his horse, and said, "Fair brother, when came ye hither?" As soon as Sir Lionel saw him he said, "Ah, Sir Bohort, make ye no false show, for, as for you, I might have been slain, for ye left me in peril of death to go help a gentlewoman; and for that misdeed I now ensure you but death, for ye have right well deserved it."

When Sir Bohort perceived his brother's wrath, he knelt down to the earth and cried him mercy, holding up both his hands, and prayed him to forgive him. "Nay," said Sir Lionel, "thou shalt have but death for it, if I have the upper hand; therefore leap upon thy horse and protect thyself; and if thou do not, I will run upon thee there, while you stand on foot, and so the shame shall be mine, and the harm thine, but of that I care not." When Sir Bohort saw that he must fight with his brother or else die, he knew not what to do. Then his heart counseled him not to do so, inasmuch as Sir Lionel was his elder brother, wherefore he ought to show him reverence. Yet kneeled he down before Sir Lionel's horse's feet, and said, "Fair brother, have mercy upon me and slay me not." But Sir Lionel cared not, for the fiend had brought in him such a will that he should slay him. When he saw that Sir Bohort would not rise to give him battle, he rushed over him, so that he smote him with his horse's feet to the earth, and hurt him sore so, that he swooned of distress. When Sir Lionel saw this, he alighted from his horse to smite off his head; and so he took him by the helm, and would have rent it from his head. But it happened that Sir Colgrevance, a knight of the Round Table, came at that time thither, as it was our Lord's will; and then he beheld how Sir Lionel would have slain his brother, and he knew Sir Bohort, whom he loved right well. Then leapt he down from his horse, and took Sir Lionel by the shoulders, and drew him strongly back from Sir Bohort, and said, "Sir Lionel, will ye slay your brother?" "Why," said Sir Lionel, "will ye slay me? If ye interfere in this, I will slay you, and him after." Then he ran upon Sir Bohort, and would have smitten him; but Sir Colgrevance ran between them, and said, "If ye persist to do so anymore, we two shall meddle together." Then Sir Lionel defied him, and gave him a great stroke through the helm. Then he drew his sword, for he was a passing good knight, and defended himself right manfully. So long endured the battle, that Sir Bohort rose up all anguishly, and beheld Sir Colgrevance, the good knight, fight with his brother for his quarrel. Then was he full sorry and heavy, and thought that, if Sir Colgrevance slew his brother, he should never have joy, and if his brother slew Sir Colgrevance, the shame should ever be his.

Then he would have risen to have parted them, but he had not so much strength as to stand on his feet; so he stayed so long that Sir Colgrevance had the worse, for Sir Lionel was of great chivalry and right hardy. Then cried Sir Colgrevance, "Ah, Sir Bohort, why come ye not to bring me out of peril of death, wherein I have put me to help you?" With that, Sir Lionel smote off his helm, and bore him to the earth. And when he had slain Sir Colgrevance, he ran upon his brother as a friendly man, and gave him such a stroke that he made him stoop. And he that was full of humility prayed him, "For God's sake leave this battle, for if it befell, fair brother, that I slew you, or ye me, we should be dead of that sin." "Pray ye not me for mercy," said Sir Lionel. Then Sir Bohort, all weeping, drew his sword, and said, "Now God have mercy upon me, though I defend my life against my brother." With that Sir Bohort lifted up his sword, and would have stricken his brother. Then heard he a voice that said, "Flee, Sir Bohort, and touch him not." Right so alighted a cloud between them, in the likeness of a fire, and a marvelous flame, so that they both fell to the earth, and lay there a great while in a swoon. And when they came to themselves, Sir Bohort saw that his brother had no harm; and he was right glad, for he dread sore that God had taken vengeance upon him. Then Sir Lionel said to his brother, "Brother, forgive me, for God's sake, all that I have trespassed against you." And Sir Bohort answered, "God forgive it thee, and I do."

Never Use Force Against a Woman

From Sir Thomas Malory,
Le Morte D'Arthur

Now we turn unto Sir Lancelot who rode with the damosel on a fair highway.

"Sir," said the damosel, "here by this way lurks a knight who distresses all ladies and gentlewomen; at the least he robbeth them or lieth by them."

"What?" said Sir Lancelot. "Is he a thief and a knight, and a ravisher of women? He doth shame unto the Order of Knighthood, contrary to his oath. It is a pity that he liveth! But fair damosel, ye shall ride on ahead by yourself and I will keep myself under cover. If he troubles you or distresses you, I shall be your rescue and teach him to be ruled as a knight."

So the maiden rode on by the way at a soft ambling pace; within a while that knight came out on horseback, out of the wood and his page with him. He pulled the damosel from her horse, and then she cried out. With that, Lancelot came as fast as he might till he reached the knight, saying, "Oh, thou false knight and traitor unto knight-hood, who taught thee to distress ladies and gentlewomen?"

When the knight saw Sir Lancelot thus rebuking him he answered not, but drew his sword and rode unto Sir Lancelot. Sir Lancelot threw his spear from him, drew out his sword, and struck the knight such a buffet on the helmet that he split his head and neck unto the throat.

"Now thou hast thy payment which long thou hast deserved!"

"That is truth," said the damosel, "for just as Tarquine watched to destroy good knights, so did this knight lie in wait to destroy and distress ladies."

Attraction to Beauty Is No Excuse

From Sir Thomas Malory,
Le Morte D'Arthur

Tristram and Isoude encounter a host with a strange way of making his guests feel welcome.

They sailed on till by fortune they came near a castle that was called Pleure. There they arrived to repose themselves, thinking it a good harbor for them. But as soon as Sir Tristram was within the castle, they were taken prisoner; the custom of the castle was such that whoever rode by that castle and brought any lady must needs fight with the lord, who was called Breunor. And if Breunor won the field, then the knight-stranger and his lady could be put to death, whoever they were. But if the knight-stranger won the field from Sir Breunor, then he and his lady both could die. This custom was used for many winters; wherefore it was called the Castle Pleure: that is to say, the "Weeping Castle."

When Sir Tristram and La Belle Isoude were thus in prison it happened that a knight and a lady came to them where they were to cheer them; then Sir Tristram said unto the knight and the lady "What is the reason the lord of this castle holdeth us in prison? It was never the custom of any castle of worship that I ever came in, when a knight and a lady asked lodging and the lord received them, afterward to distress those who were his guests."

"Sir," said the knight, "this is the old custom of this castle: when a knight cometh here he must needs fight with our lord, and he who is weaker must lose his head. When that is done, if the lady whom the knight bringeth is uglier than our lord's wife, she must lose her head; but if she is proved fairer than our lady, then the lady of this castle shall lose her head."

"So help me God," said Sir Tristram, "this is a foul and a shameful custom. But one advantage I have: I have a lady who is fair enough—fairer I never saw in all my life-days—and I doubt that for lack of beauty she shall lose her head. And rather than lose my head, I will fight for it in a fair field. Wherefore, sir knight, I pray you tell your lord that I will be ready to-morn—my lady and myself—to do battle, if I may have my horse and my armor."

"Sir," said the knight, "I undertake to see that your desire will be sped right well. Therefore take your rest and see that ye are up betimes to make ready with your lady, for you shall lack nothing that to you behooveth."

Therewith he departed. On the morn betimes that same knight came to Sir Tristram and fetched him out with his lady, brought him the horse and armor that was his own, and bade him make ready for the field. All the estates and commons of that lordship were already there to behold that battle and judgment.

Then Sir Breunor came, the lord of that castle, with his lady muffled, and asked Sir Tristram where his lady was, "for, if thy lady is fairer than mine, with thy sword smite off my lady's head; but if my lady is fairer than thine, with my sword I must strike off her head. And if I may beat thee, thy lady shall be mine and thou shalt lose thy head."

"Sir," said Sir Tristram, "this is a foul and horrible custom; rather than that my lady should lose her head, I had rather lose my own head."

"Nay, nay!" said Sir Breunor. "The ladies shall be first shown together, and one of them shall have her judgment."

"Nay, I will not agree," said Sir Tristram, "for none is here who will give righteous judgment. But I doubt not that my lady is fairer than thine, and that I will prove and make good with my hands. And whoever will say the contrary, I will prove it on his head!"

Therewith Sir Tristram showed forth La Belle Isoude and turned her thrice about with his naked sword in his hand. When Sir Breunor saw that, he did in the same wise turn his lady. But when Sir Breunor beheld La Belle Isoude, he thought that he never saw a fairer lady; thus he feared that his lady's head would be cut off. Then all the people who were present there gave judgment that La Belle Isoude was the fairer lady and the better made.

"How now?" said Sir Tristram. "Meseemeth it were a pity that your lady should lose her head, but because thou and she for a long time have used this wicked custom—and by you both have many good knights and ladies been destroyed—for that cause it would be no loss to destroy you both."

"So help me God," said Sir Breunor, "to tell the truth thy lady is fairer than mine, and that I sorely repent. I hear the people privily say so, for of all women I saw none so fair. Therefore, if thou wilt, slay my lady. I doubt not but I shall slay thee and have thy lady."

"Thou shalt win her," said Sir Tristram, "as dearly as ever knight won lady. But because of thy own judgment and what thou would have done to my lady if she had been uglier, and because of this evil custom, give me thy lady." Therewith Sir Tristram strode unto him and took his lady from him, and with a back-handed stroke he smote off her head.

"Well, knight," said Sir Breunor, "now hast thou done me a spite. Take thy horse, and since I am now ladyless I will win thy lady if I may."

Then they took their horses and came together as if it had been thunder, and Sir Tristram smote Sir Breunor right from his horse. Quickly he rose up and as Sir Tristram came back by him he thrust his horse through both the shoulders, so that the horse ran here and there and fell dead to the ground. Sir Breunor ran quickly to slay Sir Tristram, but he was quick and nimble and left his horse rapidly. Still, before Sir Tristram could dress his shield and his sword, the other gave him three or four heavy strokes.

Then they rushed together like two boars, tracking and traversing mightily and wisely like two noble knights. For this Sir Breunor was a proved knight; he had been ere then the death of so many good knights that it was a pity that he had so long endured. Thus they fought, hurtling here and there, nigh two hours and each was wounded sorely. Then at last Sir Breunor rushed upon Sir Tristram and took him in his arms, for he attributed much to his strength. But Sir Tristram was called the strongest knight of the world, for he was stronger than Sir Lancelot—but Sir Lancelot was better in endurance—so Sir Tristram soon thrust Sir Breunor down groveling. And then he unlaced his helmet and struck off his head.

At that, all those who belonged to the castle came to Tristram and did him homage and fealty, praying him that he would stay there a little while longer to undo that foul custom. This request Sir Tristram granted.

Every Man Thinketh
His Own Lady Fairest

From Sir Thomas Malory,
Le Morte D'Arthur

A fight over Queen Guenever is narrowly avoided.

So Sir Lamorak departed from them and within a while he met Sir Melyagaunt. Sir Lamorak asked him why he loved Queen Guenever, "for I was not far from you when you made your complaint by the chapel."

"Did ye so?" said Sir Melyagaunt. "Then I will abide by it. I love Queen Guenever."

"What will ye do about it?"

"I will prove and make it good that she is the fairest lady of most beauty in the world."

"As to that," said Sir Lamorak, "I say nay thereto. For Queen Morgause of Orkney, mother to Sir Gawain, is the fairest queen and lady who beareth the life."

"That is not so," said Sir Melyagaunt. "And that I will prove with my hands upon thy body!"

"Will ye so?" said Sir Lamorak. "And in a better quarrel I look not to fight."

Then they parted each from the other in great wrath, and they came riding together as if it had been thunder; each smote the other so sorely that their horses fell backward to the earth. Then they left their horses, dressed their shields, and drew their swords.

They hurtled together like wild boars, and thus they fought a great while. For Sir Melyagaunt was a good man and of great might, but Sir Lamorak was too strong for him and put him always back; but each had wounded the other sorely. As they stood thus fighting, by fortune Sir Lancelot and Sir Bleoberys came riding by. Sir Lancelot rode between them and asked them for what cause they fought together, "and ye are both knights of King Arthur."

"Sir," said Melyagaunt, "I shall tell you for what cause we do this battle. I praised my lady Queen Guenever and said she was the fairest lady of the world. But Sir Lamorak said nay thereto, for he said Queen Morgause of Orkney was fairer than she and of more beauty."

"Ah," said Sir Lancelot, "Sir Lamorak, why sayest thou so? It is not thy part to dispraise thy princess when thou art under her obeisance, as we all are." Therewith he alighted on foot and said, "For this quarrel make thee ready. I will prove upon thee that Queen Guenever is the fairest lady and most of beauty in the world."

"Sir," said Sir Lamorak, "I am loath to have ado with you in this quarrel, for every man thinketh his own lady fairest; and though I praise the lady that I love most, ye should not be wroth. For though my lady Queen Guenever is fairest in your eye, wit ye well Queen Morgause is fairest in my eye; so every knight thinketh his own lady fairest. And wit ye well, sir, ye are the man in the world—except Sir Tristram—with whom I am most loath to have ado. But if ye must needs fight with me, I shall endure you as long as I may."

Then Sir Bleoberys spoke and said, "My lord Sir Lancelot, I knew you never so misadvised as ye are now, for Sir Lamorak sayeth to you but reason, and knightly. For I assure you I have a lady and methinketh that she is the fairest lady of the world. Would this be a great reason that ye should be wroth with me for such language? Well ye know that Sir Lamorak is as noble a knight as any I know living, and he hath ever owed you and us all good will. Therefore, I pray you, be good friends."

Then Sir Lancelot said unto Sir Lamorak, "I pray you, forgive me my offense and evil will. And if I was misadvised, I will make amends."

"Sir," said Sir Lamorak, "the amends are soon made between you and me."

How a Man Can Increase and Decrease a Lady's Love

From Andreas Capellanus,
The Art of Courtly Love

The readiness to grant requests is, we say, the same thing in women as overvoluptuousness in men—a thing which all agree should be a total stranger in the court of Love. For he who is so tormented by carnal passion that he cannot embrace anyone in heartfelt love, but basely lusts after every woman he sees, is not called a lover but a counterfeiter of love and a pretender, and he is lower than a shameless dog. Indeed the man who is so wanton that he cannot confine himself to the love of one woman deserves to be considered an impetuous ass. It will therefore be clear to you that you are bound to avoid an overabundance of passion and that you ought not to seek the love of a woman who you know will grant easily what you seek.

A lover should always offer his services and obedience freely to every lady, and he ought to root out all his pride and be very humble. Then, too, he must keep in mind the general rule that lovers must not neglect anything that good manners demand or good breeding suggest, but they should be very careful to do everything of this sort. Love may also be retained by indulging in the sweet and delightful solaces of the flesh, but only in such manner and in such number that they may never seem wearisome to the loved one. Let the lover strive to practice gracefully and manfully any act or mannerism which he has noticed is pleasing to his beloved. A cleric should not, of course, affect the manners or the dress of the laity, for no one is likely to please his beloved, if she is a wise woman, by wearing strange clothing or by practicing manners that do not suit his status. Furthermore a lover should make every attempt to be constantly in the company of good men and to avoid completely the society of the wicked. For association with the vulgar makes a lover who joins them a thing of contempt to his beloved.

Now let us see in what ways love may be decreased. Too many

opportunities for exchanging solaces, too many opportunities of seeing the loved one, too much chance to talk to each other all decrease love, and so does an uncultured appearance or manner of walking on the part of the lover or the sudden loss of his property. Love decreases, too, if the woman finds that her lover is foolish and indiscreet, or if he seems to go beyond reasonable bounds in his demands for love, or if she sees that he has no regard for her modesty and will not forgive her bashfulness. Love decreases, too, if the woman considers that her lover is cowardly in battle, or sees that he is unrestrained in his speech or spoiled by the vice of arrogance.

Stalkers Beware!

From Sir Thomas Malory,
Le Morte D'Arthur

Camping outside the gate of a woman who doesn't want you is not only shameful but stupid—and dangerous.

"Sir," said the Damosel Lynet unto Sir Beaumains, "now ye should be strong and quick, for yonder is your deadly enemy. And at yonder window is my lady, my sister Dame Lyones."

"Where?" said Beaumains.

"Yonder," said the damosel and pointed with her finger.

"That is truth," said Beaumains. "She seemeth from afar the fairest lady that I ever looked upon. And truly I ask no better quarrel than now to do battle. For she shall be my lady, and for her I will fight." He looked steadily up to the window with glad countenance, and the Lady Lyones made a curtsy to him down to the earth, holding up both her hands.

With that, the Red Knight of the Red Lands called to Sir Beaumains, "Leave, sir knight, thy beholding and look at me, I counsel thee. For I warn thee well she is my lady and for her I have done many strong battles."

"If thou have done so,"said Beaumains, "it seems to me it was but wasted labor, for she loveth not thy fellowship. And for thou to love one who loveth not thee is but great folly. If I understood that she were not glad of my coming, I would take thought ere I did battle for her. But I understand from the siege before this castle that she wishes to forgo thy fellowship. Therefore wit thou well, thou Red Knight of the Red Lands, I love her and will rescue her, or else I will die."

"Sayest thou that?" said the Red Knight. "It seems to me that in reason thou ought to be warned by the knights whom thou sawest hanging upon yonder trees."

"Fie, for shame," said Beaumains, "that ever thou shouldest say so or do such evil, for in that thou shamest thyself and all knighthood. And thou may be sure no lady will love thee who knoweth thy wicked customs. And now thou thinkest that the sight of these hanged knights should frighten me? Nay, truly not so. That shameful sight causeth me to have courage and hardiness against thee, much more than I would have had against thee if thou were a well-ruled knight."

Advice to Husbands:
Don't Use Your Wife to Bait a Trap

From Thomas Bulfinch,
Bulfinch's Mythology

And Sir Lancelot rode through many strange countries, till, by fortune, he came to a fair castle; and as he passed beyond the castle, he thought he heard two bells ring. And then he perceived how a falcon came flying over his head toward a high elm; and she had long lines about her feet and she flew unto the elm to take her perch, and the lines got entangled in a bough; and when she would have taken her flight, she hung by the legs fast, and Sir Lancelot saw how she hung and beheld the fair falcon entangled, and he was sorry for her. Then came a lady out of the castle and cried aloud, "O Lancelot, Lancelot, as thou art the flower of all knights, help me to get my hawk; for if my hawk be lost, my lord will slay me, he is so hasty." "What is your lord's name?" said Sir Lancelot. "His name is Sir Phelot, a knight that belongeth to the king of North Wales." "Well, fair lady, since ye know my name and require me of knighthood to help you, I will do what I may to get your hawk; and yet, in truth, I am an ill climber and the tree is passing high and few boughs to help me." And therewith Sir Lancelot alighted and tied his horse to a tree, and prayed the lady to unarm him. And when he was unarmed, he put off his jerkin, and with might and force he clomb up to the falcon, and tied the lines to a rotten bough, and threw the hawk down with it; and the lady got the hawk in her hand. Then suddenly there came out of the castle her husband all armed, and with his naked sword in his hand, and said, "O Knight Lancelot, now have I got thee as I would;" and stood at the bottom of the tree to slay him. "Ah, lady!" said Sir Lancelot, "why have ye betrayed me?" "She hath done," said Sir Phelot, "but as I commanded her; and therefore there is none other way but thine hour is come, and thou must die." "That were shame unto thee," said Sir Lancelot; "thou an armed knight to slay a naked man by treason." "Thou gettest none other grace," said Sir Phelot, "and therefore help thyself if thou canst." "Alas!" said Sir Lancelot, "that ever a knight should die weaponless!" And therewith he turned his eyes upward and downward; and over his head he saw a big bough leafless, and he brake it off from the trunk. And then he came lower, and watched how his own horse stood; and suddenly he leapt on the further side of his horse from the knight. Then Sir Phelot lashed at him eagerly, meaning to have slain him. But Sir Lancelot put away the stroke with the big bough, and smote Sir Phelot therewith on the side of the head, so that he fell down in a swoon to the ground. Then Sir Lancelot took his sword out of his hand and struck his head from the body. Then said the lady, "Alas! Why hast thou slain my husband?" "I am not the cause," said Sir Lancelot, "for with falsehood ye would have slain me, and now it is fallen on yourselves." Thereupon Sir Lancelot got all his armor and put it upon him hastily for fear of more resort, for the knight's castle was so nigh. And as soon as he might, he took his horse and departed, and thanked God he had escaped that adventure.

The Death of Robin Hood

From Thomas Bulfinch,
Bulfinch's Mythology

Robin Hood returned to Sherwood Forest, and there met his death. For one day, being wounded in a fight, he fled out of the battle with Little John. And being at some distance, Robin Hood said to his lieutenant, "Now truly I cannot shoot even one shot more, for the arrows will not fly. For I am sore wounded. So I will go to my cousin, the abbess, who dwells near here in Kirkley Hall, and she shall bleed me, that I may be well again." So Robin Hood left Little John, and he went his way to Kirkley; and reaching the Hall, his strength nearly left him, yet he knocked heavily at the door. And his cousin came down first to let him in. And when she saw him she knew that it was her cousin Robin Hood, and she received him with a joyful face. Then said Robin, "You see me, my cousin, how weak I am. Therefore I pray you to bleed me, that I may be whole again." And his cousin took him by the hand, and led him into an upper room, and laid him on a bed, and she bled him. But the treacherous woman tied not up the vein again, but left him so that his life began to flow from him. And he, finding his strength leaving him, thought to escape; but he could not, for the door was locked, and the casement window was so high that he might not leap down from it. Then, knowing that he must die, he reached forth his hand to his bugle horn, which lay by him on the bed. And setting the horn to his mouth, he blew weakly, though with all his strength, three blasts upon it. And Little John, as he sat under the tree in the greenwood, heard his blowing, and he said, "Now must Robin be near death, for his blast is very weak."

And he got up and ran to Kirkley Hall as fast as he might. And coming to the door, he found it locked; but he broke it down, and so came to Robin Hood. And coming to the bed, he fell upon his knees and said, "Master, I beg a boon of thee—that thou lettest me burn down Kirkley Hall and all the nunnery." "Nay," quoth Robin Hood; "nay, I cannot grant you your boon; for never in my life did I hurt woman, or man in woman's company, nor shall it be done when I die. But for me, give me my long bow, and I will let fly an arrow, and where you shall find the arrow, there bury me. And make my grave long and broad, that I may rest easily; and place my head upon a green sod, and place my bow at my side." And these words Little John readily promised him, so that Robin Hood was pleased. And they buried him as he had asked, an arrow-shot from Kirkley Hall.

Revenge Against Women Is Shameful

From Sir Thomas Malory,
Le Morte D'Arthur

Sir Lancelot rode in many wild ways throughout the moors and marshes, and as he rode in a valley he saw a knight chasing a lady with a naked sword in order to slay her. But just as this knight would have slain this lady, she cried to Sir Lancelot and prayed him to rescue her. When he saw that mischief, he took his horse and rode between them, saying, "Knight, fie, for shame! Why wilt thou slay this lady? Thou dost shame unto thee and all knights."

"What hast thou to do between me and my wife?" said the knight. "I will slay her despite my head."

"That shall ye not," said Sir Lancelot, "for instead we two will have ado together."

"Sir Lancelot," said the knight, "thou dost not thy part, for this lady hath betrayed me."

"It is not so," said the lady. "Truly he sayeth wrong about me. Because I love and cherish my cousin-germane, he is jealous; but as I shall answer to God, there was never sin between us. But, sir, as thou art called the most worshipful knight of the world I require thee of true knighthood to help me and save me. For whatsoever he says, he will slay me; he is without mercy."

"Have ye no fear," said Lancelot. "It shall not lie in his power."

"Sir," said the knight, "in your sight I will be ruled as ye will have me."

So Sir Lancelot rode with the knight on one side and the lady on the other. They had ridden only a short while when the knight bade Sir Lancelot turn and look behind him, and said, "Sir, yonder come men of arms riding after us."

So Sir Lancelot turned and suspected no treason. But therewith the knight went to his lady's side, and suddenly he cut off her head. When Sir Lancelot had spied what he had done, he said, "Traitor, thou hast shamed me forever!" And suddenly he alighted from his horse and pulled out his sword to slay the knight. But therewith he fell flat to the earth and gripped Sir Lancelot by the thighs and cried mercy.

"Fie on thee!" said Sir Lancelot. "Thou shameful knight, thou maist have no mercy; therefore arise and fight with me."

"Nay," said the knight, "I will never arise till ye grant me mercy."

"Now I will offer thee fairly," said Lancelot. "I will unarm myself to my shirt, and I will have nothing upon me but my shirt and my sword in my hand. Then if thou canst slay me, thou art quit forever."

"Nay, sir, that will I never do."

"Well," said Sir Lancelot, "take this lady and her head and bear them with thee. And here thou shalt swear upon my sword to bear them always upon thy back and never to rest till thou come to Queen Guenever."

"Sir," said he, "that I will do, by the faith of my body."

"Now," said Lancelot, "tell me, what is your name?"

"Sir, my name is Pedyvere."

"In a shameful hour thou were born," said Lancelot.

So Pedyvere departed with the dead lady and the head, and found the queen with King Arthur at Winchester. There he told all the truth.

"Sir knight," said the queen, "this is a horrible and shameful deed, and a great rebuke for Sir Lancelot; but, not withstanding, his worship is known in many diverse countries. I shall give you this as penance; make ye as good shift as ye can: ye shall bear this lady with you on horseback unto the Pope of Rome, and from him receive your penance for your foul deeds. And ye shall never rest one night where ye rest another; if ye go to any bed, the dead body shall lie with you."

He made his oath and so departed. As it telleth in the French book, when he came to Rome the Pope bade him go back unto Queen Guenever; and in Rome his lady was buried by the Pope's commandment. Later this knight, Sir Pedyvere, fell into great goodness and was a holy man and a hermit.

What Women *Really* Want in a Man

From Thomas Bulfinch,
Bulfinch's Mythology

In this tale, Sir Gawain performs the ultimate act of chivalry.

Once upon a time King Arthur held his court in merry Carlisle, when a damsel came before him and craved a boon. It was for vengeance upon a knight, who had made her lover captive and despoiled her of her lands. King Arthur commanded to bring him his sword, Excalibar, and to saddle his steed, and rode forth without delay to right the lady's wrong. Ere long he reached the castle of the grim baron, and challenged him to the conflict. But the castle stood on magic ground, and the spell was such that no knight could tread thereon but straight his courage fell and his strength decayed. King Arthur felt the charm, and before a blow was struck his sturdy limbs lost their strength, and his head grew faint. He was fain to yield himself prisoner to the churlish knight, who refused to release him except upon condition that he should return at the end of a year, and bring a true answer to the question, "What thing is it which women most desire?" or in default thereof surrender himself and his lands. King Arthur accepted the terms, and gave his oath to return at the time appointed. During the year the king rode east, and he rode west, and inquired of all whom he met what thing it was which all women most desire. Some told him riches; some pomp and state; some mirth; some flattery; and some a gallant knight. But in the diversity of answers he could find no sure dependence. The year was well nigh spent when, one day, as he rode thoughtfully through a forest, he saw sitting beneath a tree a lady of such hideous aspect that he turned away his eyes and when she greeted him in seemly sort made no answer. "What wretch art thou," the lady said, "that will not speak to me? It may chance that I may resolve thy doubts, though I be not fair of aspect." "If thou wilt do so," said King Arthur, "choose what reward thou wilt, thou grim lady, and it shall be given thee." "Swear me this upon thy faith," she said, and Arthur swore it. Then the lady told him the secret, and demanded her reward, which was that the king should find some fair and courtly knight to be her husband.

King Arthur hastened to the grim baron's castle and told him one by one all the answers which he had received from his various advisers, except the last, and not one was admitted as the true one. "Now yield thee, Arthur," the giant said, "for thou hast not paid thy ransom, and thou and thy lands are forfeited to me." Then King Arthur said:

"Yet hold thy hand, thou proud baron,
I pray thee hold thy hand.
And give me leave to speak once more,
In rescue of my land.
This morn, as I came over a moor,
I saw a lady set,
Between an oak and a green holly,
All clad in red scarlet.
She says *all women would have their will*
This is their chief desire;
Now yield, as thou art a baron true,
That I have paid my hire."

"It was my sister that told thee this," the churlish baron exclaimed. "Vengeance light on her! I will some time or other do her as ill a turn."

King Arthur rode homeward, but not light of heart; for he remembered the promise he was under to the loathly lady to give her one of his young and gallant knights for a husband. He told his grief to Sir Gawain, his nephew, and he replied, "Be not sad, my lord, for I will marry the loathly lady." King Arthur replied:

"Now nay, now nay, good Sir Gawain,
My sister's son ye be;
The loathly lady's all too grim,
And all too foule for thee."

But Gawain persisted, and the king at last, with sorrow of heart, consented that Gawain should be his ransom. So, one day, the king and his knights rode to the forest, met the loathly lady, and brought her to the court. Sir Gawain stood the scoffs and jeers of his companions as he best might, and the marriage was solemnized, but not with the usual festivities.

"There was no joye, ne fest at alle;
There n'as but hevinesse and mochel sorwe,
For prively he wed her on the morwe,
And all day after hid him as an owle,
So wo was him his wife loked so foule!"

When night came, and they were alone together, Sir Gawain could not conceal his aversion; and the lady asked him why he sighed so heavily, and turned away his face. He candidly confessed it was on account of three things, her age, her ugliness, and her low degree. The lady, not at all offended, replied with excellent arguments to all his objections. She showed him that with age is discretion, with ugliness security from rivals, and that all true gentility depends, not upon the accident of birth, but upon the character of the individual.

Sir Gawain made no reply; but, turning his eyes on his bride, what was his amazement to perceive that she wore no longer the unseemly aspect that had so distressed him. She then told him that the form she had worn was not her true form, but a disguise imposed upon her by a wicked enchanter, and that she was condemned to wear it until two things should happen; one, that she should obtain some young and gallant knight to be her husband. This having been done, one half of the charm was removed. She was now at liberty to wear her true form for half the time, and she bade him choose whether he would have her fair by day and ugly by night, or the reverse. Sir Gawain would fain have had her look her best by night, when he alone should see her, and show her repulsive visage, if at all, to others. But she reminded him how much more pleasant it would be to her to wear her best looks in the throng of knights and ladies by day. Sir Gawain yielded, and gave up his will to hers. This alone was wanting to dissolve the charm. The lovely lady now with joy assured him that she should change no more; but as she now was so would she remain by night as well as by day.

"Sweet blushes stayned her rud-red cheek,
Her eyen were black as sloe,
The ripening cherrye swelled her lippe,
And all her neck was snow.
Sir Gawain kist that ladye faire
Lying upon the sheete,
And swore, as he was true knight,
The spice was never so swete."

Stick Your Neck Out
and Close Your Eyes

From Geoffrey Chaucer,
The Canterbury Tales

Chanticleer the rooster tries to recover his hen's good opinion after being frightened by his dream of a fox. From the classic of early English poetry.

"Alas!" said she, "fie upon your timidness!
"Alas!" said she, "for, by that God above,
Now have you lost my heart and all my love.
I cannot love a coward, by my faith!
For certainly, whatever any woman says,
We all desire, if it might be,
To have husbands hardy, wise and free,
And discreet, not a niggard, nor a fool,
Nor one that is terrified of every tool,
Nor a boaster, by that God above!
How dare you say, for shame, to your love
That anything might make you afraid?
Have you no man's heart, but have a beard?
Alas! and are you afraid of dreams?"

And with that word he flew down from the beams,
For it was day, and so did his hens all,
And with a cluck, he began to call
For he had found some corn which lay in the yard.

Regal he was, he was no more afraid.
He feathered Pertelot twenty times,
And trod her just as often, before it was nine.
He looked as if he were a grim lion,
And on his toes he roamed up and down,
He deigned not to put his foot upon the ground.
He clucks whenever he finds some corn,

And then to him, run his wives all.
Thus regal, as a prince is in his hall.

This Chanticleer stood high upon his toes,
Stretching his neck, and held his eyes closed,
And began to crow loudly for the occasion
Master Russell, the fox, sprang up at once,
And by the throat seized Chanticleer,
And on his back toward the wood him bore,
For, as yet, no man pursued.
O destiny, that may not be eschewed!
Alas, that Chanticleer flew from the beams!
Alas, his wife thought nothing of dreams!

Can a Businessman Make a Good Lover?

From Andreas Capellanus,
The Art of Courtly Love

The Man says: "I know well that Love is not in the habit of differentiating men with titles of distinction, but that he obligates all equally to serve in his army, making no exceptions for beauty or birth and making no distinctions of sex or of inequality of family, considering only this, whether anybody is fit to bear Love's armor. Love is a thing that copies Nature herself, and so lovers ought to make no more distinction between classes of men than Love himself does. Just as love inflames men of all classes, so lovers should draw no distinctions of rank, but consider only whether the man who asks for love has been wounded by Love. Supported by this unanswerable argument, I may select for my beloved any woman I choose so long as I have no depravity of character to debase me."

The Woman says: "Who are you that ask for such great gifts? I know well enough what you look like, and the family you come from is obvious. But where can one find greater effrontery than in a man who for the space of a whole week devotes all his efforts to the various gains of business and then on the seventh day, his day of rest, tries to enjoy the gifts of love and to dishonor Love's commands and confound the distinctions of classes established among men from of old? It is not without cause or reason that this distinction of rank has been found among men from the very beginning; it is so that every man will stay within the bounds of his own class and be content with all things therein and never presume to arrogate to himself the things that were naturally set aside as belonging to a higher class, but will leave them severely alone. Who are you, then, to try to defile such ancient statutes and under the pretense of love to attempt to subvert the precepts of our ancestors and so presumptuously go beyond the limits of your own class?"

The Man says: "Although I am repulsed by what you say, still as long as I live I shall not give up the idea of your love, because even if I am never to get the result I hope for, the mere hope I have gained from the greatness of my heart will cause my body to lead a tranquil life, and ultimately, perhaps, God will put into your mind a cure for my pain."

The Woman says: "May God give you reward suited to your effort."

The Man says: "That word alone shows me that my hope is bearing fruit, and I pray to God that you may always be interested in the care of my health and that my sails may find a quiet haven."

The Testimony of a Disappointed Wife

From Geoffrey Chaucer,
The Canterbury Tales

My husband is to me the worst man
That ever was since the world began.
But since I am a wife, it does not become me
To tell anyone of our privacy,
Neither in bed, nor in any other place;
God forbid, I should not tell it, by his grace!
A wife should say nothing of her husband
But to his honor, as I understand;

But to you, this much I will tell:
So help me God, he is worth, not at all,
In no degree the value of a fly.
But yet what grieves me most, he is niggardly.
And well you know that women naturally
Desire six things, and so do I:
They would have their husbands be
Hardy, and wise, and rich, and therefore free,
And obedient to their wives, and fresh in bed.

The Wife of Bath Has the Last Word

From Geoffrey Chaucer,
The Canterbury Tales

Silence was commanded of them all
So that the knight should tell the audience
What thing worldly women love the best.
This knight did not stand silent like a beast,
But to this question answered speedily,
With manly voice, so all the court could hear,
"My liege lady, generally," said he,
"Women desire to have sovereignty
As well over their husband as their lover
And to be in mastery their men above.
This is your greatest desire, though me you kill
Do as you please; I am here at your will."
In all the court there was no wife, or maid,
Or widow, that contradicted what he said.

Sigh No More, Ladies

From William Shakespeare,
Much Ado About Nothing

Sigh no more, ladies, sigh no more!
Men were deceivers ever,
One foot in sea, and one on shore;
To one thing constant never.
Then sigh not so,
But let them go,
And be you blithe and bonny,
Converting all your sounds of woe
Into Hey nonny, nonny.
Sing no more ditties, sing no moe,
Of dumps so dull and heavy!
The fraud of men was ever so,
Since summer first was leavy.
Then sigh not so, &c.

THE ROMANTIC MAN

Pyramus and Thisbe

From Thomas Bulfinch,
Bulfinch's Mythology

A tragic error leads to an immortal love.

Pyramus was the handsomest youth, and Thisbe the fairest maiden, in all Babylonia, where Semiramis reigned. Their parents occupied adjoining houses; and neighborhood brought the young people together, and acquaintance ripened into love. They would gladly have married, but their parents forbade. One thing, however, they could not forbid—that love should glow with equal ardor in the bosoms of both. They conversed by signs and glances, and the fire burned more intensely for being covered up. In the wall that parted the two houses there was a crack, caused by some fault in the structure. No one had remarked it before, but the lovers discovered it. What will not love discover! It afforded a passage to the voice; and tender messages used to pass backward and forward through the gap. As they stood, Pyramus on this side, Thisbe on that, their breaths would mingle. "Cruel wall," they said, "why do you keep two lovers apart? But we will not be ungrateful. We owe you, we confess, the privilege of transmitting loving words to willing ears." Such words they uttered on different sides of the wall; and when night came and they must say farewell, they pressed their lips upon the wall, she on her side, he on his, as they could come no nearer.

Next morning, when Aurora had put out the stars, and the sun had melted the frost from the grass, they met at the accustomed spot. Then, after lamenting their hard fate, they agreed that next night, when all was still, they would slip away from the watchful eyes, leave their dwellings and walk out into the fields; and to insure a meeting, repair to a well-known edifice standing outside the city's bounds, called the Tomb of Ninus, and that the one who came first should await the other at the foot of a certain tree. It was a white mulberry tree, and stood near a cool spring. All was agreed on, and they waited impatiently for the sun to go down beneath the waters and night to rise up from them. Then cautiously Thisbe stole forth, unobserved by the family, her head covered with a veil, made her way to the monument and sat down under the tree. As she sat alone in the dim light of the evening she descried a lioness, her jaws reeking with recent slaughter, approaching the fountain to slake her thirst. Thisbe fled at the sight, and sought refuge in the hollow of a rock. As she fled she dropped her veil. The lioness after drinking at the spring turned to retreat to the woods, and seeing the veil on the ground, tossed and rent it with her bloody mouth.

Pyramus, having been delayed, now approached the place of meeting. He saw in the sand the footsteps of the lion, and the color fled from his cheeks at the sight. Presently he found the veil all rent and bloody. "O hapless girl," said he, "I have been the cause of thy death! Thou, more worthy of life than I, hast fallen the first victim. I will follow. I am the guilty cause, in tempting thee forth to a place of such peril, and not being myself on the spot to guard thee. Come forth, ye lions, from the rocks, and tear this guilt body with your teeth." He took up the veil, carried it with him to the appointed tree, and covered it with kisses and with tears. "*My* blood also shall stain your texture," said he, and drawing his sword plunged it into his heart. The blood spurted from the wound, and tinged the white mulberries of the tree all red; and sinking into the earth reached the roots, so that the red color mounted through the trunk to the fruit.

By this time Thisbe, still trembling with fear, yet wishing not to disappoint her love, stepped cautiously forth, looking anxiously for the youth, eager to tell him the danger she had escaped. When she came to the spot and saw the changed color of the mulberries she doubted whether it was the same place. While she hesitated she saw the form of one struggling in the agonies of death. She started back, a shudder ran through her frame as a ripple on the face of the still water when a sudden breeze sweeps over it. But as soon as she recognized her lover, she screamed and beat her breast, embracing the lifeless body, pouring tears into its wounds, and imprinting kisses on the cold lips. "O Pyramus," she cried, "what has done this? Answer me, Pyramus, it is your own Thisbe that speaks. Hear me, dearest, and lift that drooping head!" At the name of Thisbe Pyramus opened his eyes, then closed them again. She saw her veil stained with blood and the scabbard empty of its sword. "Thy own hand has slain thee, and for my sake," she said. "I too can be brave for once, and my love is as strong as thine. I will follow thee in death, for I have been the cause; and death which alone could part us shall not prevent my joining thee. And ye, unhappy parents of us both, deny us not our united request. As love and death have joined us, let one tomb contain us. And thou, tree, retain the marks of slaughter. Let thy berries still serve for memorials of our blood." So saying she plunged the sword into her breast. Her parents ratified her wish, the gods also ratified it. The two bodies were buried in one sepulcher, and the tree ever after brought forth purple berries, as it does to this day.

Emile and Sophy

From Jean-Jacques Rousseau, Emile

Beginning with Rousseau (1712–1778), the Romantic writers tried to restore the chivalric conception of love to compensate for an increasingly materialistic, self-interested modern age. In Rousseau's Emile, *the young man of the title perfects his own character through his devotion to Sophy, a young woman he admires from afar. In her, he sees the virtues that he wishes to cultivate in himself, and his longing to be worthy of Sophy, to be esteemed by her, gives him the impetus to strive harder to perfect himself. For her part, Sophy has always hoped to meet a young man like Homer's Telemachus. The flat-souled young men of the bourgeois era don't interest her; she is looking for a young hero, and in Emile she believes she may have found him.*

All women would be alike to a man who had no idea of virtue or beauty, and the first comer would always be the most charming. Love does not spring from nature, far from it; it is the curb and law of her desires; it is love that makes one sex indifferent to the other, the loved one alone excepted.

We wish to inspire the preference; we feel love must be mutual. To be loved we must be worthy of love; to be preferred we must be more worthy than the rest, at least in the eyes of our beloved. Hence we begin to look around among our fellows; we begin to compare ourselves with them, there is emulation, rivalry, and jealousy. A heart full to overflowing loves to make itself known; from the need of a mistress there soon springs the need of a friend. He who feels how sweet it is to be loved, desires to be loved by everybody; and there could be no preferences if there were not many that fail to find satisfaction. With love and friendship there begin dissensions, enmity, and hatred. I behold deference to other people's opinions enthroned among all these diverse passions, and foolish mortals, enslaved by her power, base their very existence merely on what other people think.

The first sentiment of which the well-trained youth is capable is not love but friendship. The first work of his rising imagination is to make known to him his fellows; the species affects him before the sex. Here is another advantage to be gained from prolonged innocence; you may take advantage of his dawning sensibility to sow the first seeds of humanity in the heart of the young adolescent. This advantage is all the greater because this is the only time in his life when such efforts may be really successful.

Do you desire to stimulate and nourish the first stirrings of awakening sensibility in the heart of a young man, do you desire to incline his disposition toward kindly deed and thought, do not cause the seeds of pride, vanity, and envy to spring up in him through the misleading picture of the happiness of mankind; do not show him to begin with the pomp of courts, the pride of palaces, the delights of pageants; do not take him into society and into brilliant assemblies; do not show him the outside of society till you have made him capable of estimating it at its true worth. To show him the world before he is acquainted with men is not to train him but to corrupt him; not to teach, but to mislead.

By nature men are neither kings, nobles, courtiers, nor millionaires. All men are born poor and naked, all are liable to the sorrows of life, its disappointments, its ills, its needs, its suffering of every kind; and all are condemned at length to die. This is what it really means to be a man, this is what no mortal can escape. Begin then with the study of the essentials of humanity, that which really constitutes mankind.

I will go further and maintain that virtue is no less favorable to love than to other rights of nature, and that it adds as much to the power of the beloved as to that of the wife or mother. There is no real love without enthusiasm, and no enthusiasm without an object of perfection real or supposed, but always present in the imagination. What is there to kindle the hearts of lovers for whom this perfection is nothing, for whom the loved one is merely the means to sensual pleasure? Nay, not thus is the heart kindled, not thus does it abandon itself to those sublime transports which form the rapture of lovers and the charm of love. Love is an illusion, I grant you, but its reality consists in the feelings it awakes, in the love of true beauty which it inspires. That beauty is not to be found in the object of our affections, it is the creation of our illusions. What matter! Do we not still sacrifice all those baser feelings to the imaginary model? And we still feed our hearts on the virtues we attribute to the beloved, we still withdraw ourselves from the baseness of human nature. What lover is there who would not give his life for his mistress? What gross and sensual passion is there in a man who is willing to die? We scoff at the knights of old; they knew the meaning of love; we know nothing but debauchery. When the teachings of romance began to seem ridiculous, it was not so much the work of reason as of immorality.

The harder and more important the duties, the stronger and clearer must be the reasons on which they are based. There is a sort of pious talk about the most serious subjects which is dinned in vain into the ears of young people. This talk, quite unsuited to their ideas and the small importance they attach to it in secret, inclines them to yield readily to their inclinations, for lack of any reasons for resistance drawn from the facts themselves. No doubt a girl brought up to goodness and piety has strong weapons against temptation; but one whose heart, or rather her ears, are merely filled with the jargon of piety, will certainly fall prey to the first skillful seducer who attacks her. A young and beautiful girl will never despise her body, she will never really deplore sins which her beauty leads men to commit, she will never lament earnestly in the sight of God that she is an object of desire, she will never be convinced that the tenderest feeling is an invention of the Evil One. Give her other and more pertinent reasons for her own sake, for these will have no effect. It will be worse to instill, as is often done, ideas which contradict each other, and after having humbled and degraded her person and her charms as the stain of sin, to bid her reverence that same vile body as the temple of Jesus Christ. Ideas too sublime and too humble are equally ineffective and they cannot both be true. A reason adapted to her age and sex is what is needed. Considerations of duty are of no effect unless they are combined with some motive for the performance of our duty.

If you would inspire young people with a love of good conduct avoid saying, "Be good;" make it in their interest to be good; make them feel the value of goodness and they will love it. It is not enough to show this effect in the distant future, show it now, in the relations of the present, in the character of their lovers. Describe a good man, a man of worth, teach them to recognize him when they see him, to love him for their own sake; convince them that such a man alone can make them happy as friend, wife, or mistress. Let reason lead the way to virtue; make them feel that the empire of their sex and all the advantages derived from it depend not merely on the right conduct, the morality, of women, but also on that of men; that they have little hold over the vile and base, and that the lover is incapable of serving his mistress unless he can do homage to virtue. You may then be sure that when you describe the manners of our age you will inspire them with a genuine disgust; give them a distaste for their maxims, an aversion to their sentiments, and a scorn for their empty gallantry; you will arouse a nobler ambition, to reign over great and strong souls, the ambition of the Spartan women to rule over men. A bold, shameless, intriguing woman, who can only attract her lovers by coquetry and retain them by her favors, wins a servile obedience in common things; in weighty and important matters she has no influence over them. But the woman who is both virtuous, wise, and charming, she who, in a word, combines love and esteem can send them at her bidding to the end of the world, to war, to glory, and to death at her behest. This is a fine kingdom and worth the winning.

Sophy loves virtue; this love has come to be her ruling passion; she loves virtue because there is nothing fairer in itself, she loves it because it is a woman's glory and because a virtuous woman is little lower than the angels; she loves virtue as the only road to real happiness, because she sees nothing but poverty, neglect, unhappiness, shame, and disgrace in the life of a bad woman; she loves virtue because it is dear to her revered father and to her tender and worthy mother; they are not content to be happy in their own virtue, they desire hers; and she finds her chief happiness in the hope of making them happy. All these feelings inspire an enthusiasm which stirs her heart and keeps all its budding passions in subjection to this noble enthusiasm. Sophy will be chaste and good till her dying day; she has vowed it in her secret heart, and not before she knew how hard it would be to keep her vow; she made this vow at a time when she should have revoked it had she been the slave of her senses.

Sophy is not so fortunate as to be a charming French woman, cold-hearted and vain, who would rather attract attention than give pleasure, who seeks amusement rather than delight. She suffers from a consuming desire for love; it even disturbs and troubles her heart in the midst of festivities; she has lost her former liveliness and her taste for merry games; far from being afraid of the tedium of solitude she desires it. Her thoughts go out to him who will make solitude sweet to her. She finds strangers tedious, she wants a lover, not a circle of admirers. She would rather give pleasure to one good man than be a general favorite, or win that applause of society which lasts but a day and tomorrow is turned to scorn.

Husband and wife should choose each other. A mutual liking should be the first bond between them. They should follow the guidance of their own eyes and heads; when they are married their first duty will be to love one another, and as love and hatred do not depend on ourselves, this duty brings another with it, and they must begin to love each other before marriage. That is the law of nature, and no power can abrogate it; those who have fettered it by so many legal restrictions have given heed rather to the outward show of order than to the happiness of marriage or the morals of the citizen. You see, my dear Sophy, we do not preach a harsh morality. It tends to make you your own mistress and to make us leave the choice of your husband to yourself.

Sophy was in love with Telemachus, and loved him with a passion which nothing could cure. When her father and mother became aware of her infatuation, they laughed at it and tried to cure her by reasoning with her. They were mistaken, reason was not altogether on their side; Sophy had her own reason and knew how to use it. Many a time did she reduce them to silence by turning their own arguments against them, by showing them that it was all their own fault for not having trained her to suit the men of that century; that she would be compelled to adopt her husband's way of thinking or he must adopt hers, that they had made the former course impossible by the way she had been brought up, and that the latter was just what she wanted. "Give me," said she, "a man who holds the same opinions as I do, or one who will be willing to learn them from me, and I will marry him; but until then, why do you scold me? Pity me; I am miserable, but not mad. Is the heart controlled by the will? Did my father not ask that very question? Is it my fault if I love what has no existence? I am no visionary; I desire no prince, I seek no Telemachus, I know he is only an imaginary person; I seek someone like him. And why should there be no such person, since there is such a person as I, I who feel that my heart is like his? No, let us not wrong humanity so greatly, let us not think that an amiable and virtuous man is a figment of the imagination. He exists, he lives."

● ● ●

At the name of Sophy you would have seen Emile give a start. His attention is arrested by this dear name, and he awakes all at once and looks eagerly at one who dares to bear it. "Sophy! Are you the Sophy whom my heart is seeking? Is it you that I love?" He looks at her; he watches her with a sort of fear and self-distrust. The face is not quite what he pictured; he cannot tell whether he likes it more or less. He studies every feature, he watches every movement, every gesture; he has a hundred fleeting interpretations for them all; he would give half his life if she would but speak. He looks at me anxiously and uneasily; his eyes are full of questions and reproaches. His every glance seems to say, "Guide me while there is yet time; if my heart yields itself and is deceived, I shall never get over it."

Consider my Emile over twenty years of age, well formed, well developed in mind and body, strong, healthy, active, skillful, robust, full of sense, reason, kindness, humanity, possessed of good morals and good taste, loving what is beautiful, doing what is good, free from the sway of cruel passions, released from the tyranny of popular prejudices, but subject to the law of wisdom, and easily guided by the voice of a friend; gifted with so many useful and pleasant accomplishments, caring little for wealth, able to earn a living with his own hands, and not afraid of lacking bread, whatever may come. Behold him in the intoxication of a growing passion; his heart opens to the first beams of love; its pleasant fancies reveal to him a whole world of new delights and enjoyments; he loves a sweet woman, whose character is even more delightful than her person; he hopes, he expects the reward which he deserves.

Their first attachment took its rise in mutual affection, in community of honorable feelings; therefore this affection is lasting. It abandons itself, with confidence, with reason, to the most delightful madness, without fear, regret, remorse, or any other disturbing thought, but that which is inseparable from all happiness. What lacks there yet? Behold, inquire, imagine what still is lacking, that can be combined with present joys. Every happiness which can exist in combination is already present; nothing could be added without taking away from what there is; he is as happy as man can be. Shall I choose this time to cut short so sweet a period: Shall I disturb such pure enjoyment? The happiness he enjoys is my life's reward. What could I give that could outweigh what I should take away? Even if I set the crown to his happiness I should destroy its greatest charm. That supreme joy is a hundredfold greater in anticipation than in possession; its savor is greater while we wait for it then when it is ours. O worthy Emile! Love and be loved! Prolong your enjoyment before it is yours; rejoice in your love and in your innocence, find your paradise upon earth, while you await your heaven. I shall not cut short this happy period of life. I will draw out its enchantments, I will prolong them as far as possible. Alas! It must come to an end and that soon; but it shall at least linger in your memory, and you will never repent of its joys.

The Sorrows of Youth

From Johann Wolfgang von Goethe,
The Sorrows of Young Werther

Goethe's novel is nearly perfect in its depiction of a troubled young man wholly absorbed in romantic passion. Werther longs for a woman he knows he cannot have, and it destroys him. An early classic of Romanticism by the famed philosopher and poet (1775).

Why don't I write to you? You ask me that though you are also numbered among the scholars! You should be able to divine that I am well, and indeed—in short, I have met someone in whom my heart is interested. I have—I do not know.

To tell you in proper order how it happened that I made the acquaintance of one of the most charming of beings will be no easy matter; I am content and happy, so am not likely to be a satisfactory narrator.

An angel! By Heaven, everybody says that of his mistress! Doesn't he? And yet I am incapable of telling you how perfect she is, or why she is perfect, enough, she has taken complete possession of my mind.

So much naivety combined with such intelligence, such kindness and such resolve, such tranquillity of soul in such an active life.

This is all hopeless twaddle that I am saying about her, mere abstractions which fail to express a single feature of her real self. Another time—no, not another time, I will tell you now, immediately. If I don't do it now, I never shall. For, between ourselves, since I began this letter I have been three times on the verge of laying down my pen, saddling my horse and riding off though I vowed early this morning that I would not—and yet every minute I go to the window to see how high the sun stands . . .

I could not help it, I had to go out to her. I am back once more, Wilhelm, and will eat my supper and finish this letter. How it enraptures my soul to see her among the dear happy children, her eight brothers and sisters.

If I continue like this, you will be no wiser at the end than you were at the beginning, so listen, I will force myself to give you details.

I wrote to you recently that I had made the acquaintance of the bailiff S., and that he had invited me to come and visit him soon at his hermitage, or rather his little kingdom. I neglected to do so and would perhaps never have gone, if there had not been revealed to me by accident the treasure concealed in that tranquil spot.

The young people here had arranged a ball in the country, and I gladly agreed to go. I offered my escort to a nice, good-looking, but not otherwise interesting girl in this town, and it was settled that I was to hire a coach to drive out to the scene of the festivities with my partner and her cousin, and that we were to pick up Charlotte S. on the way. "You will make the acquaintance of a beautiful girl," my partner said, as we drove through a broad avenue in the wood toward the hunting lodge. "Take care," her cousin added, "that you don't fall in love." "What do you mean" I asked. "She is already betrothed," the former replied, "to a very worthy man who has gone to put his affairs in order after his father's death and to apply for an important post." The information did not interest me particularly.

The sun was still a quarter of an hour from the hilltop when we reached the lodge gate; it was very sultry and the ladies expressed their anxiety lest we should be overtaken by a storm which we could see gathering in heavy, whitish-gray little clouds round the horizon. I relieved their fears by pretending to a knowledge of the weather, though I began myself to have a foreboding that our festivities would be interrupted.

I had alighted, and a maid who came to the gate begged us to wait a moment, Mamselle Lotthe would be with us straightway. I went across the courtyard to the well-built house and, when I had ascended the steps in front and entered at the door, I caught sight of the most charming scene that I have ever witnessed. In the entrance hall there swarmed six children, from two to eleven years of age, round a handsome girl of middle height, who wore a simple white frock with pink bows on the breast and arms. She was holding a loaf of black bread and cutting a slice for each of the children round her in proportion to its age and appetite, offering it with such an amiable air and each one crying "Thank you!" so artlessly, after he had stretched his little hands up as high as he could before his slice was cut, and then springing away contentedly with his supper or, if he was of a quieter nature, walking tranquilly toward the gate to see the strangers and the coach in which their Lotte was to drive away. "I beg your pardon," she said, "for giving you the trouble of coming in and making the ladies wait. While I was dressing and making all sorts of arrangements for the house in my absence, I forgot to give my children their supper, and they won't have their bread cut by anyone but me." I paid her some harmless compliment while my whole soul was absorbed in the contemplation of her figure, her voice, her bearing, and I had just time to recover from my surprise when she ran into the room to fetch her gloves and fan. The children kept at a little distance, casting sidelong glances at me, and I went up to the youngest who was a most pleasant-looking child. He had just drawn back when Lotte appeared in the doorway and said, "Louis shake hands with your cousin." The boy did so with a very frank air, and I could not refrain from kissing him heartily in spite of his dirty little nose. "Cousin?" I said, as I offered her my hand. "Do you consider that I deserve the happiness of being related to you?" "Oh!" she said, with a roguish smile, "our circle of cousins is very extensive, and I should be very sorry if you were the least worthy among them." As we went she ordered Sophie, the next oldest sister to herself, a girl of about eleven, to keep an eye on the little ones, and greet their father when he came back from his ride. The little ones she admonished to obey their sister Sophie as they would herself, and some of them expressly promised to do so. A pert little blonde, however, of about six years, said, "But it isn't you, after all, Lottchen! We like you better." The two eldest boys had climbed up behind the coach, and at my request she allowed them to travel with us until we reached the edge of the wood, so long as they promised not to tease each other and to hold on firmly.

Hardly had we fitted ourselves in and the ladies greeted one another, each in turn expressing her views abut the others' costumes, particularly bonnets, and duly passing in review the company that they expected to meet, when Lotte stopped the coach for her brothers to descend; they asked to kiss her hand once more and the older one did so with all the delicacy that could be expected of a boy of fifteen, the other with impetuousness and levity. She bade them give her love once more to the little ones, and the coach rolled on.

The cousin enquired whether she had finished the book she had recently sent her. "No," said Lotte.

"I do not like it; you can have it back. The one you sent me before was no better." When I asked what the books were, I was amazed at her reply. There was so much character in all she said, and with every word I discovered fresh charms, saw new flashes of intelligence lighting up her features, which appeared gradually to brighten with pleasure because she felt that I understood her.

"When I was younger," she said, "I liked nothing so much as novels. Heaven knows I felt happy when I could sit in some corner on Sundays and share with my whole heart the fortune or distress of some Miss Jenny. Nor do I deny that this kind of romance still has some charm for me. But since I now seldom have time for a book, it must be suited to my taste. And the author I most prefer is the one in whom I find my own world again, who describes happenings such as I see around me and yet whose story I find as interesting, as sympathetic as my own domestic existence, which is, to be sure, not a Paradise, but nevertheless on the whole a source of inexpressible bliss."

I did my best to conceal my emotions at these words. I was not, it is true, very successful, for when I heard her speak incidentally, but with such truth, about the Vicar of Wakefield and about—, I lost my control and told her everything that forced itself to my lips, and only noticed after some time, when Lotte directed her remarks to the others, that these had been sitting there the whole time with wide-open eyes, as though they were not there at all. The cousin looked at me more than once with a mocking air, which however was of little consequence to me.

The conversation turned upon the pleasure of dancing. "If this passion is a fault," said Lotte, "I willingly confess I know nothing that excels dancing. And when I have something on my mind and drum out a quadrille on my squeaky old harpsichord, then everything is all right again."

How I gazed into her black eyes as she spoke, how her vivacious lips and her fresh, lively mien drew my whole soul on, how totally absorbed I became in the glorious feeling of listening to her, so that I often did not even hear the words by which she expressed herself! Of this you can have some idea, since you know me. In short, I descended from the coach as though in a dream when we came to a halt in front of the summer house, and I was still so immersed in dreams amid the darkling world around me that I hardly noticed the music which was wafted down to us from the brightly lit hall.

Two gentlemen named Audran and a certain N.N.—who can remember everybody's name!—who were the partners of Lotte and the cousin, met us at the coach door, took charge of the ladies, and I escorted mine upstairs.

We glided round one another in minuets, I engaged one lady after another, and it was just the least attractive ones who could not manage to change hands and end the figure. Lotte and her partner began an English quadrille, and you can imagine how happy I was when the turn came for her to begin the figure with us. You should see her dance! She is so absorbed in it, heart and soul, her whole body *one* harmony, as carefree, as unaffected, as though nothing else mattered, as though she thought or felt nothing else, and it is certain that at such moments everything else has ceased to exist for her.

I asked her for the second quadrille, but she promised me the third, and with the most charming ingenuousness in the world she assured me that she was very fond of dancing in the German way. "It is the fashion here," she continued, "that each couple who are together remain together in the German dance, but my partner is an indifferent waltzer and he will be grateful if I relieve him of the labor. Your lady can't waltz either and doesn't like it, and I saw during the quadrille that you waltz well; if you care to be my partner for the German dance, go and ask leave of my partner while I go and ask your lady." I agreed, and it was soon arranged that her partner should sit out the waltz with mine.

We then began, and took delight in interlacing our arms in diverse ways. What charm, what fleetness of movement! And when we came to the waltz, and the dancers revolved round each other like planets, there was at first a certain amount of confusion since very few are expert at it. We were prudent and let them wear themselves out, and when the clumsiest couples had left the floor we joined in and held out valiantly to the end together with another pair, Audran and his partner. Never have I danced so easily. I was no longer a mortal. To have the most charming creature in the world in my arms and to fly around with her like lightning, so that everything round about ceased to exist and—Wilhelm, to be candid, I *did* vow that the girl I loved, on whom I had claims, should never waltz with another, even if it meant the end of me. You understand!

We took a turn or two round the room after the dance in order to recover our breath. Then she sat down, and the lemons I had stolen when the punch was being brewed, which were now the only ones left and which I brought her cut into slices with sugar, had an excellent refreshing effect, except that with every slice the lady sitting next to her took out of the cup a stab went through my heart, though for the sake of decency I had to offer it to her also.

In the third quadrille we were the second couple. As we danced through the ranks and I, God knows with what rapture, kept my eyes, as she hung upon my arm, fixed upon hers, in which shone the sincerest expression of frank and pure enjoyment, we reached a lady who had attracted my attention on account of her sympathetic mien, though her face was no longer exactly young. She looked at Lotte with a smile, lifted a minatory finger, and mentioned the name Albert twice with considerable emphasis as she whirled past.

"Who is Albert," I asked Lotte, "if it is not presumption on my part?" She was about to reply when we had to separate to make the figure of eight, and it seemed to me that I saw a certain pensiveness shade her brow as we crossed in front of each other. "Why should I keep it from you," she said, as she gave me her hand for the promenade. "Albert is a worthy man to whom I am as good as betrothed." This was not news to me, for the girls had told me in the carriage, and yet it *was* entirely new to me, since I had not thought of it in connection with her who had come to mean so much to me in such a short time. Enough—I became confused, forgot the steps, and danced in between the wrong couple so that everything became mixed up and Lotte's whole presence of mind and pulling and tugging were necessary to restore order.

The dance had not yet come to an end when the flashes of lightning, which we had for some time seen gleaming on the horizon and which I had pretended were sheet lightning, began to grow more pronounced and the thunder drowned the music. Three ladies ran out of the ranks, followed by their partners, confusion became general, and the music ceased. It is natural, when our pleasure is interrupted by an accident or something terrifying, that the impression made upon us should be stronger than usual, partly because of the contrast which is felt so vividly, partly and even more because our senses are susceptible and receive an impression all the more quickly. To these causes must be attributed the wondrous grimaces which I saw appear on the faces of several ladies. The wisest of them sat down in a corner with her back to the window and held her hands over her ears, another knelt down and buried her face in the lap of the first one, a third pushed her way in between them both and clasped her little sisters to her with a thousand tears. Some wanted to drive home, others, who were even less aware what they were doing, had not sufficient presence of mind to avoid the impertinences of some of the young gentlemen who had had a little to drink, and who appeared to be busily engaged in capturing from the lips of the beauties in distress the timorous prayers which were meant for Heaven. Some of the gentlemen had gone downstairs to smoke a quiet pipe, and the rest of the company did not refuse when the hostess hit upon the clever idea of showing us into a room which had curtains and shutters. Hardly had we entered when Lotte began to arrange chairs in a circle, to seat the guests and suggest a game.

I saw more than one gentleman purse his lips and stretch his limbs in expectation of a luscious forfeit. "We are going to play at Counting," she said, "so pay attention. I am going round in a circle from right to left, and each of you must also count round the number that comes to him, but it must go like wildfire, and whoever hesitates or makes a mistake receives a box on the ears, and so on to a thousand." It was merry sight. She went round the circle with her arm stretched out. "One", cried the first, his neighbour "two", "three" the next and so on. Then she began to go more quickly, more and more quickly. One man missed his number and *smack*! And more and more quickly. I received two slaps on the face myself, and with secret pleasure I thought I felt that they were harder than those she gave the others. A general uproar and outburst of laughter brought the game to an end before the thousand was counted. Those who were most intimate with each other drew aside, the storm was over, and I followed Lotte into the ballroom. On the way she said, "During the ear-boxing they forgot the weather and everything!" I did not know what to reply. "I was one of the most timorous," she said, "and by pretending to be brave in order to give the others courage I became courageous myself." We stepped to the window, the thunder could be heard away to the side, and the glorious rain was pattering down onto the earth, while the most refreshing fragrance rose up to us in a full, warm vapor. She stood leaning on her elbow, her gaze searching the landscape; she looked up to the heavens and then at me, I saw her eyes fill with tears, she put her hand on mine and murmured—*Klopstock*! I became submerged in the flood of emotions which this name let loose upon me. I could not bear it, I bent over her hand and kissed it amidst the most ecstatic tears. And looked up again into her eyes—Noble Poet! Would that thou hadst seen thy apotheosis in that gaze, and would that I might never hear again thy so oft desecrated name!

The Spread of Wertherism Among Young Men

Karl Hillebrand

Goethe's Werther was such a success that young men all over Germany embraced gloominess, torment, and alienation as the coolest way to be miserable. Karl Hillebrand was a respected nineteenth-century authority on German Romanticism.

The whole generation bore with impatience the yoke of the established order, of authority under whatever form, whether the fetters were those of literary convention or social prejudice, of the state or the church. The *ego* affirmed its absolute, inalienable right; it strove to manifest itself according to its caprices, and refused to acknowledge any check. Individual inspiration was a sacred thing, which reality with its rules and prejudices could only spoil and deflower. Now, according to the temperament of each, they rose violently against society and its laws, or resigned themselves silently to a dire necessity. The one in Titanic effort climbed Olympus, heaving Pelion on Ossa; the other wiped a furtive tear out of his eye, and, aspiring to deliverance, dreamed of an ideal happiness. Sometimes in the same poet the two dispositions succeed each other.

"Cover thy sky with vapor and clouds, O Zeus," exclaims Goethe's Prometheus, "and practice thy strength on tops of oaks and summits of mountains like the child who beheads thistles. Thou must, nevertheless, leave me my earth and my hut, which thou hast not built, and my hearth, whose flame thou enviest. Is it not my heart, burning with a sacred ardor, which alone has accomplished all? And should I thank thee, who wast sleeping whilst I worked?"

The same young man who had put into the mouth of the rebellious Titan this haughty and defiant outburst, at other moments, when he was discouraged and weary of the struggle, took refuge within himself. Like Werther, "finding his world within himself, he spoils and caresses his tender heart, like a sickly child, all whose caprices we indulge." One or the other of those attitudes toward reality, the active and the passive, were soon taken by the whole youth of the time; and just as Schiller's *Brigands* gave birth to a whole series of wild dramas, *Werther* left in the novels of the time a long line of tears. More than that, even in reality Karl Moor found imitators who engaged in an open struggle against society, and one met at every corner languishing Siegwarts, whose delicate soul was hurt by the cruel contact of the world.

What strikes us most in this morbid sentimentality is the eternal melancholy sighing after nature. Ossian's cloudy sadness and Young's dark Nights veil every brow. They fly into the solitudes of the forests in order to dream freely of a less brutal world. They must, indeed, have been very far from nature to seek for it with such avidity. Many, in fact, of these ardent, feverish young men became in the end a prey, some to madness, others to suicide. A species of moral epidemic, like that which followed upon the apparent failure of the Revolution in 1799, had broken out. The germ of Byronism may be clearly detected already in the Wertherism of those times. Exaggerated and over-strained imaginations found insufficient breathing-room in the world, and met on all sides with boundaries to their unlimited demands. Hearts, accustomed to follow the dictates of their own inspiration alone, bruised themselves against the sharp angles of reality. The thirst for action which consumed their ardent youth could not be quenched, in fact, in the narrow limits of domestic life; and public life did not exist. Frederick had done great things, but only, like the three hundred other German governments, to exclude the youth of the middle classes from active life. Thence the general uneasiness. *Werther* was as much an effect as a cause of this endemic disease; above all, it was the expression of a general state of mind. It is this which constitutes its historical importance, while the secret of its lasting value is to be found in its artistic form.

"Oh," exclaimed old Goethe fifty years later in conversation with young Felix Mendelssohn, "oh, if I could but write a fourth volume of my life! It should be a history of the year 1755, which no one knows or can write better than I. How the nobility, feeling itself outrun by the middle classes, began to do all it could not to be left behind in the race; how liberalism, Jacobinism, and all that devilry awoke; how a new life began; how we studied and poetized, made love and wasted our time; how we young folk, full of life and activity, but awkward as we could be, scoffed at the aristocratic propensities of Messrs. Nicolai and Co., in Berlin, who at that time reigned supreme." "Ah, yes, that was a spring, when everything was budding and shooting, when more than one tree was yet bare, while others were already full of leaves. All that in the year 1775!"

The way opened by Herder, although partly and temporarily abandoned during the classical period which intervened, was followed again by the third generation of the founders of German culture, the so-called Romanticists, and by all the great scholars, who, in the first half of this century, revived the historical sciences in Germany. Herder's ideas have, indeed, penetrated our whole thought to such a degree, while his works are so unfinished and disconnected, that it is hardly possible for us to account for the extraordinary effect these ideas and works produced in their day, except by marking the contrast which they present with the then reigning methods and habits as well as the surprising influence exercised by Herder personally. From his twenty-fifth year, indeed, he was a sovereign. His actual and uncontested sway was not, it is true, prolonged beyond a period of about sixteen years, albeit his name figured to a much later time on the list of living potentates. It is also true that when the seeds thrown by him had grown luxuriantly, and were bearing fruit, the sower was almost entirely forgotten or willfully ignored. The generation however, of the "*Stuermer und Draenger*," or, as they were pleased to denominate themselves, the "original geniuses," looked up to Herder as their leader and prophet. Some of them turned from him later on and went back to the exclusive worship of classical antiquity; but their very manner of doing homage to it bore witness to Herder's influence. The following generation threw itself no less exclusively into the Middle Ages; but what, after all, was it doing if not following Herder's example, when it raked up Dantes and Calderns out of the dust in order to confront them with and oppose them to Vergils and Racines? However they might repudiate, nay, even forget, their teacher, his doctrines already pervaded the whole intellectual atmosphere of Germany, and men's minds breathed them in with the very air they inhaled. Today they belong to Europe.

Man is the last and highest link in nature; his task is to understand what she aims at in him and then to fulfill her intentions. This view of Herder's was Goethe's starting-point in the formation of his *Weltanschauung* (or general view of things).

"All the world," says one of the characters in *Wilhelm Meister*, "lies before us, like a vast quarry before the architect. He does not deserve the name if he does not compose with these accidental natural materials an image whose source is in his mind, and if he does not do it with the greatest possible economy, solidity, and perfection. All that we find outside of us, nay, within us, is object-matter; but deep within us lives also a power capable of giving an ideal form to this matter. This creative power allows us no rest till we have produced that ideal form in one or the other way, either without us in finished works or in our own life."

Lotte! Lotte, Farewell!

From Johann Wolfgang von Goethe,
The Sorrows of Young Werther

Werther's suicide note to Lotte revels in the "ecstasy of death," and details his preferred funeral arrangements.

He spent much time turning out his papers during the evening, tore many of them up and threw them in the stove, and sealed a number of packages which he addressed to Wilhelm. They contained small essays and disconnected ideas, several of which I have seen. After having the fire made up and a flask of wine brought in, he sent his servant, who slept some distance away, as did the other domestics, to bed. The boy lay down in his clothes in order to be at hand at an early hour, for his master had told him that the coach horses would be at the door before six.

All is so still around me and my soul so calm. I thank thee, Lord, for these last moments of strength and ardor.

I step to the window, my dearest, and still see some stars shining through the fleeting storm-clouds. No, you will not fall! The Eternal One bears you at his heart, and me. I saw the wheeler stars of Charles's Wain, the loveliest of all the constellations. When I left you at night, as I went out at the gate, it was in front of me. With what intoxication have I so often gazed at it, raised aloft my hands and made it a symbol, a sacred token of the bliss I felt, and still— Oh! Lotte, what is there that does not remind me of you! Are you not about me always! And have I not always, like a child, insatiably, seized every trifle that your saintly hands had touched!

Beloved silhouette! I now return it to you at my death, Lotte, and beg you to hold it in honor. I have pressed a thousand, thousand kisses on it, waved a thousand greetings to it when I went out or returned.

I have left a note for your father entreating him to protect my body. In the churchyard there are two lime trees, at the back in a corner, toward the field, and there I wish to lie. He can and will do this for his friend. Add your entreaties to mine. I will not ask pious Christians to allow their bodies to rest beside that of a poor wretch. Oh! I could wish to be buried by the wayside, or in the lonely valley, that priest and Levite might cross themselves as they passed by the stone which marked the spot, and the Samaritan shed a tear.

Here, Lotte! I do not shudder to take the dread cold cup from which I am to drink the ecstasy of death! It is you who have handed it to me, and I do not fear. All! All! Thus are all the desires and hopes of my life fulfilled! To knock so cold, so stiff, at the brazen gate of death.

That I might have been granted the happiness to die for you! To sacrifice myself for you, Lotte! I would die with a stout heart, I would die gladly, if I could restore the tranquillity, the rapture of your life. But alas! It was granted to but few noble souls to shed their blood for those they loved, and by their deaths to kindle for them a new life enhanced an hundredfold.

I wish to be buried in these clothes, Lotte. You have touched and sanctified them. I have asked your father to grant me this favor. My soul will hover over my coffin. Let them not search my pockets. This pink bow which you wore on your bosom, when I met you first among your children—Oh! Kiss them a thousand times and tell them the fate of their unhappy friend. The darlings, how they swarm about me. Oh! How I attached myself to you, could not keep away from you from the first moment! Let this bow be buried with me. You gave it me on my birthday! How eagerly I accepted it all! Alas, I did not think that the way would lead to this! Be calm! I beg you, be calm!

They are loaded—it is striking twelve!—So be it then. Lotte! Lotte, farewell! Farewell!

The Age of Innocence

Edith Wharton

The delicacy of courtly love still surfaces in the more pragmatic world of American democracy. Edith Wharton's 1921 novel The Age of Innocence *is an unforgettable story of a respectable young man's unfulfilled passion for a not-quite-respectable European lady of American origins, Countess Olenska.*

That evening, after Mr. Jackson had taken himself away, and the ladies had retired to their chintz-curtained bedroom, Newland Archer mounted thoughtfully to his own study. A vigilant hand had, as usual, kept the fire alive and the lamp trimmed; and the room, with its rows and rows of books, its bronze and steel statuettes of "The Fencers" on the mantelpiece and its many photographs of famous pictures, looked singularly homelike and welcoming.

As he dropped into his armchair near the fire his eyes rested on a large photograph of May Welland, which the young girl had given him in the first days of their romance, and which had now displaced all the other portraits on the table. With a new sense of awe he looked at the frank forehead, serious eyes and gay innocent mouth of the young creature whose soul's custodian he was to be. That terrifying product of the social system he belonged to and believed in, the young girl who knew nothing and expected everything, looked back at him like a stranger through May Welland's familiar features; and once more it was borne in on him that marriage was not the safe anchorage he had been taught to think, but a voyage on uncharted seas.

The case of the Countess Olenska had stirred up old settled convictions and set them drifting dangerously through his mind. His own exclamation: "Women should be free—as free as we are," struck to the root of a problem that it was agreed in his world to regard as nonexistent. "Nice" women, however wronged, would never claim the kind of freedom he meant, and generous-minded men like himself were therefore—in the heat of argument—the more chivalrously ready to concede it to them. Such verbal generosities were in fact only a humbugging disguise of the inexorable conventions that tied things together and bound people down to the old pattern. But here he has pledged to defend, on the part of his betrothed's cousin, conduct that, on this own wife's part, would justify him in calling down on her all the thunders of Church and State. Of course the dilemma was purely hypothetical; since he wasn't a blackguard Polish nobleman, it was absurd to speculate what his wife's rights would be if he *were.* But Newland Archer was too imaginative not to feel that, in his case and May's, the tie might gall for reasons far less gross and palpable. What could he and she really know of each other, since it was his duty, as a "decent" fellow, to conceal his past from her, and hers, as a marriageable girl, to have no past to conceal? What if, for some one of the subtler reasons that would tell with both of them, they should tire of each other, misunderstand or irritate each other? He reviewed his friends' marriages—the supposedly happy ones—and saw none that answered, even remotely, to the passionate and tender comradeship which he pictured as his permanent relation with May Welland. He perceived that such a picture presupposed, on her part, the experience, the versatility, the freedom of judgment, which she had been carefully trained not to possess; and with a shiver of foreboding he saw his marriage becoming what most of the other marriages about him were: a dull association of material and social interests held together by ignorance on the one side and hypocrisy on the other. Lawrence Lefferts occurred to him as the husband who had most completely realized this enviable ideal. As became the high priest of form, he had formed a wife so completely to his own convenience that, in the most conspicuous moments of his frequent love affairs with other men's wives, she went about in smiling unconsciousness, saying that "Lawrence was so frightfully strict"; and had been known to blush indignantly, and avert her gaze, when someone alluded in her presence to the fact that Julius Beaufort (as became a "foreigner" of doubtful origin) had what was known in New York as "another establishment."

Archer tried to console himself with the thought that he was not quite such an ass as Larry Lefferts, nor May such a simpleton as poor Gertrude; but the difference was after all one of intelligence and not of standard. In reality they all lived in a kind of hieroglyphic world, where the real thing was never said or done or even thought, but only represented by a set of arbitrary signs; as when Mrs. Welland, who knew exactly why Archer had pressed her to announce her daughter's engagement at the Beaufort ball (and had indeed expected him to do no less), yet felt obliged to simulate reluctance, and the air of having had her hand forced, quite as, in the books on Primitive Man that people of advanced culture were beginning to read, the savage bride is dragged with shrieks from her parents' tent.

The result, of course, was that the young girl who was the center of this elaborate system of mystification remained the more inscrutable for her very frankness and assurance. She was frank, poor darling, because she had nothing to conceal, assured because she knew of nothing to be on her guard against; and with no better preparation than this, she was to be plunged overnight into what people evasively called "the facts of life."

The young man was sincerely but placidly in love. He delighted in the radiant good looks of his betrothed, in her health, her horsemanship, her grace and quickness at games, and the shy interest in books and ideas that she was beginning to develop under his guidance. (She had advanced far enough to join him in ridiculing the "Idyls of the King," but not to feel the beauty of "Ulysses" and the "Lotus Eaters.") She was straightforward, loyal and brave; she had a sense of humor (chiefly proved by her laughing at *his* jokes); and he suspected, in the depths of her innocently gazing soul, a glow of feeling that it would be a joy to waken. But when he had gone the brief round of her he returned discouraged by the thought that all this frankness and innocence were only an artificial product. Untrained human nature was not frank and innocent; it was full of the twists and defenses of an instinctive guile. And he felt himself oppressed by this creation of factitious purity, so cunningly manufactured by a conspiracy of mothers and aunts and grandmothers and long-dead ancestresses, because it was supposed to be what he wanted, what he had a right to, in order that he might exercise his lordly pleasure in smashing it like an image made of snow.

There was a certain triteness in these reflections: they were those habitual to young men on the approach of their wedding day. But they were generally accompanied by a sense of compunction and self-abasement of which Newland Archer felt no trace. He could not deplore (as Thackeray's heroes so often exasperated him by doing) that he had not a blank page to offer his bride in exchange for the unblemished one she was to give to him. He could not get away from the fact that if he had been brought up as she had they would have been no more fit to find their way about than the Babes in the Wood; nor could he, for all his anxious citations, see any honest reason (any, that is, unconnected with his own momentary pleasure, and the passion of masculine vanity) why his bride should not have been allowed the same freedom of experience as himself.

Such questions, at such an hour, were bound to drift through his mind; but he was conscious that their uncomfortable persistence and precision were due to the inopportune arrival of the Countess Olenska. Here he was, at the very moment of his betrothal—a moment for pure thoughts and cloudless hopes— pitchforked into a coil of scandal which raised all the special problems he would have preferred to let lie. "Hang Ellen Olenska!" he grumbled, as he covered his fire and began to undress. He could not really see why her fate should have the least bearing on his; yet he dimly felt that he had only just begun to measure the risks of the championship which his engagement had forced upon him.

Years after their flirtation with having an affair, having succumbed to the expectations of his family and class and made a good marriage, Newland Archer visits Paris with his son and considers visiting the Countess. He makes it to her building, but cannot bring himself to go up. After all these years of wondering if he made the right decision, he realizes the memory of what might have been is more beautiful than the reality.

Newland Archer, looking out of his hotel window at the stately gaiety of the Paris streets, felt his heart beating with the confusion and eagerness of youth.

It was long since it had thus plunged and reared under his widening waistcoat, leaving him, the next minute, with an empty breast and hot temples. He wondered if it was thus that his son's conducted itself in the presence of Miss Fanny Beaufort—and decided that it was not. "It functions as actively, no doubt, but the rhythm is different," he reflected, recalling the cool composure with which the young man had announced his engagement, and taken for granted that his family would approve.

"The difference is that these young people take it for granted that they're going to get whatever they want, and that we almost always took it for granted that we shouldn't. Only, I wonder—the thing one's so certain of in advance: can it ever make one's heart beat as wildly?"

It was the day after their arrival in Paris, and the spring sunshine held Archer in his open window, above the wide silvery prospect of the Place Vendome. One of the things he had stipulated—almost the only one—when he had agreed to come abroad with Dallas, was that, in Paris, he shouldn't be made to go to one of the new-fangled "palaces."

"Oh, all right—of course," Dallas good-naturedly agreed. "I'll take you to some jolly old-fashioned place—the Bristol say—" leaving his father speechless at hearing that the century-long home of kings and emperors was now spoken of as an old-fashioned inn, where one went for its quaint inconveniences and lingering local color.

Archer had pictured often enough, in the first impatient years, the scene of his return to Paris; then the personal vision had faded, and he had simply tried to see the city as the setting of Madame Olenska's life. Sitting alone at night in his library, after the household had gone to bed, he had evoked the radiant outbreak of spring down the avenues of horse-chestnuts, the flowers and statues in the public gardens, the whiff of lilacs from the flower-carts, the majestic roll of the river under the great bridges, and the life of art and study and pleasure that filled each mighty artery to bursting. Now the spectacle was before him in its glory, and as he looked out on it he felt shy, old-fashioned, inadequate: a mere gray speck of a man compared with the ruthless magnificent fellow he had dreamed of being. . . .

Dallas's hand came down cheerily on his shoulder. "Hullo, Father: this is something like, isn't it?" They stood for a while looking out in silence, and then the young man continued: "By the way, I've got a message for you: the Countess Olenska expects us both at half-past five."

He said it lightly, carelessly, as he might have imparted any casual item of information, such as the hour at which their train was to leave for Florence the next evening. Archer looked at him, and thought he saw in his gay young eyes a gleam of his great-grandmother Mingott's malice.

"Oh, didn't I tell you?" Dallas pursued. "Fanny made me swear to do three things while I was in Paris: get her the score of the last Debussy songs, go to the Grand-Guignol, and see Madame Olenska. You know she was awfully good to Fanny when Mr. Beaufort sent her over from Buenos Aires to the Assomption. Fanny hadn't any friends in Paris, and Madame Olenska used to be kind to her and trot her about on holidays. I believe she was a great friend of the first Mrs. Beaufort's. And she's our cousin, of course. So I rang her up this morning before I went out, and told her you and I were here for two days and wanted to see her."

Archer continued to stare at him. "You told her I was here?"

"Of course—why not?" Dallas's eyebrows went up whimsically. Then, getting no answer, he slipped his arm through his father's with a confidential pressure.

"I say, Father: what was she like?"

Archer felt his color rise under his son's unabashed gaze.

"Come, own up: you and she were great pals, weren't you? Wasn't she most awfully lovely?"

"Lovely? I don't know. She was different."

"Ah—there you have it! That's what it always comes to, doesn't it? When she comes, *she's different*—and one doesn't know why. It's exactly what I feel about Fanny."

His father drew back a step, releasing his arm. "About Fanny? But, my dear fellow—I should hope so! Only I don't see—"

"Dash it, Dad, don't be prehistoric. Wasn't she—once—your Fanny?"

Dallas belonged body and soul to the new generation. He was the firstborn of Newland and May Archer, yet it had never been possible to inculcate in him even the rudiments of reserve. "What's the use of making mysteries? It only makes people want to nose 'em out," he always objected when enjoined to discretion. But Archer, meeting his eyes, saw the filial light under their banter.

"My Fanny—?"

"Well, the woman you'd have chucked everything for: only you didn't," continued his surprising son.

"I didn't," echoed Archer with a kind of solemnity.

"No: you date, you see, dear old boy. But Mother said . . . "

"Your mother?"

"Yes: the day before she died. It was when she sent for me alone—you remember? She said she knew we were safe with you, and always would be, because once, when she asked you to, you'd given up the thing you most wanted."

Archer received this strange communication in silence. His eyes remained unseeingly fixed on the thronged sunlit square below the window. At length he said in a low voice: "She never asked me."

"No. I forgot. You never did ask each other anything, did you? And you never told each other anything. You just sat and watched each other, and guessed at what was going on underneath. A deaf-and-dumb asylum, in fact. Well, I back your generation for knowing more about each other's private thoughts than we ever have time to find out about our own. I say, Dad," Dallas broke off, "you're not angry with me? If you are, let's make it up and go and lunch at Henri's. I've got to rush out to Versailles afterward."

Archer did not accompany his son to Versailles. He preferred to spend the afternoon in solitary roamings through Paris. He had to deal all at once with the packed regrets and stifled memories of an inarticulate lifetime.

After a little while he did not regret Dallas's indiscretion. It seemed to take an iron band from his heart to know that, after all, someone had guessed and pitied. . . . And that it should have been his wife moved him indescribably. Dallas, for all his affectionate insight, would not have understood that. To the boy, no doubt, the episode was only a pathetic instance of vain frustration, of wasted forces. But was it really no more? For a long time Archer sat on a bench in the Champs Elysees and wondered, while the stream of life rolled by. . . .

A few streets away, a few hours away, Ellen Olenska waited. She had never gone back to her husband, and when he had died, some years before, she had made no change in her way of living. There was nothing now to keep her and Archer apart—and that afternoon he was to see her.

He got up and walked across the Place de la Concorde and the Tuileries gardens to the Louvre. She had once told him that she often went there, and he had a fancy to spend the intervening time in a place where he could think of her as perhaps having lately been. For an hour or more he wandered from gallery to gallery through the dazzle of afternoon light, and one by one the pictures burst on him in their half-forgotten splendor, filling his soul with the long echoes of beauty. After all, his life had been too starved. . . .

Suddenly, before an effulgent Titian, he found himself saying —But I'm only fifty-seven" and then he turned away. For such summer dreams it was too late; but surely not of a quiet harvest of friendship, of comradeship, in the blessed hush of her nearness.

He went back to the hotel, where he and Dallas were to meet; and together they walked again across the Place de la Concorde and over the bridge that leads to the Chamber of Deputies.

Dallas, unconscious of what was going on in his father's mind, was talking excitedly and abundantly of Versailles. He had had but one previous glimpse of it, during a holiday trip in which he had tried to pack all the sights he had been deprived of when he had had to go with the family to Switzerland; and tumultuous enthusiasm and cocksure criticism tripped each other up on his lips.

As Archer listened, his sense of inadequacy and inexpressiveness increased. The boy was not insensitive, he knew; but he had the facility and self-confidence that came of looking at fate not as a master but as an equal. "That's it: they feel equal to things—they know their way about," he mused, thinking of his son as the spokesman of the new generation which had swept away all the old landmarks, and with them the sign-posts and the danger-signal.

Suddenly Dallas stopped short, grasping his father's arm. "Oh, by Jove," he exclaimed.

They had come out into the great tree-planted space before the Invalides. The dome of Mansart floated ethereally above the budding trees and the long gray front of the building: drawing up into itself all the rays of afternoon light, it hung there like the visible symbol of the race's glory.

Archer knew that Madame Olenska lived in a square near one of the avenues radiating from the Invalides; and he had pictured the quarter as quiet and almost obscure, forgetting the central splendor that lit it up. Now, by some queer process of association, that golden light became for him the pervading illumination in which she lived. For nearly thirty years, her life—of which he knew so strangely little—had been spent in this rich atmosphere that he already felt to be too dense and yet too stimulating for his lungs. He thought of the theaters she must have been to, the pictures she must have looked at, the sober and splendid old houses she must have frequented, the people she must have talked with, the incessant stir of ideas, curiosities, images, and associations thrown out by an intensely social race in a setting of immemorial manners; and suddenly he remembered the young Frenchman who had once said to him: "Ah, good conversation—there is nothing like it, is there?"

Archer had not seen M. Riviere, or heard of him, for nearly thirty years; and that fact gave the measure of his ignorance of Madame Olenska's existence. More than half a lifetime divided them, and she had spent the long interval among people he did not know, in a society he but faintly guessed at, in conditions he would never wholly understand. During that time he had been living with his youthful memory of her; but she had doubtless had other and more tangible companionship. Perhaps she too had kept her memory of him as something apart; but if she had, it must have been like a relic in a small dim chapel, where there was not time to pray every day. . . .

They had crossed the Place des Invalides, and were walking down one of the thoroughfares flanking the building. It was a quiet quarter, after all, in spite of its splendor and its history; and the fact gave one an idea of the riches Paris had to draw on, since such scenes as this were left to the few and the indifferent.

The day was fading into a soft sun-shot haze, pricked here and there by a yellow electric light, and passers were rare in the little square into which they had turned. Dallas stopped again, and looked up.

"It must be here," he said, slipping his arm through his father's with a movement from which Archer's shyness did not shrink; and they stood together looking up at the house.

It was a modern building, without distinctive character, but many-windowed, and pleasantly balconied up its wide cream-colored front. On one of the upper balconies, which hung well above the rounded tops of the horse-chestnuts in the square, the awnings were still lowered, as though the sun had just left it.

"I wonder which floor—?" Dallas conjectured and moving toward the *porte-cochère* he put his head into the porter's lodge, and came back to say, "The fifth. It must be the one with the awnings."

Archer remained motionless, gazing at the upper windows as if the end of their pilgrimage had been attained.

"I say, you know, it's nearly six," his son at length reminded him.

The father glanced away at an empty bench under the trees.

"I believe I'll sit there a moment," he said.

"Why—aren't you well?" his son exclaimed.

"Oh, perfectly. But I should like you, please, to go up without me."

Dallas paused before him, visibly bewildered. "But, I say, Dad: do you mean you won't come up at all?"

"I don't know," said Archer slowly.

"If you don't she won't understand."

"Go, my boy; perhaps I shall follow you."

Dallas gave him a long look through the twilight.

"But what on earth shall I say?"

"My dear fellow, don't you always know what to say?" his father rejoined with a smile.

"Very well. I shall say you're old-fashioned, and prefer walking up the five flights because you don't like lifts."

His father smiled again. "Say I'm old-fashioned: that's enough."

Dallas looked at him again, and then, with an incredulous gesture, passed out of sight under the vaulted doorway.

Archer sat down on the bench and continued to gaze at the

awninged balcony. He calculated the time it would take his son to be carried up in the lift to the fifth floor, to ring the bell, and be admitted to the hall, and then ushered into the drawing room. He pictured Dallas entering that room with his quick assured step; and his delightful smile, and wondered if the people were right who said that his boy "took after him."

Then he tried to see the persons already in the room—for probably at that sociable hour there would be more than one—and among them a dark lady, pale and dark, who would look up quickly, half rise, and hold out a long thin hand with three rings on it. . . . He thought she would be sitting in a sofa-corner near the fire, with azaleas banked behind her on a table.

"It's more real to me here than if I went up," he suddenly heard himself say; and the fear lest that last shadow of reality should lose its edge kept him rooted to his seat as the minutes succeeded each other.

He sat for a long time on the bench in the thickening dusk, his eyes never turning from the balcony. At length a light shone through the windows, and a moment later a man-servant came out on the balcony, drew up the awnings, and closed the shutters.

At that, as if it had been the signal he waited for, Newland Archer got up slowly and walked back alone to his hotel.

2

THE GENTLEMAN

WHAT DOES IT MEAN TO BE A GENTLEMAN? MOST OF US WOULD associate the idea with a certain standard of exterior refinement. A gentleman dresses well, has perfect, unobtrusive manners. He is urbane, an excellent conversationalist, and can put others at their ease. He is well informed about art, literature, music, and current events. True gentlemen are often said to exhibit the signs of good "breeding"—an old-fashioned word that historically had as much to do with innate character and instinct as with class or inherited privilege. Traditional interpreters of manliness, as the readings in this section make very clear, have always pointed to signs of natural ability and refinement, rather than background, as the hallmarks of a gentleman.

A gentleman, then, is one who knows, in any circumstances, just how to act. His dress, bearing, and knowledge are worn lightly, never ostentatiously. A gentleman does not call attention to himself by flaunting his superiority. In conversation, for example, he will say something if he has something worthwhile to contribute; yet if he happens to be an expert on any given topic, he will never resort to showing off. Confidence, self-assurance, modesty, and consideration are equally apportioned in his character, and in the end his quiet, judicious contributions will leave his companions duly impressed.

Gentlemanliness, in short, is about what's on the inside, not on the outside. True gentlemanliness should not be confused with mere surface polish, foppery, flattery, or dandyism. A man may be genteel, Samuel Johnson observed, and yet immoral: "Many of his vices may be committed very genteelly, a man may debauch his friend's wife most genteely, he may cheat at cards most genteelly." It is important to distinguish between the true gentleman and his counterfeit, the man of shallow charm or sophistication. The counterfeit gentleman is nothing but surfaces, while a true gentleman's outward graciousness stems from inward virtues of mind and temperament. In this section, readers can sample a wide variety of commentary on the gentlemanly character, and how this character reveals itself in conduct.

Edmund Burke has described a gentleman as one who possesses a "most perfect vigor" and maturity in thought, and who actively cultivates in himself thoughts of kindness, generosity, and honesty. To this, Ralph Waldo Emerson adds that a gentleman is a creature of sense, of grace, of accomplishment, and of social power. Though the true gentleman is commonly a man of cultivation and learning, in the end neither intellect nor education alone will carry the day: Even the most brilliant scientists or philosophers can be callous or selfish, faithless or even ruthless. As Daniel Defoe puts it, "A man that understands everybody is understood by nobody." The intellect that develops entirely on its own, without guidance from sentiment or character, runs the risk of becoming detached, cold, even inhuman. That is why Aristotle, in the *Nicomachean Ethics*, stresses that a virtuous man needs friends with whom he can cooperate in some honorable enterprise. A gentleman is generous in recognizing the merits of his friends, and he wants friends whose honor is worth having.

Finally, a gentleman is "gentle" not merely in the sense of gracious bearing and a soft-spoken presence, but in the deeper sense of compassion for those who suffer. As Thomas Dekker wrote in 1604, he is patient, humble, and of tranquil spirit. Perhaps this aspect of manliness is best summed up by Cardinal Newman, who included in *The Idea of a University* an observation compelling in its simplicity and difficult to deny: "It is almost the definition of a gentleman," he writes, "that he is one who never inflicts pain."

A WELL-BRED MAN

Austen on Gentlemanliness

From Jane Austen, Emma

In Jane Austen's 1816 novel, Emma Woodhouse and her protégé Harriet Smith discuss the merits and drawbacks of the different varieties of gentleman. Emma believes Harriet is too good to marry a young farmer, Robert Martin. He isn't a gentleman like Emma's friend Mr. Knightley. Won't she find a farmer's life too narrow and uncultured? Emma believes a clergyman, Mr. Elton, is the right match for Harriet. When Robert Martin sends Harriet a letter of proposal, Emma persuades her to turn him down. But Mr. Knightley reproaches Emma for her meddling and snobbery.

They met Mr. Martin the very next day, as they were walking on the Donwell road. He was on foot, and after looking very respectfully at her, looked with most unfeigned satisfaction at her companion. Emma was not sorry to have such an opportunity of survey; and walking a few yards forward, while they talked together, soon made her quick eye sufficiently acquainted with Mr. Robert Martin. His appearance was very neat, and he looked like a sensible young man, but his person had no other advantage; and when he came to be contrasted with gentlemen, she thought he must lose all the ground he had gained in Harriet's inclination. Harriet was not insensible of manner; she had voluntarily noticed her father's gentleness with admiration as well as wonder. Mr. Martin looked as if he did not know what manner was.

They remained but a few minutes together, as Miss Woodhouse must not be kept waiting; and Harriet then came running to her with a smiling face, and in a flutter of spirits, which Miss Woodhouse hoped very soon to compose.

"Only think of our happening to meet him! How very odd! It was quite a chance, he said, that he had not gone round by Randalls. He did not think we ever walked this road. He thought we

walked toward Randalls most days. He has not been able to get the
'Romance of the Forest' yet. He was so busy the last time he was at
Kingston that he quite forgot it, but he goes again tomorrow. So
very odd we should happen to meet! Well, Miss Woodhouse, is he
like what you expected? What do you think of him? Do you think
him so very plain?"

"He is very plain, undoubtedly—remarkably plain: but that is
nothing, compared with his entire want of gentility. I had no right
to expect much, and I did not expect much; but I had no idea that
he could be so very clownish, so totally without air. I had imagined
him, I confess, a degree or two nearer gentility."

"To be sure," said Harriet, in a mortified voice, "he is not so
genteel as real gentlemen."

"I think, Harriet, since your acquaintance with us, you have
been repeatedly in the company of some, such very real gentlemen,
that you must yourself be struck with the difference in Mr. Martin. At
Hartfield you have had very good specimens of well-educated, well-
bred men. I should be surprised if, after seeing them, you could be in
company with Mr. Martin again without perceiving him to be a very
inferior creature—and rather wondering at yourself for having ever
thought him at all agreeable before. Do not you begin to feel that
now? Were not you struck? I am sure you must have been struck by his
awkward look and abrupt manner—and the uncouthness of a voice,
which I heard to be wholly unmodulated as I stood here."

"Certainly, he is not like Mr. Knightley. He has not such a fine
air and way of walking as Mr. Knightley. I see the difference plain
enough. But Mr. Knightley is so very fine a man!"

"Mr. Knightley's air is so remarkably good, that it is not fair to
compare Mr. Martin with *him*. You might not see one in a hundred,
with *gentleman* so plainly written as in Mr. Knightley. But he is not
the only gentleman you have been lately used to. What say you to
Mr. Weston and Mr. Elton? Compare Mr. Martin with either of *them*.
Compare their manner of carrying themselves; of walking; of
speaking; of being silent. You must see the difference."

"Oh, yes! There is a great difference. But Mr. Weston is almost
an old man. Mr. Weston must be between forty and fifty."

"Which makes his good manners the more valuable. The older
a person grows, Harriet, the more important it is that their manners should not be bad—the more glaring and disgusting any loud-
ness, or coarseness, or awkwardness become. What is passable in
youth, is detestable in later age. Mr. Martin is now awkward and
abrupt; what will he be at Mr. Weston's time of life?"

"There is no saying, indeed!" replied Harriet, rather solemnly.

"But there may be pretty good guessing. He will be a completely gross, vulgar farmer—totally inattentive to appearances, and thinking of nothing but profit and loss."

"Will he, indeed? that will be very bad."

"How much his business engrosses him already, is very plain from the circumstance of his forgetting to inquire for the book you recommended. He was a great deal too full of the market to think of anything else—which is just as it should be, for a thriving man. What has he to do with books? And I have no doubt that he *will* thrive and be a very rich man in time—and his being illiterate and coarse need not disturb *us*."

"I wonder he did not remember the book" was all Harriet's answer, and spoken with a degree of grave displeasure which Emma thought might be safely left to itself. She, therefore, said no more for some time. Her next beginning was,

"In one respect, perhaps, Mr. Elton's manners are superior to Mr. Knightley's or Mr. Weston's. They have more gentleness. They might be more safely held up as a pattern. There is an openness, a quickness, almost a bluntness in Mr. Weston, which everybody likes in *him* because there is so much good humor with it—but that would not do to be copied. Neither would Mr. Knightley's downright, decided, commanding sort of manner—though it suits *him* very well; his figure and look, and situation in life seem to allow it; but if any young man were to set about copying him, he would not be sufferable. On the contrary, I think a young man might be very safely recommended to take Mr. Elton as a model. Mr. Elton is good humored, cheerful, obliging, and gentle. He seems to me to be grown particularly gentle of late. I do not know whether he has any design of ingratiating himself with either of us, Harriet, by additional softness, but it strikes me that his manners are softer than they used to be. If he means anything, it must be to please you. Did not I tell you what he said of you the other day?"

She then repeated some warm personal praise which she had drawn from Mr. Elton, and now did full justice to; and Harriet blushed and smiled, and said she had always thought Mr. Elton very agreeable.

Mr. Elton was the very person fixed on by Emma for driving the young farmer out of Harriet's head. She thought it would be an excellent match; and only too palpably desirable, natural, and probable, for her to have much merit in planning it. She feared it was what everybody else must think of and predict. It was not likely, however, that anybody should have equaled her in the date of the plan, as it had entered her brain during the very first evening of Harriet's coming to Hartfield. The longer she considered it, the greater was her sense of its expediency. Mr. Elton's situation was most suitable, quite the gentleman himself, and without low connections; at the same time not of any family that could fairly object to the doubtful birth of Harriet. He had a comfortable home for her, and Emma imagined a very sufficient income; for though the vicarage of Highbury was not large, he was known to have some independent property; and she thought very highly of him as a good-humored, well-meaning, respectable young man, without any deficiency of useful understanding or knowledge of the world.

She had already satisfied herself that he thought Harriet a beautiful girl, which she trusted, with such frequent meetings at Hartfield, was foundation enough on his side; and on Harriet's, there could be little doubt that the idea of being preferred by him would have all the usual weight and efficacy. And he was really a very pleasing young man, a young man whom any woman not fastidious might like.

The very day of Mr. Elton's going to London produced a fresh occasion for Emma's services toward her friend. Harriet had been at Hartfield, as usual, soon after breakfast; and after a time, had gone home to return again to dinner: she returned, and sooner than had been talked of, and with an agitated, hurried look announcing something extraordinary to have happened which she was longing to tell. Half a minute brought it all out. She had heard, as soon as she got back to Mrs. Goddard's, that Mr. Martin had been there an hour before, and finding she was not at home, nor particularly expected, had left a little parcel for her from one of his sisters, and gone away; and on opening this parcel, she had actually found, besides the two songs which she had lent Elizabeth to copy, a letter to herself; and this letter was from him, from Mr. Martin, and contained a direct proposal of marriage. "Who could have thought it! She was so surprised she did not know what to do. Yes, quite a proposal of marriage; and a very good letter, at least she thought so. And he wrote as if he really loved her very much—but she did not know—and so, she was come as fast as she could to ask Miss Woodhouse what she should do." Emma was half ashamed of her friend for seeming so pleased and so doubtful.

"Upon my word," she cried, "the young man is determined not to lose anything for want of asking. He will connect himself well if he can."

"Will you read the letter?" cried Harriet. "Pray do. I'd rather you would."

Emma was not sorry to be pressed. She read, and was surprised. The style of the letter was much above her expectation. There were not merely no grammatical errors, but as a composition it would not have disgraced a gentleman; the language, though plain, was strong and unaffected, and the sentiments it conveyed very much to the credit of the writer. It was short, but expressed good sense, warm attachment, liberality, propriety, even delicacy of feeling. She paused over it, while Harriet stood anxiously watching for her opinion, with a "Well, well," and was at last forced to add, "Is it a good letter? Or is it too short?"

"Yes, indeed, a very good letter," replied Emma rather slowly— "so good a letter, Harriet, that everything considered, I think one of his sisters must have helped him. I can hardly image the young man whom I saw talking with you the other day could express himself so well, if left quite to his own powers, and yet it is not the style of a woman; no, certainly, it is too strong and concise; not diffuse enough for a woman. No doubt he is a sensible man, and I suppose may have a natural talent for—thinks strongly and clearly—and when he takes a pen in hand, his thoughts naturally find proper words. It is so with some men. Yes, I understand the sort of mind. Vigorous, decided, with sentiments to a certain point, not coarse. A better written letter, Harriet (returning it), than I had expected."

"Well," said the still waiting Harriet;—"well—and—and what shall I do?"

"Dear affectionate creature! —*You* banished to Abbey-Mill Farm!—*You* confined to the society of the illiterate and vulgar all your life! I wonder how the young man could have the assurance to ask it. He must have a pretty good opinion of himself."

"I do not think he is conceited either, in general," said Harriet, her conscience opposing such censure; "at least he is very good natured, and I shall always feel much obliged to him, and have a great regard for—but that is quite a different thing from—and you know, though he may like me, it does not follow that I should—and certainly I must confess that since my visiting here I have seen people—and if one comes to compare them, person and manners, there is no comparison at all, *one* is so very handsome and agreeable. However, I do really think Mr. Martin a very amiable young man, and have a great opinion of him; and his being so attached to me—and his writing such a letter—but as to leaving you, it is what I would not do upon any consideration."

"Thank you, thank you, my own sweet little friend. We will not be parted. A woman is not to marry a man merely because she is asked, or because he is attached to her, and can write a tolerable letter."

"Oh! No; and it is but a short letter too."

Emma felt the bad taste of her friend, but let it pass with a "very true; and it would be a small consolation to her, for the clownish manner which might be offending her every hour of the day, to know that her husband could write a good letter."

Mr. Knightley tells Emma that Robert Martin is the right match for Harriet. He is in for a shock.

"Robert Martin is the man. Her visit to Abbey-Mill, this summer, seems to have done his business. He is desperately in love and means to marry her."

"He is very obliging," said Emma; "but is he sure that Harriet means to marry him?"

"Well, well, means to make her an offer then. Will that do? He came to the Abbey two evenings ago, on purpose to consult me about it. He knows I have a thorough regard for him and all his family. And, I believe, considers me as one of his best friends. He came to ask me whether I thought it would be imprudent in him to settle so early; whether I thought her too young: in short, whether I approved his choice altogether; having some apprehension perhaps of her being considered (especially since *your* making so much of her) as in a line of society above him. I was very much pleased with all that he said. I never hear better sense from anyone than Robert Martin. He always speaks to the purpose; open, straightforward, and very well judging. He told me everything; his circumstances and plans, and what they all proposed doing in the event of his marriage. He is an excellent young man, both as son and brother. I had no hesitation in advising him to marry. He proved to me that he could afford it; and that being the case, I was convinced he could not do better. I praised the fair lady too, and altogether sent him away very happy. If he had never esteemed my opinion before, he would have thought highly of me then; and, I daresay, left the house thinking me the best friend and counselor man ever had. This happened the night before last. Now, as we may fairly suppose, he would not allow much time to pass before he spoke to the lady, and as he does not appear to have spoken yesterday, it is not unlikely that he should be at Mrs. Goddard's today;

and she may be detained by a visitor, without thinking him at all a tiresome wretch."

"Pray, Mr. Knightley," said Emma, who had been smiling to herself through a great part of this speech, "how do you know that Mr. Martin did not speak yesterday?"

"Certainly," replied he, surprised, "I do not absolutely know it; but it may be inferred. Was not she the whole day with you?"

"Come," said she, "I will tell you something, in return for what you have told me. He did speak yesterday—that is, he wrote and was refused."

This was obliged to be repeated before it could be believed and Mr. Knightley actually looked red with surprise and displeasure, as he stood up, in tall indignation, and said,

"Then she is a greater simpleton than I ever believed her. What is the foolish girl about?"

"Oh! To be sure," cried Emma, "it is always incomprehensible to a man that a woman should ever refuse an offer of marriage. A man always imagines a woman to be ready for anybody who asks her."

"Nonsense! A man does not imagine any such thing. But what is the meaning of this? Harriet Smith refuse Robert Martin? Madness, if it is so; but I hope you are mistaken."

"I saw her answer, nothing could be clearer."

"You saw her answer! You wrote her answer too. Emma, this is your doing. You persuaded her to refuse him."

"And if I did (which, however, I am far from allowing), I should not feel that I had done wrong. Mr. Martin is a very respectable young man, but I cannot admit him to be Harriet's equal and am rather surprised indeed that he should have ventured to address her. By your account, he does seem to have had some scruples. It is a pity that they were ever got over."

"Not Harriet's equal!" exclaimed Mr. Knightley loudly and warmly; and with calmer asperity, added, a few moments afterward, "No, he is not her equal indeed, for he is as much her superior in sense as in situation. Emma, your infatuation about that girl blinds you. What are Harriet Smith's claims, either of birth, nature, or education, to any connection higher than Robert Martin? She is the natural daughter of nobody knows whom, with probably no settled provision at all, and certainly no respectable relations. She is known only as parlor-boarder at a common school. She is not a sensible girl, nor a girl of any information. She has been taught nothing useful, and is too young and too simple to have acquired anything herself. At her age she can have no experience, and with her little wit, is not very likely ever to have any that can avail her. She is pretty, and she is good tempered, and that is all. My only scruple in advising the match was on his account, as being beneath his deserts, and a bad connection for him. I felt that, as to fortune, in all probability he might do much better; and that as to a rational companion or useful helpmate, he could not do worse. But I could not reason so to a man in love, and was willing to trust to there being no harm in her, to her having that sort of disposition, which, in good hands, like his, might be easily led aright and turn out very well. The advantage of the match I felt to be all on her side; and had not the smallest doubt (nor have I now) that there would be a general cry-out upon her extreme good luck. Even *your* satisfaction I made sure of. It crossed my mind immediately that you would not regret your friend's leaving Highbury, for the sake of her being set-tled so well. I remember saying to myself, 'Even Emma, with all her partiality for Harriet, will think this a good match.'"

"I cannot help wondering at your knowing so little of Emma as to say such a thing. What! Think a farmer (and with all his sense and all his merit Mr. Martin is nothing more) a good match for my intimate friend! Not regret her leaving Highbury for the sake of marrying a man whom I could never admit as an acquaintance of my own! I wonder you should think it possible for me to have such feelings. I assure you mine are very different. I must think your statement by no means fair. You are not just to Harriet's claims. They would be estimated very differently by others as well as myself; Mr. Martin may be the richest of the two, but he is undoubtedly her inferior as to rank in society. The sphere in which she moves is much above his. It would be a degradation."

"A degradation to illegitimacy and ignorance, to be married to a respectable, intelligent gentleman-farmer!"

"As to the circumstances of her birth, though in a legal sense she may be called Nobody, it will not hold in common sense. She is not to pay for the offense of others, by being held below the level of those with whom she is brought up. There can scarcely be a doubt that her father is a gentleman—and a gentleman of fortune.—Her allowance is very liberal; nothing has ever been grudged for her improvement or comfort. That she is a gentleman's daughter, is indubitable to me; that she associates with gentlemen's daughters, no one, I apprehend, will deny. She is superior to Mr. Robert Martin."

"Whoever might be her parents," said Mr. Knightley, "whoever may have had the charge of her, it does not appear to have been any part of their plan to introduce her into what you would call good society. After receiving a very indifferent education she is left in Mrs. Goddard's hands to shift as she can; to move, in short, in Mrs. Goddard's line, to have Mrs. Goddard's acquaintance. Her friends evidently thought this good enough for her; and it *was* good enough. She desired nothing better herself. Till you chose to turn her into a friend, her mind had no distaste for her own set, nor any ambition beyond it. She was as happy as possible with the Martins in the summer. She had no sense of superiority then. If she has it now, you have given it. You have been no friend to Harriet Smith, Emma. Robert Martin would never have proceeded so far, if he had not felt persuaded of her not being disinclined to him. I know him well. He has too much real feeling to address any woman on the haphazard of selfish passion. And as to conceit, he is the furthest from it of any man I know. Depend upon it he had encouragement."

It was most convenient to Emma not to make a direct reply to his assertion; she chose rather to take up her own line of the subject again.

"You are a very warm friend to Mr. Martin; but, as I said before, are unjust to Harriet. Harriet's claims to marry well are not so contemptible as you represent them. She is not a clever girl, but she has better sense than you are aware of, and does not deserve to have her understanding spoken of so slightingly. Waiving that point, however, and supposing her to be, as you describe her, only pretty and good natured, let me tell you, that in the degree she possesses them, they are not trivial recommendations to the world in general, for she is, in fact, a beautiful girl, and must be thought so by ninety-nine people out of a hundred; and till it appears that men are much more philosophic on the subject of beauty than they are generally supposed; till they do fall in love with well-informed minds instead of handsome faces, a girl, with such loveliness as Harriet, has a certainty of being admired and sought after, of having the power of choosing from among many, consequently a claim to be nice. Her good nature, too, is not so very slight a claim, comprehending, as it does, real, thorough sweetness of temper and manner, a very humble opinion of herself, and a great readiness to be pleased with other people. I am very much mistaken if your sex in general would think such beauty, and such temper, the highest claims a woman could possess."

"Upon my word, Emma, to hear you abusing the reason you have, is almost enough to make me think so too. Better be without sense, than misapply it as you do."

A Gentleman Avoids Vulgarity

From Lord Chesterfield,
The Letters of Lord Chesterfield to His Son

Lord Chesterfield's letters show us how a father can combine affection for his son with demanding standards of decency, learning, and manners. Chesterfield (1694–1773), who never intended these letters to be seen by others, achieved posthumous fame upon their publication by his son's widow.

A vulgar man is captious and jealous; eager and impetuous about trifles. He suspects himself to be slighted, thinks everything that is said is meant at him; if the company happens to laugh, he is persuaded they laugh at him; he grows angry and testy, says something very impertinent, and draws himself into a scrape, by showing what he calls a proper spirit, and asserting himself. A man of fashion does not suppose himself to be either the sole or principal object of the thoughts, looks, or words of the company; and never suspects that he is either slighted or laughed at, unless he is conscious that he deserves it. And if (which very seldom happens) the company is absurd or ill-bred enough to do either, he does not care two-pence, unless the insult be so gross and plain as to require satisfaction of another kind. As he is above trifles, he is never vehement and eager about them; and, wherever they are concerned, rather acquiesces than wrangles. A vulgar man's conversation always savors strongly of the lowness of his education and company. It turns chiefly upon his domestic affairs, his servants, the excellent order he keeps in his own family, and the little anecdotes of the neighborhood; all which he relates with emphasis, as interesting matters. He is a man gossip.

There is an incontinency of friendship among young fellows, who are associated by their mutual pleasures only, which has, very frequently, bad consequences. A parcel of warm hearts and inexperienced heads, heated by convivial mirth, and possibly a little too much wine, vow, and really mean at the time, eternal friendship to each other, and indiscreetly pour out their whole souls in common, and without the least reserve. These confidences are as indiscreetly repealed as they were made: for new pleasures and new places soon dissolve this ill-cemented connection; and then very ill uses are made of these rash confidences. Bear your part, however, in young companies; nay, excel if you can in all the social and convivial joy and festivity that become youth. Trust them with your love-tales, if you please, but keep your serious views secret. Trust those only to some tried friend more experienced than yourself, and who, being in a different walk of life from you, is not likely to become your rival; for I would not advise you to depend so much upon the heroic virtue of mankind as to hope or believe that your competitor will ever be your friend, as to the object of that competition.

There is nothing so delicate as your moral character, and nothing which it is your interest so much to preserve pure. Should you be suspected of injustice, malignity, perfidy, lying, etc., all the parts and knowledge in the world will never procure you esteem, friendship, or respect. A strange concurrence of circumstances has sometimes raised very bad men to high stations; but they have been raised like criminals to a pillory, where their persons and their crimes, by being more conspicuous, are only the more known, the more detested, and the more pelted and insulted. If, in any case whatsoever, affectation and ostentation are pardonable, it is in the case of morality; though, even there, I would not advise you to a pharisaical pomp of virtue. But I will recommend to you a most scrupulous tenderness for your moral character, and the utmost care not to say or do the least thing that may, ever so slightly, taint it. Show yourself, upon all occasions, the advocate, the friend, but not the bully, of Virtue. Colonel Chartres, whom you have certainly heard of (who was, I believe, the most notorious blasted rascal in the world, and who had, by all sorts of crimes, amassed immense wealth), was so sensible of the disadvantage of a bad character, that I heard him once say, in his impudent profligate manner, that, though he would not give one farthing for virtue, he would give ten thousand pounds for a character; because he should get a hundred thousand by it: whereas he was so blasted that he had no longer an opportunity of cheating people. Is it possible then that an honest man can neglect what a wise rogue would purchase so dear?

These amiable accomplishments are all to be acquired by use and imitation; for we are, in truth, more than half what we are, by imitation. The great point is, to choose good models, and to study them with care. People insensibly contract, not only the air, the manners, and the vices, of those with whom they commonly converse, but their virtues too, and even their way of thinking. This is so true, that I have known very plain understandings catch a certain degree of wit, by constantly conversing with those who had a great deal. Persist, therefore, in keeping the best company, and you will insensibly become like them; but if you add attention and observation, you will very soon be one of them. This inevitable contagion of company, shows you the necessity of keeping the best, and avoiding all other; for in every one, something will stick. You have hitherto, I confess, had very few opportunities of keeping polite company. Westminster school is, undoubtedly, the seat of illiberal manners and brutal behavior. Leipsig, I suppose, is not the seat of refined and elegant manners. Venice, I believe, has done something; Rome, I hope, will do a great deal more; and Paris will, I daresay, do all that you want: always supposing, that you frequent the best companies, and in the intention of improving and forming yourself; for, without that intention, nothing will do.

Many people lose a great deal of their time by laziness; they loll and yawn in a great chair, tell themselves that they have not time to begin anything then, and that it will do as well another time. This is a most unfortunate disposition, and the greatest obstruction to both knowledge and business. At your age, you have no right nor claim to laziness as I have, if I please, being *emeritus*. You are but just listed in the world, and must be active, diligent, indefatigable. If ever you propose commanding with dignity, you must serve up to it with diligence. Never put off till tomorrow what you can do today.

For instance: do you use yourself to carve, eat, and drink genteelly, and with ease? Do you take care to walk, sit, stand, and present yourself gracefully? Are you sufficiently upon your guard against awkward attitudes, and illiberal, ill-bred, and disgusting habits; such as scratching yourself, putting your fingers in your mouth, nose, and ears? Tricks always acquired at schools, often too much neglected afterward; but, however, extremely ill-bred and nauseous. For I do not conceive that any man has a right to exhibit, in company, any one excrement, more than another. Do you dress well, and think a little of the *brillant* in your person? That too is necessary, because it is *prévenant*. Do you aim at easy, engaging, but at the same time civil or respectful manners, according to the company you are in? These, and a thousand other things, which you will observe in people of fashion, better than I can describe them, are absolutely necessary for every man; but still more for you, than for almost any man living. The showish, the shining, the engaging parts of the character of a fine gentleman, should (considering your destination) be the principal objects of your present attention.

The Sun King

From the Duke of Saint-Simon, The Memoirs of the Duke of Saint-Simon

Not without flaws, Louis XIV nevertheless displayed great refinement of manners. From a secret diary of the Sun King's court by Louis de Rouvroy, Duc de Saint Simon (1675–1755), published posthumously in 1829.

At twenty-three years of age he entered the great world as King, under the most favorable auspices. His ministers were the most skillful in all Europe; his generals the best; his Court was filled with illustrious and clever men, formed during the troubles which had followed the death of Louis XIII.

Louis XIV was made for a brilliant Court. In the midst of other men, his figure, his courage, his grace, his beauty, his grand mien, even the tone of his voice and the majestic and natural charm of all his person, distinguished him till his death as the King Bee, and showed that if he had only been born a simple private gentlemen, he would equally have excelled in fêtes, pleasures, and gallantry, and would have had the greatest success in love. The intrigues and adventures which early in life he had been engaged in—when the Comtesse de Soissons lodged at the Tuileries, as superintendent of the Queen's household, and was the center figure of the Court group—had exercised an unfortunate influence upon him: he received those impressions with which he could never after successfully struggle. From this time, intellect, education, nobility of sentiment, and high principle, in others, became objects of suspicion to him, and soon of hatred. The more he advanced in years the more this sentiment was confirmed in him. He wished to reign by himself. His jealousy on this point unceasingly became weakness.

Never did man give with better grace than Louis XIV, or augmented so much, in this way, the price of his benefits. Never did man sell to better profit his words, even his smiles, nay, his looks. Never did disobliging words escape him; and if he had to blame, to reprimand, or correct, which was very rare, it was nearly always with goodness, never, except on one occasion (the admonition of Courtenvaux, related in its place), with anger or severity. Never was man so naturally polite, or of a politeness so measured, so graduated, so adapted to person, time, and place. Toward women his politeness was without parallel. Never did he pass the humblest petticoat without raising his hat; even to chambermaids, that he knew to be such, as often happened at Marly. For ladies he took his hat off completely, but to a greater or less extent; for titled people, half off, holding it in his hand or against his ear some instants, more or less marked. For the nobility he contented himself by putting his hand to his hat. He took it off for the Princes of the blood, as for the ladies. If he accosted ladies he did not cover himself until he had quitted them. All this was out of doors, for in the house he was never covered. His reverences, more or less marked, but always light, were incomparable for their grace and manner; even his mode of half raising himself at supper for each lady who arrived at table. Though at last this fatigued him, yet he never ceased it; the ladies who were to sit down, however, took care not to enter after supper had commenced.

If he was made to wait for anything while dressing, it was always with patience. He was exact to the hours that he gave for all his day, with a precision clear and brief in his orders. If in the bad weather of winter, when he could not go out, he went to Madame de Maintenon's a quarter of an hour earlier than he had arranged (which seldom happened), and the captain of the guards was not on duty, he did not fail afterward to say that it was his own fault for anticipating the hour, not that of the captain of the guards for being absent. Thus, with this regularity which he never deviated from, he was served with the utmost exactitude.

The Importance of Good Grooming and Good Company

From Lord Chesterfield,
The Letters of Lord Chesterfield to His Son

But I must remind you, at the same time, that it will be to very little purpose for you to frequent good company, if you do not conform to, and learn, their manners; if you are not attentive to please, and well bred, with the easiness of a man of fashion. As you must attend to your manners, so you must not neglect your person; but take care to be very clean, well dressed, and genteel; to have no disagreeable attitudes, nor awkward tricks, which many people use themselves to, and then cannot leave them off. Do you take care to keep your teeth very clean, by washing them constantly every morning, and after every meal? This is very necessary, both to preserve your teeth a great while, and to save you a great deal of pain. Mine have plagued me long, and are now falling out, merely for want of care when I was your age.

The next thing to the choice of your friends, is the choice of your company. Endeavor, as much as you can, to keep company with people above you. There you rise, as much as you sink with people below you; for (as I have mentioned before) you are, whatever the company you keep is. Do not mistake, when I say company above you, and think that I mean with regard to their birth; that is the least consideration: but I mean with regard to their merit, and the light in which the world considers them.

But what I do, and ever shall, regret, is the time which, while young, I lost in mere idleness, and in doing nothing. This is the common effect of the inconsideracy of youth, against which I beg you will be most carefully upon your guard. The value of moments, when cast up, is immense, if well employed; if thrown away, their loss is irrecoverable. Every moment may be put to some use, and that with much more pleasure than if unemployed.

The characteristic of a well-bred man is, to converse with his inferiors without insolence, and with his superiors with respect and with ease. He talks to kings without concern; he trifles with women of the first condition, with familiarity, gaiety, but respect; and converses with his equals, whether he is acquainted with them or not, upon general, common topics, that are not, however, quite frivolous, without the least concern of mind, or awkwardness of body; neither of which can appear to advantage, but when they are perfectly easy.

You are now come to an age capable of reflection, and I hope you will do, what, however, few people at your age do, exert it, of your own sake, in the search of truth and sound knowledge. I will confess (for I am not unwilling to discover my secrets to you) that it is not many years since I have presumed to reflect for myself. Till sixteen or seventeen, I had no reflection; and, for many years after that, I made no use of what I had. I adopted the notions of the books I read, or the company I kept, without examining whether they were just or not; and I rather chose to run the risk of easy error, than to take the time and trouble of investigating truth. Thus, partly from laziness, partly from dissipation, and partly from the *mauvaise honte* of rejecting fashionable notions, I was (as I have since found) hurried away by prejudices, instead of being guided by reason; and quietly cherished error, instead of seeking for truth. But since I have taken the trouble of reasoning for myself, and have had the courage to own that I do so, you cannot imagine how much my notions of things are altered, and in how different a light I now see them, from that in which I formerly viewed them through the deceitful medium of prejudice or authority. Nay, I may possibly still retain many errors, which from long habit, have perhaps grown into real opinions; for it is very difficult to distinguish habits, early acquired and long entertained, from the result of our reason and reflection.

What I have now said, together with your own good sense, is I hope sufficient to arm you against the seduction, the invitations, or the profligate exhortations (for I cannot call them temptations) of these unfortunate young people. On the other hand, when they would engage you in these schemes content yourself with a decent but steady refusal; avoid controversy upon such plain points. You are too young to convert them, and I trust too wise to be converted by them. Shun them, not only in reality, but even in appearance, if you would be well received in good company; for people will always be shy of receiving a man who comes from a place where the plague rages, let him look ever so healthy. There are some expressions, both in French and English, and some characters, both in those two and in other countries, which have, I daresay, misled many young men to their ruin. *Une honnête débauche, une jolie débauche; an agreeable rake, a man of pleasure.* Do not think that this means debauchery and profligacy; nothing like it. It means at most the accidental and unfrequent irregularities of youth and vivacity, in opposition to dullness, formality, and want of spirit. A *commerce galant* insensibly formed with a woman of fashion; a glass of wine or two too much unwarily taken in the warmth and joy of good company, or some innocent frolic by which nobody is injured, are the utmost bounds of that life of pleasure which a man of sense and decency, who has a regard for his character, will allow himself, or be allowed by others. Those who transgress them in the hopes of shining, miss their aim, and become infamous or at least contemptible.

The Boor

From Theophrastus, The Characters

Student of Aristotle and an illustrious teacher and scholar in his own right, Theophrastus (372–288 B.C.) gives us a rich diagnosis of human baseness in The Characters.

Boorishness would appear to be an unseemly lack of cultured behavior. Your typical boor will walk into a public assembly after eating a garlic mixture and claim that it smells every bit as good as myrrh. In addition, he wears shoes two sizes too large and talks in a loud voice. Also, he will not trust family or friends but instead asks the servants what they think about any really important question; and out on the farm he treats the hired men to a full description of everything that went on in the town meeting.

He will sit, moreover, with his clothes tucked far above the knee so that he leaves himself exposed. Nothing else in town makes any impression on him, but at the sight of a cow or donkey or goat in the street he stands gawking. And when he fetches food from the pantry shelf he takes a bite of it every time; or if he has a drink he gulps it down. Besides that, he tries to seduce the kitchen-maid when nobody's around, and then helps her grind meal for himself and the servants. He eats his breakfast and pitches hay to the oxen at the same time, too. What's more, he answers your knock himself; and when he comes to the door he will call the dog, take him by the muzzle, and tell you, "Here's the fellow who watches our house and yard."

Again, when somebody tries to give him a coin in payment he says it's worn too thin and demands another. Or if he has let a neighbor borrow his plow or sickle, or a sack or basket, spends a sleepless night thinking about them. Or on his way into town he will ask the first person he meets how hides and salt fish were selling, and whether it's market-day. He can't wait, either, to announce that he means to get his hair cut in town and bring back some salt fish from Archias's, seeing as how it's right on the way. He sings in the public bath-house, besides, and hammers hobnails into his shoes.

The Art of Good Manners

Jonathan Swift,
On Good Manners and Good Breeding

This essay by the famed Irish-born satirist (1667–1775) is a good example of his sometimes ferocious irony.

Good manners is the art of making those people easy with whom we converse.

Whoever makes the fewest persons uneasy is the best bred in the company.

As the best law is founded upon reason, so are the best manners. And as some lawyers have introduced unreasonable things into common law, so likewise many teachers have introduced absurd things into common good manners.

One principal point of this art is to suit our behavior to the three several degrees of men; our superiors, our equals, and those below us.

For instance, to press either of the two former to eat or drink is a breach of manners; but a farmer or tradesman must be thus treated, or else it will be difficult to persuade them that they are welcome.

Pride, ill nature, and want of sense are the three great sources of ill manners; without some one of these defects, no man will behave himself ill for want of experience; or of what, in the language of fools, is called knowing the world.

I defy anyone to assign an incident wherein reason will not direct us what we are to say or do in company, if we are not misled by pride or ill nature.

Therefore I insist that good sense is the principal foundation of good manners but because the former is a gift which very few among mankind are possessed of, therefore all the civilized nations of the world have agreed upon fixing some rules for common behavior, best suited to their general customs, or fancies, as a kind of artificial good sense, to supply the defects of reason. Without which the gentlemanly part of dunces would be perpetually at cuffs, as they seldom fail when they happen to be drunk, or engaged in squabbles about women or play. And, God be thanked, there hardly happens a duel in a year, which may not be imputed to one of those three motives. Upon which account, I should be exceedingly sorry to find the legislature make any new laws against the practice of dueling; because the methods are easy and many for a wise man to avoid a quarrel with honor, or engage in it with innocence. And I can discover no political evil in suffering bullies, sharpers, and rakes to rid the world of each other by a method of their own; where the law hath not been able to find an expedient.

As the common forms of good manners were intended for regulating the conduct of those who have weak understandings; so they have been corrupted by the persons for whose use they were contrived. For these people have fallen into a needless and endless way of multiplying ceremonies, which have been extremely troublesome to those who practice them, and insupportable to everybody else: insomuch that wise men are often more uneasy at the overcivility of these refiners, than they could possibly be in the conversations of peasants or mechanics.

The impertinencies of this ceremonial behavior are nowhere better seen than at those tables where ladies reside, who value themselves upon account of their good breeding; where a man must reckon upon passing an hour without doing any one thing he has a mind to; unless he will be so hardy as to break through all the settled decorum of the family. She determines what he loves best, and how much he shall eat; and if the master of the house happens to be of the same disposition, he proceeds in the same tyrannical manner to prescribe in the drinking part: at the same time you are under the necessity of answering a thousand apologies for your entertainment. And although a good deal of this humor is pretty well worn off among many people of the best fashion, yet too much of it still remains, especially in the country; where an honest gentleman assured me, that having been kept four days, against his will at a friend's house, with all the circumstances of hiding his boots, locking up the stable, and other contrivances of the like nature, he could not remember, from the moment he came into the house to the moment he left it, any one thing, wherein his inclination was not directly contradicted; as if the whole family had entered into a combination to torment him.

But, besides all this, it would be endless to recount the many foolish and ridiculous accidents I have observed among these unfortunate proselytes to ceremony. I have seen a duchess fairly knocked down, by the precipitancy of an officious coxcomb running to save her the trouble of opening a door. I remember, upon a birthday at court, a great lady was utterly desperate by a dish of sauce let fall by a page directly upon her headdress and brocade, while she gave a sudden turn to her elbow upon some point of ceremony with the person who sat next her. Monsieur Buys, the Dutch envoy, whose politics and manners were much of a size, brought a son with him, about thirteen years old, to a great table at court. The boy and his father, whatever they put on their plates, the first offered round in order, to every person in the company; so that we could not get a minute's quiet during the whole dinner. At last their two plates happened to encounter, and with so much violence, that, being china, they broke in twenty pieces, and stained half the company with wet sweetmeats and cream.

There is a pedantry in manners, as in all arts and sciences; and sometimes in trades. Pedantry is properly the overrating any kind of knowledge we pretend to. And if that kind of knowledge be a trifle in itself, the pedantry is the greater. For which reason I look upon fiddlers, dancing-masters, heralds, masters of the ceremony, &c. to be greater pedants than Lipsius, or the elder Scaliger. With these kind of pedants, the court, while I knew it, was always plentifully stocked; I mean from the gentleman usher (at least) inclusive, downward to the gentleman porter; who are, generally speaking, the most insignificant race of people that this island can afford, and with the smallest tincture of good manners, which is the only trade they profess. For being wholly illiterate, and conversing chiefly with each other, they reduce the whole system of breeding within the forms and circles of their several offices; and as they are below the notice of ministers, they live and die in court under all revolutions with great obsequiousness to those who are in any degree of favor or credit, and with rudeness or insolence to everybody else. Whence I have long concluded, that good manners are not a plant of the court growth: for if they were, these people who have understandings directly of a level for such acquirements, and who have served such long apprenticeships to nothing else, would certainly have picked them up. For as to the great officers, who attend the prince's person or councils, or preside in his family, they are a transient body, who have no better a title to good manners than their neighbors, nor will probably have recourse to gentlemen ushers for instruction. So that I know little to be learned at court upon this head, except in the material circumstance of dress; wherein the authority of the maids of honor must indeed be allowed to be almost equal to that of a favorite actress.

I remember a passage my Lord Bolingbroke told me, that going to receive Prince Eugene of Savoy at his landing, in order to conduct him immediately to the Queen, the prince said, he was much concerned that he could not see her Majesty that night; for Monsieur Hoffman (who was then by) had assured his Highness that he could not be admitted into her presence with a tied-up periwig; that his equipage was not arrived; and that he had endeavored in vain to borrow a long one among all his valets and pages. My lord turned the matter into a jest, and brought the Prince to her Majesty; for which he was highly censured by the whole tribe of gentlemen ushers; among whom Monsieur Hoffman, an old dull resident of the Emperor's, had picked up this material point of ceremony; and which, I believe, was the best lesson he had learned in five-and-twenty years' residence.

I make a difference between good manners and good breeding; although, in order to vary my expression, I am sometimes forced to confound them. By the first, I only understand the art of remembering and applying certain settled forms of general behavior. But good breeding is of a much larger extent; for besides an uncommon degree of literature sufficient to qualify a gentleman for reading a play, or a political pamphlet, it takes in a great compass of knowledge; no less than that of dancing, fighting, gaming, making the circle of Italy, riding the great horse, and speaking French; not to mention some other secondary, or subaltern accomplishments, which are more easily acquired. So that the difference between good breeding and good manners lies in this, that the former cannot be attained to by the best understandings, without study and labor; whereas a tolerable degree of reason will instruct us in every part of good manners, without other assistance.

I can think of nothing more useful upon this subject, than to point out some particulars, wherein the very essentials of good manners are concerned, the neglect or perverting of which doth very much disturb the good commerce of the world, by introducing a traffic of mutual uneasiness in most companies.

First, a necessary part of good manners is a punctual observance of time at our own dwellings, or those of others, or at third places; whether upon matter of civility, business, or diversion; which rule, though it be a plain dictate of common reason, yet the greatest minister I ever knew was the greatest trespasser against it; by which all his business doubled upon him, and placed him in a continual arrear. Upon which I often used to rally him, as deficient in point of good manners. I have known more than one ambassador, and secretary of state with a very moderate portion of intellectuals, execute their offices with good success and applause, by the mere force of exactness and regularity. If you duly observe time for the service of another, it doubles the obligation; if upon your own account, it would be manifest folly, as well as ingratitude, to neglect it. If both are concerned, to make your equal or inferior attend on you, to his own disadvantage, is pride and injustice.

Ignorance of forms cannot properly be styled ill manners; because forms are subject to frequent changes; and consequently, being not founded upon reason, are beneath a wise man's regard. Besides, they vary in every country; and after a short period of time, very frequently in the same; so that a man who travels, must needs be at first a stranger to them in every court through which he passes; and perhaps at his return, as much a stranger in his own; and after all, they are easier to be remembered or forgotten than faces or names.

Indeed, among the many impertinencies that superficial young men bring with them from abroad, this bigotry of forms is one of the principal, and more prominent than the rest; who look upon them not only as if they were matters capable of admitting of choice, but even as points of importance; and are therefore zealous on all occasions to introduce and propagate the new forms and fashions they have brought back with them. So that, usually speaking, the worst-bred person in the company is a young traveler just returned from abroad.

A Club Man

From Sir Richard Steele,
The Spectator Club

Male bonding has a long history. Poet, playwright, politician, and wit, Sir Richard Steele is best known for founding the Tatler *in 1711, a journal of social, moral, and literary observation from which this essay is taken.*

The first of our society is a gentleman of Worcestershire, of an ancient descent, a baronet, his name Sir Roger de Coverley. His great-grandfather was inventor of that famous country-dance which is called after him. All who know that shire are very well acquainted with the parts and merits of Sir Roger. He is a gentleman that is very singular in his behavior, but his singularities proceed from his good sense, and are contradictions to the manners of the world, only as he thinks the world is in the wrong. However, this humor creates him no enemies, for he does nothing with sourness or obstinacy; and his being unconfined to modes and forms makes him but the readier and more capable to please and oblige all who know him. When he is in town he lives in Soho Square. It is said he keeps himself a bachelor by reason he was crossed in love by a perverse beautiful widow of the next county to him. Before this disappointment, Sir Roger was what you call a fine gentleman, had often supped with my Lord Rochester and Sir George Etherege, fought a duel upon his first coming to town, and kicked bully Dawson in a public coffeehouse for calling him youngster. But being ill-used by the above-mentioned widow, he was very serious for a year and a half; and though, his temper being naturally jovial, he at last got over it, he grew careless of himself and never dressed afterward. He continues to wear a coat and doublet of the same cut that were in fashion at the time of his repulse, which, in his merry humors, he tells us, has been in and out twelve times since he first wore it. It is said Sir Roger grew humble in his desires after he had forgot his cruel beauty, insomuch that it is reported he has frequently offended with beggars and gypsies; but this is looked upon, by his friends, rather as matter of raillery than truth. He is now in his fifty-sixth year, cheerful, gay, and hearty; keeps a good house both in town and country; a great lover of mankind; but there is such a mirthful cast in his behavior, that he is rather beloved than esteemed. His tenants grow rich, his servants look satisfied, all the young women profess love to him, and the young men are glad of his company. When he comes into a house, he calls the servants by their names, and talks all the way upstairs to a visit. I must not omit that Sir Roger is a justice of the quorum; that he fills the chair at a quarter-session with great abilities, and three months ago gained universal applause, by explaining a passage in the Game Act.

The gentleman next in esteem and authority among us is another bachelor, who is a member of the inner Temple, a man of great probity, wit, and understanding; but he has chosen his place of residence rather to obey the direction of an old humorsome father than in pursuit of his own inclinations. He was placed there to study the laws of the land, and is the most learned of any of the house in those of the stage. Aristotle and Longinus are much better

understood by him than Littleton or Coke. The father sends up
every post questions relating to marriage-articles, leases, and
tenures, in the neighborhood; all which questions he agrees with
an attorney to answer and take care of in the lump. He is studying
the passions themselves, when he should be inquiring into the
debates among men which arise from them. He knows the argument of each of the orations of Demosthenes and Tull, but not one
case in the reports of our own courts. No one ever took him for a
fool; but none, except his intimate friends, know he has a great
deal of wit. This turn makes him at once both disinterested and
agreeable. As few of his thoughts are drawn from business they are
most of them fit for conversation. His taste for books is a little too
just for the age he lives in; he has read all, but approves of very few.
His familiarity with the customs, manners, actions, and writings of
the ancients, makes him a very delicate observer of what occurs to
him in the present world. He is an excellent critic, and the time of
the play is his hour of business; exactly at five he passes through
New-Inn, crosses through Russell-Court, and takes a turn at Will's
till the play begins; he has his shoes rubbed and his periwig pow-
dered at the barber's as you go into the Rose. It is for the good of
the audience when he is at the play, for the actors have an ambition
to please him.

The person of next consideration is Sir Andrew Freeport, a
merchant of great eminence in the city of London; a person of
indefatigable industry, strong reason, and great experience. His
notions of trade are noble and generous, and (as every rich man
has usually some sly way of jesting, which would make no great figure were he not a rich man) he calls the sea the British Common.
He is acquainted with commerce in all its parts, and will tell you
that it is a stupid and barbarous way to extend dominion by arms;
for true power is to be got by arts and industry. He will often argue
that, if this part of our trade were well cultivated, we should gain
from one nation; and if another, from another. I have heard him
prove that diligence makes more lasting acquisitions than valor,
and that sloth has ruined more nations than the sword. He
abounds in several frugal maxims, amongst which the greatest
favorite is, "A penny saved is a penny got." A general trader of good
sense is pleasanter company than a general scholar; and Sir
Andrew having a natural unaffected eloquence, the perspicuity of
his discourse gives the same pleasure that wit would in another
man. He has made his fortune himself; and says that England may
be richer than other kingdoms by as plain methods as he himself is

richer than other men; though at the same time I can say this of him, that there is not a point in the compass but blows home a ship in which he is an owner.

Next to Sir Andrew in the clubroom sits Captain Sentry, a gentleman of great courage, good understanding, but invincible modesty. He is one of those that deserve very well, but are very awkward at putting their talents within the observation of such as should take notice of them. He was some years a captain, and behaved himself with great gallantry in several engagements and at several sieges; but having a small estate of his own, and being next heir to Sir Roger, he has quitted a way of life in which no man can rise suitably to his merit, who is not something of a courtier as well as a soldier. I have heard him often lament that, in a profession where merit is placed in so conspicuous a view, impudence should get the better of modesty. When he has talked to this purpose, I never heard him make a sour expression, but frankly confess that he left the world, because he was not fit for it. A strict honesty and an even regular behavior are in themselves obstacles to him that must press through crowds, who endeavor at the same end with himself, the favor of a commander. He will, however, in his way of talk excuse generals for not disposing according to men's dessert, or inquiring into it; for, says he, that great man who has a mind to help me has as many to break through to come to me as I have to come at him: therefore he will conclude that the man who would make a figure, especially in a military way, must get over all false modesty, and assist his patron against the importunity of all other pretenders, by a proper assurance in his own vindication. He says it is a civil cowardice to be backward in asserting what you ought to expect, as it is a military fear to be slow in attacking when it is your duty. With this candor does the gentleman speak of himself and others. The same frankness runs through all his conversation. The military part of his life had furnished him with many adventures, in the relating of which he is very agreeable to the company; for he is never overbearing, though accustomed to command men in the utmost degree below him; nor ever too obsequious, for an habit of obeying men highly above him.

But that our society may not appear a set of humorists, unacquainted with the gallantries and pleasures of the age, we have amongst us the gallant Will Honeycomb, a gentleman who, according to his years, should be in the decline of his life; but having ever been very careful of his person, and always had a very easy fortune, time has made but a very little impression either by wrinkles on his forehead, or traces on his brain. His person is well turned, and of a good height. He is very ready at that sort of discourse with which men usually entertain women. He has all his life dressed very well, and remembers habits as others do men. He can smile when one speaks to him, and laughs easily. He knows the history of every mode, and can inform you from which of the French king's wenches our wives and daughters had this manner of curling their hair, that way of placing their hoods; whose frailty was covered by such a sort of a petticoat, and whose vanity to show her foot made that part of the dress so short in such a year. In a word, all his conversation and knowledge have been in the female world. As other men of his age will take notice to you what such a minister said upon such and such an occasion, he will tell you when the Duke of Monmouth danced at court, such a woman was then smitten, another was taken with him at the head of his troop in the park. In all these important relations, he has ever about the same time received a kind glance, or a blow of a fan from some celebrated beauty, mother of the present Lord Such-a-one. If you speak of a young commoner that said a lively thing in the House, he starts up, "He has good blood in his veins; Tom Mirabel begot him; the rogue cheated me in that affair; that young fellow's mother used me more like a dog than any woman I ever made advances to." This way of talking of his very much enlivens the conversation among us of a more sedate turn, and I find there is not one of the company, but myself, who rarely speak at all, but speaks of him as of that sort of a man who is usually called a well-bred fine gentleman. To conclude his character, where women are not concerned, he is an honest worthy man.

I cannot tell whether I am to account him, whom I am next to speak of, as one of our company; for he visits us but seldom, but when he does, it adds to every man else a new enjoyment of himself. He is a clergyman, a very philosophic man, of general learning, great sanctity of life, and the most exact good breeding. He has the misfortune to be of a very weak constitution, and consequently cannot accept of such cares and business as preferments in his function would oblige him to; he is therefore among divines what a chamber-counselor is among lawyers. The probity of his mind, and the integrity of his life, create him followers, as being eloquent or loud advances others. He seldom introduces the subject he speaks upon; but we are so far gone in years that he observes, when he is among us, an earnestness to have him fall on some divine topic, which he always treats with much authority, as one who has no interest in this world, as one who is hastening to the object of all his wishes, and conceives hope from his decays and infirmities. These are my ordinary companions.

The Country Gentleman

From Anthony Trollope, Phineas Finn

Lord Chiltern, more accustomed to a country life than to citified refinement, is a little clumsy at declaring his love to Violet Effingham. From Trollope's 1869 novel.

The reader has been told that Lord Chiltern was a red man, and that peculiarity of his personal appearance was certainly the first to strike a stranger. It imparted a certain look of ferocity to him, which was apt to make men afraid of him at first sight. Women are not actuated in the same way, and are accustomed to look deeper into men at the first sight than other men will trouble themselves to do. His beard was red, and was clipped, so as to have none of the softness of waving hair. The hair on his head also was kept short, and was very red, and the color of his face was red. Nevertheless he was a handsome man, with well-cut features, not tall, but very strongly built, and with a certain curl in the corner of his eyelids which gave to him a look of resolution, which perhaps he did not possess. He was known to be a clever man, and when very young had had the reputation of being a scholar. When he was three-and-twenty grey-haired votaries of the turf declared that he would make his fortune on the race course, so clear-headed was he as to odds, so excellent a judge of a horse's performance, and so gifted with a memory of events. When he was five-and-twenty he had lost every shilling of a fortune of his own, had squeezed from his father more than his father ever chose to name in speaking of his affairs to anyone, and was known to be in debt. But he had sacrificed himself on one or two memorable occasions in conformity with turf laws of honor, and men said of him, either that he was very honest or very chivalric, in accordance with the special views on the subject of the man who was speaking. It was reported now that he no longer owned horses on the turf; but this was doubted by some who could name the animals which they said that he owned, and which he ran in the name of Mr. Macnab, said some; of Mr. Pardoe, said others; of Mr. Chickerwick, said a third set of informants. The fact was that Lord Chiltern at this moment had no interest of his own in any horse upon the turf.

But all the world knew that he drank. He had taken by the throat a proctor's bulldog when he had been drunk at Oxford, had nearly strangled the man, and had been expelled. He had fallen through his violence into some terrible misfortune at Paris, had been brought before a public judge, and his name and his infamy had been made notorious in every newspaper in the two capitals. After that he had fought a ruffian at Newmarket, and had really killed him with his fists. In reference to this latter affray it had been proved that the attack had been made on him, that he had not been to blame, and that he had not been drunk. After a prolonged investigation he had come forth from that affair without disgrace. He would have done so, at least, if he had not been heretofore disgraced. But we all know how the man well spoken of may steal a horse, while he who is of evil repute may not look over a hedge. It was asserted widely by many who were supposed to know all about everything that Lord Chiltern was in a fit of delirium tremens when he killed the ruffian at Newmarket. The worst of that latter affair was that it produced the total estrangement which now existed between Lord Brentford and his son. Lord Brentford would not believe that his son was in that matter more sinned against than sinning. "Such things do not happen to other men's sons," he said, when Lady Laura pleaded for her brother. Lady Laura could not induce her father to see his son, but so far prevailed that no sentence of banishment was pronounced against Lord Chiltern. There was nothing to prevent the son sitting at his father's table if he so pleased. He never did so please, but nevertheless he continued to live in the house in Portman Square; and when he met the Earl, in the hall, perhaps, or on the staircase, would simply bow to him. Then the Earl would bow again, and shuffle on, and look very wretched, as no doubt he was. A grown-up son must be the greatest comfort a man can have, if he be his father's best friend; but otherwise he can hardly be a comfort. As it was in this house, the son was a constant thorn in his father's side.

"What does he do when we leave London?" Lord Brentford once said to his daughter.

"He stays here, Papa."

"But he hunts still?"

"Yes, he hunts, and he has a room somewhere at an inn, down in Northamptonshire. But he is mostly in London. They have trains on purpose."

"What a life for my son!" said the Earl. "What a life! Of course no decent person will let him into his house." Lady Laura did not know what to say to this, for in truth Lord Chiltern was not fond of staying at the houses of persons whom the Earl would have called decent.

General Effingham, the father of Violet, and Lord Brentford had been the closest and dearest of friends. They had been young men in the same regiment, and through life each had confided in the other. When the General's only son, then a youth of seventeen, was killed in one of our grand New Zealand wars, the bereaved father and the Earl had been together for a month in their sorrow. At that time Lord Chiltern's career had still been open to hope, and the one man had contrasted his lot with the other. General Effingham lived long enough to hear the Earl declare to him that his lot was the happier of the two. Now the General was dead, and Violet, the daughter of a second wife, was all that was left of the Effinghams. This second wife had been a Miss Plummer, a lady from the city with much money, whose sister had married Lord Baldock. Violet in this way had fallen to the care of the Baldock people, and not into the hands of her father's friends. But, as the reader will have surmised, she had ideas of her own of emancipating herself from Baldock thraldom.

Twice before that last terrible affair at Newmarket, before the quarrel between the father and the son had been complete, Lord Brentford had said a word to his daughter, merely a word, of his son in connection with Miss Effingham.

"If he thinks of it I shall be glad to see him on the subject. You may tell him so." That had been the first word. He had just then resolved that the affair in Paris should be regarded as condoned, as among the things to be forgotten. "She is too good for him; but if he asks her let him tell her everything." That had been the second word, and had been spoken immediately subsequent to a payment of twelve thousand pounds made by the Earl toward the settlement of certain Doncaster accounts. Lady Laura in negotiating for the money had been very eloquent in describing some honest, or shall we say chivalric, sacrifice which had brought her brother into this special difficulty. Since that the Earl had declined to interest himself in his son's matrimonial affairs; and when Lady Laura had once again mentioned the matter, declaring her belief that it would be the means of saving her brother Oswald, the Earl had desired her to be silent. "Would you wish to destroy the poor child?" he had said. Nevertheless Lady Laura felt sure that if she were to go to her father with a positive statement that Oswald and Violet were engaged, he would relent and would accept Violet as his daughter. As for the payment of Lord Chiltern's present debts; she had a little scheme of her own about that.

Miss Effingham, who had been already two days in Portman Square, had not as yet seen Lord Chiltern. She knew that he lived in the house, that is, that he slept there, and probably ate his breakfast in some apartment of his own; but she knew also that the habits of the house would not by any means make it necessary that they should meet. Laura and her brother probably saw each other daily, but they never went into society together, and did not know the same sets of people. When she had announced to Lady Baldock her intention of spending the first fortnight of her London season with her friend Lady Laura, Lady Baldock had as a matter of course "jumped upon her," as Miss Effingham would herself call it.

"You are going to the house of the worst reprobate in all England," said Lady Baldock.

"What; dear old Lord Brentford, whom Papa loved so well!"

"I mean Lord Chiltern, who, only last year, murdered a man!"

"That is not true, Aunt."

"There is worse than that, much worse. He is always tipsy, and always gambling, and always—but it is quite unfit that I should speak a word more to you about such a man as Lord Chiltern. His name ought never to be mentioned."

"Then why did you mention it, Aunt?"

Lady Baldock's process of jumping upon her niece, in which I think the aunt had generally the worst of the exercise, went on for some time, but Violet of course carried her point.

"If she marries him there will be an end of everything," said Lady Baldock to her daughter Augusta.

"She has more sense than that, Mamma," said Augusta.

"I don't think she has any sense at all," said Lady Baldock; "not in the least. I do wish my poor sister had lived; I do indeed."

Lord Chiltern was now in the room with Violet, immediately upon that conversation between Violet and his sister as to the expediency of Violet becoming his wife. Indeed his entrance had interrupted the conversation before it was over. "I am so glad to see you, Miss Effingham," he said. "I came in thinking that I might find you."

"Here I am, as large as life," she said, getting up from her corner on the sofa and giving him her hand. "Laura and I have been discussing the affairs of the nation for the last two days, and have nearly brought our discussion to an end." She could not help looking, first at his eye and then at his hand, not as wanting evidence to the truth of the statement which his sister had made, but because the idea of a drunkard's eye and a drunkard's hand had been brought before her mind. Lord Chiltern's hand was like the hand of any other man, but there was something in his eye that almost frightened her. It looked as though he would not hesitate to wring his wife's neck round, if ever he should be brought to threaten to do so. And then his eye, like the rest of him, was red. No; she did not think that she could ever bring herself to marry him. Why take a venture that was double-dangerous, when there were so many ventures open to her, apparently with very little of danger attached to them? "If it should ever be that I loved him, I would do it all the same," she said to herself.

"If I did not come and see you here, I suppose that I should never see you," said he, seating himself. "I do not often go to parties and when I do you are not likely to be there."

"We might make our little arrangements for meeting," said she, laughing. "My aunt, Lady Baldock, is going to have an evening next week."

"The servants would be ordered to put me out of the house."

"Oh no. You can tell her that I invited you."

"I don't think that Oswald and Lady Baldock are great friends," said Lady Laura.

"Or he might come and take you and me to the Zoo on Sunday. That's the proper sort of thing for a brother and a friend to do."

"I hate that place in the Regent's Park," said Lord Chiltern.

"When were you there last?" demanded Miss Effingham.

"When I came home once from Eton. But I won't go there again till I can come home from Eton again." Then he altered his tone as he continued to speak. "People would look at me as if I were the wildest beast in the whole collection."

"Then," said Violet, "if you won't go to Lady Baldock's or to the Zoo, we must confine ourselves to Laura's drawing-room; unless, indeed, you like to take me to the top of the Monument."

"I'll take you to the top of the Monument with pleasure."

"What do you say, Laura?"

"I say that you are a foolish girl," said Lady Laura, "and that I will have nothing to do with such a scheme."

"Then there is nothing for it but that you should come here; and as you live in the house, and as I am sure to be here every morning, and as you have no possible occupation for your time, and as we have nothing particular to do with ours, I daresay I shan't see you again before I go to my aunt's in Berkeley Square."

"Very likely not," he said.

"And why not, Oswald?" asked his sister.

He passed his hand over his face before he answered her. "Because she and I run in different grooves now, and are not such meet playfellows as we used to be once. Do you remember my taking you away right through Saulsby Wood once on the old pony, and not bringing you back till teatime, and Miss Blink going and telling my father?"

"Do I remember it? I think it was the happiest day in my life. His pockets were crammed full of gingerbread and Everton toffy, and we had three bottles of lemonade slung on to the pony's saddlebows. I thought it was a pity that we should ever come back."

"It was a pity," said Lord Chiltern.

"But, nevertheless, substantially necessary," said Lady Laura.

"Failing our power of reproducing the toffy, I suppose it was," said Violet.

"You were not Miss Effingham then," said Lord Chiltern.

"No, not as yet. These disagreeable realities of life grow upon one; do they not? You took off my shoes and dried them for me at a woodman's cottage. I am obliged to put up with my maid's doing those things now. And Miss Blink the mild is changed for Lady Baldock the martinet. And if I rode about with you in a wood all day I should be sent to Coventry instead of to bed. And so you see everything is changed as well as my name."

"Everything is not changed," said Lord Chiltern, getting up from his seat. "I am not changed, at least not in this, that as I then loved you better than any being in the wold, better even than Laura there—so do I love you now infinitely the best of all. Do not look so surprised at me. You knew it before as well as you do now; and Laura knows it. There is no secret to be kept in the matter among us three."

"But, Lord Chiltern," said Miss Effingham, rising also to her feet, and then pausing, not knowing how to answer him. There had been a suddenness in his mode of addressing her which had, so to say, almost taken away her breath; and then to be told by a man of his love before his sister was in itself, to her, a matter so surprising, that none of those words came at her command which will come, as though by instinct, to young ladies on such occasions.

"You have known it always," said he, as though he were angry with her.

"Lord Chiltern," she replied, "you must excuse me if I say that you are, at the least, very abrupt. I did not think when I was going back so joyfully to our old childish days that you would turn the tables on me in this way."

"He has said nothing that ought to make you angry," said Lady Laura.

"Only because he has driven me to say that which will make me appear to be uncivil to himself. Lord Chiltern, I do not love you with that love of which you are speaking now. As an old friend I have always regarded you, and I hope that I may always do so." Then she got up and left the room.

"Why were you so sudden with her, so abrupt, so loud?" said his sister, coming up to him and taking him by the arm almost in anger.

"It would make no difference," said he. "She does not care for me."

"It makes all the difference in the world," said Lady Laura. "Such a woman as Violet cannot be had after that fashion. You must begin again."

"I have begun and ended," he said.

"That is nonsense. Of course you will persist. It was madness to speak in that way today. You may be sure of this, however, that there is no one she likes better than you. You must remember that you have done much to make any girl afraid of you."

"I do remember it."

"Do something now to make her fear you no longer. Speak to her softly. Tell her of the sort of life which you would live with her. Tell her that all is changed. As she comes to love you, she will believe no one else on that matter."

"Am I to tell her a lie?" said Lord Chiltern, looking his sister full in the face. Then he turned upon his heel and left her.

Gentlemanly Reserve

From William Shenstone, On Reserve

Although such beliefs are not much in fashion today, our ancestors believed reserve was essential to gentlemanly behavior. The essays of William Shenstone (1714–1763) were celebrated for their stylistic grace and discriminating judgment.

Taking an evening's walk with a friend in the country, among many grave remarks, he was making the following observation: "There is not," says he, "any one quality so inconsistent with respect as what is commonly called familiarity. You do not find one in fifty whose regard is proof against it. At the same time, it is hardly possible to insist upon such a deference as will render you ridiculous, if it be supported by common-sense. Thus much at least is evident, that your demands will be so successful as to procure a greater share than if you had made no such demand. I may frankly own to you, Leander, that I frequently derived uneasiness from a familiarity with such persons as despised everything they could obtain with ease. Were it not better therefore to be somewhat frugal of our affability, at least to allot it only to few persons of discernment who can make the proper distinction betwixt real dignity and pretended: to neglect those characters which, being impatient to grow familiar, are at the same time very far from familiarity-proof: to have posthumous fame in view, which affords us the most pleasing landscape: to enjoy the amusement of reading, and the consciousness that reading paves the way to general esteem: to preserve a constant regularity of temper, and also of constitution, for the most part but little consistent with a promiscuous intercourse with men: to shun all illiterate, though ever so jovial assemblies, insipid, perhaps, when present, and upon reflection painful: to meditate on those absent or departed friends, who value or valued us for those qualities with which they were best acquainted: to partake with such a friend as you the delights of a studious and rational retirement—are not these the paths that lead to happiness?"

In answer to this (for he seemed to feel some late mortification) I observed that what we lost by familiarity in respect was generally made up to us by the affection it procured and that an absolute solitude was so very contrary to our natures, that were he excluded from society but for a single fortnight, he would be exhilarated at the sight of the first beggar he saw.

What follows were thoughts thrown out in our further discourse upon the subject without order or connection, as they occur to my remembrance.

Some reserve is a debt to prudence; as freedom and simplicity of conversation is a debt to good nature.

There would not be any absolute necessity for reserve, if the world were honest: yet, even then, it would prove expedient. For, in order to attain any degree of deference, it seems necessary that people should imagine you have more accomplishments than you discover.

It is on this depends one of the excellences of the judicious Vergil. He leaves you something ever to imagine: and such is the constitution of the human mind, that we think so highly of nothing as of that whereof we do not see the bounds. This, as Mr. Burke ingeniously observes, affords the pleasure when we survey a cylinder; and Sir John Suckling says:

"They who know all the wealth they have are poor;
He's only rich who cannot tell his store."

A person who would secure to himself great deference will, perhaps, gain his point by silence as effectually as by anything he can say.

To be, however, a niggard of one's observation is so much worse than to hoard up one's money, as the former may be both imparted and retained at the same time.

Men oftentimes pretend to proportion their respect to real desert; but a supercilious reserve and distance weary them into a compliance with more. This appears so very manifest to many persons of the lofty character that they use no better means to acquire respect than like highwaymen to make a demand of it. They will, like Empedocles, jump into the fire rather than betray the mortal part of their character.

Virtues, like essences, lose their fragrance when exposed. They are sensitive plants, which will not bear too familiar approaches.

Let us be careful to distinguish modesty, which is ever amiable, from reserve, which is only prudent. A man is hated sometimes for pride, when it was an excess of humility gave the occasion.

What is often termed shyness is nothing more than refined sense, and an indifference to common observations.

The reserved man's intimate acquaintance are, for the most part, fonder of him than the persons of a more affable character, *i.e.*, he pays them a greater compliment than the other can do his, as he distinguishes them more.

It is indolence, and the pain of being upon one's guard, that makes me hate an artful character.

The most reserved of men, who would not exchange two syllables together in an English coffeehouse, should they meet at Ispahan, would drink sherbet and eat a mess of rice together.

The man of show is vain: the reserved man is proud more properly. The one has greater depth: the other a more lively imagination. The one is more frequently respected: the other more generally beloved. The one a Cato; the other a Caesar.

A reserved man often makes it a rule to leave company with a good speech: and I believe sometimes proceeds so far as to leave company because he has made one. Yet it is fate often, like the mole, to imagine himself deep when he is near the surface.

Were it prudent to decline this reserve, and this horror of disclosing foibles; to give up a part of character to secure the rest? The world will certainly insist upon having some part to pull to pieces. Let us throw out some follies to the envious; as we give up counters to a highwayman, or a barrel to a whale, in order to save one's money and one's ship: to let it make exceptions to one's head of hair, if one can escape being stabbed in the heart.

The reserved man should drink double glasses.

Prudent men lock up their motives; letting familiars have a key to their heart as to their garden.

A reserved man is in continual conflict with the social part of his nature; and even grudges himself the laugh into which he is sometimes betrayed.

"Seldom he smiles—

And smiles in such a sort as he disdained

Himself—that could be moved to smile at anything."

"A fool and his words are soon parted;" for so should the proverb run.

Modesty often passes for errant haughtiness; as what is deemed spirit in a horse proceeds from fear.

The higher character a person supports, the more he should regard his minutest actions.

The reserved man should bring a certificate of his honesty, before he be admitted into company.

Reserve is no more essentially connected with understanding than a church organ with devotion, or wine with good nature.

The Ugly Club

From Sir Richard Steele, The Ugly Club

Not every man can be a "hunk": Homely men must make the best of it. They have nowhere to go but up.

Since our persons are not of our own making, when they are such as appear defective or uncomely, it is, methinks, an honest and laudable fortitude to dare to be ugly; at least to keep ourselves from being abashed with a consciousness of imperfections which we cannot help, and in which there is no guilt. I would not defend a haggard beau for passing away much time at a glass, and giving softness and languishing graces to deformity: all I intend is, that we ought to be contented with our countenance and shape, so far as never to give ourselves an uneasy reflection on that subject. It is to the ordinary people, who are not accustomed to make very proper remarks on any occasion, matter of great jest if a man enters with a prominent pair of shoulders into an assembly, or is distinguished by an expansion of mouth, or obliquity of aspect. It is happy for a man that has any of these oddnesses about him, if he can be as merry upon himself as others are apt to be upon that occasion. When he can possess himself with such a cheerfulness, women and children, who are at first frightened at him, will afterward be as much pleased with him. As it is barbarous in others to rally him for natural defects, it is extremely agreeable when he can jest upon himself for them.

MANLY CHARACTER
AND CONDUCT

The Rules of Harvard College
(1643)

Who could pass this SAT today?

1. When any scholar is able to understand Tully or such like classical author *extempore,* and make and speak true Latin in verse and prose, *suo ut aiunt marte,* and decline perfectly the paradigms of nouns and verbs in the Greek tongue: let him then, and not before, be capable of admission into the College.

2. Let every student be plainly instructed and earnestly pressed to consider well, the main end of his life and studies is, "to know God and Jesus Christ which is eternal life," John 17:3, and therefore to lay Christ in the bottom, as the only foundation of all sound knowledge and learning.

And seeing the Lord only giveth wisdom, let everyone seriously set himself by prayer in secret to seek it of Him, Prov. 2:3.

3. Everyone shall so exercise himself in reading the scriptures twice a day, that he shall be ready to give such an account of his proficiency therein, both in theoretical observations of the language, and logic, and in practical and spiritual truths, as his tutor shall require, according to his ability; seeing "the entrance of the Word giveth light, it giveth understanding to the simple," Psalm 119:130.

4. That they, eschewing all profanation of God's name, attributes, word, ordinances, and times of worship, do study with good conscience, carefully to retain God, and the love of His truth in their minds. Else, let them know, that (notwithstanding their learning) God may give them up "to strong delusions," and in the end "to a reprobate mind," 2 Thes. 2:11, 12; Rom. 1:28.

5. That they studiously redeem the time; observe the general hours appointed for all the students, and the special hours for their

own classes; and then diligently attend the lectures, without any disturbance by word or gesture. And if in anything they doubt, they shall inquire, as of their fellows, so (in the case of "nonsatisfaction"), modestly of their tutors.

6. None shall, under any pretense whatsoever, frequent the company and society of such men as lead an unfit and dissolute life.

Nor shall any without his tutor's leave, or (in his absence) the call of parents or guardians, go abroad to other towns.

7. Every scholar shall be present in his tutor's chamber at the seventh hour in the morning, immediately after the sound of the bell, at his opening the scripture and prayer; so also at the fifth hour at night, and then give account of his own private reading, as aforesaid in particular the third, and constantly attend lectures in the hall at the hours appointed. But if any (without necessary impediment) shall absent himself from prayer or lectures, he shall be liable to admonition, if he offend above once a week.

8. If any scholar shall be found to transgress any of the laws of God, or the school, after twice admonition, he shall be liable, if not *adultus*, to correction; if *adultus*, his name shall be given up to the overseers of the College, that he may be admonished at the public monthly act.

A Travel Guide for Young Men

Francis Bacon, Essays

Bacon's tips for young men traveling in Europe:

1. *Take along "some tutor or grave servant" who will make sure you keep up with your studies.*
2. *It's fine to attend "masks and feasts," but don't go out of your way to find them.*
3. *Make sure you visit lots of libraries, churches, and monuments!*
4. *Learn the language and keep a diary of your experiences.*
5. *Don't spend the whole time hanging around with kids from your own country.*

6. *Don't bore people by talking about your trip endlessly when you get home.*

From Bacon's essay, Of Travel.

Travel in the younger sort is a part of education; in the elder, a part of experience. He that travelleth into a country before he hath some entrance into the language goeth to school, and not to travel. That young men travel under some tutor or grave servant, I allow well; so that he be such a one that hath the language, and hath been to the country before, whereby he may be able to tell them what things are worthy to be seen in the country where they go, what acquaintances they are to seek, what exercises or discipline the place yieldeth. For else young men shall go hooded, and look abroad little. It is a strange thing that in sea voyages, where there is nothing to be seen but sky and sea, men should make diaries, but in land-travel, wherein so much is to be observed, for the most part they omit it, as if chance were fitter to be registered than observation. Let diaries therefore be brought in use. The things to be seen and observed are: the courts of princes, specially when they give audience to ambassadors; the courts of justice, while they sit and hear causes, and so of consistories ecclesiastic; the churches and monasteries, with the monuments which are therein extant; the walls and fortifications of cities and towns, and so the havens and harbors; antiquities and ruins; libraries; colleges, disputation, and lectures, where any are; shipping and navies; houses and gardens of state and pleasure near great cities; armories; arsenals; magazines; exchanges; burses; warehouses; exercises of horsemanship, fencing, training of soldiers, and the like; comedies, such whereunto the better sort of persons do resort; treasuries of jewels and robes; cabinets and rarities; and, to conclude, whatsoever is memorable in the places where they go. After all which the tutors or servants ought to make diligent inquiry. As for triumphs, masks, feasts, weddings, funerals, capital executions, and such shows, men need not to be put in mind of them, yet are they not to be neglected. If you will have a young man to put his travel into a little room, and in short time to gather much, this you must do. First as was said, he must have some entrance into the language before he goeth. Then he must have such a servant or tutor as knoweth the country, as was likewise said. Let him carry with him also some card or book describing the country where he travelleth, which will be a good key to his inquiry. Let him keep also a diary. Let him not stay long in one city or town; more or less as the place deserveth, but not long; nay, when he stayeth in one city or town, let him change his lodging from one end and part of the town to another, which is a great adamant of acquaintance. Let him sequester himself from the company of his countrymen, and diet in such places where there is good company of the nation where he travelleth. Let him upon his removes from one place to another procure recommendation to some person of quality residing in the place whither he removeth, that he may use his favor in those things he desireth to see or know. Thus he may abridge his travel with much profit. As for the acquaintance which is to be sought in travel, that which is most of all profitable is acquaintance with the secretaries and employed men of ambassadors, for so in traveling in one country he shall suck the experience of many. Let him also see and visit eminent persons in all kinds, which are of great name abroad, that he may be able to tell how the life agreeth with the fame. For quarrels, they are with care and discretion to be avoided. They are commonly for mistresses, healths, place, and words. And let a man beware how he keepeth company with choleric and quarrelsome persons, for they will engage him into their own quarrels. When a traveler returneth home, let him not leave the countries where he hath traveled altogether behind him, but maintain a correspondence by letters with those of his acquaintance which are of most worth. And let his travel appear rather in his discourse than in his apparel or gesture, and in his discourse let him be rather advised in his answers than forward to tell stories, and let it appear that he doth not change his country manners for those of foreign parts, but only prick in some flowers of that he hath learned abroad into the customs of his own country.

Pride and Prejudice

From Jane Austen,
Pride and Prejudice

Sometimes women are the best authority on what it means to be a man. In Jane Austen's Pride and Prejudice, when Mr. Darcy first proposes marriage to Elizabeth Bennet, she angrily rejects the gesture for its conspicuous lack of

chivalry and even simple politeness, both of which are consumed by his
intolerable pride. To Elizabeth, Mr. Darcy appears to believe he would be
doing her a favor to marry her. Her antipathy is deepened by what she per-
cieves to be Darcy's obstruction of her sister's relationship with his friend Mr.
Bingley, and his apparent injustice to Mr. Wickham.

When they were gone, Elizabeth, as if intending to exasperate
herself as much as possible against Mr. Darcy, chose for her employment the examination of all the letters which Jane had written to
her since her being in Kent. They contained no actual complaint,
nor was there any revival of past occurrences, or any communication of present suffering. But in all, and in almost every line of
each, there was a want of that cheerfulness which had been used to
characterize her style and which, proceeding from the serenity of a
mind at ease with itself, and kindly disposed toward everyone, had
been scarcely ever clouded. Elizabeth noticed every sentence con-
veying the idea of uneasiness, with an attention which it had hardly
received on the first perusal. Mr. Darcy's shameful boast of what
misery he had been able to inflict, gave her a keener sense of her
sister's sufferings. It was some consolation to think that his visit to
Rosings was to end on the day after the next, and a still greater, that
in less than a fortnight she should herself be with Jane again, and
enabled to contribute to the recovery of her spirits, by all that affection could do.

She could not think of Darcy's leaving Kent, without remembering that his cousin was to go with him; but Colonel Fitzwilliam
had made it clear that he had no intentions at all, and agreeable as
he was, she did not mean to be unhappy about him.

While settling this point, she was suddenly roused by the
sound of the doorbell, and her spirits were a little fluttered by the
idea of its being Colonel Fitzwilliam himself, who had once before
called late in the evening, and might now come to enquire particularly after her. But this idea was soon banished, and her spirits were
very differently affected, when, to her utter amazement, she saw
Mr. Darcy walk into the room. In a hurried manner he immediately began an enquiry after her health, imputing his visit to a wish of
hearing that she were better. She answered him with cold civility.
He sat down for a few moments, and then getting up walked about
the room. Elizabeth was surprised, but said not a word. After a
silence of several minutes he came toward her in an agitated manner, and thus began,

"In vain have I struggled. It will not do. My feelings will not be repressed. You must allow me to tell you how ardently I admire and love you."

Elizabeth's astonishment was beyond expression. She stared, colored, doubted, and was silent. This he considered sufficient encouragement, and the avowal of all that he felt and had long felt for her, immediately followed. He spoke well, but there were feelings besides those of the heart to be detailed, and he was not more eloquent on the subject of tenderness than of pride. His sense of her inferiority—of its being a degradation—of the family obstacles which judgment had always opposed to inclination, were dwelt on with a warmth which seemed due to the consequence he was wounding, but was very unlikely to recommend his suit.

In spite of her deeply rooted dislike, she could not be insensible to the compliment of such a man's affection, and though her intentions did not vary for an instant, she was at first sorry for the pain he was to receive; till, roused to resentment by his subsequent language, she lost all compassion in anger. She tried, however, to compose herself to answer him with patience, when he should have done. He concluded with representing to her the strength of that attachment which, in spite of all his endeavors, he had found impossible to conquer; and with expressing his hope that it would now be rewarded by her acceptance of his hand. As he said this, she could easily see that he had no doubt of a favorable answer. He *spoke* of apprehension and anxiety, but his countenance expressed real security. Such a circumstance could only exasperate further, and when he ceased, the color rose into her cheeks, and she said,

"In such cases as this, it is, I believe, the established mode to express a sense of obligation for the sentiments avowed, however unequally they may be returned. It is natural that obligation should be felt, and if I could *feel* gratitude, I would now thank you. But I cannot—I have never desired your good opinion, and you have certainly bestowed it most unwillingly. I am sorry to have occasioned pain to anyone. It has been most unconsciously done, however, and I hope will be of short duration. The feelings which, you tell me, have long prevented the acknowledgment of your regard, can have little difficulty in overcoming it after this explanation."

Mr. Darcy, who was leaning against the mantlepiece with his eyes fixed on her face, seemed to catch her words with no less resentment than surprise. His complexion became pale with anger, and the disturbance of his mind was visible in every feature. He was struggling for the appearance of composure, and would not open his lips, till he believed himself to have attained it. The pause was to

Elizabeth's feelings dreadful. At length, in a voice of forced calmness, he said,

"And this is all the reply which I am to have the honor of expecting! I might, perhaps, wish to be informed why, with so little *endeavor* at civility, I am thus rejected. But it is of small importance."

"I might as well enquire," replied she, "why with so evident a design of offending and insulting me, you chose to tell me that you liked me against your will, against your reason, and even against your character? Was not this some excuse for incivility, if I *was* uncivil? But I have other provocations. You know I have. Had not my own feelings decided against you, had they been indifferent, or had they even been favorable, do you think that any consideration would tempt me to accept the man, who has been the means of ruining, perhaps forever, the happiness of a most beloved sister?"

As she pronounced these words, Mr. Darcy changed color; but the emotion was short, and he listened without attempting to interrupt her while she continued.

"I have every reason in the world to think ill of you. No motive can excuse the most unjust and ungenerous part you acted *there*. You dare not, you cannot deny that you have been the principal, if not the only means of dividing them from each other, of exposing one to the censure of the world for caprice and instability, the other to its derision for disappointed hopes, and involving them both in misery of the acutest kind."

She paused, and saw with no slight indignation that he was listening with an air which proved him wholly unmoved by any feeling of remorse. He even looked at her with a smile of affected incredulity.

"Can you deny that you have done it?" she repeated.

With assumed tranquillity he then replied, "I have no wish of denying that I did everything in my power to separate my friend from your sister, or that I rejoice in my success. Toward *him* I have been kinder than toward myself."

Elizabeth disdained the appearance of noticing this civil reflection, but its meaning did not escape, nor was it likely to conciliate her.

"But it is not merely this affair," she continued, "on which my dislike is founded. Long before it had taken place, my opinion of you was decided. Your character was unfolded in the recital which I received many months ago from Mr. Wickham. On this subject, what can you have to say? In what imaginary act of friendship can you here defend yourself? Or under what misrepresentation, can you here impose upon others?"

"You take an eager interest in that gentleman's concerns," said Darcy in a less tranquil tone, and with a heightened color.

"Who that knows what his misfortunes have been, can help feeling an interest in him?"

"His misfortunes!" repeated Darcy contemptuously; "yes, his misfortunes have been great indeed."

"And of your infliction," cried Elizabeth with energy. "You have reduced him to his present state of poverty, comparative poverty. You have withheld the advantages, which you must know to have been designed for him. You have deprived the best years of his life, of that independence which was no less his due than his desert. You have done all this! And yet you can treat the mention of his misfortunes with contempt and ridicule."

"And this," cried Darcy, as he walked with quick steps across the room, "is your opinion of me! This is the estimation in which you hold me! I thank you for explaining it so fully. My faults, according to this calculation, are heavy indeed! But perhaps," added he, stopping in his walk, and turning toward her, "these offenses might have been overlooked, had not your pride been hurt by my honest confession of the scruples that had long prevented my forming any serious design. These bitter accusations might have been suppressed, had I with greater policy concealed my struggles, and flattered you into the belief of my being impelled by unqualified, unalloyed inclination; by reason, by reflection, by everything. But disguise of every sort is my abhorrence. Nor am I ashamed of the feelings I related. They were natural and just. Could you expect me to rejoice in the inferiority of your connections? To congratulate myself on the hope of relations, whose condition in life is so decidedly beneath my own?"

Elizabeth felt herself growing more angry every moment; yet she tried to the utmost to speak with composure when she said,

"You are mistaken, Mr. Darcy, if you suppose that the mode of your declaration affected me in any other way, than as it spared me the concern which I might have felt in refusing you, had you behaved in a more gentleman-like manner."

She saw him start at this, but he said nothing, and she continued,

"You could not have made me the offer of your hand in any possible way that would have tempted me to accept it."

Again his astonishment was obvious; and he looked at her with an expression of mingled incredulity and mortification. She went on.

"From the very beginning, from the first moment I may almost say, of my acquaintance with you, your manners impressing me with the fullest belief of your arrogance, your conceit, and your selfish disdain of the feelings of others, were such as to form that groundwork of disapprobation, on which succeeding events have built so immovable a dislike; and I had not known you a month before I felt that you were the last man in the world whom I could ever be prevailed on to marry."

"You have said quite enough, madam. I perfectly comprehend your feelings, and have now only to be ashamed of what my own have been. Forgive me for having taken up so much of your time, and accept my best wishes for your health and happiness."

And with these words he hastily left the room, and Elizabeth heard him the next moment open the front door and quit the house.

The tumult of her mind was now painfully great. She knew not how to support herself, and from actual weakness sat down and cried for half an hour. Her astonishment, as she reflected on what had passed, was increased by every review of it. That she should receive an offer of marriage from Mr. Darcy! That he should have been in love with her for so many months! So much in love as to wish to marry her in spite of all the objections which had made him prevent his friend's marrying her sister, and which must appear at least with equal force in his own case, was almost incredible! It was gratifying to have inspired unconsciously so strong an affection. But his pride, his abominable pride, his shameless avowal of what he had done with respect to Jane, his unpardonable assurance in acknowledging, though he could not justify it, and the unfeeling manner in which he had mentioned Mr. Wickham, his cruelty toward whom he had not attempted to deny, soon overcame the pity which the consideration of his attachment had for a moment excited.

She continued in very agitating reflections till the sound of Lady Catherine's carriage made her feel how unequal she was to encounter Charlotte's observation, and hurried her away to her room.

When Darcy proposes for a second time, both he and Elizabeth acknowledge the faults they displayed during his first proposal. Each has shown a measure of pride and prejudice alike toward the other. Darcy, moreover, has redeemed himself by proving correct in his low opinion of Mr. Wickham, and by helping the Bennetts deal with the scandal of Wickham's elopement with Elizabeth's foolish younger sister, Lydia.

The gentlemen arrived early; and, before Mrs. Bennet had time to tell him of their having seen his aunt, of which her daughter sat in momentary dread, Bingley, who wanted to be alone with Jane, proposed their all walking out. It was agreed to. Mrs. Bennet was not in the habit of walking, Mary could never spare time, but the remaining five set off together. Bingley and Jane, however, soon allowed the others to outstrip them. They lagged behind, while Elizabeth, Kitty, and Darcy, were to entertain each other. Very little was said by either; Kitty was too much afraid of him to talk; Elizabeth was secretly forming a desperate resolution; and perhaps he might be doing the same.

They walked toward the Lucases, because Kitty wished to call upon Maria; and as Elizabeth saw no occasion for making it a general concern, when Kitty left them, she went boldly on with him alone. Now was the moment for her resolution to be executed, and, while her courage was high, she immediately said,

"Mr. Darcy, I am a very selfish creature; and, for the sake of giving relief to my own feelings, care not how much I may be wounding yours. I can no longer help thanking you for your unexampled kindness to my poor sister. Ever since I have known it, I have been most anxious to acknowledge to you how gratefully I feel it. Were it known to the rest of my family, I should not have merely my own gratitude to express."

"I am sorry, exceedingly sorry," replied Darcy, in a tone of surprise and emotion, "that you have ever been informed of what may, in a mistaken light, have given you uneasiness. I did not think Mrs. Gardiner was so little to be trusted."

"You must not blame my aunt. Lydia's thoughtlessness first betrayed to me that you had been concerned in the matter; and, of course, I could not rest till I knew the particulars. Let me thank you again and again, in the name of all my family, for that generous compassion which induced you to take so much trouble, and bear so many mortifications, for the sake of discovering them."

"If you *will* thank me," he replied, "let it be for yourself alone. That the wish of giving happiness to you, might add force to the other inducements which led me on, I shall not attempt to deny. But your *family* owe me nothing. Much as I respect them, I believe, I thought only of *you*."

Elizabeth was too much embarrassed to say a word. After a short pause, her companion added, "You are too generous to trifle with me. If your feelings are still what they were last April, tell me so at once. *My* affections and wishes are unchanged, but one word from you will silence me on this subject forever."

Elizabeth, feeling all the more than common awkwardness and anxiety of his situation, now forced herself to speak; and immediately, though not very fluently, gave him to understand, that her sentiments had undergone so material a change, since the period to which he alluded, as to make her receive with gratitude and pleasure, his present assurances. The happiness which this reply produced, was such as he had probably never felt before; and he expressed himself on the occasion as sensibly and as warmly as a man violently in love can be supposed to do. Had Elizabeth been able to encounter his eye, she might have seen how well the expression of heartfelt delight, diffused over his face, became him; but, though she could not look, she could listen, and he told her of feelings, which, in proving of what importance she was to him, made his affection every moment more valuable.

They walked on, without knowing in what direction. There was too much to be thought, and felt, and said, for attention to any other objects. She soon learned that they were indebted for their present good understanding to the efforts of his aunt, who *did* call on him in her return through London, and there relate her journey to Longbourn, its motive, and the substance of her conversation with Elizabeth; dwelling emphatically on every expression of the latter, which, in her ladyship's apprehension, peculiarly denoted her perverseness and assurance, in the belief that such a relation must assist her endeavors to obtain that promise from her nephew, which *she* had refused to give. But, unluckily for her ladyship, its effect had been exactly contrariwise.

"It taught me to hope," said he, "as I had scarcely ever allowed myself to hope before. I knew enough of your disposition to be certain, that, had you been absolutely, irrevocably decided against me, you would have acknowledged it to Lady Catherine, frankly and openly."

Elizabeth colored and laughed as she replied, "Yes, you know enough of my *frankness* to believe me capable of *that*. After abusing you so abominably to your face, I could have no scruple in abusing you to all your relations."

"What did you say of me, that I did not deserve? For, though your accusations were ill founded, formed on mistaken premises, my behavior to you at the time, had merited the severest reproof. It was unpardonable. I cannot think of it without abhorrence."

"We will not quarrel for the greater share of blame annexed to that evening," said Elizabeth. "The conduct of neither, if strictly examined, will be irreproachable; but since then, we have both, I hope, improved in civility."

"I cannot be so easily reconciled to myself. The recollection of what I then said, of my conduct, my manners, my expressions during the whole of it, is now, and has been many months, inexpressibly painful to me. Your reproof, so well applied, I shall never forget: 'had you behaved in a more gentleman-like manner.' These were your words. You know not, you can scarcely conceive, how they have tortured me; though it was some time, I confess, before I was reasonable enough to allow their justice."

"I was certainly very far from expecting them to make so strong an impression. I had not the smallest idea of their being ever felt in such a way."

"I can easily believe it. You thought me then devoid of every proper feeling, I am sure you did. The turn of your countenance I shall never forget, as you said that I could not have addressed you in any possible way, that would induce you to accept me."

"Oh! Do not repeat what I then said. These recollections will not do at all. I assure you, that I have long been most heartily ashamed of it."

Darcy mentioned his letter. "Did it," said he, "did it *soon* make you think better of me? Did you, on reading it, give any credit to its contents?"

She explained what its effect on her had been, and how gradually all her former prejudices had been removed.

"I knew," said he, "that what I wrote must give you pain, but it was necessary. I hope you have destroyed the letter. There was one part especially, the opening of it, which I should dread your having the power of reading again. I can remember some expressions which might justly make you hate me."

"The letter shall certainly be burned, if you believe it essential to the preservation of my regard; but, though we have both reason to think my opinions not entirely unalterable, they are not, I hope, quite so easily changed as that implies."

"When I wrote that letter," replied Darcy, "I believed myself perfectly calm and cool, but I am since convinced that it was written in a dreadful bitterness of spirit."

"The letter, perhaps, began in bitterness, but it did not end so.

The adieu is charity itself. But think no more of the letter. The feelings of the person who wrote, and the person who received it, are now so widely different from what they were then, that every unpleasant circumstance attending it, ought to be forgotten. You must learn some of my philosophy. Think only of the past as its remembrance gives you pleasure."

"I cannot give you credit for any philosophy of the kind. *Your* retrospections must be so totally void of reproach, that the contentment arising from them, is not of philosophy, but what is much better, of ignorance. But with *me*, it is not so. Painful recollections will intrude, which cannot, which ought not to be repelled. I have been a selfish being all my life, in practice, though not in principle. As a child I was taught what was *right*, but I was not taught to correct my temper. I was given good principles, but left to follow them in pride and conceit. Unfortunately an only son (for many years an only *child*), I was spoiled by my parents, who though good themselves (my father particularly, all that was benevolent and amiable), allowed, encouraged, almost taught me to be selfish and overbearing, to care for none beyond my own family circle, to think meanly of all the rest of the world, to *wish* at least to think meanly of their sense and worth compared with my own. Such I was, from eight to eight-and-twenty; and such I might still have been but for you, dearest, loveliest Elizabeth! What do I not owe you! You taught me a lesson, hard indeed at first, but most advantageous. By you, I was properly humbled. I came to you without a doubt of my reception. You shewed me how insufficient were all my pretensions to please a woman worthy of being pleased."

"Had you then persuaded yourself that I should?"

"Indeed I had. What will you think of my vanity? I believed you to be wishing, expecting my addresses."

"My manners must have been in fault, but not intentionally I assure you. I never meant to deceive you, but my spirits might often lead me wrong. How you must have hated me after *that* evening."

"Hate you! I was angry perhaps at first, but my anger soon began to take a proper direction."

"I am almost afraid of asking what you thought of me; when we met at Pemberley. You blamed me for coming?"

"No indeed; I felt nothing but surprise."

"Your surprise could not be greater than *mine* in being noticed by you. My conscience told me that I deserved no extraordinary politeness, and I confess that I did not expect to receive *more* than my due."

"My object *then*," replied Darcy, "was to shew you, by every civility in my power, that I was not so mean as to resent the past; and I hoped to obtain your forgiveness, to lessen your ill opinion, by letting you see that your reproofs had been attended to."

Do Not Be a Rake

From Lord Chesterfield,
The Letters of Lord Chesterfield to His Son

An uninterrupted life of pleasures is as insipid as contemptible. Some hours given every day to serious business, must whet both the mind and the senses, to enjoy those of pleasure. A surfeited glutton, an emaciated sot, and an enervated rotten whoremaster never enjoy the pleasures to which they devote themselves; they are only so many human sacrifices to false gods. The pleasures of low life are all of this mistaken, merely sensual, and disgraceful nature; whereas those of high life, and in good company (though possibly in themselves not more moral), are more delicate, more refined, less dangerous, and less disgraceful; and, in the common course of things, not reckoned disgraceful at all. In short, pleasure must not, nay, cannot, be the business of a man of sense and character; but it may be, and is, his relief, his reward.

Nothing sinks a young man into low company, both of women and men, so surely as timidity, and diffidence of himself. If he thinks that he shall not, he may depend upon it, he will not please. But with proper endeavors to please, and a degree of persuasion that he shall, it is almost certain that he will. How many people does one meet with everywhere, who with very moderate parts, and very little knowledge, push themselves pretty far, singly by being sanguine, enterprising, and persevering? They will take no denial from man or woman; difficulties do not discourage them; repulsed twice or thrice, they rally, they charge again, and nine times in ten prevail at last. The same means will much sooner, and more certainly, attain the same ends, with your parts and knowledge. You have a fund to be sanguine upon, and good forces to rally. In business (talents supposed) nothing is more effectual, or successful, than a good, though concealed, opinion of one's self, a firm resolution, and an unwearied perseverance. None but madmen attempt impossibilities; and whatever is possible, is one way or another to be brought about. If one method fails, try another, and suit your methods to the characters you have to do with.

Having mentioned the word rake, I must say a word or two more on that subject, because young people too frequently, and always fatally, are apt to mistake that character for that of a man of pleasure; whereas, there are not in the world two characters more different. A rake is a composition of all the lowest, most ignoble, degrading, and shameful vices; they all conspire to disgrace his character and to ruin his fortune; while wine and the pox contend which shall soonest and most effectually destroy his constitution. A dissolute, flagitious footman or porter makes full as good a rake as a man of the first quality. By the bye, let me tell you that in the wildest part of my youth I never was a rake, but on the contrary, always detested and despised the character.

For, as I have often formerly observed to you, nobody but a father can take the liberty to reprove a young fellow grown up, for those kind of inaccuracies and improprieties of behavior. The most intimate friendship, unassisted by the paternal superiority, will not authorize it. I may truly say, therefore, that you are happy in having me for a sincere, friendly, and quick-sighted monitor. Nothing will escape me; I shall pry for your defects, in order to correct them, as curiously as I shall seek for your perfections, in order to applaud and reward them; with this difference only, that I shall publicly mention the latter, and never hint at the former, but in a letter to, or a *tête-à-tête* with you.

John Grey, the Worthy Man

From Anthony Trollope,
Can You Forgive Her?

Alice Vavasor has a problem. A man with no character flaws of any kind whatsoever has proposed marriage. Trollope's 1864 novel chronicles Alice's vacillations between two suitors—the somewhat too flawless John Grey and her charming but unreliable cousin, George Vavasor.

Mr. Grey's answer to Alice Vavasor's letter, which was duly sent by return of post and duly received on the morning after Lady Macleod's visit, may perhaps be taken as giving a sample of his worthiness. It was dated from Nethercoats, a small countryhouse in Cambridgeshire which belonged to him, at which he already spent much of his time, and at which he intended to live altogether after his marriage.

> *Nethercoats, June, 186–*
> *Dearest Alice,*
> *I am glad you have settled your affairs, foreign affairs, I mean, so much to your mind. As to your home affairs they are not, to my thinking, quite so satisfactorily arranged. But as I am a party interested in the latter my opinion may perhaps have an undue bias. Touching the tour, I quite agree with you that you and Kate would have been uncomfortable alone. It's a very fine theory, that of women being able to get along without men as well as with them; but, like other fine theories, it will be found very troublesome by those who first put it in practise. Gloved hands, petticoats, feminine softness, and the general homage paid to beauty, all stand in the way of success. These things may perhaps someday be got rid of, and possibly with advantage; but while young ladies are still encumbered with them a male companion will always be found to be a comfort. I don't quite know whether your cousin George is the best possible knight you might have chosen. I should consider myself to be infinitely preferable, had my going been upon the cards. Were you in danger of meeting Paynim foes, he, no doubt, would kill them off much quicker than I could do, and would be much more serviceable in liberating you from the dungeons of oppressors, or even from stray tigers in the Swiss forests. But I doubt his being punctual with the luggage. He will want you or Kate to keep the accounts, if any are kept. He will be slow in getting you glasses of water at the railway stations, and will always keep you waiting at breakfast. I hold that a man with two ladies on a tour should be an absolute slave to them, or they will not fully enjoy themselves. He should simply be an upper servant, with the privilege of sitting at the same table with his mistresses. I have my doubts as to whether your cousin is fit for the place; but, as to myself, it is just the thing that I was made for. Luckily, however, neither you nor Kate are without wills of your own, and perhaps you may be able to reduce Mr. Vavasor to obedience.*
> *As to the home affairs I have very little to say here, in this letter. I shall of course run up and see you before you start, and shall proba-*

*bly stay a week in town. I know I ought not to do so, as it will be a
week of idleness, and yet not a week of happiness. I'd sooner have an
hour with you in the country than a whole day in London. And I
always feel in town that I've too much to do to allow of my doing anything. If it were sheer idleness I could enjoy it, but it is a feverish idleness, in which one is driven here and there, expecting some gratification which not only never comes, but which never even begins to come.
I will, however, undergo a week of it, say the last seven days of this
month, and shall trust to you to recompense me by as much of yourself
as your town doings will permit.*

*And now again as to those home affairs. If I say nothing now I
believe you will understand why I refrain. You have cunningly just
left me to imply, from what you say, that all my arguments have been
of no avail; but you do not answer them, or even tell me that you
have decided. I shall therefore imply nothing, and still trust to my personal eloquence for success. Or rather not trust—not trust, but hope.*

*The garden is going on very well. We are rather short of water,
and therefore not quite as bright as I had hoped; but we are preparing
with untiring industry for future brightness. Your commands have
been obeyed in all things, and Morrison always says, "The mistress
didn't mean this," or "The mistress did intend that." God bless the
mistress is what I now say, and send her home, to her own home, to
her flowers, and her fruit, and her house, and her husband, as soon
as may be, with no more of these delays which are to me so grievous,
and which seem to me to be so unnecessary. That is my prayer.*

Yours ever and always,

J.G.

"I didn't give commands," Alice said to herself, as she sat with
the letter at her solitary breakfast-table. "He asked me how I liked
the things, and of course I was obliged to say. I was obliged to seem
to care, even if I didn't care." Such were her first thoughts as she
put the letter back into its envelope, after reading it the second
time. When she opened it, which she did quickly, not pausing a
moment lest she should suspect herself of fearing to see what
might be its contents, her mind was full of that rebuke which her
aunt had anticipated, and which she had almost taught herself to
expect. She had torn the letter open rapidly, and had dashed at its
contents with quick eyes. In half a moment she had seen what was
the nature of the reply respecting the proposed companion of her
tour, and then she had completed her reading slowly enough. "No;
I gave no commands," she repeated to herself, as though she might

thereby absolve herself from blame in reference to some possible future accusations, which might perhaps be brought against her under certain circumstances which she was contemplating.

Then she considered the letter bit by bit, taking it backward, and sipping her tea every now and then amidst her thoughts. No; she had no home, no house, there. She had no husband; not as yet. He spoke of their engagement as though it were a betrothal, as betrothals used to be of yore; as though they were already in some sort married. Such betrothals were not made nowadays. There still remained, both to him and to her, a certain liberty of extricating themselves from this engagement. Should he come to her and say that he found that their contemplated marriage would not make him happy, would not she release him without a word of reproach? Would not she regard him as much more honorable in doing so than in adhering to a marriage which was distasteful to him? And if she would so judge him, judge him and certainly acquit him, was it not reasonable that she under similar circumstances should expect a similar acquittal? Then she declared to herself that she carried on this argument within her own breast simply as an argument, induced to do so by that assertion on his part that he was already her husband, that his house was even now her home. She had no intention of using that power which was still hers. She had no wish to go back from her pledged word.

She thought that she had no such wish. She loved him much, and admired him even more than she loved him. He was noble, generous, clever, good, so good as to be almost perfect; nay, for aught she knew he was perfect. Would that he had some faults! Would that he had! Would that he had! How could she, full of faults as she knew herself to be, how could she hope to make happy a man perfect as he was! But then there would be no doubt as to her present duty. She loved him, and that was everything. Having told him that she loved him, and having on that score accepted his love, nothing but a change in her heart toward him could justify her in seeking to break the bond which bound them together. She did love him, and she loved him only.

But she had once loved her cousin. Yes, truly it was so. In her thoughts she did not now deny it. She had loved him, and was tormented by a feeling that she had had a more full delight in that love than in this other that had sprung up subsequently. She had told herself that this had come of her youth; that love at twenty was sweeter than it could be afterward. There had been a something of rapture in that earlier dream which could never be repeated, which could never live, indeed, except in a dream. Now, now that she was older and perhaps wiser, love meant a partnership, in which each partner would be honest to the other, in which each would wish and strive for the other's welfare, so that thus their joint welfare might be insured. Then, in those early girlish days, it had meant a total abnegation of self. The one was of earth, and therefore possible. The other had been a ray from heaven, and impossible, except in a dream.

And she had been mistaken in her first love. She admitted that frankly. He whom she had worshiped had been an idol of clay, and she knew that it was well for her to have abandoned that idolatry. He had not only been untrue to her, but, worse than that, had been false in excusing his untruth. He had not only promised falsely, but had made such promises with a deliberate, premeditated falsehood. And he had been selfish, coldly selfish, weighing the value of his own low lusts against that of her holy love. She had known this, and had parted from him with an oath to herself that no promised contrition on his part should ever bring them again together. But she had pardoned him as a man, though never as a lover, and had bade him welcome again as a cousin and as her friend's brother. She had again become very anxious as to his career, not hiding her regard, but professing that anxiety aloud. She knew him to be clever, ambitious, bold, and she believed even yet, in spite of her own experience, that he might not be bad at heart. Now, as she told herself that in truth she loved the man to whom her troth was plighted, I fear that she almost thought more of that other man from whom she had torn herself asunder.

"Why should he find himself unhappy in London?" she said, as she went back to the letter. "Why should he pretend to condemn the very place which most men find the fittest for all their energies? Were I a man, no earthly consideration should induce me to live elsewhere. It is odd how we differ in all things. However brilliant might be his own light, he would be contented to hide it under a bushel!"

And at last she recurred to that matter as to which he had been so anxious when she first opened her lover's letter. It will be remembered how assured she had expressed herself that Mr. Grey would not condescend to object to her traveling with her cousin. He had not so condescended. He had written on the matter with a pleasant joke, like a gentleman as he was, disdaining to allude to the past passages in the life of her whom he loved, abstaining even from expressing anything that might be taken as a permission on his part. There had been in Alice's words, as she told him of their proposed plan, a something that had betrayed a tremor in her thoughts. She had studiously striven so to frame her phrases that her tale might be told as any other simple statement, as though there had been no trembling in her mind as she wrote. But she had failed, and she knew that she had failed. She had failed; and he had read all her effort and all her failure. She was quite conscious of this; she felt it thoroughly: and she knew that he was noble and a gentleman to the last drop of his blood. And yet—yet—yet there was almost a feeling of disappointment in that he had not written such a letter as Lady Macleod had anticipated.

During the next week Lady Macleod still came almost daily to Queen Anne Street, but nothing further was said between her and Miss Vavasor as to the Swiss tour; nor were any questions asked about Mr. Grey's opinion on the subject. The old lady of course discovered that there was no quarrel, or, as she believed, any probability of a quarrel; and with that she was obliged to be contented. Nor did she again on this occasion attempt to take Alice to Lady Midlothian's. Indeed, their usual subjects of conversation were almost abandoned, and Lady Macleod's visits, though they were as constant as heretofore, were not so long. She did not dare to talk about Mr. Grey, and because she did not so dare, was determined to regard herself as in a degree ill-used. So she was silent, reserved, and fretful. At length came the last day of her London season, and her last visit to her niece. "I would come because it's my last day," said Lady Macleod; "but really I'm so hurried, and have so many things to do, that I hardly know how to manage it."

"It's very kind," said Alice, giving her aunt an affectionate squeeze of the hand.

"I'm keeping the cab, so I can just stay twenty-five minutes. I've marked the time accurately, but I know the man will swear it's over the half-hour."

"You'll have no more trouble about cabs, Aunt, when you are back in Cheltenham."

"The flies are worse, my dear. I really think they're worse. I pay the bill every month, but they've always one down that I didn't have. It's the regular practice, for I've had them from all the men in the place."

"It's hard enough to find honest men anywhere, I suppose."

"Or honest women either. What do you think of Mrs. Green wanting to charge me for an extra week, because she says I didn't give her notice till Tuesday morning? I won't pay her, and she may stop my things if she dares. However, it's the last time. I shall never come up to London again, my dear."

"Oh, Aunt, don't say that!"

"But I do say it, my dear. What should an old woman like me do, trailing up to town every year, merely because it's what people choose to call the season."

"To see your friends, of course. Age doesn't matter when a person's health is so good as yours."

"If you knew what I suffer from lumbago, though I must say coming to London always does cure that for the time. But as for friends! Well, I suppose one has no right to complain when one gets to be as old as I am; but I declare I believe that those I love best would sooner be without me than with me."

"Do you mean me, Aunt?"

"No, my dear, I don't mean you. Of course my life would have been very different if you could have consented to remain with me till you were married. But I didn't mean you. I don't know that I meant anyone. You shouldn't mind what an old woman like me says."

"You're a little melancholy because you're going away."

"No, indeed. I don't know why I stayed the last week. I did say to Lady Midlothian that I thought I should go on the twentieth; and, though I know that she knew that I really didn't go, she has not once sent to me since. To be sure they've been out every night; but I thought she might have asked me to come and lunch. It's so very lonely dining by myself in lodgings in London."

"And yet you never will come and dine with me."

"No, my dear; no. But we won't talk about that. I've just one word more to say. Let me see. I've just six minutes to stay. I've made up my mind that I'll never come up to town again, except for one thing."

"And what's that, Aunt?" Alice, as she asked the question, well knew what that one thing was.

"I'll come for your marriage, my dear. I do hope you will not keep me long waiting."

"Ah! I can't make any promise. There's no knowing when that may be."

"And why should there be no knowing? I always think that when a girl is once engaged the sooner she's married the better. There may be reasons for delay on the gentleman's part."

"There very often are, you know."

"But, Alice, you don't mean to say that Mr. Grey is putting it off?"

Alice was silent for a moment, during which Lady Macleod's face assumed a look of almost tragic horror. Was there something wrong on Mr. Grey's side of which she was altogether unaware? Alice, though for a second or two she had been guilty of a slight playful deceit, was too honest to allow the impression to remain. "No Aunt," she said; "Mr. Grey is not putting it off. It has been left to me to fix the time."

"And why don't you fix it?"

"It is such a serious thing! After all it is not more than four months yet since I—I accepted him. I don't know that there has been any delay."

"But you might fix the time now, if he wishes it."

"Well, perhaps I shall, some day, Aunt. I'm going to think about it, and you mustn't drive me."

"But you should have some one to advise you, Alice."

"Ah! That's just it. People always do seem to think it so terrible that a girl should have her own way in anything. She mustn't like anyone at first; and then, when she does like someone, she must marry him directly she's bidden. I haven't much of my own way at present; but you see, when I'm married I shan't have it at all. You can't wonder that I shouldn't be in a hurry."

"I am not advocating anything like hurry, my dear. But, goodness gracious me! I've been here twenty-eight minutes, and that horrid man will impose upon me. Good-bye; God bless you! Mind you write." And Lady Macleod hurried out of the room more intent at the present moment upon saving her sixpence than she was on any other matter whatsoever.

And then John Grey came up to town, arriving a day or two after the time that he had fixed. It is not, perhaps, improbable that Alice had used some diplomatic skill in preventing a meeting between Lady Macleod and her lover. They both were very anxious to obtain the same object, and Alice was to some extent opposed to their views. Had Lady Macleod and John Grey put their forces together she might have found herself unable to resist their joint endeavors. She was resolved that she would not at any rate name any day for her marriage before her return from Switzerland; and she may therefore have thought it wise to keep Mr. Grey in the country till after Lady Macleod had gone, even though she thereby cut down the time of his sojourn in London to four days. On the occasion of that visit Mr. Vavasor did a very memorable thing. He dined at home with the view of welcoming his future son-in-law. He dined at home, and asked, or rather assented to Alice's asking,

George and Kate Vavasor to join the dinner-party. "What an auspicious omen for the future nuptials!" said Kate, with her little sarcastic smile. "Uncle John dines at home, and Mr. Grey joins in the dissipation of a dinner-party. We shall all be changed soon, I suppose, and George and I will take to keeping a little cottage in the country."

"Kate," said Alice, angrily, "I think you are about the most unjust person I ever met. I would forgive your raillery, however painful it might be, if it were only fair."

"And to whom is it unfair on the present occasion; to your father?"

"It was not intended for him."

"To yourself?"

"I care nothing as to myself; you know that very well."

"Then it must have been unfair to Mr. Grey."

"Yes; it was Mr. Grey whom you meant to attack. If I can forgive him for not caring for society, surely you might do so."

"Exactly; but that's just what you can't do, my dear. You don't forgive him. If you did you might be quite sure that I should say nothing. And if you choose to bid me hold my tongue I will say nothing. But when you tell me all your own thoughts about this thing you can hardly expect but that I should let you know mine in return. I'm not particular; and if you are ready for a little good, wholesome, useful hypocrisy, I won't balk you. I mayn't be quite so dishonest as you call me, but I'm not so wedded to truth but what I can look, and act, and speak a few falsehoods if you wish it. Only let us understand each other."

"You know I wish for no falsehood, Kate."

"I know it's very hard to understand what you do wish. I know that for the last year or two I have been trying to find out your wishes, and, upon my word, my success has been very indifferent. I suppose you wish to marry Mr. Grey, but I'm by no means certain. I suppose the last thing on earth you'd wish would be to marry George."

"The very last. You're right there at any rate."

"Alice! Sometimes you drive me too hard; you do, indeed. You make me doubt whether I hate or love you most. Knowing what my feelings are about George, I cannot understand how you can bring yourself to speak of him to me with such contempt!" Kate Vavasor, as she spoke these words, left the room with a quick step, and hurried up to her own chamber. There Alice found her in tears, and was driven by her friend's real grief into the expression of an apology, which she knew was not properly due from her. Kate was acquainted with all the circumstances of that old affair between her brother and Alice. She had given in her adhesion to the propriety of what Alice had done. She had allowed that her brother George's behaviors had been such as to make any engagement between them impossible. The fault, therefore, had been hers in making any reference to the question of such a marriage. Nor had it been by any means her first fault of the same kind. Till Alice had become engaged to Mr. Grey she had spoken of George only as her brother, or as her friend's cousin, but now she was constantly making allusion to those past occurrences, which all of them should have striven to forget. Under these circumstances was not Lady Macleod right in saying that George Vavasor should not have been accepted as a companion for the Swiss tour?

The little dinner-party went off very quietly; and if no other ground existed for charging Mr. Grey with London dissipation than what that afforded, he was accused most unjustly. The two young men had never before met each other; and Vavasor had gone to his uncle's house, prepared not only to dislike but to despise his successor in Alice's favor. But in this he was either disappointed or gratified, as the case may be. "He has plenty to say for himself," he said to Kate on his way home.

"Oh yes; he can talk."

"And he doesn't talk like a prig either, which was what I expected. He's uncommonly handsome."

"I thought men never saw that in each other. I never see it in any man."

"I see it in every animal—in men, women, horses, dogs, and even pigs. I like to look on handsome things. I think people always do who are ugly themselves."

"And so you're going into raptures in favor of John Grey."

"No, I'm not. I very seldom go into raptures about anything. But he talks in the way I like a man to talk. How he bowled my uncle over about those actors; and yet if my uncle knows anything about anything it is about the stage twenty years ago." There was nothing more said then about John Grey; but Kate understood her brother well enough to be aware that this praise meant very little. George Vavasor spoke sometimes from his heart, and did so more frequently to his sister than to any one else; but his words came generally from his head.

On the day after the little dinner in Queen Anne Street, John Grey came to say good-bye to his betrothed; for his betrothed she certainly was, in spite of those very poor arguments which she had used in trying to convince herself that she was still free if she wished to claim her freedom. Though he had been constantly with Alice during the last three days, he had not hitherto said anything as to the day of their marriage. He had been constantly with her alone, sitting for hours in that ugly green drawing-room, but he had never touched the subject. He had told her much of Switzerland, which she had never yet seen but which he knew well. He had told her much of his garden and house, whither she had once gone with her father, whilst paying a visit nominally to the colleges at Cambridge. And he had talked of various matters, matters bearing in an immediate way upon his own or her affairs; for Mr. Grey was a man who knew well how to make words pleasant; but previous to this last moment he had said nothing on that subject on which he was so intent.

"Well, Alice," he said, when the last hour had come, "and about that question of home affairs?"

"Let us finish off the foreign affairs first."

"We have finished them; haven't we?"

"Finished them! Why we haven't started yet."

"No; you haven't started. But we've had this discussion. Is there any reason why you'd rather not have this thing settled?"

"No, no special reason."

"Then why not let it be fixed? Do you fear coming to me as my wife?"

"No."

"I cannot think that you repent your goodness to me."

"No; I don't repent it; what you call my goodness? I love you too entirely for that."

"My darling!" And now he passed his arm round her waist as they stood near the empty fireplace. "And if you love me . . . "

"I do love you."

"Then why should you not wish to come to me?"

"I do wish it. I think I wish it."

"But, Alice, you must have wished it altogether when you consented to be my wife."

"A person may wish for a thing altogether, and yet not wish for it instantly."

"Instantly! Come; I have not been hard on you. This is still June. Will you say the middle of September, and we shall still be in time for warm pleasant days among the lakes? Is that asking for too much?"

"It is not asking for anything."

"Nay, but it is, love. Grant it, and I will swear that you have granted me everything."

She was silent, having things to say but not knowing in what words to put them. Now that he was with her she could not say the things which she had told herself that she would utter to him. She could not bring herself to hint to him that his views of life were so unlike her own, that there could be no chance of happiness between them, unless each could strive to lean somewhat toward the other. No man could be more gracious in word and manner than John Grey; no man more chivalrous in his carriage toward a woman; but he always spoke and acted as though there could be no question that his manner of life was to be adopted, without a word or thought of doubting, by his wife. When two came together, why should not each yield something, and each claim something? This she had meant to say to him on this day; but now that he was with her she could not say it.

"John," she said at last, "do not press me about this till I return."

"But then you will say the time is short. It would be short then."

"I cannot answer you now; indeed, I cannot. That is I cannot answer in the affirmative. It is such a solemn thing."

"Will it ever be less solemn, dearest?"

"Never, I hope never."

He did not press her further then, but kissed her and bade her farewell.

The Knight

From Geoffrey Chaucer, The Canterbury Tales

A knight there was, and that a worthy man,
That from the time he first began
To ride out, he loved chivalry,
Truth and honor, generosity and courtesy.
Full worthy was he in his lord's wars
And to them he had ridden, no man farther,

As well in Christiandom as in heathenness,
And ever honored for his worthiness.

And always he had the highest praise,
And though that he were worthy, he was wise,
And bore himself as meekly as a maid.
He never yet a vile thing said
In all his life to anyone of any kind.
He was a truly perfect, gentle knight.

Honor and Reputation

From Francis Bacon, Essays

From Bacon's essay, Of Honor and Reputation.

The winning of honor is but the revealing of a man's virtue and worth without disadvantage. For some in their actions do woo and affect honor and reputation, which sort of men are commonly much talked of, but inwardly little admired. And some, contrariwise, darken their virtue in the shew of it, so as they be undervalued in opinion. If a man perform that which hath not been attempted before, or attempted and given over, or hath been achieved, but not with so good circumstance, he shall purchase more honor than by effecting a matter of greater difficulty or virtue, wherein he is but a follower. If a man so temper his actions as in some one of them he doth content every faction or combination of people, the music will be the fuller. A man is an ill husband of his honor that entereth into any action, the failing wherein may disgrace him more than the carrying of it through can honor him. Honor that is gained and broken upon another hath the quickest reflexion, like diamonds cut with facets. And therefore let a man contend to excel any competitors of his in honor, in outshooting them, if he can, in their own bow. Discreet followers and servants help much to reputation.

Temperance

From Baldesar Castiglione, The Book of the Courtier

A gentleman must possess all the virtues: prudence, justice, liberality, magnificence, honor, gentleness, pleasantness, and affability. Temperance, according to Ottaviano, is the basis for them all.

My lord Ottaviano was continuing his discourse further, but the Magnifico Giuliano interrupted him and said:

"If I heard rightly, my lord Ottaviano, you said that continence is an imperfect virtue because it has a grain of passion in it. But when there is a struggle waging in our minds between reason and appetite, I think that the virtue which battles and gives reason the victory, ought to be esteemed more perfect than that which conquers without opposition of lust or passion; for there the mind seems not to abstain from evil by force of virtue, but to refrain from doing evil because it has no inclination thereto."

Then my lord Ottaviano said:

"Which captain would you deem of greater worth, the one who fighting openly puts himself in danger and yet conquers the enemy, or the one who by his ability and skill deprives them of their strength, reducing them to such straits that they cannot fight, and thus conquers them without any battle or danger whatever?"

"The one," said the Magnifico Giuliano, "who more safely conquers is without doubt more to be praised, provided this safe victory of his does not proceed from the cowardice of the enemy."

My lord Ottaviano replied:

"You have judged rightly; and hence I tell you that continence may be likened to a captain who fights manfully, and although the enemy be strong and powerful, still conquers them, albeit not without great difficulty and danger. While temperance unperturbed is like that captain who conquers and rules without opposition, and having not only abated but quite extinguished the fire of lust in the mind where she abides, like a good prince in time of civil strife, she destroys her seditious enemies within, and gives reason the sceptre and whole dominion.

"Thus this virtue does not compel the mind, but infusing it by

very gentle means with a vehement belief that inclines it to righteousness, renders it calm and full of rest, in all things equal and
well measured, and disposed on every side by a certain self-accord
which adorns it with a tranquillity so serene that it is never ruffled,
and becomes in all things very obedient to reason and ready to
turn its every act thereto and to follow wherever reason may wish to
lead it, without the least unwillingness; like a tender lambkin,
which always runs and stops and walks near its mother, and moves
only with her.

"This virtue, then, is very perfect and especially befitting to
princes, because from it spring many others."

Then messer Cesare Gonzaga said:

"I do not know what virtues befitting to a lord can spring from
this temperance, if it is the one which removes the passions from
the mind, as you say. Perhaps this would be fitting in a monk or
hermit; but I am by no means sure whether it would befit a prince
(who was magnanimous, liberal and valiant in arms) never to feel,
whatever might be done to him, either wrath or hate or good will
or scorn or lust or passion of any kind, and whether he could without this wield authority over citizens or soldiers."

My lord Ottaviano replied:

"I did not say that temperance wholly removes and uproots
the passions from the human mind, nor would it be well to do this,
for even the passions contain some elements of good; but it
reduces to the sway of reason that which is perverse in our passions
and resistant to right. Therefore it is not well to extirpate the passions altogether, in order to be rid of disturbance; for this would be
like making an edict that no one must drink wine, in order to be
rid of drunkenness, or forbidding everyone to run, because in running we sometimes fall. You know that those who tame horses do
not keep them from running and leaping, but would have them do
so seasonably and in obedience to the rider.

"Thus, when moderated by temperance, the passions are helpful to virtue, like the wrath that aids strength, hatred of evil-doers
aids justice, and likewise the other virtues are aided by the passions;
which, if they were wholly removed, would leave reason very weak
and languid, so that it could effect little, like the master of a vessel
abandoned by the winds in a great calm.

"Now do not marvel, messer Cesare, if I have said that many
other virtues are born of temperance, for when a mind is attuned
to this harmony, it then through reason easily receives true

strength, which makes it bold, and safe from every peril, and almost superior to human passions. Nor is this less true of justice (unspotted virgin, friend of modesty and good, queen of all the other virtues), because she teaches us to do that which it is right to do, and to shun that which it is right to shun; and therefore she is most perfect, because the other virtues perform their works through her, and because she is helpful to whomsoever possesses her, both to himself and to others: without whom (as it is said) Jove himself could not rule his kingdom rightly. Magnanimity also follows these and enhances them all; but she cannot stand alone, for whoever has no other virtue, cannot be magnanimous. Then the guide of these virtues is foresight, which consists in a certain judgment in choosing well. And in this happy chain are joined liberality, magnificence, thirst for honour, gentleness, pleasantness, affability and many others which there is not now time to name.

"But if our Courtier will do that which we have said, he will find them all in his prince's mind, and will daily see spring therefrom beautiful flowers and fruits, such as all the delightful gardens in the world do not contain."

Then my lord Gaspar said:

"I should much like to know what virtues are useful and necessary in war, and what ones are righteous in peace."

My lord Ottaviano replied:

"All virtues are good and helpful, because they tend to a good end; but of special utility in war is that true courage which so frees the mind from the passions that it not only fears no dangers, but even pays no heed to them; likewise steadfastness, and that enduring patience, with a mind staunch and undisturbed by all the shocks of fortune. It is also fitting in war, and always, to have all the virtues that make for right,—like justice, continence, temperance; but much more in time of peace and ease, because men placed in prosperity and ease, when good fortune smiles upon them, often become unjust, intemperate, and allow themselves to be corrupted by pleasures: hence those who are in such case have very great need of these virtues, for ease too readily engenders evil behaviour in human minds. Therefore it was anciently said as a proverb, slaves should be given no ease and it is believed that the pyramids of Egypt were made to keep the people busy, because it is very good for everyone to be accustomed to bear toil.

"There are still many other virtues that are all helpful, but let it suffice for the present that I have spoken until now; for if I knew how to teach my prince and instruct him in this kind of worthy education such as we have planned, merely by so doing I should deem myself to have attained sufficiently well the aim of the good Courtier."

The Man Without Moral Feeling

From Theophrastus, The Characters

Lack of moral feeling is willingness to do or say what is disgraceful. The man without moral feeling is the kind who will take an oath with no sense of responsibility, since he does not mind letting himself in for hard words or even downright abuse. By nature he is a base kind of person, lacking the most elementary sense of decency and capable of absolutely anything. Dead sober, he will do a belly dance when he is supposed to be part of a comic chorus; and at a puppet show he goes around collecting the penny admission from everybody and arguing with pass-holders who think they have a right to watch free. Very likely he runs a shady hotel or a whorehouse, too, or collects taxes. Town crier, gambler, cook—no trade is too disgraceful for this fellow. He leaves his mother without support in her old age; he gets hauled into court for petty theft and knows the inside of the town jail better than his own house.

[This man also seems to be the sort who gets a crowd around him and lectures his listeners in a loud, cracked voice, trading arguments and abuse. And some of them arrive in the middle of his tirade, while others leave without bothering to hear it all; but he obliges with a summary of whatever is left out, convinced that there's no occasion so proper for a display of his lack of moral feeling as when he has an audience.]

In court, moreover, he is capable of playing any role: defendant, plaintiff, or witness. Sometimes he gets out of testifying by swearing ignorance; or he may appear in court as a witness, with stacks of evidence inside his coat and whole handfuls of documents. He knows a good many rascals, and he will not disqualify even the worst of them from high office. More than that, he lends money to these fellows the moment they ask for the loan—collecting interest, to be sure, at a rate of three obols in twelve, not yearly or monthly but daily. He gets the interest from their businesses, too, and makes the rounds of bakers and fishmongers with the money stuffed into his cheek.

[They are a troublesome lot, always ready with an insult and talking so loudly that the market-place and the shops echo.]

Practice Makes Perfect

From John Locke, Of Practice and Habits

John Locke (1632–1704) was perhaps the single most influential English philosopher. His views on individual liberty, religious tolerance, and liberal education were influential in America as well.

We are born with faculties and powers capable almost of anything, such at least as would carry us further than can be easily imagined; but it is only the exercise of those powers which gives us ability and skill in anything, and leads us towards perfection.

A middle-aged ploughman will scarce ever be brought to the carriage and language of a gentleman, though his body be as well proportioned, and his joints as supple, and his natural parts not any way inferior. The legs of a dancing-master, and the fingers of a musician, fall as it were naturally, without thought or pains, into regular and admirable motions. Bid them change their parts, and they will in vain endeavor to produce like motions in the members not used to them, and it will require length of time and long practice to attain but some degrees of a like ability. What incredible and astonishing actions do we find rope-dancers and tumblers bring their bodies to! Not but that sundry in almost all manual arts are as wonderful; but I name those which the world takes notice of for such, because, on that very account, they give money to see them. All these admired motions, beyond the reach, and almost the conception, of unpracticed spectators, are nothing but the mere effects of use and industry in men whose bodies have nothing different in them from those of the amazed lookers-on.

As it is in the body, so it is in the mind; practice makes it what it is: and most, even of those excellencies which are looked on as natural endowments, will be found, when examined into more narrowly, to be the product of exercise, and to be raised to that pitch only by repeated actions. Some men are remarked for pleasantness in raillery; others for apologues and apposite diverting stories. This is apt to be taken for the effect of pure nature, and that the rather, because it is not got by rules; and those who excel in either of them never purposely set themselves to the study of it as an art to be learned. But yet it is true that at first some lucky hit which took with somebody, and gained him commendation, encouraged him to try again, inclined his thoughts and endeavors that way, till at last he insensibly got a facility in it without perceiving how; and that is attributed wholly to nature, which was much more the effect of use and practice. I do not deny that natural disposition may often give the first rise to it; but that never carries a man far without use and exercise, and it is practice alone that brings the powers of the mind, as well as those of the body, to their perfection. Many a good poetic vein is buried under a trade, and never produces anything, for want of improvement. We see the ways of discourse and reasoning are very different, even concerning the same matter at court and in the university. And he that will go but from Westminster Hall to the Exchange will find a different genius and turn in their ways of talking: and yet one cannot think that all whose lot fell in the city were born with different parts from those who were bred at the university or inns of court.

To what purpose all this, but to show that the difference so observable in men's understandings and parts does not arise so much from the natural faculties as acquired habits? He would be laughed at that should go about to make a fine dancer out of a country hedger at past fifty. And he will not have much better success who shall endeavor at that age to make a man reason well, or speak handsomely, who has never been used to it, though you should lay before him a collection of all the best precepts of logic or oratory. Nobody is made anything by hearing of rules, or laying them up in his memory; practice must settle the habit of doing, without reflecting on the rule: and you may as well hope to make a good painter or musician extempore by a lecture and instruction in the arts of music and painting, as a coherent thinker, or strict reasoner, by a set of rules showing him wherein right reasoning consists.

This being so, that defects and weakness in men's understandings, as well as other faculties, come from a want of a right use of their own minds, I am apt to think the fault is generally mislaid upon nature, and there is often a complaint of want of parts, when the fault lies in want of a due improvement of them. We see men frequently dexterous and sharp enough in making a bargain, who, if you reason with them about matters of religion, appear perfectly stupid.

On Friendship

From Aristotle, The Nicomachean Ethics

A gentleman takes pleasure in the esteem of a friend whom he esteems in return.

The duties which we owe to our friends seem analogous to those which each individual willingly pays to himself. We ought, it is said, to wish their good, or what appears to us to be such, and to promote it to our best ability, merely on their own account. With this kind of disinterested affection mothers are animated towards their children, and those friends towards each other, between whom some disgust has arisen which, though it interrupts their intercourse, does not destroy their mutual kindness. Others say that friends must spend much of their time together, have the same inclinations and pursuits, and sympathize with each other in their joy as well as in their sorrow. On whichever or how many soever of those conditions friendship principally depends, we shall find that all of them belong to the affections by which a good man is animated towards himself; and by which all men are animated in proportion as they either approximate, or only think they approximate, to an honorable and praiseworthy character; which, in questions concerning human nature, is justly considered as the sole unerring standard. The virtuous man only is at peace within himself, since all the powers of his mind are actuated by the same motives, and conspire to the same end: always aiming at good, real and intrinsic, the good of his intellectual part. To him existence is a benefit, which he earnestly wishes may be preserved, especially the existence of the thinking principle within him, which is peculiarly himself; for every individual strives after its own good, real or apparent, which in the virtuous man only coincide: but could an individual love its change into something quite different from itself, the good of the latter would be to the former a matter of slight concern. In Deity all goods are accumulated, because he is ever and invariably that which he is; and in man the thinking principle is the part that is properly and permanently himself. He who pursues the good of his mind is pleased in his own company, being delighted with the recollection of the past as well as animated with the prospect of the future; and having ever at command innumerable speculations, in which he exercises himself with the most exquisite pleasure. Both his joys and his sorrows are respectively consistent with themselves, since they invariably proceed from fixed and regular causes; for he does not delight at one time in what will excite his repentance at another; and thus harmonized within his own breast, he is similarly affected towards his friend, whom he considers as a second self; and his sympathy for whom, when it reaches the highest perfection, resembles that internal concord which is experienced in his own mind, when the various principles of his nature coalesce into one movement, and flow in the same homogeneous stream of virtuous energy.

Yet many men of very irregular lives seem to be highly satisfied with themselves. Is this because they mistake their own characters? It should seem so, since the complete villain is always visibly at variance with himself; and all others are similarly affected in proportion to their progress in wickedness; willing one thing, yet desiring and preferring another as those who allow themselves to be subdued by vicious pleasure, and who may be said, with their eyes open, to rush into voluntary destruction. In the same manner others, through laziness or cowardice, avoid that conduct which they know most likely to promote their happiness. When men proceed to the last stage of depravity, they become as odious to themselves as they are detestable to others, and therefore often destroy their own lives; and even before they arrive at this deplorable condition, they fly from and avoid themselves; preferring any kind of society to that of their own reflections; the past crimes which haunt their memory, and the meditated guilt which is continually occurring to their fancy. As they have nothing in them that is amiable, they cannot be the objects of their own love. Neither their joys nor their sorrows are consistent. Their whole soul is in sedition, distracted between contending principles, the pleasure of one giving pain to another; and when the worst principle prevails, a foundation is laid for the bitterest remorse. If such be the wretchedness of wickedness, how strenuously ought we to exert ourselves to become good men, that we may live in friendship with ourselves, and be worthy of the friendship of others!

The Lover of Bad Company

From Theophrastus, The Characters

Love of bad company and rascally behavior is a passion for the vicious. It makes the kind of man who imagines that he will find out what life is really about and become a terror if he associates with people convicted of crimes against the state. Or when you describe somebody as respectable this fellow will reply, "So it would appear . . ." and then go on to argue that really nobody can claim respectability—people are all alike. A remark like "What a respectable man so-and-so is" he turns into a joke.

Moreover it's the rascal, he argues, who turns out to be the real gentleman if you put him to the test. Some of what you hear about such men is true, he admits, but other things aren't. "They're clever and good-natured, the kind who won't let a friend down," he maintains; and he champions anyone like this with all his might as the most capable person he ever met. In addition, he listens sympathetically whenever a rascal is bing prosecuted in a court of law or called on to make a public defence of his record. "Remember, you're trying the case, not the man," he will say to the jury every time; and he calls the defendant a watchdog of the people's interests, on the look-out against lawbreakers. "We won't have anybody left to worry about good government," he adds, "if we don't stand by fellows like this."

You also find him playing the protector of worthless men, or trying to get a jury packed for dirty work in the courtroom. And if he is called in to give an individual opinion, he puts the arguments of the opposing sides in an unfavorable light.

It could be said generally that sympathy with rascally behavior represents the next thing to rascality itself; and there is some truth in the old saying about birds of a feather.

3

THE WISE MAN

Few thoughtful people would contest the notion that manliness includes, indeed requires, a quotient of wisdom. But the connection between the two is elusive and has sparked a lively and even fierce debate over the centuries. What do we mean by wisdom? The abstract, purely intellectual rigor of academia? The grand contemplative speculations and metaphysical doctrines of philosophers from Plato to Hegel? The search by natural scientists for ever greater clarity about the universe, the beautiful complexities of pure mathematics, the jeweler's-eye precision of the logician? Or is wisdom something deeper, more universal?

The readings in this section examine the question of wisdom from many perspectives. It may be helpful to keep in mind that the word *wise* suggests a different human quality from the intellectual connotations of words like *brilliant* or *smart*. As Aristotle tells us, a young man can be a brilliant metaphysician or mathematician, and yet lack enough experience of the world to be wise in civic affairs, family relations, and ethical behavior. Wisdom—as opposed to braininess or brilliance—suggests character tested and tempered by time, challenged by adversity and fortified by the earned insights of experience. The best recipe for happiness, Aristotle concludes, involves a balance of contemplative and active virtues—a teaching that weaves a golden thread throughout every period of reflection on the meaning of manliness.

It is this broader kind of wisdom that we explore in this section: what it means to be wise in the affairs of one's fellow citizens, but also what it means for a man to embark on an *inner* journey of self-awareness and spiritual evolution, reflecting on life's hardships and disappointments, reversals and rewards.

It was Cato who observed that wise men learn more from fools than fools do from wise men, for wise men can avoid the errors of fools while fools rarely profit from the examples of the wise. This sharp distinction between the wise and the foolish does not sit well with our democratic instincts, but it is often amply justified by everyday experience. Men we know to be wise learn from every source available in life: from their elders, from their peers, from family and loved ones—above all, they learn by example. A wise man is cautious and deliberate, reserving judgment and taking nothing for granted. Among his qualities are a commitment to open-mindedness and an ability to look beyond the conventional wisdom of the status quo. As Thoreau put it, "The wisest man preaches no doctrines, he has no scheme, he sees no rafter, not even a cobweb, against the heavens. It is clear sky." Wisdom has more to do with an appetite to learn than with a blind faith in one's own judgment; the wise man never mistakes his opinion for a fixed and unalterable truth. In this sense, wisdom is intrinsically connected with intellectual modesty. As Thomas Jefferson wrote (echoing Socrates), a wise man is the best expert on his own weaknesses and failings, for he recognizes how little he truly knows.

THE WISE MAN OF AFFAIRS

Where Do You Shop for Wisdom?

From Diogenes Laertius,
Lives of the Philosophers

Xenophon, son of Gryllus, was an Athenian citizen and belonged to the deme Erchia. He was an extremely handsome man, yet possessed an unusual modesty. There is a story that once Socrates on meeting him in a narrow passage stretched out his stick, barring his way, and asked him where different kinds of food might be bought. When Xenophon answered, Socrates asked another question, "And where do men become good and honorable?" Xenophon was too puzzled to reply. "Then follow me," said Socrates, "and learn." Thence forward Xenophon was a pupil of Socrates.

My Son, Be Admonished!

From Ecclesiastes (11:9–12; 12)

Rejoice, O young man, in thy youth; and let thy heart cheer thee in the days of thy youth, and walk in the ways of thine heart, and in the sight of thine eyes: but know thou, that for all these things God will bring thee into judgment. Therefore remove sorrow from thy heart, and put away evil from thy flesh: for youth and the prime of life are vanity. Remember also thy Creator in the days of thy youth, or ever the evil days come, and the years draw nigh, when thou shalt say, I have no pleasure in them; or ever the sun, and the light, and the moon, and the stars, be darkened, and the clouds return after the rain: in the day when the keepers of the house shall tremble, and the strong men shall bow themselves, and the grinders cease because they are few, and those that look out of the windows be darkened, and the doors shall be shut in the street; when the sound of the grinding is low, and one shall rise up at the voice of a bird, and all the daughters of music shall be brought low; yea, they shall be afraid of *that which is high,* and terrors *shall be* in the way; and the almond tree shall blossom, and the grasshopper shall be a burden, and the caper-berry shall fail: because man goeth to his long home, and the mourners go about the streets: or ever the silver cord be loosed, or the golden bowl be broken, or the Pitcher be broken at the fountain, or the wheel broken at the cistern; and the dust return to the earth as it was, and the spirit return unto God who gave it. Vanity of vanities, saith the Preacher; all is vanity.

And further, because the Preacher was wise, he still taught the people knowledge; yea, he pondered, and sought out, *and* set in order many proverbs. The Preacher sought to find out acceptable words, and that which was written uprightly, *even* words of truth. The words of the wise are as goads, and as nails well fastened are *the words of* the masters of assemblies, *which* are given from one shepherd. And furthermore, my son, be admonished: of making many books there is no end; and much study is a weariness of the flesh. *This is* the end of the matter; all hath been heard: fear God, and keep his commandments; for this is the whole *duty* of man. For God shall bring every work into judgment, with every hidden thing, whether it be good or whether it be evil.

How Should a Young Man Live?

From Plato, The Republic

How should a young man live? Should he devote himself to justice, moderation and the other virtues? Or should he get all the pleasures he can out of life—limitless sex, wealth, power, and glory? In Plato's Republic, *we see two promising young men, Glaucon and Adeimantos—the brothers of Plato—wrestling with this dilemma, as common to teenagers then as it is now. According to Glaucon, some influential thinkers argue that justice is only an artificial convention to protect the weak from the strong. By contrast, exploiting and taking advantage of others is the natural way for a man to live if he has the brains and guts to get away with it. The proof: Give any so-called law-abiding citizen a magic ring that would make him invisible, and he would immediately begin living "naturally" by plundering and ravishing everyone in sight. If people weren't afraid of being caught for breaking the law, in other words, everyone would do it. Glaucon challenges Socrates: Prove that justice really is a happier life than a life of tyrannical pleasure, not just something we do because we're slaves of convention.*

"I am perplexed when I hear the voices of Thrasymachus and myriads of others dinning in my ears; and, on the other hand, I have never yet heard the superiority of justice to injustice maintained by anyone in a satisfactory way. I want to hear justice praised in respect of itself; then I shall be satisfied, and you are the person from whom I think that I am most likely to hear this; and therefore I will praise the unjust life to the utmost of my power, and my manner of speaking will indicate the manner in which I desire to hear you too praising justice and censuring injustice. Will you say whether you approve of my proposal?"

"Indeed I do; nor can I imagine any theme about which a man of sense would oftener wish to converse."

"I am delighted," he replied, "to hear you say so, and shall begin by speaking, as I proposed, of the nature and origin of justice.

"They say that to do injustice is, by nature, good; to suffer injustice, evil; but that the evil is greater than the good. And so when men have both done and suffered injustice and have had experience of both, not being able to avoid the one and obtain the other, they think that they had better agree among themselves to have neither; hence there arise laws and mutual covenants; and that which is ordained by law is termed by them lawful and just. This they affirm to be the origin and nature of justice; it is a mean or compromise between the best of all, which is to do injustice and not be punished, and worst of all, which is to suffer injustice without the power of retaliation; and justice being at a middle point between the two, is tolerated not as a good, but as the lesser evil, and honored by reason of the inability of men to do injustice. For no man who is worthy to be called a man would ever submit to such an agreement if he were able to resist; he would be mad if he did. Such is the received account, Socrates, of the nature and origin of justice.

"Now that those who practice justice do so involuntarily and because they have not the power to be unjust will best appear if we imagine something of this kind: having given both to the just and the unjust power to do what they will, let us watch and see whither desire will lead them; then we shall discover in the very act the just and unjust man to be proceeding along the same road, following their interest, which all natures deem to be their good, and are only diverted into the path of justice by the force of law. The liberty which we are supposing may be most completely given to them in the form of such a power as is said to have been possessed by Gyges the ancestor of Croesus the Lydian. According to the tradition, Gyges was a shepherd in the service of the king of Lydia; there was a great storm, and an earthquake made an opening in the earth at the place where he was feeding his flock. Amazed at the sight, he descended into the opening, where, among other marvels, he beheld a hollow brazen horse, having doors, at which he stooping and looking in saw a dead body of stature, as appeared to him, more than human, and having nothing on but a gold ring; this he took from the finger of the dead and reascended. Now the shepherds met together, according to custom, that they might send their monthly report about the flocks to the king; into their assembly he came having the ring on his finger, and as he was sitting among them he chanced to turn the collet of the ring inside his hand, when instantly he became invisible to the rest of the company and they began to speak of him as if he were no longer present.

He was astonished at this, and again touching the ring he turned the collet outward and reappeared; he made several trials of the ring, and always with the same result–when he turned the collet inward he became invisible, when outward he reappeared. Whereupon he contrived to be chosen one of the messengers who were sent to the court; where as soon as he arrived he seduced the queen, and with her help conspired against the king and slew him, and took the kingdom. Suppose now that there were two such magic rings, and the just put on one of them and the unjust the other; no man can be imagined to be of such an iron nature that he would stand fast in justice. No man would keep his hands off what was not his own when he could safely take what he liked out of the market, or go into houses and lie with anyone at his pleasure, or kill or release from prison whom he would, and in all respects be like a God among men. Then the actions of the just would be as the actions of the unjust; they would both come at last to the same point. And this we may truly affirm to be a great proof that a man is just, not willingly or because he thinks that justice is any good to him individually, but of necessity, for whenever anyone thinks that he can safely be unjust, then he is unjust. For all men believe in their hearts that injustice is far more profitable to the individual than justice, and if a man argues as I have been supposing, he will say that they are right. If you could imagine anyone obtaining this power of becoming invisible, and never doing any wrong or touching what was another's, he would be thought by the lookers-on to be a most wretched idiot, although they would praise him to one another's faces, and keep up appearances with one another from a fear that they too might suffer injustice. Enough of this.

"Now, if we are to form a real judgment of the life of the just and unjust, we must isolate them; there is no other way; and how is the isolation to be effected? I answer: Let the unjust man be entirely unjust and the just man entirely just; nothing is to be taken away from either of them, and both are to be perfectly furnished for the work of their respective lives. First, let the unjust be like other distinguished masters of craft; like the skillful pilot or physician, who knows intuitively his own powers and keeps within their limits, and who, if he fails at any point, is able to recover himself. So let the unjust make his unjust attempts in the right way, and lie hidden if he means to be great in his injustice (he who is found out is nobody): for the highest reach of injustice is: to be deemed just when you are not. Therefore I say that in the perfectly unjust man we must assume the most perfect injustice; there is to be no deduction, but we must allow him while doing the most unjust acts, to have acquired the greatest reputation for justice. If he has taken a false step he must be able to recover himself; he must be one who can speak with effect, if any of his deeds come to light, and who can force his way where force is required by his courage and strength, and command of money and friends. And at his side let us place the just man in his nobleness and simplicity, wishing, as Aeschylus says, to be and not to seem good. There must be no seeming, for if he seem to be just he will be honored and rewarded, and then we shall not know whether he is just for the sake of justice or for the sake of honors and rewards; therefore, let him be clothed in justice only, and have no other covering; and he must be imagined in a state of life the opposite of the former. Let him be the best of men, and let him be thought the worst; then he will have been put to the proof; and we shall see whether he will be affected by the fear of infamy and its consequences. And let him continue thus to the hour of death; being just and seeming to be unjust. When both have reached the uttermost extreme, the one of justice and the other of injustice, let judgment be given which of them is the happier of the two."

"Heavens! My dear Glaucon," I said, "how energetically you polish them up for the decision, first one and then the other, as if they were two statues."

"I do my best," he said. "And now that we know what they are like there is no difficulty in tracing out the sort of life which awaits either of them. This I will proceed to describe; but as you may think the description a little too coarse, I ask you to suppose, Socrates, that the words which follow are not mine. Let me put them into the mouths of the eulogists of injustice: They will tell you that the just man who is thought unjust will be scourged, racked, bound—will have his eyes burned out; and, at last, after suffering every kind of evil, he will be impaled: Then he will understand that he ought to seem only, and not to be, just; the words of Aeschylus may be more truly spoken of the unjust than of the just. For the unjust is pursuing a reality; he does not live with a view to appearances—he wants to be really unjust and not seem only:

'His mind has a soil deep and fertile,
Out of which spring his prudent counsels.'

"In the first place, he is thought just, and therefore rules in the city; he can marry whom he will, and give in marriage to whom he will; also he can trade and deal where he likes, and always to his own advantage, because he has no misgivings about injustice; and at every contest, whether in public or private, he gets the better of his antagonists, and gains at their expense, and is rich, and out of his gains he can benefit his friends, and harm his enemies; moreover, he can offer sacrifices, and dedicate gifts to the gods abundantly and magnificently, and can honor the gods or any man whom he wants to honor in a far better style than the just, and therefore he is likely to be dearer than they are to the gods. And thus, Socrates, gods and men are said to unite in making the life of the unjust better than the life of the just."

Daedalus and Icarus

From Thomas Bulfinch,
Bulfinch's Mythology

The ancient legend of Daedalus and his son Icarus, who flew too high. Scientific and technical knowledge can bring great rewards, but unless governed by moderation, they can also bring destruction.

The labyrinth from which Theseus escaped by means of the clew of Ariadne was built by Daedalus, a most skillful artificer. It was an edifice with numberless winding passages and turnings opening into one another, and seeming to have neither beginning nor end, like the River Maeander, which returns on itself, and flows now onward, now backward, in its course to the sea. Daedalus built the labyrinth for King Minos, but afterward lost the favor of the king, and was shut up in a tower. He contrived to make his escape from his prison, but could not leave the island by sea, as the king kept strict watch on all the vessels, and permitted none to sail without being carefully searched. "Minos may control the land and sea," said Daedalus, "but not the regions of the air. I will try that way." So he set to work to fabricate wings for himself and his young son Icarus. He wrought feathers together, beginning with the smallest and adding larger, so as to form an increasing surface. The larger ones he secured with thread and the smaller with wax, and gave the whole a gentle curvature like the wings of a bird. Icarus, the boy, stood and looked on, sometimes running to gather up the feathers which the wind had blown away, and then handling the wax and working it over with his fingers, by his play impeding his father in his labors. When at last the work was done, the artist, waving his wings, found himself buoyed upward, and hung suspended, poising himself on the beaten air. He next equipped his son in the same manner and taught him how to fly, as a bird tempts her young ones from the lofty nest into the air. When all was prepared for flight he said, "Icarus, my son, I charge you to keep at a moderate height, for if you fly too low the damp will clog your wings, and if too high the heat will melt them. Keep near me and you will be safe." While he gave him these instructions and fitted the wings to his shoulders, the face of the father was wet with tears, and his hands trembled. He kissed the boy, not knowing that it was for the last time. Then rising on his wings, he flew off, encouraging him to follow, and looked back from his own flight to see how his son managed his wings. As they flew the ploughman stopped his work to gaze, and the shepherd leaned on his staff and watched them, astonished at the sight, and thinking they were gods who could thus cleave the air.

They passed Samos and Delos on the left and Lebynthos on the right, when the boy, exulting in his career, began to leave the guidance of his companion and soar upward as if to reach heaven. The nearness of the blazing sun softened the wax which held the feathers together, and they came off. He fluttered with his arms, but no feathers remained to hold the air. While his mouth uttered cries to his father, it was submerged in the blue waters of the sea, which henceforth was called by his name. His father cried, "Icarus, Icarus, where are you?" At last he saw the feathers floating on the water, and bitterly lamenting his own arts, he buried the body and called the land Icaria in memory of his child. Daedalus arrived safe in Sicily, where he built a temple to Apollo, and hung up his wings, an offering to the god.

The Man of Discipline

From The Bhagavad-Gita

In this great Hindu poem of the first century A.D. *King Arjuna, about to lead his army into battle, despairs of finding a reason to perform his earthly duties when religion teaches us to flee the world for a higher realm of perfection. Although most of this anthology is from Western sources, there are equally rich traditions of manly virtue in non-Western civilizations.*

Why go to war or govern if the world of mortals is an illusion? The great god Krishna suspends time on the eve of the battle as Arjuna is paralyzed by these doubts. There must be a balance, Lord Krishna teaches, between our duties in life and the perfection of our inner selves through renouncing worldly ambition and willfulness.

Doing our duty without regard for the rewards both helps us to shed our worldly selves and to fulfill our worldly duties.

Krishna:
Therefore, whoever does work rightful to do,
Not seeking gain from work, that man, O Prince!
Is Renouncer and man of holy discipline—both in one.
And he is neither who does not light the flame
Of sacrifice, nor sets his hands to work.

Regard as a true Renouncer he who makes
Worship by work, for he who renounces not,
Works not with Holy Discipline. So it is well said:
"By works the votary rises to faith,
And sainthood is the ceasing from all works;"
Because the perfect self-disciplined worker acts—but acts
Unmoved by passions and unbound by deeds,
Setting result aside.

Let each man raise
Himself by Soul, but not by trampling down his Self,
For Soul, which is Self's friend, can become Self's enemy.
Soul is Self's friend when Self controls itself,

But Self becomes Soul's enemy if Soul's own Self
Hates Self as not part of itself.

The sovereign soul
Of he who lives self-governed and at peace
Is centered in itself, impartial alike to
Pleasure and pain; heat and cold; glory and shame.
He is a man of holy discipline, glad
With joy of light and truth; dwelling apart
Upon a peak, with senses subjugated.
To him a clod of earth, a rock, and glistening gold
Show all as one. By this sign he is known:
Being of equal grace to comrades, friends,
Chance-comers, strangers, lovers, enemies,
Aliens and kinsmen; loving all alike,
Evil or good.

Sequestered, he should sit,
Steadfastly meditating, solitary,
His thoughts controlled, his passions put away,
Rid of possessions. Let him abide
In a fair, still spot—not too much raised,
Nor yet too low—His goods:
A cloth, a deerskin, and the grass.
There, focusing his mind upon The One,
Restraining heart and senses, silent and calm,
Let him accomplish self-discipline and achieve
Pureness of soul, holding immovable
Body and neck and head, his gaze absorbed
Upon the tip of his nose, oblivious to all around him,
Tranquil in spirit, free of fear, intent
Upon his vow of chastity, devout,
Musing on Me, lost in the thought of Me.
That man of self-discipline, so devoted, so controlled,
Comes to the peace beyond,—My peace, the peace
Of high Nirvana!

But for earthly needs,
Piety is not his who fasts too much
Or feasts too much, nor his who sleeps away
An idle mind; nor his who wears himself down,
Wasting his strength in vigils. Nay! Arjuna! Call

That the true piety which most removes
Earthly aches and ills, where one is moderate
In eating and in resting, and in sport;
Moderate in wish and in act; sleeping early,
Waking early for duty.

When a man,
So living, centers on his soul, his thought
Tightly restrained—untouched within
By stress of sense—then he achieves true discipline. See!
Like an unwavering lamp which burns sheltered from the wind;
Such is the steadiness of the disciplined mind
Freed from the storms of sense and burning bright to Heaven.
When mind broods calmly, soothed with holy discipline;
When Self contemplates Self, and in itself
Has comfort; when it knows the nameless joy
Beyond all scope of sense, revealed to soul—
Only to soul! and, knowing, wavers not,
True to the farther Truth; when, holding this,
It deems no other treasure comparable,
But, harbored there, cannot be stirred or shook
By any gravest grief, call that state "peace,"
That happy severance from suffering; call that man
The perfect man of self-discipline.

Steadfastly the will
Must toil thereto, until its efforts end in ease,
And thought has passed from thinking. Shaking off
All longings bred by dreams of fame and gain,
Shutting the doorways of the senses, closed
With watchful guard; so, step by step, he comes
To the gift of peace assured and heart calmed,
When the mind dwells self-wrapped, and the soul broods
Unencumbered. But as often as the heart
Breaks—wild and wavering—from control, so often
Let him re-curb it, let him rein it back in
To the soul's mastery; for perfect bliss
Grows only in the bosom tranquillized,
The spirit passionless, purged from offence,
Vowed to the Infinite. He who thus vows
His soul to the Supreme Soul, quitting sin,
Passes unhindered to the endless bliss

Of unity with Brahma. He so vowed,
So blended, sees the Life-Soul resident
In all things living, and all living things
In that Life-Soul contained. And whoever thus
Discerns Me in all, and all in Me,
I never let him go; nor does he loosen his
Hold upon Me; but, dwell he where he may,
Whatever his life, in Me he dwells and lives,
Because he knows and worships Me, I who dwell
In all which lives, and cleaves to me in all.
Arjuna! If a man sees everywhere—
Taught by his own similitude to all—one Life
One Essence in the Evil and the Good,
Behold in him a man of holy discipline, yes! well perfected!

Virtue or Vice?

From Plato, The Republic

In Plato's Republic, *Adeimantus adds another dimension to the quandary of how a young man should live. Figures of authority rarely give young people a clear message in their upbringing. On the one hand, the poets going back to Homer say a man should be virtuous and pious, should restrain his passions, should be a good family man and a decent citizen. On the other hand, an ambition for preeminence in war, politics, and business is held up as admirable. Life is a contest and a real man must fight for his place in the sun. The poets say virtue is difficult and doesn't necessarily bring happiness, while vice is easy and pleasant and doesn't necessarily get punished. Why then would any sane man chose virtue over vice? Moreover, the gods are depicted as indifferent to good or bad behavior among men, or—worse—capable of being won over to the side of the wicked by lavish sacrifices and worship. How can a young man know how to live when he is told to be moderate and obedient and at the same time to aim for triumph over others?*

I was going to say something in answer to Glaucon, when Adeimantus, his brother, interposed: "Socrates," he said, "you do not suppose that there is nothing more to be urged?"

"Why, what else is there?" I answered.

"The strongest point of all has not been even mentioned," he replied.

"Well, then, according to the proverb, 'Let brother help brother'—if he fails in any part do you assist him; although I must confess that Glaucon has already said quite enough to lay me in the dust, and take from me the power of helping justice."

"Nonsense," he replied. "But let me add something more: There is another side to Glaucon's argument about the praise and censure of justice and injustice, which is equally required in order to bring out what I believe to be his meaning. Parents and tutors are always telling their sons and their wards that they are to be just; but why? not for the sake of justice, but for the sake of character and reputation; in the hope of obtaining for him who is reputed just some of those offices, marriages, and the like of which Glaucon has enumerated among the advantages accruing to the unjust from the reputation of justice. More, however, is made of appearances by this class of persons than by the others; for they throw in the good opinion of the gods, and will tell you of a shower of benefits which the heavens, as they say, rain upon the pious; and this accords with the testimony of the noble Hesiod and Homer, the first of whom says, that the gods make the oaks of the just:

'To bear acorns at their summit, and bees in the middle;
and the sheep are bowed down with the weight of their
fleeces.'

and many other blessings of a like kind are provided for them. And Homer has a very familiar strain; for he speaks of one whose fame is:

'As the fame of some blameless king who, like a god,
maintains justice; to whom the black earth brings forth
Wheat and barley, whose trees are bowed with fruit, and his
sheep never fail to bear, and the sea gives him fish.'

"Still grander are the gifts of heaven which Musaeus and his son vouchsafe to the just; they take them down into the world below, where they have the saints lying on couches at a feast, everlastingly drunk, crowned with garlands; their idea seems to be that an immortality of drunkenness is the highest meed of virtue. Some extend their rewards yet further; the posterity, as they say, of the faithful and just shall survive to the third and fourth generation. This is the style in which they praise justice. But about the wicked there is another strain; they bury them in a slough in Hades, and make them carry water in a sieve; also while they are yet living they bring them to infamy, and inflict upon them the punishments which Glaucon described as the portion of the just who are reputed to be unjust; nothing else does their invention supply. Such is their manner of praising the one and censuring the other.

"Once more, Socrates, I will ask you to consider another way of speaking about justice and injustice, which is not confined to the poets, but is found in prose writers. The universal voice of mankind is always declaring that justice and virtue are honorable, but grievous and toilsome; and that the pleasures of vice and injustice are easy of attainment, and are only censured by law and opinion. They say also that honesty is for the most part less profitable than dishonesty; and they are quite ready to call wicked men happy, and to honor them both in public and private when they are rich or in any other way influential, while they despise and overlook those who may be weak and poor, even though acknowledging them to be better than the others. But most extraordinary of all is their mode of speaking about virtue and the gods: they say that the gods apportion calamity and misery to many good men, and good and happiness to the wicked. And mendicant prophets go to rich men's doors and persuade them that they have a power committed to them by the gods of making an atonement for a man's own or his ancestor's sins by sacrifices or charms, with rejoicings and feasts; and they promise to harm an enemy, whether just or unjust, at a small cost; with magic arts and incantations binding heaven, as they say, to execute their will. And the poets are the authorities to whom they appeal, now smoothing the path of vice with the words of Hesiod:

'Vice may be had in abundance without trouble; the way is
smooth and her dwelling-place is near. But before virtue
the gods have set toil.'

and a tedious and uphill road: then citing Homer as a witness that the gods may be influenced by men; for he also says:

'The gods, too, may be turned from their purpose; and men
pray to them and avert their wrath by sacrifices and
soothing entreaties, and by libations and the odor of fat,
when they have sinned and transgressed.'

"And they produce a host of books written by Musaeus and Orpheus, who were children of the Moon and the Muses—that is what they say—according to which they perform their ritual, and persuade not only individuals, but whole cities, that expiations and atonements for sin may be made by sacrifices and amusements which fill a vacant hour, and are equally at the service of the living and the dead; the latter sort they call mysteries, and they redeem us from the pains of hell, but if we neglect them no one knows what awaits us.

"And now," he proceeded, "when the young hear all this said about virtue and vice, and the way in which gods and men regard them, how are their minds likely to be affected, my dear Socrates—those of them, I mean, who are quick-witted, and, like bees on the wing, light on every flower, and from all that they hear are prone to draw conclusions as to what manner of persons they should be and in what way they should walk if they would make the best of life? Probably the youth will say to himself in the words of Pindar:

'Can I by justice or by crooked ways of deceit ascend a
loftier tower which may be a fortress to me all my days?'

"For what men say is that, if I am really just and am not also thought just, profit there is none, but the pain and loss on the other hand are unmistakable. But if, though unjust, I acquire the reputation of justice, a heavenly life is promised to me. Since then, as philosophers prove, appearance tyrannizes over truth and is lord of happiness, to appearance I must devote myself. I will describe around me a picture and shadow of virtue to be the vestibule and exterior of my house; behind I will trail the subtle and crafty fox, as Archilochus, greatest of sages, recommends. But I hear someone exclaiming that the concealment of wickedness is often difficult; to which I answer, Nothing great is easy. Nevertheless, the argument indicates this, if we would be happy, to be the path along which we should proceed. With a view to concealment we will establish secret brotherhoods and political clubs. And there are professors of rhetoric who teach the art of persuading courts and assemblies; and so, partly by persuasion and partly by force, I shall make unlawful gains and not be punished. Still I hear a voice saying that the gods cannot be deceived, neither can they be compelled. But what if there are no gods? or, suppose them to have no care of human things—why in either case should we mind about concealment? And even if there are gods, and they do care about us, yet we know of them only from tradition and genealogies of the poets; and these are the very persons who say that they may be influenced and turned by 'sacrifices and soothing entreaties and by offerings.' Let us be consistent then, and believe both or neither. If the poets speak truly, why then we had better be unjust, and offer of the fruits of injustice; for if we are just, although we may escape the vengeance of heaven, we shall lose the gains of injustice; but if we are unjust, we shall keep the gains, and by our sinning and praying, and praying and sinning, the gods will be propitiated and we shall not be punished. 'But there is a world below in which either we or our posterity will suffer for our unjust deeds.' Yes, my friend, will be the reflection, but there are mysteries and atoning deities, and these have great power. That is what mighty cities declare; and the children of the gods, who were their poets and prophets, bear a like testimony.

"On what principle, then, shall we any longer choose justice rather than the worst injustice? When, if we only unite the latter with a deceitful regard to appearances, we shall fare to our mind both with gods and men, in life and after death, as the most numerous and the highest authorities tell us. Knowing all this, Socrates, how can a man who has any superiority of mind or person or rank or wealth, be willing to honor justice; or indeed to refrain from laughing when he hears justice praised? And even if there should be some one who is able to disprove the truth of my words, and who is satisfied that justice is best, still he is not angry with the unjust, but is very ready to forgive them, because he also knows that men are not just of their own free will; unless, peradventure, there be someone whom the divinity within him may have inspired with a hatred of injustice, or who has attained knowledge of the truth— but no other man. He only blames injustice who, owing to cowardice or age or some weakness, has not the power of being unjust. And this is proved by the fact that when he obtains the power, he immediately becomes unjust as far as he can be.

"The cause of all this, Socrates, was indicated by us at the beginning of the argument, when my brother and I told you how astonished we were to find that of all the professing panegyrists of justice—beginning with the ancient heroes of whom any memorial has been preserved to us, and ending with the men of our own time—no one has ever blamed injustice or praised justice except with a view to the glories, honors, and benefits which flow from them. No one has ever adequately described either in verse or prose the true essential nature of either of them abiding in the soul, and invisible to any human or divine eye; or shown that of all the things of a man's soul which he has within him, justice is the greatest good, and injustice the greatest evil. Had this been the universal strain, had you sought to persuade us of this from our youth upward, we should not have been on the watch to keep one another from doing wrong, but every one would have been his own watchman, because afraid, if he did wrong, of harboring in himself the greatest of evils. I daresay that Thrasymachus and others would seriously hold the language which I have been merely repeating, and words even stronger than these about justice and injustice, grossly, as I conceive, perverting their true nature. But I speak in this vehement manner, as I must frankly confess to you, because I want to hear from you the opposite side; and I would ask you to show not only the superiority which justice has over injustice, but what effect they have on the possessor of them which makes the one to be a good and the other an evil to him. And please, as Glaucon requested of you, exclude reputations; for unless you take away from each of them his true reputation and add on the false, we shall say that you do not praise justice, but the appearance of it; we shall think that you are only exhorting us to keep injustice dark, and that you really agree with Thrasymachus in thinking that justice is another's good and the interest of the stronger, and that injustice is a man's own profit and interest, though injurious to the weaker. Now as you have admitted that justice is one of that highest class of goods which are desired indeed for their results, but in a far greater degree for their own sakes—like sight or hearing or knowledge or health, or any other real and natural and not merely conventional good—praise this aspect of justice."

The Value of Study

From Francis Bacon, Essays

Studies serve for delight, for ornament, and for ability. Their chief use for delight, is in privateness and retiring; for ornament, is in discourse; and for ability, is in the judgment and disposition of business. For expert men can execute, and perhaps judge of particulars, one by one; but the general counsels, and the plots and marshaling of affairs, come best, from those that are learned. To spend too much time in studies is sloth; to use them too much for ornament, is affectation; to make judgment wholly by their rules, is the humor of a scholar. They perfect nature, and are perfected by experience: for natural abilities are like natural plants, that need pruning, by study; and studies themselves, do give forth directions too much at large, except they be bounded in by experience. Crafty men condemn studies, simple men admire them, and wise men use them; for they teach not their own use; but that is a wisdom without them, and above them, won by observation. Read not to contradict and confute; nor to believe and take for granted; nor to find talk and discourse; but to weigh and consider. Some books are to be tasted, others to be swallowed, and some few to be chewed and digested; that is, some books are to be read only in parts; others to be read, but not curiously; and some few to be read wholly, and with diligence and attention. Some books also may be read by deputy, and extracts made of them by others; but that would be only in the less important arguments, and the meaner sort of books, else distilled books are like common distilled waters, flashy things. Reading maketh a full man; conference a ready man; and writing an exact man. And therefore, if a man write little, he had need have a great memory; if he confer little, he had need have a present wit: and if he read little, he had need have much cunning, to seem to know, that he doth not. Histories make men wise; poets witty; the mathematics subtle; natural philosophy deep; moral grave; logic and rhetoric able to contend. Studies turn into manners. Nay, there is no obstacle or impediment in the wit, but may be wrought out by fit studies; like as diseases of the body, may have appropriate exercises. Bowling is good for the stone and kidneys; shooting for the lungs and breast; gentle walking for the stomach; riding for the head; and the like. So if a man's wit be wandering, let him study the mathematics; for in demonstrations, if his wit be called away never so little, he must begin again. If his wit be not apt to distinguish or find differences, let him study the Schoolmen; for they are hair-splitters. If he be not apt to beat over matters, and to call up one thing to prove and illustrate another, let him study the lawyers' cases. So every defect of the mind may have a special recipe.

Why a Man Must Be Liberally Educated If He Is to Gain Eternal Fame

From Baldesar Castiglione, The Book of the Courtier

"And if I were speaking with them, or with others who had an opinion contrary to mine, I should strive to show them how useful and necessary letters are to our life and dignity, having indeed been granted by God to men as a crowning gift. Nor should I lack instances of many excellent commanders of antiquity, who all added the ornament of letters to the valour of their arms.

"Thus you know Alexander held Homer in such veneration that he always kept the Iliad by his bedside; and he devoted the greatest attention not only to these studies but to philosophical speculation under Aristotle's guidance. Alcibiades enlarged his natural aptitudes and made them greater by means of letters and the teachings of Socrates. The care that Caesar gave to study is also attested by the surviving works that he divinely wrote. It is said that Scipio Africanus always kept in his hand the works of Xenophon, wherein the perfect king is portrayed under the name of Cyrus. I could tell you of Lucullus, Sulla, Pompey, Brutus, and many other Romans and Greeks; but I will merely remind you that Hannibal, the illustrious commander,—although fierce by nature and a stranger to all humanity, faithless and a despiser of both men and gods,—yet had knowledge of letters and was conversant with the Greek language; and if I mistake not, I once read that he even left a book composed by him in Greek.

"However it is superfluous to tell you this, for I well know that you all see how wrong the French are in thinking that letters are injurious to arms. You know that glory is the true stimulus to great and hazardous deeds of war, and whoso is moved thereto by gain or other motive, besides doing nothing good, deserves not to be called a gentleman, but a base trafficker. And true glory is that which is preserved in the sacred treasure-house of letters, as everyone may understand except those unfortunates who have never enjoyed them.

"What soul is there so abject, timid and humble, that when he reads the deeds of Caesar, Alexander, Scipio, Hannibal, and many others, is not inflamed by an ardent desire to be like them, and does not make small account of this frail two days' life, in order to win the almost eternal life of fame, which in spite of death makes him live in far greater glory than before? But he who does not feel the delight of letters, cannot either know how great is the glory they so long preserve, and measures it by the life of one man or two, because his memory runs no further. Hence he cannot esteem this short-lived glory so much as he would that almost eternal glory if knowledge of it were unhappily not denied him, and as he does not esteem it so much, we may reasonably believe that he will not run such danger to pursue it as one who knew it would.

Men's Happiness or Misery Is Mostly of Their Own Making

From John Locke, Some Thoughts Concerning Education

A sound mind in a sound body is a short but full description of a happy state in this world. He that has these two has little more to wish for, and he that wants either of them will be but little the better for anything else. Men's happiness or misery is most part of their own making. He whose mind directs not wisely will never take the right away, and he whose body is crazy and feeble will never be able to advance in it. I confess there are some men's constitutions of body and mind so vigorous and well framed by nature that they need not much assistance from others, but by the strength of their natural genius, they are from their cradles carried toward what is excellent; and by the privilege of their happy constitutions, are able to do wonders. But examples of this kind are but few, and I think I may say, that of all the men we meet with, nine parts of ten are what they are, good or evil, useful or not, by their education. It is that which makes the great difference in mankind. The little or almost insensible impressions on our tender infancies have very important and lasting consequences. And there it is, as in the fountains of some rivers, where a gentle application of the hand turns the flexible waters into channels, that make them take quite contrary courses; and by this little

direction, given them at first in the source, they receive different tendencies, and arrive at last at very remote and distant places.

Those that intend ever to govern their children should begin
it whilst they are very little, and look that they perfectly comply with
the will of their parents. Would you have your son obedient to you
when past a child, be sure then to establish the authority of a father
as soon as he is capable of submission, and can understand in
whose power he is. If you would have him stand in awe of you,
imprint it in his infancy; and as he approaches more to a man,
admit him nearer to your familiarity, so shall you have him your
obedient subject (as is fit) whilst he is a child, and your affectionate
friend when he is a man. For methinks they mightily misplace the
treatment due to their children, who are indulgent and familiar
when they are little, but severe to them, and keep them at a distance when they are grown up. For liberty and indulgence can do
no good to children; their want of judgment makes them stand in
need of restraint and discipline; and, on the contrary, imperviousness and severity is but an ill way of treating men who have reason
of their own to guide them, unless you have a mind to make your
children, when grown up, weary of you, and secretly to say within
yourselves, "When will you die, Father?"

The child's natural genius and constitution must be considered
in a right education. We must not hope wholly to change their original tempers, nor make the gay pensive and grave, nor the melancholy sportive, without spoiling them. God has stamped certain characters upon men's minds, which, like their shapes, may perhaps be a
little mended, but can hardly be totally altered and transformed into
the contrary. He, therefore, that is about children should well study
their natures and aptitudes, and see by often trials what turn they easily take, and what becomes them, observe what their native stock is,
how it may be improved, and what it is fit for. He should consider
what they want, whether they be capable of having it wrought into
them by industry, and incorporated there by practice, and whether it
be worthwhile to endeavor it. For in many cases all that we can do, or
should aim at, is to make the best of what nature has given, to prevent
the vices and faults to which such a constitution is most inclined, and
give it all the advantages it is capable of. Everyone's natural genius
should be carried as far as it could; but to attempt the putting
another upon him will be but labor in vain; and what is so plastered
on will at best fit but untowardly, and have always hanging to it the
ungracefulness of constraint and affectation.

Of all the ways whereby children are to be instructed and their manners formed, the plainest, easiest, and most efficacious is to set before their eyes the examples of those things you would have them do or avoid, which, when they are pointed out to them, in the practice of persons within their knowledge, with some reflections on their beauty and unbecomingness, are of more force to draw or deter their imitation, than any discourses which can be made to them. Virtues and vices can by no words be so plainly set before their understandings as the actions of other men will show them, when you direct their observation, and bid them view this or that good or bad quality in their practice. And the beauty or uncomeliness of many things, in good and ill breeding, will be better learned, and make deeper impressions on them, in the examples of others, than from any rules or instructions which can be given about them. This is a method to be used, not only whilst they are young, but to be continued even as long as they shall be under another's tuition or conduct; nay, I know not whether it be not the best way to be used by a father, as long as he should think fit, on any occasion, to reform anything he wishes mended in his son; nothing sinking so gently, and so deep, into men's minds, as example. And what ill they either overlook or indulge in themselves they cannot but dislike, and be ashamed of, when it is set before them in another.

The great work of a governor is to fashion the carriage, and form the mind; to settle in his pupil good habits, and the principles of virtue and wisdom; to give him by little and little a view of mankind, and work him into a love and imitation of what is excellent and praiseworthy; and in the prosecution of it, to give him vigor, activity, and industry. The studies which he sets him upon are but as it were the exercises of his faculties and employment of his time, to keep him from sauntering and idleness, to teach him application, and accustom him to take pains, and to give him some little taste of what his own industry must perfect.

Latin I look upon as absolutely necessary to a gentleman; and indeed custom, which prevails over everything, has made it so much a part of education that even those children are whipped to it, and made spend many hours of their precious time uneasily in Latin, who, after they are once gone from school, are never to have more to do with it as long as they live. Can there be anything more ridiculous than that a father should waste his own money and his son's time in setting him to learn the Roman language, when at the same time he designs him for a trade, wherein he, having no use for Latin, fails not to forget that little which he brought from school, and which it is ten to one he abhors for the ill-usage it procured him?

The great skill of a teacher is to get and keep the attention of his scholar; whilst he has that, he is sure to advance as fast as the learner's abilities will carry him; and without that, all his bustle and pudder will be to little or no purpose. To attain this, he should make the child comprehend (as much as may be) the usefulness of what he teaches him, and let him see, by what he has learned, that he can do something which he could not before; something which gives him some power and real advantage above others who are ignorant of it. To this he should add sweetness in all his instructions, and, by a certain tenderness in his whole carriage, make the child sensible that he loves him, and designs nothing but his good, the only way to beget love in the child, which will make him hearken to his lessons, and relish what he teaches him. Nothing but obstinacy should meet with any imperviousness, or rough usage. All other faults should be corrected with a gentle hand; and kind, engaging words will work better and more effectually upon a willing mind, and even prevent a good deal of that perverseness which rough and imperious usage often produces in well-disposed and generous minds. It is true obstinacy and willful neglects must be mastered, even though it costs blows to do it. But I am apt to think perverseness in the pupils is often the effect of forwardness in the tutor; and that most children would seldom have deserved blows, if needless and misapplied roughness had not taught them ill-nature, and given them an aversion for their teacher, and all that comes from him.

To write and speak correctly gives a grace, and gains a favorable attention to what one has to say. And since it is English that an English gentleman will have constant use of, that is the language he should chiefly cultivate, and wherein most care should be taken to polish and perfect his style. To speak or write better Latin than English may make a man be talked of, but he will find it more to his purpose to express himself well in his own tongue that he uses every moment, than to have the vain commendation of others for a very insignificant quality. This I find universally neglected, nor no care taken anywhere to improve young men in their own language, that they may thoroughly understand and be masters of it. If anyone among us have a facility or purity more than ordinary in his mother tongue, it is owing to chance, or his genius, or anything, rather than to his education, or any care of his teacher. To mind what English his pupil speaks or writes is below the dignity of one bred up amongst

Greek and Latin, though he have but little of them himself. These are the learned languages, fit only for learned men to meddle with and teach; English is the language of the illiterate vulgar.

The Contemplative Man and the Active Man

From Aristotle, The Nicomachean Ethics

Unfortunately, not everyone longs to achieve wisdom. In addition to beautiful words about virtue, the constraint of law and even punishment is always required to prod some young men along the right path. That's why a man concerned with virtue must also be concerned with education, and in turn must take part in civic affairs to make sure that society at large supports the aims of an education in virtue for children. The best recipe for happiness, Aristotle concludes in the Nicomachean Ethics, *is the right balance of active and contemplative virtues—contemplation is nobler, but the life of an active citizen can achieve happiness in its own right. With this hierarchy of virtues, Aristotle crystallizes a teaching that weaves throughout every period of reflection on the meaning of manliness, stretching through medieval chivalry and the Renaissance gentleman down to the present.*

Of all human things, habitual energies of virtue are the most stable; they are more permanent than even the sciences; and of the virtues themselves, the most valuable are the firmest; forming the continual meditation and delight of those whom they adorn. For this reason, they alone are not liable to be forgotten or lost; but are an immovable property in the thoughts and life of a good man; who, whatever may befall him, will behave gracefully; approving his conduct exact, square, and blameless. Slight misfortunes are unable to shake his well-balanced happiness; but, in the use of a great prosperity, his excellence will shine more conspicuous: and when persecuted by painful and afflicting calamity, which not only impedes his present exertions but darkens his future prospects, his worth will irradiate the gloom, while he resists and surmounts the severest sufferings, not by stupid insensibility, but by generous magnanimity; for, if our own actions be the sovereign arbiters of our lot, a virtuous man can never be wretched; because he will never render himself an object either of hatred or contempt. Of the circumstances in which he is placed, he will always make the best and most honorable use; as a good general, and a good artist, employs the forces, and the materials, with which they are respectively entrusted, always to the best advantage. A happiness, founded on such a basis, can never sink into misery; although it must be shaken by tragic misfortunes, from which it will not soon recover its natural state. Yet, in consequence of virtuous exertions, continued through a sufficient length of time, a good man, competently furnished with the accommodations of life, will resume his wonted serenity; and may be pronounced happy, notwithstanding the vicissitudes to which he is still exposed; at least possessed of such happiness as is consistent with the condition of humanity.

Happiness, then, cannot consist in mere recreative pastime; for it is absurd to think that all our serious exertions and strenuous labors should terminate in so frivolous an end. We do not labor that we may be idle; but, as Anarchis justly said, we are idle that we may labor with more effect; that is, we have recourse to sports and amusements as refreshing cordials after contentious exertions, that, having reposed in such diversions for a while, we may recommence our labors with increased vigor. The weakness of human nature requires frequent remissions of energy; but these rests and pauses are only the better to prepare us for enjoying the pleasures of activity. The amusements of life, therefore, are but preludes to its business, the place of which they cannot possibly supply; and its happiness, because its business, consists in the exercise of those virtuous energies which constitute the worth and dignity of our nature. Inferior pleasures may be enjoyed by the fool and the slave as completely as by the hero or the sage. But who will ascribe the happiness of a man to him, who by his character and condition, is disqualified for manly pursuits?

If happiness consists in virtuous energies, the greatest human happiness must consist in the exercise of the greatest virtue in man, which must be the virtue or perfection of his best part, whether this be intellect, or whatever principle it be, that is destined to command and bear sway; having knowledge of things beautiful and divine, as being either divine itself, or at least that principle in us which most approximates to divinity. The greatest human happiness, then, is theoretic and intellectual, which well accords with the properties which we formerly found, by investigation, to be essentially inherent in that most coveted object. The intellect is the best principle in man; its energies are the strongest, and the objects about which it is conversant are far the most sublime. The energies of intellect are also the longest and most continuous, since we can persevere in theorizing and thinking much longer than in performing any action whatever. Pleasure, it was observed, must be an ingredient in happiness; but contemplative wisdom offers pleasures the most admirable in purity and stability, and the pleasures of knowledge continually increase in proportion to our improvement in it; certainty concerning the sublimest truths affording still higher delight in proportion to the intense efforts of intellect by which they were discovered. That all-sufficiency, which we remarked as a property of happiness, belongs to intellectual energies more than to any other; for though the sage, as well as the moralist or the patriot, stands in need of bodily accommodations, yet in exerting his highest excellencies he is not like them dependent on fortune, both for his objects and his instruments; for objects towards whom he may exercise his virtues, and instruments which may enable him to effectuate his ends. Even unassisted and alone, though perhaps better with assistants, he can still think and theorize, possessing in the energies of his own mind the purest and most independent enjoyments. These enjoyments are valuable peculiarly on their own account, since they terminate completely in themselves; whereas all practical virtue has, beside the practice itself, some distinct and separate end in view. The tranquillity of leisure is naturally more agreeable than the bustle of business; we toil for the sake of quiet, and make war for the sake of peace.

But the practical virtues are most conspicuously exercised in political and military functions, the latter of which none but the most savage and sanguinary minds would submit to from choice, converting friends into enemies for the mere pleasure of fighting with them. Politics, too, forms an onerous and troublesome occupation, which would not be undertaken from the sole love of exercising political functions, independently of distinct and separate ends; power, wealth, and honor; in one word, prosperity to ourselves, friends, or fellow-citizens. But intellectual energies are complete and perfect in themselves, supplying an exhaustless stream of pure and perennial pleasure, which in its turn invigorates and enlivens the energies, and thus increases and refines the source from which it unceasingly springs; all sufficient, peaceful, and permanent, as far as is compatible with the condition of humanity. Were unalterable permanency added to such a life, its happiness

would be more than human; but even within a limited term, its
inestimable delights may be enjoyed by those who attain the perfection of their age and faculties; living not merely as partners with
a frail and compound nature, but according to the simple and
divine principle within them, whose energies and virtues as far
transcend all others as the intellectual substance in which they
reside excels all other substances of which our frame is composed.
We ought not, therefore, according to the vulgar exhortation,
though mortal, to regard only mortal things; but, as far as possible,
to put on immortality, exerting ourselves to taste the joys of the
intellectual life. This is living according to the best part of what we
call ourselves, which, though seemingly small in bulk, is incomparably greater in power and in value than all things besides. The
intellect, indeed, is the best and sovereign part of our constitution,
and therefore strictly and properly ourselves. It is absurd, therefore, to prefer any other life to our own. What was above observed
will apply here. The pleasure and good of each individual must
consist in that which is most congenial to his nature. The intellectual life, therefore, must be the best and happiest for man; since
the intellect is that which is peculiarly himself.

Having thus delineated virtue, friendship, and pleasure, ought
we to consider our undertaking as now finished? Or ought we
rather to consider, as has been already said, that in practical matters, practice, and not theory, is the main object; and that, independently of good actions, the mere speculative knowledge of
virtue is not of any avail. The important question then is, how men
may be rendered virtuous? If moral discourses sufficed for this purpose, they could not be purchased, as Theognis says, at too high a
price. But the influence of such lessons extends only over the liberal minds of ingenuous and well-disciplined youths, who may thereby be retained within the paths of honor and duty: they are too feeble to control the multitude, whose wickedness is to be restrained,
not through the dread of shame, but through the fear of punishment; since the many, being enslaved by their appetites, make it the
business of their lives to pursue sensual pleasures, and to avoid
bodily pains; having no taste nor perception of refined and laudable enjoyments. What eloquence can persuade, what words can
transform men thus brutified? It is impossible, at least hardly possible, for reasoning to extract the evils which custom has riveted; and
when all favorable circumstances concur, the felicity of those is still
worthy of envy, who, through the combined energy of conspiring
causes, are retained and confirmed in the practice of virtue. This

inestimable possession some ascribe to the bounty of nature; others think that they have acquired it by custom; and a third class acknowledge themselves indebted for it to instruction. The virtue bestowed by nature evidently depends not on our own exertions; it is given by a certain divine disposal, to those whose lot is surely beyond that of all other men most fortunate. Instruction and reasoning will not succeed, unless the mind is previously wrought on by custom, as a field is ploughed and prepared for receiving and nourishing the good seed: for those who are not habituated to love what is amiable, and to detest what is odious, would neither listen to, nor understand, exhortations to virtue; because their affections lead them not beyond the pursuit of coarse animal gratifications, the unrestrained appetite for which is of too stubborn a nature to yield to mere reason; and which, when no contrary passion intervenes, can be checked only by force.

Before virtue, therefore, can be acquired, affections congenial to it must be implanted; the love of beauty and excellence, the hatred of baseness and deformity; which preparatory discipline cannot take place, except in those states which are governed by good laws; for a life of soberness and self-command is irksome to the multitude, and peculiarly unpleasing to the headstrong impetuosity of youthful passions, which must, therefore, be bridled by the authority of law; that what is painful by nature may become pleasant through custom. The superintending aid of discipline ought not to be confined to children, but must extend to adolescence and manhood; the greater proportion of human kind remaining through life rather slaves to necessity, than subjects of reason; and more susceptible of the fear of punishment, than sensible to the charms of moral excellence. Legislators, therefore, it is said, ought to employ admonitions and chastisements, as well as punishments that are final; admonitions, for those whose character and morals render them open to conviction; chastisements, for those whose immoderate and beastly passion for selfish pleasures must be subdued and corrected by coarse bodily pains (the pains inflicted on them standing as nearly as possible in direct opposition to the pleasures which they unlawfully pursued); and total extermination, or perpetual banishment, for the extreme evils of incurable profligacy and incorrigible villainy. Since, then, the condition of the greater proportion of mankind is such that to be kept within the bounds of propriety and virtue they require not only the benefits of early instruction, but the watchfulness of perpetual discipline through life, good laws become essentially necessary for upholding this discipline by their coercive authority. The influence

of fathers over their children is too feeble for that purpose; or indeed
the influence of any individuals not invested with public authority.
Law has a compulsive and necessary force, since it is acknowledged as
the commanding voice of prudence and reason; and its power is not
invidious, like that of men, who are apt to offend us when they
oppose, even most justly, our favorite propensities. In Lacedaemon,
the legislator, with the assistance of a few friends, established a regular plan of public education and moral discipline; things neglected in
the greater part of states, where men, in these particulars, live like the
Cyclops:

"By whom no statutes and no rights are known,
No council held, no monarch fills the throne;
Each rules his race, his neighbor not his care,
Heedless of others, to his own severe."

Iliad, ix. v. 127

A public education, when good, is doubtless preferable to a
private one; but what is omitted by the public, individuals ought, as
far as possible, to supply.

The Dream of Scipio

From Cicero, On the Commonwealth

Cicero's On the Commonwealth *beautifully expresses the classical ideal
of manliness. The Roman statesman and general Scipio Africanus the
Younger is a brilliant success in public life, but reserves his greatest respect
for the life of learning. In his formulation, to be a man is not only to be vigorous in service of the common good, but to be refined, gracious, and
learned, familiar with the sublime beauties of art, music, and philosophy. In
the magnificent Dream of Scipio, the noble Roman is given a vision of the
afterlife in which eternal celestial bliss is the reward of serving one's country,
parents, and kindred here on earth.*

*Maurus Tullius Cicero (106–43 B.C.) was one of the greatest men of
the Roman Republic. As a statesman, he defended constitutional govern-*

ment against the despotic ambitions of Julius Caesar. His philosophical and
oratorical writings are among the most influential in European history.

After my arrival in Africa—where, as you know, I served under
Manius Manilius as military tribune of the fourth legion—my first
desire was to meet King Masinissa, who, for very good reasons, was
a close friend of our family. When I met him, the aged prince
embraced me and burst into tears. After a brief space he looked up
into the sky and said: "To thee, O mighty Sun, and to you, ye other
dwellers in heaven, I give thanks because, ere I depart this life, I
behold in my kingdom and within this palace Publius Cornelius
Scipio whose very name gives me new life. So constantly does my
heart muse on the memory of his grandfather, that excellent man
and invincible general." Then I questioned him about his kingdom, and he asked me about the condition of our commonwealth;
and we spent the day together in lengthy conversation.

I was then entertained with princely splendor, and we prolonged our discussion late into the night. For the venerable man
spoke of nothing except Africanus, and recalled not only all that he
had done but even all that he had said. I was exhausted both by my
journey and by the lateness of the hour. Accordingly, when we separated to retire, a deeper sleep than usual took me in its embrace.
What ensued had its origin, I suppose, in the matter of our conversation. For quite regularly the subjects of our thought and discourse suggest our dreams, as Ennius writes that he dreamed of
Homer, who no doubt was frequently the theme of his waking
thought and conversation. Thus it happened that Africanus
appeared to me, in a form which was more familiar from his death
mask than from the man himself. When I recognized him, I confess
that I was stricken with fear. But he said, "Be calm, Scipio; banish
your fears, and inscribe my words in your memory."

"Do you see that city?" From a lofty station, bright and glittering and filled with stars, he pointed out Carthage. "Do you see that
city which I forced to obey the Roman people, but which now
begins anew those ancient wars and cannot be at peace? Although
you who now come to besiege it are as yet hardly a soldier, in three
years you will be consul and will overthrow it, and the cognomen
which now you inherit from me you will then have won for yourself
by your own achievements. After you have destroyed Carthage, celebrated your triumph, been censor, and traveled on an embassy
through Egypt, Syria, Asia and Greece, a second time you will be
chosen consul, though absent from Rome, and by destroying

Numanthia you will bring to a close Rome's greatest war. But when you have been borne to the Capitol in your triumphal chariot, you will find the commonwealth thrown into utter confusion by the designs of my grandson."

"Then, Africanus, you must show to your country the light of your courage, your character, and your wisdom. But I see, as it were, the course of your destiny then becoming uncertain. For when your life has passed through eight times seven yearly revolutions of the sun, and when these two numbers, seven and eight— each of which is considered perfect for a special reason—have by their natural cycle completed the span allotted you by destiny, then to you alone, because of your renown, the whole state will turn. On you the senate, all patriotic citizens, the allies, and the Latins will fix their eyes. On you alone the safety of the state will rest. In a word, you must be dictator and must set the state in order—if only you escape the godless hands of your kindred."

At an exclamation from Laelius and at the deeper groans of the others, Scipio gently smiled. "Hush," said he, "pray, do not break my slumber. Hear yet a little longer what remains for me to tell."

"Yet Africanus, that you may be more zealous in guarding your country, be assured of this: All men who have saved or benefited their native land, or have enhanced its power, are assigned an especial place in heaven where they may enjoy a life of eternal bliss. For the supreme god who rules the entire universe finds nothing, at least among earthly objects, more pleasing than the societies and groups of men, united by law and right, which are called states. The rulers and saviors of states set forth from that place and to that place return."

At these words I was greatly frightened, less by fear of death than by the thought of treachery at the hands of my kindred. Nevertheless, I asked Africanus whether he and my father Paulus and the others whom we supposed dead were still living. "In truth, he replied, "only those are alive who have escaped the bondage of the flesh as from a prison, while that which you call life is in reality death. Do you not behold your father Paulus coming toward you?" When I saw him, I poured forth a flood of tears, but Paulus embraced me and bade me not to weep.

As soon as I mastered my tears and regained the power of speech, I said, "O father most excellent and holy, since true life is here, as Africanus tells me, why, I ask you, do I linger upon earth? Why may I not hasten to come to you?" "That may not be," he replied, "for, until God, to whom belongs this whole world before your eyes, shall free you from the body's prison, you may not enter this place. For the human race was born subject to the condition that they should guard the sphere which you see in the center of the heavens and which is called earth. To them souls were given, drawn from those eternal fires which you name constellations and stars. These heavenly bodies are round like spheres. They are quickened by divine intelligences and complete their cycles and rotations with wonderful swiftness. For this reason, Publius, you and all loyal men must retain the soul in its fleshly prison, and unless he who has bestowed the soul upon you so commands, you must not abandon human life, lest you seem to have deserted the earthly tasks imposed by God.

"But even as your grandfather here before you, even as I who begot you, so do you, Scipio, cultivate justice and loyalty, which is a noble spirit when shown toward parents and kindred, but noblest when shown toward your country. Such a life is the way to heaven and to the company of those whose life on earth is done and who released from the body, inhabit the region which you behold, and which, after the Greeks, you name the Milky Way."

The place was a glittering circle that shone with exceeding brilliance in the midst of fiery stars. As I gazed down from it all other objects seemed dazzling and wonderful. There were stars which we have never seen from this earth of ours, and all of them had magnitudes such as we have never supposed to exist. The smallest of them was situated most remote from the heaven (of the fixed stars) and nearest to the earth, and shone with borrowed light. Moreover, the stars appeared so small that I felt ashamed of our empire, by which we cover a point, as it were, upon its surface.

Since I was observing the earth more intently than aught else, Africanus said, "How long, I ask you, will your thoughts be fixed upon the earth? Do you not perceive the heavenly spaces into which you have come? The universe is formed of nine circles or spheres, as we should more properly call them. One of these is the heaven (of the fixed stars); it is on the exterior of the universe, embracing all the other orbs, and is the supreme god himself who constrains and includes the remaining spheres. In it are placed the eternal courses of the rolling stars. Beneath this outer circle are the seven orbs which revolve in a direction opposite to that of the heavens. The outermost of these spheres belongs to the planet which men on earth call Saturn. The next is the luminary called Jupiter, benign and propitious to the human race, and next the ruddy star, feared by earth, which you call Mars. Below Mars comes the sun, which holds almost the mid-region (between the earth and the heavens) and is the leader, chief, and director of the other stars, and the mind which keeps the universe in balance. Such is his greatness that he encompasses and fills the whole world with his light. In the sun's train, like comrades, follow the spheres of Venus and Mercury. The lowest globe carries the moon, which is kindled by the rays of the sun. All below the moon is mortal and transitory, except the souls which the gods have bestowed on man, while all above the moon is immortal. The earth, which occupies the ninth position, is the center of the universe. It does not move, it is the lowest of the spheres, and all heavy bodies are swept to it by gravity."

When I recovered from the astonishment with which I was gazing upon this spectacle, I asked, "What is this mighty yet delightful sound which fills my ears?" "That," he replied, "is the melody produced by the swift movement of the spheres themselves."

Though I was filled with awe at the celestial harmonies, I kept turning my eyes constantly toward the earth. "I see," said Africanus, "that you still contemplate the abode and home of man. If the earth appears insignificant to you—as indeed it is—ever lift up your eyes to these heavenly realms and despise the concerns of men. For what fame can you win among men or what renown worthy of your striving?"

"If, then, you give up the hope of returning to this place where all blessings await great and distinguished men, how puerile is the renown conferred by man, lasting as it does for only a small portion of a single year! But if you wish to look on high and to contemplate this abode and eternal home, you will not yield to the flattery of the rabble or set your hopes upon the rewards that men may give. Excellence itself, by its own inherent charm, must draw you toward true glory. What others say about you must be their concern; nothing will prevent their talking. All that they may say, however, is confined to the narrow limits you perceive; it is never lasting in the case of any man, but is obscured when men die and is blotted out when posterity forgets."

After he had spoken thus, I answered: "Since, Africanus, there is, as it were, a path which leads to heaven and which lies open to men who have earned their country's gratitude, I shall strive for so glorious a reward even more earnestly than I have. And yet from boyhood I have followed in my father's footsteps and in yours and have not tarnished your glory." "Strive earnestly," he replied, "and be assured that only this body of yours, and not your real self, is mortal. For you are not the mere physical form that you appear to be; but the real man is the soul and not that physical body which men can point to. Know, then, that your true nature is divine, if indeed it is a divine principle which lives, feels, remembers, and foresees, and which rules, guides, and activates the body beneath its sway, even as the supreme god directs the universe. And as the world, which is in part mortal, is stirred to motion by God Himself, who lives forever, so the frail body is quickened by an immortal soul.

"Now the noblest concerns of the soul have to do with the security of your country, and the soul which is employed and disciplined in such pursuits will fly more speedily to this abode, its natural home. This journey it will make the swifter, if it looks abroad, while still imprisoned in the flesh, and if, by meditating upon that which lies beyond it, it divorces itself as far as may be from the body. For the souls of men who have surrendered themselves to carnal delights, who have made themselves as it were slaves of the passions, and who have been prompted by lust to violate the laws of gods and men, wander about near the earth itself, after their escape from the body, and do not return hither until they have been driven about for many ages."

He departed; I awoke from sleep.

A Man of Principles

From John Locke, Of Principles

There is another fault that stops or misleads men in their knowledge, which I have also spoken something of, but yet is necessary to mention here again, that we may examine it to the bottom, and see the root is springs from, and that is the custom of taking up with principles that are not self-evident, and very often not so much as true. It is not unusual to see men rest their opinions upon foundations that have no more certainty nor solidity than the propositions built on them, and embraced for their sake. Such foundations are these, and the like, namely: The founders or leaders of my party are good men, and therefore their tenets are true; it is the opinion of a sect that is erroneous, therefore it is false; it hath been long received in the world, therefore it is true; or, it is new, and therefore false.

These, and many the like, which are by no means the measures of truth and falsehood, the generality of men make the standards by which they accustom their understanding to judge. And thus, they falling into a habit of determining of truth and falsehood by such wrong measures, it is no wonder they should embrace error for certainty, and be very positive in things they have no ground for.

There is not any who pretends to the least reason, but when any of these his false maxims are brought to the test, must acknowledge them to be fallible, and such as he will not allow in those that differ from him; and yet, after he is convinced of this, you shall see him go on in the use of them, and the very next occasion that offers, argue again upon the same grounds. Would one not be ready to think that men are willing to impose upon themselves, and mislead their own understanding, who conduct them by such wrong measures, even after they see they cannot be relied on? But yet, they will not appear so blamable as may be thought at first sight; for I think there are a great many that argue thus in earnest, and do it not to impose on themselves or others. They are persuaded of what they say, and think there is weight in it, though, in a like case, they have been convinced there is none; but men would be intolerable to themselves, and contemptible to others, if they should embrace opinions without any ground, and hold what they could give no manner of reason for. True or false, solid or sandy, the mind must have some foundation to rest itself upon; and, as I have remarked in another place, it no sooner entertains any proposition, but it presently hastens to some hypothesis to bottom it on: till then it is unquiet and unsettled. So much do our own very tempers dispose us to a right use of our understandings, if we would follow as we should the inclinations of our nature.

In some matters of concernment, especially those of religion, men are not permitted to be always wavering and uncertain, they must embrace and profess some tenets or other; and it would be a shame, nay, a contradiction too heavy for anyone's mind to lie constantly under, for him to pretend seriously to be persuaded of the truth of any religion, and yet not to be able to give any reason of his belief, or to say anything for his preference of this to any other opinion; and, therefore, they must make use of some principles or other, and those can be no other than such as they have and can manage; and to say they are not in earnest persuaded by them, and do not rest upon those they make use of, is contrary to experience, and to allege that they are not misled when we complain they are.

If this be so, it will be urged why, then, do they not rather make use of sure and unquestionable principles, rather than rest on such grounds as may deceive them, and will, as is visible, serve to support error as well as truth?

To this I answer, the reason why they do not make use of better and surer principles is because they cannot: but this inability proceeds not from want of natural parts (for those few whose case that is, are to be excused), but for want of use and exercise. Few men are from their youth accustomed to strict reasoning, and to trace the dependence of any truth in a long train of consequences to its remote principles, and to observe its connection; and he that by frequent practice has not been used to this employment of his understanding, it is no more wonder that he should not, when he is grown into years, be able to bring his mind to it, than that he should not be on a sudden able to grave or design, dance on the ropes, or write a good hand, who has never practiced either of them.

Nay, the most of men are so wholly strangers to this, that they do not so much as perceive their want of it; they dispatch the ordinary business of their callings by rote, as we say, as they have learned it; and if at any time they miss success, they impute it to anything rather than want of thought or skill; that, they conclude (because they know no better), they have in perfection: or, if there be any subject that interest or fancy has recommended to their thoughts, their reasoning about it is still after their own fashion, be it better or worse; it serves their turns, and is the best they are acquainted with; and, therefore, when they are led by it into mistakes, and their business succeeds accordingly, they impute it to any cross accident or default of others, rather than to their own want of understanding; that is what nobody discovers or complains of in himself. Whatsoever made his business to miscarry, it was not want of right thought or judgment in himself: he sees no such defect in himself, but is satisfied that he carries on his designs well enough by his own reasoning; or, at least, should have done, had it not been for unlucky traverses not in his power. Thus, being content with this short and very imperfect use of his understanding, he never troubles himself to seek out methods of improving his mind, and lives all his life without any notion of close reasoning, in a continued connection of a long train of consequences from sure foundations, such as is requisite for the making out and clearing most of the speculative truths most men own to believe and are most concerned in. Not to mention here what I shall have occasion to insist on by and by more fully, namely, that, in many cases, it is not one series of consequences will serve the turn, but many different and opposite deductions must be examined and laid together, before a man can come to make a right judgment of the point in question. What, then, can be expected from men that neither see the want of any such kind of reasoning as this; nor, if they do, know they how to set about it, or could perform it? You may as well set a countryman, who scarce knows the figures, and never casts up a sum of three particulars, to state a merchant's long account, and find the true balance of it.

What, then, should be done in the case? I answer, we should always remember what I said above, that the faculties of our souls are improved and made useful to us, just after the same manner as our bodies are. Would you have a man write or paint, dance or fence well, or perform any other manual operation dexterously and with ease, let him have never so much vigor and activity, suppleness and address, naturally, yet nobody expects this from him unless he has been used to it, and has employed time and pains in fashioning and forming his hand, or outward parts, to these motions. Just so it is in the mind—would you have a man reason well, you must use him to it betimes, exercise his mind in observing the connection of ideas, and following them in train. Nothing does this better than mathematics, which, therefore, I think, should be taught all those who have the time and opportunity; not so much to make them mathematicians, as to make them reasonable creatures; for though we all call ourselves so, because we are born to it, if we please, yet we may truly say, nature gives us but the seeds of it; we are born to be, if we please, rational creatures, but it is use and exercise only that make us so, and we are indeed so no further than industry and application have carried us. And, therefore, in ways of reasoning which men have not been used to, he that will observe the conclusions they take up must be satisfied they are not at all rational.

This has been the less taken notice of because everyone in his private affairs uses some sort of reasoning or other, enough to denominate him reasonable. But the mistake is that he that is found reasonable in one thing is concluded to be so in all; and to think or say otherwise is thought so unjust an affront, and so senseless a censure, that nobody ventures to do it. It looks like the degradation of a man below the dignity of his nature. It is true that he that reasons well in any one thing has a mind naturally capable of reasoning well in others, and to the same degree of strength and clearness, and possibly much greater, had his understanding been so employed. But it is as true that he who can reason well today about one sort of matters cannot at all reason today about others, though perhaps a year hence he may. But wherever a man's rational faculty fails him, and will not serve him to reason, there we cannot say he is rational, how capable soever he may be by time and exercise to become so.

Try in men of low and mean education, who have never elevated their thoughts above the spade and the plough, nor looked beyond the ordinary drudgery of a day laborer. Take the thoughts of such a one, used for many years to one tract, out of that narrow compass he has been all his life confined to, you will find him no more capable of reasoning than almost a perfect natural. Some one or two rules, on which their conclusions immediately depend, you will find, in most men, have governed all their thoughts; these, true or false, have been the maxims they have been guided by— take these from them, and they are perfectly at a loss; their compass and pole-star then are gone, and their understanding is perfectly at a nonplus: and, therefore, they either immediately return to their old maxims again as the foundations of all truth to them, notwithstanding all that can be said to show their weakness; or if they give them up to their reasons, they with them give up all truth and further inquiry, and think there is no such thing as certainty. For if you would enlarge their thoughts, and settle them upon more remote and surer principles, they either cannot easily apprehend them, or, if they can, know not what use to make of them; for long deductions from remote principles is what they have not been used to, and cannot manage.

What then! Can grown men never be improved or enlarged in their understandings? I say not so; but this I think I may say, that it will not be done without industry and application, which will require more time and pains than grown men, settled in their course of life, will allow to it, and therefore very seldom is done. And this very capacity of attaining it by use and exercise only brings us back to that which I laid down before, that it is only practice that improves our minds as well as bodies, and we must expect nothing from our understandings any further than they are perfected by habits.

The Americans are not at all born with worse understandings than the Europeans, though we see none of them have such reaches in the arts and sciences. And among the children of a poor countryman the lucky chance of education and getting into the world gives one infinitely the superiority in parts over the rest, who continuing at home, had continued also just of the same size with his brethren.

He that has to do with young scholars, especially in mathematics, may perceive how their minds open by degrees, and how it is exercise alone that opens them. Sometimes they will stick a long time at a part of a demonstration, not for want of will or application, but really for want of perceiving the connection of two ideas; that, to one whose understanding is more exercised, is as visible as anything can be. The same would be with a grown man beginning to study mathematics—the understanding, for want of use, often sticks in a very plain way—and he himself that is so puzzled, when he comes to see the connection, wonders what it was he stuck at in a case so plain.

How a Grown Man Should Live

From Plato, The Republic

Socrates's answer to how man should live is as profound as it is simple. The passions must be governed by a well-ordered soul, and a well-ordered soul parallels a well-ordered city. Civic-spiritedness is higher than economic productivity, and both must be governed by wisdom. There can be no conflict between virtue and happiness. Virtue cannot be enforced, it must be satisfying. Happiness cannot be a life of degraded hedonism. If a man is moderate, he will be spared the toil and pain of gratifying endless and unlimited desires, and in this way happier than a tyrant or hedonist. The aim of education is to cultivate the soul so that it mirrors the beautiful harmony and orderly proportionality of the cosmos. A man should not aspire merely to master others, but should turn his ambition inward and master his own unruly impulses. If we believe the world as a whole is orderly and intelligible, we will behave in the same way. If we believe the world is chaotic and irrational, we will in turn be governed by impulse and passion. The issue of the attitude of the epic poets is brought into focus here: it is contended that their world is one of irrational chance—a world of absurdity. As a result, a figure like Achilles careens between extremes of frenzied daring and hopeless-

ness. Achilles must be replaced, it is argued, with a new model for young men: a moderate Guardian of the common good, whose gracious repose and consistency mirror the rationality of the cosmic order. Being a guardian probably isn't as much fun as being the wild, moody, beautiful and charismatic demi-god of youth Achilles. But, while Socratic manliness may not match the glorious excesses of Achilles's daring, neither does it lead to the adolescent self-pity, fury, and pointless aggression of his lot. Under Socrates's influence, "courage"—which in ancient Greek was literally a synonym for "manliness"—becomes primarily a quality of soul, mind, and will, not of brute strength or martial prowess.

We must beg Homer and the other poets not to be angry if we strike out these and similar passages, not because they are unpoetical, or unattractive to the popular ear, but because the greater the poetical charm of them, the less are they meet for the ears of boys and men who are meant to be free, and who should fear slavery more than death.

Then we will once more entreat Homer and the other poets not to depict Achilles, who is the son of a goddess, first lying on his side, then on his back, and then on his face; then starting up and sailing in a frenzy along the shores of the barren sea; now taking the sooty ashes in both his hands and pouring them over his head, or weeping and wailing in the various modes which Homer has delineated. Nor should he describe Priam the kinsman of the gods as praying and beseeching,

"Rolling in the dirt, calling each man loudly by his name."

For if, my sweet Adeimantus, our youth seriously listen to such unworthy representations of the gods, instead of laughing at them as they ought, hardly will any of them deem that he himself, being but a man, can be dishonored by similar actions; neither will he rebuke any inclination which may arise in his mind to say and do the like. And instead of having any shame or self-control, he will be always whining and lamenting on slight occasions.

And then, again, to make the wisest of men say that nothing in his opinion is more glorious than:

"When the tables are full of bread and meat, and the
cupbearer carries round wine which he draws from the
bowl and pours into the cups."

Is it fit or conducive to temperance for a young man to hear such words? Or the verse:

"The saddest of fates is to die and meet destiny from hunger."

What would you say again to the tale of Zeus, who, while other gods and men were asleep and he the only person awake, lay devising plans, but forgot them all in a moment through his lust, and was so completely overcome at the sight of Hera that he would not even go into the hut, but wanted to lie with her on the ground, declaring that he had never been in such a state of rapture before, even when they first met one another

"without the knowledge of their parents."

or that other tale of how Hephaestus, because of similar goings on, cast a chain around Ares and Aphrodite?

Loving Homer as I do, I hardly like to say that in attributing these feelings to Achilles, or in believing that they are truly attributed to him, he is guilty of downright impiety. As little can I believe the narrative of his insolence to Apollo, where he says,

"Thou hast wronged me, O far-darter, most abominable of deities. Verily I would be even with thee, if I had only the power,"

or his insubordination to the river-god, on whose divinity he is ready to lay hands; or his offering to the dead Patroclus of his own hair, which had been previously dedicated to the other river-god Spercheius, and that he actually performed this vow; or that he dragged Hector round the tomb of Patroclus, and slaughtered the captives at the pyre; of all this I cannot believe that he was guilty, any more than I can allow our citizens to believe that he, the wise Cheiron's pupil, the son of a goddess and of Peleus who was the gentlest of men and third in descent from Zeus, was so disordered in his wits as to be at one time the slave of two seemingly inconsistent passions, meanness, not untainted by avarice, combined with overweening contempt of gods and men.

If I am not mistaken, we shall have to say that about men poets and storytellers are guilty of making the gravest misstatements when they tell us that wicked men are often happy, and the good miserable; and that injustice is profitable when undetected, but that justice is a man's own loss and another's gain—these things we shall forbid them to utter, and command them to sing and say the opposite.

Suppose, that a just and good man in the course of a narration comes on some saying or action of another good man,—I should imagine that he will like to impersonate him, and will not be ashamed of this sort of imitation: he will be most ready to play the part of the good man when he is acting firmly and wisely; in a less degree when he is overtaken by illness or love or drink, or has met with any other disaster. But when he comes to a character which is unworthy of him, he will not make a study of that; he will disdain such a person, and will assume his likeness, if at all, for a moment only when he is performing some good action; at other times he will be ashamed to play a part which he has never practiced, nor will he like to fashion and frame himself after the baser models; he feels the employment of such an art, unless in jest, to be beneath him, and his mind revolts at it.

Like those who take colts amid noise and tumult to see if they are of a timid nature, so must we take our youth amid terrors of some kind, and again pass them into pleasures, and prove them more thoroughly than gold is proved in the furnace, that we may discover whether they are armed against all enchantments, and of a noble bearing always, good guardians of themselves and of the music which they have learned, and retaining under all circumstances a rhythmical and harmonious nature, such as will be most serviceable to the individual and to the State. And he who at every age, as boy and youth and in mature life has come out of the trial victorious and pure, shall be appointed a ruler and guardian of the State; he shall be honored in life and death, and shall receive sepulchre and other memorials of honor, the greatest that we have to give.

A WISE MAN WITHIN

The Child Is Father of the Man

William Wordsworth

From the quintessential Romantic poet (1770–1850).

My heart leaps up when I behold
A rainbow in the sky:
So was it when my life began;
So is it now I am a man;
So be it when I shall grow old,
Or let me die!
The child is father of the man;
And I could wish my days to be
Bound each to each by natural piety.

The Painful Path to Manhood

From St. Augustine, Confessions

In the Confessions, *St. Augustine describes his upbringing, education, and search for a successful occupation and marriage. In all these pursuits, he laments, he was motivated by fleshly longings and a vain craving for worldly distinction. Through a painful process of inner deepening, he gradually came to realize how shallow was the world's definition of happiness and success in comparison with the true inner repose offered by faith in God.*
Born in 345 A.D. *in the Roman providence of Numidia, Augustine*

became the Bishop of Hippo and the author of timeless works of Christian reflection.

My God, what miseries and mockeries I experienced at that age! I was told that in order to get ahead in the world, a boy my age should be obedient and achieve excellence in the arts of language and rhetoric. For this would gain me reputation among men, and deceitful riches! So I was sent to school to get learning. Little did I know what profit I might gain from it, wretch that I was. But if I neglected my studies, I was soon beaten for it. For this form of discipline was recommended by our ancestors. Those who had passed the same way before us, laid out this troublesome course for us, which we were forced to follow in our turn, thus multiplying the labor and sorrow of the sons of Adam.

Yet we observed, Oh Lord, that some men prayed to you, and we learned from them to think of you, insofar as we could understand, as some Great One who—although not perceived by our senses—was able to both hear and help us. Though still a boy, I began to pray to you, my Help and Refuge. Even then, I wore out my tongue in praying to you. Although still a little boy, I prayed to you with great devotion that I would not be beaten at school. And when you did not hear my prayers—which were folly, although I did not think so then—my punishments, which I then thought were my greatest and most grievous affliction, were laughed at by my elders, yes, and by my own parents who wished that no harm befall me. Is there any man, Oh Lord, of such great spirit, attached to you with such devotion, that he can fear those racks and hooks and other instruments of torture so little—to avoid which men all over the world pray to you with so much fear—that he can laugh at those who most bitterly fear them, as our parents laughed at those tortures which we school boys suffered at the hands of our masters? Is there any man, I say, whose devotion is so strong? For otherwise, even callous indifference might be enough.

We were just as much afraid of the strap and prayed just as earnestly to escape it, as others have prayed to escape torture. But for all our fears, we played truant all too often, either in writing or reading or thinking about our lessons less than was required. It was not, Oh Lord, that we lacked either memory or capacity (of which it had pleased you to give us enough for our age). It was that our minds were set upon playing, for which we were beaten by those same masters who were doing much the same thing themselves.

But older people's idleness is called "business." When children do the same thing, these same men must punish them. Yet no one pities either the children or the men, or both. However, perhaps some impartial judge might think that it was just for me to be beaten for playing ball when I was a boy, because playing that sport was distracting me from my studies, with the consequence of my playing the fool all the more unbecomingly when I became a man. Is this not what my master who beat me did, when, if thwarted by another school master over some trifling matter, was soon more racked by rage and envy toward him, than I was when I lost a tennis match to my playfellow?

I will now call to mind my impurities and the carnal corruptions of my soul, which I passed over before, not because I love them, Oh my God. I do it for love of your love, repeating in the very bitterness of my memories my most wicked ways, so that only you may grow sweet to me. Your sweetness is never deceptive, but is happy and secure! I remember myself in my broken condition, in which I was torn to pieces, when turning away from you alone, I squandered myself away on vanities.

In my youth, I even burned to take my fill of hell. I even dared to grow wild with various shady loves. My beauty withered away. I even stank in your eyes. But all this while I was pleased with myself and desired to please the eyes of men.

What was it that I delighted in but to love and be loved? But I did not restrict my love to the moderation of one mind loving another, which is the bright path of friendship. But out of the foul desirousness of my flesh, mists and delusions of youth reeked up, which so obscured and overcast my heart that I could not distinguish the beauty of pure affection from the fog of impure lust. Both boiled confusedly within me, and my youthful instability swept me away over the precipice of impure desires, and drenched me over head and ears in the whirlpool of wicked impurities. All this time, your anger with me grew, and I knew it not. By now I had grown deaf from the continual clanking of the chains of my mortality: your punishment for the pride in my soul. I strayed further from you, and you let me go. I was tumbled up and down. I was even split and poured out. Yes, and I boiled over in my fornications, and you remained silent. Oh my tardy Joy! You remained silent then, and I wandered still further and further from you, sowing more and more fruitless seeds of sorrow with proud dejection and untried weariness.

Wretch that I was, I seethed with wickedness and still pursued the violent course of my own stream, forsaking you utterly. I broke all your laws, but did not escape your lashes, for what mortal can avoid them? For you were with me at every turn—mercifully angry, and flavoring all my unlawful pleasures with most bitter discontent—in order to lead me to seek pleasures that are not accompanied by discontent. I could not find any, except for you, Oh Lord: you who teach your commandments through pain and wound us so that you may heal us, yes, and slay us so that we may not die away from you. Where was I, how far was I banished from the delights of your house in the sixteenth year of the age of my flesh? At that age, the madness of raging lust—in which human shamelessness takes too much liberty despite being forbidden by your laws—exercised such supreme domination over me that I put all my efforts into it. My parents took no care to save me from ruin, by marriage. All they cared about was that I learn to make a powerful speech and prove a most persuasive speaker.

I desired honours, wealth and marriage, and you laughed at me. From these desires I suffered most bitter hardships. You were all the more gracious to me, the less you allowed anything but you to seem sweet to me. Behold now my heart, Oh Lord, who wills that I remember this, so that I might confess it to you now. Let my soul cling tightly to you, for you have freed it from the tight-clinging snare of death. How wretched I was then! You probed my wound to the quick, so that forsaking all other things, I might turn to you who are above all.

You did this, I say, so that I might turn and be healed, for without you all things would turn to nothing. Therefore, how miserable I was! How you dealt with me, to make me aware of my misery! The same day that I was preparing a speech in praise of the Emperor, in which I was to deliver many lies, and be applauded for my lies, even by those who knew that I lied. Walking along one of the streets of Milan, while my heart panted with these cares and boiled again with the feverishness of these consuming thoughts, I observed a poor beggar. I believe he was half drunk and with a belly full of food, for he was joyous and merry. I looked at him sadly, however, and spoke to my friends who were with me about the many sorrows brought about by our own madness. For the goal of all our efforts is nothing but to gain joy without care. Yet the efforts I labored under then, goaded by the spurs of desire, only increased the burden of my own unhappiness which I dragged along behind me, and increased by dragging. That beggar had already reached that joy which we, perhaps, might never reach at all. For what he had gained by means of a few coins he had begged, I was still scheming for by many a tortuous twisting and turning. Namely, to know the joy of a temporary happiness.

In truth, that beggar did not enjoy true happiness. But I, with my ambitious designs, chased after a happiness more uncertain still. For he was merry, but I was perplexed; he was without care but I was full of fears. But if someone had asked me whether I would rather be merry or fearful, I would answer, merry. Again, if I were asked whether I would rather be in that beggar's shoes or in my own? At that time I would have chosen my own, although I was overwhelmed with cares and fears. Was this out of perversity? Was it for any true reason? For I ought not to prefer myself over that beggar because I was more learned than he, seeing that my learning did not make me happy. Instead, I sought to please others with it: not to instruct them, but merely to delight them. For this reason you broke even my bones with the rod of your correction.

The Man of Eternal Renunciation

From The Bhagavad-Gita

Arjuna:
Yet Krishna! at one time you praise
Renunciation of works, but, at another time
Service through work. Of these two, plainly tell
Which is the better way?
Krishna:
To renounce works
Is well, and to do works with holiness
Is well; and both lead to supreme bliss;
But of these two, the better way is
Working piously, not refraining from works.

The true Renouncer is firm and fixed,
Seeking nothing, rejecting nothing – living proof
Against the opposites of joy and sorrow, success and failure;
So doing, one escapes easily from all deeds:
It is the neophyte who thinks
renunciation and disciplined action are separate.
Wise men know
He who cultivates one, plucks golden fruit from both!

Youth

From John Woolman, Journal

John Greenleaf Whittier called this Quaker's account of his search for God "a classic of the inner life." John Woolman (1720–1772) traveled the New England colonies for thirty years, preaching the Quaker faith and advocating temperance and the abolition of slavery.

I have often felt a motion of love to leave some hints of my experience of the goodness of God; and pursuant thereto, in the thirty-sixth year of my age, I begin this work.

I was born in Northampton, in Burlington county, in West Jersey, in the year of our Lord 1720; and before I was seven years old I began to be acquainted with the operations of divine love. Through the care of my parents, I was taught to read near as soon as I was capable of it; and as I went from school one seventh-day, I remember, while my companions went to play by the way, I went forward out of sight, and setting down, I read the twenty-second chapter of the Revelations: "He showed me a pure river of water of life, clear as crystal, proceeding out of the throne of God and of the lamb," etc.; and in the reading of it, my mind was drawn to seek after that pure habitation, which I then believed God had prepared for His servants. The place where I sat, and the sweetness that attended my mind, remain fresh in my memory.

This, and the like gracious visitations, had that effect upon me, that when boys used ill language, it troubled me, and through the continued mercies of God, I was preserved from it. The pious instructions of my parents were often fresh in my mind when I happened to be among wicked children, and were of use to me.

My parents, having a large family of children, used frequently, on first days after meeting, to put us to read in the holy scriptures, or some religious books, one after another, the rest sitting by without much conversation; which I have since often thought was a good practice. From what I had read, I believed there had been in past ages, people who walked in uprightness before God in a degree exceeding any that I knew, or heard of, now living; and the apprehension of there being less steadiness and firmness amongst people in this age than in past ages, often troubled me while I was still young.

I had a dream about the ninth year of my age as follows: I saw the moon rise near the West, and run a regular course Eastward, so swift that in about a quarter of an hour, she reached our meridian, when there descended from her a small cloud on direct line to the earth, which lighted on a pleasant green about twenty yards from the door of my father's house (in which I thought I stood) and was immediately turned into a beautiful green tree. The moon appeared to run on with equal swiftness, and soon set in the East, at which time the sun arose at the place where it commonly doth in the summer, and shining with full radiance in a serene air, it appeared as pleasant a morning as ever I saw.

All this time I stood still in the door, in an awful frame of mind, and I observed that as heat increased by the rising sun, it wrought so powerfully on the little green tree, that the leaves gradually withered, and before noon it appeared dry and dead. There then appeared a being, small of size, moving swift from the North Southward, called a sun worm.

(Though I was a child, this dream was instructive to me.)

Another thing remarkable in my childhood was, that once, as I went to a neighbor's house, I saw, on the way, a robin sitting on her nest; and as I came near she went off, but having young ones, flew about, and with many cries expressed her concern for them. I stood and threw stones at her, till one striking her, she fell down dead. At first I was pleased with the exploit, but after a few minutes was seized with horror, as having in a sportive way killed an innocent creature while she was careful for her young. I beheld her lying dead, and thought those young ones for which she was so careful must now perish for want of their dam to nourish them; and after some painful considerations on the subject, I climbed up the tree, took all the young birds, and killed them—supposing that better than to leave them to pine away and die miserably: and believed in this case, that scripture proverb was fulfilled, "The tender mercies of the wicked are cruel." I then went on my errand, but, for some hours, could think of little else but (the cruelties I had committed, and was much troubled).

Thus He, whose tender mercies are over all His works, hath placed that in the human mind, which incites to exercise goodness toward every living creature, and this singly attended to, people become tender-hearted and sympathizing; but being frequently and totally rejected, the mind shuts itself up in a contrary disposition.

About the twelfth year of my age, my father being abroad, my mother reproved me for some misconduct, to which I made an undutiful reply; and the next first-day, as I was with my father returning from meeting, he told me he understood I had behaved amiss to my mother, and advised me to be more careful in future. I knew myself blamable, and in shame and confusion remained silent. Being thus awakened to a sense of wickedness, I felt remorse in my mind, and getting home, I retired and prayed to the Lord to forgive me; and I do not remember that I ever, after that, spoke unhandsomely to either of my parents, however foolish in some other things.

Having attained the age of sixteen, I began to love wanton company: and though I was preserved from profane language or scandalous conduct, still I perceived a plant in me which produced such wild grapes. Yet my merciful Father forsook me not utterly, but at times, through His grace, I was brought seriously to consider my ways; and the sight of my backsliding affected me with sorrow: but for want of rightly attending to the reproofs of instruction, vanity was added to vanity, and repentance. Upon the whole, my mind was more and more alienated from the truth, and I hastened toward destruction. While I meditate on the gulf toward which I traveled, and reflect on my youthful disobedience, my heart is affected with sorrow.

Advancing in age, the number of my acquaintance increased, and thereby my way grew more difficult. Though I had heretofore found comfort in reading the holy scriptures, and thinking on heavenly things, I was now estranged therefrom. I knew I was going from the flock of Christ, and had no resolution to return; hence serious reflections were uneasy to me, and youthful vanities and diversions my greatest pleasure. Running in this road I found many like myself; and we associated in that which is reverse to true friendship. But in this swift race it pleased God to visit me with sickness, so that I doubted of recovering: and then did darkness, horror, and amazement, with full force seize me, even when my pain and distress of body was very great. I thought it would have been better for me never to have had a being, than to see the day which I now saw. I was filled with confusion; and in great affliction both of mind and body, I lay and bewailed myself. (I had not confidence to lift up my cries to God, whom I had thus offended; but in a deep sense of my great folly, I was humbled before Him,) and at length, that Word which is as a fire and a hammer, broke and dissolved my rebellious heart, and then my cries were put in contrition, and in the multitude of His mercies I found inward relief, and felt a close engagement, that if He was pleased to restore my health, I might walk humbly before Him.

After my recovery, this exercise remained with me a considerable time, but, by degrees, giving way to youthful vanities, they gained strength, and getting with wanton young people I lost ground. The Lord had been very gracious, and spoke peace to me in the time of my distress, and I now most ungratefully turned again to folly, on which account, at times, I felt sharp reproof, but did not get low enough to cry for help. I was not so hardy as to commit things scandalous, but to exceed in vanity, and promote mirth, was my chief study. Still I retained a love and esteem for pious people, and their company brought an awe upon me. My dear parents several times admonished me in the fear of the Lord, and their admonition entered into my heart, and had a good effect for a season; but not getting deep enough to pray rightly, the tempter, when he came, found entrance. I remember once, having spent a part of a day in wantonness, as I went to bed at night, there lay in a window near my bed a Bible, which I opened, and first cast my eye on the text, "we lie down in our shame, and our confusion covers us." This I knew to be my case, and meeting with so unexpected a reproof, I was somewhat affected with it, and went to bed under remorse of conscience, which I soon cast off again.

Thus time passed on, my heart was replenished with mirth and wantonness, while pleasing scenes of vanity were presented to my imagination, till I attained the age of eighteen years, near which time I felt the judgments of God in my soul like a consuming fire, and looking over my past life, the prospect was moving. I was often sad, and longed to be delivered from those vanities; then again my heart was strongly inclined to them, and there was in me a sore conflict. At times I turned to folly, and then again sorrow and confusion took hold of me. In a while, I resolved totally to leave off some of my vanities, but there was a secret reserve in my heart, of the more refined part of them, and I was not low enough to find true peace. Thus for some months, I had great troubles and disquiet, there remaining in me an unsubjected will, which rendered my labors fruitless, till at length, through the merciful continuance of heavenly visitations, I was made to bow down in spirit before the Most High. I remember one evening I had spent some time in reading a pious author, and walking out alone, I humbly prayed to the Lord for His help, that I might be delivered from those vanities which so ensnared me. . . . Thus, being brought low, He helped me, and as I learned to bear the cross, I felt refreshment to come from His presence: but not keeping in that strength which gave victory, I lost ground again, the sense of which greatly afflicted me; and I sought deserts and lonely places, and there with tears did confess my sins to God, and humbly craved help of Him. And I may say with reverence, He was near to me in my troubles, and in those times of humiliation opened my ear to discipline.

I was now led to look seriously at the means by which I was drawn from the pure truth, and I learned this: that if I would live in the life which the faithful servants of God lived in, I must not go into company as heretofore, in my own will; but all the cravings of sense must be governed by a divine principle. In times of sorrow and abasement, these instructions were sealed upon me, and I felt the power of Christ prevail over all selfish desires, so that I was preserved in a good degree of steadiness; and being young and believing at that time that a single life was best for me, I was strengthened to keep from such company as had often been a snare to me.

I kept steady to meetings; spent first-days in the afternoon chiefly in reading the scriptures and other good books; and was early convinced in my mind that true religion consisted in an inward life, wherein the heart doth love and reverence God the Creator, and learn to exercise true justice and goodness, not only toward all men, but also toward the brute creatures. That as the mind was moved by an inward principle to love God as an invisible, incomprehensible Being, by the same principle it was moved to love Him in all His manifestations in the visible world. That, as by His breath the flame of life was kindled in all animal and sensible creatures, to say we love God as unseen, and at the same time exercise cruelty toward the least creature moving by His life, or by life derived from him, was a contradiction in itself.

I found no narrowness respecting sects and opinions; but believe that sincere, upright-hearted people, in every society, who truly love God, were accepted of Him.

As I lived under the cross, and simply followed the openings of truth, my mind from day to day was more enlightened; my former acquaintance were left to judge of me as they would, for I found it safest for me to live in private and keep these things sealed up in my own breast. While I silently ponder on that change which was wrought in me, I find no language equal to it, not any means to convey to another a clear idea of it. I looked upon the works of God in this visible creation, and an awfulness covered me: my heart was tender and often contrite, and a universal love to my fellow creatures increased in me. This will be understood by such who have trodden in the same path.

Some glances of real beauty is perceivable in their faces, who dwell in true meekness. Some tincture of true harmony in the sound of that voice to which divine love gives utterance, and some appearance of right order in their temper and conduct, whose passions are fully regulated; yet all these do not fully show forth that inward life to such as have not felt it; but this white stone and new name is known rightly to such only who have it. . . .

The Four Ages of Man

W. B. Yeats

From the great Irish symbolist poet (1865–1939).

He with body waged a fight,
But body won; it walks upright.

Then he struggled with the heart;
Innocence and peace depart.

Then he struggled with the mind;
His proud heart he left behind.

Now his wars on God begin;
At stroke of midnight God shall win.

Reflections on a Man's Success

William James, The Varieties of Religious Experience

In The Varieties of Religious Experience, *the American Pragmatic philosopher William James (1842–1910) reflects on how a man who builds his sense of self on his successes and accomplishments will inevitably look back on his life and be disappointed. To illustrate, James cites Martin Luther and Goethe as they looked back on their respective lives.*

To begin with, how *can* things so insecure as the successful experiences of this world afford a stable anchorage? A chain is no stronger than its weakest link, and life is after all a chain. In the healthiest and most prosperous existence, how many links of illness, danger, and disaster are always interposed? Unsuspectedly from the bottom of every fountain of pleasure, as the old poet said, something bitter rises up: a touch of nausea, a falling dead of the delight, a whiff of melancholy, things that sound a knell, for fugitive as they may be, they bring a feeling of coming from a deeper region and often have an appalling convincingness. The buzz of life ceases at their touch as a piano-string stops sounding when the damper fall upon it.

Of course the music can commence again—and again and again—at intervals. But with this the healthy-minded consciousness is left with an irremediable sense of precariousness. It is a bell with a crack; it draws its breath on sufferance and by an accident.

Even if we suppose a man so packed with healthy-mindedness as never to have experienced in his own person any of these sobering intervals, still, if he is a reflecting being, he must generalize and class his own lot with that of others; and, in doing so, he must see that his escape is just a lucky chance and no essential difference. He might just as well have been born to an entirely different fortune. And then indeed the hollow security! What kind of a frame of things is it of which the best you can say is, "Thank God, it has let me off clear this time!" Is not its blessedness a fragile fiction? Is not your joy in it a very vulgar glee, not much unlike the snicker of any rogue at his success? If indeed it were all success, even on such terms as that! But take the happiest man, the one most envied by the world, and in nine cases out of ten his inmost consciousness is one of failure. Either his ideals in the line of his achievements are pitched far higher than the achievement themselves, or else he has secret ideals of which the world knows nothing, and in regard to which he inwardly knows himself to be found wanting.

When such a conquering optimist as Goethe can express himself in this wise, how must it be with less successful men?

"I will say nothing," writes Goethe in 1824, "against the course of my existence. But at bottom it has been nothing but pain and burden, and I can affirm that during the whole of my 75 years, I have not had four weeks of genuine well-being. It is but the perpetual rolling of a rock that must be raised up again forever."

What single-handed man was ever on the whole as successful as Luther? yet when he had grown old, he looked back on his life as if it were an absolute failure.

"I am utterly weary of life. I pray the Lord will come forthwith and carry me hence. Let him come, above all, with his last Judgment: I will stretch out my neck, the thunder will burst forth, and I shall be at rest." —And having a necklace of white agates in his hand at the time he added: "O God, grant that it may come without delay. I would readily eat up this necklace today, for the Judgment to come tomorrow." —The Electress Dowager, one day when Luther was dining with her, said to him: "Doctor, I wish you may live forty years more, I would give up my chance of Paradise."

Failure, then, failure! So the world stamps us at every turn. We strew it with our blunders, our misdeeds, our lost opportunities, with all the memorials of our inadequacy to our vocation. And with what a damning emphasis does it then blot us out! No easy fine, no mere apology or formal expiation, will satisfy the world's demands, but every pound of flesh exacted is soaked with all its blood. The subtlest forms of suffering known to man are connected with the poisonous humiliations incidental to these results.

And they are pivotal human experiences. A process so ubiquitous and everlasting is evidently an integral part of life. "There is indeed one element in human destiny," Robert Louis Stevenson writes, "that not blindness itself can controvert: whatever else we are intended to do, we are not intended to succeed; failure is the fate allotted." And our nature being thus rooted in failure, is it any wonder that theologians should have held it to be essential, and thought that only through the personal experience of humiliation which it engenders the deeper sense of life's significance is reached?

But this is only the first stage of the world sickness. Make the human being's sensitiveness a little greater, carry him a little farther over the misery-threshold, and the good quality of the successful moments themselves when they occur is spoiled and vitiated. All natural goods perish. Riches take wings; fame is a breath; love is a cheat; youth and health and pleasure vanish. Can things whose end is always dust and disappointment be the real goods which our souls require? Back of everything is the great specter of universal death, the all-encompassing blackness:

"What profit hath a man of all his labor which he taketh under the sun? I looked on all the works that my hands had wrought, and, behold, all *was* vanity and vexation of spirit. For that which befalleth the sons of men befalleth beasts; as the one dieth, so dieth the other; all are of the dust, and all turn to dust again. . . . The dead know not any thing, neither have they any more a reward; for the memory of them is forgotten. Also their love, and their hatred, and their envy, is now perished; neither have they any more a portion forever in any*thing* that is done under the sun. . . . Truly the light *is* sweet, and a pleasant *thing it is* for the eyes to behold the sun: but if a man live many years, and rejoice in them all; yet let him remember the days of darkness; for they shall be many."

In short, life and its negation are beaten up inextricably together. But if the life be good, the negation of it must be bad. Yet the two are equally essential facts of existence; and all natural happiness thus seems infected with a contradiction. The breath of the sepulcher surrounds it.

To a mind attentive to this state of things and rightly subject to the joy-destroying chill which such a contemplation engenders, the only relief that healthy-mindedness can give is by saying: "Stuff and nonsense, get out into the open air!" or "Cheer up, old fellow, you'll be all right erelong, if you will only drop your morbidness!" But in all seriousness, can such bald animal talk as that be treated as a rational answer? To ascribe religious value to mere happy-go-lucky contentment with one's brief chance at natural good is but the very consecration of forgetfulness and superficiality. Our troubles lie indeed too deep for *that* cure. The fact that we *can* die, that we *can* be ill at all, is what perplexes us; the fact that we now for a moment live and are well is irrelevant to that perplexity. We need a life not correlated with death, a health not liable to illness, a kind of good that will not perish, a good in fact that flies beyond the Goods of nature.

It all depends on how sensitive the soul may become to discords. "The trouble with me is that I believe too much in common happiness and goodness," said a friend of mine whose consciousness was of this sort, "and nothing can console me for their transiency. I am appalled and disconcerted at its being possible." And so with most of us: a little cooling down of animal excitability and instinct, a little loss of animal toughness, a little irritable weakness and descent of the pain-threshold, will bring the worm at the core of all our usual springs of delight into full view, and turn us into melancholy metaphysicians. The pride of life and glory of the world will shrivel. It is after all but the standing quarrel of hot youth and hoary eld. Old age has the last word: the purely naturalistic look at life, however enthusiastically it may begin, is sure to end in sadness.

This sadness lies at the heart of every merely positivistic, agnostic, or naturalistic scheme of philosophy. Let sanguine healthy-mindedness do its best with its strange power of living in the moment and ignoring and forgetting, still the evil background is really there to be thought of, and the skull will grin in at the banquet. In the practical life of the individual, we know how his whole gloom or glee about any present fact depends on the remoter schemes and hopes with which it stands related. Its significance and framing give it the chief part of its value. Let it be known to lead nowhere, and however agreeable it may be in its immediacy, its glow and gilding vanish. The old man, sick with an insidious internal disease, may laugh and quaff his wine at first as well as ever, but he knows his fate now, for the doctors have revealed it; and the knowledge knocks the satisfaction out of all these functions. They are partners of death and the worm is their brother, and they turn to a mere flatness.

The luster of the present hour is always borrowed from the background of possibilities it goes with. Let our common experiences be enveloped in an eternal moral order; let our suffering have an immortal significance; let Heaven smile upon the earth, and deities pay their visits; let faith and hope be the atmosphere which man breathes in;—and his days pass by with zest; they stir with prospects, they thrill with remoter values. Place round them on the contrary the curdling cold and gloom and absence of all permanent meaning which for pure naturalism and the popular science evolutionism of our time are all that is visible ultimately, and the thrill stops short, or turns rather to an anxious trembling.

For naturalism, fed on recent cosmological speculations, mankind is in a position similar to that of a set of people living on a frozen lake, surrounded by cliffs over which there is no escape, yet knowing that little by little the ice is melting, and the inevitable day drawing near when the last film of it will disappear, and to be drowned ignominiously will be the human creature's portion. The merrier the skating, the warmer and more sparkling the sun by day, and the ruddier the bonfires at night, the more poignant the sadness with which one must take in the meaning of the total situation.

A Man Must Stand Erect

From Marcus Aurelius, Meditations

For the great Roman emperor and stoic philosopher Marcus Aurelius, "a man must stand erect, not be kept erect by others." Happiness comes from understanding that a virtuous soul participates in eternity, while everything else—power, riches, prestige—vanish with our mortal shells. True strength is the inner strength of self-mastery. A man who knows this will neither be intoxicated by his earthly authority nor overwhelmed by its frustrations and failures.

Begin the morning by saying to thyself, I shall meet with the busybody, the ungrateful, arrogant, deceitful, envious, unsocial. All these things happen to them by reason of their ignorance of what is good and evil. But I who have seen the nature of the good that it is beautiful, and of the bad that it is ugly, and the nature of him who does wrong, that it is akin to me, not (only) of the same blood or seed, but that it participates in (the same) intelligence and (the same) portion of the divinity, I can neither be injured by any of them, for no one can fix on me what is ugly, nor can I be angry with my kinsman, nor hate him. For we are made for cooperation, like feet, like hands, like eyelids, like the rows of the upper and lower teeth. To act against one another then is contrary to nature; and it is acting against one another to be vexed and to turn away.

Whatever this is that I am, it is a little flesh and breath, and the ruling part. Throw away thy books; no longer distract thyself: it is not allowed; but as if thou was now dying, despise the flesh; it is blood and bones and a network, a contexture of nerves, veins, and arteries. See the breath also, what kind of a thing it is, air and not always the same, but every moment sent out and again sucked in. The third then is the ruling part: consider thus: Thou art an old man; no longer let this be a slave, no longer be pulled by the strings like a puppet to unsocial movements, no longer be either dissatisfied with thy present lot, or shrink from the future.

All that is from the gods is full of providence. That which is from fortune is not separated from nature or without an interweaving and involution with the things which are ordered by providence. From thence all things flow; and there is besides necessity, and that which is for the advantage of the whole universe, of which thou art a part. But that is good for every part of nature which the nature of the whole brings, and what serves to maintain this nature. Now the universe is preserved, as by the changes of the elements so by the changes of things compounded of the elements. Let these principles be enough for thee, let them always be fixed opinions. But cast away the thirst after books, that thou mayest not die murmuring, but cheerfully, truly, and from thy heart thankful to the gods.

Remember how long thou hast been putting off these things, and how often thou hast received an opportunity from the gods, and yet dost not use it. Thou must now at last perceive of what universe thou are a part, and of what administrator of the universe thy existence is a efflux, and that a limit of time is fixed for thee, which if thou dost not use for clearing away the clouds from thy mind, it will go and thou wilt go, and it will never return.

Every moment think steadily as a Roman and a man to do what thou hast in hand with perfect and simple dignity, and feeling of affection, and freedom, and justice; and to give thyself relief from all other thoughts. And thou wilt give thyself relief, if thou doest every act of thy life as if it were the last, laying aside all carelessness and passionate aversion from the commands of reason, and all hypocrisy, and self-love, and discontent with the portion which has been given to thee. Thou seest how few the things are, the which if a man lays hold of, he is able to live a life which flows in quiet, and is like the existence of the gods; for the gods on their part will require nothing more from him who observes these things.

Do wrong to thyself, do wrong to thyself, my soul; but thou wilt no longer have the opportunity of honoring thyself. Every man's life is sufficient. But thine is nearly finished, though thy soul reverences not itself, but places thy felicity in the souls of others.

Do the things external which fall upon thee distract thee? Give thyself time to learn something new and good, and cease to be whirled around. But then thou must also avoid being carried about the other way. For those too are triflers who have wearied themselves in life by their activity, and yet have no object to which to direct every movement, and, in a word, all their thoughts.

Through not observing what is in the mind of another a man has seldom been seen to be unhappy; but those who do not observe the movements of their own minds must of necessity be unhappy.

This thou must always bear in mind, what is the nature of the whole, and what is my nature, and how is this related to that, and what kind of a part it is of what kind of a whole; and that there is no one who hinders thee from always doing and saying the things which are according to the nature of which thou art a part.

Theophrastus, in his comparison of bad acts—such a comparison as one would make in accordance with the common notions of mankind—says, like a true philosopher, that the offenses which are committed through desire are more blamable than those which are committed though anger. For he who is excited by anger seems to turn away from reason with a certain pain and unconscious contraction; but he who offends through desire, being overpowered by pleasure, seems to be in a manner more intemperate and more womanish in his offenses. Rightly then, and in a way worthy of philosophy, he said that the offense which is committed with pleasure is more blamable than that which is committed with pain; and on the whole the one is more like a person who has been first wronged and through pain is compelled to be angry; but the other is moved by his own impulse to do wrong, being carried toward doing something by desire.

Since it is possible that thou mayest depart from life this very moment, regulate every act and thought accordingly. But to go away from among men, if there are gods, is not a thing to be afraid of, for the gods will not involve thee in evil; but if indeed they do not exist, or if they have no concern about human affairs, what is it to me to live in a universe devoid of gods or devoid of providence? But in truth they do exist, and they do care for human things, and they have put all the means in man's power to enable him not to fall into real evils. And as to the rest, if there was anything evil, they would have provided for this also, that it should be altogether in a man's power not to fall into it. Now that which does not make a man worse, how can it make a man's life worse? But neither through ignorance, nor having the knowledge, but not the power to guard against or correct these things, is it possible that the nature of the universe has overlooked them; nor is it possible that it has made so great a mistake, either through want of power or want of skill, that good and evil should happen indiscriminately to the good and the bad. But death certainly, and life, honor and dishonor, pain and pleasure, all these things equally happen to good men and bad, being things which make us neither better nor worse. Therefore they are neither good nor evil.

How quickly all things disappear, in the universe the bodies themselves, but in time the remembrance of them; what is the nature of all sensible things, and particularly those which attract with the bait of pleasure or terrify by pain, or are noised abroad by vapory fame; how worthless, and contemptible, and sordid, and perishable, and dead they are—all this it is the part of the intellectual faculty to observe. To observe too who these are whose opinions and voices give reputation; what death is, and the fact that, if a man looks at it in itself, and by the abstractive power of reflection resolves into their parts all the things which present themselves to the imagination in it, he will then consider it to be nothing else than an operation of nature; and if anyone is afraid of an operation of nature, he is a child. This, however, is not only an operation of nature, but it is also a thing which conduces to the purposes of nature. To observe too how man comes near to the deity, and by what part of him, and when this part of man is so disposed.

Nothing is more wretched than a man who traverses everything in a round, and pries into the things beneath the earth, as the poet says, and seeks by conjecture what is in the minds of his neighbors, without perceiving that it is sufficient to attend to the daemon within him, and to reverence it sincerely. And reverence of the daemon consists in keeping it pure from passion and thoughtlessness, and dissatisfaction with what comes from gods and men. For the things from the gods merit veneration for their excellence; and the things from men should be dear to us by reason of kinship; and sometime even, in a manner, they move our pity by reason of men's ignorance of good and bad; this defect being not less than that which deprives us of the power of distinguishing things that are white and black.

Though thou shouldest be going to live three thousand years, and as many times ten thousand years, still remember that no man loses any other life than this which he now lives, nor lives any other life than this which he now loses. The longest and shortest are thus brought to the same. For the present is the same to all, though that which perishes is not the same; and so that which is lost appears to be a mere moment. For a man cannot lose either the past or the future: for what a man has not how can anyone take this from him? These two things then thou must bear in mind; the one, that all things from eternity are of like forms and come round in a circle, and that it makes no difference whether a man shall see the same things during a hundred years or two hundred, or an infinite time; and the second, that the longest liver and he who will die soonest lose just the same. For the present is the only thing of which a man can be deprived, if it is true that this is the only thing which he has, and that a man cannot lose a thing if he has it not.

Remember that all this is opinion. For what was said by the Cynic Monimus is manifest: and manifest too is the use of what was said, if a man receives what may be got out of it as far as it is true.

The soul of man does violence to itself, first of all, when it becomes an abscess and, as it were, a tumor on the universe, so far as it can. For to be vexed at anything which happens is a separation of ourselves from nature, in some part of which the natures of all other things are contained. In the next place, the soul does violence to itself when it turns away from any man, or even moves toward him with the intention of injuring, such as are the souls of those who are angry. In the third place, the soul does violence to itself when it is overpowered by pleasure or by pain. Fourthly, when it plays a part, and does or says anything insincerely and untruly. Fifthly, when it allows any act of its own and any movement to be without an aim, and does anything thoughtlessly and without considering what it is, it being right that even the smallest things be done with reference to an end; and the end of rational animals is to follow the reason and the law of the most ancient city and polity.

Of human life the time is a point, and the substance is in a flux, and the perception dull, and the composition of the whole body subject to putrefaction, and the soul a whirl, and fortune hard to divine, and fame a thing devoid of judgment. And, to say all in a word, everything which belongs to the body is a stream, and what belongs to the soul is a dream and vapor, and life is a warfare and a stranger's sojourn, and after-fame is oblivion. What then is that which is able to conduct a man? One thing and only one, philosophy. But this consists in keeping the daemon within a man free from violence and unharmed, superior to pains and pleasures doing nothing without a purpose, nor yet falsely and with hypocrisy, not feeling the need of another man's doing or not doing anything; and besides, accepting all that happens, and all that is allotted, as coming from thence, wherever it is, from whence he himself came; and, finally, waiting for death with a cheerful mind, as being nothing else than a dissolution of the elements of which every living being is compounded. But if there is no harm to the elements themselves in each continually changing into another, why should a man have any apprehension about the change and dissolution of all the elements? For it is according to nature, and nothing is evil which is according to nature.

Labor not unwillingly, nor without regard to the common interest, nor without due consideration, nor with distraction; nor let studied ornament set off thy thoughts, and be not either a man of many words, or busy about too many things. And further, let the deity which is in thee be the guardian of a living being, manly and of ripe age, and engaged in matter political, and a Roman, and a ruler, who has taken his post like a man waiting for the signal which summons him from life, and ready to go, having need neither of oath nor of any man's testimony. Be cheerful also, and seek not external help nor the tranquillity which others give. A man then must stand erect, not be kept erect by others.

If thou workest at that which is before thee, following right reason seriously, vigorously, calmly, without allowing anything else to distract thee, but keeping thy divine part pure, as if thou shouldst be bound to give it back immediately; if thou holdest to this, expecting nothing, fearing nothing, but satisfied with thy present activity according to nature, and with heroic truth in every word and sound which thou utterest, thou wilt live happy. And there is no man who is able to prevent this.

Soon, very soon, thou wilt be ashes, or a skeleton, and either a name or not even a name; but name is sound and echo. And the things which are much valued in life are empty and rotten and trifling, and [like] little dogs biting one another, and little children quarreling, laughing, and then straightway weeping. But fidelity and modesty and justice and truth are fled,

Up to Olympus from the wide-spread earth.

What then is there which still detains thee here? If the objects of sense are easily changed and never stand still, and the organs of perception are dull and easily receive false impressions; and the poor soul itself is an exhalation from blood. But to have good repute amidst such a world as this is an empty thing.

Why then dost thou not wait in tranquillity for thy end, whether it is extinction or removal to another state? And until that time comes, what is sufficient? Why, what else than to venerate the gods and bless them, and to do good to men, and to practice tolerance and self-restraint; but as to everything which is beyond the limits of the poor flesh and breath, to remember that this is neither thine nor in thy power.

Intimations of Immortality from Recollections of Childhood

William Wordsworth

The child is father of the man;
And I could wish my days to be
Bound each to each by natural piety.

I

There was a time when meadow, grove, and stream,
The earth, and every common sight,
To me did seem
Apparelled in celestial light,
The glory and the freshness of a dream.
It is not now as it hath been of yore;—
Turn whersoe'er I may,
By night or day,
The things which I have seen I now can see no more.

II

The Rainbow comes and goes,
And lovely is the rose,
The moon doth with delight
Look round her when the heavens are bare,
Waters on a starry night
Are beautiful and fair;
The sunshine is a glorious birth;

But yet I know, where'er I go,
That there hath past away a glory from the earth.

III

Now, while the birds thus sing a joyous song,
And while the young lambs bound
As to the tabor's sound,
To me alone there came a thought of grief:
A timely utterance gave that thought relief,
And I again am strong:
The cataracts blow their trumpets from the steep;
No more shall grief of mine the season wrong;
I hear the echoes through the mountains throng,
The winds come to me from the fields of sleep,
And all the earth is gay;
Land and sea
Give themselves up to jollity,
And with the heart of May
Doth every beast keep holiday;
Thou child of joy,
Shout round me, let me hear thy shouts, thou happy
shepherd-boy!

IV

Ye blessed creatures, I have heard the call
Ye to each other make; I see
The heavens laugh with you in your jubilee;
My heart is at your festival,
My head hath its coronal,
The fulness of your bliss, I feel—I feel it all.
Oh evil day! if I were sullen
While earth herself is adorning,
This sweet May-morning,
And the children are culling
On every side,
In a thousand valleys far and wide,
Fresh flowers; while the sun shines warm,
And the babe leaps up on his mother's arm:—
I hear, I hear, with joy, I hear!

—But there's a tree, of many, one,
A single field which I have looked upon,
Both of them speak of something that is gone:
The pansy at my feet
Doth the same tale repeat:
Whither is fled the visionary gleam?
Where is it now, the glory and the dream?

V

Our birth is but a sleep and a forgetting:
The soul that rises with us, our life's star,
Hath had elsewhere its setting,
And cometh from afar:
Not in entire forgetfulness,
And not in utter nakedness,
But trailing clouds of glory do we come
From God, who is our home:
Heaven lies about us in our infancy!
Shades of the prison-house begin to close
Upon the growing boy,
But he beholds the light, and whence it flows,
He sees it in his joy;
The youth, who daily farther from the east
Must travel, still is nature's priest,
And by the vision splendid
Is on his way attended;
At length the man perceives it die away,
And fade into the light of common day.

VI

Earth fills her lap with pleasures of her own;
Yearnings she hath in her own natural kind,
And, even with something of a mother's mind,
And no unworthy aim,
The homely nurse doth all she can
To make her foster-child, her inmate man,
Forget the glories he hath known,
And that imperial palace whence he came.

VII

Behold the child among his new-born blisses,
A six years' darling of a pigmy size!
See, where 'mid work of his own hand he lies,
Fretted by sallies of his mother's kisses,
With light upon him from his father's eyes!
See, at his feet, some little plan or chart,
Some fragment from his dream of human life,
Shaped by himself with newly-learned art;
A wedding or a festival,
A mourning or a funeral;
And this hath now his heart,
And unto this he frames his song:
Then will he fit his tongue
To dialogues of business, love, or strife;
But it will not be long
Ere this be thrown aside,
And with new joy and pride
The little actor cons another part;
Filling from time to time his "humorous stage"
With all the persons, down to palsied age,
That life brings with her in her equipage;
As if his whole vocation
Were endless imitation.

VIII

Thou, whose exterior semblance doth belie
Thy soul's immensity;
Thou best philosopher, who yet dost keep
Thy heritage, thou eye among the blind,
That, deaf and silent, read'st the eternal deep,
Haunted for ever by the eternal mind,—
Mighty prophet! Seer blest!
On whom those truths do rest,
Which we are toiling all our lives to find,
In darkness lost, the darkness of the grave;
Thou, over whom thy immortality
Broods like the day, a master o'er a slave,
A presence which is not to be put by;

Thou little child, yet glorious in the might
Of heaven-born freedom on thy being's height,
Why with such earnest pains dost thou provoke
The years to bring the inevitable yoke,
Thus blindly with thy blessedness at strife?
Full soon thy soul shall have her earthly freight,
And custom lie upon thee with a weight,
Heavy as frost, and deep almost as life!

IX

O joy! that in our embers
Is something that doth live,
That nature yet remembers
What was so fugitive!
The thought of our past years in me doth breed
Perpetual benediction: not indeed
For that which is most worthy to be blest;
Delight and liberty, the simple creed
Of childhood, whether busy or at rest,
With new-fledged hope still fluttering in his breast:—
Not for these I raise
The song of thanks and praise;
But for those obstinate questionings
Of sense and outward things,
Fallings from us, vanishings;
Blank misgivings of a creature
Moving about in worlds not realised,
High instincts before which our mortal nature
Did tremble like a guilty thing surprised:
But for those first affections,
Those shadowy recollections,
Which, be they what they may,
Are yet the fountain-light of all our day,
Are yet a master-light of all our seeing;
Uphold us, cherish, and have power to make
Our noisy years seem moments in the being
Of the eternal silence: truths that wake,
To perish never:
Which neither listlessness, nor mad endeavour,
Nor man nor boy,

Nor all that is at enmity with joy,
Can utterly abolish or destroy.
Hence in a season of calm weather
Though inland far we be,
Our souls have sight of that immortal sea
Which brought us hither,
Can in a moment travel thither,
And see the children sport upon the shore,
And hear the mighty waters rolling evermore.

X

Then sing, ye birds, sing, sing a joyous song!
And let the young lambs bound
As to the tabor's sound!
We in thought will join your throng,
Ye that pipe and ye that play,
Ye that through your hearts to-day
Feel the gladness of the May!
What though the radiance which was once so bright
Be now for ever taken from my sight,
Though nothing can bring back the hour
Of splendour in the grass, of glory in the flower;
We will grieve not, rather find
Strength in what remains behind;
In the primal sympathy
Which having been must ever be;
In the soothing thoughts that spring
Out of human suffering;
In the faith that looks through death,
In years that bring the philosophic mind.

XI

And O, ye fountains, meadows, hills, and groves,
Forebode not any severing of our loves!
Yet in my heart of hearts I feel your might;
I only have relinquished one delight
To live beneath your more habitual sway.
I love the brooks which down their channels fret,

Even more than when I tripped lightly as they;
The innocent brightness of a new-born day
Is lovely yet;
The clouds that gather round the setting sun
Do take a sober colouring from an eye
That hath kept watch o'er man's mortality;
Another race hath been, and other palms are won.
Thanks to the human heart by which we live,
Thanks to its tenderness, its joys, and fears,
To me the meanest flower that blows can give
Thoughts that do often lie too deep for tears.

Death Is Not to Be Feared

Desiderius Erasmus,
The Education of a Christian Prince

*At once learned humanist and devout Christian, Erasmus of Rotterdam
(1466–1530) was a Renaissance thinker of enormous depth and breadth,
from theology to education, statesmanship, and humor.*

The tutor should first see that his pupil loves and honors
virtue as the finest quality of all, the most felicitous, the most fitting
a prince; and that he loathes and shuns moral turpitude as the
foulest and most terrible of things. Lest the young prince be accustomed to regard riches as an indispensable necessity, to be gained
by right or wrong, he should learn that those are not true honors
which are commonly acclaimed as such. True honor is that which
follows on virtue and right action of its own will. The less affected it
is, the more it redounds to fame. The low pleasures of the people
are so far beneath a prince, especially a Christian prince, that they
hardly become any man. There is another kind of pleasure which
will endure, genuine and true, all through life. Teach the prince
that nobility, statues, wax masks, family-trees, all the pomp of heralds, over which the great mass of people stupidly swell with pride,
are only empty terms unless supported by deeds worth while. The
prestige of a prince, his greatness, his majesty, must be not devel-

oped and preserved by fortune's wild display, but by wisdom, solidarity, and good deeds.

Death is not to be feared, nor should we wail when it comes to others, unless it was a foul death. The happiest man is not the one who has lived the longest, but the one who has made the most of his life. The span of life should be measured not by years but by our deeds well performed. Length of life has no bearing on a man's happiness. It is how well he lived that counts. Surely virtue is its own reward. It is the duty of a good prince to consider the welfare of his people, even at the cost of his own life if need be. But that prince does not really die who loses his life in such a cause. All those things which the common people cherish as delightful, or revere as excellent, or adopt as useful, are to be measured by just one standard—worth. On the other hand, whatever things the common people object to as disagreeable, or despise as lowly, or shun as pernicious, should not be avoided unless they are bound up with dishonor.

The True Spirit of Man

From The Bhagavad-Gita

Krishna:
Men call the tree of life,—the Banyan-tree,—
Which has its branches beneath, its roots above,—
the ever-holy tree. Yes! for its leaves
Are green and waving hymns which whisper Truth!
Whoever knows the tree of life, knows holy lore.

Its branches shoot to heaven and sink to earth,
Like the deeds of men, which take their birth
From qualities: its silver sprays and blooms,
And all the eager verdure of its girth
Leap to quick life at the kiss of sun and air,
As men's lives quicken to the fair temptations
Of wooing sense: its hanging rootlets seek
The soil beneath, helping to hold it there

As actions wrought amid this world of men
Bind them by ever-tightening bonds again.
If you know well the teaching of the Tree,
What its shape says; and whence it springs; and, then

How it must end, and all the ills of it,
You would sharpen the ax of sharp Detachment,
And sever the clinging snaky roots, and lay
This tree of sense-life low,—to set

New growths upspringing to that happier sky,—
Which those who reach shall have no day to die,
Nor fade away, nor fall—to Him, I mean,
FATHER and FIRST, Who made the mystery

Of old Creation; for to Him come those
Who break away from passing and from dreams;
Who part the bonds constraining them to flesh,
And—worshipping always Him, the Highest—

No longer grow at the mercy of whatever breeze
Of summer pleasure stirs the sleeping trees,
Whatever blast of tempest tears them, bough and stem:
To the eternal world pass such as these!

Another Sun gleams there! another Moon!
Another Light,—not Dusk, nor Dawn, nor Noon—
They who once behold it return no more;
They have attained My rest, life's Utmost boon!

When, in this world of manifested life,
The undying Spirit, setting forth from Me,
Takes on form, it draws to itself
From Being's storehouse,—which contains all,—
Senses and intellect both. The Sovereign Soul
Thus entering the flesh, or quitting it,
Gathers these up, as the wind gathers scents,
Blowing above the flower beds. Ear and Eye,
And Touch and Taste, and Smelling, these it takes,—
Yes, and a sentient mind;—linking itself
To sense-things so.

The unenlightened ones
Do not perceive Spirit when he goes or comes,
Nor when he takes his pleasure in the form,
Conjoined with these qualities; but those see plain
Who have the eyes to see. Holy souls see Spirit
When they strive to see. Enlightened, they perceive
That Spirit in themselves; but foolish ones,
without holy discipline,
Even though they strive, discern not, having hearts
Unkindled, ill-informed!

Know, too, from Me
Shines the gathered glory of the suns
Which lighten all the world: from Me the moons
Draw silvery beams, and fire draws fierce loveliness.
I penetrate the clay, and lend all shapes
Their living force; I glide into the plant—
Root, leaf, and bloom—to make the woodlands green
With springing sap. Becoming vital warmth,
I glow in glad, respiring frames, and pass,
With outward and with inward breath, to feed
The body with all nourishment.

For in this world
Being is twofold: the Divided, one;
The Undivided, one. All things that live
Are "the Divided." That which sits apart, is
"The Undivided."

Higher still is He,
The Highest, holding all, whose Name is LORD,
The Eternal, Sovereign, First! Who fills all worlds,
Sustaining them. And—dwelling thus beyond
Divided being and Undivided—I
Am called by men and by holy lore, Life Supreme,
The TRUE SPIRIT OF MAN.

Who knows Me thus,
With mind unclouded, knows all, dear Prince!
And with his whole soul forever worships Me.

Now is the sacred, secret Mystery
Declared to thee! Whoever comprehends this
Has wisdom! He is freed from works, in bliss!

The Two Paths

St. Augustine, The City of God

Not everyone admired the classical ideal of wisdom. With Christianity came new beliefs about man's foremost duties. Godliness and humility became far more important than a concern with worldly success and intellect. The classical ideal of manhood had subordinated civic virtue to the life of the mind in a harmonious hierarchy, but in The City of God, *St. Augustine insists one must choose between two irreconcilable ways of life—the city of the flesh and the city of the spirit. A life devoted to worldly ambition, he claims, is vain, exploitive, arrogant, and restless. A life devoted to God is moderate, modest, peaceable, and allows a man to be at peace with himself. Faith becomes the new model for manliness. Being a Stoic is preferable to being a hedonist, but both schools of thought are mistaken in believing that wisdom and happiness are possible though man's efforts alone, without faith in God.*

Is it reasonable and wise to glory in the extent and greatness of the empire when you can in no way prove that there is any real happiness in men perpetually living amid the horrors of war, perpetually wading in blood?—Does it matter whether it is the blood of their fellow citizens or the blood of their enemies? It is still human blood, in men perpetually haunted by the gloomy specter of fear and driven by murderous passions. The happiness arising from such conditions is a thing of glass, of mere glittering brittleness. One can never shake off the horrible dread that it may suddenly shiver into fragments.

In order to be perfectly clear on this point, we must not be carried away by hollow verbal blasts and allow our judgment to be confused by the high-sounding words of prattlers about nations, kingdoms, and provinces. Let us imagine two individuals—for each man, like a letter in a word, is an integral part of a city or of a kingdom, however extensive. Of these two men, let us suppose that one is poor, or, better, in moderate circumstances; the other, extremely wealthy. But, our wealthy man is haunted by fear, heavy with cares, feverish with greed, never secure, always restless, breathless from endless quarrels with his enemies. By these miseries, he adds to possessions beyond measure, but he also piles up for himself a mountain of distressing worries. The man of modest means is content with a small and compact patrimony. He is loved by his own, enjoys the sweetness of peace in his relations with kindred, neighbors, and friends, is religious and pious, of kindly disposition, healthy in body, self-restrained, chaste in morals, and at peace with his conscience.

I wonder if there is anyone so senseless as to hesitate over which of the two to prefer. What is true of these two individuals is likewise true of two families, two nations, two kingdoms; the analog holds in both cases. If we apply it with care and correct our judgment accordingly, it will be easy to see on which side lies folly and on which true happiness.

Hence, if the true God is adored, and if He is given the service of true sacrifice and of an upright life, then it is beneficial for good men to extend their empire far and wide and to rule for a long time. This is beneficial, not so much for themselves as for their subjects. Fear of God, and uprightness, God's great gifts, are enough for the true happiness of rulers, since this will enable them to spend this life well and thus win life eternal. On this earth, therefore, rule by good men is a blessing bestowed, not so much on themselves as upon mankind. But the rule of wicked men brings greater harm to themselves, since they ruin their own souls by the greater ease with which they can do wrong.

As for their subjects, only their own villainy can harm them. For, whatever injury wicked masters inflict upon good men is to be regarded, not as a penalty for wrongdoing, but as a test for their virtues. Thus, a good man, though a slave, is free; but a wicked man, though a king, is a slave. For he serves, not one man alone, but what is worse, as many masters as he has vices. For, it is in reference to vice that the Holy Scripture says: "For by whom a man is overcome, of the same also he is the slave."

In the absence of justice, what is sovereignty but organized brigandage? For, what are bands of brigands but petty kingdoms? They also are groups of men, under the rule of a leader, bound together by a common agreement, dividing their booty according to a settled principle. And even though a crooked world came to admit that men should be honored only according to merit, even humans' honor would be of no great value. It is smoke that weighs nothing. The reward of the saints is altogether different. They were men who, while on earth, suffered reproaches for the City of God which is so much hated by the lovers of this world. That City is eternal. There, no one is born because no one dies. There, there reigns that true and perfect happiness which is not a goddess, but a gift of God—toward whose beauty we can but sigh in our pilgrimage on earth, though we hold the pledge of it by faith. In that City, the sun does not "rise upon the good and bad" for the Sun of Justice cherishes the good alone. There, where the Truth is a treasure shared by all, there is no need to pinch the poor to fill the coffers of the state.

When it is considered how short is the span of human life, does it really matter to a man whose days are numbered what government he must obey, so long as he is not compelled to act against God or his conscience?

Those philosophers who regard virtue as the ultimate human good try to make those others feel ashamed of themselves who think highly enough of the virtues, but who subordinate them to physical pleasure, making pleasure an end in itself and virtues merely a means to this end. They do this by picturing Pleasure enthroned like a high-born queen, surrounded by ministering virtues who watch her every nod, ready to do whatever she bids them. Thus, she bids Prudence to examine carefully in what way Pleasure may be both supreme and safe. She commands Justice to render whatever services she can in the interest of friendships which are necessary for bodily comfort and to avoid doing wrong, lest pleasure might be jeopardized by the breaking of laws. She bids Fortitude keep her mistress, Pleasure, very much in mind, so that, when the body suffers some affliction, short of death, the memory of former pleasures may mitigate the pangs of present pain. She orders Temperance to take just so much of food or of other pleasant things that health may not be endangered by any excess, or Pleasure (which, for the Epicureans, is mainly a matter of bodily health) be seriously checked.

Thus, the virtues with all the glory of their dignity are made to minister to Pleasure, like the servants of an imperious but ill-famed mistress. The Stoics are right when they say that no picture could be more ugly and ignominious and difficult for good people to look at than this. But I do not see how the picture becomes much more beautiful if we imagine the virtues ministering to human glory. For, if Glory is not exactly a lovely lady, she has a certain vanity and inanity about her. Certainly, it ill becomes the gravity and solidity of the virtues to be her servants; so that, apart from pleasing men and serving their vainglory, Prudence should make no provision, Justice should share nothing. Ugly as this picture is, it fits those self-complacent and seeming philosophers who, in the guise of despising glory, pay no heed to what others think. Their virtue, if they have any, is just as much a slave to glory.

The Myth of the Cave

From Plato, The Republic

Perhaps the single most powerful and influential allegory for the soul's ascent from the darkness of passion and prejudice to the sunlight of wisdom: Socrates teaches young Glaucon to prefer the enduring pleasures of the mind to the empty pleasures of tyranny.

"And now," I said, "let me show in a figure how far our nature is enlightened or unenlightened: Behold! Human beings living in an underground den, which has a mouth open toward the light and reaching all along the den; here they have been from their childhood, and have their legs and necks chained so that they cannot move, and can only see before them, being prevented by the chains from turning round their heads. Above and behind them a fire is blazing at a distance, and between the fire and the prisoners there is a raised way; and you will see, if you look, a low wall built along the way, like the screen which marionette players have in front of them, over which they show the puppets."

"I see."

"And do you see," I said, "men passing along the wall all sorts of vessels, and statues and figures of animals made of wood and stone and various materials, which appear over the wall? Some of them are talking, others silent."

"You have shown me a strange image, and they are strange prisoners."

"Like ourselves," I replied; "and they see only their own shadows, or the shadows of one another, which the fire throws on the opposite wall of the cave?"

"True," he said; "how could they see anything but the shadows if they were never allowed to move their heads?"

"And of the objects which are being carried in like manner they would only see the shadows?"

"Yes," he said.

"And if they were able to converse with one another, would they not suppose that they were naming what was actually before them?"

"Very true."

"And suppose further that the prison had an echo which came from the other side, would they not be sure to fancy when one of the passers-by spoke that the voice which they heard came from the passing shadow?"

"No question," he replied.

"To them," I said, "the truth would be literally nothing but the shadows of the images."

"That is certain."

"And now look again, and see what will naturally follow if the prisoners are released and disabused of their error. At first, when any of them is liberated and compelled suddenly to stand up and turn his neck round and walk and look toward the light, he will suffer sharp pains; the glare will distress him, and he will be unable to see the realities of which in his former state he had seen the shadows; and then conceive someone saying to him, that what he saw before was an illusion, but that now, when he is approaching nearer to being and his eye is turned toward more real existence, he has a clearer vision, what will be his reply? And you may further imagine that his instructor is pointing to the objects as they pass and requiring him to name them, will he not be perplexed? Will he not fancy that the shadows which he formerly saw are truer than the objects which are now shown to him?"

"Far truer."

"And if he is compelled to look straight at the light, will he not have a pain in his eyes which will make him turn away to take refuge in the objects of vision which he can see, and which he will conceive to be in reality clearer than the things which are now being shown to him?"

"True," he said.

"And suppose once more, that he is reluctantly dragged up a steep and rugged ascent, and held fast until he is forced into the presence of the sun himself, is he not likely to be pained and irritated? When he approaches the light his eyes will be dazzled, and he will not be able to see anything at all of what are now called realities."

"Not all in a moment," he said.

"He will require to grow accustomed to the sight of the upper world. And first he will see the shadows best, next the reflections of men and other objects in the water, and then the objects themselves; then he will gaze upon the light of the moon and the stars and the spangled heaven; and he will see the sky and the stars by night better than the sun or the light of the sun by day?"

"Certainly."

"Last of all he will be able to see the sun, and not mere reflections of him in the water, but he will see him in his own proper place, and not in another; and he will contemplate him as he is.

"This entire allegory," I said, "you may now append, dear Glaucon, to the previous argument; the prison-house is the world of sight, the light of the fire is the sun, and you will not misapprehend me if you interpret the journey upward to be the ascent of the soul into the intellectual world according to my poor belief, which, at your desire, I have expressed—whether rightly or wrongly God knows. But, whether true or false, my opinion is that in the world of knowledge the idea of good appears last of all, and is seen only with an effort; and, when seen, is also inferred to be the universal author of all things beautiful and right, parent of light and of the lord of light in this visible world, and the immediate source of reason and truth in the intellectual; and that this is the power upon which he who would act rationally either in public or private life must have his eye fixed."

"I agree," he said, "as far as I am able to understand you."

Levin Wonders About the Meaning of Life

From Leo Tolstoy, Anna Karenina

There are quiet heroes of peace as well as heroes of war, and perhaps the former are more impressive. In this moving scene from Tolstoy's Anna Karenina *(1876), Levin is plunged by the death of his beloved brother into wondering what meaning his life has as a man. He concludes that the philosophy and theology he learned as a young man amount to little more than vanity and con-*

ceit. Instead, he realizes that it is his daily obligations as a husband and a father that give his life meaning—his duty to his wife and children, to their extended families, and to the people who work for him.

From the moment when, at the sight of his dying brother, Levin had for the first time looked at the questions of life and death through his new convictions, as he called them, convictions which, in the period between his twentieth and thirty-sixth year had imperceptibly taken the place of his childish beliefs, he had become horrified, not so much at death, as at life, without the least conception whence it came, what it was for, and what it meant. The organism, its dissolution, the indestructibility of matter, the law of the conservation of energy, evolution, were the words that had taken the place of his former beliefs. These words and the conceptions they stood for satisfied his mental requirements, but they gave him nothing for life, and he suddenly began to feel himself in the position of a man who has given up his fur coat in exchange for a gauze garment, and at the first approach of the frost realizes that he is little better than naked, and must inevitably die a painful death.

Levin continued to live as before, but was constantly tormented on account of his ignorance. He had a vague feeling that what he called his convictions was not only ignorance, but that it actually stood in the way of the knowledge that he needed.

In the early days of his marriage his new joys and duties had completely drowned these thoughts, but later, after his wife's confinement, when he had lived in Moscow without occupation, the question began to present itself more and more frequently, demanding a solution.

It presented itself in this way: "If I do not accept the explanation offered me by Christianity on the problem of my existence, where shall I find others?" He scrutinized the whole arsenal of his scientific convictions and found no answer whatsoever to this question. He was in the position of a man who seeks to find food in a toy shop or a gun shop.

Involuntarily and unconsciously he sought now in every book, in every conversation, in every person he met, some sympathy with the subject that absorbed him.

What surprised and puzzled him most was the fact that the majority of men of his circle, who had, like himself, substituted science for religion, did not experience the least moral suffering, and were perfectly contented and happy. Were they sincere, or did science give them a clearer answer to these troublesome questions?

And he took to studying these men and books that might contain the solution that he desired.

He discovered that he had made a gross error in taking up the idea of his university friends, that religion had outlived its day and no longer existed. The best people he knew were believers—the old prince, Lvov, for whom he had taken such a liking, Sergei Ivanovitch, all the women, including his wife, who believed, just as he had done when he was a child, nine-tenths of the Russian people—the part of the nation whose lives inspired him with the greatest respect, were believers.

Another strange thing was that, as he read many books, he became convinced that the materialists whose opinions he shared did not attach any importance to these questions. Far from explaining them, they set them aside and took up others of no interest to him, such as, for instance, the evolution of organisms, the mechanical explanation of the soul, and so forth.

Moreover, during his wife's illness an extraordinary event had occurred. He, an unbeliever, had prayed fervently, in full faith. But as soon as the danger was over he was unable to give that spiritual experience any place in his life.

He could not admit that he had known the truth then and was mistaken now, for the moment he began to think of it calmly everything went to pieces. Nor could he admit that he had been mistaken then, for he thought too highly of that experience, and if he assumed it to have been a weakness, he was defiling those precious moments. He was in painful discord with himself, and strained all his mental powers in order to put himself right.

There were days when these thoughts tormented him more than others, but they never left him entirely. The more he read and thought, the further he felt himself from the aim he was pursuing.

Having convinced himself that he could get no answer from the materialists, he turned to Plato, Spinoza, Kant, Schelling, Hegel, Schopenhauer—all those philosophers who did not give a materialistic explanation of life.

The ideas seemed to him fruitful, particularly as a refutation of the materialistic teaching, but the moment he reflected on the solution of the important question, he found the same thing repeated again and again. Following the definition given to obscure words such as spirit, will, freedom, substance, and purposely allowing himself to be caught in the word-trap, he seemed to understand something, but he need only forget the artificial chain of thoughts and return to what satisfied him, and the whole edifice fell to pieces like a house of cards.

When reading Schopenhauer one day he substituted the word "love" for "will," and for a short time this new philosophy consoled him, but even that fell like the rest when dissected and brought into the domain of real life.

His brother advised him to read the theological works of Horniakov, and the second volume, in spite of its polemical, brilliant, elegant style, which at first repelled him, impressed him deeply by its Church doctrine. He was struck by the idea that the attainment of divine truth was not given to one man, but to the totality of men, embodied in the Church. He rejoiced at the thought that it was easier to believe in an existing, living church embracing all the creeds of men with God at its head, than to begin with some distant, mysterious, unknown God.

Later, when he read a history of the Church by a Catholic writer, and another by a Greek Orthodox writer, and saw that both Churches, infallible in their essence, denied each other, he was again disappointed in Horniakov's doctrine, and this structure, too, fell to pieces just as the philosophical teachings had done.

The spring was a most difficult time for Levin, and he lived through some terrible moments.

"Without knowing who I am and why I am here life is impossible. And I cannot know it, consequently I cannot live," he would say to himself.

"In endless time and space, in the infinitude of matter, an organic bubble separated itself, will hold together a while, and burst. And that bubble am I."

It was an agonizing untruth, but it was the result of centuries of labor of the human mind in that direction.

It was the last belief on which was reared all human inquiry, in all its branches. It was the reigning conviction, and Levin had involuntarily adopted it out of all other explanations, as being the most clear.

But it was only an untruth—a cruel sarcasm of some evil power, impossible to submit to.

It was necessary to free oneself from that power, and each man held his liberation in his own hands. There was only one means to do this, and that was death.

And though in good health and happily married, Levin was several times so near to killing himself that he had to hide a rope so as not to hang himself, and would not go out with a gun for fear of shooting himself.

But he did neither the one nor the other, and still continued living.

When Levin puzzled over what he was and where he came from, he found no answer and fell into despair, but when he ceased worrying about it he seemed to know definitely why he was there, and acted accordingly. Latterly his life had even assumed a more definite purpose than before.

On his return to the country at the beginning of June, he returned also to his customary occupations. The farm, his relations with the peasants and the neighboring gentry, his home affairs, his brother's and sister's affairs, his relation with his wife and her relatives, his care for the child, the new bee-keeping that had fascinated him since the spring, and a hundred other things, absorbed all his time.

These matters interested him not because he justified them by some general principle as he had done formerly; on the contrary, having become disenchanted by the failure of his various undertakings for the common good, he now busied himself for no other reason than because it seemed to him that he could not do otherwise.

Formerly, whenever he had tried to do anything for the good of humanity, for Russia, for the village, he had observed that the idea itself was agreeable, but the work senseless. There was no full conviction that it was absolutely necessary, and from at first appearing great, it grew smaller and smaller, until it reached the point of impossibility. Since his marriage, however, he had begun to confine his life more strictly to himself, and though he no longer experienced the same joy at the thought of his activity, he felt more certain of its usefulness, saw that it proceeded much better than before, and that it grew larger instead of smaller.

Almost against his will he buried himself deeper and deeper into the soil, so that he could not get out of it without opening a furrow.

To live as his father and grandfathers had lived, to carry out their work so as to hand it on to his children, seemed to him a plain duty. It was as necessary as eating when one is hungry. And for that, just as one had to prepare a meal, one had to keep the farm at Pokrovsky in such a manner as to make it profitable. Just as it was necessary to pay one's debts, so it was necessary to manage the estate in such a manner that when his son inherited it from him, he would be as grateful as Levin himself had been when he had received it from his grandfather. And so he looked after his cows, fields and manures, and planted forests.

He could not help attending to the affairs of Sergei Ivanovitch and his sister, and the peasants had become so accustomed to coming to him for advice that he had not the heart to cast them off. Then he had to see to the comforts of his sister-in-law and her children, whom he had invited to stay with them, and to that of his wife and child; he had to be with them at least a small part of the day.

Taken all together, Levin's life was fully occupied, yet it had no meaning for him whenever he thought of it.

Not only did Levin see clearly what it was he had to do, but he saw also how he must do it, and what part was of paramount importance.

He knew that it was necessary to hire laborers as cheaply as possible, but that he ought not to enslave them by advancing them money in order to get them below market price. There was no harm in selling peasants straw when they had no food for their cattle, but the wine and the dramshop had to be abolished, even though they brought in an income. Wood-stealing he would punish most severely, but he would take no fines for cattle driven on to his land, much to the disgust of his own herds.

Peter, who was paying a moneylender ten per cent a month, was to get a loan in order to save him, but no mercy was to be shown to those peasants who did not pay their rents. His bailiff was not to be forgiven for having delayed mowing a small meadow and thus losing the grass for nothing; on the other hand, the eighty acres where new trees had been planted were not to be mowed at all. No mercy was to be shown to a laborer who went away during working time because his father had died, no matter how much he was to be pitied, and he was to be paid less for the valuable time he had lost; at the same time, he could not refuse giving a monthly allowance to old, worthless servants.

Upon returning home he knew that he had to go to his wife even though some peasants had been waiting for him for hours, yet he would forego the pleasure of hiving a swarm of bees to talk to the peasants who came to find him at the apiary.

He did not know whether he was doing right or wrong, indeed he had ceased thinking about the question. He dreaded any reflection that would have given rise to doubts and obscured the clear and accurate view he had taken of his duties. But an infallible judge was ever present in his soul who decided which of two possible acts was the better one, and instantly let him know the moment he did not act as was proper.

Thus he lived, not knowing and not seeing the remotest possibility of knowing what he was and for what purpose he had been placed in the world. He was tormented by this ignorance to the extent of fearing suicide, yet at the same time was laying out for himself a definite path in life.

The day on which Sergei Ivanovitch reached Pokrovsky was one full of torment for Levin. It was at that hurried, busy season of the year when the peasantry put forth an extraordinary amount of effort and show an endurance quite unknown in any other conditions of life—an endurance that would be prized more highly were it not repeated every year, and if it did not produce such very simple results. Digging, sowing, mowing, reaping, harvesting, threshing—these are labors that seem simple and commonplace, but to accomplish them in the short time accorded by nature, every one, old and young, must set to work. For three or four weeks they must be content with the simplest fare, such as black bread, garlic, and kvas, and must haul the ricks at night and not get more than two or three hours' sleep a day. And this is done every year throughout the whole of Russia.

Having lived the greater part of his life in the country in close relations with the people, Levin always felt the electric feeling of this particular time communicate itself to him.

Early in the morning he went out to see the first sowing of the rye and the oats that were being hauled to the lots, and returning home, he drank his coffee with his wife and sister-in-law, and afterwards departed on foot to the outfarm, where they were to start a newly erected threshing-machine for the preparation of the seeds.

All that day while talking with his bailiff, the peasants, or at home with his wife, Dolly, the children, and his father-in-law, Levin kept thinking of the one and only thing that interested him at that time, in spite of all his farm cares. "What am I? where am I? and why am I?" he asked himself.

Standing in the cold-room of the newly thatched kiln, he watched the dust thrown off by the threshing-machine flying about in the air, the chaff settling down on the sunny grass, while the swallows took refuge under the roof and the laborers hurried about in the dark interior. A strange idea came into his head.

"What is this all done for?" he thought. "Why do I stand here compelling them to work? What makes them bustle so and try to show their zeal in my presence? Why does that old woman Matriona work so hard? I remember curing her once when she was struck down by a beam during a fire." He was looking at the haggard old woman who was trotting about on her sunburnt feet over the rough, uneven threshing floor, turning the grain over with a rake. "She recovered then, but to-day, or to-morrow, or in ten years, she will be dead and buried, and nothing will be left of her. And that pretty woman in the red blouse, who is so nimbly separating the grain from the chaff, will share the same fate. She, too, will be buried, and so will that horse," he thought, as he gazed at the piebald gelding that was breathing heavily through its dilated nostrils as it walked in the tread-mill. "The horse will be buried and so will Fiodor, the feeder, with his curly beard full of chaff and the shirt that is torn over the shoulder. And I, too, will be buried and nothing will be left. What is it all for?"

During these thoughts he kept a steady watch in order to calculate how much work they would do in an hour. He had to know that in order to fix the task of the day.

"An hour has nearly gone and they are only on the third rick," Levin thought. He walked over to the feeder, and raising his voice above the rumble of the machine, ordered him to feed it more evenly.

"You put too much at a time, Fiodor! You see, it catches and goes more slowly. Try and make it more even!"

Fiodor, his face black from perspiration and dust, shouted something in reply, but still did not do what Levin wanted him to.

Levin walked over to the drum, and pushing Fiodor aside began feeding it himself.

He worked until the peasant dinner hour, then went out of the kiln with the feeder, and stopped to talk to him at the yellow stack of cut rye.

The man came from a distant village, where Levin had once let land on the company system. Now it was let to the innkeeper.

Levin questioned Fiodor about this land, and asked whether Platon, a rich merchant of that village, would not take it for the coming year.

"The price is high, Konstantin Dmitritch; Platon cannot make it pay," the peasant replied, picking off the ears of rye from his perspiring bosom.

"But how does Kirillov make it pay?"

"Oh, Mityuha could make anything pay!" (Mityuha was a nickname the innkeeper was known by in the village.) "He will squeeze a fellow and get what he wants. He will not spare a Christian. As for Uncle Fokanitch" (thus he called Platon), "he is different. To some he gives on credit, and on others he loses. Sometimes he does not get back his own. He is a good man."

"But why doesn't he insist on getting his own?"

"People are different; one man lives for himself alone, like Mityuha, who only thinks of filling his belly, but Fokanitch is an honest man; he lives for his soul. He thinks of God."

"What do you mean by that? How does he live for his soul?" Levin almost shouted.

"It's quite simple, according to the truth, according to God's work. There are all kinds of people. Take yourself, for example, you would not hurt any one . . . "

"Yes, yes, good-bye!" Levin said, hastily, and turned away. He took his cane and walked rapidly towards the house, in a state of great agitation. The peasant's simple words about Fokanitch living for his soul, according to God's word, set a whole chain of thoughts whirling in his brain, blinding him with their light.

Levin walked along the highway with long strides, excited, not so much by his thoughts, as by his strange mental condition—a condition he had never experienced before.

The words uttered by the peasant were like an electric spark, that suddenly transformed and blended into a whole series of heterogeneous, impotent, disconnected thoughts, that had never ceased interesting him. They had been with him even when he had spoken to the peasant about the land.

He felt that something new was taking place in his soul, and though he did not yet know what it was, he felt a pleasurable excitement in the feeling.

"Not to live for oneself, but for God. For what God? Could any one have said anything more stupid? According to Fiodor one must live not for one's own needs, that is, for what we want, what we understand, but for some incomprehensible God whom nobody knows or can define. Well? Did I not understand the meaning of Fiodor's words? Did I doubt their justice? Did I find them senseless, incomprehensible, insignificant? I understood them just as Fiodor understood them. I understand them more clearly and fully than anything in life, and never have I doubted them, or could have doubted them. Not I alone, but everybody, the whole world understands them fully; in this alone men have no doubts, and are in complete accord. Fiodor said that Kirillovitch the innkeeper lives only for his stomach. That is comprehensible and sensible. All sensible people cannot help but live for their stomachs. And suddenly this same Fiodor says that it is bad to live for one's stomach, that one ought to live for truth, for God, and I understand him. And the millions of people who lived centuries back, and those who are living now, peasants, the poor in spirit, and the wise, those who have thought and written about it, those who say the same in their own simple language—all are agreed on this one point, and know what it is we should live for, and what is good. With all people in common, I have one firm, indubitable piece of knowledge—a knowledge that cannot be explained through reason, because it is beyond the sphere of reason, a knowledge that has no causes and can have no effects. If good has a cause, it is no longer good if it has an effect—rewards—it is again not good. Consequently good must be beyond the law of cause and effect.

"I know this and we all know it.

"I wanted a miracle to convince me. But here it is, the only possible, existing miracle, surrounding me on all sides, and I did not even observe it! What greater miracle can there be?

"Is it possible that I have found the solution to everything? Is it possible that all my sufferings have come to an end?" Levin asked himself, as he continued on his way along the dusty road, oblivious to heat and fatigue, with a sensation as though an old pain had suddenly left him. The sensation was so joyous that it seemed almost incredible to him. He was so overcome by emotion that he was unable to proceed, and leaving the road, he turned aside into the forest. He took off his hat and sank down on the rich, luxurious grass, under the shade of the aspens.

"Yes, I must consider it carefully," he thought, gazing at the untrodden grass in front of him, and watching the movements of a little green caterpillar that was climbing up a blade of couch-grass. "What is it I have discovered?" he asked himself, bending another blade of grass for the caterpillar to crawl on. "Why am I so pleased? What have I discovered?

"Formerly I used to say that in my body, in this grass, in this caterpillar, a transmutation of matter takes place according to physical, chemical, and physiological laws. And in all of us, in these aspens, in the clouds, evolution is going on. Evolution from what, to what? An eternal evolution and struggle? As if there could be any direction and struggle in the infinite! And in spite of all the efforts of my reason in that direction, until now, the meaning of life, the meaning of my own impulses and strivings were not revealed to me. Now I know that life consists in living for God, for the soul.

"I have not discovered anything; I have merely found what I knew already. I have come to understand the power that gave me life in the past, that gives me life in the present. I have freed myself from deception and found the master."

He reviewed briefly the whole progress of his thoughts of the last two years, thoughts that had first been aroused by the sight of his sick, dying brother. Then, for the first time, had he clearly comprehended that for every man, and himself too, there was nothing ahead but suffering, death, eternal oblivion. He had decided that it was impossible to live thus, that it was necessary to explain life in a more sane way or else shoot himself. But he had done neither the one nor the other; he had continued to live, think, and feel. He even married during that time, experienced many joys, and was happy so long as he tried to shut his eyes to the meaning of life.

What did it mean? It meant that he was living well and thinking badly.

He had been living unconsciously on the spiritual truths he had imbibed with his mother's milk, yet in his thoughts he had not only refused to acknowledge them, but had cautiously avoided them altogether.

Now it was clear to him that he could only live according to the beliefs in which he had been brought up.

"What should I have been, how should I have passed my life had it not been for those beliefs, had I not known that one must live for God and not for one's own needs? I might have robbed, lied, and killed. What are now the chief joys of my life would never have existed for me." And try as he would he was unable to picture to himself the bestial creature he would have been had he not known what he was living for.

"I have been seeking an answer to my question, but reason could not give it to me. It was life itself gave me the answer, through my knowledge of good and bad. This knowledge I have not acquired in any way; it was given me from the beginning, given me because I could not get it anywhere.

"Where did it come from? Was it reason that told me it was necessary to love my neighbor? It was told to me in my childhood, and I gladly believed it, because it was already in my soul. Who discovered it? Not reason; reason discovered the theory of the struggle of existence and the law demanding that I should gratify my own desires at the cost of others. To love my neighbor could not have been discovered by reason, because it is unreasonable."

Levin recalled a recent scene between Dolly and her children. When left alone one day the children began amusing themselves by making raspberry jam in a tea-cup over a lighted candle, and throwing milk into each other's faces. Their mother, catching them in the act, began scolding them before Levin. She tried to impress on them the idea that what they were destroying had cost their elders a large amount of labor, performed for their sakes, also saying that if they broke the cups they would have nothing from which to drink their tea, and that if they spilled the milk they would have nothing to eat, and would have to go hungry.

Levin was struck by the indifference and scepticism with which the children listened to their mother's words. They did not believe what she said, and were merely sorry to have their interesting game interrupted. They did not believe because they did not know the value of what they were playing with, and did not understand that they were destroying their own means of subsistence.

"That is all very well," they thought, "but these things are not so important, for they have always been and always will be. We needn't worry about that, that is all ready for us. We want to invent something new. It was quite a nice idea to make raspberry jam in a cup over a candle, and to pour milk into each other's mouths as from a fountain. It was very jolly, and not in any way worse than drinking it out of a cup.

"Are we not doing the same?" Levin thought. "Have I not done it by trying to discover the meaning of the forces of nature and human life through reason? And is not the same done by all philosophical theories that lead us by strange paths to the knowledge that we already have? Can we not see clearly in the development of the theory of any philosopher that he knows in advance, just as much as Fiodor did, what is the real meaning of life?

"If we were to let the children get things for themselves, make the dishes, milk the cows, and so forth, what would happen? They would starve, probably. In the same way if we were let loose with our passions and ideas, without any conception of a God, a Creator, of what is good or evil, we should only destroy just as the children do. For without the idea of a God we cannot build up anything.

"From whence did this joyful knowledge come to me, a knowledge that I have in common with the peasant Fiodor, which alone gives me peace of mind? Here am I, a Christian, brought up in the faith, surrounded by the blessings of Christianity, living upon these spiritual blessings without being conscious of them, and failing to understand them, destroying that by which I live. And the moment anything important in life occurs I run to Him as children run to their mother when they are cold and hungry.

"Yes, what I know has not come to me through reason, it has been given to me, revealed to me; I know it with my heart, by my faith in the teachings of the Church.

"The Church? The Church?" Levin repeated to himself as he rolled over on his other side and, leaning on his arm, looked away into the distance, beyond the cattle going down to the river.

"But can I believe in all that the Church teaches?" he said, in order to test himself, and bring up everything that might destroy his present feeling of security. He purposely brought to mind the part of the Church teaching that had seemed to him strange and had most alienated him. "Creation? Yes, how did I explain existence? By existence? By nothing? The devil, and sin? But how did I explain evil? The Redeemer? . . .

"But I know nothing, nothing, and cannot know other than what I have been told with the rest."

It seemed to him now that not one of these Church dogmas was inimical to the great objects of life—faith in God and goodness. On the contrary, all tended to produce the greatest of miracles; enabling the world with its millions of human beings, young and old, Lvov, Kitty, peasants, and kings, to comprehend the same great truths, so as to live the life of the soul—the only life that is worth living.

Lying on his back he looked up into the high, cloudless sky.

"Do I not know that that is endless space and not a vault of blue stretching over me? But however much I may strain my sight I can only see a vaulted dome; and in spite of my knowledge of infinite space I am unquestionably right when I see it like that, far more right than when I try to probe into the beyond."

Levin stopped thinking, and listened intently to the mysterious joyful voices that seemed to be talking about him.

"Is it faith?" he thought, afraid to believe his own happiness.

"My God, I thank thee!" he cried, swallowing the sobs that rose within him, and brushing the tears from his eyes.

4

THE FAMILY MAN

PERHAPS THERE IS NO MORE COMPLEX SET OF RELATIONSHIPS FOR A man than that of family life. At different stages and in different spheres of his life, a man relates to his family as a son, grandson, brother, cousin, nephew, husband, father, uncle, and grandfather. The demands and rewards, triumphs and heartbreaks of the web of family relationships are almost endless in their variety. In all the stages and spheres I've just listed, a boy and later a man can experience the most astonishing range of emotions—achingly intense love for a parent, spouse, child or relation combined with feelings of disappointment, envy, betrayal, or rejection, and sorrow and grief should illness, pain, or misfortune befall any of those family members.

Family life, for these reasons, is a lifelong school for a man in developing his own inner resources, fortitude under adversity, compassion, understanding, and patience. Aristotle believed that the successful head of a household must possess what he termed "the proper art of household management"—the virtuous organization of the family to sustain it economically and, at a higher level, to raise children in partnership with their mother so as to prepare them for their future duties as citizens and family members. As G. K. Chesterton has observed, the family is the most demanding test of a man's freedom because it is the only situation that a man is more or less free to succeed at or bungle all on his own. For many men family life is the source of their chief satisfactions, and most men at some point find themselves contemplating the meaning of life in a larger religious or philosophical context chiefly as the result of the reversals, torments, and puzzles of family love.

Of course, the very reasons that family life offers such intense satisfactions can also make us bitter enemies of the institution. Because we are so vulnerable to the wounds that parents, spouses, and children can inflict on us, some men long to flee the responsibilities of family altogether. "Sacred family!" cries a character in one of Strindberg's plays, "the supposed home of all the virtues, where innocent children are tortured into their first falsehoods, where wills are broken by parental tyranny, and self-respect smothered by crowded jostling egos." Some men find friendships outside of the family more satisfying than blood ties because they can choose a friend or lover freely, without the obligations implied by a biological kinship. But for most men the family is, for better or worse, their best shot at personal happiness; even the most prestigious and rewarding job is unlikely to give one a comparable feeling of inner contentment and peace.

Being the father of a family can be likened to governing the affairs of a small, self-contained country. It requires great reserves of prudence—an ability to alternate between reticence and candor, and between exerting too much authority and too little. According to the great French humanist Michel de Montaigne, governing a private family is in fact hardly less challenging than governing a whole kingdom—and even more complicated in our era, when we are no likelier to accept a king in private life than in public. The Chinese proverb puts it wisely: the family man should "govern his family as you would cook a small fish—very carefully."

BOYS INTO MEN

Telemachus's Search for a Father

From Homer, The Odyssey

Homer's Odyssey *is a search within a search. While Odysseus is making his slow way home from Troy, his son Telemachus embarks on a voyage of his own to search for his missing father and bring him back. Spiritually as well as literally, Telemachus is a fatherless young man searching for that missing guide in his life. In the course of searching for his father, he becomes more mature. By pursuing a father who, absent for twenty years, is really more of an ideal for Telemachus than a flesh-and-blood reality, Telemachus raises himself in the light of this ideal, trying to become the man he thinks his father would want him to be. Both Odysseus and Telemachus are under the protection of Athena, the goddess of sage counsel. Her intelligence, subtlety, and curiosity mirror Odysseus's own. Her partnership with Odysseus and his son suggests a new vision of manliness, in which male and female traits deepen and temper each other.*

Almost nothing is known of Homer, who may or may not have been born in the middle of the 9th century B.C. in Ionia. But the ancient Greeks firmly believed he was the author of both the Odyssey *and its companion poem, the* Iliad. *Their influence on Western literature is immeasurable.*

Early in the Odyssey, *young Telemachus laments the twenty-year absence of his father. How can the boy protect his mother Penelope from the rapacious suitors who are eating her out of house and home? Is he man enough to take on his adult responsibilities? He confides his worries to Athena, who appears in human guise at the palace.*

Now far the first to see Athene was godlike Telemachus, as he sat among the suitors, his heart deep grieving within him, imagining in his mind his great father, how he might come back and all throughout the house might cause the suitors to scatter, and hold his rightful place and be lord of his own possessions. With such thoughts, sitting among the suitors, he saw Athene and went straight to the forecourt, the heart within him scandalized that a guest should still be standing at the doors. He stood beside her and took her by the right hand, and relieved her of the bronze spear, and spoke to her and addressed her in winged words: "Welcome, stranger. You shall be entertained as a guest among us. Afterward, when you have tasted dinner, you shall tell us what your need is."

Then the haughty suitors came in, and all of them straightway took their places in order on chairs and along the benches, and their heralds poured water over their hands for them to wash with, and the serving maids brought them bread heaped up in the baskets, and the young men filled the mixing bowls with wine for their drinking. They put their hands to the good things that lay ready before them. But when they had put away their desire for eating and drinking, the suitors found their attention turned to other matters, the song and the dance; for these things come at the end of the feasting. A herald put the beautifully wrought lyre in the hands of Phemios, who sang for the suitors, because they made him. He played his lyre and struck up a fine song. Meanwhile Telemachus talked to Athene of the gray eyes, leaning his head close to hers, so that none of the others might hear him:

"Dear stranger, would you be scandalized at what I say to you? This is all they think of, the lyre and the singing. Easy for them,

since without penalty they eat up the substance of a man whose
white bones lie out in the rain and fester somewhere on the main-
land, or roll in the wash of the breakers. If they were ever to see
him coming back to Ithaka all the prayer of them all would be to be
lighter on their feet instead of to be richer men for gold and clothing. As it is, he has died by an evil fate, and there is no comfort left
for us, not even though someone among mortals tells us he will
come back. His day of homecoming has perished."

"Now I have come," Athene replied. "They told me he was
here in this country, your father, I mean. But no. The gods are
impeding his passage. For no death on the land has befallen the
great Odysseus, but somewhere, alive on the wide sea, he is held
captive, on a sea-washed island, and savage men have him in their
keeping, rough men, who somehow keep him back, though he is
unwilling. Now, I will make you a prophecy, in the way the immortals put it into my mind, and as I think it will come out, though I am
no prophet, nor do I know the ways of birds clearly. He will not
long be absent from the beloved land of his fathers, even if the
bonds that hold him are iron, but he will be thinking of a way to
come back, since he is a man of many resources. But come now tell
me this and give me an accurate answer. Are you, big as you are, the
very child of Odysseus? Indeed, you are strangely alike about the
head, the fine eyes, as I remember; we used to meet so often
together before he went away to Troy, where others beside him and
the greatest of the Argives went in their hollow vessels. Since that
time I have not seen Odysseus nor has he seen me."

Then the thoughtful Telemachus said to her in answer: "See, I
will accurately answer all that you ask me. My mother says indeed I
am his. I for my part do not know. Nobody really knows his own
father."

Then the thoughtful Telemachus said to his mother:

"Why, my mother, do you begrudge this excellent singer his
pleasing himself as the thought drives him? It is not the singers who
are to blame, it must be Zeus is to blame, who gives out to men who
eat bread, to each and all, the way he wills it. There is nothing
wrong in his singing the sad return of the Danaans. People, surely,
always give more applause to that song which is the latest to circu-
late among the listeners. So let your heart and let your spirit be
hardened to listen. Odysseus is not the only one who lost his homecoming day at Troy. There were many others who perished, besides
him. Go therefore back in the house, and take up your own work,
the loom and the distaff, and see to it that your handmaidens ply

their work also; but the men must see to discussion, all men, but I most of all. For mine is the power in this household."

But the suitors all through the shadowy halls were raising a tumult, and all prayed for the privilege of lying beside her, until the thoughtful Telemachus began speaking among them:

"You suitors of my mother, overbearing in your rapacity, now let us dine and take our pleasure, and let there be no shouting, since it is a splendid thing to listen to a singer who is such a singer as this man is, with a voice such as gods have. Then tomorrow let us all go to the place of assembly, and hold a session, where I will give you my forthright statement, that you go out of my palace and do your feasting elsewhere, eating up your own possessions, taking turns, household by household. But if you decide it is more profitable and better to go on, eating up one man's livelihood, without payment, then spoil my house. I will cry out to the gods everlasting in the hope that Zeus might somehow grant a reversal of fortunes. Then you may perish in this house, with no payment given."

The suitors, men from noble families, want Penelope to give Odysseus up for dead and marry one of them so as to preserve dynastic and social stability. Telemachus takes his complaint about them to the Assembly. The suitors threaten to usurp his father's rightful place. As son and heir, it is his duty to resist them.

"I have lost a noble father, one who was king once over you here, and was kind to you like a father; and now here is a greater evil, one which presently will break up the whole house and destroy all my livelihood. For my mother, against her will, is beset by suitors, own sons to the men who are greatest hereabouts. These shrink from making the journey to the house of her father Ikarios, so that he might take bride gifts for his daughter and bestow on her the one he wished, who came as his favorite; rather, all their days, they come and loiter in our house and sacrifice our oxen and our sheep and our fat goats and make a holiday feast of it and drink the bright wine recklessly. Most of our substance is wasted. We have no man here such as Odysseus was, to drive this curse from the household.

"We ourselves are not the men to do it; we must be weaklings in such a case, not men well seasoned in battle. I would defend myself if the power were in me. No longer are the things endurable that have been done, and beyond all decency my house has been destroyed. Even you must be scandalized and ashamed before the neighboring men about us, the people who live around our land; fear also the gods' anger, lest they, astonished by evil actions, turn against you. I supplicate you: by Zeus the Olympian and by Themis who breaks up the assemblies of men and calls them in session; let be, my friends, and leave me alone with my bitter sorrow to waste away; unless my noble father Odysseus at some time in anger did evil to the strong-greaved Achaians, for which angry with me in revenge you do me evil in setting these on me. But for me it would be far better for you to eat away my treasures and eat my cattle. If you were to eat them, there might be a recompense someday, for we could go through all the settlement, with claims made public asking for our goods again, until it was all regiven. But now you are heaping me with troubles I cannot deal with."

So he spoke in anger, and dashed to the ground the scepter in a stormburst of tears; and pity held all the people.

Educating Boys

From Michel de Montaigne, Essays

Don't make a boy "a prisoner to schooling," writes the great sixteenth-century French humanist, by cooping him up all day to learn by rote. Encourage him to relate his learning to life's grandeur and adversities, and let his experience of life and the company of others motivate him to learn more. The test of a boy's education is the goodness, justice, and prudence of his actions.

Let the tutor demand of him an account not only of the words of his lesson, but of their meaning and substance, and let him estimate the profit he has gained, not by the testimony of his memory, but of his life. Let him show what he has just learned from a hundred points of view, and adapt it to as many different subjects, to see if he has yet rightly taken it in and made it his own, taking stock of his progress according to Plato's disciplinary method. It is a sign of crudeness and indigestion to disgorge meat as it has been swallowed. The stomach has not performed its operation, unless it has altered the form and condition of what has been given to it to cook.

Our mind only works on trust, bound and compelled to follow the appetite of another's fancy, a slave and captive to the authority of his teaching. We have been so much subjected to leading-strings, that we no longer have the power of walking freely. Our vigor and liberty are extinct. *They never cease to be under guardianship* (Seneca).

Silence and modesty are very becoming qualities in social intercourse. Our boy will be trained to save and husband his accomplishments, when he has acquired them; not to take exception at the stories and foolish things that may be spoken in his presence, for he is an uncivil and tiresome person who falls foul of everything that is not to his liking. Let him be satisfied with correcting himself, and not to appear to reprove in others all that he declines to do, and be a censor of public morals: *He may be wise without ostentation, without exciting envy* (Seneca). Let him avoid those authoritative and unmannerly airs and that puerile ambition of trying to appear more clever, because he is different, and to gain a reputation for being critical and original. As it is becoming only in great poets to indulge in poetical license, so to assume unconventional priviliges is tolerable only in great and illustrious souls. *If Socrates and Aristippus have failed to observe the rules of good conduct and custom, let him not imagine that he is licensed to do the same; their great and divine merits authorized that liberty* (Cicero).

He shall be taught to enter into no dispute or argument but where he sees a champion worthy to wrestle with, and even then not to employ all the turns that may serve him, but only those that may serve him best. He shall be taught to be particular in choosing and sifting his reasons, to prefer pertinence, and consequently brevity. Instruct him above all to quit his arms and surrender in the face of truth as soon as he perceives it, whether it appears in his opponent's arguments or in his own, through being better advised. For he will not be sitting in a professor's chair to read a prepared lecture.

Let his conscience and his virtue shine forth in his speech, and be guided solely by reason. Make him understand that to confess the error he discovers in his own reasoning, though he himself alone perceive it, is a mark of judgment and honesty, which are the chief qualities he aims at; that obstinacy and contention are vulgar qualities, most apparent in the basest minds; that to correct oneself and change one's mind, and in the heat of ardor to abandon a weak position, is a sign of strong, rare, and philosophical qualities.

Let him be advised, when in company, to have his eyes everywhere, for I have found that the chief places are commonly seized upon by the least capable men, and that greatness of fortune is seldom combined with ability. I have observed that whilst at the high end of a table the conversation has turned upon the beauty of a tapestry or the flavor of a Malmsey wine, many witty things spoken at the other end have been lost to them.

He will sound the depths of every man: a neatherd, a mason, a passing stranger; he should utilize and borrow from each according to his wares, for everything is of use in the household; he will learn something even from the follies and weaknesses of others. By observing the graces and manners of each, he will plant in himself the seeds of emulation of the good, and contempt of the bad.

Suggest to his fancy an honest curiosity that will make him inquire into all things; he should see everything uncommon in his surroundings: a building, a fountain, a man, the scene of an ancient battle, the passage of Caesar or of Charlemagne.

His intercourse with men will comprise, as I understand it, and principally, those who live only in the memory of books. Through the medium of histories he will hold converse with the great souls of the best ages. That is an empty study, if a man list, but also, if a man list, it is a study of inestimable fruit, and the only study, as Plato tells us, that the Lacedaemonians had reserved for their share. What profit will he not reap, to that end, by reading the Lives of our Plutarch? But let my tutor remember the object of his charge, and impress upon his pupil not so much the date of the ruin of Carthage as the character of Hannibal and Scipio, not so much where Marcellus died, as why it was unworthy of his duty to die there. Let him not so much teach him history as to give his opinions on it.

The great world, which some yet multiply as a species under one genus, is the mirror wherein we are to behold ourselves, in order to know ourselves from the right point of view. In a word, I should wish it to be my pupil's book. So many ways of looking at things, so many sects, judgments, opinions, laws and customs, teach us to form a sound estimate of our own, and teach our judgment to discover its own imperfections and its natural feebleness; and that is no small apprenticeship. So many disturbances of State and changes in public fortune instruct us to make no great miracle of our own. So many names, so many victories and conquests buried in oblivion, render ridiculous the hope of eternalizing our name by the capture of half a score of arquebusiers or of a wretched hovel that is only known to those that took it. The pride and arrogance of so many foreign pomps and ceremonies, the inflated majesty of so many courts and grandeurs, assures and fortifies our eyes to bear, without blinking, the brilliance of ours. So many millions of men interred before our time, encourage us to have no fear of finding as good company in the other world; and so with the rest.

The tutor will give him this new lesson: That the grandeur and value of true virtue lies in the facility, the pleasure, and usefulness of its practice: it is so far from being difficult that children as well as men, the simple as well as the subtle, may possess it. The means of attaining it is moderation, not effort. Socrates, her first favorite, consciously abandons effort, to glide toward her by easy and natural stages. She is the nursing-mother of human joys. By making them righteous she makes them pure and certain. By moderating them she keeps them in breath and appetite. By curtailing those she denies, she whets our desire for those she allows, and like a mother abundantly leaves us all that nature requires, even to satiety, if not to lassitude (unless peradventure we mean to say that the regimen that stops the toper before he is drunk, the glutton before he is surfeited, the lecher before he loses his hair, is an enemy to our pleasures). If she misses the happy lot of the vulgar she will escape its consequences; or she will do without them and will invent others, wholly her own, no longer fleeting and unsteady. She can be rich and powerful and learned, and lie on perfumed mattresses. She loves life, she loves beauty and glory and health. But her own particular duty is to know how to use these blessings temperately, and to lose them bravely: a duty much more noble than laborious, without which the whole course of life is unnatural, turbulent, and deformed, and such a life is more really dotted with those dangerous reefs, thickets and monsters.

For all those reasons I would not have this youth kept a prisoner; I would not hand him over to the melancholy humors of a hot-tempered schoolmaster. I would not break his spirit by keeping him, as some others do, to hard labor and the torture for fourteen or fifteen hours a day, like a porter. Nor should I think it well, if, in consequence of a disposition to solitude and melancholy, he were found to be addicted to a too close application to his books, to encourage that tendency in him: that renders them unfit for society and conversation, and diverts them from better occupations. How many men have I not seen in my time dulled by this injudicious avidity for learning! Carneades was so infatuated with it that he had no leisure to comb his hair and pare his nails.

He should not so much say his lesson, as do it. He should repeat it in his actions. We shall see if there is prudence in his enterprises, if there is goodness and justice in his behaviour, if there is judgment and grace in his speaking, manliness in his maladies, soberness in his play, temperance in his pleasures, indifference in his tastes, whether meat, fish, wine, or water, order in his economy.

For the rest, this education is to be conducted with a mild severity, contrary to the usual practice. Instead of making study attractive to children, they only suggest to their minds horrors and cruelties. Away with violence and compulsion! There is nothing to my mind more calculated to deaden and brutalize a generous nature. If you wish him to fear shame and chastisement do not harden him to them. Harden him to sweat and cold, wind and sun, and the dangers that he is to despise; wean him from all effeminacy and delicacy in clothing and bedding, in eating and drinking; accustom him to everything. Let him not be a pretty and namby-pamby youth, but a fresh and sturdy boy. As boy and man I have ever been of this belief and opinion, and am so still in my old age.

But, among other things, I have always disliked the discipline of most of our colleges. They would perhaps have failed less disastrously by inclining to the side of indulgence. It is a regular jail of imprisoned youth. They become undisciplined by being punished before they are so. Go there at lesson time: you will hear nothing but crying and shouting, both of boys under execution and of masters drunk with rage. What a way to arouse an appetite for learning in those tender and timid souls, to drive them to it with a terrifying scowl and hands armed with rods! An iniquitous and pernicious system! Besides that, as Quintilian has very well observed, this imperious authority is attended with dangerous consequences, and especially in the matter of punishment. How much more becomingly would their class-room be strewn with flowers and green boughs, instead of with bloody stumps of birch! I would have pictures of Joy and Gladness, of Flora and the Graces, such as the philosopher Speusippus had in his school. Where their profit is, there let also their recreation be. The viands that are wholesome for children should be sweetened, and the harmful ones made bitter with gall.

The Value of a Fair Fight

From Thomas Hughes,
Tom Brown's School Days

Tom Brown's School Days (1881) is one of the best-loved accounts of how a boy grows into a man by experiencing the trials of homesickness and the rewards of fair play and friendship. Fighting isn't necessarily a bad thing, Tom learns, if you choose the right fight.

Let those young persons who stomachs are not strong, or who think a good set-to with the weapons which God has given us all, an uncivilized, unchristian, or ungentlemanly affair, just skip this chapter at once, for it won't be to their taste.

It was not at all usual in those days for two School-house boys to have a fight. Of course there were exceptions, when some cross-grained hard-headed fellow came up who would never be happy unless he was quarreling with his nearest neighbors, or when there was some class-dispute, between the fifth-form and the fags for instance, which required blood-letting; and a champion was picked out on each side tacitly, who settled the matter by a good hearty mill. But for the most part the constant use of those surest keepers of the peace, the boxing-gloves, kept the School-house boys from fighting one another. Two or three nights in every week the gloves were brought out, either in the hall or fifth-form room; and every boy who was ever likely to fight at all knew all his neighbor's prowess perfectly well, and could tell to a nicety what chance he would have in a stand-up fight with any other boy in the house. But of course no such experience could be gotten as regarded boys in other houses; and as most of the other houses were more or less jealous of the School-house, collisions were frequent.

After all, what would life be without fighting, I should like to know? From the cradle to the grave, fighting, rightly understood, is the business, the real, highest, honestest, business of every son of man. Every one who is worth his salt has his enemies, who must be beaten, be they evil thoughts and habits in himself, or spiritual wickedness in high places, or Russians, or Border-ruffians, or Bill,

Tom, or Harry, who will not let him live his life in quiet till he has thrashed them.

It is no good for Quakers, or any other body of men, to uplift their voices against fighting. Human nature is too strong for them, and they don't follow their own precepts. Every soul of them is doing his own piece of fighting, somehow and somewhere. The world might be a better world without fighting, for anything I know, but it wouldn't be our world; and therefore I am dead against crying peace when there is no peace, and isn't meant to be. I am as sorry as any man to see folk fighting the wrong people and the wrong things, but I'd a deal sooner see them doing that, than that they should have no fight in them.

And now, boys all, three words before we quit the subject. I have put in this chapter on fighting of malice prepense, partly because I want to give you a true picture of what every-day school life was in my time, and not a kid-glove and go-to-meeting coat picture; and partly because of the cant and twaddle that's talked of boxing and fighting with fists now-a-days. Even Thackeray has given in to it; and only a few weeks ago there was some rampant stuff in the *Times* on the subject, in an article on field sports.

Boys will quarrel, and when they quarrel will sometimes fight. Fighting with fists is the natural and English way for English boys to settle their quarrels. What substitute for it is there, or ever was there, amongst any nation under the sun? What would you like to see take its place?

Learn to box, then, as you learn to play cricket and football. Not one of you will be the worse, but very much the better for learning to box well. Should you never have to use it in earnest, there's no exercise in the world so good for the temper, and for the muscles of the back legs.

As to fighting, keep out of it if you can, by all means. When the time comes, if it ever should, that you have to say "Yes" or "No" to a challenge to fight, say, "No" if you can—only take care you make it clear to yourselves why you say "No." It's a proof of the highest courage, if done from true Christian motives. It's quite right and justifiable, if done from a simple aversion to physical pain and danger. But don't say "No" because you fear a licking, and say or think it's because you fear God, for that's neither Christian nor honest. And if you do fight, fight it out; and don't give in while you can stand and see.

Telemachus Finds His Father

From Homer, The Odyssey

*As he begins his journey in search of his father, Athena guides Telemachus
to some of the legendary figures from the Trojan War—Nestor, Menelaos,
and Helen, all of whom knew and admired Odysseus. Hearing them talk
about his father, Telemachus absorbs the heritage of the* Iliad *and lessons of
war that his father would otherwise have imparted to him.*

Telemachus stepped out of the ship, but Athene went first,
and it was the gray-eyed goddess Athene who first spoke to him:

"Telemachus, there is no more need at all of modesty; for this
was why you sailed on the open sea, to find news of your father,
what soil covers him, what fate he has met with. So come now, go
straight up to Nestor, breaker of horses, for we know what intelligence is hidden inside him. You yourself must entreat him to speak
the whole truth to you. He will not tell you any falsehood; he is too
thoughtful."

Then the thoughtful Telemachus said to her in answer:

"Mentor, how shall I go up to him, how close with him? I have
no experience in close discourse. There is embarrassment for a
young man who must question his elder."

Then in turn the gray-eyed goddess Athene answered him:

"Telemachus, some of it you yourself will see in your own
heart, and some the divinity will put in your mind. I do not think
you could have been born and reared without the gods' will."

*Menelaos laments the many men who died in the Trojan War, and especial-
ly the unknown fate of Odysseus.*

"But for none of all these, sorry as I am, do I grieve so much as
for one, who makes hateful for me my food and my sleep, when I
remember, since no one of the Achaians labored as much as
Odysseus labored and achieved, and for him the end was grief for
him, and for me a sorrow that is never forgotten for his sake, how
he is gone so long, and we knew nothing of whether he is alive or
dead. The aged Laertes and temperate Penelope must surely be

grieving for him, with Telemachus whom he left behind in his house, a young child."

He spoke, and stirred in Telemachus the longing to weep for his father, and the tears fell from his eyes to the ground when he heard his father's name, holding with both hands the robe that was stained with purple up before his eyes. And Menelaos perceived it, and how he pondered two ways within, in mind and in spirit whether he would leave it to him to name his father, or whether he should speak first and ask and inquire about everything.

While he was pondering these things in his heart and his spirit, Helen came out of her fragrant high-roofed bedchamber, looking like Artemis of the golden distaff. At once she spoke to her husband and questioned him about everything:

"Do we know, Menelaos beloved of Zeus, who these men announce themselves as being, who have come into our house now? Shall I be wrong, or am I speaking the truth? My heart tells me to speak, for I think I never saw such a likeness, neither in man nor woman, and wonder takes me as I look on him, as this man has a likeness to the son of the great-hearted Odysseus, Telemachus, who was left behind in his house, a young child by that man when, for the sake of shameless me, the Achaians went beneath Troy, their hearts intent upon reckless warfare."

Then in answer fair-haired Menelaos said to her:

"I also see it thus, my wife, the way you compare them, for Odysseus's feet were like this man's, his hands were like this, and the glances of his eyes and his head and the hair growing. Now too I was remembering things about Odysseus and spoke of him, what misery he had in his hard work for me; and he let fall a heavy tear from under his eyelids, holding before his eyes the robe that was stained with purple."

Then the thoughtful Telemachus said to him in answer:

"Great Menelaos, son of Atreus, leader of the people, I have come to see if you could tell me some news of my father, for my home is being eaten away, the rich fields are ruined, and the house is full of hateful men, who now forever slaughter my crowding sheep and lumbering horn-curved cattle, these suitors of my mother, overbearing in their rapacity. That is why I come to your knees now, in case you might wish to tell me of his dismal destruction, whether you saw it perhaps with your own eyes, or heard the tale from another who wandered too. His mother bore this man to be wretched. Do not soften it because you pity me and are sorry for me, but fairly tell me all that your eyes have witnessed. I implore you, if ever noble Odysseus, my father, undertook any kind of word or work and fulfilled it for you, in the land of the Trojans where all you Achaians suffered, tell me these things from your memory. And tell me the whole truth."

Then deeply angered fair-haired Menelaos said to him:

"Oh for shame, it was in the bed of a bold and strong man they wished to lie, they themselves being all unwarlike. As when a doe has brought her fawns to the lair of a lion and put them there to sleep, they are newborn and still suckling, then wanders out into the foothills and the grassy corners, grazing there, but now the lion comes back to his own lair and visits a shameful destruction on both mother and children; so Odysseus will visit shameful destruction on these men."

At first, Telemachus cannot believe his eyes when he finally sees his father back home. Then they fall into each other's arms weeping, man and boy reunited at last. Through the lessons of his travels and trials, as guided by Athena, Telemachus knows he has proven himself worthy of his long-lost father, an ideal he carried around in his heart during every moment of his journey.

"Son of Laertes and seed of Zeus, resourceful Odysseus, it is time now to tell your son the story; no longer hide it, so that, contriving death and doom for the suitors, you may go to the glorious city. I myself shall not be long absent from you in my eagerness for the fighting."

So spoke Athene, and with her golden wand she tapped him. First she made the mantle and the tunic that covered his chest turn bright and clean; she increased his strength and stature. His dark color came back to him again, his jaws firmed, and the beard that grew about his chin turned black. Athene went away once more, having done her work, but Odysseus went back into the shelter. His beloved son was astonished and turned his eyes in the other direction, fearing this must be a god, and spoke aloud to him and addressed him in winged words:

"Suddenly you have changed, my friend, from what you were formerly; your skin is no longer as it was, you have other clothing. Surely you are one of the gods who hold the high heaven. Be gracious, then: so we shall give you favored offerings and golden gifts that have been well wrought. Only be merciful."

Then in turn long-suffering great Odysseus answered him:

"No I am not a god. Why liken me to the immortals? But I am

your father, for whose sake you are always grieving as you look for violence from others, and endure hardships."

So he spoke, and kissed his son, and the tears running down his cheeks splashed on the ground. Until now, he was always unyielding. But Telemachus, for he did not yet believe that this was his father, spoke to him once again in answer, saying:

"No, you are not Odysseus my father, but some divinity beguiles me, so that I must grieve the more and be sorry. For no man who was mortal could ever have so contrived it by his own mind alone, not unless some immortal, descending on him in person, were likely to make him a young or an old man. For even now you were an old man in unseemly clothing, but now you resemble one of the gods who hold wide heaven."

Then resourceful Odysseus spoke in turn and answered him:

"Telemachus, it does not become you to wonder too much at your own father when he is here, nor doubt him. No other Odysseus than I will ever come back to you. But here I am, and I am as you see me, and after hardships and suffering much I have come, in the twentieth year, back to my own country. But here you see the work of Athene, the giver of plunder, who turns me into whatever she pleases, since she can do this; and now she will make me look like a beggar, but then the next time like a young man, and wearing splendid clothes on my body; and it is a light thing for the gods who hold wide heaven to glorify any mortal man, or else to degrade him."

So he spoke, and sat down again, but now Telemachus folded his great father in his arms and lamented, shedding tears, and desire for mourning rose in both of them; and they cried shrill in a pulsing voice, even more than the outcry of birds.

The New Kid in Town

From Mark Twain,
The Adventures of Tom Sawyer

Writing as Mark Twain, Samuel Clemens (1835–1910) chronicles life in
rural and frontier America with gentle humor and irony.

A new-comer of any age or either sex was an impressive curiosity in the poor little shabby village of St. Petersburg. This boy was
well dressed, too—well dressed on a week-day. This was simply
astounding. His cap was a dainty thing, his close buttoned blue
cloth roundabout was new and natty, and so were his pantaloons.
He had shoes on—and it was only Friday. He even wore a necktie, a
bright bit of ribbon. He had a citified air about him that ate into
Tom's vitals. The more Tom stared at the splendid marvel, the
higher he turned up his nose at his finery and the shabbier and
shabbier his own outfit seemed to him to grow. Neither boy spoke.
If one moved, the other moved—but only sidewise, in a circle; they
kept face to face and eye to eye all the time. Finally Tom said:
"I can lick you!"
"I'd like to see you try it."
"Well, I can do it."
"No, you can't, either."
"Yes I can."
"No you can't."
"I can."
"You can't."
"Can!"
"Can't!"
An uncomfortable pause. Then Tom said:
"What's your name?"
"'Tisn't any of your business, maybe."
"Well I 'low I'll *make* it my business."
"Well why don't you?"
"If you say much, I will."
"Much—much—*much*. There now."
"Oh, you think you're mighty smart, *don't* you?

"I could lick you with one hand tied behind me, if I wanted to."

"Well why don't you *do* it? You *say* you can do it."

"Well I *will*, if you fool with me."

"Oh yes—I've seen whole families in the same fix."

"Smarty! You think you're *some*, now, *don't* you? Oh, what a hat!"

"You can lump that hat if you don't like it. I dare you to knock it off—and anybody that'll take a dare will suck eggs."

"You're a liar!"

"You're another."

"You're a fighting liar and dasn't take it up."

"Aw—take a walk!"

"Say—if you give me much more of your sass I'll take and bounce a rock off'n your head."

"Oh, of *course* you will."

"Well I *will*."

"Why don't you *do* it then? What do you keep *saying* you will for? Why don't you *do* it? It's because you're afraid."

"I ain't afraid."

"You are."

"I ain't."

"You are."

Another pause, and more eying and sidling around each other. Presently they were shoulder to shoulder. Tom said:

"Get away from here!"

"Go away yourself!"

"I won't."

"*I* won't either."

So they stood, each with a foot placed at an angle as a brace, and both shoving with might and main, and glowering at each other with hate. But neither could get an advantage. After struggling till both were hot and flushed, each relaxed his strain with watchful caution, and Tom said:

"You're a coward and a pup. I'll tell my big brother on you, and he can thrash you with his little finger, and I'll make him do it, too."

"What do I care for your big brother? I've got a brother that's bigger than he is—and what's more, he can throw him over that fence, too."

(Both brothers were imaginary.)

"That's a lie."

"*Your* saying so don't make it so."

Tom drew a line in the dust with his big toe, and said:

"I dare you to step over that, and I'll lick you till you can't stand up. Anybody that'll take a dare will steal sheep."

The new boy stepped over promptly, and said:

"Now you said you'd do it, now let's see you do it."

"Don't you crowd me now; you better look out."

"Well, you *said* you'd do it—why don't you do it?"

"By jingo! For two cents I *will* do it."

The new boy took two broad coppers out of his pocket and held them out with derision. Tom struck them to the ground. In an instant both boys were rolling and tumbling in the dirt, gripped together like cats; and for the space of a minute they tugged and tore at each other's hair and clothes, punched and scratched each other's noses, and covered themselves with dust and glory. Presently the confusion took form and through the fog of battle Tom appeared, seated astride the new boy, and pounding him with his fists.

"Holler 'nuff!" said he.

The boy only struggled to free himself. He was crying—mainly from rage.

"Holler 'nuff!"—and the pounding went on.

At last the stranger got out a smothered "'Nuff!" and Tom let him up and said:

"Now that'll learn you. Better look out who you're fooling with next time."

The new boy went off brushing the dust from his clothes, sobbing, snuffling and occasionally looking back and shaking his head and threatening what he would do to Tom the "next time he caught him out." To which Tom responded with jeers, and started off in high feather, and as soon as his back was turned the new boy snatched up a stone, threw it and hit him between the shoulders and then turned tail and ran like an antelope. Tom chased the traitor home, and thus found out where he lived. He then held a position at the gate for some time, daring the enemy to come outside, but the enemy only made faces at him through the window and declined. At last the enemy's mother appeared, and called Tom a bad, vicious, vulgar child, and ordered him away. So he went away, but he said he "'lowed" to "lay" for that boy.

He got home pretty late, that night, and when he climbed cautiously in at the window, he uncovered an ambuscade, in the person of his aunt; and when she saw the state his clothes were in her resolution to turn his Saturday holiday into captivity at hard labor became adamantine in its firmness.

The Education of Cyrus

From Xenophon, The Education of Cyrus

The classical ideal of manhood called for a lifelong commitment to moral and intellectual education. One of the most famous accounts comes to us from Xenophon's Education of Cyrus, *an idealized account of the life of Cyrus the Great. In the Persian Republic, the boys were educated throughout all the stages of childhood and youth to prefer the common good to their own selfish desires. Xenophon says that special care must be taken during adolescence to teach boys self-control and keep them occupied all day long with their duties and games—"for this time of life, it seems, demands the most watchful care."*

He was educated in conformity with the laws of the Persians; and these laws appear in their care for the common weal not to start from the same point as they do in most states. For most states permit everyone to train his own children just as he will, and the older people themselves to live as they please; and then they command them not to steal and not to rob, not to break into anybody's house, not to strike a person whom they have no right to strike, not to commit adultery, not to disobey an officer, and so forth; and if a man transgress any one of these laws, they punish him. The Persian laws, however, begin at the beginning and take care that from the first their citizens shall not be of such a character as ever to desire anything improper or immoral; and the measures they take are as follows.

They have their so-called "Free Square," where the royal palace and other government buildings are located. The hucksters with their wares, their cries, and their vulgarities are excluded from this and relegated to another part of the city, in order that their tumult may not intrude upon the orderly life of the cultured. This square, enclosing the government buildings, is divided into four parts; one of these belongs to the boys, one to the youths, another to the men of mature years, and another to those who are past the age for military service. And the laws require them to come daily to their several quarters—the boys and the full-grown men at daybreak; but the elders may come at whatever time it suits each one's convenience, except that they must present themselves on certain specified days. But the youths pass the night also in light armor about the government buildings—all except those who are married; no inquiry is made for such, unless they be especially ordered in advance to be there, but it is not proper for them to be absent too often.

Over each of these divisions there are twelve officers, for the Persians are divided into twelve tribes. To have charge of the boys, such are chosen from the ranks of the elders as seem likely to make out of the boys the best men; to have charge of the youths, such are chosen from the ranks of the mature men as seem most likely on their part to develop the youths best; to preside over the mature men, those are selected who seem most likely to fit them best to execute the orders and requirements of the highest authorities; and of the elders also chiefs are selected who act as overseers to see that those of this class also do their duty. And what duties are assigned to each age to perform we shall now set forth, that it may be better understood what pains the Persians take that their citizens may prove to be the very best.

The boys go to school and spend their time in learning justice; and they say that they go there for this purpose; just as in our country they say that they go to learn to read and write. And their officers spend the greater part of the day in deciding cases for them. For, as a matter of course, boys also prefer charges against one another, just as men do, of theft, robbery, assault, cheating, slander, and other things that might naturally come up; and when they discover anyone committing any of these crimes they punish him; and they punish also anyone whom they find accusing another falsely. And they bring one another to trial also charged with an offense for which people hate one another most but go to law least, namely, that of ingratitude; and if they know that anyone is able to return a favor and fails to do so, they punish him also severely. For they think that the ungrateful are likely to be most neglectful of their duty toward their gods, their parents, their country, and their friends; for it seems that shamelessness goes hand in hand with ingratitude; and it is that, we know, which leads the way to every moral wrong.

They teach the boys self-control also; and it greatly conduces to their learning self-control that they see their elders also living temperately day by day. And they teach them likewise to obey the officers; and it greatly conduces to this also that they see their elders implicitly obeying their officers. And besides, they teach them self-restraint in eating and drinking; and it greatly conduces to this also that they see that their elders do not leave their posts to satisfy their hunger until the officers dismiss them; and the same end is promoted by the fact that the boys do not eat with their mothers but with their teachers, from the time the officers so direct. Furthermore, they bring from home bread for their food, cress for a relish, and for drinking, if any one is thirsty, a cup to draw water from the river. Besides this, they learn to shoot and to throw the spear.

This, then, is what the boys do until they are sixteen or seventeen years of age, and after this they are promoted from the class of boys and enrolled among the young men.

Now the young men in their turn live as follows: for ten years after they are promoted from the class of boys they pass the nights, as we said before, about the government buildings. This they do for the sake of guarding the city and of developing their powers of self-control; for this time of life, it seems, demands the most watchful care.

And when they have completed the five-and-twenty years, they are, as one would expect, somewhat more than fifty years of age; and then they come out and take their places among those who really are, as they are called, the "elders."

Now these elders, in their turn, no longer perform military service outside their own country, but they remain at home and try all sorts of cases, both public and private. They try people indicted for capital offenses also, and they elect all the officers. And if anyone, either among the youths or among the mature men, fail in any one of the duties prescribed by law, the respective officers of that division, or anyone else who will, may enter complaint, and the elders, when they have heard the case, expel the guilty party; and the one who has been expelled spends the rest of his life degraded and disfranchised.

An Early Critic of Rock Music?

From Jacopo Sadoleto,
On the Education of Boys

Born in 1477, this Renaissance humanist wrote an influential dialogue on educating boys.

What correctness or beauty can the music which is now in vogue possess? It has scarcely any real and stable foundation in word or thought. If it should have for its subject a maxim or proverb, it would obscure and hamper the sense and meaning by abruptly cutting and jerking the sounds in the throat—as though music were designed not to soothe and control the spirit, but merely to afford a base pleasure to the ears, mimicking the cries of birds and beasts, which we should be sorry to resemble. This is to turn soul into body, and weaken self-control. From this Plato most properly shrank in horror, and refused a place in his ideal state for such music as this. For when flaccid, feeble, sensual ideas are rendered in similar music, in kindred modulation of the voice, weakly yielding to lust, languishing in grief, or rushing in frenzied agitation toward the sudden passions of a disordered mind, what ruin to virtue, what wreckage of character, do you suppose, must ensue?

Bringing Up a Prince

From Desiderius Erasmus,
The Education of a Christian Prince

In this celebrated treatise, the Renaissance philosopher and man of letters stresses the importance of instilling good habits in a boy from the earliest age—especially when he is destined to rule a Kingdom.

There is no better time to shape and improve a prince than when he does not yet realize himself a prince. This time must be diligently employed, not only to the end that for a while he may be kept away from base associations, but also that he may be imbued with certain definite moral principles. If diligent parents raise with great care a boy who is destined to inherit only an acre or two, think how much interest and concern should be given to the education of one who will succeed not to a single dwelling, but to so many peoples, to so many cities, yea, to the world, either as a good man for the common gain of all, or an evil one, to the great ruination of all! It is a great and glorious thing to rule an empire well, but none-the-less glorious to pass it on to no worse a ruler: nay, rather it is the main task of a good prince to see that he does not become a bad one. So conduct your rule as if this were your aim: "My equal shall never succeed me!" In the meantime, raise your children for future rule as if it were your desire to be succeeded by a better prince. There can be no more splendid commendation of a worthy prince than to say that he left such a successor to the state, that he himself seemed average by comparison. His own glory cannot be more truly shown than to be so obscured. The worst possible praise is that a ruler who was intolerable during his life is longingly missed as a good and beneficial prince each time a worse man ascends the throne.

He should not be allowed to associate with whatever playmates appear, but only with those boys of good and modest character; he should be reared and trained most carefully and as becomes a gentleman. That whole crowd of wantons, hard drinkers, filthy-tongued fellows, especially flatterers, must be kept far from his sight and hearing while his mind is not yet fortified with precepts to the contrary. Since the natures of so many men are inclined toward the ways of evil, there is no nature so happily born that it cannot be corrupted by wrong training. What do you expect except a great fund of evil in a prince, who, regardless, of his native character (and a long line of ancestors does not necessarily furnish a mind, as it does a kingdom), is beset from his very cradle by the most inane opinions; is raised in the circle of senseless women; grows to boyhood among naughty girls, abandoned playfellows, and the most abject flatterers, among buffoons and mimes, drinkers and gamesters, and worse than stupid and worthless creators of wanton pleasures. In the company of all these he hears nothing, learns nothing, absorbs nothing except pleasures, amusements, arrogance, haughtiness, greed, petulance, and tyranny—

and from this school he will soon progress to the government of his kingdom! Although each one of all the great arts is very difficult, there is none finer nor more difficult than that of ruling well. Why in the case of this one thing alone do we feel the need of no training, but deem it sufficient to have been born for it? To what end except tyranny do they devote themselves as men, who as boys played at nothing except as tyrants?

The teacher, into whose care the state has given its prince, shall give much careful thought to discover his leanings. Sometimes, too, at this early age it can be discovered by certain signs whether the prince is more prone to petulance or arrogance, to a desire for popularity or a thirst for fame, to licentiousness or dicing or greed, to defense or war, to rashness or tyranny. When he has found the prince's weak spot, there he should strengthen him with goodly doctrines and suitable teachings and try to lead into better ways a spirit still prone to follow. On the other hand, if he finds a nature prone to the good things of life, or at any rate to only those vices which are readily turned to virtue, e.g., ambition and prodigality, he should work the harder and assist advantages of nature with refinement. It is not enough just to hand out precepts to restrain the prince from vices or to incite him to a better course—they must be impressed, crammed in, inculcated, and in one way and another be kept before him, now by a suggestive thought, now by a fable, now by analogy, now by example, now by maxims, now by a proverb. They should be engraved on rings, painted on pictures, appended to the wreaths of honor, and, by using any other means by which that age can be interested, kept always before him. The deeds of famous men fire the minds of noble youths, but the opinions with which they become imbued is a matter of far greater importance, for from these sources the whole scheme of life is developed. In the case of a mere boy, we must immediately be on guard, to see that he gets only the virtuous and helpful ideas and that he be fortified as by certain efficacious drugs against the poisoned opinions of the common people. But if the prince happens to be somewhat tinged with the thoughts of the common people, then the first effort must be to rid him of them little by little, to weed out the seeds of trouble and replace them by wholesome ones.

Those shores which receive the severest pounding of the waves we are wont to bulwark most carefully. Now there are countless things which can turn the minds of princes from the true course— great fortune, worldly wealth in abundance, the pleasures of luxurious extravagance, freedom to do anything they please, the precedents of great but foolish princes, the storms and turmoils of human affairs themselves, and above all else, flattery, spoken in the guise of faith and frankness. On this account must the prince be the more sincerely strengthened with the best of principles and the precedents of praiseworthy princes.

When the little fellow has listened with pleasure to Aesop's fable of the lion and the mouse or of the dove and the ant, and when he has finished his laugh, then the teacher should point out the *new* moral: the first fable teaches the prince to despise no one, but to seek zealously to win to himself by kindnesses the heart of even the lowest peasant (*plebs*), for no one is so weak but that on occasion he may be a friend to help you. Or an enemy to harm you, even though you be the most powerful. When he has had his fun out of the eagle, queen of the birds, that was almost completely done for by the beetle, the teacher should again point out the meaning: not even the most powerful prince can afford to provoke or overlook even the humblest enemy. Often those who can inflict no harm by physical strength can do much by the machinations of their minds. When he has learned with pleasure the story of Phaeton, the teacher should show that he represents a prince, who while still headstrong with the ardor of youth, but with no supporting wisdom, seized the reins of government and turned everything into ruin for himself and the whole world. When he has finished the story of the Cyclops who was blinded by Ulysses, the teacher should say in conclusion that the prince who has great strength of body, but not of mind, is like Polyphemus.

What is more stupid than to judge a prince on the following accomplishments: his ability to dance gracefully, dice expertly, drink with a gusto, swell with pride, plunder the people with kingly grandeur, and do all the other things which I am ashamed even to mention, although there are plenty who are not ashamed to do them? The common run of princes zealously avoid the dress and manner of living of the lower classes. Just so should the true prince be removed from the sullied opinions and desires of the common folk. The one thing which he should consider base, vile, and unbecoming to him is to share the opinions of the common people who never are interested in anything worthwhile. How ridiculous it is for one adorned with gems, gold, the royal purple, attended by courtiers, possessing all the other marks of honor, wax images and statues, wealth that clearly is not his, to be so far superior to all because of them, and yet in the light of real goodness of spirit to be found inferior to many born from the very dregs of society.

The boy should be instructed to turn to his own advantage those titles to which he is forced to listen. He hears (himself called) "Father of his Country": let him think that no title could ever be given to princes which more perfectly accords (with the nature of) a good prince than does that of "Father of his Country." He must then act in such a way as to appear worthy of that title. If he thinks of it in that way, it will be a warning; but if he takes it otherwise, it will be fawning adulation.

If the prince is called "The unconquerable," let him think how ridiculous it is for one to be called unconquerable who is conquered by wrath, who daily is a slave to passion, and whom ambition pulls and leads as a captive whither she will. He is truly unconquerable who gives way to no passion and under no pretext can be deflected from the course of honor.

The first matter is the selection of authors, for the sort of books the boy first reads and absorbs is of prime importance. Wicked conversations ruin the mind, and in no less a degree do wicked books. Those mute letters are transformed into manners and moods, especially if they come upon a native character that is prone to some weakness. A boy that is wild and impetuous by nature would easily be incited to tyranny, if without forewarning he should read about Achilles, Alexander the Great, Xerxes, or Julius Caesar. But today we see many a one taking delight in the tales of Arthur and Lancelot, and other tales of similar nature which are not only about tyrants but are also very poorly done, stupid, and fit to be "old wives' tales," so that it would be more advisable to put in one's time, reading the comedies or the legends of the poets instead of nonsense of that sort. But if any should desire to make use of my plan, as soon as the elements of language have been taught, he should set forth the *Proverbs* of Solomon, *Ecclesiasticus,* and the *Book of Wisdom,* not with the idea that the boy may be tormented with the four senses of the theologian by a vaunting interpreter, but that he may fitly show in a few words whatever pertains to the functions of a good prince. First a love for the author and his work must be inculcated. You are destined to rule, he (the author) explains the art of ruling. You are the son of a king, yourself a future king you will hear what the wisest king of all teaches his own son, whom he is preparing to be his successor. Later take the Gospels. There the means by which the spirit of the boy is kindled with a love for the writer and his work is of great importance, for no small part will depend upon the cleverness and opportunism of the one interpreting, to explain briefly, clearly, plausibly, and vividly,

not everything, but just those points which have most to do with the
office of the prince and those that will cause (the young prince) to
rid his mind of the undermining ideas common to the general run
of princes. In the third place, read the *Apophthegmata* of Plutarch
and then his *Morals*, for nothing can be found purer than these
works. I should also prefer his *Lives* to those of anyone else. After
Plutarch, I would readily assign the next place to Seneca, whose
writings are wonderfully stimulating and excite one to enthusiasm
for (a life of) moral integrity, raise the mind of the reader from sordid cares, and especially decry tyranny everywhere. From the *Politics* of Aristotle and from the *Offices* of Cicero many passages that
are worth knowing can well be culled out. But Plato is the most venerable source of such things—in my opinion at least.

Now I shall not deny that a great fund of wisdom may be gathered from reading the historians, but you will also draw out the
very essence of destruction from these same sources unless you are
forearmed and read with discretion. Be on guard lest the names of
writers and leaders celebrated by the approval of centuries deceive
you. Herodotus and Xenophon were both pagans and often set
forth the worst types of prince, even if they did write history, the
one to give pleasure through his narrative, the other to show the
picture of an exceptional leader. Sallust and Livy tell us many
things very clearly and everything very learnedly to be sure, but
they do not weigh all that they tell, and they approve some things
which are by no means to be approved for a Christian prince.
When you hear about Achilles, Xerxes, Cyrus, Darius, and Julius
Caesar, do not be carried away and deluded by the great names.
You are hearing about raging robbers, for that is what Seneca has
called them on various occasions.

A prince who is about to assume control of the state must be
advised at once that the main hope of a state lies in the proper education of its youth. This Xenophon wisely taught in his *Cyropaedia*.
Pliable youth is amenable to any system of training.

The Lion and the Mouse

Aesop

Recommended reading by Erasmus for a boy Prince. The Fables *are traditionally ascribed to Aesop, a Greek slave in the 6th century* B.C.

A Lion was awakened from sleep by a Mouse running over his face. Rising up in anger, he caught him and was about to kill him, when the Mouse piteously entreated, saying: "If you would only spare my life, I would be sure to repay your kindness." The Lion laughed and let him go. It happened shortly after this that the Lion was caught by some hunters, who bound him by strong ropes to the ground. The Mouse, recognizing his roar, came up, and gnawed the rope with his teeth, and setting him free, exclaimed: "You ridiculed the idea of my ever being able to help you, not expecting to receive from me any repayment of your favor; but now you know that it is possible for even a Mouse to confer benefits on a Lion."

It Is Held That Schools Corrupt the Morals

From Quintillian, On Public and Private Instruction

Marcus Fabius Quintillianus (born around 35 A.D.) was a celebrated professor of rhetoric, attorney, and personal tutor of the Emperor Domitian's great-nephews. His reflections on educating boys are remarkable for their level-headed and sympathetic understanding.

It is held that schools corrupt the morals. It is true that this is sometimes the case. But morals may be corrupted at home as well. There are numerous instances of both, as there are also of the preservation of a good reputation under either circumstance. The nature of the individual boy and the care devoted to his education make all the difference. Given a natural bent toward evil or negligence in developing and watching over modest behavior in early years, privacy will provide equal opportunity for sin. The teacher employed at home may be of bad character, and there is just as much danger in associating with bad slaves as there is with immodest companions of good birth. On the other hand if the natural bent be towards virtue, and parents are not afflicted with a blind and torpid indifference, it is possible to choose a teacher of the highest character (and those who are wise will make this their first object), to adopt a method of education of the strictest kind and at the same time to attach some respectable man or faithful freedman to their son as his friend and guardian, that his unfailing companionship may improve the character even of those who gave rise to apprehension.

Yet how easy were the remedy for such fears. Would that we did not too often ruin our children's character ourselves! We spoil them from the cradle. That soft upbringing, which we call kindness, saps all the sinews both of mind and body. If the child crawls on purple, what will he not desire when he comes to manhood? Before he can talk he can distinguish scarlet and cries for the very best brand of purple. We train their palates before we teach their lips to speak. They grow up in litters: if they set foot to earth, they are supported by the hands of attendants on either side. We rejoice if they say something impudent, and words which we should not tolerate from the lips even of an Alexandrian page are greeted with laughter and a kiss. We have no right to be surprised. It was we that taught them: they hear us use such words, they see our mistresses and minions; every dinner party is loud with foul songs, and things are presented to their eyes of which we should blush to speak. Hence springs habit, and habit in time becomes second nature. The poor children learn these things before they know them to be wrong. They become luxurious and effeminate, and far from acquiring such vices at schools, introduce them into the schools themselves.

I now turn to the objection that one master can give more attention to one pupil. In the first place there is nothing to prevent the principle of "one teacher, one boy" being combined with school education. And even if such a combination should prove impossible, I should still prefer the broad daylight of a respectable school to the solitude and obscurity of a private education. For all the best teachers pride themselves on having a large number of

pupils and think themselves worthy of a bigger audience. On the
other hand, in the case of inferior teachers a consciousness of their
own defects not seldom reconciles them to being attached to a single pupil and playing the part—for it amounts to little more—of a
mere baby-sitter.

But let us assume that influence, money or friendship succeed
in securing a paragon of learning to teach the boy at home. Will he
be able to devote the whole day to one pupil? Or can we demand
such continuous attention on the part of the learner? The mind is
as easily tired as the eye, if given no relaxation. Moreover by far the
larger proportion of the learner's time ought to be devoted to private study. The teacher does not stand over him while he is writing
or thinking or learning by heart. While he is so occupied the intervention of anyone, whoever he may be, is a hindrance. Further, not
all reading requires to be first read aloud or interpreted by a master. If it did, how would the boy ever become acquainted with all
the authors required of him? A small time only is required to give
purpose and direction to the day's work, and consequently individual instruction can be given to more than one pupil. There are
moreover a large number of subjects in which it is desirable that
instruction should be given to all the pupils simultaneously. I say
nothing of the analyses and declamations of the professors of
rhetoric: in such cases there is no limit to the number of the audience, as each individual pupil will in any case receive full value.
The voice of a lecturer is not like a dinner which will only suffice
for a limited number; it is like the sun which distributes the same
quantity of light and heat to all of us. So too with the teacher of literature. Whether he speak of style or expound disputed passages,
explain stories or paraphrase poems, everyone who hears him will
profit by his teaching. But, it will be urged, a large class is unsuitable for the correction of faults or for explanation. It may be inconvenient: one cannot hope for absolute perfection; but I shall shortly contrast the inconvenience with the obvious advantages.

Still I do not wish a boy to be sent where he will be neglected.
But a good teacher will not burden himself with a larger number
of pupils than he can manage, and it is further of the very first
importance that he should be on friendly and intimate terms with
us and make his teaching not a duty but a labor of love. Then there
will never be any question of being swamped by the number of our
fellow-learners. Moreover any teacher who has the least tincture of
literary culture will devote special attention to any boy who shows
signs of industry and talent; for such a pupil will redound to his

own credit. But even if large schools are to be avoided, a proposition from which I must dissent if the size be due to the excellence
of the teacher, it does not follow that all schools are to be avoided.
It is one thing to avoid them, another to select the best.

Having refuted these objections, let me now explain my own
views. It is above all things necessary that our future public speaker,
who will have to live in the utmost publicity and in the broad daylight of public life, should become accustomed from his childhood
to move in society without fear and habituated to a life far removed
from that of the pale student, the solitary and recluse. His mind
requires constant stimulus and excitement, whereas retirement
such as has just been mentioned induces languor and the mind
becomes mildewed like things that are left in the dark, or else flies
to the opposite extreme and becomes puffed up with empty conceit; for he who has no standard of comparison by which to judge
his own powers will necessarily rate them too high. Again when the
fruits of his study have to be displayed to the public gaze, our
recluse is blinded by the sun's glare, and finds everything new and
unfamiliar, for though he has learnt what is required to be done in
public, his learning is but the theory of a hermit. I say nothing of
friendships which endure unbroken to old age having acquired the
binding force of a sacred duty: for initiation in the same studies has
all the sanctity of initiation in the same mysteries of religion. And
where shall he acquire that instinct which we call common feeling,
if he secludes himself from that intercourse which is natural not
merely to mankind but even to dumb animals?

Further, at home he can only learn what is taught to himself,
while at school he will learn what is taught others as well. He will
hear many merits praised and many faults corrected every day: he
will derive equal profit from hearing the indolence of a comrade
rebuked or his industry commended. Such praise will incite him to
emulation, he will think it a disgrace to be outdone by his contemporaries and a distinction to surpass his seniors. All such incentives
provide a valuable stimulus, and though ambition may be a fault in
itself, it is often the mother of virtues. I remember that my own
master had a practice which was not without advantages. Having
distributed the boys in classes, they made the order in which they
were to speak depend on their ability, so that the boy who had
made most progress in his studies had the privilege of declaiming
first. The performances on these occasions were criticized. To win
commendation was a tremendous honor, but the prize most eagerly coveted was to be the leader of the class. Such a position was not

permanent. Once a month the defeated competitors were given a fresh opportunity of competing for the prize. Consequently, success did not lead the victor to relax his efforts, while the vexation caused by defeat served as an incentive to wipe out the disgrace. I will venture to assert that to the best of my memory this practice did more to kindle our oratorical ambitions then all the exhortations of our instructors, the watchfulness of our teachers and the prayers of our parents. Further, while emulation promotes progress in the more advanced pupils, beginners who are still of tender years derive greater pleasure from imitating their comrades than their masters, just because it is easier. For children still in the elementary stages of education can scarcely hope to reach that complete eloquence which they understand to be their goal: their ambition will not soar so high, but they will imitate the vine which has to grasp the lower branches of the tree on which it is trained before it can reach the topmost boughs. So true is this that it is the master's duty as well, if he is engaged on the task of training unformed minds and prefers practical utility to a more ambitious programme, not to burden his pupils at once with tasks to which their strength is unequal, but to curb his energies and refrain from talking over the heads of his audience. Vessels with narrow mouths will not receive liquids if too much be poured into them at a time, but are easily filled if the liquid is admitted in a gentle stream or, it may be, drop by drop; similarly you must consider how much a child's mind is capable of receiving: the things which are beyond their grasp will not enter their minds, which have not opened out sufficiently to take them in. It is a good thing therefore that a boy should have companions whom he will desire first to imitate and then to surpass: thus he will be led to aspire to higher achievement. I would add that the instructors themselves cannot develop the same intelligence and energy before a single listener as they can when inspired by the presence of a numerous audience.

For eloquence depends in the main on the state of the mind, which must be moved, conceive images and adapt itself to suit the nature of the subject which is the theme of speech. Further, the loftier and the more elevated the mind, the more powerful will be the forces which move it: consequently praise gives it growth and effort increase, and the thought that it is doing something great fills it with joy. The duty of stooping to expend that power of speaking which has been acquired at the cost of such effort upon an audience of one gives rise to a silent feeling of disdain, and the teacher is ashamed to raise his voice above the ordinary conversa-

tional level. Imagine the air of a declaimer, or the voice of an orator, his gait, his delivery, the movements of his body, the emotions
of his mind, and, to go no further, the fatigue of his exertions, all
for the sake of one listener! Would he not seem little less than a
lunatic? No, there would be no such thing as eloquence, if we
spoke only with one person at a time.

The skilful teacher will make it his first care, as soon as a boy is
entrusted to him, to ascertain his ability and character. The surest
indication in a child is his power of memory. The characteristics of
a good memory are twofold: it must be quick to take in and faithful
to retain impressions of what it receives. The indication of next
importance is the power of imitation: for this is a sign that the child
is teachable: but he must imitate merely what he is taught, and
must not, for example, mimic someone's gait or bearing or defects.
For I have no hope that a child will turn out well who loves imitation merely for the purpose of raising a laugh. He who is really gifted will also above all else be good. For the rest, I regard slowness of
intellect as preferable to actual badness. But a good boy will be
quite unlike the dullard and the sloth. My ideal pupil will absorb
instruction with ease and will even ask some questions; but he will
follow rather than anticipate his teacher. Precocious intellects
rarely produce sound fruit. By the precocious I mean those who
perform small tasks with ease and, thus emboldened, proceed to
display all their little accomplishments without being asked: but
their accomplishments are only of the most obvious kind: they
string words together and trot them out boldly and undeterred by
the slightest sense of modesty. Their actual achievement is small,
but what they can do they perform with ease. They have no real
power and what they have is but of shallow growth: it is as when we
cast seed on the surface of the soil: it springs up too rapidly, the
blade apes the loaded ear, and yellows ere harvest time, but bears
no grain. Such tricks please us when we contrast them with the per-
former's age, but progress soon stops and our admiration withers
away.

Such indications once noted, the teacher must next consider
what treatment is to be applied to the mind of his pupil. There are
some boys who are slack, unless pressed on; others again are impatient of control: some are amenable to fear, while others are para-
lysed by it: in some cases the mind requires continued application
to form it, in others this result is best obtained by rapid concentration. Give me the boy who is spurred on by praise, delighted by success and ready to weep over failure. Such a one must be encouraged

by appeals to his ambition; rebuke will bite him to the quick; honor will be a spur, and there is no fear of his proving indolent.

Still, all our pupils will require some relaxation, not merely because there is nothing in this world that can stand continued strain (and even unthinking and inanimate objects are unable to maintain their strength, unless given intervals of rest), but because study depends on the good will of the student, a quality that cannot be secured by compulsion. Consequently, if restored and refreshed by a holiday they will bring greater energy to their learning and approach their work with greater spirit of a kind that will not submit to be driven. I approve of play in the young; it is a sign of a lively disposition; nor will you ever lead me to believe that a boy who is gloomy and in a continual state of depression is ever likely to show alertness of mind in his work, lacking as he does the impulse most natural to boys of his age. Such relaxation must not however be unlimited: otherwise the refusal to give a holiday will make boys hate their work, while excessive indulgence will accustom them to idleness. There are moreover certain games which have an educational value for boys, as for instance when they compete in posing each other all kinds of questions which they take turns asking. Games too reveal character in the most natural way, at least that is so if the teacher will bear in mind that there is no child so young as to be unable to learn to distinguish between right and wrong, and that the character is best moulded, when it is still guiltless of deceit and most susceptible to instruction: for once a bad habit has become engrained, it is easier to break than bend. There must be no delay, then, in warning a boy that his actions must be unselfish, honest, self-controlled, and we must never forget the words of Virgil,

"So strong is custom formed in early years."

I disapprove of flogging, although it is the regular custom and meets with the acquiescence of Chrysippus, because in the first place it is a disgraceful form of punishment and fit only for slaves, and is in any case an insult, as you will realise if you imagine its infliction at a later age. Secondly, if a boy is so insensible to instruction that reproof is useless, he will, like the worst type of slave, merely become hardened to blows. Finally, there will be absolutely no need of such punishment if the master is a thorough disciplinarian. As it is, we try to make amends for the negligence of the boy's instructor, not by forcing him to do what is right, but by punishing him for not doing what is right. And though you may compel a child with blows, what are you to do with him when he is a young man no longer amenable to such threats and confronted

with tasks of far greater difficulty? Moreover, when children are
beaten, pain or fear frequently have results of which it is not pleasant to speak and which are likely subsequently to be a source of
shame, a shame which unnerves and depresses the mind and leads
the child to shun and loathe the light. Further, if inadequate care is
taken in the choices of respectable governors and instructors, I
blush to mention the shameful abuse which scoundrels sometimes
make of their right to administer corporal punishment or the
opportunity not infrequently offered to others by the fear thus
caused in the victims. I will not linger on this subject; it is more
than enough if I have made my meaning clear. I will content myself
with saying that children are helpless and easily victimised, and that
therefore no one should be given unlimited power over them.

The Boy and the Filberts

Aesop

A Boy put his hand into a pitcher full of filberts. He grasped as
many as he could possibly hold, but when he endeavored to pull
out his hand, he was prevented from doing so by the neck of the
pitcher. Unwilling to lose his filberts, and yet unable to withdraw
his hand, he burst into tears, and bitterly lamented his disappointment. A bystander said to him, "Be satisfied with half the quantity,
and you will readily draw out your hand."

Do not attempt too much at once.

Shame Is Good in a Boy

From Jacopo Sadoleto,
On the Education of Boys

A boy's ability to blush shows that he is capable of shame, therefore of virtue.

The blush is the pledge of a good disposition and of the virtue we look for in a boy, so that there seems much fitness in the saying "He blushed—all's well." For shame itself is a habit of taking precaution against the occurrence of anything which may cause a blush: and while it is appropriate to any time of life, it is the chief grace of youth: nor should we be wrong in describing it as the averter of crime and the bulwark of temperance and virtue. And I would urge upon any parents, with whom my influence is likely to have weight, that they delay not to cherish and increase in their children this root of shame which nature has planted in their fresh minds. They can rely upon reaping a rich harvest for their pains. For though a sense of shame may not actually be virtue itself, it is the chief support to virtue: since it is the dread of an evil name and of disgrace: and this is a stern and vigilant guardian of virtue. So those who call shame a kind of divine timidity seem to me to get nearer the right definition of this emotion. It alone dreads the loss of that one well-nigh divine possession, which we win from high honor and office—to wit, our credit and good repute.

The Hare and the Tortoise

Aesop

A Hare one day ridiculed the short feet and slow pace of the Tortoise. The latter, laughing, said: "Though you be swift as the wind, I will beat you in a race." The Hare, deeming her assertion to be simply impossible, assented to the proposal; and they agreed that the Fox should choose the course, and fix the goal. On the day appointed for the race they started together. The Tortoise never for a moment stopped, but went on with a slow but steady pace straight to the end of the course. The Hare, trusting to his native swiftness cared little about the race, and lying down by the wayside, fell fast asleep. At last waking up, and moving as fast as he could, he saw the Tortoise had reached the goal, and was comfortably dozing after her fatigue.

A Father's Advice: Neither a Borrower nor a Lender Be

From William Shakespeare, Hamlet

Yet here, Laertes? Aboard, aboard, for shame!
The wind sits in the shoulder of your sail,
And you are stayed for. There—my blessing with thee,
And these few precepts in thy memory
Look thou character. Give thy thoughts no tongue,
Nor any unproportioned thought his act.
Be thou familiar, but by no means vulgar.
Those friends thou hast, and their adoption tried,
Grapple them unto thy soul with hoops of steel,
But do not dull thy palm with entertainment
Of each new-hatched, unfledged courage. Beware
Of entrance to a quarrel; but being in,
Bear't that th' opposed may beware of thee.
Give every man thine ear, but few thy voice;
Take each man's censure, but reserve thy judgment.
Costly thy habit as thy purse can buy,
But not expressed in fancy; rich, not gaudy,
For the apparel oft proclaims the man,
And they in France of the best rank and station
Are of a most select and generous chief in that.
Neither a borrower nor a lender be,
For loan oft loses both itself and friend,

And borrowing dulleth edge of husbandry.
This above all, to thine own self be true,
And it must follow as the night the day
Thou canst not then be false to any man.
Farewell. My blessing season this in thee!

Boys and Teachers Are Honorable Foes

From Thomas Hughes,
Tom Brown's School Days

"Only what one has always felt about the masters is, that it's a fair trial of skill and last between us and them—like a match at football, or a battle. We're natural enemies in school, that's the fact. We've got to learn so much Latin and Greek and do so many verses, and they've got to see that we do it. If we can slip the collar and do so much less without getting caught, that's one to us. If they can get more out of us, or catch us shirking, that's one to them. All's fair in war, but lying. If I run my luck against theirs, and go into school without looking at my lessons, and don't get called up, why am I a snob or a sneak? I don't tell the master I've learned it. He's got to find out whether I have or not, what's he paid for? If he calls me up, and I get floored, he makes me write it out in Greek and English.

"Very good, he's caught me, and I don't grumble. I grant you, if I go and snivel to him, and tell him I've really tried to learn it but found it so hard without a translation, or say I've had a toothache, or any humbug of that kind, I'm a snob. That's my school morality; it's served me—and you too, Tom, for the matter of that—these five years. And it's all clear and fair, no mistake about it. We understand it, and they understand it, and I don't know what we're to come to with any other."

A Boy Should Be
His Own Best Critic

From Jacopo Sadoleto,
On the Education of Boys

The early training and discipline will hold good. The boy himself will be a sterner critic of his own action than his father, will have less mercy on himself, and will feel much pain at the prayers and admonitions of the parent whom he dearly loves. If, however (though I should be reluctant to say a word of ill augury, since in such a family with such a character it is incredible that anything should befall contrary to our desires)—if, I say there be any grave misconduct, a father must take stringent measures and use more serious language; not to the extent of breaking out into the violent anger which disorders voice and feature, and hampers all the gestures of a speaker, impairs his dignity, and is always unseemly in a man of his position; but he will copy the old man of Terence, who apparently rebuked his son with sufficient sternness: "Now do you really suppose" (said he) "that you can be allowed while I your father am alive to do this sort of thing any longer? to have a mistress almost in the position of a wife? You are mistaken if you think that, Cleinias, and do not know me. I like you to be called my son so long as you behave in a manner worthy of yourself: otherwise I shall find a way of dealing with you worthy of myself." That kind of language seems likely to move any erring son, and so much the more if it has been preceded by the training and issues from the lips of a father such as I have described above—a man who has never set his son a bad example to follow. But if the matter be so serious as to require it, there will be a remedy, not, however, to be adopted save in an extreme case. The father will show himself estranged from his son and refuse to deal with him in the old way; he will little by little curtail his former generosity and indulgence to him; for either that will have the desired effect or he will have to take other measures.

Cyrus Visits His Grandfather

From Xenophon, The Education of Cyrus

The boy Cyrus visits his grandfather, the ruler of Media, and is invited to extend his stay. Cyrus's mother warns the precocious boy not to get uppity.

His mother asked Cyrus whether he wished to stay or go. And he did not hesitate but said at once that he wished to stay. And when he was asked again by his mother why he wished to stay, he is said to have answered: "Because at home, Mother, I am and have the reputation of being the best of those of my years both in throwing the spear and in shooting with the bow; but here I know that I am inferior to my fellows in horsemanship. And let me tell you, Mother," said he, "this vexes me exceedingly. But if you leave me here and I learn to ride, I think you will find, when I come back to Persia, that I shall easily surpass the boys over there who are good at exercises on foot, and when I come again to Media, I shall try to be a help to my grandfather by being the best of good horsemen."

"But my boy," said his mother, "how will you learn justice here, while your teachers are over there?"

"Why Mother," Cyrus answered, "that is one thing that I understand thoroughly."

"How so?" said Mandane.

"Because," said he, "my teacher appointed me on the ground that I was already thoroughly versed in justice, to decide cases for others also. And so, in one case," said he, "I once got a flogging for not deciding correctly. The case was like this: a big boy with a little tunic, finding a little boy with a big tunic on, took it off him and put his own tunic on him, while he himself put on the other's. So, when I tried their case, I decided that it was better for them both that each should keep the tunic that fitted him. And thereupon the master flogged me, saying that when I was a judge of a good fit, I should do as I had done; but when it was my duty to decide whose tunic it was, I had this question, he said, to consider—whose title was the rightful one; whether it was right that he who took it away by force should keep it, or that he who had had it made for himself or had bought it should own it. And since, he said, what is lawful is right and what is unlawful is wrong, he bade the judge always render his verdict on the side of the law. It is in this way, Mother, you see, that I already have a thorough understanding of justice in all its bearings; and" he added, "if I do require anything more, my grandfather here will teach me that."

"Yes, my son,'" said she; "but at your grandfather's court they do not recognize the same principles of justice as they do in Persia. For he has made himself master of everything in Media, but in Persia equality of rights is considered justice. And your father is the first one to do what is ordered by the State and to accept what is decreed, and his standard is not his will but the law. Mind, therefore, that you not be flogged within an inch of your life, when you come home, if you return with a knowledge acquired from your grandfather here of the principles not of kingship but of tyranny, one principle of which is that it is right for one to have more than all."

The Duties and Education of Children

From Leon Battista Alberti,
On the Duties and Education of Children

A young man owes respect and gratitude to his father and elders. Thoughts from the Renaissance humanist and architect (1407–1472).

The young, then, must respect the old, especially their fathers, who well deserve it for their age and for many other reasons. From your father you have received life and instruction on how to acquire virtue. With his labor, solicitude, and zeal, your father has brought you to manhood and to that state and condition in which you find yourself. If you owe gratitude to those who help you when in need and misery, you will certainly owe more to the one who, insofar as he could, did not let you want in the least. If you must share every thought, possession, and fortune with your friends and undergo inconveniences, hardships, and fatigue for those who love you, you certainly owe much more to your father, who loves you more than anyone else, and toward whom you have almost more obligations than to your very self. If your friends and acquaintances must enjoy a goodly part of your wealth and possessions, your father is entitled to much more, for you received

your life, if not your wealth, from him; not only life, but your nourishment for so long a time, or if not your nourishment, your being and
your name. It is the duty of the young, therefore, to share with their
fathers and elders their every wish, thought, and plan and to ask counsel of many on everything, especially of those who, to our knowledge,
love and cherish us more than others. They must listen to them willingly because of their prudence and experience and cheerfully follow
the teachings of those who are older and wiser. Let the young not be
slow in helping all elders in their age and weakness; they should hope
that in their own old age they will receive from youth the same respect
and kindness they themselves have shown their elders. Let them,
therefore, be diligent and prompt in giving them comfort, pleasure,
and rest in their tired old age. Let them not think there is any greater
pleasure or happiness for the old than seeing their young virtuous and
deserving of love. And I tell you there is no greater comfort for the old
than to see that those in whom they have placed all their hopes and
expectations, those for whom they have been ever solicitous and full
of care, are esteemed, loved, and honored for their customs and
virtues. Those men are happy who in their old age see their children
entering upon a peaceful and honorable life. A peaceful life shall be
the reward of men of irreproachable customs; an honorable one, that
of virtuous men. Nothing so much as vice disturbs the life of mortals.

So then, young men, let it be your duty to try to satisfy your
fathers and elders in this as in all things which bring you praise and
glory and give your family happiness and joy. Thus, my children,
pursue virtue, avoid vice, respect your elders, try to make yourselves
liked, and strive to live free, happy, honored, and loved. The first
step toward becoming honored is to make oneself loved; the first
step in gaining love is to be virtuous and honest; and the first step
to becoming virtuous is to hate vice and avoid the wicked. You
must, then, always be with those who are good, praised, and
esteemed and never abandon those from whom you can learn and
acquire virtue and good customs through their teaching and example. You must love and respect them and take pleasure in being
known by all to be without fault. Do not be obstinate, difficult, and
irresponsible, but willing and amenable and as serious and
thoughtful as your age demands. Try as hard as you can to be agreeable to everyone and respectful and obedient with your elders.
Courtesy, gentleness, moderation, and modesty in the young are
praised. But even more pleasing and necessary is the respect of the
young for their elders.

The Shepherd's Boy and Wolf

Aesop

A Shepherd-boy who watched a flock of sheep near a village, brought out the villagers three or four times by crying out, "Wolf! Wolf!" and when his neighbors came to help him, laughed at them for their pains. The Wolf, however, did truly come at last. The Shepherd-boy, now really alarmed, shouted in an agony of terror: "Pray, do come and help me; the Wolf is killing the sheep;" but no one paid any heed to his cries, nor rendered any assistance. The Wolf, having no cause of fear, took it easily, and lacerated or destroyed the whole flock.

There is no believing a liar, even when he speaks the truth.

Youth Must Respect Age

From Jacopo Sadoleto, On the Education of Boys

By respecting his parents, a boy learns deference to tradition and friendship between the generations. An older man can become like a father to a youth who is not his biological child, out of kindness and a concern for his welfare.

And the tender spirit of the child should be trained by them in habits of respect to his parents in such sort that the father should hold up the mother, and the mother the father, and all the members of the household and acquaintance should hold up both to the dutiful regard and veneration of the son. Nor should this tribute of honor on the part of children stop with the parents: it should extend also to his grandparents and all other ancestors, if they are still living: for in them the source of all those benefits which we have received from our parents may be seen in a yet more august and venerable form. Furthermore, from this reverence toward parents and grandparents, this due and dutiful observance, flows—as from a full source of good feeling—the general respect and common deference paid to age, to office, and to ripe years. It is a fit and appropriate tribute to pay to old age, which not improperly claims the title of father: for in their first years children, warned by the aspect of age, give the name of father to persons whom they are not yet able accurately and exactly to distinguish by their lineaments and features: and then afterward their affectionate and almost brotherly relations with those of their own age and their friends' fathers. Indeed, at that age a man, whoever he may be, may become the father of a child or youth in virtue not of kindred, but of kindly counsel.

The Right Kind of Boy: Brave and Tender

From Theodore Roosevelt, The Americanism of Theodore Roosevelt

Even though American democracy might weaken the authority of the father as paterfamilias, *Americans continued to think that manly pride, honor, and striving were important. Theodore Roosevelt (1858–1919)—writer, explorer, soldier, and President—was especially eloquent on the importance of manliness to a vigorous sense of citizenship and meritocracy. And yet, Roosevelt reserves his highest praise for the kind of manliness that combines tenderness with honor. In this we hear an echo of traditional notions of manly civility and refinement hearkening back to the ancients. For, although Roosevelt admires courage in battle and in the opening of the American frontier, he is even more admiring of the steadiness and affection of a good husband and father.*

I want to see you game, boys; I want to see you brave and manly; and I also want to see you gentle and tender. In other words, you should make it your object to be the right kind of boys at home, so that your family will feel a genuine regret, instead of a sense of relief, when you stay away; and at the same time you must be able to hold your own in the outside world. You cannot do that if you have not manliness, courage in you. It does no good to have either or those two sets of qualities if you lack the other. I do not care how nice a little boy you are, how pleasant at home, if when you are out you are afraid of other little boys lest they be rude to you; for if so you will not be a very happy boy nor grow up a very useful man. When a boy grows up I want him to be of such a type that when somebody wrongs him he will feel a good, healthy desire to show the wrongdoers that he cannot be wronged with impunity. I like to have the man who is a citizen feel, when a wrong is done to the community by anyone, when there is an exhibition of corruption or betrayal of trust, or demagogy or violence, or brutality, not that he is shocked and horrified and would like to go home; but I want to have him feel the determination to put the wrongdoer down, to make the man who does wrong aware that the decent man is not only his superior in decency, but his superior in strength; not necessarily physical strength, but strength of character, the kind of strength that makes a good and forceful citizen.

The place in which each of you should try to be most useful is his own home, and each of you should wish for and should practice in order to have courage and strength, so that they can be used in protecting the gentle, in protecting the weak, against those who would wrong weakness and gentleness. The boy who will maltreat either a smaller child, a little boy or a little girl, or a dumb animal, is just about the meanest boy that you can find anywhere in the world. You should be brave and able to hold your own just because you should be able to put down such a bully. It should be your pride to be the champion of the weak. You will find a certain number of boys who have strength and who pride themselves in it, and who misuse it. The boy who will torture something harmless, who will oppress the boy or girl who is weak, or do wrong to those who cannot resist, almost always proves to have a weak streak in him, and not to have the stuff in him that would make him stand up to an equal foe under punishment. That boy has not real courage, real strength; and much though I dislike seeing a boy who is timid, who is afraid, who cannot hold his own, I dislike infinitely more, I abhor, the boy who uses strength and courage to oppress those who cannot help themselves.

To all who have known really happy family lives, that is to all who have known or have witnessed the greatest happiness which there can be on this earth, it is hardly necessary to say that the highest ideal of the family is attainable only where the father and mother stand to each other as lovers and friends, with equal rights. In these homes the children are bound to father and mother by ties of love, respect, and obedience, which are simply strengthened by the fact that they are treated as reasonable beings with rights of their own, and that the rule of the household is changed to suit the changing years, as childhood passes into manhood and womanhood. In such a home the family is not weakened; it is strengthened. This is no unattainable ideal. Everyone knows hundreds of homes where it is more or less perfectly realized, and it is an ideal incomparably higher than the ideal of the beneficent autocrat which it has so largely supplanted.

To be a good husband or good wife, a good neighbor and friend, to be hardworking and upright in business and social relations, to bring up many healthy children—to be and to do all this is to lay the foundations of good citizenship as they must be laid. But we cannot stop even with this. Each of us has not only his duty to himself, his family, and his neighbors, but his duty to the State and to the Nation.

The Value of a Boy's Friendships

From Thomas Hughes,
Tom Brown's School Days

Tom learns the importance of sharing his inner life with a trusted friend, East. He also grows into manliness by taking responsibility for a younger boy, Arthur—as the school's headmaster had always intended he should.

The fact is, that in the stage of his inner life at which Tom had lately arrived, his intimacy with and friendship for East could not have lasted if he had not made him aware of, and a sharer in, the thoughts that were beginning to exercise him. Nor indeed could the friendship have lasted if East had shown no sympathy with these thoughts; so that it was a great relief to have unbosomed himself, and to have found that his friend could listen.

Tom had always had a sort of instinct that East's levity was only skin-deep, and this instinct was a true one. East had no want of reverence for anything he felt to be real: but his was one of those natures that burst into what is generally called recklessness and impiety the moment they feel that anything is being poured upon them for their good, which does not come home to their inborn sense of right, or which appeals to anything like self-interest in them. Daring and honest by nature, and outspoken to an extent which alarmed all respectabilities, with a constant fund of animal health and spirits which he did not feel bound to curb in any way, he had gained for himself with the steady part of the School (including as well those who wished to appear steady as those who really were so), the character of a boy whom it would be dangerous to be intimate with; while his own hatred of everything cruel, or underhand, or false, and his hearty respect for what he could see to be good and true, kept off the rest.

Tom, besides being very like East in many points of character, had largely developed in his composition the capacity for taking the weakest side. This is not putting it strongly enough; it was a necessity with him; he couldn't help it any more than he could eating or drinking. He could never play on the strongest side with any heart at football or cricket, and was sure to make friends with any boy who was unpopular, or down on his luck.

Now though East was not what is generally called unpopular, Tom felt more and more every day, as their characters developed, that he stood alone, and did not make friends among their contemporaries, and therefore sought him out. Tom was himself much more popular, for his power of detecting humbug was much less acute, and his instincts were much more sociable. He was at this period of his life, too, largely given to taking people for what they gave themselves out to be; but his singleness of heart, fearfulness and honesty were just what East appreciated, and thus the two had been drawn into greater intimacy.

This intimacy had not been interrupted by Tom's guardianship of Arthur.

East had often, as has been said, joined them in reading the Bible; but their discussions had almost always turned upon the characters of the men and women of whom they read, and not become personal to themselves. In fact, the two had shrunk from personal religious discussion, not knowing how it might end; and fearful of risking a friendship very dear to both, and which they felt somehow, without quite knowing why, would never be the same, but either tenfold stronger or sapped at its foundation, after such a communing together.

What a bother all this explaining is! I wish we could get on without it. But we can't. However, you'll all find, if you haven't found it out already, that a time comes in every human friendship, when you must go down into the depths of yourself, and lay bare what is there to your friend, and wait in fear for his answer. A few moments may do it; and it may be (most likely will be, as you are English boys) that you never do it but once. But done it must be, if the friendship is to be worth the name. You must find what is there, at the very root and bottom of one another's hearts; and if you are at once there, nothing on earth can, or at least ought to sunder you.

East had remained lying down until Tom finished speaking, as if fearing to interrupt him; he now sat up at the table, and leaned his head on one hand, taking up a pencil with the other, and working little holes with it in the tablecover. After a bit he looked up, stopped the pencil and said, "Thank you very much, old fellow; there's no other boy in the house would have done it for me but you or Arthur. I can see well enough," he went on after a pause, "all the best big fellows look on me with suspicion; they think I'm a devil-may-care, reckless young scamp. So I am—eleven hours out of twelve—but not the twelfth. Then all our contemporaries worth knowing follow suit, of course; we're very good friends at games and all that, but not a soul of them but you and Arthur ever tried to break through the crust, and see whether there was anything at the bottom of me; and then the bad ones I won't stand, and they know that."

"I wonder where Arthur can be," said Tom at last, looking at his watch: "why, it's nearly half-past nine already."

"Oh, he is comfortably at supper with the eleven, forgetful of his oldest friends," said the master. "Nothing has given me greater pleasure," he went on, "than your friendship for him; it has been the making of you both."

"Of me, at any rate," answered Tom; "I should never have been here now but for him. It was the luckiest chance in the world that sent him to Rugby, and made him my chum."

"Why do you talk of lucky chances?" said the master; "I don't know that there are any such things in the world; at any rate there was neither luck nor chance in that matter."

Tom looked at him inquiringly, and he went on.

"Do you remember when the Doctor lectured you and East at the end of one half-year, when you were in the shell, and had been getting into all sorts of scrapes?"

"Yes, well enough," said Tom; "it was the half-year before Arthur came."

"Exactly so," answered the master. "Now, I was with him a few minutes afterward, and he was in great distress about you two. And, after some talk, we both agreed that you in particular wanted some object in the School beyond games and mischief; for it was quite clear that you never would make the regular school work your first object. And so the Doctor, at the beginning of the next half-year, looked out the best of the new boys, and separated you and East, and put the young boy into your study, in the hope that when you had somebody to lean on you, you would begin to stand a little steadier yourself, and get manliness and thoughtfulness. And I can assure you he has watched the experiment ever since with great satisfaction. Ah! not one of you boys will ever know the anxiety you have given him, or the care with which he has watched over every step in your school lives."

THE MANLY FATHER

Phaeton Aims Too High

From Thomas Bulfinch, Bulfinch's Mythology

This ancient myth poses a troubling question. Should a son aim to match his father's success if he destroys himself in the process?

Phaeton was the son of Apollo and the nymph Clymene. One day a schoolfellow laughed at the idea of his being the son of the god, and Phaeton went in rage and shame and reported it to his mother. "If," said he, "I am indeed of heavenly birth, give me, Mother, some proof of it, and establish my claim to the honor." Clymene stretched forth her hands toward the skies, and said, "I call to witness the Sun which looks down upon us, that I have told you the truth. If I speak falsely, let this be the last time I behold his light. But it needs not much labor to go and inquire for yourself; the land whence the Sun rises lies next to ours. Go and demand of him whether he will own you as a son." Phaeton heard with delight. He traveled to India, which lies directly in the regions of sunrise; and, full of hope and pride, approached the goal whence his parent begins his course.

The palace of the Sun stood reared aloft on columns, glittering with gold and precious stones, while polished ivory formed the ceilings, and silver the doors. The workmanship surpassed the material; for upon the walls Vulcan had represented earth, sea, and skies, with their inhabitants. In the sea were the nymphs, some sporting in the waves, some riding on the backs of fishes, while others sat upon the rocks and dried their sea-green hair. Their faces were not all alike, nor yet unlike, but such as sisters' ought to be. The earth had its towns and forests and rivers and rustic divinities. Over all was carved the likeness of the glorious heaven; and on the silver doors the twelve signs of the zodiac, six on each side.

Clymene's son advanced up the steep ascent, and entered the halls of his disputed father. He approached the paternal presence, but stopped at a distance, for the light was more than he could bear. Phoebus, arrayed in purple vesture, sat on a throne, which glittered as with diamonds. On his right hand and his left stood the Day, the Month, and the Year, and, at regular intervals, the Hours. Spring stood with her head crowned with flowers, and Summer, with garment cast aside, and a garland formed of spears of ripened grain, and Autumn, with his feet stained with grape-juice, and icy Winter, with his hair stiffened with hoar frost. Surrounded by these attendants, the Sun with the eye that sees everything, beheld the youth dazzled with the novelty and splendour of the scene, and inquired the purpose of his errand. The youth replied, "O light of the boundless world, Phoebus, my father—if you permit me to use that name—give me some proof, I beseech you, by which I may be known as yours." He ceased; and his father, laying aside the beams that shone all around his head, bade him approach, and embracing him, said, "My son, you deserve not to be disowned, and I confirm what your mother has told you. To put an end to your doubts, ask what you will, the gifts shall be yours. I call to witness that dreadful lake, which I never saw, but which we gods swear by in our most solemn engagements." Phaeton immediately asked to be permitted for one day to drive the chariot of the sun. The father repented of his promise, thrice and four times he shook his radiant head in warning. "I have spoken rashly," said he; "this is the only request I would fain deny. I beg you to withdraw it. It is not a safe boon, nor one, my Phaeton, suited to your youth and strength. Your lot is mortal, and you ask what is beyond a mortal's power. In your ignorance you aspire to do that which not even the gods themselves may do. None but myself may drive the flaming car of day. Not even Jupiter, whose terrible right arm hurls the thunderbolts. The first part of the way is steep; and such as the horses when fresh in the morning can hardly climb; the middle is high up in the heavens, whence I myself can scarcely, without alarm, look down and behold the earth and sea stretched beneath me. The last part of the road descends rapidly, and requires most careful driving. Tethys, who is waiting to receive me, often trembles for me lest I should fall headlong. Add to all this, the heaven is all the time turning round and carrying the stars with it. I have to be perpetually on my guard lest that movement, which sweeps everything else along, should hurry me also away. Suppose I should lend you the chariot, what would you do? Could you keep your course while the sphere was revolving under you? Perhaps you think that there are forests and cities, the abodes of gods, and palaces and temples on the way. On the contrary, the road is through the midst of frightful monsters. You pass by the horns of the Bull, in front of the Archer, and near the Lion's jaws, and where the Scorpion stretches its arms in one direction and the Crab in another. Nor will you find it easy to guide those horses, with their mouths and nostrils. I can scarcely govern them myself, when they are unruly and resist the reins. Beware, my son, lest I be the donor of a fatal gift; recall your request while yet you may. Do you ask me for a proof that you are sprung from my blood? I give you a proof in my fears for you. Look at my face—I would that you could look into my breast, you would there see all a father's anxiety. Finally," he continued, "look round the world and choose whatever you will of what earth or sea contains most precious—ask it and fear no refusal. This only I pray you not to urge. It is not honor, but destruction you seek. Why do you hang round my neck and still entreat me? You shall have it if you persist—the oath is sworn and must be kept—but I beg you to choose more wisely."

He ended; but the youth rejected all admonition and held to his demand. So, having resisted as long as he could, Phoebus at last led the way to where stood the lofty chariot.

It was of gold, the spokes of silver. Along the seat were rows of chrysolites and diamonds which reflected all around the brightness of the sun. While the daring youth gazed in admiration, the early Dawn threw open the purple doors of the east, and showed the pathway strewn with roses. The stars withdrew, marshaled by the Day-star, which last of all retired also. The father, when he saw the earth beginning to glow, and the Moon preparing to retire, ordered the Hours to harness up the horses. They obeyed, and led forth from the lofty stalls the steeds full fed with ambrosia, and attached the reins. Then the father bathed the face of his son with a powerful unguent, and made him capable of enduring the brightness of the flame. He set the rays on his head, and, with a foreboding sigh, said, "If, my son, you will in this at least heed my advice, spare the whip and hold tight the reins. They go fast enough of their own accord; the labor is to hold them in. You are not to take the straight road directly between the five circles, but turn off to the left. Keep within the limit of the middle zone, and avoid the northern and the southern alike. You will see the marks of the wheels, and they will serve to guide you. And, that the skies and the earth may each receive their due share of heat, go not too high, or you will burn the heavenly dwellings, not too low, or you will set the earth on fire; the middle course is safest and best. And now I leave you to your chance, which I hope will plan better for you than you have done for yourself. Night is passing out of the western gates and we can delay no longer. Take the reins; but if at last your heart fails you, and you will benefit by my advice, stay where you are in safety, and suffer me to light and warm the earth." The agile youth sprang into the chariot, stood erect, and grasped the reins with delight, pouring out thanks to his reluctant parent.

Meanwhile, the horses fill the air with their snortings and fiery breath, and stamp the ground impatiently. Now the bars are let down, and the boundless plain of the universe lies open before them. They dart forward and cleave the opposing clouds, and outrun the morning breezes which started from the same eastern goal. The steeds soon perceived that the load they drew was lighter than usual; and as a ship without ballast is tossed hither and thither on the sea, so the chariot, without its accustomed weight, was dashed about as if empty. They rush headlong and leave the traveled road. He is alarmed, and knows not how to guide them; nor, if he knew, has he the power. Then, for the first time, the Great and Little Bear were scorched with heat, and would fain, if it were possible, have plunged into the water; and the Serpent which lies coiled up round the north pole, torpid and harmless, grew warm, and with warmth felt its rage revive. Boötes, they say, fled away, though encumbered with his plough, and all unused to rapid motion.

When hapless Phaeton looked down upon the earth, now spreading in vast extent beneath him, he grew pale and his knees shook with terror. In spite of the glare all around him, the sight of his eyes grew dim. He wished he had never touched his father's horses, never learned his parentage, never prevailed in his request. He is borne along like a vessel that flies before a tempest, when the pilot can do no more and betakes himself to his prayers. What shall he do? Much of the heavenly road is left behind, but more remains before. He turns his eyes from one direction to the other; now to the goal whence he began his course, now to the realms of sunset which he is not destined to reach. He loses his self-command, and knows not what to do—whether to draw tight the reins or throw them loose; he forgets the names of the horses. He sees with terror the monstrous forms scattered over the surface of heaven. Here the Scorpion extended his two great arms, with his tail and crooked claws stretching over two signs of the zodiac. When the boy beheld him, reeking with poison and menacing with his fangs, his courage failed, and the reins fell from his hands. The horses, when they felt them loose on their backs, dashed headlong, and unrestrained went off into unknown regions of the sky, in among the stars, hurling the chariot over pathless places, now up in high heaven, now down almost to the earth. The moon saw with astonishment her brother's chariot running beneath her own. The clouds begin to smoke, and the mountain tops take fire; the fields are parched with heat, the plants wither, the trees with their leafy branches burn, the harvest is ablaze! But these are small things. Great cities perished, with their walls and towers; whole nations with their people were consumed to ashes! The forest-clad mountains burned, Athos and Taurus and Tmolus and Oete; Ida, once celebrated for fountains, but now all dry; the Muses' mountain Helicon, and Haemus; Aetna, with fires within and without, and Parnassus, with his two peaks, and Rhodope, forced at last to part with his snowy crown. Her cold climate was no protection to Scythia, Caucasus burned, and Osa and Pindus, and, greater than both, Olympus; the Alps high in air, and the Apennines crowned with clouds.

Then Phaeton beheld the world on fire, and felt the heat intolerable. The air he breathed was like the air of a furnace and full of burning ashes, and the smoke was of a pitchy darkness. He dashed forward he knew not whither. Then, it is believed, the people of Ethiopia became black by the blood being forced so suddenly to the surface, and the Libyan desert was dried up to the condition in which it remains to this day. The Nymphs of the fountains, with disheveled hair, mourned their waters, nor were the rivers safe beneath their banks: Tanais smoked, and Caicus, Xanthus, and Meander; Babylonian Euphrates and Ganges. Tagus with golden sands, and Cayster where the swans resort. Nile fled away and hid his head in the desert, and there it still remains concealed. Where he used to discharge his waters through seven mouths into the sea, there seven dry channels alone remained. The earth cracked open, and through the chinks light broke into Tartarus, and frightened the king of shadows and his queen. The sea shrank up. Where before was water, it became a dry plain; and the mountains that lie beneath the waves lifted up their heads and became islands. The fishes sought the lowest depths, and the dolphins no longer ventured as usual to sport on the surface. Even Nereus, and his wife Doris, with the Nereids, their daughters, sought the deepest caves for refuge. Thrice Neptune essayed to raise his head above the surface, and thrice was driven back by the heat. Earth, surrounded as she was by waters, yet with head and shoulders bare, screening her face with her hand, looked up to heaven, and with a husky voice called on Jupiter:

"O ruler of the gods, if I have deserved this treatment, and it is your will that I perish with fire, why withhold your thunderbolts? Let me at least fall by your hand. Is this the reward of my fertility, of my obedient service? Is it for this that I have supplied herbage for cattle, and fruits for men, and frankincense for your altars? But if I am unworthy of regard, what has my brother Ocean done to deserve such a fate? If neither of us can excite your pity, think, I pray you, of your own heaven, and behold how both the poles are smoking which sustain your palace, which must fall if they be destroyed. Atlas faints, and scarce holds up his burden. If sea, earth, and heaven perish, we fall into ancient Chaos. Save what yet remains to us from the devouring flame. O, take thought for our deliverance in this awful moment!"

Thus spoke Earth, and overcome with heat and thirst, could say no more. Then Jupiter omnipotent, calling to witness all the gods, including him who had lent the chariot, and showing them that all was lost unless some speedy remedy were applied, mounted the lofty tower from whence he diffuses clouds over the earth, and hurls the forked lightnings. But at that time not a cloud was to be found to interpose for a screen to earth, nor was a shower remaining unexhausted. He thundered, and brandishing a lightning bolt in his right hand launched it against the charioteer, and struck him at the same moment from his seat and from existence! Phaeton, with his hair on fire, fell headlong, like a shooting star which marks the heavens with its brightness as it falls, and Eridanus, the great river, received him and cooled his burning frame. The Italian Naiads reared a tomb for him, and inscribed these words upon the stone:

"Driver of Phoebus' chariot, Phaeton,
Struck by Jove's thunder, rests beneath this stone.
He could not rule his father's car of fire,
Yet it was much so nobly to aspire."

A Father and Son Discuss Education

From Jacopo Sadoleto, On the Education of Boys

In this charming and instructive Renaissance dialogue, Paulo asks his father Jacopo to sum up everything his father taught him since childhood, so that "from it I might learn to fashion myself to the pattern of goodness—to become what you wish me to be." In reviewing what he has tried to teach his son, Jacopo also sums up the kind of man he has tried to be for his boy. The fact that he and his son can have this conversation is the best proof that Paulo has grown up well.

Jacopo. What is it then that you look for from me? Come, tell me, for it will never be my wish to say no to your right desire.
Paulo. I know that, even without your assurance, Father. Your actions prove that. But just now when your servant told me, on my asking, that you were at leisure, I thought it was not an unsuitable moment to beg you to put together, in a single discourse, all the counsels which you have been in the habit of giving, in scattered and fragmentary form, upon the subject of the right training of youth; for I long to have, if I may so call it, a compendium of your opinions in this kind; from it I might learn to fashion myself to the pattern of goodness—to become what you would wish me to be. But only if this is not troublesome to you, and if you do not feel that something else has a first claim.
Jac. Troublesome to me? And shall I put anything before such a task? Is there anything in all the world that I should more fervently covet than that you should be good and learned. For I think I

understand your request—you want me to expound everything
that concerns the training of character and the establishment of
sound learning.

Paul. Yes, it is just that; that is my wish.

Jac. But consider, Paullus; if we are to take the matter in hand and
follow it out in its proper sequence, we must make a beginning
with childhood itself. For no one can be properly trained as a
youth, who has been badly brought up as a child; for as the character and quality of a tree come from its roots, so a well-condi-
tioned, well-balanced youth is the fruit of childhood. It is remarkable that this early stage of life, in which a slip and a mistake are
most easily made, has been less than any other handled and considered by our present laws; no care is taken to ensure the cultivation of childhood as a public duty, though it is on this and no
other foundation that the character of our citizens, and the
soundness of our states is based.

Our system of education, then, falls into two divisions—the
first deals with moral, the second with literary training. Moral training sets out with the object of ensuring that all our words and
actions may be marked by moderation, and may keep a fit and
proper rule of conduct, the correct beauty of which may delight not
only the mind of the learned but even the eyes of the ignorant and
constrain them to admiring imitation. Now the power, the quality of
literature and of what we call humane studies in this: We receive
from Nature what is central in ourselves, what indeed makes us truly
and individually what we are, but in a rough and unfinished form; it
is the function of letters to bring this to its highest perfection and to
work out in it a beauty comparable to its divine original.

It is inappropriate, nay, impossible, for that precise and subtle
idea of virtue to be instilled into the youthful mind, and when a
man attains it even in advanced age we rightly call him blessed. But
in your childhood, and even in your youth, you should receive in
place of knowledge and understanding a certain conviction, to
make you trust and obey your elders, who, as you can see, are held
in high esteem; for public opinion never approves or admires for
long what is at variance with goodness and truth.

There are, of course, many tendencies at this time of life which
make rather for vice than for virtue; this is inevitable, because of the
vehemence of the passions, particularly at that age, for in boys and
youths a firm footing has not yet been won by reason, which even in
its mature development seems scarcely able to keep men of advanced

years from every kind of error and misdeed. So a father should carefully see that he bring much fairness and patience to the task of guiding and directing the slippery steps of youth and should sharply note any violation of the law of virtue or duty, and consider whether the fault be of a kind to corrupt good character, or whether it is the result of a kind of fermentation of youth.

We must lead our youths to a position from which, not content with following the footsteps of others, they will learn to look, as if from a watchtower, with their own eyes, choosing their goal and selecting the path toward it under the command of their own judgment and will. Therefore, as soon as a boy has learned to speak correctly, to bring out his words clearly and with precision, and to throw out some little sparks of boyish wit, his father should most carefully lead him to the notion and the desire of learning to read. This can be very effectively done, if he invites some small boys, a little in advance of his own age, who have made some progress in reading; he will listen to them, and in the hearing of his own boy, praise their performance, and caress them, and perhaps give them some little present or prize—for the ambition of a child will be kindled for those studies in which he sees another winning such approbation; and he himself will ask, nay, he will beg for those same writing tablets, and those very exercises to be given to him. And those which are to be given to him must be themselves beautiful and pleasant and written in clear letters, so that by every attraction which can move children of that age, the boy may be allured to a passionate love for reading. For we must always carefully make sure that appetite for reading is present and so keen that a feeling of surfeit may never follow.

I Have a Boy of Five Years Old

William Wordsworth

I have a boy of five years old;
His face is fair and fresh to see;
His limbs are cast in beauty's mould,
And dearly he loves me.

One morn we strolled on our dry walk,
Our quiet home all full in view,
And held such intermitted talk
As we are wont to do.

My thoughts on former pleasures ran;
I thought of Kilve's delightful shore,
Our pleasant home when spring began,
A long, long year before.

A day it was when I could bear
Some fond regrets to entertain;
With so much happiness to spare,
I could not feel a pain.

The green earth echoed to the feet
Of lambs that bounded through the glade,
From shade to sunshine, and as fleet
From sunshine back to shade.

Birds warbled round me—and each trace
Of inward sadness had its charm;
Kilve, thought I, was a favored place,
And so is Liswyn farm.

My boy beside me tripped, so slim
And graceful in his rustic dress!
And, as we talked, I questioned him,
In every idleness.

"Now tell me, had you rather be,"
I said, and took him by the arm,
"On Kilve's smooth shore, by the green sea,
Or here at Liswyn farm?"

In careless mood he looked at me,
While still I held him by the arm,
And said, "At Kilve I'd rather be
Than here at Liswyn farm."

"Now, little Edward, say why so:
My little Edward, tell me why."—

"I cannot tell, I do not know."—
"Why, this is strange," said I;

"For here are woods, hills smooth and warm:
There surely must some reason be
Why you would change sweet Liswyn farm
For Kilve by the green sea."

At this my boy hung down his head,
He blushed with shame, nor made reply;
And three times to the child I said,
"Why, Edward, tell me why?"

His head he raised—there was in sight
It caught his eye, he saw it plain—
Upon the house-top, glittering bright,
A broad and gilded vane.

Then did the boy his tongue unlock,
And eased his mind with this reply:
"At Kilve there was no weather-cock;
And that's the reason why."

O dearest, dearest boy! my heart
For better lore would seldom yearn,
Could I but teach the hundredth part
Of what from thee I learn.

The Farmer and His Son

Aesop

A Farmer being on the point of death wished to ensure from his sons the same attention to his farm as he had himself given it. He called them to his bedside, and said, "My sons, there is a great treasure hid in one of my vineyards." The sons after his death took their spades and mattocks, and carefully dug over every portion of their land. They found no treasure, but the vines repaid their labor by an extraordinary and superabundant crop.

Apply Yourself, My Boy

From Lord Chesterfield,
The Letters of Lord Chesterfield to His Son

Son, I would never want the fact that I could cut you off without a penny to influence in any way your behavior and your wish to please me.

Dear Boy,

I was very sorry that Mr. Maittaire did not give me such an account of you yesterday as I wished and expected. He takes so much pains to teach you, that he well deserves from you the returns of care and attention. Besides, pray consider, now that you have justly got the reputation of knowing much more than other boys of your age do, how shameful it would be for you to lose it, and to let other boys, that are now behind you, get before you. If you would but have attention, you have quickness enough to conceive, and memory enough to retain: but, without attention while you are learning, all the time you employ at your book is thrown away; and your shame will be the greater if you should be ignorant, when you had such opportunities of learning. An ignorant man is insignificant and contemptible; nobody cares for his company, and he can just be said to live, and that is all. There is a very pretty French epigram upon the death of such an ignorant, insignificant fellow; the sting of which is, that all that can be said of him is, that he was once alive, and that he is now dead.

Though I employ so much of my time in writing to you, I confess I have often my doubts whether it is to any purpose. I know how unwelcome advice generally is; I know that those who want it most, like it and follow it least; and I know, too, that the advice of parents, more particularly, is ascribed to the moroseness, the imperiousness, or the garrulity of old age. But then, on the other hand, I flatter myself, that as your own reason, though too young as yet to suggest much to you of itself, is, however, strong enough to enable you, both to judge of, and receive plain truths: I flatter myself (I say) that your own reason, young as it is, must tell you, that I can have no interest but yours in the advice I give you; and that, consequently, you will at least weigh and consider it well: in which case, some of it will, I hope, have its effect. Do not think that I mean to dictate as a parent; I only mean to advise as a friend, and an indulgent one too: and do not apprehend that I mean to check your pleasures; of which, on the contrary, I only desire to be the guide, not the censor. Let my experience supply your want of it, and clear your way, in the progress of your youth, of those thorns and briars which scratched and disfigured me in the course of mine. I do not, therefore, so much as hint to you, how absolutely dependent you are upon me; that you neither have, nor can have a shilling in the world but from me; and that, as I have no womanish weakness for your person, your merit must, and will, be the only measure of my kindness. I say, I do not hint these things to you, because I am convinced that you will act right, upon more noble and generous principles: I mean, for the sake of doing right, and out of affection and gratitude to me.

I have so often recommended to you attention and application to whatever you learn, that I do not mention them now as duties; but I point them out to you as conducive, nay, absolutely necessary to your pleasures; for can there be greater pleasure than to be universally allowed to excel those of one's own age and manner of life? And, consequently, can there be anything more mortifying than to be excelled by them? In this latter case, your shame and regret must be greater than anybody's, because everybody knows the uncommon care which has been taken of your education, and the opportunities you have had of knowing more than others of your age. I do not confine the application which I recommend, singly to the view and emulation of excelling others (though that is a very sensible and a very warrantable pride); but I mean likewise to excel in the thing itself; for, in my mind, one may as well not know a thing at all, as know it but imperfectly. To know a little of anything gives neither satisfaction nor credit; but often brings disgrace or ridicule.

Let me, therefore, most earnestly recommend to you to hoard up, while you can, a great stock of knowledge; for though, during the dissipation of your youth, you may not have occasion to spend much of it, yet you may depend upon it, that a time will come when you will want it to maintain you. Public granaries are filled in plentiful years; not that it is known that the next, or the second, or third year will prove a scarce one; but because it is known, that, sooner or later, such a year will come, in which the grain will be wanted.

Pleasure is the rock which most young people split upon; they launch out with crowded sails in quest of it, but without a compass to direct their course, or reason sufficient to steer the vessel; for want of which, pain and shame, instead of Pleasure, are the returns of their voyage. Do not think that I mean to snarl at Pleasure, like a Stoic, or to preach against it, like a parson; no, I mean to point it out a great deal; and my only view is to hinder you from mistaking it.

A Father Pays Attention All the Time

From Leon Battista Alberti,
On the Duties and Education of Children

A boy needs to be paid attention to at every stage of his development. A father shouldn't be overly familiar or try to be his son's pal. But, by the same token, he can only maintain his authority through love, never through fear.

A father's duties do not consist solely in filling the granary and the cradle, as they say. The head of a family must be vigilant and observant above all. He must know all the family's acquaintances, examine all customs both within and without the house, and correct and mend the evil ways of any member of the family with words of reason rather than anger. He must use a father's authority rather than despotism, and counsel where it is of more value than commanding. He must be severe, firm, and stern when necessary, and he must always keep in mind the well-being, peace, and tranquillity of his entire family as the ultimate purpose of all his efforts and counsels for the guidance of the family in virtue and honor. As sailors take advantage of favorable winds and currents, so must a father know how to use the favor and benevolence of his fellow citizens in order to reach a harbor of honor, respect, and authority. Once there, he must know how to pause and lower his sails at the proper time. In stormy weather, ill-winds, and unfortunate shipwreck, such as our house has been unjustly suffering for twenty-two years, he must strengthen the spirit of the young and prevent them from giving in to the blows of Fortune or remaining prostrate. He must never allow them to attempt any foolhardy or mad enterprise to avenge themselves or to carry out a youthful and unwise plan. He must not allow them to abandon the rudder of reason and the ways of wisdom when Fortune seems benign or neutral, and more so in stormy weather. He must foresee and prepare himself for the fog of envy, the clouds of hatred, and the thunderbolts of enmity on the part of his fellow citizens. He must be prepared for opposing winds and all perils and reefs against which the vessel might strike. He must be like the experienced helmsman, keeping in mind with what winds others have sailed, with what sails, and how they saw and avoided every danger. Nor must he forget that in our state no one ever unfurled all his sails, no matter how great, without having to lower them afterward torn and in tatters. Thus he will learn that the losses incurred in sailing unskillfully once are greater than the success gained by reaching a safe harbor a thousand times. Envy disappears if one shows modesty rather than pomp; hatred is lessened if one is affable rather than haughty; enmity disappears if one arms himself with gentleness and charm rather than scorn and anger. The family elders must keep their eyes and minds open and give great thought to all these matters. They must be ready to foresee and learn everything. They must strive with great care and diligence to make the young members of the family always more honest, virtuous, and pleasing to our fellow citizens.

I am certain that a father does not have to be afraid of disobedience or stubbornness in his sons if he is always alert and tries to prevent vices, and if at the first sign he proceeds diligently to eradicate them and shows care and foresight by not waiting for them to become so rooted and widespread that they will cast the shadow of infamy over the entire family. If through negligence and indolence a son's vice grows and spreads its branches, I advise the father not to cut it in such a way that it will crash down on his family's fortune and honor. He must not send the son away or disown him, as some irascible and impetuous men do. For in such a case the licentious young man, full of vices and burdened by need, will stoop to vile and dangerous enterprises and will bring infamy upon himself and his family. The head of the family must first of all be on the watch for the first sparks of vice to appear among his children's appetites and must put them out immediately if he does not wish to be compelled later to extinguish the flames of corrupt desire at greater cost, with sorrow and tears.

The proverb says that the right path must be taken where it

begins. A father must see where his son is headed from the earliest age and must not allow him to proceed on an unsafe and little-praised path. He must not allow his sons to have their way against his wishes or become accustomed to dishonest ways. The father must always appear as a father; he must be severe, but not hateful, loving, but not too familiar. Let all fathers and elders remember that authority maintained through force is always less stable than that maintained through love. No fear can last forever; love is long enduring. Fear loses its power with time, but love grows from day to day. Who, then, is so mad as to believe that one must show himself strict and harsh in all things? Severity without humaneness breeds hatred, rather than authority. The more loving and free from harshness kindness is, the more benevolence and good will it acquires. Excessive curiosity in everything is not what I should call diligence; it resembles a tyrant's ways more than a father's. Austerity and harshness make one angry and scornful toward his elders more often than obedient. A noble spirit suffers when treated as a servant rather than as a son. It is better at times not to want to know something rather than not to correct the faults that you have shown you have noticed. It does less harm for a son to think that his father is ignorant of something than to find him negligent. Those who become accustomed to deceive their own father will not think twice before betraying someone else. Let us, then, strive to be thought of as fathers by our sons at all times, whether we are with them or away. To accomplish this, diligence is most useful. It is diligence that makes us loved and respected by our sons.

A Father's Parting Advice

From Thomas Hughes,
Tom Brown's School Days

Squire Brown's advice as he sends his son Tom off to school.

"And now, Tom, my boy," said the Squire, "remember you are going, at your own earnest request, to be chucked into this great school, like a young bear with all your troubles before you—earlier than we should have sent you perhaps. If schools are what they were in my time, you'll see a great many cruel blackguard things done, and hear a deal of foul bad talk. But never fear. You tell the truth, keep a brave and kind heart, and never listen to or say anything you wouldn't have your mother and sister hear, and you'll never feel ashamed to come home, or we to see you."

The allusion to his mother made Tom feel rather chokey, and he would have liked to have hugged his father well, if it hadn't been for the recent stipulation.

As it was, he only squeezed his father's hand, and looked bravely up and said, "I'll try, Father."

"I know you will, my boy. Is your money all safe?"

"Yes," said Tom, diving into one pocket to make sure.

"And your keys?" said the Squire.

"All right," said Tom, diving into the other pocket.

"Well then, good night. God bless you! I'll tell Boots to call you, and be up to see you off."

Tom was carried off by the chambermaid in a brown study, from which he was roused in a clean little attic by that buxom person calling him a little darling, and kissing him as she left the room, which indignity he was too much surprised to resent. And still thinking of his father's last words, and the look with which they were spoken, he knelt down and prayed, that, come what might, he might never bring shame or sorrow on the dear folk at home.

Indeed, the Squire's last words deserved to have their effect, for they had been the result of much anxious thought. All the way up to London he had pondered what he should say to Tom by way of parting advice, something that the boy could keep in his head ready for use. By way of assisting meditation, he had even gone the length of taking out his flint and steel and tinder, and hammering away for a quarter of an hour till he had manufactured a light for a long Trichinopoli cheroot, which he silently puffed; to the no small wonder of Coachee, who was an old friend, and an institution on the Bath road; and who always expected a talk on the prospects and doings, agricultural and social, of the whole country when he carried the Squire.

To condense the Squire's meditation, it was somewhat as follows: "I won't tell him to read his Bible and love and serve God; if he don't do that for his mother's sake and teaching, he won't for mine. Shall I go into the sort of temptations he'll meet with? No, I can't do that. Never do for an old fellow to go into such things with a boy. He won't understand me. Do him more harm than good, ten to one. Shall I tell him to mind his work, and say he's sent to school to make himself a good scholar? Well, but he isn't sent to school for that—at any rate, not for that mainly. I don't care a straw for Greek particles, or the digamma, no more does his mother. What is he sent to school for? Well, partly because he wanted so to go. If he'll only turn out a brave, helpful, truth-telling Englishman, and a gentleman, and a Christian, that's all I want," thought the Squire; and upon this view of the case framed his last words of advice to Tom, which were well enough suited to his purpose.

Cyrus's Father Advises Him on Governing

From Xenophon, The Education of Cyrus

After the young Cyrus has completed his education in the Persian Republic, his father Cambyses advises him that if he wants men to respect his leadership, he will have to prove that he is willing to endure the hardships he asks of them, and that he knows what he's talking about.

"And then in regard to keeping the soldiers in a state of obedience, I think, Father, that I am not inexperienced in that direction; for you instructed me in obedience from my very childhood on, compelling me to obey you. Then you surrendered me to the charge of my teachers, and they pursued the same course; and when we were in the class of young men, the officer in charge paid especial attention to this same point; and most of the laws seem to me to teach these two things above all else, to govern and to be governed. And now, when I think of it, it seems to me that in all things the chief incentive to obedience lies in this: praise and honor for the obedient, punishment and dishonor for the disobedient."

"This, my son, is the road to compulsory obedience, indeed, but there is another road, a short cut, to what is much better— namely, to willing obedience. For people are only too glad to obey the man who they believe takes wiser thought for their interests than they themselves do. And you might recognize that this is so in many instances but particularly in the case of the sick: how readily they call in those who are able to prescribe what they must do; and at sea how cheerfully the passengers obey the captain; and how earnestly travelers desire not to get separated from those who they think are better acquainted with the road than they are. But when people think that they are going to get into trouble if they obey, they will neither yield very much for punishment nor will they be moved by gifts; for no one willingly accepts even a gift at the cost of trouble to himself."

"You mean to say, Father, that nothing is more effectual toward keeping one's men obedient than to seem to be wiser than they?"

"Yes," said he, "that is just what I mean."

"And how, pray, Father, could one most quickly acquire such a reputation for oneself?"

"There is no shorter road, my son," said he, "than really to be wise in those things which you wish to seem to be wise; and when you examine concrete instances, you will realize that what I say is true. For example, if you wish to seem to be a good farmer when you are not, or a good rider, doctor, flute-player, or anything else that you are not, just think how many schemes you must invent to keep up your pretensions. And even if you should persuade any number of people to praise you, in order to give yourself a reputation, and if you should procure a fine outfit for each of your professions, you would soon be found to have practiced deception; and not long after, when you were giving an exhibition of your skill, you would be shown up and convicted, too, as an imposter."

"But how could one become really wise in foreseeing that which will prove to be useful?"

"Obviously, my son," said he, "by learning all that it is possible to acquire by learning."

At the end of his life, Cyrus offers some advice to his own sons.

"My sons, and all you my friends about me, the end of my life is now at hand; I am quite sure of this for many reasons; and when I am dead, you must always speak and act in regard to me as one blessed of fortune. For when I was a boy, I think I plucked all the fruits that among boys count for the best; when I became a youth, I enjoyed what is accounted best among young men; and when I became a mature man, I had the best that men can have. And as time went on, it seemed to me that I recognized that my own strength was always increasing with my years, so that I never found my old age growing any more feeble than my youth had been; and, so far as I know, there is nothing that I ever attempted or desired and yet failed to secure.

"Moreover, I have lived to see my friends made prosperous and happy through my efforts and my enemies reduced by me to subjection; and my country, which once played no great part in Asia, I now leave honored above all. Of all my conquests, there is not one that I have not maintained. Throughout the past I have fared even as I have wished; but a fear that was ever at my side, lest in the time to come I might see or hear or experience something unpleasant, would not let me become overweeningly proud or extravagantly happy.

"But now, if I die, I leave you, my sons, whom the gods have given me, to survive me, and I leave my friends and country happy; and so why should I not be justly accounted blessed and enjoy an immortality of fame?

"Nay, by our fathers' gods I implore you, my sons, honor one another, if you care at all to give me pleasure. For assuredly, this one thing, so it seems to me, you do not know clearly, that I shall have no further being when I have finished this earthly life; for not even in this life have you seen my soul, but you have detected its existence by what it accomplished.

"Next to the gods, however, show respect also to all the race of men as they continue in perpetual succession; for the gods do not hide you away in darkness but your works must ever live on in the sight of all men; and if they are pure and untainted with unrighteousness, they will make your power manifest among all mankind. But if you conceive any unrighteous schemes against each other, you will forfeit in the eyes of all men your right to be trusted. For no one would be able any longer to trust you—not even if he very much desired to do so—if he saw either of you wronging that one who has the first claim to the other's love.

"Now, if I am giving you sufficient instructions as to what manner of men you ought to be one toward the other—well and good; if not, then you must learn it from the history of the past, for this is the best source of instruction. For, as a rule, parents have always been friends to their children, brothers to their brothers; but ere now some of them have been at enmity one with another. Whichever, therefore, of these two courses you shall find to have been profitable, choose that, and you would counsel well."

The Father and His Sons

Aesop

A father had a family of sons who were perpetually quarreling among themselves. When he failed to heal their disputes by his exhortations, he determined to give them a practical illustration of the evils of disunion; and for this purpose he one day told them to bring him a bundle of sticks. When they had done so, he placed the faggot into the hands of each of them in succession, and ordered them to break it in pieces. They each tried with all their strength, and were not able to do it. He next unclosed the faggot, and took the sticks separately, one by one, and again put them into their hands, on which they broke them easily. He then addressed them in these words: "My sons, if you are of one mind, and unite to assist each other, you will be as this faggot, uninjured by all the attempts of your enemies; but if you are divided among yourselves, you will be broken as easily as these sticks."

A Real Man Loathes Cruelty and Injustice

From Theodore Roosevelt,
The Letters of Theodore Roosevelt

Theodore Roosevelt hopes to pass on to his son what he learned from his own father—that a real man eschews cruelty, and combines courage with tenderness.

1901 To Edward Sanford Martin Roosevelt Mss
Albany, November 26, 1900
Dear Dan:
I shall write to Bangs and thank him.
Now, about small Ted's fighting. I believe you will find that

he is not quarrelsome, and that above all, he is not a bully. I think it has been in amicable wrestling and boxing bouts that in your boy's words he has "licked all the boys in his form." In a measure, I am responsible for some of his fighting proclivities, but most of them came naturally. For instance, my two youngest small boys are not in the least fighters like Ted, although I think I have succeeded in instilling into them the theory that they ought not to shirk any quarrel forced upon them.

Now, do you want to know the real underlying feeling which has made me fight myself and want Ted to fight? Well, I summed it up to Ted once or twice when I told him, apropos of lessons of virtue, that he could be just as virtuous as he wished *if only he was prepared to fight.* Fundamentally this has been my own theory. I am not naturally at all a fighter. So far as any man is capable of analyzing his own impulses and desires, mine incline me to amicable domesticity and the avoidance of effort and struggle and any kind of roughness and to the practice of home virtues. Now, I believe that these are good traits, not bad ones. But I also believe that if unsupported by something more virile, they may tend to evil rather than good. The man who merely possesses these traits, and in addition is timid and shirks effort, attracts and deserves a good deal of contempt. He attracts more, though he deserves less, contempt than the powerful, efficient man who is not at all virtuous, but is merely a strong, selfish, self-indulgent brute; the latter being the type. . . . I was fortunate enough in having a father whom I have always been able to regard as an ideal man. It sounds a little like cant to say what I am going to say, but he really did combine the strength and courage and will and energy of the strongest man with the tenderness, cleanness and purity of a woman. I was a sickly and timid boy. He not only took great and loving care of me—some of my earliest remembrances are of nights when he would walk up and down with me for an hour at a time in his arms when I was a wretched mite suffering acutely with asthma—but he also most wisely refused to coddle me, and made me feel that I must force myself to hold my own with other boys and prepare to do the rough work of the world. I cannot say that he ever put it into words, but he certainly gave me the feeling that I was always to be both decent and manly, and that if I were manly nobody would long laugh at my being decent. In all my childhood he never laid a hand

on me but once, but I always knew perfectly well that in case it
became necessary he would not have the slightest hesitancy to
do so again, and alike from my love and respect, and in a certain sense, from my fear of him, I would have hated and
dreaded beyond measure to have him know that I had been
guilty of a lie, or of cruelty, or of bullying, or of uncleanness, or
of cowardice. Gradually I grew to have the feeling on my own
account, and not merely on his. There were many things I tried
to do because he did them, which I found afterward were not
in my line. For instance, I taught Sunday school all through
college, but afterward gave it up, just as on experiment I could
not do the charitable work which he had done. In doing my
Sunday school work I was very much struck by the fact that the
other men who did it only possessed one side of his character.
. . . My ordinary companions in college would I think have had
a tendency to look down upon me for doing Sunday school
work if I had not also been a corking boxer, a good runner,
and a genial member of the Porcellian Club. I went in for boxing and wrestling a good deal, and I really think that while this
was partly because I like them as sports, it was even more
because I intended to be a middling decent fellow, and I did
not intend that anyone should laugh at me with impunity
because I was decent. It is exactly the same thing with history.
In most countries the "Bourgeoisie"—the moral, respectable,
commercial, middle class—is looked upon with a certain contempt which is justified by their timidity and unwarlikeness.
But the minute a middle class produces men like Hawkins and
Frobisher on the seas, or men such as the average Union soldier in the civil war, it acquires the hearty respect of others
which it merits.

Well, I have wanted to pass on to my boys some of what I
got from my own father. I loathe cruelty and injustice. To see a
boy or man torture something helpless whether in the shape of
a small boy or little girl or dumb animal makes me rage. So far
as I know my children have never been cruel, though I have
had to check a certain amount of bullying. Ted is a little fellow,
under the usual size, and wears spectacles, so that strange boys
are rather inclined to jump on him first. When in addition to
this I have trained him so that he objects strongly to torturing
cats or hurting little girls, you can see that there are chances
for life to be unpleasant for him when among other boys. Now
I have striven to make him feel that if he only fights hard

enough he is perfectly certain to secure the respect of all his associates for his virtues. I do not believe he is quarrelsome. I do not think your little boy has found him so. I do not think he oppresses smaller boys, but he does hold his own. When his aunt goes to see him at school, he flings his arms around her neck and is overjoyed with her companionship and has the greatest difficulty to keep from crying when she goes away. Now there are certain of his companions who would be inclined to think him a mollycoddle for betraying such emotion over a female relative; but they won't think him a mollycoddle if he shows an instantaneous readiness to resent hostile criticism on the subject.

Of course, there are dangers in any such training. Every now and then Ted gets an attack of the big head and has to have it reduced, usually by his own associates, occasionally by his affectionate father. Moreover, I know perfectly well that all my training him will only amount to one element out of the many which will go to determine what he is in the future. As you say in your last article, the mother has much more to do than the father with the children's future.

By the way, Mrs. Roosevelt and I laughed all the way down in the cars the other day over that article, I suppose "Jonas" is Ted's schoolfellow. Your account of the father's function in sickness so exactly reproduced our experience that it made me feel guilty and Mrs. Roosevelt decorously exultant. So with my tendency to be a little late at meals, and the tuition of my wife toward the children on the subject.

There I have written you much longer than I had any idea I was going to. With hearty regards, *Faithfully yours*

P.S. I have just received your second note. I have rarely read a more touching letter than Mrs. Moore's. What a fine woman she must be and what a fine son she must have had! I return her letter herewith. If you think she would not mind it, I wish you would give her my most respectful and sincere sympathy.

A Father Sets the Example

From Leon Battista Alberti, The Duties
and Education of Children

In The Duties and Education of Children, *Alberti stresses that a father must serve as a model of the virtues for his children. In other words, practice what you preach—don't expect your son to grow up well unless you exemplify the behavior you want from him. A father is entitled to a son's respect, but he has to earn it. Your son will be good if he respects you and wants to earn your affection by living up to the example you set for him.*

I do not deny that fathers, more than others, must strive with their whole being, with all their diligence and wisdom, to make their children honest and high-principled. They must do so because they will be rendering a service to them, since principles in a young man are not esteemed less than wealth. They will also bring honor to their house, their country, and themselves, for virtuous children bear witness to their fathers' diligence and honor them. If I am not mistaken, it is thought better for a country to have virtuous and honest citizens than rich and powerful ones. In truth, unprincipled children must be the cause of great sorrow to a sensitive father. This is not only because a father dislikes to see vice and wickedness in his child, but also because there can be no doubt that a son's dishonesty redounds to his father's shame. The more so in that everyone knows it is mainly up to the father to make the children honest, virtuous, and honorable. No one denies that fathers can accomplish as much as they wish with their children. A good horseman will make a horse gentle and obedient; a less skillful and diligent one could not even bridle the same horse. In the same way, a solicitous father will make his children modest and courteous. Those whose sons are wicked and lost in iniquity shall not avoid shame or escape blame for negligence.

As Lorenzo said, therefore, the elders' first care and thought should be to make the young as virtuous and high-principled as possible.

Fathers can easily see their children's inclination through many signs. No man is so experienced and accomplished or so sly and shrewd in hiding his appetites, desires, and passions that you cannot see his secret vices if you observe his actions and ways for several days. Plutarch writes that Arpallus immediately realized how avaricious Demosthenes was simply by noticing how he glanced at certain foreign vases. Thus a gesture, an action, a word often allows you to look within a man's soul. This is more easily done with children than with men, who are wiser through age and slyness, for children do not know how to hide their thoughts through feigning and dissimulating. I believe it is a sign of a good mind in children if they rarely remain idle and if they want to do what they see others do. It is a sign of a good and mild nature when they are easily quieted and forget an injury, when they are not obstinate, give way to the opinion of others without harshness and desire of vengeance, and when they do not insist on having their own way. It is a sign of a virile spirit when a boy is ready and quick to answer and courageous and willing to appear among men without timidity and boorish elusiveness. It seems that custom and habit greatly help in this. It will, therefore, be useful not to shelter them in one's room and lap as some mothers do, but to accustom them to be with people and respectful toward all. They must not be left alone or allowed to languish in womanly idleness and vegetate among women. Plato used to reproach his Dion for being solitary, saying that solitude is the companion of stubbornness. Cato, seeing a young man alone and idle, asked him what he was doing. The latter answered that he was conversing with himself. "Take care," said Cato, "that you do not converse with an evil man." He was a most prudent man, for he knew how in young minds desires corrupted by lust, wrath, or evil thoughts are more powerful than reason. He knew that this young man, busy in answering and listening to himself, was more apt to listen to his desires and appetites than to honesty, and less likely to believe in continence and avoiding lust than in the pleasures and delight he desired. With idleness and solitude one becomes stubborn, strange, and full of vices.

From the very beginning, boys must be accustomed to being among men, where they may learn more virtues than vices. They must be made manly from an early age, by making them exercise in matters as great and magnificent as their age allows, and they must be steered away from womanly customs and ways. The Spartans made their boys walk along graves in the darkness of night to teach them not to be afraid or believe old wives' tales. They knew, and no wise man doubts this, that custom is powerful throughout life, and more so during childhood than at any other time. Every praiseworthy deed not beyond their strength will seem light and easy to undertake to those who have been reared in manly arts from an early age. One must, therefore, accustom boys to taxing and arduous tasks where, with diligence and effort, they may seek and hope for true praise and favor. It is useful for them to exercise their minds and bodies, nor can one sufficiently praise the value and necessity of exercises in all things.

Through idleness the mind becomes dull and foggy and all spiritual virtues become weak and inert. Exercise, on the other hand, is very useful. One becomes more lively, the nerves become accustomed to labor, the limbs are strengthened, the blood is thinned, one puts on firm flesh, and the mind is alert and cheerful.

It is not necessary at this point to speak of how useful and necessary exercise is for everyone, particularly the young. Notice how boys who are raised in the country, working under the sun's rays, are stronger and more robust than ours who grow up in idleness and in the shade, and to whom, as Columella said, death can add nothing of its own. They sit around, thin, pale, all eyes and sniffles. It is useful, therefore, to accustom them to work and engage in manly tasks, to strengthen them as well as prevent them from being overcome by idleness and inertia. I also praise those who accustom their children to endure cold with bare heads and feet, stay up late at night, rise before the sun, and for the rest give them only what propriety requires and what the body needs to grow and become strong. In short, one must accustom them to these privations, thus making them as manly as possible, for this can do no harm while it may result in much good. Herodotus, that ancient Greek known as the father of history, writes that after the Persians, led by their King Cambyses, had won a battle over the Egyptians, the bones of the many dead were gathered. Although in time the bones of Egyptians and the Persians had been mingled together, they could still be easily recognized, for the skulls of the Persians would crumble at the slightest touch, while those of the Egyptians were very hard and resisted the strongest blows. He states that the reason for this was that the Persians were more delicate and always kept their heads covered, while the Egyptians, from the time they were children, accustomed themselves to going bare-headed under the hot sun and in the rain, and also at night, whether the sky was clear or stormy. We must, then, consider the value of these customs, for he also says that the Persians are almost never bald. Lycurgus, that most prudent king of the Spartans, decreed that his citizens be accustomed from an early age, not to delicacies, but to labor, not to games in the city, but to tilling the soil in the fields and to military exercises. How well he knew the value of exercise. Have not some of our citizens become skilled and strong who once were weak and awkward? And have not some who at first were clumsy and inept become excellent runners and jumpers and skilled in hurling weights or the javelin?

It is a father's duty to test his sons' intellect in many ways. He must be alert and notice his sons' every act and indication, encouraging and praising the children when they are manly and good, and correcting them when lazy and dissolute. He must make them exercise according to their needs and at the proper time. It is said that it is harmful to engage in bodily exercise immediately after meals. To be active and become somewhat tired before eating does no harm, but it is not helpful to become extremely fatigued. To exercise one's intellect and spirit in the pursuit of virtue at any time and in any place and in all things has always been praiseworthy. Let fathers, then, consider this task not troublesome, but pleasant. You go hunting in the forest, tire yourself, sweat, spend the night in the cold and wind and the day in the sun and dust in order to see dogs run after animals and hunt them down. Is there any less pleasure in seeing two or more minds vie in the pursuit of virtue? Is it less useful for you to adorn your children with good habits and manners through your worthy and just efforts than to return home tired and hot with whatever game you have killed? Let fathers take pleasure, then, in inciting their sons to pursue virtue and fame. Let them encourage them to vie for honors. Let them praise the victor and enjoy having sons who are alert and thirst for well-deserved praise and honor.

If our sons will not want for any necessities, we shall be leaving them considerable wealth. They will be wealthy indeed if we leave them enough so that they will not have to use that phrase so bitter and hateful to a noble spirit, "I beg you." It will, however, be a greater inheritance for our sons if we educate them so that they will prefer to endure poverty rather than descend to begging or serving in order to accumulate wealth. An inheritance is large enough if it satisfies not only all our necessities, but our desires. By desires I mean only honest wishes; those of a dishonest character have always seemed to me to be madness or the vice of a corrupt spirit, rather than just desires. If you leave excessive wealth to your sons it will be a burden to them and a father does not show his love by burdening his children, but by lightening their load. Every excessive burden is difficult to support; what cannot be supported easily falls, and there is nothing more fragile than wealth. A gift which entails servitude and vexation is not worthy of a father toward his child. Let us give burdensome and disagreeable things to enemies; to our friends we shall give happiness and freedom. I shall not consider wealth anything which entails servitude and worry, as is the case with excessive riches. It is better for our sons to have to fend for themselves than to lose all their wealth, the useful part as well as the superfluous, as happens without doubt to those who do not know how to manage their fortune. Whatever your sons will be unable to manage will be superfluous and a burden to them. One must, therefore, teach his sons virtue, make them learn how to govern themselves and curb their appetites and desires, educate them so that they will know how to acquire praise, benevolence, and favor more than wealth, and make them learned in the art of preserving their honor and the goodwill of others, as well as in all other matters. Those who know how to adorn themselves with glory and dignity in this manner will certainly be learned and skilled in acquiring and preserving all other lesser things.

Cato, that good man of antiquity, was not ashamed, and it did not seem a burden to him, to teach his son swimming, fencing, and other civil and military skills in addition to letters, and he believed it was a father's duty to teach his children all the virtues worthy of free men. He did not think it just to call anyone free who lacked any of these virtues. And he himself wanted to be their teacher, thinking no one else should be given preference for this task since no one could be found who would show greater solicitude toward his children than he himself. Moreover, he thought his children would not learn as willingly from others as they would from their own father. A father's love, care, and zeal are more effective in making children virtuous than the great doctrine of a most learned man. As for me, I should like to follow the example of Cato and the other good men of antiquity who were teachers and guides to their children in everything they knew and wanted above all to correct their vices personally and make them virtuous. In addition they placed their children with those whose culture and friendship might help them acquire excellence in learning and virtue.

It is a father's duty, therefore, to punish his children and make them wise and virtuous. We must be like the farmer in his fields who does not fear to trample some good grass in order to destroy harmful weeds. In the same manner, let not a father hesitate to treat a son more harshly than his nature and love dictate in order to make him better. But perhaps there are some who not only do not eradicate bad habits, but implant a thousand vices in their children. How harmful do you think it is for the young to associate with a father who is ill-mannered, haughty, and bestial in words and deeds, who shouts and blusters, swears and blasphemes endlessly? He rages, and his children believe they should and can imitate the customs of their elders. Through the fault and negligence of those who take care of the young, we have come to the point where gluttonous babies ask for capon and partridge even before they know what to call them and demand rare delicacies before they have all their teeth with which to chew them. A father, therefore, who is a glutton given to pleasures will easily give in to the desires of those dear to him and will allow them to enjoy those same pleasures. This sort of dissolute fathers can have only one reason for not daring to punish their children in order to instill honesty and good habits in them. They are afraid that if their children grow up virtuous they will then reproach them for their vices, as is often the case. There are some who do not like to see in others the vices in which they themselves indulge: they stuff themselves, yet hate gluttons; they perjure themselves, yet scorn liars; they are obstinate in everything, yet they condemn the stubborn. For this reason they become excessively stern disciplinarians, punishing in their children those vices for which they themselves are infamous. They beat their children to give vent to their wrath and ill humor. These fathers are most unjust, for they do not first correct in themselves what they hate in others. To these one can say: "O foolish, mad fathers, how do you expect your little children not to have learned what you, with your hoary locks, have taught them by persisting in your vices?"

But we must also overcome all evil inclinations through our zeal and diligence. Wise men judge that it is bad habits and intemperance that lead to vice, rather than any natural appetite or urge. We often see young men who are quiet, humble, and modest by nature become shameless, haughty, and impetuous because of evil companions and the frequenting of dishonest places. And in similar matters we observe that habit has greater power for instilling vice in us than our own natural appetite; for instance, an abundance of well-prepared foods strengthens lust in a man. From this came the ancient proverb, "Without Bacchus and Ceres, Venus lies cold."

Let fathers see to it that their sons pursue the study of letters assiduously and let them teach them to understand and write correctly. Let them not think they have taught them if they do not see that their sons have learned to read and write perfectly, for in this it is almost the same to know badly as not to know at all. Then let the children learn arithmetic and gain a sufficient knowledge of geometry, for these are enjoyable sciences suitable to young minds and of great use to all regardless of age or social status. Then let them turn once more to the poets, orators, and philosophers.

Fathers should know that a knowledge of letters never does any harm, but is useful to all professions. Of the many excellent and esteemed men of letters in our family, none proved to be less useful in other matters because of his love of letters. It is not necessary to continue to discuss at this time how a knowledge of letters is always useful in all matters and in acquiring fame. I do not want you to think, however, that I want fathers to keep their sons continuously imprisoned with their books, Adovardo. On the contrary, I want boys to amuse themselves as much as is necessary for relaxation. But let all their games be manly, honest, and without the least suspicion of vice or reproach. Let them play those games which the good ancients enjoyed.

A Father Must Be His Son's Guide to Maturity

From Lord Chesterfield,
The Letters of Lord Chesterfield to His Son

Dear Boy,

Let us resume our reflection upon men, their characters, their manners; in a word, our reflection upon the world. They may help you to form yourself and to know others. A knowledge very useful at all ages, very rare at yours; it seems as if it were nobody's business to communicate it to young men. Their masters teach them, singly, the languages or the sciences of their several departments; and are indeed generally incapable of teaching them the world; their parents are often so too, or at least neglect doing it, either from avocations, indifference, or from an opinion that throwing them into the world (as they call it) is the best way of teaching it them. This last notion is in a great degree true; that is, the world can doubtless never be well known by theory; practice is absolutely necessary; but surely, it is of great use to a young man, before he sets out for that country, full of mazes, windings, and turnings, to have at least a general map of it, made by some experienced traveler.

It seems extraordinary, but it is very true, that my anxiety for you increases in proportion to the good accounts which I receive of you from all hands. I promise myself so much from you, that I dread the least disappointment. You are now so near the port, which I have so long wished and labored to bring you safe into, that my concern would be doubled, should you be shipwrecked within sight of it. The object, therefore, of this letter is (laying beside all the authority of a parent) to conjure you as a friend, by the affection you have for me (and surely you have reason to have some), and by the regard you have for yourself, to go on, with assiduity and attention, to complete that work, which of late you have carried on so well, and which is now so near being finished. My wishes and my plan were to make you shine, and distinguish yourself equally in the learned and the polite world. Few have been able to do it. Deep learning is generally tainted with pedantry, or at least unadorned by manners; as, on the other hand, polite manners, and the turn of the world, are too often unsupported by knowledge, and consequently end contemptibly in the frivolous dissipation of drawing-rooms and *ruelles*. You are now got over the dry and difficult parts of learning; what remains, requires much more time than trouble.

In short, I give you fair warning, that when we meet, if you are absent in mind, I will soon be absent in body; for, it will be impossible for me to stay in the room; and if at table you throw down your knife, plate, bread, etc., and hack the wing of a chicken for half an hour, without being able to cut it off, and your sleeve all the time in another dish, I must rise from table to escape the fever you would certainly give to me. Good God! how I should be shocked if you came into my room, for the first time, with two left legs, presenting yourself with all the graces and dignity of a tailor, and your clothes hanging upon you like those in Monmouth Street, upon tenter-hooks! whereas I expect, and require, to see you present yourself with the easy and genteel air of a man of fashion who has kept good company. I expect you not only well dressed, but very well dressed; I expect a gracefulness in all your motions, and something particularly engaging in your address. All this I expect, and all this it is in your power, by care and attention, to make me find out; but, to tell you the plain truth, if I do not find it, we shall not converse very much together; for I cannot stand inattention and awkwardness; it would endanger my health.

Son, What Have I Done to Deserve This?

From *William Shakespeare,* Henry IV, Part One

Shakespeare's Henry IV *presents a striking example of the familiar tension between the gravity of age and the impetuosity of youth, compounded by the tension between a father and a son who also happen to be the King of England and the heir to the throne. There could hardly be a better illustration of how a flawed relationship between a father and a son in private life can have profoundly important consequences for the wider sphere of society and politics. The scene begins with Henry asking his noblemen to leave the room so that he can have some private words with the Prince. Like a father taking his son to his room to upbraid him beyond the view of his friends and the rest of the family, Henry chastises Hal severely for being such a wastrel and layabout. His are the kind of words disappointed fathers have said to rebellious sons throughout history: What have I done to deserve this? Don't you have any feeling for me?*

King.   Lords, give us leave: the Prince of Wales and I
Must have some private conference; but be near at hand,
For we shall presently have need of you.
Exeunt Lords.
I know not whether God will have it so
For some displeasing service I have done,
That, in his secret doom, out of my blood
He'll breed revengement and a scourge for me;
But thou dost in thy passages of life
Make me believe that thou art only marked
For the hot vengeance and the rod of heaven
To punish my mistreadings. Tell me else,
Could such inordinate and low desires,

Such poor, such bare, such lewd, such mean attempts,
Such barren pleasures, rude society,
As thou art matched withal and grafted to,
Accompany the greatness of thy blood
And hold their level with thy princely heart?
Prince.   So please your Majesty, I would I could
Quit all offenses with as clear excuse
As well as I am doubtless I can purge
Myself of many I am charged withal.
Yet such extenuation let me beg
As, in reproof of many tales devised,
Which oft the ear of greatness needs must hear
By smiling pickthanks and base newsmongers,
I may, for some things true wherein my youth
Hath faulty wand'red and irregular
Find pardon on my true submission.
King.   God pardon thee! Yet let me wonder, Harry,
At thy affections, which do hold a wing
Quite from the flight of all thy ancestors.
Thy place in council thou hast rudely lost,
Which by thy young brother is supplied,
And art almost an alien to the hearts
Of all the court and princes of my blood.
The hope and expectation of thy time
Is ruined, and the soul of every man
Prophetically do forethink thy fall.
Had I so lavish of my presence been,
So common-hackneyed in the eyes of men,
So stale and cheap to vulgar company,
Opinion that did help me to the crown,
Had still kept loyal to possession
And left me in reputeless banishment,
A fellow of no mark nor likelihood.
By being seldom seen, I could not stir
But, like a comet, I was wond'red at;
That men would tell their children, "This is he!"
Others would say, "Where? Which is Bolingbroke?"
And then I stole all courtesy from heaven,
And dressed myself in such humility
That I did pluck allegiance from men's hearts,
Loud shouts and salutations from their mouths
Even in the presence of the crowned King.

Thus did I keep my person fresh and new,
My presence, like a robe pontifical,
Ne'er seen but wond'red at; and so my state,
Seldom but sumptuous, showed like a feast
And won by rareness such solemnity.
The skipping King, he ambled up and down
With shallow jesters and rash bavin wits,
Soon kindled and soon burnt; carded his state;
Mingled his royalty with cap'ring fools;
Had his great name profaned with their scorns
And gave his countenance, against his name,
To laugh at gibing boys and stand the push
Of every beardless vain comparative,
Grew a companion to the common streets,
Enfeoffed himself to popularity;
That, being daily swallowed by men's eyes,
They surfeited with honey and began
To loathe the taste of sweetness, whereof a little
More than a little is by much too much.
So, when he had occasion to be seen,
He was but as the cuckoo is in June,
Heard, not regarded—seen, but with such eyes
As, sick and blunted with community,
Afford no extraordinary gaze,
Such as is bent on sunlike majesty
When it shines seldom in admiring eyes;
but rather drowsed and hung their eyelids down,
Slept in his face, and rend'red such aspect
As cloudy men use to their adversaries,
Being with his presence glutted, gorged, and full.
And in that very line, Harry, standest thou;
For thou hast lost thy princely privilege
With vile participation. Not an eye
But is aweary of thy common sight,
Save mine, which hath desired to see thee more;
Which now doth that I would not have it do—
Make blind itself with foolish tenderness.
Prince. I shall hereafter, my thrice-gracious lord,
Be more myself.

But the political dimension makes their private tension much graver. Henry tells Hal: You are like Richard II, the unworthy ruler I deposed, while your cousin Hotspur is like I was when I was your age. Your undignified, dishonorable way of life makes you unfit to succeed to the throne. In the unkindest cut, Henry tells his son he isn't even sure that Hal won't desert to the other side in the civil war with the Percys. Hal pleads with his father for a chance to redeem himself—to prove to his father that he truly is his son.

King.   For all the world,
As thou art to this hour was Richard then
When I from France set foot at Ravenspurgh;
And even as I was then is Percy now.
Now, by my scepter, and my soul to boot,
He hath more worthy interest to the state
Than thou the shadow of succession;
For of no right, nor color like to right,
He doth fill fields with harness in the realm,
Turns head against the lion's armed jaws.
Why, Harry, do I tell thee of my foes,
Which art my nearest and dearest enemy?
Thou that art like enough, through vassal fear,
Base inclination, and the start of spleen,
To fight against me under Percy's pay,
To dog his heels and curtsy at his frowns,
To show how much thou art degenerate.
Prince.   Do not think so, you shall not find it so.
And God forgive them that so much have swayed
Your Majesty's good thoughts away from me.
I will redeem all this on Percy's head
And, in the closing of some glorious day,
Be bold to tell you that I am your son.

On the Affection of Fathers for Their Children

From Michel de Montaigne, Essays

When should a man marry? When should he pass his property to his children? Can a man be friends with his children? From two essays by Montaigne on friendship and paternal affection.

There is nothing to which Nature seems so much to have inclined us as to society. And Aristotle says that good lawgivers had more respect to friendship than to justice. Now the supreme point of its perfection is this. For, speaking generally, all those amities that are created and nourished by pleasure or profit, public or private needs, are so much the less noble and beautiful, and so much the less friendship, as they introduce some other cause and design and fruit into friendship, than itself.

That of children to their fathers is rather respect. Friendship is kept alive by communication, which, by reason of too great disparity, cannot exist between them, and would haply conflict with natural duties. For neither can all the secret thoughts of the father be communicated to his son, in order not to beget an unseemly familiarity, nor can the admonitions and corrections, which are among the first offices of friendship, be administered by the son to the father. There have been nations where it was the custom for children to kill their fathers, and others where the fathers killed their children, to avoid their becoming at some time a hindrance to each other; and by the law of Nature the one depends on the destruction of the other. Some philosophers have been known to disdain their natural tie: witness Aristippus, who, being close pressed about the affection he owed to his children, as being come out of him, began to spit, saying that that had also come out of him, and that we also breed lice and worms. And that other whom Plutarch tried to reconcile with his brother: "I do not think any better of him, he said, for having come out of the same orifice."

Truly the name of brother is a beautiful name, and full of affection, and on that model did he and I form our alliance. But that intervention of worldly goods, those divisions, and the fact that the wealth of the one is the other's poverty, have a wonderful effect in softening and loosening the brotherly solder. Brothers having to conduct the progress of their advancement along the same path and at the same rate, they must of necessity often jostle and clash with one another. Moreover, the agreement and the relation which beget those true and perfect friendships, why should they be found in natural brothers? The father and son may be of entirely different dispositions, and brothers too. He is my son, he is my kinsman, but he is sullen, ill-natured, or a fool. And besides, the more these friendships are imposed upon us by law and natural obligation, the less is there of our voluntary choice and freedom. And our voluntary freedom produces nothing more properly its own than affection and friendship. Not but that I have experienced on that side all that can possibly be experienced, having had the best father that ever was, and the most indulgent, even in his extreme old age; and one who from father to son was descended from a family famed and exemplary in this respect of brotherly concord:

Known
For loving-kindness father-like
To all his brothers shown (Horace).

As concerning marriage, besides that it is a bargain to which only the entrance is free (its continuance being forced and constrained; and depending on something other than our will), a bargain moreover that is usually concluded to other ends, there supervene a thousand extraneous entanglements to unravel, sufficient to break the thread and disturb the course of a lively affection; whereas in friendship there is no traffic or business except with itself.

A father is indeed miserable who holds the affection of his children only through the need they have of his assistance, if that may be called affection. He should make himself worthy of respect by his virtue and abilities, and worthy of love by his kindness and gentle manners. Even the ashes of a rich matter have their price; and we have been accustomed to hold in respect and reverence the bones and relics of persons of honor.

No old age can be so decrepit and musty in a person who has lived an honorable life, but it should be revered, especially by his children, whose minds he should have trained to their duty by reason, not by want and the need that they have of him, nor by harshness and compulsion:

He greatly errs who thinks a father's rule
Can be upheld with more stability
By stern, unbending measures than
By any loving kindness (Terrence).

I condemn all harsh measures in the bringing-up of a tender soul that is being trained for honor and freedom. There is a something that savors of slavishness in severity and compulsion; and I hold that what cannot be done by reason, by wisdom and tact, can never be done by force. I was brought up in that way. They tell me that in all my early childhood I did not taste the rod but twice, and very gently. I owed the same treatment to the children I have had. I lost them all as infants in their nurses' arms; but Leonor, an only daughter who escaped that misfortune, has reached the age of six years or more, without our ever employing for her guidance and for the chastisement of her childish faults (her mother's indulgence readily conforming thereto), any but words, and very gentle ones. And if I should be disappointed in my hopes of her, there are other causes enough to blame, without condemning my educational methods, which I know to be right and natural. I should in this respect have been much more scrupulous with boys, who are not so much born for service, and of a freer condition. I should have loved to make their hearts big with free and noble sentiments. I have never known any other effect of the rod but to render the soul more cowardly and more deceitfully obstinate.

Do we wish to be loved by our children? Would we take from them all occasion to desire our death (although no cause for so dreadful a desire can be either right or excusable—*no crime is founded on reason* [Livy])? Let us reasonably furnish their lives with what is in our power. To do that we should not marry so young that our age will be almost confounded with theirs. For this inconvenience plunges us into many great difficulties. I refer specially to the nobility, who are of a leisurely condition, living, as they say, on their rents only. For in other classes where they have to earn their living, the plurality, and company of children are an additional resource to the household, and so many new tools and instruments wherewith to grow rich.

I married at thirty-three, and concur in Aristotle's opinion, which is said to have recommended thirty-five.

In a certain region of the Spanish Indies the men were not permitted to marry until after they were forty; and yet the girls were allowed to marry at ten.

For a gentleman of thirty-five it is too soon to make way for his son of twenty: he is yet able to cut a good figure both in warlike expeditions and at the court of his prince. He has need of all his resources, and he ought certainly to share them, but not to the extent of neglecting himself for another. And such a man may rightly make use of the answer that fathers usually have on their lips: "I have no desire to undress until I go to bed."

But a father, stricken with years and infirmities, barred by his weakness and poor health from the ordinary society of his fellow-men, wrongs himself and his family by brooding unprofitably over a great hoard of wealth. He has come to that state when, if he is wise, he will wish to strip, not to his shirt, but to a nice warm night-gown, to go to bed. The remaining pomps, for which he has no further use, he should willingly bestow on those to whom, by the order of Nature, they should belong. It is only right that he should leave to them the enjoyment which Nature denies him: otherwise he is surely moved by envy and malice.

I do not mean to say that we should give our property up to them by means of a bond which cannot be recalled. I, who am old enough to play this part, would resign to them the enjoyment of my house and property, but with liberty to repent if they should give me occasion. I should leave them the use thereof, because it would be no longer convenient to me, but would reserve to myself as much as I thought good of the management of affairs in general, having ever been of opinion that it must be a great satisfaction to an aged father, himself to put his children in the way of managing his affairs, and to have the power, during his lifetime, of controlling their behavior, giving them instruction and advice according to the experience he has of them, and of personally directing the ancient honor and order of his house in the hands of his successors, and so make himself responsible for the hopes he may conceive of their future conduct.

And to this end I would not fly their company: I would observe them near at hand and join, as far as my age would permit, in their mirth and their pastimes. If I did not live in the midst of them (which I could not do without trespassing on their gatherings, by reason of the peevishness of my old age and the exigencies of my infirmities, and without besides straining and breaking through the regularity of the habits and mode of living that I should then have adopted), I would at least live near them in a corner of my house, not the most showy, but the most comfortable.

It is also foolish and wrong not to admit them to familiarity with their fathers when they are grown up, and to try to maintain toward them an austere and scornful gravity, hoping thereby to keep them in awe and obedience. For that is a very futile pretense, which makes fathers distasteful and, what is worse, ridiculous to their children. They are in possession of youth and vigor, and consequently enjoy the goodwill and favor of the world; and receive with mockery those fierce and tyrannical looks of a man who has no longer any blood in his heart or his veins: regular scarecrows in a hempfield!

Even though I could inspire fear I would much rather inspire love.

The King's Son and the Painted Lion

Aesop

You can't protect them from everything.

A king who had one only son, fond of martial exercises, had a dream in which he was warned that his son would be killed by a lion. Afraid lest the dream should prove true, he built for his son a pleasant palace, and adorned its walls for his amusement with all kinds of animals of the size of life, among which was the picture of a lion. When the young Prince saw this, his grief at being thus confined burst out afresh, and standing near the lion, he thus spoke: "O you most detestable of animals! through a lying dream of my father's, which he saw in his sleep, I am shut up on your account in this palace as if I had been a girl: what shall I now do to you?" With these words he stretched out his hands toward a thorn-tree, meaning to cut a stick from its branches that he might beat the lion, when one of its sharp prickles pierced his finger, and caused great pain and inflammation, so that the young Prince fell down in a fainting fit. A violent fever suddenly set in, from which he died not many days later.

We had better bear our troubles bravely than try to escape them.

A Roman Father

From Plutarch,
Lives of the Noble Greeks and Romans

Plutarch's lives of eminent Greeks and Romans abundantly illustrate the classical ideal of manliness. Cato the Elder, despite his famous moral rectitude, was also a loving husband and a good father. He expected much of his son, but because the boy had a delicate physique, he relaxed the physical requirements of his education. The boy rewarded his father's careful attention to his education and his understanding attitude by distinguishing himself in battle.

Cato was also a good father, an excellent husband to his wife, and an extraordinary household manager. And since he did not manage his affairs of this kind carelessly, or treat them as things of no importance, I think I ought to record a little further whatever was commendable in him in this regard. He married a wife whose nobility exceeded her wealth, being of the opinion that the rich and the high-born are equally haughty and proud, but that those of noble blood would be more ashamed of base behavior, and consequently more obedient to their husbands in all that was fitting and right. Cato said that a man who beat his wife or child laid violent hands on what was most sacred, and in his view a good husband was more worthy of praise than a great senator. He admired the ancient Socrates more than anything else for having lived a temperate and contented life in spite of having a wife who was a scold and children who were half-witted.

As soon as his son was born, unless Cato was occupied by the most urgent affairs of state, he would be on hand when his wife washed it and dressed it in its swaddling clothes. For she herself suckled it, and she often gave her breast to her servants' children, to produce in them, by suckling the same milk, a kind of brotherly love for her son. When their son began to mature, Cato himself would teach him to read, although he had a servant, a very good grammarian, called Chilo, who taught many others. But Cato thought it not fit, as he himself said, to have his son reprimanded by a slave, or pulled by the ears when found tardy in his lesson: nor would he have him owe to a servant the obligation of so great a thing as his learning. Cato himself, therefore, taught his son grammar, law, and his gymnastic exercises. Not only did he show him, as well, how to throw a dart, to fight in armor, and to ride, but also how to box and to endure both heat and cold, and to swim in the most rapid and rough rivers. Cato tells us that he wrote histories, in large letters, with his own hand, so that his son, without stirring out of the house, might learn to know about his countrymen and forefathers. He never said anything obscene in front of his son, no more than if he had been in the presence of the holy Vestal Virgins. Nor would he ever go into the bath with him, although this seems to have been the common custom of the Romans. In earlier times, sons-in-law used to avoid bathing with fathers-in-law, ashamed to see one another naked. But later on, having learned from the Greeks to strip before men, they have since taught the Greeks to do it even with the women themselves.

Thus, like an excellent piece of work, Cato formed and fashioned his son to virtue, and he never had occasion to find fault with him, since the boy was always eager and never docile. But because he proved to have too weak a constitution for undergoing hardships, Cato did not insist on requiring of him any very austere way of living. However, though delicate in health, he proved a stout man in the field, and behaved himself valiantly when Paulus Æmilius fought against Perseus. When his sword was struck from him by a blow, or rather slipped out of his hand by reason of its moistness, he so keenly resented it, that he turned to some of his friends about him, and taking them along with him again fell upon the enemy; and having by a long fight and such force cleared the place, at length found his sword among great heaps of arms, and the dead bodies of friends as well as enemies piled one upon the other. Upon which Paulus, his general, much commended the youth; and there is a letter of Cato's to his son, which highly praised his honorable eagerness for the recovery of his sword. Afterwards he married Tertia, Æmilius Paulus's daughter, and sister to Scipio. He was admitted into this family as much for his own worth as his father's. So Cato's care over his son's education was fittingly rewarded.

Cato was old, when Carneades the Academic, and Diogenes the Stoic, came as deputies from Athens to Rome, pleading for

release from a fine of five hundred talents laid on the Athenians in
a law suit. The Athenians had not contested the law suit, in which
the Oropians were plaintiffs and Sicyonians judges. All the most
studious youth immediately waited on these philosophers, admired
them and frequently heard them speak. The gracefulness of
Carneades's oratory, whose ability was really greatest, and his reputation equal to it, gathered large and favourable audiences, and
before long filled, like a wind, all the city with the sound of it. So
that it soon began to be said that a Greek, famous and admired,
winning and carrying all before him, had impressed so strange a
love upon the young men, that they had abandoned all their pleasures and pastimes and ran mad, as it were, after philosophy.
Indeed, this greatly pleased the Romans in general, since they
enjoyed seeing their young men respond to Greek literature so
enthusiastically, and frequent the company of learned men. But
Cato, on the other hand, seeing the passion for words flowing into
the city, opposed it from the beginning, fearing that Roman youth
would be diverted and would prefer the glory of speaking well over
the glory of arms and behaving virtuously. And when the fame of
the philosophers increased in the city, and Caius Acilius, a person
of distinction, at his own request, became their interpreter to the
senate at their first audience, Cato resolved, under some specious
pretence, to have all philosophers cleared out of the city. Coming
into the senate, he blamed the magistrates for letting these
deputies stay in the city for so long a time. He argued that since
they were persons who could easily persuade people to accept any
argument they pleased, a decision should therefore be reached
quickly about their petition. Then they could go home again to
their own schools, and display their oratory to the sons of Greece,
and leave the Roman youth to be obedient, as hitherto, to their
own laws and authorities.

Yet he did this not out of any anger, as some think, toward
Carneades, but because he completely despised philosophy, and
out of a kind of patriotic pride scoffed at Greek studies and literature. For example, he would say that Socrates was a seditious wind-
bag, who did his best to tyrannize over his country, undermine the
ancient customs, and seduce the citizens into holding opinions
contrary to the laws. Ridiculing the school of Isocrates, he said that
his students grew into old men before they had finished studying
with him, as if they were to use their art to plead causes in the court

of Minos in the next world. To frighten his son away from anything that was Greek, he pronounced as if he were an oracle—and in a more vehement tone than was seemly for a man his age—that the Romans would certainly be destroyed if they were ever infected with Greek culture. Time indeed has shown the vanity of this prophecy. For, in truth, the city of Rome has risen to the height of its good fortune since it came to embrace Greek learning.

Fathers Must Earn Their Authority

From Jacopo Sadoleto,
On the Education of Boys

According to Sadoleto, a father must provide for his son a model of decency, learning, and good manners. He doesn't actually have to possess all the virtues he encourages in his son. But by setting an example, he can hope that his son will grow up to be a better man than himself—which all fathers naturally desire.

The next main principle in a child's training . . . is that a father, who desires to bring his son up as a good and noble man, should himself afford a pattern to be copied. No training can be better than that. In saying this I do not deny that there are many graces of life that ought daily to be increased in a child, though his father may not possess them: for example, letters and the pursuit and study of those Arts which are called Liberal, the knowledge of civil or ecclesiastical law, practice and understanding of war and military matters, it may be: for while a father may by the fault of his own father or of mere mischance be wholly ignorant of these matters, he should see that his son know something of them. For there is a natural desire common to all fathers, that they should leave sons better and more illustrious than themselves. And this comes from a natural love in every man, not more for his son than for himself, due to the deeply implanted, inborn craving to prolong our life, a craving by which we are swept on to the lust for immortality; and a father always feels himself to live again in his son and to pass into his own image.

Let this, then, be the first rule for parents in regard to their children if they desire to bring them to the best fruits of good-ness—that what they long for their children to become, they must show themselves to be in their children's eyes.

Let the father then be a man of this sort: of well-balanced nature, his one vehement passion the pursuit of goodness and honor, eager to pour his whole soul through the channel of ears and eyes into the mind and spirit of his son. For the child at once begins to turn his eyes upon the father of the family as soon as he has any power of thought, and observes with a special attention all that he says and does; and so we must be more watchful, lest we carry from ourselves any infection of evil or dishonor into the life of him whom we ourselves long to mold and shape to the fair form of a rounded and complete virtue. Now as the sense of sight is prior to the sense of hearing and is earlier to develop its natural power, the first care must be to set before the eyes of the son the pattern, in the person of his father, of a manly dignity. This will express itself in dress, in every movement of body and of mind—and all the con-cerns of home life from day to day: in all these the father must observe the fashion of dress which is in general vogue, yet so that there shall be nothing over-exquisite in his apparel, and nothing again common or unkempt, which is sometimes attributed to care-lessness, but more often to meanness. As for the movements and impulses of the mind, which springing from anger, vexation, love, hate, hope, unexpected pleasure, the fear of some evil or disaster, the sudden announcement of calamity, and all the other influ-ences, the inward passions of whatever kind that buffet or shake the mind, and strive to move it from its seat, all these he must so support and govern that to a beholder he may seem to be on the lookout for these assaults, however impetuous and swift they may be, but awaiting the command of reason, not daring to make a sor-tie against them, until, and then only so far as, reason bids. This is a spectacle than which the world offers nothing more God-like. For what can the eye discover so rare, so noble, so splendid in its rounded and beautiful dignity as the sight of virtue controlling and ordering the impulses and affections of the mind, or fitly adjusting them to the rule of reason.

If a boy from his earliest years has been steeped in this tradi-tion in the example of his father, he will have taken into his heart the noble seed of a virtue which will come to a splendid fruition in his own character.

But this ordered self-control of the mind is accompanied by a certain slowness shown in every movement and gesture of the body—not of course the heaviness or slackness which is generally the sign of indolence and inertness of mind, and sometimes even of a gross stupidity—I mean rather that slowness which accords with acknowledged dignity of character and is curbed by the same checks and enjoys the same freedom as the mind itself; when occasion calls for quick decision and rapid action, the quick and ready service of the body, with hand and foot, the keen glance, the sharp tone of voice, are not forbidden, yet each seems to have been held at the disposal of reason and judgment for use when use was urgent.

This art of moderation, which, as I said, is the supreme ornament of life, decorating it and illuminating it in every part, this knowledge of what is fit in every circumstance, on every occasion, under every condition, is the gift, the work of philosophy. Philosophy alone makes this art self-consistent everywhere, and for every stage of life; though no doubt it gets aid from age and wide experience, and from that shrewd observation of what has commonly befallen or is at the moment taking place in the world and among men, which affords to philosophy both her materials and her instruments and by itself, apart from philosophy, can achieve in one naturally intelligent and good the appearance of a wise man, though it cannot produce complete and perfect wisdom.

In conduct of this sort there is always the note, the quality of grave and assured command; it is a supreme and constant illustration of dignity, of a kind to foster a certain loftiness and magnificence of temper and spirit. For we must graft upon the mind and disposition of the boy that sense of what is noble and honorable, which will keep him from any failure in grave courtesy in his relations with the great, and yet prevent him from loss of tender clemency in governing those who are in subordinate positions—a sense, the exhibition of which is at once most charming and most difficult. And yet the first lines of such a character a father must trace upon the heart of his son with his own example for his instrument: experience and the convention of the best society will deepen the impression; and philosophy will give it its final distinction.

Dignity, of course, must always be kept; a father should never let himself sink to the level of familiarity or become the boon companion of his son—that merely breeds contempt and self-confidence in the youth, who, feeling himself curbed by no law, comes to pursue with headstrong passion whatever takes his fancy. On the other hand he should be no formal or rigid moralist, afraid of giving his son ample proof of courteous and warm-hearted consideration, or shy of taking affectionately and even with a certain rapture to his heart the child, who is a living image of himself, than which nothing in life is sweeter to a parent. But if he must control his affection, lest the child spoiled by excessive indulgence cast away all respect and reverence for his father, he must take even more strenuous pains to avoid violent and rough severity; that crushes out love from the child's heart and brings him to the purpose and passion of hating whatever in himself he knows to be pleasing to his father.

This Fair Child of Mine

William Shakespeare

When forty winters shall beseige thy brow
And dig deep trenches in thy beauty's field,
Thy youth's proud livery, so gazed on now,
Will be a tottered weed of small worth held:
Then being asked where all thy beauty lies,
Where all the treasures of thy lusty days,
To say within thine own deep-sunken eyes
Were an all-eating shame and thriftless praise.
How much more praise deserved thy beauty's use
If thou couldst answer, "This fair child of mine
Shall sum my count and make my old excuse,"
Proving his beauty by succession thine.
This were to be new made when thou art old
And see thy blood warm when thou feel'st it cold.

A MAN'S JOURNEY

The Seven Ages of Man

From William Shakespeare, As You Like It

All the world's a stage,
And all the men and women merely players;
They have their exits and their entrances,
And one man in his time plays many parts,
His acts being seven ages. At first, the infant,
Mewling and puking in the nurse's arms.
Then the whining schoolboy, with his satchel
And shining morning face, creeping like snail
Unwillingly to school. And then the lover,
Sighing like furnace, with a woeful ballad
Made to his mistress' eyebrow. Then a soldier,
Full of strange oaths and bearded like the pard,
Jealous in honor, sudden and quick in quarrel,
Seeking the bubble reputation
Even in the cannon's mouth. And then the justice,
In fair round belly with good capon lined,
With eyes severe and beard of formal cut,
Full of wise saws and modern instances;
And so he plays his part. The sixth age shifts
Into the lean and slippered pantaloon,
With spectacles on nose and pouch on side;
His youthful hose, well saved, a world too wide
For his shrunk shank, and his big manly voice,
Turning again toward childish treble, pipes
And whistles in his sound. Last scene of all,
That ends this strange eventful history,
Is second childishness and mere oblivion,
Sans teeth, sans eyes, sans taste, sans everything.

Odysseus Comes Home

From Homer, The Odyssey

Upon Odysseus's return to Ithaca in disguise after twenty years of wandering, his wife Penelope tricks him into revealing himself by making him jealous. Years before, he had made their bed out of a giant tree that grew right into their bedroom. She makes him jealous by leading him to think another man has rearranged his bed in his absence. Once she realizes it's really him, they embrace and he weeps at the thought of what this extraordinary woman has been through, ruling in his absence, fighting off the suitors and bringing up their son on her own. They hug for a long time—after twenty years, she doesn't want to let him go.

So she spoke to her husband, trying him out, but Odysseus spoke in anger to his virtuous-minded lady:

"What you have said, dear lady, has hurt my heart deeply. What man has put my bed in another place? But it would be difficult for even a very expert one, unless a god, coming to help in person, were easily to change its position. But there is no mortal man alive, no strong man, who lightly could move the weight elsewhere. There is one particular feature in the bed's construction. I myself, no other man, made it. There was the bole of an olive tree with long leaves growing strongly in the courtyard, and it was thick like a column. I laid down my chamber around this, and built it, until I finished it, with close-set stones. And roofed it well over, and added the compacted doors, fitting closely together. Then I cut away the foliage of the long-leaved olive, and trimmed the trunk from the roots up, planing it with a brazen adze, well and expertly, and trued it straight to a chalkline, making a bed post of it, and bored all holes with an auger. I began with this and built my bed, until it was finished, and decorated it with gold and silver and ivory. Then I lashed it with thongs of oxhide, dyed bright with purple. There is its character, as I tell you; but I do not know now, dear lady, whether my bed is still in place, or if some man has cut underneath the stump of the olive, and moved it elsewhere."

So he spoke, and her knees and the heart within her went slack as she recognized the clear proofs that Odysseus had given;

but then she burst into tears and ran straight to him, throwing her arms around the neck of Odysseus, and kissed his head, saying:

"Do not be angry with me, Odysseus, since, beyond other men, you have the most understanding. The gods granted us misery, in jealousy over the thought that we two, always together, should enjoy our youth, and then come to the threshold of old age. But now, since you have given me accurate proof describing our bed, which no other mortal man beside has ever seen, but only you and I, and there is one serving woman Aktor's daughter, whom my father gave me when I came here, who used to guard the doors for us in our well-built chamber; so you persuade my heart, though it has been very stubborn."

She spoke, and still more roused in him the passion for weeping. He wept as he held his lovely wife, whose thoughts were virtuous. And as when the land appears welcome to men who are swimming after Poseidon has smashed their strong-built ship on the open water, pounding it with the weight of wind and the heavy seas, and only a few escape the gray water landward by swimming, with a thick scurf of salt coated upon them, and gladly they set foot on the shore, escaping the evil; so welcome was her husband to her as she looked upon him, and she could not let him go from the embrace of her white arm.

Meanwhile, the bed chamber has been prepared. After their lovemaking, they sit up all night telling each other of what each has endured during their long separation. Husband and wife are the only ones who can understand each other. Did they tell everything?

Now as these two were conversing thus with each other, meanwhile the nurse and Eurynome were making the bed up with soft coverings, under the light of their flaring torches. Then when they had worked and presently had a firm bed made, the old woman went away back to bed in her own place, while Eurynome, as mistress of the chamber, guided them on their way to the bed, and her hands held the torch for them. When she had brought them to the chamber she went back. They then gladly went together to bed, and their old ritual.

At this time Telemachus and the oxherd and swineherd stopped the beat of their feet in the dance, and stopped the women, and they themselves went to bed in the shadowy palace.

When Penelope and Odysseus had enjoyed their lovemaking, they took their pleasure in talking, each one telling his story. She, shining among women, told of all she had endured in the palace, as she watched the suitors, a ravening company, who on her account were slaughtering many oxen and fat sheep, and much wine was being drawn from the wine jars. But shining Odysseus told of all the cares he inflicted on other men, and told too of all that in his misery he had toiled through. She listened to him with delight, nor did any sleep fall upon her eyes until he had told her everything.

The Halcyon Birds

From Thomas Bulfinch, Bulfinch's Mythology

The gods take pity on a husband's and wife's devotion to each other.

Ceyx was king of Thessaly, where he reigned in peace, without violence or wrong. He was son of Hesporus, the Day-star, and the glow of his beauty reminded one of his father. Halcyone, the daughter of Aeolus, was his wife, and devotedly attached to him. Now Ceyx was in deep affliction for the loss of his brother, and direful prodigies following his brother's death made him feel as if the gods were hostile to him. He thought best, therefore, to make a voyage to Carlos in Ionia, to consult the oracle of Apollo. But as soon as he disclosed his intention to his wife Halcyone, a shudder ran through her frame, and her face grew deadly pale. "What fault of mine, dearest husband, has turned your affection from me? Where is that love of me that used to be uppermost in your thoughts? Have you learned to feel easy in the absence of Halcyone? Would you rather have me away?" She also endeavored to discourage him, by describing the violence of the winds, which she had known familiarly when she lived at home in her father's house—Aeolus being the god of the winds, and having as much as he could do to restrain them. "They rush together," said she, "with such fury that fire flashes from the conflict. But if you must go," she added, "dear husband, let me go with you, otherwise I shall suffer not only the real evils which you must encounter, but those also which my fears suggest."

These words weighed heavily on the mind of King Ceyx, and it was no less his own wish than hers to take her with him, but he could not bear to expose her to the dangers of the sea. He answered, therefore, consoling her as well as he could, and finished with these words: "I promise, by the rays of my father the Daystar, that if fate permits I will return before the moon shall have twice rounded her orb." When he had thus spoken, he ordered the vessel to be drawn out of the shiphouse, and the oars and sails to be put aboard. When Halcyone saw these preparations she shuddered, as if with a presentiment of evil. With tears and sobs she said farewell, and then fell senseless to the ground.

Ceyx would still have lingered, but now the young men grasped their oars and pulled vigorously through the waves, with long and measured strokes. Halcyone raise her streaming eyes, and saw her husband standing on the deck, waving his hand to her. She answered his signal till the vessel had receded so far that she could no longer distinguish his form from the rest. When the vessel itself could no more be seen, she strained her eyes to catch the last glimmer of the sail, till that too disappeared. Then, retiring to her chamber, she threw herself on her solitary couch.

Meanwhile they glide out of the harbor, and the breeze plays among the ropes. The seamen draw in their oars, and hoist their sails. When half or less of their course was passed, as night drew on, the sea began to whiten with swelling waves, and the east wind to blow a gale. The master gave the word to take in sail, but the storm forbade obedience, for such is the roar of the winds and waves his orders are unheard. The men, of their own accord, busy themselves to secure the oars, to strengthen the ship, to reef the sail. While they thus do what to each one seems best, the storm increases. The shouting of the men, the rattling of the shrouds, and the dashing of the waves, mingle with the roar of the thunder. The swelling sea seems lifted up to the heavens, to scatter its foam among the clouds; then sinking away to the bottom assumes the color of the shoal—a Stygian blackness.

The vessel shares all these changes. It seems like a wild beast that rushes on the spears of the hunters. Rain falls in torrents, as if the skies were coming down to unite with the sea. When the lightning ceases for a moment, the night seems to add its own darkness to that of the storm; then comes the flash, rending the darkness asunder, and lighting up all with a glare. Skill fails, courage sinks, and death seems to come on every wave. The men are stupefied with terror. The thought of parents, and kindred, and pledges left at home, comes over their minds. Ceyx thinks of Halcyone. No name but hers is on his lips, and while he yearns for her, he yet rejoices in her absence. Presently the mast is shattered by a stroke of lightning, the rudder broken, and the triumphant surge curling ever looks down upon the wreck, then falls, and crushes it to fragments. Some of the seamen, stunned by the stroke, sink, and rise no more; others cling to fragments of the wreck. Ceyx, with the hand that used to grasp the sceptre, holds fast to a plank, calling for help—alas, in vain—upon his father and his father-in-law. But oftenest on his lips was the name of Halcyone. To her his thoughts cling. He prays that the waves may bear his body to her sight, and that it may receive burial at her hands. At length the waters overwhelm him, and he sinks. The Day-star looked dim that night. Since it could not leave the heavens, it shrouded its face with clouds.

In the meanwhile Halcyone, ignorant of all these horrors, counted the days till her husband's promised return. Now she gets ready the garments which he shall put on, and now what she shall wear when he arrives. To all the gods she offers frequent incense, but more than all to Juno. For her husband, who was no more, she prayed incessantly: that he might be safe; that he might come home; that he might not, in his absence, see anyone that he would love better than her. But of all these prayers, the last was the only one destined to be granted. The goddess, at length, could not bear any longer to be pleaded with for one already dead, and to have hands raised to her altars that ought rather to be offering funeral rites. So, calling Iris, she said, "Iris, my faithful-messenger, go to the drowsy dwelling of Somnus, and tell him to send a vision to Halcyone in the form of Ceyx, to make known to her the event."

Iris puts on her robe of many colors, and tinging the sky with her bow, seeks the palace of the King of Sleep. Near the Cimmerain country, a mountain cave is the abode of the dull god Somnus. Here Phoebus dares not come, either rising, at midday, or setting. Clouds and shadows are exhaled from the ground, and the light glimmers faintly. The bird of dawning, with crested head, never there calls aloud to Aurora, nor watchful dog, nor more sagacious goose disturbs the silence. No wild beast, nor cattle, nor branch moved with the wind, nor sound of human conversation, breaks the stillness. Silence reigns there; but from the bottom of the rock the River Lethe flows, and by its murmur invites to sleep. Around him lie dreams, resembling all various forms, as many as the harvest bears stalks, or the forest leaves, or the seashore sand grains.

As soon as the goddess entered and brushed away the dreams that hovered around her, her brightness lit up all the cave. The god, scarce opening his eyes, and ever and anon dropping his beard upon his breast, at last shook himself free from himself, and leaning on his arm, inquired her errand—for he knew who she was. She answered, "Somnus, gentlest of the gods, tranquilizer of minds and soother of careworn hearts, Juno sends you her commands that you despatch a dream to Halcyone, in the city of Trachine, representing her lost husband and all the events of the wreck."

Having delivered her message, Iris hasted away, for she could not longer endure the stagnant air, and as she felt drowsiness creeping over her, she made her escape, and returned by her bow the way she came. Then Somnus called one of his numerous sons—Morpheus—the most expert in counterfeiting forms, and in imitating the walk, the countenance, and mode of speaking, even the clothes and attitudes most characteristic of each. But he only imitates men, leaving it to another to personate birds, beasts, and serpents. Him they call Icelos; and Phantasos is a third, who turns himself into rocks, waters, woods, and other things without life. These wait upon kings and great personages in their sleeping hours, while others move among the common people. Somnus chose from all the brothers, Morpheus, to perform the command of Iris; then laid on his pillow and yielded himself to grateful repose.

Morpheus flew, making no noise with his wings, and soon came to the Haemonian city, where, laying aside his wings, he assumed the form of Ceyx. Under that form, but pale like a dead man, naked, he stood before the couch of the wretched wife. His beard seemed soaked with water, and water trickled from his drowned locks. Leaning over the bed, tears streaming from his eyes, he said, "Do you recognize your Ceyx, unhappy wife, or has death too much changed my visage? Behold me, know me, your husband's shade, instead of himself. Your prayers, Halcyone, availed me nothing. I am dead. No more deceive yourself with vain hopes of my return. The stormy winds sunk my ship in the Aegean Sea, waves filled my mouth while it called aloud on you. No uncertain messenger tells you this, no vague rumor brings it to your ears. I come in person, a shipwrecked man, to tell you my fate. Arise! give me tears, give me lamentations, let me not go down to Tartarus unwept." To these words Morpheus added the voice, which seemed to be that of her husband; he seemed to pour forth genuine tears; his hands had the gestures of Ceyx.

Halcyone, weeping, groaned, and stretched out her arms in her sleep, striving to embrace his body, but grasping only the air. "Stay!"

she cried; "whither do you fly? let us go together." Her own voice awakened her. Starting up, she gazed eagerly around, to see if he was still present. The servants, alarmed by her cries, had brought a light. When she found him not, she smote her breast and rent her garments. She cares not to unbind her hair, but tears it wildly. Her nurse asks what is the cause of her grief. "Halcyone is no more," she answers, "she perished with her Ceyx. Utter not words of comfort, he is shipwrecked and dead. I have seen him, I have recognized him. I stretched out my hands to seize him and detain him. His shade vanished, but it was the true shade of my husband. Not with the accustomed features, not with the beauty that was his, but pale, naked, and with his hair wet with sea water, he appeared to wretched me. Here, in this very spot, the sad vision stood"—and she looked to find the mark of his footsteps. "This it was, this that my presaging mind foreboded, when I implored him not to leave me, to trust himself to the waves. Oh, how I wish, since thou wouldst go, thou hadst taken me with thee! It would have been far better. Then I should have had no remnant of life to spend without thee, nor a separate death to die. If I could bear to live and struggle to endure, I should be more cruel to myself than the sea has been to me. But I will not struggle, I will not be separated from thee, unhappy husband. This time, at least, I will keep thee company. In death, if one tomb may not include us, one epitaph shall; if I may not lay my ashes with thine, my name, at least, shall not be separated." Her grief forbade more words, and these were broken with tears and sobs.

It was now morning. She went to the seashore, and sought the spot where she last saw him, on his departure. "While he lingered here, and cast off his tacklings, he gave me his last kiss." While she reviews every object, and strives to recall every incident, looking out over the sea, she descries an indistinct object floating in the water. At first she was in doubt what it was, but by degrees the waves bore it nearer, and it was plainly the body of a man. Though unknowing of whom, yet, as it was of some shipwrecked one, she was deeply moved, and gave it her tears, saying, "Alas! unhappy one, and unhappy, if such there be, thy wife!" Borne by the waves, it came nearer. As she more and more nearly views it, she trembles more and more. Now, now it approaches the shore. Now marks that she recognizes appear. It is her husband! Stretching out her trembling hands toward it, she exclaims, "O dearest husband, is it thus you return to me?"

There was built out from the shore a mole, constructed to break the assaults of the sea, and stem its violent ingress. She leaped upon this barrier and (it was wonderful she could do so) she flew, and striking the air with wings produced on the instant, skimmed along the surface of the water, an unhappy bird. As she flew, her throat poured forth sounds full of grief, and like the voice of one lamenting. When she touched the mute and bloodless body, she enfolded its beloved limbs with her new-formed wings, and tried to give kisses with her horny beak. Whether Ceyx felt it, or whether it was only the action of the waves, those who looked on doubted, but the body seemed to raise its head. But indeed he did feel it, and by the pitying gods both of them were changed into birds. They mate and have their young ones. For seven placid days, in wintertime, Halcyone broods over her nest, which floats upon the sea. Then the way is safe to seamen. Aeolus guards the winds and keeps them from disturbing the deep. The sea is given up, for the time, to his grandchildren.

Hektor and Andromache
on the Walls of Troy

From Homer, The Iliad

In contrast with the Greek hero Achilles, the Trojan prince Hektor is as much concerned with family life as with glory. From the beginning of history, men have been torn between their love for their families and their duty to the common good. In this touching scene, Andromache begs her husband to avoid the battle and not leave his child an orphan and her a widow. But he has no choice—he must fight for his country. Standing on the walls of Troy, they enjoy a moment of laughter when their baby son cries in fright at the sight of his father's plumed helmet. In the midst of war and despite a foreboding of tragedy, they retain their vibrant integrity as a family.

Hektor smiled in silence as he looked on his son, but she, Andromache, stood close beside him, letting her tears fall, and clung to his hand and called him by name and spoke to him:

"Dearest, your own great strength will be your death, and you have no pity on your little son, nor on me, ill-starred, who soon must be your widow; for presently the Achaians, gathering together, will set upon you and kill you; and for me it would be far better to sink into the earth when I have lost you, for there is no other consolation for me after you have gone to your destiny—only grief; since I have no father, no honored mother. Hektor, thus you are father to me, and my honored mother, you are my brother, and you it is who are my young husband. Please take pity upon me then, stay here on the rampart, that you may not leave your child an orphan, your wife a widow, but draw your people up by the fig tree, there where the city is openest to attack, and where the wall may be mounted."

Then tall Hektor of the shining helm answered her: "All these things are in my mind also, lady; yet I would feel deep shame before the Trojans, and the Trojan women with trailing garments, if like a coward I were to shrink aside from the fighting; and the spirit will not let me, since I have learned to be valiant and to fight always among the foremost ranks of the Trojans, winning for my own self great glory, and for my father. For I know this thing well in my heart, and my mind knows it: there will come a day when sacred Ilion shall perish, and Priam, and the people of Priam of the strong ash spear. But it is not so much the pain to come of the Trojans that troubles me, not even of Priam the king nor Hekabe, not the thought of my brothers who in their numbers and valor shall drop in the dust under the hands of men who hate them, as troubles me the thought of you, when some bronze-armored Achaian leads you off, taking away your day of liberty, in tears; and in Argos you must work at the loom of another, and carry water from the spring Messeis or Hypereia, all unwilling, but strong will be the necessity upon you; and someday seeing you shedding tears a man will say of you; 'This is the wife of Hektor, who was ever the bravest fighter of the Trojans, breakers of horses, in the days when they fought about Ilion.'

"So will one speak of you; and for you it will be yet a fresh grief, to be widowed of such a man who could fight on the day of your slavery. But may I be dead and the piled earth hide me under before I hear you crying and know by this that they drag you captive."

So speaking glorious Hektor held out his arms to his baby, who shrank back to his fair-girdled nurse's bosom screaming, and frightened at the aspect of his own father, terrified as he saw the bronze and the crest with its horse-hair, nodding dreadfully, as he thought, from the peak of the helmet. Then his beloved father laughed out, and his honored mother, and at once glorious Hektor lifted from his head the helmet and laid it in all its shining upon the ground. Then taking up his dear son he tossed him about in his arms, and kissed him, and lifted his voice in prayer to Zeus and the other immortals: "Zeus, and you other immortals, grant that this boy, who is my son, may be as I am, preeminent among the Trojans, great in strength, as am I and rule strongly over Ilion; and some day let them say of him: 'He is better by far than his father,' as he comes in from the fighting; and let him kill his enemy and bring home the blooded spoils, and delight the heart of his mother."

Can a Man Be Too Honest?

William Shakespeare

My mistress' eyes are nothing like the sun;
Coral is far more red than her lips' red;
If snow be white, why then her breasts are dun;
If hairs be wires, black wires grow on her head.
I have seen roses damasked, red and white,
But no such roses see I in her cheeks;
And in some perfumes is there more delight
Than in the breath that from my mistress reeks.
I love to hear her speak; yet well I know
That music hath a far more pleasing sound:
I grant I never saw a goddess go;
My mistress, when she walks, treads on the ground.
And yet, by heaven, I think my love as rare
As any she belied with false compare.

A Son's Mixed Feelings

From John Stuart Mill, Autobiography

What would it be like if a father had complete control over his son's educa-
tion? In his autobiography, the utilitarian philosopher J. S. Mill
(1806–1873) recalls that his imposing father prescribed every aspect of his
studies, a rigorous immersion in the classics, history, and science. The boy
had no playmates and no holidays to interfere with this demanding cur-
riculum. He was isolated from any exposure to religious faith so that he
would grow up as his father's ally in "the great and decisive contest against
priestly tyranny for liberty of thought." The reader senses Mill's mixed feel-
ings about his upbringing—and especially his father's lack of tenderness
toward his children.

My father, in all his teaching, demanded of me not only the
utmost that I could do, but much that I could by no possibility have
done. What he was himself willing to undergo for the sake of my
instruction, may be judged from the fact, that I went through the
whole process of preparing my Greek lessons in the same room and
at the same table at which he was writing: and as those days Greek
and English Lexicons were not, and I could make no more use of a
Greek and Latin Lexicon than could be made without having yet
begun to learn Latin, I was forced to have recourse to him for the
meaning of every word which I did not know. This incessant interruption he, one of the most impatient of men, submitted to, and
wrote under that interruption several volumes of his History and all
else that he had to write during those years.

One of the evils most liable to attend on any sort of early proficiency, and which often fatally blights its promise, my father most
anxiously guarded against. This was self-conceit. He kept me, with
extreme vigilance, out of the way of hearing myself praised, or of
being led to make self-flattering comparisons between myself and
others. From his own intercourse with me I could derive none but
a very humble opinion of myself; and the standard of comparison
he always held up to me, was not what other people did, but what a
man could and ought to do. He completely succeeded in preserving me from the sort of influences he so much dreaded. I was not at

all aware that my attainments were anything unusual at my age. If I accidentally had my attention drawn to the fact that some other boy knew less than myself—which happened less often than might be imagined—I concluded, not that I knew much, but that he, for some reason or other, knew little, or that his knowledge was of a different kind from mine. My state of mind was not humility, but neither was it arrogance. I never thought of saying to myself, I am, or I can do, so and so. I neither estimated myself highly nor lowly: I did not estimate myself at all. If I thought anything about myself, it was that I was rather backward in my studies, since I always found myself so, in comparison with what my father expected from me. I assert this with confidence, though it was not the impression of various persons who saw me in my childhood. They, as I have since found, thought me greatly and disagreeably self-conceited; probably because I was disputatious, and did not scruple to give direct contradictions to things which I heard said. I suppose I acquired this bad habit from having been encouraged in an unusual degree to talk on matters beyond my age, and with grown persons, while I never had inculcated on me the usual respect for them. My father did not correct this ill breeding and impertinence, probably from not being aware of it, for I was always too much in awe of him to be otherwise than extremely subdued and quiet in his presence. Yet with all this I had no notion of any superiority in myself; and well was it for me that I had not.

It is evident that this, among many other of the purposes of my father's scheme of education, could not have been accomplished if he had not carefully kept me from having any great amount of intercourse with other boys. He was earnestly bent upon my escaping not only the ordinary corrupting influence which boys exercise over boys, but the contagion of vulgar modes of thought and feeling; and for this he was willing that I should pay the price of inferiority in the accomplishments which schoolboys in all countries chiefly cultivate. The deficiencies in my education were principally in the things which boys learn from being turned out to shift for themselves, and from being brought together in large numbers. From temperance and much walking, I grew up healthy and hardy, though not muscular; but I could do no feats of skill or physical strength, and knew none of the ordinary bodily exercises. It was not that play, or time for it, was refused me. Though no holidays were allowed, lest the habit of work should be broken, and a taste for idleness acquired, I had ample leisure in every day to amuse myself; but as I had no boy companions, and the animal need of physical activity was satisfied by walking, my amusements, which were mostly solitary, were in general of a quiet, if not a bookish turn, and gave little stimulus to any other kind even of mental activity than that which was already called forth by my studies. I consequently remained long, and in a less degree have always remained, inexpert in anything requiring manual dexterity; my mind, as well as my hands, did its work very lamely when it was applied, or ought to have been applied, to the practical details which, as they are the chief interest of life to the majority of men are also the things in which whatever mental capacity they have, chiefly shews itself.

It would have been wholly inconsistent with my father's ideas of duty, to allow me to acquire impressions contrary to his convictions and feelings respecting religion: and he impressed upon me from the first, that the manner in which the world came into existence was a subject on which nothing was known: that the question "Who made me?" cannot be answered, because we have no experience or authentic information from which to answer it; and that any answer only throws the difficulty a step further back, since the question immediately presents itself, Who made God? He, at the same time, took care that I should be acquainted with what had been thought by mankind on these impenetrable problems. I have mentioned at how early an age he made me a reader of ecclesiastical history; and he taught me to take the strongest interest in the Reformation, as the great and decisive contest against priestly tyranny for liberty of thought. I am thus one of the very few examples, in this country, of one who has, not thrown off religious belief, but never had it: I grew up in a negative state with no regard to it. I looked upon the modern exactly as I did upon the ancient religion, as something which in no way concerned me. It did not seem to me more strange that English people should believe what I did not, than that the men whom I read of in Herodotus should have done so. History had made the variety of opinions among mankind a fact familiar to me, and this was but a prolongation of that fact. This point in my early education had, however incidentally, one bad consequence deserving notice. In giving me an opinion contrary to that of the world, my father thought it necessary to give it as one which could not prudently be avowed to the world. This lesson of keeping my thoughts to myself, at that early age, was attended with some moral disadvantages, though my limited intercourse with strangers, especially such as were likely to speak to me on religion, prevented me from being placed in the alternative of avowal or hypocrisy. I remember two occasions in my boyhood, on which I

felt myself in this alternative, and in both cases I avowed my disbe-
lief and defended it. My opponents were boys, considerably older
than myself: one of them I certainly staggered at the time, but the
subject was never renewed between us: the other, who was surprised and somewhat shocked, did his best to convince me for
some time, without effect.

Of unbelievers (so called) as well as of believers, there are
many species, including almost every variety of moral type. But the
best among them, as no one who has had opportunities of really
knowing them will hesitate to affirm (believers rarely have that
opportunity), are more genuinely religious, in the best sense of the
word religion, than those who exclusively arrogate to themselves
the title.

He thought human life a poor thing at best, after the freshness of youth and of unsatisfied curiosity had gone by. This was a
topic on which he did not often speak, especially, it may be supposed, in the presence of young persons: but when he did it, it was
with an air of settled and profound conviction. He would sometimes say, that if life were made what it might be, by good government and good education, it would be worth having: but he never
spoke with anything like enthusiasm even of that possibility. He
never varied in rating intellectual enjoyments above all others,
even in value as pleasures, independently of their ulterior benefits.
The pleasures of the benevolent affections he placed high in the
scale; and used to say, that he had never known a happy old man,
except those who were able to live over again in the pleasures of
the young. For passionate emotions of all sorts, and for everything
which had been said or written in exaltation of them, he professed
the greatest contempt. He regarded them as a form of madness.
"The intense" was with him a bye-word of scornful disapprobation.
He regarded as an aberration of the moral standard of modern
times, compared with that of the ancients, the great stress laid
upon feeling. Feelings, as such, he considered to be no proper subjects of praise or blame. Right and wrong, good and bad, he regarded as qualities solely of conduct.

It will be admitted, that a man of the opinions, and the character, above described, was likely to leave a strong moral impression on any mind principally formed by him, and that his moral
teaching was not likely to err on the side of laxity or indulgence.
The element which was chiefly deficient in his moral relation to his
children was that of tenderness. I do not believe that this deficiency lay in his own nature. I believe him to have had much more feel-

ing than he habitually shewed, and much greater capacities of feeling than were ever developed. He resembled most Englishmen in
being ashamed of the signs of feeling, and, by the absence of
demonstration, starving the feelings themselves. If we consider further that he was in the trying position of sole teacher, and add to
this that his temper was constitutionally irritable, it is impossible
not to feel true pity for a father who did, and strove to do so much
for his children, who would have so valued their affection, yet who
must have been constantly feeling that fear of him was drying it up
at its source. This was no longer the case, later in life and with his
younger children. They loved him tenderly: and if I cannot say so
much of myself, I was always loyally devoted to him. As regards my
own education, I hesitate to pronounce whether I was more a loser
or gainer by his severity.

Married or Single?

From Francis Bacon, Essays

*When a man has a wife and children, Bacon tells us, he gives hostages to
fortune. As a contemporary arbitrageur might put it, if you're married,
you're exposed.*

He that hath wife and children hath given hostages to fortune,
for they are impediments to great enterprises, either of virtue or
mischief. Certainly the best works, and of greatest merit for the
public, have proceeded from the unmarried or childless men,
which both in affection and means have married and endowed the
public. Yet it were great reason that those that have children should
have greatest care of future times, unto which they know they must
transmit their dearest pledges. Some there are who though they
lead a single life, yet their thoughts do end with themselves, and
account future times impertinences. Nay, there are some other that
account wife and children but as bills of charges. Nay more, there
are some foolish, rich covetous, men that take pride in having no
children, because they may be thought so much the richer. For perhaps they have heard some talk, *Such an one is a great rich man,* and
another except to it, *Yea, but he hath a great charge of children,* as if it

were an abatement to his riches. But the most ordinary cause of a single life is liberty, especially in certain self-pleasing and humorous minds, which are so sensible of every restraint, as they will go near to think their girdles and garters to be bonds and shackles. Unmarried men are best friends, best masters, best servants, but not always best subjects, for they are light to run away; and almost all fugitives are of that condition.

Is It for Fear to Wet a Widow's Eye?

William Shakespeare

Is it for fear to wet a widow's eye
That thou consum'st thyself in single life?
Ah, if thou issueless shalt hap to die,
The world will wail thee like a makeless wife;
The world will be thy widow, and still weep
That thou no form of thee hast left behind,
When every private widow well may keep,
By children's eyes, her husband's shape in mind.
Look what an unthrift in the world doth spend
Shifts but his place, for still the world enjoys it;
But beauty's waste hath in the world an end,
And, kept unused, the user so destroys it:
No love toward others in that bosom sits
That on himself such murd'rous shame commits.

The Joys of Parents Are Secret

From Francis Bacon, Essays

From Francis Bacon's essay, Of Parents and Children.

The joys of parents are secret; and so are their griefs and fears. They cannot utter the one, nor they will not utter the other. Children sweeten labors, but they make misfortunes more bitter. They increase the cares of life, but they mitigate the remembrance of death. The perpetuity by generation is common to beasts, but memory, merit, and noble works are proper to men. And surely a man shall see the noblest works and foundations have proceeded from childless men, which have sought to express the images of their minds, where those of their bodies have failed. So the care of posterity is most in them that have no posterity.

A Childless Man Can Be a Father

From Leon Battista Alberti, On the Duties
and Education of Children

There's no stronger love than that of a father for a son. But a childless man can feel fatherly affection for a boy in his care, and a biological father has a duty to extend his paternal care beyond his immediate family to the children of his relatives and friends.

"Who can judge," said Adovardo, "how great and strong is a father's love for his children, if he himself has not experienced it? All loves seem strong to me. Many have been seen to risk their wealth, their lives, and all their fortunes, and to endure extreme hardship, danger, and injuries in order to show their devotion to their friends. Others, it is said, loved some things so much that when they thought they had lost them they could no longer endure life. The histories and traditions of men are filled with stories of the power of these passions which many have experienced. But I believe there is no love so powerful, so constant, so complete, and so great as to equal a father's love for his children. I should certainly agree with Plato that his four frenzies, of prophecy, divine mysteries, poetry and love, are most powerful in the souls and minds of mortals. And it seems to me that erotic love is in itself more violent and tempestuous than all others. But we often see that it wanes and perishes through wrath, desuetude, new desires, or other causes, and it nearly always leaves a feeling of disgust. Nor should I deny that true friendship is bound by complete and strong love. But I do not believe that in it there is a greater, more devoted, and more ardent love than that which grows spontaneously in a father's heart, unless you are of a different opinion.

Lionardo: I cannot judge what love a father feels for his children, for I do not know, Adovardo, what pleasure and sweetness there may be in having children. But from what I understand, it seems to me one can justly hold your opinion and say that in many ways a father's love is most powerful. And this conjecture of mine is based on many observations, in addition to my seeing with what zeal and love Lorenzo just recommended his children to us. He did so, not because he thought he had to make these young men more dear to us, for he knows how we love them, but because he was carried away by paternal love and because it seemed to him that no one, no matter how solicitous, watchful, and prudent, could give as much care and counsel to another's children as a loving father might wish. To tell you the truth, Lorenzo's words had only one effect upon me: they convinced me how just and reasonable it is to care for the orphans and young men of one's house with great diligence. Yet at times I could not hold back my tears; and seeing that you were so pensive, it seemed to me that your thoughts went far beyond mine.

Adovardo: The truth is that every word Lorenzo uttered moved me to pity and compassion. Being a father myself, could I treat any differently than my own children those whom I must hold dear because of blood-ties, and who are the sons of a good, loving relative and friend, especially after they have been recommended to us? If I did not consider them as my very own children, Lionardo, I should not be a good relative or a true friend. In fact, you would consider me merciless, false, and of vile character, and I should be scorned and reproached for it. Who could feel no pity for orphans? Who could do anything but always remember the father of these orphans and the last words with which, at the point of death, this dear friend and relative recommended his dearest possessions, his children, to us? He trusted us and left his children in our lap, in our arms. As for me, my dear Lionardo, I am determined that I will let my own children want for everything before I let these boys suffer the least discomfort. I alone am the judge of my own children's needs, but every good man, every merciful and wise person has the right to judge any faults of mine toward those who have been entrusted to me. I believe it is our duty to look after their reputation, honor, habits, and well-being. I believe that if through avarice or negligence someone allows a mind capable of attaining honor and esteem to perish, he deserves not only reproach, but severe punishment. It is shameful to neglect, and not properly keep an ox or horse, or to let any animal, no matter how useless perish through one's negligence. If this is the case with animals, shall we not condemn one who crushes a man's mind with the burdens of need, sadness, and dishonor, and who scorns him and allows him to perish because of his disinterest or avarice? Shall he not deserve infamy and the hatred of all good men? Oh, let such a man beware of his cruelty, let him fear the wrath of God, let him pay heed to that proven and true proverb which states: "He who cares not for another's family shall not see his own flourish."

Lionardo: I clearly see what a responsibility it is to be a father. It seems to me that Lorenzo's words have moved you much more than I thought. Your words have made me think of what I believe is in your own mind: your children. And while you spoke just now, a doubt grew in my mind as to whether the zeal and solicitude of fathers toward their children is greater than their pleasure and satisfaction in raising them. I have no doubts regarding the labors involved, and it seems to me that this is not the least important reason why they become so dear to you. I see that it is natural for everyone, the painter, the writer, the poet, to love his creations, and I believe a father loves his children even more, for in order to raise them he endures trials even more necessary and of longer duration. Everyone wants his creations to be appreciated and praised by many and to last eternally, insofar as possible.

I can easily believe it is the same with you fathers as with everything else. I see that nature is always solicitous in seeing to it that everything created survives and receives nourishment and aid from its creator so that it may continue in life and develop its qual-

ities. In plants and trees I see how the roots gather and offer nourishment to the trunk, the trunk to the branches, and the branches
to the leaves and fruit. Thus, perhaps, it is to be deemed natural
that fathers should not spare any efforts to nourish and maintain
those who were born of them and because of them. And I admit
that it is just for you fathers to show great solicitude and care in
properly raising your children.

The age that follows [infancy] brings laughter and delight to
all. The young children begin to speak and partly disclose their
desires with their words. The whole house listens, all the neighbors hear, and no one fails to discuss, praise, and interpret with
great delight what the child has said and done. In that springlike
age, one sees in the child's expression, words, and ways great signs
of subtle intellect, excellent memory, and good hopes already budding. And so everyone says that children are a father's comfort
and the solace of the old. Nor do I think there is a father so busy
or burdened with thoughts that he does not find his children's
presence most delightful. It is said that Cato, that good man of
ancient times who was deemed and called wise, and was so firm
and severe in everything, often abandoned weighty public and private affairs during the day and returned home many times to see
his little children. For having children did not seem a cause of bitterness and sorrow for him. He thought it sweet and delightful to
see the smile and hear the words of children and enjoy the
enchanting ways and the simplicity and charm which fills the
expression of children at that pure and sweet age.

Advice to a Young Man
on Marrying Early

From Benjamin Franklin, Essays Humorous,
Moral and Literary

*Scientist, moralist, and diplomat, Benjamin Franklin (1706-1780) was an
early authority on virtuous living for colonial America.*

To John Alleyn, Esq.

Dear Jack,

You desire, you say, my impartial thoughts on the subject of an early marriage, by way of answer to the numberless objections that have been made by numerous persons to your own. You may remember, when you consulted me on the occasion, that I thought youth on both sides to be no objection. Indeed, from the marriages that have fallen under my observation, I am rather inclined to think, that early ones stand the best chance of happiness. The temper and habits of the young are not yet become so stiff and uncomplying, as when more advanced in life; they form more easily to each other, and hence, many occasions of disgust are removed. And if youth has less of that prudence which is necessary to manage a family, yet the parents and elder friends of young married persons are generally at hand to afford their advice, which amply supplies that defect; and, by early marriage, youth is sooner formed to regular and useful life; and possibly some of those accidents or connections, that might have injured the constitution, or reputation, or both, are thereby happily prevented. Particular circumstances of particular persons may possibly sometimes make it prudent to delay entering into that state: but, in general, when nature has rendered our bodies fit for it, the presumption is in nature's favor, that she has not judged amiss in making us desire it. Late marriages are often attended, too, with this further inconvenience, that there is not the same chance that the parents should live to see their offspring educated. "Late children," says the Spanish proverb, "are early orphans." A melancholy reflection to those whose case it may be. With us in America, marriages are generally in the morning of life; our children are therefore educated and settled in the world by noon; and thus, our business being done, we have an afternoon and evening of cheerful leisure to ourselves, such as our friend at present enjoys. By these early marriages we are blessed with more children; and from the mode among us, founded by nature, of every mother suckling and nursing her own child, more of them are raised. Thence the swift progress of population among us, unparalleled in Europe. In fine, I am glad you are married, and congratulate you most cordially upon it. You are now in the way of becoming a useful citizen; and you have escaped the unnatural state of celibacy for life—the fate of many here, who never intended it, but who having too long postponed the change of their conditions, find, at length, that it is too late to think of it, and so live all their lives in a situation that greatly lessens a man's value. An odd volume of a set of books bears not the value of its proportion to the set; what think you of the odd half of a pair of scissors; it can't well cut any thing; it may possibly serve to scrape a trencher.

Pray make my compliments and best wishes acceptable to your bride. I am old and heavy, or should ere this have presented them in person. I shall make but small use of the old man's privilege, that of giving advice to younger friends. Treat your wife always with respect; it will procure respect to you, not only from her, but from all that observe it. Never use a slighting expression to her, even in jest; for slights in jest, after frequent bandyings, are apt to end in angry earnest. Be studious in your profession and you will be learned. Be industrious and frugal, and you will be rich. Be sober and temperate, and you will be healthy. Be in general virtuous, and you will be happy. At least, you will, by such conduct, stand the best chance for such consequences. I pray God to bless you both! being ever your affectionate friend,

B. Franklin

My Wife Is My Best Friend

From John Stuart Mill, Autobiography

Mill's moving tribute to his wife and "most valuable friend" Harriet Parker suggests that he found in marriage an emotional wholeness and an intellectual openness denied to him in childhood—and a partner and mentor for every sphere of his life. His marriage to this "eminently meditative and poetic" woman made him a deeper man, one whose life work was not a solitary labor but "the fusion of two minds."

It was at the period of my mental progress which I have now reached that I formed the friendship which has been the honor and chief blessing of my existence, as well as the source of a great part of all that I have attempted to do, or hope to effect hereafter, for human improvement. My first introduction to the lady who, after a friendship of twenty years, consented to become my wife, was in 1830, when I was in my twenty-fifth and she in her twenty-third year. With her husband's family it was the renewal of an old acquaintanceship. His grandfather lived in the next house to my father's in Newington Green, and I had sometimes when a boy been invited to play in the old gentleman's garden. He was a fine specimen of the old Scotch puritan; stern, severe, and powerful, but very kind to children, on whom such men make a lasting impression. Although it was years after my introduction to Mrs. Taylor before my acquaintance with her became at all intimate or confidential, I very soon felt her to be the most admirable person I had ever known. It is not to be supposed that she was, or that anyone, at the age at which I first saw her, could be, all that she afterward became. Least of all could this be true of her, with whom self-improvement, progress in the highest and in all senses, was a law of nature; a necessity equally from the ardor with which she sought it, and from the spontaneous tendency of faculties which could not receive an impression or an experience without making it the source or the occasion of an accession of wisdom. Up to the time when I first saw her, her rich and powerful nature had chiefly unfolded itself according to the received type of feminine genius. To her outer circle she was a beauty and a wit, with an air of natural distinction, felt by all who approached her: to the inner, a woman of deep and strong feeling, of penetrating and intuitive intelligence, and of an eminently meditative and poetic nature. Married at a very early age, to a most upright, brave, and honorable man, of liberal opinions and good education, but without the intellectual or artistic tastes which would have made him a companion for her—though a steady and affectionate friend, for whom she had true esteem and the strongest affection through life, and whom she most deeply lamented when dead; shut out by the social disabilities of women from any adequate exercise of her highest faculties in action on the world without; her life was one of inward meditation, varied by familiar intercourse with a small circle of friends, of whom one only (long since deceased) was a person of genius, or of capacities of feeling or intellect kindred with her own, but all had more or less of alliance with her in sentiments and opinions. Into this circle I had the good fortune to be admitted, and I soon perceived that she possessed, in combination, the qualities which in all other persons whom I had known I had been only too happy to find singly. In her, complete emancipation from every kind of superstition (including that which attributes a pretended perfection to the order of nature and the universe), and an earnest protest against many things which are still part of the established constitution of society, resulted not from the hard intellect but from strength of noble and elevated feeling, and coexisted with a highly reverential nature. In general spiritual characteristics, as well as in temperament and organization, I have often compared her, as she was at this time, to Shelley: but in thought and intellect, Shelley, so far as his powers were developed in his short life, was but a child compared with what she ultimately became. Alike in the highest regions of speculation and in the smallest practical concerns of daily life, her mind was the same perfect instrument, piercing to the very heart and marrow of the matter; always seizing the essential idea or principle. The same exactness and rapidity of operation, pervading as it did her sensitive as well as her mental faculties, would with her gifts of feeling and imagination have fitted her to be a consummate artist, as her fiery and tender soul and her vigorous eloquence would certainly have made her a great orator, and her profound knowledge of human nature and discernment and sagacity in practical life, would in the times when such a *carriere* was open to women, have made her eminent among the rulers of mankind. Her intellectual gifts did but minister to a moral character at once the noblest and the best balanced which I have ever met with in life. Her unselfishness was not that of a taught system of duties, but of a heart which thoroughly identified itself with the feeling of others, and often went to excess in consideration for them, by imaginatively investing their feelings with the intensity of its own. The passion of justice might have been thought to be her strongest feeling, but for her boundless generosity, and a lovingness every ready to pour itself forth upon any or all human beings who were capable of giving the smallest feeling in return. The rest of her moral characteristics were such as naturally accompany these qualities of mind and heart: the most genuine modesty combined with the loftiest pride; a simplicity and sincerity which were absolute, toward all who were fit to receive them; the utmost scorn of whatever was mean and cowardly, and a burning indignation at everything brutal or tyrannical, faithless or dishonorable in conduct and character; while making the broadest distinction between *mala in se* and mere *mala prohibita*—between acts giving evidence of intrinsic badness in feeling and character, and those which are only violations of conventions either good or bad, violations which whether in themselves right or wrong, are capable of being committed by persons in every other respect loveable or admirable.

To be admitted into any degree of mental intercourse with a being of these qualities, could not but have a most beneficial influence on my development; though the effect was only gradual, and many years elapsed before her mental progress and mine went forward in the complete companionship they at last attained. The benefit I received was far greater than any which I could hope to give; though to her, who had at first reached her opinions by the moral intuition of a character of strong feeling, there was doubtless help as well as encouragement to be derived from one who had arrived at many of the same results by study and reasoning; and in the rapidity of her intellectual growth, her mental activity, which converted everything into knowledge, doubtless drew from me, as it did from other sources, many of its materials. What I owe, even intellectually, to her, is, in its detail, almost infinite; of its general character, a few words will give some, though a very imperfect, idea. With those who, like all the best and wisest of mankind, are dissatisfied with human life as it is, and whose feelings are wholly identified with its radical amendment, there are two main regions of thought. One is the region of ultimate aims; the constituent elements of the highest realizable ideal of human life. The other is that of the immediately useful and practically attainable. In both these departments I have acquired more from her teaching, than from all other sources taken together. And, to say truth, it is in these two extremes principally, that real certainty lies. My own strength lay wholly in the uncertain and slippery intermediate region, that of theory, or moral and political science: respecting the conclusions of which, in any of the forms in which I have received or originated them, whether as political economy, analytic psychology, logic, philosophy of history, or anything else, it is not the least of my intellectual obligations to her that I have derived from her a wise skepticism, which, while it has not hindered me from following out the honest exercise of my thinking faculties to whatever conclusions might result from it, has put me on my guard against holding or announcing those conclusions with a degree of confidence which the nature of such speculations does not warrant, and has kept my mind not only open to admit it, but prompt to welcome and eager to seek, even the questions on which I have most meditated, any prospect of clearer perceptions and better evidence. I have often received praise, which in my own right I only partially deserve, for the greater practicality which is supposed to be found in my writings, compared with those of most thinkers who have been equally addicted to large generalizations. The writings in which this quality had been observed, were not the work of one mind, but of the fusion of two, one of them as preeminently practical in its judgments and perceptions of things present, as it was high and bold in its anticipations for a remote futurity.

At His Brother's Grave

From Robert G. Ingersoll, Select Orations

Robert G. Ingersoll was a nationally known lecturer, humanist critic of Biblical revelation, and a staunch Illinois Republican.

My friends: I am going to do that which the dead oft promised he would do for me.

The loved and loving brother, husband, father, friend, died where manhood's morning almost touches noon, and while the shadows still were falling toward the west.

He had not passed on life's highway the stone that marks the highest point, but, being weary for a moment, lay down by the wayside, and using his burden for a pillow, fell into that dreamless sleep that kisses down his eyelids still. While yet in love with life and raptured with the world, he passed to silence and pathetic dust.

Yet, after all, it may be best, just in the happiest, sunniest hour of all the voyage, while eager winds are kissing every sail, to dash against the unseen rock, and in an instant hear the billows roar above a sunken ship. For, whether in midsea or 'mong the breakers of the farther shore, a wreck at last must mark the end of each and all. And every life, no matter if its every hour is rich with love and every moment jeweled with a joy, will at its close become a tragedy as sad and deep and dark as can be woven of the warp and woof of mystery and death.

This brave and tender man in every storm of life was oak and rock, but in the sunshine he was vine and flower. He was the friend of all heroic souls. He climbed the heights and left all superstitions far below, while on his forehead fell the golden dawning of the grander day.

He loved the beautiful, and was with color, form, and music

touched to tears. He sided with the weak, and with a willing hand gave alms; with loyal heart and with purest hands he faithfully discharged all public trusts.

He was a worshiper of liberty, a friend of the oppressed. A thousand times I have heard him quote these words: "For justice all place a temple, and all seasons, summer." He believed that happiness was the only good, reason the only torch, justice the only worship, humanity the only religion, and love the only priest. He added to the sum of human joy; and were every one to whom he did some loving service to bring a blossom to his grave, he would sleep tonight beneath a wilderness of flowers.

Life is a narrow vale between the cold and barren peaks of two eternities. We strive in vain to look beyond the heights. We cry aloud, and the only answer is the echo of our wailing cry. From the voiceless lips of the unreplying dead there comes no word; but in the night of death, hope sees a star, and listening love can hear the rustle of a wing.

He who sleeps here, when dying, mistaking the approach of death for the return of health, whispered with his last breath, "I am better now." Let us believe, in spite of doubts and dogmas, and tears and fears, that these dear words are true of all the countless dead.

And now to you who have been chosen, from among the many men he loved, to do the last sad office for the dead, we give his sacred dust. Speech cannot contain our love. There was, there is, no greater, stronger, manlier man.

Mother o' Mine

Rudyard Kipling

If I were hanged on the highest hill,
Mother o' mine, O mother o' mine!
I know whose love would follow me still,
Mother o' mine, O mother' o' mine!
If I were drowned in the deepest sea,
Mother o' mine, O mother o' mine!

I know whose tears would come down to me,
Mother o' mine, O mother o' mine!
If I were damned of body and soul,
I know whose prayers would make me whole,
Mother o' mine, O mother o'mine!

A Man and His Wife

Aesop

A man had a wife who made herself hated by all the members of his household. He wished to find out if she had the same effect on the persons in her father's house. He therefore made some excuse to send her home on a visit to her father. After a short time she returned, when he inquired how she had got on, and how the servants had treated her. She replied, "The neatherds and shepherds cast on me looks of aversion." He said, "O Wife, if you were disliked by those who go out early in the morning with their flocks, and return late in the evening, what must have been felt toward you by those with whom you passed the whole of the day!"

Straws show how the wind blows.

Youth Versus Age

Francis Bacon, Essays

Young men are bold, impetuous, and drawn to extremes, Bacon tells us. Older men are cautious, garrulous, and tend to carp. What age gains in understanding, it loses in willpower.

A man that is young in years may be old in hours, if he have lost no time. But that happeneth rarely. Generally youth is like the first cogitations, not so wise as the second. For there is a youth in thoughts, as well as in ages. And yet the invention of young men is more lively than that of old; and imaginations stream into their minds better, and as it were more divinely. Natures that have much heat and great and violent desires and perturbations are not ripe for action till they have passed the meridian of their years, as it was with Julius Caesar and Septimius Severus. Of the latter of whom it is said, *Juventutem egit erroribus, imo furoribus, plenam* ["He spent his youth in folly, nay in madness"]. And yet he was the ablest emperor, almost of all the list. But reposed natures may do well in youth. As it is seen in Augustus Caesar, Cosmus, Duke of Florence, Gaston de Fois, and others. On the other side, heat and vivacity in age is an excellent composition for business. Young men are fitter to invent than to judge, fitter for execution than for counsel, and fitter for new projects than for settled business. For the experience of age, in things that fall within the compass of it, directeth them, but in new things abuseth them. The errors of young men are the ruin of business, but the errors of aged men amount but to this, that more might have been done, or sooner. Young men in the conduct and manage of actions embrace more than they can hold; stir more than they can quiet; fly to the end, without consideration of the means and degrees; pursue some few principles which they have chanced upon absurdly; [are careless in their innovations], which draws unknown inconveniences; use extreme remedies at first; and that which doubleth all errors, will not acknowledge or retract them, like an unready horse that will neither stop nor turn. Men of age object too much, consult too long, adventure too little, repent too soon, and seldom drive business home to the full period, but content themselves with a mediocrity of success. Certainly it is good to compound employments of both, for that will be good for the present, because the virtues of either age may correct the defects of both; and good for succession, that young men may be learners, while men in age are actors; and, lastly, good for extern[al] accidents, because authority followeth old men, and favor and popularity youth. But for the moral part, perhaps youth will have the preeminence, as age hath for the politic. A certain rabbi, upon the text, *Your young men shall see visions, and your old men shall dream dreams,* inferreth that young men are admitted nearer to God than old, because vision is a clearer revelation than a dream. And certainly the more a man drinketh of the world, the more it intoxicateth, and age doth profit rather in the powers of understanding than in the virtues of the will and affections.

Why Should Not Old Men Be Mad?

William Butler Yeats

Why should not old men be mad?
Some have known a likely lad
That had a sound fly-fisher's wrist
Turn to a drunken journalist;
A girl that knew all Dante once
Live to bear children to a dunce;
A Helen of social welfare dream
Climb on a wagonette to scream.
Some think it a matter of course that chance
Should starve good men and bad advance,
That if their neighbors figured plain,
As though upon a lighted screen,
No single story would they find
Of an unbroken happy mind,
A finish worthy of the start.
Young men know nothing of this sort,
Observant old men know it well;
And when they know what old books tell,
And that no better can be had,
Know why an old man should be mad.

5

THE
STATESMAN

FOR THE ANCIENT GREEKS AND ROMANS, MANLINESS COULD NOT BE understood apart from a full-time devotion to the duties of public life and the cultivation of the civic virtues. As Aristotle had it in his famous axiom from the *Politics*, "Man is by nature a political animal." In our times, this statement might at first strike us as strange: We have professional politicians, after all, who are elected to concern themselves with public affairs on a full-time basis, while the rest of us devote our efforts to trying to be a good man in other areas of life besides politics—by being a good husband, father, or friend, good at one's job or vocation, or by contributing to the community through myriad other channels.

Yet when the ancients identified manliness with the civic virtues, they were not thinking of politics in the narrow way we sometimes do today. For them, politics was more than just a realm for brokering private interests. The civic association was not just a contract among individuals to protect its members from crime or foreign invasion and enable them to get on with their private lives in peace. For the ancients, the city or *polis* was an all-encompassing association. To be a citizen was a source not only of security and freedom from unjust treatment, but of aesthetic and cultural satisfaction through the community's shared traditions, and even of religious fulfillment through its common faith. By serving the common good, according to the ancients, we exercise our moral and intellectual virtues in a way that would not be possible in private life alone. By deliberating together with our fellow citizens on the great issues of war and peace, justice and injustice, nobility and baseness, we give our natures room to flower and blossom. Family life is crucially important to a republic of virtuous men because it provides children with their first habituation to good behavior, preparing them for their future lives as citizens. But, in the end, a man's public life might be said to possess an even higher dignity and importance than his private life as a husband and father. The cardinal virtues of justice, moderation, courage, liberality, and wisdom can only be expressed at their fullest through our lives as citizens.

The readings in this section, then, are about man as statesman. The Greek word for statesman, *politikos,* meant "citizen" in
the fullest sense—not someone who sits passively by while the great
affairs of state unfold, but one who takes an active part in deciding
their course, whether jointly with his peers or by taking a role at the
helm of affairs. Of course, there is always the danger that a man
convinced of his ability to lead will become overbearing and intolerant of dissenting opinions, or jealous of the talents of others;
what starts out as statesmanship can degenerate into tyranny. For
manly pride and honor have both good and bad potential. At its
highest levels it can involve an energetic commitment to justice at
home and, when necessary, the defense of one's country from
external threats. And yet unchecked pride can lead to overweening
arrogance, ambition and dreams of imperialism, and at worst to a
base desire to overthrow the common good and rule as tyrant,
indulging one's own self-serving desires at the expense of others.
Many of the readings in this section explore this problem: how can
masculine ambition be channeled away from tyrannical selfishness
and redirected toward honorable citizenship?

For these reasons, statesmanship has always been closely connected with moral and intellectual education. According to Plato's
Republic, in a just and well-ordered society, the soul of the individual citizen will mirror the virtues of the community as a whole, and
the community in turn will enable the individual citizen to exercise
his potential for excellence. Both within the individual soul and
the structure of the community at large, there must be a hierarchy
in which reason governs the passions. To achieve this harmony
within the individual soul and between the citizen and the community he serves, government must take the lead in providing a civic
education.

Young men need an education that will instill in their characters a sense of order, of harmony and justice that seems to mirror
the order of the cosmos itself. If a man's soul participates in this
pattern in the heavens, he will be steady, sober, gracious, and self-
restrained—a true gentleman. The aim of Platonic education is to
harness manly ambition and turn it away from extravagance and
profligacy toward civic virtue and the life of the mind. In his dialogues we encounter perplexed young men who want to be good,
but who are tempted by a life of pleasure or domination, and troubled by the lack of a clear moral direction from their parents,
teachers, or other authorities. Everyone tells them to be good, but

to do everything necessary to get ahead in the world and be successful! Socrates, by contrast, characterized the life of the soul as an ascent from bodily pleasures to the higher pleasures of the mind, pleasures that include the love of family and further ennoble family life by directing it toward the even higher purposes of the common good.

Readers of this section will find many variations on this fundamental classical ideal of citizenship, which identifies true manliness with the sobriety, thoughtfulness, and steadfastness required by civic affairs and a respect for learning. It is captured well by Cicero's portrait of Scipio Africanus the Younger, the great Roman general and statesman. Scipio perfectly embodies the classical hierarchy of active and contemplative virtues. To be a man, his example shows, one must demonstrate civic virtue, including military prowess, in the service of one's country and thereby reap the deserved reward of public honor. But worthy as the civic virtues and public honor are, the life of learning, art, and culture is even worthier. The intellectual virtues should govern the civic virtues so that both may flourish. Political and military prowess that might otherwise make a man too harsh and proud will be tempered by their subordination to the nobler virtues of learning and culture. A true man is strong, but in a quiet way. He is modest, generous and affable, not a boaster or a bully. This ideal of statesmanship as a balance between active and contemplative virtues endures throughout all the ages of the West, down to the American Founding Fathers and great men of the present century like Churchill.

On reflection, then, the classical ideal of statesmanship is not quite so alien to us as it might first appear. For much of that ideal of citizenship and governing is familiar to us through the influence of its modern admirers, Thomas Jefferson, Alexis de Tocqueville, and Theodore Roosevelt among them. Its influence is still with us and shapes us deeply, even if we might have lost our immediate day-to-day connection with this heritage. For even in our most pessimistic mood about the careerism or posturing of modern politicians—or over the failure of some of our own leaders to demonstrate the maturity and honesty that we might rightly expect—we can still feel inspired to recall the classical ideal. It's not all that distant, the image of strong yet just, forceful yet reflective leadership. As Jefferson tells us in a reading appearing later in this anthology, a free people must be liberally educated in the same moral and intellectual virtues praised by the ancients if they are not to lose their freedom to a demagogue. As long as free peoples and self-governing republics exist, men must aspire to rise above being mere politicians to being statesmen. For, as Dwight D. Eisenhower once wrote, "Only our individual faith in freedom can keep us free."

THE KINGLY MAN

Two Kings Clashing: Achilles and Agamemnon

From Homer, The Iliad

Anger is necessary in a warrior, but when mixed with jealousy and wounded honor it can lead to a dangerous instability. When the Greek king of kings, Agamemnon, deprives the Greeks' greatest fighter, Achilles, of his war prize, the young warrior withdraws from the army. Achilles, a king in his own right, believes he is a better man than his lawful commander in chief, and is ready to sacrifice his own side's safety and success against the Trojans to avenge his wounded pride. It's an age-old conflict of youth versus age, and natural merit versus authority. For his part, Agamemnon has long resented Achilles' resistance to his supreme authority, as their heated argument makes plain. The ultimate consequence of Achilles' desertion of the Greeks is that the Trojans come close to defeating them, while Achilles' best friend Patroclus dies in his place. Thus Homer demonstrates that overreaching anger and pride are due for a fall. Achilles wanted the Greeks to suffer so they would realize how much they needed him. He got his wish, but at an awful price.

Sing, goddess, the anger of Paleus's son Achilleus and its devastation, which put pains thousandfold upon the Achaians, hurled in their multitudes to the house of Hades strong souls of heroes, but gave their bodies to be the delicate feasting of dogs, of all birds, and the will of Zeus was accomplished since that time when first there stood in division of conflict Atreus's son, the lord of men and brilliant Achilleus.

Then in answer again spoke brilliant swift-footed Achilleus:

"Son of Atreus, most lordly, greediest for gain of all men, how shall the great-hearted Achaians give you a prize now? There is no great store of things lying about I know of. But what we took from the cities by storm has been distributed; it is unbecoming for the people to call back things once given. No, for the present give the girl back to the god; we Achaians thrice and four times over will repay you, if ever Zeus gives into our hands the strong-walled citadel of Troy to be plundered."

Then in answer again spoke powerful Agamemnon:

"Not that way, good fighter though you be, godlike Achilleus, strive to cheat, for you will not deceive, you will not persuade me. What do you want? To keep your own prize and have me sit here lacking one? Are you ordering me to give this girl back? Either the great-hearted Achaians shall give me a new prize chosen according to my desire to atone for the girl lost, or else if they will not give me one I myself shall take her, your own prize, or that of Aias, or that of Odysseus."

Then looking darkly at him Achilleus of the swift feet spoke:

"O wrapped in shamelessness, with your mind forever on profit, how shall any one of the Achaians readily obey you either to go on a journey or to fight men strongly in battle? I for my part did not come here for the sake of the Trojan spearmen to fight against them, since to me they have done nothing. Never yet have they driven away my cattle or my horses, never in Phthia where the soil is rich and men grow great did they spoil my harvest, since indeed there is much that lies between us, the shadowy mountains and the echoing sea; but for your sake, o great shamelessness, we followed, to do you a favor, you with the dog's eyes, to win your honor and Menelaos's from the Trojans. You forget all this or else you care nothing. And now my prize you threaten in person to strip from me, for whom I labored much, the gift of the sons of the Achaians. Never, when the Achaians sack some well-founded citadel of the Trojans, do I have a prize that is equal to your prize. Always the greater part of the painful fighting is the work of my hands; but when the time comes to distribute the booty yours is far the greater reward, and I with some small thing yet dear to me go back to my ships when I am weary with fighting. Now I am returning to Phthia, since it is much better to go home again with my curved ships, and I am minded no longer to stay here dishonored and pile up your wealth and your luxury."

Then answered him in turn the lord of men Agamemnon:

"Run away by all means if your heart drives you. I will not

entreat you to stay here for my sake. There are others with me who will do me honor, and above all Zeus of the counsels. To me you are the most hateful of all the kings whom the gods love."

"Forever quarreling is dear to your heart, and wars and battles; and if you are very strong indeed, that is a god's gift. Go home then with your own ships and your own companions, be king over the Myrmidons. I care nothing about you. I take no account of your anger. But here is my threat to you. Even as Phoibos Apollo is taking away my Chryseis, I shall convey her back in my own ship, with my own followers; but I shall take the fair-cheeked Briseis, your prize, I myself going to your shelter, that you may learn well how much greater I am than you, and another man may shrink back from likening himself to me and contending against me."

David and Goliath

From 1 Samuel (16–20)

The great biblical account of how a young man's valor serves his king, but also threatens his power.

The Lord said to Samuel, "How long will you mourn for Saul because I have rejected him as king over Israel? Fill your horn with oil and take it with you; I am sending you to Jesse of Bethlehem; for I have chosen myself a king among his sons." Samuel answered, "How can I go? Saul will hear of it and kill me." "Take a heifer with you," said the Lord; "say you have come to offer a sacrifice to the Lord, and invite Jesse to the sacrifice; then I will let you know what you must do. You shall anoint for me the man whom I show you." Samuel did as the Lord had told him, and went to Bethlehem. The elders of the city came in haste to meet him, saying, "Why have you come? Is all well?" "All is well," said Samuel; "I have come to sacrifice to the Lord. Hallow yourselves and come with me to the sacrifice." He himself hallowed Jesse and his sons and invited them to the sacrifice also. They came, and when Samuel saw Eliab he thought, "Here, before the Lord, is his anointed king." But the Lord said to him, "Take no account of it if he is handsome and tall; I reject him. The Lord does not see as man sees; men judge by appearances but the Lord judges by the heart." Then Jesse called Abinadab and made him pass before Samuel, but he said, "No, the Lord has not chosen this one." Then he presented Shammah, and Samuel said, "Nor has the Lord chosen him." Seven of his sons Jesse presented to Samuel, but he said, "The Lord has not chosen any of these." Then Samuel asked, "Are these all?" Jesse answered, "There is still the youngest, but he is looking after the sheep." Samuel said to Jesse, "Send and fetch him; we will not sit down until he comes." So he sent and fetched him. He was handsome, with ruddy cheeks and bright eyes. The Lord said, "Rise and anoint him: this is the man." Samuel took the horn of oil and anointed him in the presence of his brothers. Then the spirit of the Lord came upon David and was with him from that day onward. And Samuel set out on his way back to Ramah.

The spirit of the Lord had forsaken Saul, and at times an evil spirit from the Lord would seize him suddenly. His servants said to him, "You see, sir, how an evil spirit from God seizes you; why do you not command your servants here to go and find some man who can play the harp? Then, when an evil spirit from God comes on you, he can play and you will recover." Saul said to his servants, "Find me a man who can play well and bring him to me." One of his attendants said, "I have seen a son of Jesse of Bethlehem who can play; he is a brave man and a good fighter, wise in speech and handsome, and the Lord is with him." Saul therefore sent messengers to Jesse and asked him to send him his son David, who was with the sheep. Jesse took a homer of bread, a skin of wine, and a kid, and sent them to Saul by his son David. David came to Saul and entered his service; and Saul loved him dearly, and he became his armor-bearer. So Saul sent word to Jesse: "Let David stay in my service, for I am pleased with him." And whenever a spirit from God came upon Saul, David would take his harp and play on it, so that Saul found relief; he recovered and the evil spirit left him alone.

The Philistines collected their forces for war and massed at Socoh in Judah; they camped between Socoh and Azekah at Ephes-dammim. Saul and the Israelites also massed, and camped in the Vale of Elah. They drew up their lines facing the Philistines, the Philistines occupying a position on one hill and the Israelites on another, with a valley between them. A champion came out from the Philistine camp, a man named Goliath, from Gath; he was over nine feet in height. He had a bronze helmet on his head, and he wore plate-armor of bronze, weighing five thousand shekels. On his legs were bronze greaves, and one of his weapons was a dagger of bronze. The shaft of his spear was like a weaver's beam, and its head, which was of iron, weighed six hundred shekels; and his shield-bearer marched ahead of him. The champion stood and shouted to the ranks of Israel, "Why do you come out to do battle, you slaves of Saul? I am the Philistine champion; choose your man to meet me. If he can kill me in fair fight, we will become your slaves; but if I prove too strong for him and kill him, you shall be our slaves and serve us. Here and now I defy the ranks of Israel. Give me a man," said the Philistine, "and we will fight it out." When Saul and the Israelites heard what the Philistine said, they were shaken and dismayed.

David was the son of an Ephrathite called Jesse, who had eight sons. By Saul's time he had become a feeble old man, and his three eldest sons had followed Saul to the war. The eldest was called Eliab, the next Abinadab, and the third Shammah; David was the youngest. The three eldest followed Saul, while David used to go to Saul's camp and back to Bethlehem to mind his father's flocks.

Morning and evening for forty days the Philistine came forward and took up his position. Then one day Jesse said to his son David, "Take your brothers an ephah of this parched grain and these ten loaves of bread, and run with them to the camp. These ten cream-cheeses are for you to take to the commanding officer. See if your brothers are well and bring back some token from them." Saul and the brothers and all the Israelites were in the Vale of Elah, fighting the Philistines. Early next morning David left someone in charge of the sheep, set out on his errand and went as Jesse had told him. He reached the lines just as the army was going out to take up position and was raising the war-cry. The Israelites and the Philistines drew up their ranks opposite each other. David left his things in charge of the quartermaster, ran to the line and went up to his brothers to greet them. While he was talking to them the Philistine champion, Goliath, came out from the Philistine ranks and issued his challenge in the same words as before; and David heard him. When the Israelites saw the man they ran from him in fear. "Look at this man who comes out day after day to defy Israel," they said. "The king is to give a rich reward to the man who kills him; he will give him his daughter in marriage too and will exempt his family from service due in Israel." Then David turned to his neighbors and said, "What is to be done for the man who kills this Philistine, and wipes out our disgrace? And who is he, an uncircumcised Philistine to defy the army of the living God?" The people told him how the matter stood and what was to be done for the

man who killed him. His elder brother Eliab overheard David talking with the men and grew angry. "What are you doing here?" he
asked. "And who have you left to look after those sheep in the
wilderness? I know you, you impudent young rascal; you have only
come to see the fighting." David answered, "What have I done now?
I only asked a question." And he turned away from him to someone
else and repeated his question, but everybody gave him the same
answer.

What David had said was overheard and reported to Saul, who
sent for him. David said to him, "Do not lose heart, sir. I will go and
fight this Philistine." Saul answered, "You cannot go and fight with
this Philistine; you are only a lad, and he has been a fighting man
all his life." David said to Saul, "Sir, I am my father's shepherd;
when a lion or a bear comes and carries off a sheep from the flock,
I attack it and rescue the victim from its jaws. Then if it turns on
me, I seize it by the beard and batter it to death. Lions I have killed
and bears, and this uncircumcised Philistine will fare no better
than they; he has defied the army of the living God. The Lord who
saved me from the lion and the bear will save me from this Philistine." "Go then," said Saul; "and the Lord will be with you." He put
his own tunic on David, placed a bronze helmet on his head and
gave him a coat of mail to wear; he then fastened his sword on
David over his tunic. But David hesitated, because he had not tried
them, and said to Saul, "I cannot go with these, because I have not
tried them." So he took them off. Then he picked up his stick,
chose five smooth stones from the brook and put them in a shepherd's bag which served as his pouch. He walked out to meet the
Philistine with his sling in his hand.

The Philistine came toward David, with his shield-bearer
marching ahead; and he looked David up and down and had nothing but contempt for this handsome lad with his ruddy cheeks and
bright eyes. He said to David, "Am I a dog that you come out
against me with sticks?" And he swore at him in the name of his
god. "Come on," he said, "and I will give your flesh to the birds and
the beasts." David answered, "You have come against me with sword
and spear and dagger, but I have come against you in the name of
the Lord of Hosts, the God of the army of Israel which you have
defied. The Lord will put you into my power this day; I will kill you
and cut your head off and leave your carcass and the carcasses of
the Philistines to the birds and the wild beasts; all the world shall
know that there is a God in Israel. All those who are gathered here
shall see that the Lord saves neither by sword nor spear; the battle

is the Lord's, and he will put you all into our power."

When the Philistine began moving toward him again, David ran quickly to engage him. He put his hand into his bag, took out a stone, slung it, and struck the Philistine on the forehead. The stone sank into his forehead, and he fell flat on his face on the ground. So David proved the victor with his sling and stone; he struck Goliath down and gave him a mortal wound, though he had no sword. Then he ran to the Philistine and stood over him, and grasping his sword, he drew it out of the scabbard, dispatched him and cut off his head. The Philistines, when they saw that their hero was dead, turned and ran. The men of Israel and Judah at once raised the war-cry and hotly pursued them all the way to Gath and even to the gates of Ekron. The road that runs to Shaarim, Gath, and Ekron was strewn with their dead. On their return from the pursuit of the Philistines, the Israelites plundered their camp. David took Goliath's head and carried it to Jerusalem, leaving his weapons in his tent.

Next day an evil spirit from God seized upon Saul; he fell into a frenzy in the house, and David played the harp to him as he had before. Saul had his spear in his hand, and he hurled it at David, meaning to pin him to the wall; but twice David swerved aside. After this Saul was afraid of David, because he saw that the Lord had forsaken him and was with David. He therefore removed David from his household and appointed him to the command of a thousand men. David led his men into action, and succeeded in everything that he undertook, because the Lord was with him. When Saul saw how successful he was, he was more afraid of him than ever; all Israel and Judah loved him because he took the field at their head.

Saul said to David, "Here is my elder daughter Merab; I will give her to you in marriage, but in return you must serve me valiantly and fight the Lord's battles." For Saul meant David to meet his end at the hands of the Philistines and not himself. David answered Saul, "Who am I and what are my father's people, my kinfolk, in Israel, that I should become the king's son-in-law?" However, when the time came for Saul's daughter Merab to be married to David, she had already been given to Adriel of Meholah. But Michal, Saul's other daughter, fell in love with David, and when Saul was told of this, he saw that it suited his plans. He said to himself, "I will give her to him; let her be the bait that lures him to his death at the hands of the Philistines." So Saul proposed a second time to make David his son-in-law, and ordered his courtiers to say to David privately, "The king is well disposed to you and you are dear to us all; now is the time for you to marry into the king's family." When Saul's people spoke in this way to David, he said to them, "Do you think that marrying the king's daughter is a matter of so little consequence that a poor man of no consequence, like myself, can do it?" Saul's courtiers reported what David had said, and he replied, "Tell David this: all the king wants as the brideprice is the foreskins of a hundred Philistines, by way of vengeance on his enemies." Saul was counting on David's death at the hands of the Philistines. The courtiers told David what Saul had said, and marriage with the king's daughter on these terms pleased him well. Before the appointed time, David went out with his men and slew two hundred Philistines; he brought their foreskins and counted them out to the king in order to be accepted as his son-in-law. So Saul married his daughter Michal to David. He saw clearly that the Lord was with David, and knew that Michal his daughter had fallen in love with him; and so he grew more and more afraid of David and was his enemy for the rest of his life.

The Philistine officers used to come out to offer single combat; and whenever they did, David had more success against them than all the rest of Saul's men, and he won a great name for himself.

Saul spoke to Jonathan his son and all his household about killing David. But Jonathan was devoted to David and told him that his father Saul was looking for an opportunity to kill him. "Be on your guard tomorrow morning," he said; "conceal yourself, and remain in hiding. Then I will come out and join my father in the open country where you are and speak to him about you, and if I discover anything I will tell you." Jonathan spoke up for David to his father Saul and said to him, "Sir, do not wrong your servant David; he has not wronged you; his conduct toward you has been beyond reproach. Did he not take his life in his hands when he killed the Philistine, and the Lord won great victory for Israel? You saw it, you shared in the rejoicing; why should you wrong an innocent man and put David to death without cause?" Saul listened to Jonathan and swore solemnly by the Lord that David should not be put to death. So Jonathan called David and told him all this; then he brought him to Saul, and he was in attendance on the king as before.

War broke out again, and David attacked the Philistines and dealt them such a blow that they ran out before him.

An evil spirit from the Lord came upon Saul as he was sitting in the house with his spear in his hand; and David was playing the harp. Saul tried to pin David to the wall with the spear, but he avoided the king's thrust so that Saul drove the spear into the wall. David escaped and got safely away. That night Saul sent servants to keep watch on David's house, intending to kill him in the morning, but David's wife Michal warned him to get away that night, "or tomorrow," she said, "you will be a dead man." She let David down through a window and he slipped away and escaped. Michal took their household gods and put them on the bed; at its head she laid a goat's-hair rug and covered it all with a cloak. When the men arrived to arrest David she told them he was ill. Saul sent them back to see David for themselves. "Bring him to me, bed and all," he said, "and I will kill him." When they came, there were the household gods on the bed and the goat's-hair rug at its head. Then Saul said to Michal, "Why have you played this trick on me and let my enemy get safe away?" And Michal answered, "He said to me, 'Help me escape or I will kill you.'"

Meanwhile David made good his escape and came to Samuel at Ramah, and told him how Saul had treated him.

An Insulting Gift to a Young Monarch

From William Shakespeare, Henry V

King:
What treasure, uncle?
Exeter:
Tennis balls, my liege.
King:
We are glad the Dauphin is so pleasant with us.
His present and your pains we thank you for.
When we have matched our rackets to these balls,
We will in France, by God's grace, play a set
Shall strike his father's crown into the hazard.
Tell him he hath made a match with such a wrangler
That all the courts of France will be disturbed
With chases. And we understand him well,

How he comes o'er us with our wilder days,
Not measuring what use we made of them.
We never valued this poor seat of England,
And therefore, living hence, did give ourself
To barbarous license; as 'tis ever common
That men are merriest when they are from home.
But tell the Dauphin I will keep my state,
Be like a king, and show my sail of greatness
When I do rouse me in my throne of France.
For that I have laid by my majesty
And plodded like a man for working days,
But I will rise there with so full a glory
That I will dazzle all the eyes of France,
Yea, strike the Dauphin blind to look on us.
And tell the pleasant prince this mock of his
Hath turned his balls to gunstones, and his soul
Shall stand sore charged for the wasteful vengeance
That shall fly with them; for many a thousand widows
Shall this his mock mock out of their dear husbands,
Mock mothers from their sons, mock castles down;
And some are yet ungotten and unborn
That shall have cause to curse the Dauphin's scorn.
But this lies all within the will of God,
To whom I do appeal, and in whose name,
Tell you the Dauphin, I am coming on
To venge me as I may, and to put forth
My rightful hand in a well-hallowed cause.
So get you hence in peace. And tell the Dauphin
His jest will savour but of shallow wit
When thousands weep more than did laugh at it.
Convey them with safe conduct. Fare you well.
Exeunt Ambassadors

Achilles and Agamemnon Reconciled

From Homer, The Iliad

Achilles deserted the Greeks over a personal slight, and now rejoins them to avenge a personal loss—Patroklos's death at the hands of Hektor. With the help of lavish gifts, Achilles is reconciled to Agamemnon. Odysseus, hero of Homer's next poem, makes a brief but characteristic appearance and demonstrates his reputation for prudence, the practical wisdom of a man of affairs. While Achilles wants the Greeks to rush straight into battle and smash the foe, Odysseus recommends they all have a good meal first to keep up their strength.

"Here am I to give you all those gifts, as many as brilliant Odysseus yesterday went to your shelter and promised. Or if you will, hold back, though you lean hard into the battle, while my followers take the gifts from my ship and bring them to you, so you may see what I give to comfort your spirit."

Then in answer to him spoke Achilleus of the swift feet:

"Son of Atreus, most lordly and king of men, Agamemnon, the gifts are yours to give if you wish, and as it is proper, or to keep with yourself. But now let us remember our joy in warcraft, immediately, for it is not fitting to stay here and waste time nor delay, since there is still a big work to be done. So a man can see once more Achilleus among the front fighters with the bronze spear wrecking the Trojan battalions. Therefore let each of you remember this and fight his antagonist."

Then in answer to him spoke resourceful Odysseus:

"Not that way, good fighter that you are, godlike Achilleus. Do not drive the sons of the Achaians on Ilion when they are hungry, to fight against the Trojans, since not short will be the time of battle, once the massed formations of men have encountered together, with the god inspiring fury in both sides. Rather, tell the men of Achaia here by their swift ships, to take food and wine, since these make fighting fury and warcraft. For a man will not have strength to fight his way forward all day long until the sun goes down if he is starved for food. Even though in his heart he will be very passionate for the battle, yet without his knowing it his limbs will go heavy, and hunger and thirst will catch up with him and cumber his knees as he moves on. But when a man has been well filled with wine and with eating and then does battle all day long against the enemy, why then the heart inside him is full of cheer, nor do his limbs get weary, until all are ready to give over the fighting. Come then, tell your men to scatter and bid them get ready a meal."

The Kingdom of the Lion

Aesop

The beasts of the field and forest had a Lion as their king. He was neither wrathful, cruel, nor tyrannical, but just and gentle as a king should be. He made during his reign a royal proclamation for a general assembly of all the birds and beasts, and drew up conditions for an universal league, in which the Wolf and the Lamb, the Panther and the Kid, the Tiger and the Stag, the Dog and the Hare, should live together in perfect peace and amity. The Hare said, "Oh, how I have longed to see this day, in which the weak shall take their place with impunity by the side of the strong."

The Good Prince and the Evil Prince

From Desiderius Erasmus,
The Education of a Christian Prince

Good and bad models for the moral education of a prince.

Let the teacher paint a sort of celestial creature, more like to a divine being than a mortal: complete in all the virtues; born for the common good; yea, sent by the God above to help the affairs of mortals by looking out and caring for everyone and everything; to whom no concern is of longer standing or more dear than the state; who has more than a paternal spirit toward everyone; who holds the life of each individual dearer than his own; who works and strives night and day for just one end—to be the best he can for everyone; with whom rewards are ready for all good men and pardon for the wicked, if only they will reform—for so much does he want to be of real help to his people, without thought of recompense, that if necessary he would not hesitate to look out for their welfare at great risk to himself; who considers his wealth to lie in the advantages of his country; who is ever on the watch so that everyone else may sleep deeply; who grants no leisure to himself so that he may spend his life in the peace of his country; who worries himself with continual cares so that his subjects may have peace and quiet. Upon the moral qualities of this one man alone depends the felicity of the state. Let the tutor point this out as the picture of a true prince!

Now let him bring out the opposite side by showing a frightful, loathsome beast, formed of a dragon, wolf, lion, viper, bear, and like creatures; with six hundred eyes all over it, teeth everywhere, fearful from all angles, and with hooked claws; with never satiated hunger, fattened on human vitals, and reeking with human blood; never sleeping, but always threatening the fortunes and lives of all men; dangerous to everyone, especially to the good; a sort of fatal scourge to the whole world, on which everyone who has the interests of the state at heart pours forth execration and hatred; which cannot be borne because of its monstrousness and yet cannot be overthrown without great disaster to the city because its maliciousness is hedged about with armed forces and wealth. This is the picture of a tyrant—unless there is something more odious which can be depicted. Monsters of this sort were Claudius and Caligula. The myths in the poets also showed Busyris, Pentheus, and Midas, whose names are now objects of hate to all the human race, to be of the same type.

The Good and Great
Man Beowulf

From Thomas Bulfinch, Bulfinch's Mythology

In his boyhood Beowulf gave evidence of the great feats of strength and courage which in manhood made him the deliverer of Hrothgar, King of Denmark, from the monster, Grendel, and later in his own kingdom from the fiery dragon which dealt Beowulf a mortal blow.

Beowulf's first renown followed his conquest of many seamonsters while he swam for seven days and nights before he came to the country of the Finns. Helping to defend the land of the Hetware, he killed many of the enemy and again showed his prowess as a swimmer by bringing to his ship the armor of thirty of his slain pursuers. Offered the crown of his native land, Beowulf, just entering manhood, refused it in favor of Heardred, the young son of the queen. Instead, he acted as guardian and counselor until the boy-king grew old enough to rule alone.

For twelve years, Hrothgar, King of Denmark, suffered while his kingdom was being ravaged by a devouring monster, named Grendel. This Grendel bore a charmed life against all weapons forged by man. He lived in the wastelands and nightly prowled out to visit the hall of Hrothgar, carrying off and slaughtering many of the guests.

Beowulf, hearing from mariners of Grendel's murderous visits, sailed from Geatland with fourteen stalwart companions to render Hrothgar the help of this great strength. Landing on the Danish coast, Beowulf was challenged as a spy. He persuaded the coastguards to let him pass, and he was received and feasted by King Hrothgar. When the king and his court retired for the night, Beowulf and his companions were left alone in the hall. All but Beowulf fell asleep. Grendel entered. With a stroke he killed one of Beowulf's sleeping men, but Beowulf, unarmed, wrestled with the monster and by dint of his great strength managed to tear Grendel's arm out at the shoulder. Grendel, mortally wounded, retreated, leaving a bloody trail from the hall to his lair.

All fear of another attack by Grendel allayed, the Danes returned to the hall, and Beowulf and his companions were sheltered elsewhere. Grendel's mother came to avenge the fatal injury to her monster son and carried off a Danish nobleman and Grendel's torn off paw. Following the blood trail, Beowulf went forth to despatch the mother. Armed with his sword, Hrunting, he came to the water's edge. He plunged in and swam to a chamber under the sea. There he fought with Grendel's mother, killing her with an old sword he found in the sea cavern. Nearby was Grendel's body. Beowulf cut off its head and brought it back as a trophy to King Hrothgar. Great was the rejoicing in the hall and greater was Beowulf's welcome when he returned to Geatland, where he was given great estates and many high honors.

Shortly afterward, Heardred, the boy-king, was killed in the war with the Swedes. Beowulf succeeded him to the throne.

For fifty years Beowulf ruled his people in peace and serenity. Then suddenly a dragon, furious at having his treasure stolen from his hoard in a burial mound, began to ravage Beowulf's kingdom. Like Grendel, this monster left its den at night on its errand of murder and pillage.

Beowulf, now an aged monarch, resolved to do battle, unaided, with the dragon. He approached the entrance to its den, whence boiling steam issued forth. Undaunted, Beowulf strode forward shouting his defiance. The dragon came out, sputtering flames from its mouth. The monster rushed upon Beowulf with all its fury and almost crushed him in its first charge. So fearful grew the struggle that all but one of Beowulf's men deserted and fled for their lives. Wiglaf remained to help his aged monarch. Another rush of the dragon shattered Beowulf's sword and the monster's fangs sunk into Beowulf's neck. Wiglaf, rushing into the struggle, helped the dying Beowulf to kill the dragon.

Before his death, Beowulf named Wiglaf his successor to the throne of Geatland and ordered that his own ashes be placed in a memorial shrine at the top of a high cliff commanding the sea. Beowulf's body was burned on a vast funeral pyre, while twelve Geats rode around the mound singing their sorrow and their praise for the good and great man, Beowulf.

Theseus, the Minotaur and Other Adventures

Thomas Bulfinch, Bulfinch's Mythology

Theseus was the son of Aegeus, king of Athens, and of Aethra, daughter of the king of Troezen. He was brought up at Troezen, and when arrived at manhood was to proceed to Athens and present himself to his father. Aegeus, on parting from Aethra, before the birth of his son, placed his sword and shoes under a large stone and directed her to send his son to him when he became strong enough to roll away the stone and take them from under it. When she thought the time had come, his mother led Theseus to the stone, and he removed it with ease and took the sword and shoes. As the roads were infested with robbers, his grandfather pressed him earnestly to take the shorter and safer way to his father's country—by sea; but the youth, feeling in himself the spirit and the soul of a hero, and eager to signalize himself like Hercules, with whose fame all Greece then rang, by destroying the evildoers and monsters that oppressed the country, determined on the more perilous and adventurous journey by land.

His first day's journey brought him to Epidaurus, where dwelt a man named Periphetes, a son of Vulcan. This ferocious savage always went armed with a club of iron, and all travelers stood in terror of his violence. When he saw Theseus approach he assailed him, but speedily fell beneath the blows of the young hero, who took possession of his club and bore it ever afterward as a memorial of his first victory.

Several similar contests with the petty tyrants and marauders of the country followed, in all of which Theseus was victorious. One of these evildoers was called Procrustes, or the Stretcher. He had an iron bedstead, on which he used to tie all travelers who fell into his hands. If they were shorter than the bed, he stretched their limbs to make them fit it; if they were longer than the bed, he lopped off a portion. Theseus served him as he had served others.

Having overcome all the perils of the road, Theseus at length reached Athens, where new dangers awaited him. Medea, the sorceress, who had fled from Corinth after her separation from Jason, had become the wife of Aegeus, the father of Theseus. Knowing by her arts who he was, and fearing the loss of her influence with her husband if Theseus should be acknowledged as his son, she filled the mind of Aegeus with suspicions of the young stranger, and induced him to present him a cup of poison; but at the moment when Theseus stepped forward to take it, the sight of the sword which he wore discovered to his father who he was, and prevented the fatal draught. Medea, detected in her arts, fled once more from deserved punishment, and arrived in Asia, where the country afterward called Media, received its name from her. Theseus was acknowledged by his father, and declared his successor.

The Athenians were at that time in deep affliction, on account of the tribute which they were forced to pay to Minos, king of Crete. This tribute consisted of seven youths and seven maidens, who were sent every year to be devoured by the Minotaur, a monster with a bull's body and a human head. It was exceedingly strong and fierce, and was kept in a labyrinth constructed by Daedalus, so artfully contrived that whoever was enclosed in it could by no means find his way out unassisted. Here the Minotaur roamed, and was fed with human victims.

Theseus resolved to deliver his countrymen from this calamity, or to die in the attempt. Accordingly, when the time of sending off the tribute came, and the youths and maidens were, according to custom, drawn by lot to be sent, he offered himself as one of the victims, in spite of the entreaties of his father. The ship departed under black sails, as usual, which Theseus promised his father to change for white, in case of his returning victorious. When they arrived in Crete, the youths and maidens were exhibited before Minos; and Ariadne, the daughter of the king, being present, became deeply enamored of Theseus, by whom her love was readily returned. She furnished him with a sword, with which to encounter the Minotaur, and with a spool of thread by which he might find his way out of the labyrinth. He was successful, slew the Minotaur, escaped from the labyrinth, and taking Ariadne as the companion of his way, with his rescued companions sailed for Athens. On their way they stopped at the island of Naxos, where Theseus abandoned Ariadne, leaving her asleep. His excuse for this ungrateful treatment of his benefactress was that Minerva appeared to him in a dream and commanded him to do so.

On approaching the coast of Attica, Theseus forgot the signal appointed by his father, and neglected to raise the white sails, and the old king, thinking his son had perished, put an end to his own life. Theseus thus became king of Athens.

One of the most celebrated of the adventures of Theseus is his expedition against the Amazons. He assailed them before they had recovered from the attack of Hercules, and carried off their queen Antiope. The Amazons in their turn invaded the country of Athens and penetrated into the city itself; and the final battle in which Theseus overcame them was fought in the very midst of the city. This battle was one of the favorite subjects of the ancient sculptors, and is commemorated in several works of art that are still extant.

The friendship between Theseus and Pirithous was of a most intimate nature, yet it originated in the midst of arms. Pirithous had made an irruption into the plain of Marathon, and carried off the herds of the king of Athens. Theseus went to repel the plunderers. The moment Pirithous beheld him, he was seized with admiration; he stretched out his hand as a token of peace, and cried, "Be judge thyself—what satisfaction dost thou require?" "Thy friendship," replied the Athenian, and they swore inviolable fidelity. Their deeds corresponded to their professions, and they ever continued true brothers in arms. Each of them aspired to possess a daughter of Jupiter. Theseus fixed his choice on Helen, then but a child, afterward so celebrated as the cause of the Trojan war, and with the aid of his friend he carried her off. Pirithous aspired to the wife of the monarch of Erebus; and Theseus, though aware of the danger, accompanied the ambitious lover in his descent to the underworld. But Pluto seized and set them on an enchanted rock at his palace gate, where they remained till Hercules arrived and liberated Theseus, leaving Pirithous to his fate.

After the death of Antiope, Theseus married Phaedra, daughter of Minos, king of Crete. Phaedra saw in Hippolytus, the son of Theseus, a youth endowed with all the graces and virtues of his father, and of an age corresponding to her own. She loved him, but he repulsed her advances, and her love was changed to hate. She used her influence over her infatuated husband to cause him to be jealous of his son, and he imprecated the vengeance of Neptune upon him. As Hippolytus was one day driving his chariot along the shore, a seamonster raised himself above the waters, and frightened the horses so that they ran away and dashed the chariot to pieces. Hippolytus was killed, but by Diana's assistance Aesculapius restored him to life. Diana removed Hippolytus from the power of his deluded father and false stepmother, and placed him in Italy under the protection of the nymph Egeria.

Theseus at length lost the favor of his people, and retired to the court of Lycomedes, king of Scyros, who at first received him kindly, but afterward treacherously slew him. In a later age the Athenian general Cimon discovered the place where his remains were laid, and caused them to be removed to Athens, where they were deposited in a temple called the Theseum, erected in honor of the hero.

Henry the Fifth Rallies His Troops Before the Walls of Harfleur

From William Shakespeare, Henry V

Once more unto the breach, dear friends, once more;
Or close the wall up with our English dead!
In peace, there's nothing so becomes a man,
As modest stillness, and humility;
But when the blast of war blows in our ears,
Then imitate the action of the tiger;
Stiffen the sinews, summon up the blood,
Disguise fair nature with hard-favored rage:
Then lend the eye a terrible aspect;
Let it pry through the portage of the head,
Like the brass cannon; let the brow o'erwhelm it,
As fearfully, as doth a gallèd rock
O'erhang and jutty his confounded base,
Swilled with the wild and wasteful ocean.
Now set the teeth, and stretch the nostril wide;
Hold hard the breath, and bend up every spirit
To his full height! On, on, you noblest English,
Whose blood is fet from fathers of war-proof!
Fathers, that like so many Alexanders,
Have, in these parts, from morn till even fought,
And sheathed their swords for lack of argument,
Dishonor not your mothers; now attest,
That those, whom you called fathers, did beget you!

Be copy now to men of grosser blood,
And teach them how to war! And you, good yeomen,
Whose limbs were made in England, show us here
The mettle of your pasture; let us swear
That you are worth your breeding: which I doubt not;
For there is none of you so mean and base,
That hath not noble lustre in your eyes.
I see you stand like greyhounds in the slips,
Straining upon the start. The game's afoot;
Follow your spirit: and, upon this charge,
Cry—God for Harry! England! And Saint George!

The Frogs Ask for a King

Aesop

Don't push your luck with the king of the gods.

The Frogs, grieved at having no established Ruler, sent ambassadors to Jupiter entreating for a King. He, perceiving their simplicity, cast down a huge log into the lake. The Frogs, terrified at the splash occasioned by its fall, hid themselves in the depths of the pool. But no sooner did they see that the huge log continued motionless, than they swam again to the top of the water, dismissed their fears, and came so to despise it as to climb up, and to squat upon it. After some time they began to think themselves ill-treated in the appointment of so inert a Ruler, and sent a second deputation to Jupiter to pray that he would set over them another sovereign. He then gave them an Eel to govern them. When the Frogs discovered his easy good nature, they yet a third time sent to Jupiter to beg that he would once more choose for them another King. Jupiter, displeased at their complaints, sent a Heron, who preyed upon the Frogs day by day till there were none left to croak upon the Lake.

Napoleon, Man of the World

From Ralph Waldo Emerson, Representative Men

Emerson (1803–1882) was a celebrated essayist, poet, and speaker, and the main exponent of New England Transcendentalism.

In describing the two parties into which modern society divides itself—the democrat and the conservative—I said, Bonaparte represents the democrat, or the party of men of business, against the stationary or the conservative party. I omitted then to say, what is material to the statement, namely that these two parties differ only as young and old. The democrat is a young conservative; the conservative is an old democrat. The aristocrat is the democrat ripe and gone to seed; because both parties stand on the one ground of the supreme value of property, which one endeavors to get, and the other to keep. Bonaparte may be said to represent the whole history of this party, its youth and its age; yes, and with poetic justice its fate, in his own. The counter-revolution, the counter-party, still waits for its organ and representative, in a lover and a man of truly public and universal aims.

Here was an experiment, under the most favorable conditions, of the powers of intellect without conscience. Never was such a leader so endowed and so weaponed; never leader found such aids and followers. And what was the result of this vast talent and power, of these immense armies, burned cities, squandered treasures, immolated millions of men, of this demoralized Europe? It came to no result. All passed away like the smoke of his artillery, and left no trace. He left France smaller, poorer, feebler, than he found it; and the whole contest for freedom was to be begun again. The attempt was in principle suicidal. France served him with life and limb and estate, as long as it could identify its interest with him; but when men saw that after victory was another war; after the destruction of armies, new conscriptions; and they who had toiled so desperately were never nearer to the reward—they could not spend what they had earned, nor repose on their down-beds, nor strut in their chateaux—they deserted him. Men found that his absorbing egotism was deadly to all other men. It resembled the torpedo, which inflicts a succession of shocks on anyone who takes hold of it, producing spasms which contract the muscles of the hand, so that the man cannot open his fingers; and the animal inflicts new and more violent shocks, until he paralyzes and kills his victim. So this exorbitant egotist narrowed, impoverished and absorbed the power and existence of those who served him; and the universal cry of France and of Europe in 1814 was, "Enough of him;" "*Assez de Bonaparte.*"

It was not Bonaparte's fault. He did all that in him lay to live and thrive without moral principle. It was the nature of things, the eternal law of man and of the world which baulked and ruined him; and the result, in a million experiments, will be the same. Every experiment, by multitudes or by individuals, that has a sensual and selfish aim, will fail. The pacific Fourier will be as inefficient as the pernicious Napoleon. As long as our civilization is essentially one of property, of fences, of exclusiveness, it will be mocked by delusions. Our riches will leave us sick; there will be bitterness in our laughter, and our wine will burn our mouth. Only that good profits which we can taste with all doors open, and which serves all men.

Alfred the Great,
a Model King and Man

From John Richard Green, A Short History
of the English People

A portrait of the ideal ruler, balancing valor and humanity.

Alfred was the noblest as he was the most complete embodiment of all that is great, all that is lovable, in the English temper. He combined as no other man has ever combined its practical energy, its patient and enduring force, its profound sense of duty, the reserve and self-control that steady in it a wide outlook and a restless daring, its temperance and fairness, its frank geniality, its sensitiveness to action, its poetic tenderness, its deep and passionate religion. Religion, indeed, was the groundwork of Alfred's character. His temper was instinct with piety. Everywhere throughout his writings that remain to us the name of God, the thought of God, stir him to outbursts of ecstatic adoration.

But he was no mere saint. He felt none of that scorn of the world about him which drove the nobler souls of his day to monastery or hermitage. Vexed as he was by sickness and constant pain, his temper took no touch of asceticism. His rare geniality, a peculiar elasticity and mobility of nature, gave color and charm to his life. A sunny frankness and openness of spirit breathe in the pleasant chat of his books, and what he was in his books he showed himself in this daily converse. Alfred was in truth an artist, and both the lights and shadows of his life were those of the artistic temperament. His love of books, his love of strangers, his questionings of travelers and scholars, betray an imaginative restlessness that longs to break out of the narrow world of experience which hemmed him in. At one time he jots down news of a voyage to the unknown seas of the north. At another he listens to tidings which his envoys bring back from the churches of Malabar.

And side by side with this restless outlook of the artistic nature he showed its tenderness and susceptibility, its vivid apprehension of unseen danger, its craving for affection, its sensitiveness to wrong. It was with himself rather than with his reader that he communed as thoughts of the foe without, of ingratitude and opposition within, broke the calm pages of Gregory or Boethius.

"Oh, what a happy man was he," he cries once, "that man that had a naked sword hanging over his head from a single thread; so as to me it always did!" "Desirest thou power?" he asks at another time. "But thou shalt never obtain it without sorrows—sorrows from strange folk, and yet keener sorrows from thine own kindred." "Hardship and sorrow!" he breaks out again; "not a king but would wish to be without these if he could. But I know that he cannot!"

The loneliness which breathes in words like these has often begotten in great rulers a cynical contempt of men and the judgments of men. But cynicism found no echo in the large and sympathetic temper of Alfred. He not only longed for the love of his subjects, but for the remembrance of "generations" to come. Nor did his inner gloom or anxiety check for an instant his vivid and versatile activity. To the scholars he gathered round him he seemed the very type of a scholar, snatching every hour he could find to read or listen to books read to him. The singers of his court found in him a brother singer, gathering the old songs of his people to teach them to his children, breaking his renderings from the Latin with simple verse, solacing himself in hours of depression with the music of the Psalms.

He passed from court and study to plan buildings and instruct craftsmen in gold work, to teach even falconers and dogkeepers their business. But all this versatility and ingenuity was controlled by a cool good sense. Alfred was a thorough man of business. He was careful of detail, laborious, methodical. He carried in his bosom a little handbook in which he noted things as they struck him—now a bit of family genealogy, now a prayer, now such a story as that of Ealdhelm playing minstrel on the bridge. Each hour of the day had its appointed task; there was the same order in the division of his revenue and in the division of the court.

Wide, however, and various as was the King's temper, its range was less wonderful than its harmony. Of the narrowness, of the want of proportion, of the predominance of one quality over another which go commonly with an intensity of moral purpose Alfred showed not a trace. Scholar and soldier, artist and man of business, poet and saint, his character kept that perfect balance which charms us in no other Englishman save Shakespeare. But full and harmonious as his temper was, it was the temper of a king. Every power was bent to the work of rule. His practical energy found scope for itself in the material and administrative restoration of the wasted land.

His intellectual activity breathed fresh life into education and literature. His capacity for inspiring trust and affection drew the hearts of Englishmen to a common center, and began the upbuilding of a new England. And all was guided, controlled, ennobled by a single aim. "So long as I have lived," said the King as life closed about him, "I have striven to live worthily." Little by little men came to know what such a life of worthiness meant. Little by little they came to recognize in Alfred a ruler of higher and nobler stamp than the world had seen. Never had it seen a king who lived solely for the good of his people. Never had it seen a ruler who set aside every personal aim to devote himself solely to the welfare of those whom he ruled. It was this grand self-mastery that gave him his power over the men about him. Warrior and conqueror as he was, they saw him set aside at thirty the warrior's dream of conquest; and the self-renouncement of Wedmore struck the keynote of his reign. But still more is it this height and singleness of purpose, this absolute concentration of the noblest faculties to the noblest aim, that lifts Alfred out of the narrow bounds of Wessex.

If the sphere of his action seems too small to justify the comparison of him with the few whom the world owns as its greatest men, he rises to their level in the moral grandeur of his life. And it is this which has hallowed his memory among his own English people. "I desire," said the King in some of his latest words, "I desire to leave to the men that come after me a remembrance of me in good works."

His aim has been more than fulfilled. His memory has come down to us with a living distinctness through the mists of exaggeration and legend which time gathered round it. The instinct of the people has clung to him with a singular affection. The love which he won a thousand years ago has lingered round his name from that day to this. While every other name of those earlier times has all but faded from the recollection of Englishmen, that of Alfred remains familiar to every English child.

He took his books as he found them—they were the popular manuals of his age—the *Consolation of Boethius*, the *Pastoral* of Pope Gregory, the compilation of Orosius, then the one accessible handbook of universal history, and the history of his own people by Bede. He translated these works into English, but he was far more than a translator, he was an editor for the people. Here he omitted, there he expanded. He enriched Orosius by a sketch of the new geographical discoveries in the north. He gave a West Saxon form to his selections from Bede. In one place he stops to explain his theory of government, his wish for a thicker population, his conception of national welfare as consisting in a due balance of priest, soldier, and churl. The mention of Nero spurs him to an outbreak on the abuses of power. The cold providence of Boethius gives way to an enthusiastic acknowledgment of the goodness of God.

As he writes, his large-hearted nature flings off its royal mantle, and he talks as a man to men. "Do not blame me," he prays with a charming simplicity, "if any know Latin better than I, for every man must say what he says and do what he does according to his ability."

But simple as was his aim, Alfred changed the whole front of our literature. Before him, England possessed in her own tongue one great poem and a train of ballads and battle-songs. Prose she had none. The mighty roll of the prose books that fill her libraries begins with the translations of Alfred, and above all with the chronicle of his reign.

Tyrants Will Always
Be with Us

Aesop

A Wolf meeting with a Lamb astray from the fold, resolved not to lay violent hands on him, but to find some plea, which should justify to the Lamb himself his right to eat him. He thus addressed him: "Sirrah, last year you grossly insulted me." "Indeed," bleated the Lamb in a mournful tone of voice, "I was not then born." Then said the Wolf, "You feed in my pasture." "No, good sir," replied the Lamb, "I have not yet tasted grass." Again said the Wolf, "You drink of my well." "No," exclaimed the Lamb, "I never yet drank water, for as yet my mother's milk is both food and drink to me." On which the Wolf seized him, and ate him up, saying, "Well! I won't remain supperless, even though you refute every one of my imputations."

The tyrant will always find a pretext for his tyranny.

The Outstandingly
Virtuous Prince

From Niccolo Machiavelli, The Prince

In his classic meditation on princely power (1513), the Renaissance philosopher explores a disturbing question: Are there any moral limits on what a ruler must do to make his people secure and prosperous?

Many have imagined republics and principalities which have never been seen or known to exist in reality; for how we live is so far removed from how we ought to live, that he who abandons what is done for what ought to be done, will rather learn to bring about his own ruin than his preservation. A man who wishes to make a profession of goodness in everything must necessarily come to grief among so many who are not good. Therefore it is necessary for a prince, who wishes to maintain himself, to learn how not to be good, and to use his knowledge and not use it, according to the necessity of the case.

Let no one marvel if in speaking of new dominions both as to prince and state, I bring forward very exalted instances, for men walk almost always in the paths trodden by others, proceeding in their actions by imitation. Not being always able to follow others exactly, nor attain to the excellence of those he imitates, a prudent man should always follow in the path trodden by great men and imitate those who are most excellent, so that if he does not attain to their greatness, at any rate he will get some tinge of it. He will do as prudent archers, who when the place they wish to hit is too far off, knowing how far their bow will carry, aim at a spot much higher than the one they wish to hit, not in order to reach this height with their arrow, but by help of this high aim to hit the spot they wish to.

I say then that in new dominions, where there is a new prince, it is more or less easy to hold them according to the greater or lesser ability of him who acquires them. And as the fact of a private individual becoming a prince presupposes either great ability or good fortune, it would appear that either of these things would in part mitigate many difficulties. Nevertheless those who have been less beholden to good fortune have maintained themselves best. The matter is also facilitated by the prince being obliged to reside personally in his territory, having no others. But to come to those who have become princes through their own merits and not by fortune, I regard as the greatest, Moses, Cyrus, Romulus, Theseus, and their like. And although one should not speak of Moses, he having merely carried out what was ordered him by God, still he deserves admiration, if only for that grace which made him worthy to speak with God. But regarding Cyrus and others who have acquired or founded kingdoms, they will all be found worthy of admiration; and if their particular actions and methods are examined they will not appear very different from those of Moses, although he had so great a Master. And in examining their life and deeds it will be seen that they owed nothing to fortune but the opportunity which gave them matter to be shaped into what form they thought fit; and without that opportunity their powers would have been wasted, and without their powers the opportunity would have come in vain.

It was thus necessary that Moses should find the people of

Israel slaves in Egypt and oppressed by the Egyptians, so that they were disposed to follow him in order to escape from their servitude. It was necessary that Romulus should be unable to remain in Alba, and should have been exposed at his birth, in order that he might become King of Rome and founder of that nation. It was necessary that Cyrus should find the Persians discontented with the empire of the Medes, and the Medes weak and effeminate through long peace. Theseus could not have shown his abilities if he had not found the Athenians dispersed. These opportunities, therefore, gave these men their chance, and their own great qualities enabled them to profit by them, so as to ennoble their country and augment its fortunes.

Those who by the exercise of abilities such as these become princes, obtain their dominions with difficulty but retain them easily, and the difficulties which they have in acquiring their dominions arise in part from the new rules and regulations that they have to introduce in order to establish their position securely. It must be considered that there is nothing more difficult to carry out, nor more doubtful of success, nor more dangerous to handle, than to initiate a new order of things. For the reformer has enemies in all those who profit by the old order, and only lukewarm defenders in all those who would profit by the new order, this lukewarmness arising partly from fear of their adversaries, who have the laws in their favor; and partly from the incredulity of mankind, who do not truly believe in anything new until they have had actual experience of it. Thus it arises that on every opportunity for attacking the reformer, his opponents do so with the zeal of partisans, the others only defend him half-heartedly, so that between them he runs great danger. It is necessary, however, in order to investigate thoroughly this question, to examine whether these innovators are independent, or whether they depend upon others, that is to say, whether in order to carry out their designs they have to entreat or are able to compel. In the first case they invariably succeed ill, and accomplish nothing; but when they can depend on their own strength and are able to use force, they rarely fail. Thus it comes about that all armed prophets have conquered and unarmed ones failed; for besides what has been already said, the character of peoples varies, and it is easy to persuade them of a thing, but difficult to keep them in that persuasion. And so it is necessary to order things so that when they no longer believe, they can be made to believe by force. Moses, Cyrus, Theseus, and Romulus would not have been able to keep their constitutions observed for so long had they been disarmed, as happened in our own time with Fra Girolamo Savonarola, who failed entirely in his new rules when the multitude began to disbelieve in him, and he had no means of holding fast those who had believed nor of compelling the unbelievers to believe. Therefore such men as these have great difficulty in making their way, and all their dangers are met on the road and must be overcome by their own abilities; but when once they have overcome them and have begun to be held in veneration, and have suppressed those who envied them, they remain powerful and secure, honored and happy.

The Patriot King

From Henry St. John, Viscount Bolingbroke,
The Idea of a Patriot King

It matters whether a ruler is noble or base. But the best kings are not necessarily men! From the 1749 treatise on virtuous government.

Machiavel is an author who should have great authority with the persons likely to oppose me. He proposes to princes the amplification of their power, the extent of their dominion, and the subjection of their people, as the sole objects of their policy. He devises and recommends all means that tend to these purposes, without the consideration of any duty owing to God or man, or any regard to the morality or immorality of actions. Yet even he declares the affectation of virtue to be useful to princes: he is so far on my side in the present question. The only difference between us is, I would have the virtue real: he requires no more than the appearance of it.

Kings who have weak understandings, bad hearts, and strong prejudices, and all these, as it often happens, inflamed by their passions, and rendered incurable by their self-conceit and presumption; such kings are apt to imagine, that the king and the people in free governments are rival powers, who stand in competition with one another, who have different interests, and must of course have different views: that the rights and privileges of the people are so many spoils taken from the right and prerogative of the crown; and that the rules and laws, made for the exercise and security of the former, are so many diminutions of their dignity, and restrains on their power.

A Patriot King will see all this in a far different and much truer light. The constitution will be considered by him as one law, consisting of two tables, containing the rule of his government, and the measure of his subjects' obedience; or as one system, composed of different parts and powers, but all duly proportioned to one another, and conspiring by their harmony to the perfection of the whole. He will make one, and but one, distinction between his rights, and those of his people: he will look on his to be a trust, and theirs a property. He will discern, that he can have a right to no more than is trusted to him by the constitution: and that his people, who had an original right to the whole by the law of nature, can have the sole indefeasible right to any part; and really have such a right to that part which they have reserved to themselves. In fine, the constitution will be reverenced by him as the law of God and of man; the force of which binds the king as much as the meanest subject, and the reason of which binds him much more.

Wisdom is neither left-handed, nor crooked: but the heads of some men contain little, and the hearts of others employ it wrong. To use my lord Bacon's own comparison, the cunning man knows how to pack the cards, the wise man how to play the game better: but it would be of no use to the first to pack the cards, if his knowledge stopped here, and he had no skill in the game; nor to the second to play the game better, if he did not know how to pack the cards, that he might unpack them by new shuffling. Inferior wisdom or cunning may get the better of folly: but superior wisdom will get the better of cunning. Wisdom and cunning have often the same objects; but a wise man will have more and greater in his view. The least will not fill his soul, nor ever become the principal there; but will be pursued in subservience, in subordination at least, to the other. Wisdom and cunning may employ sometimes the same means too: but the wise man stoops to these means, and the other cannot rise above them.

The true image of a free people, governed by a Patriot King, is that of a patriarchal family, where the head and all the members are united by one common interest, and animated by common spirit: and where, if any are perverse enough to have another, they will be soon borne down by the superiority of those who have the same; and, far from making a division, they will but confirm the union of the little state. That to approach as near as possible to these ideas of perfect government, and social happiness under it, is desirable in every state, no man will be absurd enough to deny. The sole question is, therefore, how near to them it is possible to attain? For, if this attempt be not absolutely impracticable, all the views of a Patriot King will be directed to make it succeed. Instead of abetting the divisions of his people, he will endeavor to unite them, and to be himself the center of their union: instead of putting himself at the head of his people in order to govern, or more properly to subdue, all parties. Now, to arrive at this desirable union, and to maintain it, will be found more difficult in some cases than in others, but absolutely impossible in none, to a wise and good prince.

Our Elizabeth was queen in a limited monarchy, and reigned over a people at all times more easily led than driven; and at that time capable of being attached to their prince and their country, by a more generous principle than any of those which prevail in our days, by affection. There was a strong prerogative then in being, and the crown was in possession of greater legal power. Popularity was, however, then, as it is now, and as it must be always in mixed government, the sole true foundation of that sufficient authority and influence, which other constitutions give the prince gratis, and independently of the people, but which a king of this nation must acquire. The wise queen saw it, and she saw too, how much popularity depends on those appearances, that depend on the decorum, the decency, the grace, and the propriety of behavior of which we are speaking. A warm concern for the interest and honor of the nation, a tenderness for their people, and a confidence in their affections, were appearances that ran through her whole public conduct, and gave life and color to it. She did great things, and she knew how to set them off according to their full value, by her manner of doing them. In her private behavior she shewed great affability, she descended even to familiarity; but her familiarity was such as could not be imputed to her weakness, and was, therefore, most justly ascribed to her goodness. Though a woman, she hid all that was womanish about her: and if a few equivocal marks of coquetry appeared on some occasions, they passed like flashes of lightning, vanished as soon as they were discerned, and imprinted no blot on her character. She had private friendships, she had favorites: but she never suffered her friends to forget she was their queen; and when her favorites did, she made them feel that she was so.

Her successor had no virtues to set off, but he had failings and vices to conceal.

Let not princes flatter themselves. They will be examined closely, in private as well as in public life: and those, who cannot pierce further, will judge of them by the appearances they give in both. To obtain true popularity, that which is founded in esteem and affection, they must, therefore, maintain their characters in both; and to that end neglect appearances in neither, but observe the decorum necessary to preserve the esteem, whilst they win the affections, of mankind. Kings, they must never forget that they are men: men, they must never forget that they are kings. The sentiments, which one of these reflections of course inspires, will give a humane and affable air to their whole behavior, and make them taste in that high elevation all the joys of social life. The sentiments, that the other reflection suggests, will be found very compatible with the former: and they may never forget that they are kings, though they do not always carry the crown on their heads, nor the scepter in their hands. Vanity and folly must entrench themselves in a constant affectation of state, to preserve regal dignity: a wise prince will know how to preserve it when he lays his majesty aside. He will dare to appear a private man, and in that character he will draw to himself a respect less ostentatious, but more real and more pleasing to him, than any which is paid to the monarch. By never saying what is unfit for him to say, he will never hear what is unfit for him to hear. By never doing what is unfit for him to do, he will never see what is unfit for him to see. Decency and propriety of manners are so far from lessening the pleasures of life, that they refine them, and give them an higher taste: they are so far from restraining the free and easy commerce of social life, that they banish the bane of it, licentiousness of behavior. Ceremony is the barrier against this abuse of liberty in public; politeness and decency are so in private: and the prince, who practices and exacts them, will amuse himself much better and oblige those, who have the honor to be in his intimacy and to share his pleasures with him, much more, than he could possibly do by the most absolute and unguarded familiarity.

That which is here recommended to princes, that constant guard on their own behavior even in private life, and that constant decorum which their example ought to exact from others, will not be found so difficult in practice as may be imagined; if they use a proper discernment in the choice of the persons whom they admit to the nearest degrees of intimacy with them. A prince should choose his companions with as great care as his ministers. If he trusts the business of his state to these, he trusts his character to those: and his character will depend on theirs much more than is commonly thought. General experience will lead men to judge that a similitude of character determined the choice; even when chance, indulgence to assiduity, good-nature, or want of reflection, had their share in the introduction of men unworthy of such favor. But, in such cases, certain it is that they, who judged wrong at first concerning him, will judge right at last. He is not a trifler, for instance. Be it so: but if he takes trifling futile creatures, men of mean characters or of no character, into his intimacy, he shews a disposition to become such; and will become such, unless he breaks these habits early, and before puerile amusements are grown up to be the business of his life. I mean, that the minds of princes, like the minds of other men, will be brought down insensibly to the tone of the company they keep.

To Be a King

Queen Elizabeth I to the House of Commons,
November 30, 1601

Mr. Speaker, we perceive your coming is to present thanks unto us. Know I accept them with no less joy than your loves can have desire to offer such a present, and do more esteem it than any treasure, or riches; for those we know how to prize, but loyalty, love, and thanks, I account them invaluable, and though God hath raised me high, yet this I account the glory of my crown, that I have reigned with your loves. This makes that I do not so much rejoice that God hath made me to be a queen, as to be a queen over so thankful a people, and to be the means under God to conserve you in safety, and preserve you from danger, yea to be the instrument to deliver you from dishonor, from shame, and from infamy, to keep you from out of servitude, and from slavery under our enemies, and cruel tyranny and vile oppression intended against us; for the better withstanding whereof, we take very acceptable their intended helps, and chiefly in that it manifesteth your loves and largeness of hearts to your sovereign. Of myself I must say this, I never was any greedy scraping grasper, nor a strict fast-holding prince, nor yet a waster, my heart was never set upon any worldly goods, but only for my subjects' good. What you do bestow on me I will not hoard up, but receive it to bestow on you again; yea mine own properties

I account yours to be expended for your good, and your eyes shall see the bestowing of it for your welfare.

Mr. Speaker, I would wish you and the rest to stand up, for I fear I shall yet trouble you with longer speech.

Mr. Speaker, you give me thanks, but I am more to thank you, and I charge you thank them of the Lower House from me; for had I not received knowledge from you, I might a' fallen into the lapse of an error, only for want of true information.

Since I was Queen, yet did I never put my pen to any grant but upon pretext and semblance made me, that it was for the good and avail of my subjects generally, though a private profit to some of my ancient servants, who have deserved well; but that my grants shall be made grievances to my people, and oppressions, to be privileged under color of our patents, our princely dignity shall not suffer it.

When I heard it, I could give no rest unto my thoughts until I had reformed it, and those varlets, lewd persons, abusers of my bounty, shall know I will not suffer it. And, Mr. Speaker, tell the House from me, I take it exceeding grateful, that the knowledge of these things are come unto me from them. And though amongst them the principal members are such as are not touched in private, and therefore need not speak from any feeling of the grief, yet we have heard that other gentlemen also of the House, who stand as free, have spoken as freely in it; which gives us to know, that no respect or interests have moved them other than the minds they bear to suffer no diminution of our honor and our subjects love unto us. The zeal of which affection tending to ease my people, and knit their hearts unto us, I embrace with a princely care far above all earthly treasures. I esteem my people's love, more than which I desire not to merit: and God, that gave me here to sit, and placed me over you, knows, that I never respected myself, but as your good was conserved in me; yet what dangers, what practices, and what perils I have passed, some if not all of you know, but none of these things do move me, or ever made me fear, but it's God that hath delivered me.

And in my governing this land, I have ever set the last judgment day before mine eyes, and so to rule as I shall be judged and answer before a higher Judge, to whose judgment seat I do appeal: in that never thought was cherished in my heart that tended not to my people's good.

And if my princely bounty have been abused; and my grants turned the hurt of my people contrary to my will and meaning, or if any in authority under me have neglected, or converted what I have committed unto them, I hope God will not lay their culps to my charge.

To be a king, and wear a crown, is a thing more glorious to them that see it than it's pleasant to them that bear it: for myself, I never was so much enticed with the glorious name of a king, or the royal authority of a queen, as delighted that God hath made me his instrument to maintain his truth and glory, and to defend this kingdom from dishonor, damage, tyranny, and oppression. But should I ascribe any of these things to myself or my sexly weakness, I were not worthy to live, and of all most unworthy of the mercies I have received at God's hands, but to God only and wholly all is given and ascribed.

The cares and troubles of a crown I cannot more fitly resemble than to the drugs of a learned physician, perfumed with some aromatical savor, or to bitter pills gilded over, by which they are made more acceptable or less offensive, which indeed are bitter and unpleasant to take; and for my own part, were it not for conscience sake to discharge the duty that God hath lay'd upon me, and to maintain his glory, and keep you in safety, in mine own disposition I should be willing to resign the place I hold to any other, and glad to be freed of the glory with the labors, for it is not my desire to live nor to reign, longer than my life and reign shall be for your good. And though you have had and may have many mightier and wiser princes sitting in this seat, yet you never had nor shall have any that will love you better.

Thus, Mr. Speaker, I commend me to your loyal loves, and yours to my best care and your further councils, and I pray you, Mr. Controuler and Mr. Secretary, and you of my council, that before these gentlemen depart into their countries, you bring them all to kiss my hand.

Who Should Pilot
the Ship of State?

From Plato, The Republic

In the famous allegory for good government from The Republic, *Socrates tells Adeimantus why the state needs a "pilot."*

Conceive now such a person as this to be the pilot of a fleet or a single ship, one who surpasses all in the ship both in bulk and strength, but is somewhat deaf, and short-sighted as well, and whose skill in nautical affairs is much of the same kind; and also that the sailors are all quarreling among each other about the pilotage, each thinking he ought to be pilot, though he never learned the art, and cannot show who was his master, nor at what time he got his learning; that besides this, they all say that the art itself cannot be taught, and are ready to cut in pieces anyone who says that it can. Imagine further, that they are constantly crowding round the pilot himself, begging, and forming all schemes to induce him to commit the helm into their hands, and that some- times even, when they do not so well succeed in persuading him as others may, they either kill these others, or throw them overboard, and after having, by mandragora or wine or something else, ren- dered the noble pilot incapable, they manage the ship by aid of the crew, and sail on, thus drinking and feasting, as may be expected of such people; and besides this, if any one be clever at assisting them in getting the management into their own hands, and either by persuasion or force, setting aside the pilot, they praise such an one, calling him sailor and pilot, and versed in navigation, but despise as useless everyone not of this character—not in the least considering that the true pilot must necessarily study the year, the seasons, the heavens, and stars, and winds, and everything belonging to his art, if he would be a real commander of a ship; but at the same time as respects the art and practice of governing men, whether some be willing or not, they think it impossible for a man to attain it in con- nection with the art of navigation. Whilst affairs are thus situated as regards ships, do you not think that the true pilot will be called by the sailors on board of ships thus regulated, a mere stargazer, trifler, and of no use to them whatever? Undoubtedly, said Adeimantus. I think then, said I, that you do not want this comparison explained, in order to see that it represents how people feel in states toward true philosophers, but that you quite understand what I mean. Perfectly, said he. First of all then, as regards this—namely, a person's wondering the philosophers are not honored in states—you must acquaint him with our comparison, and try to persuade him, that it would be much more wonderful if they were honored. I will so, replied he. And further, that it is quite true, as you were just observing, that the best of those who study philosophy are useless to the bulk of mankind: but nevertheless, for all this, they intend to lay the blame not on the philosophers, but on such as make no use of them, for it is not natural that the pilot should beg of the sailors to allow him to govern them, nor that the wise should hold attendance at the gates of the rich: and whoever wittily said this was mistaken; for this indeed is the natural method, that whoever is sick, whether rich or poor, must necessarily go to the gates of the physician, and whoever wants to be governed must wait on a person able to govern; for it is not natural that a really worthy governor should beg of the governed to subject themselves to his government. You will not be far wrong, however, in comparing our present political governors to those sailors we now mentioned, and those whom they call insignificant and star-gazers to those who are truly pilots. Quite right, said he.

The Oath of the Knights
of the Round Table

From Thomas Bulfinch,
Bulfinch's Mythology

Then the king established all his knights, and to them that were not rich he gave lands, and charged them all never to do outrage nor murder, and always to flee treason; also, by no means to be cruel, but to give mercy unto him that asked mercy, upon pain of forfeiture of their worship and lordship; and always to do ladies, damosels, and gentlewomen service, upon pain of death. Also that no man take battle in a wrongful quarrel, for no law, nor for any world's goods. Unto this were all the knights sworn of the Table Round, both old and young. And at every year were they sworn at the high feast of Pentecost.

The King of Sherwood Forest

From Rosemary Sutcliffe,
The Chronicles of Robin Hood

Robin Hood makes his men take their own Oath of Honor.

"Lead you?" cried Robin. "Then listen to me, lads, for if I am to lead you I will not have you become like the robbers who make honest men's lives a terror. Firstly, you shall harm no woman, nor any man in woman's company, for the sake of Mary the Mother of Our Lord. Secondly, you shall not rob or molest any poor man or honest yeoman who works for his bread as you and I have worked; nor any poor knight errant; nor any child. But against the rich merchants and the barons and potbellied churchmen who trample the weak beneath their feet and scoop the poor possessions of humble folk into their greedy pouches, you may do what you will. Thus, and thus only, will I be your leader. Men of the Greenwood, do you accept my terms?" His voice had grown louder as he spoke, and his last words rang through the midnight forest like a challenge to oppression and injustice.

The men answered him gladly, fiercely: "We accept your terms, and we will have you for our leader, Robin of Barnesdale." They scrambled to their feet and came to him one by one; and there, kneeling beside the fire, each man set his hands between Robin's in token of fealty and swore to be true to him and to each other, to the death if need be.

Afterward they lay down around the fire and, being worn out with the day's events, for the most part were soon asleep. But for a long time Robin lay wakeful on his back, staring up at the stars which sparkled here and there through the branches, and listening to the stealthy night-sounds of the forest.

The Midas Touch

From Thomas Bulfinch, Bulfinch's Mythology

What can happen when a king's wishes are too greedy.

Bacchus, on a certain occasion, found his old schoolmaster and foster-father, Silenus, missing. The old man had been drinking, and in that state wandered away, and was found by some peasants, who carried him to their king, Midas. Midas recognized him, and treated him hospitably, entertaining him for ten days and nights with an unceasing round of jollity. On the eleventh day he brought Silenus back, and restored him in safety to his pupil. Whereupon Bacchus offered Midas his choice of a reward, whatever he might wish. He asked that whatever he might touch should be turned into *gold.* Bacchus consented, though sorry that he had not made a better choice. Midas went his way, rejoicing in his new-acquired power, which he hastened to put to the test. He could scarce believe his eyes when he found a twig of an oak, which he plucked from the branch, become gold in his hand. He took up a stone; it changed to gold. He touched a sod; it did the same. He took an apple from the tree; you would have thought he had robbed the garden of the Hesperides. His joy knew no bounds, and as soon as he got home, he ordered the servants to set a splendid repast on the table. Then he found to his dismay that whether he touched bread, it hardened in his hand; or put a morsel to his lip, it defied his teeth. He took a glass of wine, but it flowed down his throat like melted gold.

In consternation at the unprecedented affliction, he strove to divest himself of his power; he hated the gift he had lately coveted, but all in vain; starvation seemed to await him. He raised his arms all shining with gold, in prayer to Bacchus, begging to be delivered from his glittering destruction. Bacchus, merciful deity, heard and consented. "Go," said he, "to the River Pactolus, trace the stream to its fountain-head, there plunge your head and body in, and wash away your fault and its punishment." He did so, and scarce had he touched the waters before the gold-creating power passed into them, and the river sands became changed into gold, as they remain to this day.

Thenceforth Midas, hating wealth and splendor, dwelt in the country, and became a worshipper of Pan, the god of the fields. On a certain occasion Pan had the temerity to compare his music with that of Apollo, and to challenge the god of the lyre to a trial of skill. The challenge was accepted, and Tmolus, the mountain god, was chosen umpire. The senior took his seat, and cleared away the trees from his ears to listen. At a given signal Pan blew on his pipes, and with his rustic melody gave great satisfaction to himself and his faithful follower Midas, who happened to be present. Then Tmolus turned his head toward the Sun-god, and all his trees turned with him. Apollo rose, his brow wreathed with Parnassian laurel, while his robe of Tyrian purple swept the ground. In his left hand he held the lyre, and with his right hand struck the strings. Ravished with the harmony, Tmolus at once awarded the victory to the god of the lyre, and all but Midas acquiesced in the judgment. He dissented, and questioned the justice of the award. Apollo would not suffer such a depraved pair of ears any longer to wear the human form, but caused them to increase in length, grow hairy, within and without, and movable on their roots; in short, to be on the perfect pattern of those of an ass.

Mortified enough was King Midas at this mishap; but he consoled himself with the thought that it was possible to hide his misfortune, which he attempted to do by means of an ample turban or head-dress. But his hair-dresser of course knew the secret. He was charged not to mention it, and threatened with dire punishment if he presumed to disobey. But he found it too much for his discretion to keep such a secret; so he went out into the meadow, dug a hole in the ground, and stooping down, whispered the story, and covered it up. Before long a thick bed of reeds sprang up in the meadow, and as soon as it had gained its grown, began whispering the story, and has continued to do so, from that day to this, every time a breeze passes over the place.

The Career of Charlemagne

From Francois P. G. Guizot,
History of France from the Earliest Times
to the Year 1848

*"An able warrior, an energetic legislator, a hero of poetry." From Guizot's
celebrated history of France published in 1869.*

The original and dominant characteristic of the hero of this reign, that which won for him and keeps for him after more than ten centuries, the name of great, is the striking variety of his ambition, his faculties, and his deeds. Charlemagne aspired to and attained to every sort of greatness—military greatness, political greatness, and intellectual greatness; he was an able warrior, an energetic legislator, a hero of poetry. And he united, he displayed all these merits in a time of general and monotonous barbarism when, save in the church, the minds of men were dull and barred. Those men, few in number, who made themselves a name at that epoch, rallied round Charlemagne and were developed under his patronage. To know him well and appreciate him justly, he must be examined under those various grand aspects, abroad and at home, in his wars and in his government.

We have here, it will be seen, no ordinary legislator and no ordinary laws: we see the work, with infinite variations and in disconnected form, of a prodigiously energetic and watchful master, who had to think and provide for everything, who had to be everywhere the moving and the regulating spirit. This universal and untiring energy is the grand characteristic of Charlemagne's government, and was, perhaps, what made his superiority most incontestable and his power most efficient.

The energy of Charlemagne as a warrior and a politician having thus been exhibited, it remains to say a few words about his intellectual energy. For that is by no means the least original or least grand feature of his character and his influence.

Modern times and civilized society have more than once seen despotic sovereigns filled with distrust toward scholars of exalted intellect, especially such as cultivated the moral and political sciences, and little inclined to admit them to their favor or to public office. There is no knowing whether, in our days, with our freedom of thought and of the press, Charlemagne would have been a stranger to this feeling of antipathy; but what is certain is that in his day, in the midst of a barbaric society, there was no inducement to it, and that, by nature, he was not disposed to it. His power was not in any respect questioned; distinguished intellects were very rare; Charlemagne had too much need of their services to fear their criticisms, and they, on their part, were more anxious to second his efforts than to show, toward him, anything like exaction or independence. He gave rein, therefore, without any embarrassment or misgiving, to his spontaneous inclination toward them, their studies, their labors, and their influence. He drew them into the management of affairs.

It was without effort and by natural sympathy that Charlemagne had inspired them with such sentiments; for he, too, really loved sciences, literature, and such studies as were then possible, and he cultivated them on his own account and for his own pleasure, as a sort of conquest. It has been doubted whether he could write, and an expression of Eginhard's might authorize such a doubt; but, according to other evidence, and even according to the passage in Eginhard, one is inclined to believe merely that Charlemagne strove painfully, and without much success, to write a good hand. He had learned Latin, and he understood Greek. He caused to be commenced, and, perhaps, himself commenced the drawing up of the first Germanic grammar. He ordered that the old barbaric poems, in which the deeds and wars of the ancient kings were celebrated, should be collected for posterity. He gave Germanic names to the twelve months of the year. He distinguished the winds by twelve special terms, whereas before his time they had but four designations. He paid great attention to astronomy. Being troubled one day at no longer seeing in the firmament one of the known planets, he wrote to Alcuin: "What thinkest thou of this *Mars*, which, last year, was intercepted from the sight of men by the light of the sun? Is it the regular course of his revolution? Is it the influence of the sun? Is it a miracle? Could he have been two years about performing the course of a single one?"

And at the same time that he thus took part in the great ecclesiastical questions, Charlemagne paid zealous attention to the instruction of the clergy whose ignorance he deplored. "Ah," said he one day, "if only I had about me a dozen clerics learned in all the sciences, as Jerome and Augustin were!" With all his puissance it was not in his power to make Jeromes and Augustins; but he laid the foundation, in the cathedral churches and the great monasteries, of episcopal and cloistral schools for the education of ecclesiastics, and, carrying his solicitude still further, he recommended to the bishops and abbots that, in those schools, "they should take care to make no difference between the sons of serfs and of free men, so that they might come and sit on the same benches to study grammar, music, and arithmetic." Thus, in the eighth century, he foreshadowed the extension which, in the nineteenth, was to be accorded to primary instruction, to the advantage and honor not only of the clergy, but also of the whole people.

After so much of war and toil at a distance, Charlemagne was now at Aix-la-Chapelle, finding rest in this work of peaceful civilization. He was embellishing the capital which he had founded, and which was called the king's court. He had built there a grand basilica, magnificently adorned. He was completing his own palace there. He fetched from Italy clerics skilled in church music, a pious joyance to which he was much devoted, and which he recommended to the bishops of his empire. In the outskirts of Aix-la-Chapelle "he gave full scope," says Eginhard, "to his delight in riding and hunting. Baths of naturally tepid water gave him great pleasure. Being passionately fond of swimming, he became so dexterous that none could be compared with him. He invited not only his sons, but also his friends, the grandees of the court, and sometimes even the soldiers of his guard, to bathe with him, insomuch that there were often a hundred and more persons bathing at a time."

If we sum up his designs and his achievements, we find an admirable sound idea and a vain dream, a great success and a great failure.

Charlemagne took in hand the work of placing upon a solid foundation the Frankish Christian dominion by stopping, in the north and South, the flood of barbarians and Arabs, paganism and Islamism. In that he succeeded; the inundations of Asiatic populations spent their force in vain against the Gallic frontier. Western and Christian Europe was placed, territorially, beyond reach from attacks from the foreigner and infidel. No sovereign, no human being, perhaps, ever rendered greater service to the civilization of the world.

Charlemagne formed another conception and made another attempt. Like more than one great barbaric warrior, he admired the Roman Empire that had fallen, its vastness all in one, and its powerful organization under the hand of a single master. He thought he could resuscitate it, durably, through the victory of a new people and a new faith, by the hand of Franks and Christians. With this view he labored to conquer, convert, and govern. And for a moment he appeared to have succeeded; but the appearance passed away with himself. The unity of the empire and the absolute power of the emperor were buried in his grave. The Christian religion and human liberty set to work to prepare for Europe other governments and other destinies.

We Few, We Happy Few, We Band of Brothers

From William Shakespeare, Henry V

Westmoreland:
O that we now had here
But one ten thousand of those men in England
That do no work to-day!
King:
What's he that wishes so?
My cousin Westmoreland? No, my fair cousin.
If we are marked to die, we are enow
To do our country loss; and if to live,
The fewer men, the greater share of honor.
God's will! I pray thee wish not one man more.
By Jove, I am not covetous for gold.
Nor care I who doth feed upon my cost;
It yearns me not if men my garments wear;
Such outward things dwell not in my desires:
But if it be a sin to covet honor,
I am the most offending soul alive.
No, faith, my coz, wish not a man from England.
God's peace! I would not lose so great an honor
As one man more methinks would share from me
For the best hope I have. O, do not wish one more!
Rather proclaim it, Westmoreland, through my host,
That he which hath no stomach to this fight,

Let him depart; his passport shall be made,
And crowns for convoy put into his purse.
We would not die in that man's company
That fears his fellowship to die with us.
This day is called the Feast of Crispian.
He that outlives this day, and comes safe home,
Will stand a-tiptoe when this day is named
And rouse him at the name of Crispian.
He that shall see this day, and live old age,
Will yearly on the vigil feast his neighbors
[And say, "These wounds I had on Crispin's day."]
Old men forget; yet all shall be forgot,
But he'll remember, with advantages,
What feats he did that day. Then shall our names,
Familiar in his mouth as household words—
Harry the King, Bedford and Exeter,
Warwick and Talbot, Salisbury and Gloucester—
Be in their flowing cups freshly rememb'red.
This story shall the good man teach his son;
And Crispin Crispian shall ne'er go by,
From this day to the ending of the world,
But we in it shall be remembered—
We few, we happy few, we band of brothers;
For he to-day that sheds his blood with me
Shall be my brother. Be he ne'er so vile,
This day shall gentle his condition;
And gentlemen in England now abed
Shall think themselves accursed they were not here,
And hold their manhoods cheap whiles any speaks
That fought with us upon Saint Crispin's day.

MANLY LEADERS
AND CITIZENS

The Man of Character

From Charles de Gaulle,
The Edge of the Sword

By common agreement one of the greatest statesmen of the twentieth century, Charles de Gaulle organized French resistance to the Nazi occupation of World War II from abroad, eventually returning in triumph to his liberated country and serving as its president. The Edge of the Sword *offers reflections on statesmanship remarkable for their subtlety, eloquence, and realism.*

When faced with the challenge of events, the man of character has recourse to himself. His instinctive response is to leave his mark on action, to take responsibility for it, to make it *his own business.* Far from seeking shelter behind his professional superiors, taking refuge in textbooks, or making the regulations bear the responsibility for any decision he may make, he sets his shoulders, takes a firm stand, and looks the problem straight in the face. It is not that he wishes to turn a blind eye to orders, or to sweep aside advice, but only that he is passionately anxious to exert his own will, to make up his own mind. It is not that he is unaware of the risks involved, or careless of consequences, but that he takes their measure honestly, and frankly accepts them. Better still, he embraces action with the pride of a master; for if he takes a hand in it, it will become his, and he is ready to enjoy success on condition that it is really *his own,* and that he derives no profit from it. He is equally prepared to bear the weight of failure, though not without a bitter sense of dissatisfaction. In short, a fighter who finds within himself all the zest and support he needs, a gambler more intent on success than profits, a man who pays his debts with his own money lends nobility to action. Without him there is but the dreary task of the slave; thanks to him, it becomes the divine sport of the hero.

This does not mean that he carries out his purpose unaided. Others share in it who are not without the merit of self-sacrifice and obedience, and give of their best when carrying out his orders. Some there are who even contribute to his planning—technicians or advisers. But it is character that supplies the essential element, the creative touch, the divine spark; in other words, the basic fact of initiative. Just as talent gives to a work of art a special stamp of understanding and expression, character imparts its own dynamic quality to the elements of action, and gives it personality which, when all is said, makes it live and move, just as the talent of the artist breathes life into matter.

The power to vivify an undertaking implies an energy sufficient to shoulder the burden of its consequences. The man of character finds an especial attractiveness in difficulty, since it is only by coming to grips with difficulty that he can realize his potentialities. Whether or not he proves himself the stronger is a matter between it and him. He is a jealous lover and will share with no one the prizes or the pains that may be his as a result of trying to overcome obstacles. Whatever the cost to himself, he looks for no higher reward than the harsh pleasure of knowing himself to be the man responsible.

This passion for self-reliance is obviously accompanied by some roughness in method. The man of character incorporates in his own person the severity inherent in his effort. This is felt by his subordinates, and at times they groan under it. In any event, a leader of this quality is inevitably aloof, for there can be no authority without prestige, nor prestige unless he keeps his distance. Those under his command mutter in whispers about his arrogance and the demands he makes. But once action starts, criticism disappears. The man of character then draws to himself the hopes and the wills of everyone as the magnet draws iron. When the crisis comes, it is him they follow, it is he who carries the burden on his own shoulders, even though they collapse under it. On the other hand, the knowledge that the lesser men have confidence in him exalts the man of character. The confidence of those under him gives him a sense of obligation. It strengthens his determination but also increases his benevolence, for he is a born protector. If success attends upon his efforts he distributes its advantages with a generous hand. If he meets with failure, he will not let the blame fall on anybody but himself. The security he offers is repaid by the esteem of his men.

In his relationship with his superiors he is generally at a disadvantage. He is too sure of himself, too conscious of his strength to let his conduct be influenced by a mere wish to please. The fact that he finds his powers of decision within himself, and not imposed upon him by an order, often disinclines him to adopt an attitude of passive obedience. All he asks is that he shall be given a task to do, and then be left alone to do it. He wants to be the captain of his own ship, and this many senior officers find intolerable since, temperamentally incapable of taking a wide view, they concentrate on details and draw their mental sustenance from formalities. And so it comes about that the authorities dread any officer who has the gift of making decisions and cares nothing for routine and soothing words. "Arrogant and undisciplined" is what the mediocrities say of him, treating the thoroughbred with a tender mouth as they would a donkey which refuses to move, not realizing that asperity is, more often than not, the reverse side of a strong character, that you can only lean on something that offers resistance, and that resolute and inconvenient men are to be preferred to easy-going natures without initiative.

But when the position becomes serious, when the nation is in urgent need of leaders with initiative who can be relied upon, and are willing to take risks, then matters are seen in a very different light, and credit goes to whom credit is due. A sort of a ground swell brings the man of character to the surface. His advice is listened to, his abilities are praised, and his true worth becomes apparent. To him is entrusted, as a matter of course, the difficult task, the direction of the main effort, the decisive mission. Everything he suggests is given serious consideration; all his demands are met. He, for his part, does not take advantage of this change in his fortunes, but shows a generous temperament and responds wholeheartedly when he is called upon. Scarcely, even, does he taste the sweet savor of revenge, for his every faculty is brought to bear upon the action he must take.

This rallying to character when danger threatens is the outward manifestation of an instinctive urge, for all men at heart realize the supreme value of self-reliance, and know that without it there can be no action of value. In the last resort, we must, to quote Cicero, "judge all conduct in the light of the best examples available," for nothing great has ever been achieved without that passion and that confidence which is to be found only in the man of character. Alexander would never have conquered Asia, Galileo would never have demonstrated the movement of the earth, Columbus would never have discovered America, nor Richelieu have restored the authority of the crown, had they not believed in themselves and taken full control of the task in hand. Boileau would never have established the laws of classic taste, Napoleon would never have founded an empire, Lesseps would never have pierced the isthmus of Suez, Bismarck would never have achieved German unity, nor Clemenceau have saved his country, had they hearkened to the counsels of short-sighted prudence or the promptings of fainthearted modesty. We can go further and say that those who have done great deeds have often had to take the risk of ignoring the merely routine aspects of discipline. Examples are plentiful: Pelissier at Sebastopol stuffing the Emperor's threatening dispatches into his pocket unopened and reading them only after the action was over; Lanrezac saving his army after Charleroi by breaking off the battle, contrary to orders; Lyautey keeping the whole of Morocco in 1914, in the teeth of instructions issued at a higher level. After the Battle of Jutland and the English failure to take the opportunity offered them of destroying the German fleet, Admiral Fisher, then First Sea Lord, exclaimed in a fury after reading Jellicoe's dispatch: "He has all Nelson's qualities but one: he doesn't know how to disobey!"

It goes without saying that the successes achieved by great men have always depended on their possessing many different faculties. Character alone, if unsupported by other qualities, results only in rashness and obstinacy. On the other hand, purely intellectual gifts, even of the highest order, are not sufficient. History is filled with examples of men who, though they were gifted beyond the ordinary, saw their labors brought to nothing because they were lacking in character. Whether serving, or betraying, their masters in the most expert fashion, they were entirely uncreative. Notable they may have been, but famous never.

Letter to Benjamin Franklin, August 1781

From Edmund Burke,
Selected Letters of Edmund Burke

Sometimes statesmen must reach out to each other across national boundaries. The Irish-born Member of Parliament and author Edmund Burke (1729–1797) was one of the founders of modern conservatism.

Dear Sir,

I feel as an honest man and as a good citizen ought to feel, the calamities of the present unhappy war. The only part, however, of those calamities which personally affects myself is, that I have been obliged to discontinue my intercourse with you; but that one misfortune I must consider as equivalent to many. I may, indeed, with great truth, assure you, that your friendship has always been an object of my ambition; and that, if a high and very sincere esteem for your talents and virtues could give me a title to it, I am not wholly unworthy of that honor. I flatter myself that your belief in the reality of these sentiments will excuse the liberty I take of laying before you a matter in which I have no small concern. That application I make originates wholly from myself, and has not been suggested to me by any person whatsoever.

I have lately been informed with great certainty, and with no less surprise, that the congress have made an application for the return of my friend General Burgoyne to captivity in America, at a time when the exchange of almost all the rest of the convention officers has been completed. It is true that this requisition has been for the present withdrawn; but then, it may be renewed at every instant; and no arrangement has been made or proposed, which may prevent a thing on all accounts so very disagreeable, as to see the most opposite interests conspiring in the persecution of a man, formed, by the unparalleled candor and moderation of his mind, to unite the most discordant parties in his favor.

I own this proceeding of the congress fills me with astonishment. I am persuaded that some unusually artful management, or very unexampled delusion, has operated to produce an effect which cannot be accounted for on any of the ordinary principles of nature or of policy.

I shall not enter into the particulars of the convention under which this claim is made, nor into the construction of it, nor the execution. I am not, perhaps, capable of doing justice to the merits of the cause; and if I were, I am not disposed to put them upon any ground of argument, because (whatever others might and possibly ought to do) I am not pleading a point of strict right, but appealing to your known principles of honor and generosity, with the freedom and privileges of an old friendship; and as I suppose you perfectly acquainted with the whole history of the extraordinary treatment General Burgoyne has met with, I am resolved not to show so much distrust in so sound a memory and so good a judgment as yours, as to attempt to refresh the one or to lead the other.

I am ready to admit that General Burgoyne has been and (as far as what is left him will suffer) is a very affectionate and a very jealous servant of the crown; and that in America he acted as an officer of the king (so long as fortune favored him) with great abilities, and distinguished fidelity, activity, and spirit. You, my dear sir, who have made such astonishing exertions in the cause which you espouse, and are so deeply read in human nature and in human morals, know better than anybody, that men will and that sometimes they are bound to take very different views and measures of their duty from local and from professional situation; and that we may all have equal merit in extremely different lines of conduct. You know that others may deserve the whole of your admiration in a cause, in which your judgment leads you to oppose them. But whatever may be our opinions on the origin of this fatal war, I assure you, General Burgoyne has the merit of never having driven it with violence, or fostered or kept it alive by any evil arts, or aggravated its natural mischiefs by unnecessary rigor; but has behaved on all occasions with that temper which becomes a great military character, which loves nothing so well in the profession, as the means it so frequently furnishes of splendid acts of generosity and humanity.

You have heard of the sacrifices he has made to his nice sense of honor on this side of the water—sacrifices far beyond the just demands of the principle to which they were made. This has been no advantage to the country where he was piqued to it. Shall America, too, call for sacrifices that are still more severe, and of full as little advantage to those who demand them? I know the rigor of political necessity; but I see here as little of necessity, or even expedience, as of propriety. I know the respect that is due to all public bodies; but none of them are exempt from mistake; and the most disrespectful thing that can be done toward them is to suppose them incapable of correcting an error.

If I were not fully persuaded of your liberal and manly way of thinking, I should not presume, in the hostile situation in which I stand, to make an application to you. But in this piece of experimental philosophy I run no risk of offending you. I apply not to the ambassador of America, but to Dr. Franklin, the philosopher, the friend and the lover of his species. In that light, whatever color politics may take, I shall ever have the honor to be, dear sir, etc., etc.,

Edm. Burke.

The Model Citizen

From Plutarch, Lives of the Noble Greeks
and Romans

In many ways, Marcus Brutus is Plutarch's ideal combination of active and contemplative virtues. Student of philosophy, defender of the Roman republic against ambitious usurpers like Julius Caesar, he was blessed with an extraordinary wife with whom he shared his secrets and labors. Even his enemies on the Caesarean side, such as Mark Antony, admired his nobility of character and the sincerity of his convictions. Plutarch (46–127 A.D.) wrote numerous biographies of Greek and Roman heroes and statesmen.

Marcus Brutus was descended from Junius Brutus, whose brass statue was erected by the ancient Romans in the capitol among the images of their kings. His statue has a drawn sword in its hand, in remembrance of his courage and resolution in expelling the Tarquins and destroying the monarchy. But this ancestor of Brutus had a severe and inflexible nature, like steel of too hard a temper, for his character had never been softened by study and thought. As a result, he let himself be so carried away by his rage and hatred against the tyrants that he executed even his own sons for conspiring with them. But the Brutus whose life is our present subject combined a good character with the improvements of learning and the study of philosophy. Despite a naturally grave and gentle disposition, he applied himself to business and public affairs, forging in himself a temperament that seems to have been perfectly suited for virtue. So much so, that even those who were his greatest enemies, because of his conspiracy against Caesar, said that if there had been any honorable or generous part in that whole affair, they attributed it entirely to Brutus, and attributed whatever was barbarous and cruel to Cassius, who was Brutus's relative and close friend, but not his equal in honesty and pureness of purpose.

Cato the philosopher was the brother of Brutus' mother, Servilia. Of all the Romans, this was the man his nephew most admired. Brutus strove to imitate his example, and later married his daughter, Porcia. Of all the Greek philosophers, and Brutus had heard and studied them all, the ones he admired most were the Platonists.

When Rome split into two factions, with Pompey and Caesar taking up arms against one another, and the whole empire was thrown into confusion, it was commonly thought that Brutus would take Caesar's side, since Brutus' father had been put to death by Pompey. But Brutus thought it was his duty to prefer the public interest to his own private feelings, and judging that Pompey had the better cause, sided with him. He did this even though, previously, he had refused to so much as greet or take any notice of Pompey, if he happened to meet him, for he thought it would be disgraceful to have the least conversation with his father's murderer. But now, looking upon Pompey as the general of his country, he placed himself under his command, and set sail for Cilicia as lieutenant to Sestius, who was the governor of that province.

It is reported that Caesar, when he first heard Brutus speak in public, said to his friends, "I do not know what this young man wants, but whatever he wants, he wants it vehemently." His natural strength of mind was so great that he was not easily persuaded, or moved to favor everyone who entreated his kindness, but once set into action upon motives of right reason and deliberate moral choice, whatever direction he took, he was pretty certain to stay the course, and work in such a way as to achieve his end. No flattery could ever prevail upon him to listen to unjust petitions. Although some people compliment such behaviour for its modesty and bash-fulness, Brutus thought that allowing himself to be overcome by shameless and fawning entreaties, was the worst disgrace that could befall a great man. Brutus used to say that he always felt that those who could not deny such entreaties could not have behaved well in the flush of their own youth.

Well aware of the dangers they would encounter, Brutus felt that the safety of those Romans who were most honored for their virtue, birth, or courage depended upon him. Therefore, he strove, as much as possible, when in public, to hide his uneasiness, and con-trol his thoughts; but at home, and especially at night, he was not the same man. Sometimes, against his will, his worries would make him start out of his sleep. At other times he was so absorbed in reflection and consideration of his difficulties, that his wife who lay with him, could not help but notice that he was unusually troubled, and agitated by some dangerous and perplexing matter

Porcia, as I said above, was the daughter of Cato. She was very young when she married her cousin Brutus, after the death of her first husband, by whom she had a son, named Bibulus. There still exists a little book, called Memoirs of Brutus, that was written by him. Porcia, who was addicted to philosophy, loved her husband greatly, and was full of understanding and courage. She resolved, therefore, not to inquire into Brutus's secrets before she had made this trial of herself. She turned all her attendants out of her cham-ber, and taking a little knife, of the sort they use to cut nails with, she gave herself a deep gash in the thigh. She lost a great deal of blood. This was followed by violent pains and a shivering fever, caused by the wound. At the height of her suffering, when Brutus was extremely anxious and afflicted for her, she said to him: "I, Bru-tus, being the daughter of Cato, was not given to you in marriage to share only in your bed and board, like a concubine, but to share as well in all your good and all your evil fortunes. For your part, as regards your care of me, I find no reason to complain. But what evi-dence of my love, what satisfaction can you receive from me, if I may not share with you your hidden griefs, nor be admitted to your counsels when they require secrecy and trust? I know very well that women seem to have too weak a nature to be trusted with secrets; but surely, Brutus, a virtuous birth and education, and the compa-ny of good and honorable men, help form our characters; and I can boast that I am the daughter of Cato and the wife of Brutus. I put even more confidence in this now that I have tried myself, and find that I can withstand pain." Then she showed him her wound, and told him the trial she had made of her constancy. He was astonished, and lifting up his hands to heaven begged the gods to help him be worthy of such a wife. Then he comforted his wife.

On the day Brutus planned to kill Caesar, someone came in haste from Brutus's house and told him that his wife was dying. For Porcia was extremely agitated and unable to bear her terrible anxiety. She could scarcely keep herself within doors, and at every little noise or voice she heard, she started up suddenly, like one possessed with a bacchic frenzy. She asked everyone who came in from the forum what Brutus was doing, and sent one messenger after another to inquire after him. At last, after long expectation and waiting, she could hold out no longer. Her mind was overcome with doubts and fears, until she lost the control of herself, and began to faint away. She had not time to take refuge in her chamber, but, sitting as she was amongst her women, a sudden swoon and a great stupor seized her, her color changed, and she lost the power to speak. Her women made a loud cry, and many of the neighbors ran to Brutus's door to know what was the matter. The report was soon spread abroad that Porcia was dead; though with her women's help she recovered soon and came to herself again. When Brutus received this news, he was extremely troubled, not without reason, yet was not so carried away by his private grief as to shirk his public purpose.

Cassius was a man governed by anger and passion, whose self-interest often carried him beyond the bounds of justice. He endured all the hardships of war and travel and danger most courageously in order to gain dominion for himself, and not liberty for the people. As for former disturbers of the peace of Rome, like Cinna, or Marius, or Carbo, it is clear that they treated their country as a stake for whoever could win it. They almost admitted openly that they fought for empire. But we are told that even the enemies of Brutus did not accuse him of this. No! many heard Antony himself say that Brutus was the only man who conspired against Caesar out of a sense of the glory and apparent justice of the action, but that all the rest rose up against him from private envy and malice. Moreover, it is plain from his own writings, that Brutus relied not so much upon his forces, as upon his own virtue. For he wrote in a letter to Atticus, shortly before he was to engage the enemy, that his affairs were in the best state of fortune that he could wish; that either he should prevail, and restore liberty to the people of Rome, or die which would put himself out of the reach of slavery. He wrote that while other things were certain and beyond the reach of chance, one thing was still in doubt, whether they should live or die free men. He adds further, that Mark Antony had received a just punishment for his folly, for, when he had the opportunity to have been numbered with Brutus and Cassius and Cato, he chose instead to join the likes of Octavius. He predicts that, though they would not both be defeated, they would soon fight one another. And in this he seems to have been no ill prophet.

I Come to Bury Caesar, Not to Praise Him

William Shakespeare, Julius Caesar

Be careful how you praise a departed superior—praise too fulsome or too faint can be your undoing. Marc Antony's famous oration.

Friends, Romans, Countrymen! lend me your ears.
I come to bury Caesar, not to praise him.
The evil that men do lives after them;
The good is oft interred with their bones:
So let it be with Caesar. Noble Brutus
Hath told you Caesar was ambitious:—
If it were so, it was a grievous fault;
And grievously hath Caesar answered it.
Here, under Brutus, and the rest—
For Brutus is an honorable man!
So are they all! all honorable men!—
Come I to speak in Caesar's funeral.
He was my friend, faithful and just to me,—
But Brutus says he was ambitious;
And Brutus is an honorable man.
He hath brought many captives home to Rome,
Whose ransoms did the general coffers fill:

Did this in Caesar seem ambitious?
When that the poor have cried, Caesar hath wept.
Ambition should be made of sterner stuff!—
Yet Brutus says he was ambitious,
And Brutus is an honorable man!
You all did see, that, on the Lupereal,
I thrice presented him a kingly crown,
Which he did thrice refuse: was this ambition?—
Yet Brutus says he was ambitious;
And, sure, he is an honorable man!
I speak not to disprove what Brutus spoke;
But here I am to speak what I do know.
You all did love him once; not without cause:
What cause withholds you, then, to mourn for him?
O judgment! thou art fled to brutish beasts,
And men have lost their reason! Bear with me:
My heart is in the coffin there with Caesar;
And I must pause till it come back to me.—
But yesterday, the word of Caesar might
Have stood against the world;—now lies he there,
And none so poor to do him reverence!
O masters! if I were disposed to stir
Your hearts and minds to mutiny and rage,
I should do Brutus wrong, and Cassius wrong,
Who, you all know, are honorable men!—
I will not do them wrong: I rather choose
To wrong the dead, to wrong myself and you,
Than I will wrong such honorable men!—
But here's a parchment with the seal of Caesar,—
I found it in his closet,—'tis his will!
Let but the commons hear this testament,—
Which, pardon me, I do not mean to read,—
And they would go and kiss dead Caesar's wounds,
And dip their napkins in his sacred blood
Yea, beg a hair of him for memory,
And, dying, mention it within their wills,
Bequeathing it, as a rich legacy,
Unto their issue!
If you have tears, prepare to shed them now.
You all do know this mantle: I remember
The first time ever Caesar put it on:
'Twas on a summer's evening, in his tent,—

That day he overcame the Nervii! -
Look! in this place ran Cassius' dagger through:
See what a rent the envious Casca made!—
Through this—the well-beloved Brutus stabbed,
And, as he plucked the cursed steel away,
Mark how the blood of Caesar followed it;
As rushing out of doors, to be resolved
If Brutus so unkindly knocked, or no!
For Brutus, as you know, was Caesar's angel.
Judge, O ye Gods, how dearly Caesar loved him!
This was the most unkindest cut of all!
For when the noble Caesar saw him stab,
Ingratitude, more strong than traitors' arms,
Quite vanquished him. Then burst his mighty heart—
And, in his mantle muffling up his face,
Even at the base of Pompey's statue,—
Which all the while ran blood!—great Caesar fell!
O, what a fall was there, my countrymen!
Then I, and you, and all of us fell down;
Whilst bloody treason flourished over us!
O, now you weep; and I perceive you feel
The dint of pity: these are gracious drops!
Kind souls! what! weep you when you but behold
Our Caesar's vesture wounded?—look you here!
Here is himself,—marred, as you see, by traitors!—
Good friends! sweet friends! let me not stir you up
To such a sudden flood of mutiny!
They that have done this deed are honorable.
What private griefs they have, alas! I know not,
What made them do it: they are wise and honorable,
And will, no doubt, with reasons answer you.
I come not, friends, to steal away your hearts:
I am no orator, as Brutus is,
But, as you know me all, a plain, blunt man,
That love my friend,—and that they know full well
That gave me public leave to speak of him,—
For I have neither wit, nor words, nor worth,
Action, nor utterance, nor the power of speech,
To stir men's blood: I only speak right on,
I tell you that which you yourselves do know;
Show you sweet Caesar's wounds,—poor, poor, dumb mouths—
And bid them speak for me. But, were I Brutus,

And Brutus Antony, there were an Antony
Would ruffle up your spirits, and put a tongue
In every wound of Caesar, that would move
The stones of Rome to rise and mutiny!

The Mice in Council

Aesop

The need for leadership, the danger of apathy.

The Mice summoned a council to decide how they might best devise means for obtaining notice of the approach of their great enemy the Cat. Among the many plans devised, the one that found most favor was the proposal to tie a bell to the neck of the Cat, that the Mice being warned by the sound of the tinkling might run away and hide themselves in their holes at his approach. But when the Mice further debated who among them should thus "bell the Cat," there was no one found to do it.

Prestige and the Mystique
of Manly Authority

From Charles de Gaulle,
The Edge of the Sword

How can a leader of men inspire confidence in his followers? By inspiring them with his own high ideals.

Men, in their hearts, can no more do without being controlled than they can live without food, drink, and sleep. As political animals they feel the need for organization, that is to say for an established order and for leaders. Authority may totter on its shaken foundations, but sooner or later the natural equilibrium which lies at the base of all things will provide it with new ones, better, or less good, but, in any case, firm enough to establish discipline in a new form. These new foundations are, even now, emerging into the light of day. They are apparent in the recognition given to the value of individuals, and to the ascendency of a few men. What the masses once granted to birth or office, they now give to those who can assert themselves. What legitimate prince was ever so blindly obeyed as is now the dictator who owes his rise to nothing but his own audacity? What established authority ever so left its mark upon events as does the proficiency of an engineer in the modern world? What conquerors were ever so wildly acclaimed as our athletes who owe success only to their own endeavors?

This transformation of authority cannot but have its effect upon military discipline. In the army, as elsewhere, they say: "Respect is disappearing." But in fact it has only changed its object. To be obeyed, the man in command must today rely less on his rank than on his own value. We can no longer confuse power and its attributes.

This does not, of course, mean that all of the things in which discipline used to be steeped can be dispensed with. Men do not change so quickly or so completely, nor does human nature move by leaps and bounds. Authority exercised over other people will depend to a large extent upon the aura which surrounds rank and seniority. At the same time, the ascendancy exercised by the personality of the master, and his consequent ability to ensure obedience, have always existed. But in these unsettled times, and in a society where traditions and institutions have been violently disturbed, the conventions of obedience are growing weaker, and the mainspring of command is now to be found in the personal prestige of the leader.

Prestige is largely a matter of feeling, suggestion, and impression, and it depends primarily on the possession of an elementary gift, a natural aptitude which defies analysis. The fact of the matter is that certain men have, one might almost say from birth, the quality of exuding authority, as though it were a liquid, though it is impossible to say precisely of what it consists. Even those who come under its influence frequently feel surprised by their own reactions to it. This phenomenon has something in common with the emotion of love which cannot be explained without the presence of what we call "charm," for want of a better word. Still stranger is the fact that the authority exerted by certain individuals has often nothing to do with their intrinsic gifts or abilities. It is no rare thing to find men of outstanding intellect who are without it, whereas others far less highly endowed possess it in a very high degree.

But though there is something in what we call a "natural gift of authority" which cannot be acquired, but comes from the innermost being of some individuals, and varies in each, there are also a number of constant and necessary elements on which it is possible to lay one's finger, and these can be acquired or developed. The true leader, like the great artist, is a man with an inborn propensity which can be strengthened and exploited by the exercise of his craft.

First and foremost, there can be no prestige without mystery, for familiarity breeds contempt. All religions have their holy of holies, and no man is a hero to his valet. In the designs, the demeanor, and the mental operations of a leader there must be always a "something" which others cannot altogether fathom, which puzzles them, stirs them, and rivets their attention. In saying this I do not mean that he must shut himself away in an ivory tower, remote from, and inaccessible to, his subordinates. On the contrary, if one is to influence men's minds, one must observe them carefully and make it clear that each has been marked out from among his fellows, but only on condition that this goes with a determination to give nothing away, to hold in reserve some piece of secret knowledge which may at any moment intervene, and the more effectively from being in the nature of a surprise. The latent faith of the masses will do the rest. Once the leader has been judged capable of adding the weight of his personality to the known factors of any situation, the ensuing hope and confidence will add immensely to the faith reposed in him.

It must, indeed, respond to the cravings felt by men who, imperfect themselves, seek perfection in the end they are called upon to serve. Conscious of their own limitations and restricted by nature, they give free rein to unlimited hopes, and each measuring his own littleness, accepts the need for collective action on condition that it contribute to an end which is, in itself, great. No leader will ever succeed in asserting himself unless he can touch that spring. All whose role it is to command and direct the crowd are fully aware of this fact. It is the basis of eloquence. There is not an orator but will dress up the poorest argument in the garments of greatness. It is the king post of big business: every company prospectus commends itself to the public by talking of progress. It

is the springboard of political parties, each one of which unceasingly declares that universal happiness is the end and purpose of its
program. Consequently, whatever orders the leader may give, they
must be swathed in the robes of nobility. He must aim high, show
that he has vision, act on the grand scale, and so establish his
authority over the generality of men who splash in shallow water.
He must personify contempt for contingencies, and leave it to his
subordinates to be bogged down in detail. He must put from him
all that smacks of niggling and leave it to the humdrum individuals
to be circumspect and wary. The question of virtue does not arise.
The perfection preached in the Gospels never yet built up an
empire. Every man of action has a strong dose of egotism, pride,
hardness, and cunning. But all those things will be forgiven him,
indeed, they will be regarded as high qualities, if he can make of
them the means to achieve great ends. Thus, by satisfying the secret
desires of men's hearts, by providing compensation for the
cramped condition of their lives, he will capture their imagination,
and, even should he fall by the way, will retain, in their eyes, the
prestige of those heights to which he did his best to lead them. But
he who never rises above the commonplace and is content with little, will never be of much account. At most he will be remembered
as a good servant, but never as a master who can draw to himself
the faith and the dreams of mankind.

It is, indeed, an observable fact that all leaders of men,
whether as political figures, prophets, or soldiers, all those who can
get the best out of others, have always identified themselves with
ideals, and this has given added scope and strength to their influence. Followed in their lifetime because they stand for greatness of
mind rather than self-interest, they are later remembered less for
the usefulness of what they have achieved than for the sweep of
their endeavors. Though sometimes reason may condemn them,
feeling clothes them in an aura of glory. In the concourse of great
men Napoleon will always rank higher than Parmentier. So true is
this that history gives a sort of somber magnificence to certain men
whose claim to fame rests merely on the fact that they were the
instigators of revolts and brutalities, because their crimes were
committed in the name of some high-sounding cause.

Everything That Entitles
a Man to Praise

From Cicero,
On the Commonwealth

Cicero's On the Commonwealth *beautifully expresses the classical ideal of the manly citizen. To be a man is not only to be vigorous in service of the common good, but refined, gracious, and learned, familiar with the sublime beauties of art, music, and philosophy.*

Let us count those who treat the philosophy of life as great men—as indeed they are—let us count them as scholars and teachers of truth and excellence. But at the same time let us admit the existence of an art—whether discovered by statesmen who have faced the vicissitudes of public life or studied even by your philosophers in scholarly retirement—an art which comprises the theory of politics and the government of peoples and which, in truth, is by no means to be despised. This art, when added to great natural abilities, produces, as it has often done in the past, a type of character extraordinary and divine. And when men have felt, as did the participants in this dialogue, that, to the powers of mind received from nature and developed by experience in public affairs, they should add also scholarly interests and a richer acquaintance with life, such men must be universally conceded to be superior to all others. What, indeed, can be more glorious than the union of practical experience in great affairs with an intelligent enthusiasm for the liberal arts? Can anything be imagined more perfect than the distinction of a Publius Scipio, a Gaius Laelius, or a Lucius Philus, men who, in order not to neglect anything which might bring the highest glory to illustrious men, united the rules of conduct which they learned at home and inherited from their ancestors even with a foreign philosophy derived from Socrates? Hence I hold that a man who has been able and willing to combine these two interests, and has disciplined himself both in the ways of his ancestors and in liberal culture, has attained everything that entitles a man to praise.

The Thief and
the House Dog

Aesop

Citizens must be watchful guardians.

A Thief came in the night to break into a house. He brought with him several slices of meat, that he might pacify the House Dog, so that he should not alarm his master by barking. As the Thief threw him the pieces of meat, the Dog said, "If you think to stop my mouth, you will be greatly mistaken. This sudden kindness at your hands will only make me more watchful, lest under these unexpected favors to myself, you have some private ends to accomplish for your own benefits, and for my master's injury."

Liberty Is Order,
Liberty Is Strength

From Charles James Fox,
Select Orations

As a Member of Parliament, Fox (1749–1806) was an ardent champion of liberty and the rights of man.

Liberty is order. Liberty is strength. Look round the world, and admire, as you must, the instructive spectacle. You will see that liberty not only is power and order, but that it is power and order predominant and invincible, and that it derides all other sources of strength. And shall the preposterous imagination be fostered, that men bred in liberty—the first of human kind who asserted the glorious distinction of forming for themselves their social compact—

can be condemned to silence upon their rights? Is it to be conceived that men who have enjoyed, for such a length of days, the light and happiness of freedom, can be restrained, and shut up again in the gloom of ignorance and degradation? As well, sir, might you try, by a miserable dam, to shut up the flowing of a rapid river! The rolling and impetuous tide would burst through every impediment that man might throw in its way; and the only consequence of the impotent attempt would be, that, having collected new force by its temporary suspension, enforcing itself through new channels, it would spread devastation and ruin on every side. The progress of liberty is like the progress of the stream. Kept within its bounds, it is sure to fertilize the country through which it runs; but no power can arrest it in its passage; and short-sighted, as well as wicked, must be the heart of the projector that would strive to divert its course.

To Live Up to an Ideal!

From Cicero, Letters to Atticus

The depressing contrast between true statesmanship and political reality.

You feel that I show great perturbation of spirit. I do, indeed, but not so much, perhaps, as I seem, for merely by going over the matter I get relief whether I come to some conclusion or none.

Still one may lament. This I do whole days despite the fruitlessness of such actions. Since I come to no conclusion, I fear that I may disgrace my studies and my book *On the State*. Therefore I put in all my time considering what is the dominant trait of that *ideal statesman*, whom with some care as you maintain, I have described in that book. You comprehend, do you, the ideal by which the statesman should be guided in all his acts? It is, I believe, set forth in the fifth book where Scipio is made to say: "As the helmsman presents himself with a safe journey as an ideal, the physician with health, the general with victory, so the statesman holds up before himself the happiness of the citizens that they may be strong in resources, rich in goods, honorable in virtue." In so doing, to my way of thinking, he would consummate the greatest and best task in the world.

Neither formerly nor now has Pompey bethought himself of this ideal. It is mastery that both he and Caesar have sought. Neither has striven that the state be happy and honored. Pompey did not abandon the city because he could not defend it, nor Italy because he was driven from it; but from the very beginning he had this in mind: to move everything on land and sea, to stir up the kings of the barbarians, to arm wild peoples and lead them against Italy, and to muster mighty armies. Long since, spurred on by many of his followers, he has aimed at the sort of power wielded by Sulla. "Could there have been," you will say, "no agreement between Pompey and Caesar, no compromise?" Today there can be. But the happiness of the people is the aim of neither. Both wish to reign.

At your request I have made this brief review of the case for you wanted me to set forth my sentiments concerning the prevailing troubles. I prophesy, my Atticus, not talking at random as did Cassandra whom nobody believed, but forecasting the future for a whole Iliad of troubles is imminent.

The Wolf and the House Dog

Aesop

A Wolf, meeting with a big well-fed Mastiff having a wooden collar about his neck, inquired of him who it was that fed him so well, and yet compelled him to drag that heavy log about wherever he went. "The master," he replied. Then said the Wolf: "May no friend of mine ever be in such a plight; for the weight of this chain is enough to spoil the appetite."

Comparing the Statesman
and the Soldier

From Charles de Gaulle, The Edge of the Sword

It is the task of political leaders to dominate opinion: that of the monarch, of the council, of the people, since it is from these that they draw their authority. They have no value, and can do nothing, except in the name of the sovereign power. But their abilities matter less than their skill in pleasing, and promises are more effective than arguments. The statesman, therefore, must concentrate all his efforts on captivating men's minds. He must know when to dissemble, when to be frank. He must pose as the servant of the public in order to become its master. He must outbid his rivals in self-confidence, and only after a thousand intrigues and solemn undertakings will he find himself entrusted with full power. Even when he has it in his grasp, he can never be completely open in his dealings, for he must still be concerned to please, to know how to convince prince or parliament, how to gratify popular passions and soothe the anxieties of vested interests. His authority, no matter how unquestioned, is precarious. Public opinion, that inconstant mistress, follows his lead with a capricious step, ready to stop dead should he race too far ahead, to take giant strides when he thinks it advisable to move with caution. Ungrateful, it rates at a low price the efforts he has made, and, even at the moment of success, is only too ready to listen to his opponents. But, if he makes a mistake, the pack is at his heels; if he shows signs of weakness it hurls itself upon him. What does the statesman's empire amount to? A court cabal, an intrigue in the Council, a shift of opinion in the Assembly can snatch it from him in a moment. Toppled from his pedestal he finds nothing but injustice awaiting him. Great or small, historic figure or colorless politician, he comes and goes between power and powerlessness, between prestige and public ingratitude. The whole of his life and the sum total of his work are marked by instability, restlessness, and storm, and so are very different from those of the soldier. The soldier's profession is that of arms, but the power they give him has to be strictly organized. From the moment that he embarks upon it he becomes a slave of a body of regulations, and so remains all through his active life. The army is generous but jealous. It guides his steps, supports him in his moments of weakness, develops such gifts as he may have. But it also keeps a tight hold on him, overriding his doubts and holding his enthusiasm in check. As a man he suffers much from its demands, for he must renounce his personal liberty, his chances of making money, and, sometimes, sacrifice his life, and what greater offering could there be? But at this high cost it opens the door for him to the empire of armed might. That is why, though he often grumbles at his slavery, he clings to it; nay, more, he loves it, and glories in the price he has to pay. "It is my honor!" he says.

In the company of his fellows he rises to a position of power, but by degrees, for the hierarchy of which he is a member is strict and uncompromising. For the soldier there is always yet some higher rank to attain, some recognition to be gained. On the other hand, such authority as he may wield is absolute. Supported by discipline and strengthened by tradition, it makes use of everything in the way of credit and prestige which the military order gives to him who holds command. Under the iron rod and the shield of the "regulations" he marches with a firm step along a road which, grueling though it may be, points straight ahead.

The statesman and the soldier bring, therefore, to a common task very different characters, methods, and anxieties. The former reaches his goal by roundabout ways, the later by direct approach. The one is long-sighted though his vision may be clouded, sees realities as complex, and sets himself to master them by trickery and calculation. The other sees with clear eyes what there is to be seen straight in front of his nose and thinks it simple and capable of being controlled by resolution. In dealing with immediate problems, the statesman's first concern is what people will say of him; the soldier looks for counsel to principles.

Always Be Prepared for War

From Niccolo Machiavelli, The Prince

The best way for statesmen to avoid going to war is to be always ready to wage it.

The Romans in the provinces they took, always followed this policy; they established colonies, inveigled the less powerful without increasing their strength, put down the most powerful and did not allow foreign rulers to obtain influence in them. I will adduce the province of Greece as a sole example. They made friends with the Achaeans and the Aetolians, the kingdom of Macedonia was cast down, and Antiochus driven out, nor did they allow the merits of the Achaeans or the Aetolians to gain them any increase of territory, nor did the persuasions of Philip induce them to befriend him without reducing his influence, nor could the power of Antiochus make them consent to allow him to hold any state in that province.

For the Romans did in these cases what all wise princes should do, who consider not only present but also future discords and diligently guard against them; for being foreseen they can easily be remedied, but if one waits till they are at hand, the medicine is no longer in time as the malady has become incurable; it happening with this as with those hectic fevers, as doctors say, which at their beginning are easy to cure but difficult to recognize, but in course of time when they have not at first been recognized and treated, become easy to recognize and difficult to cure. Thus it happens in matters of state; for knowing afar off (which it is only given to a prudent man to do) the evils that are brewing, they are easily cured. But when, for want of such knowledge, they are allowed to grow so that everyone can recognize them, there is no longer any remedy to be found. Therefore, the Romans, observing disorders while yet remote, were always able to find a remedy, and never allowed them to increase in order to avoid a war; for they knew that war is not to be avoided, and can be deferred only to the advantage of the other side; they therefore declared war against Philip and Antiochus in Greece, so as not to have to fight them in Italy, though they might at the time have avoided either; this they did not choose to do, never caring to do that which is now every day to be heard in the mouths of our wise men, namely to enjoy the advantages of delay, but preferring to trust their own virtue and prudence; for time brings with it all things, and may produce indifferently either good or evil.

The Wolves to the Sheep: Give Peace a Chance

Aesop

"Why should there always be this internecine and implacable warfare between us?" said the Wolves to the Sheep. "Those evil-disposed Dogs have much to answer for. They always bark whenever we approach you, and attack us before we have done any harm. If you would only dismiss them from your heels, there might soon be treaties of peace and of reconciliation between us." The Sheep, poor silly creatures! were easily beguiled, and dismissed the Dogs. The Wolves destroyed the flock at their own pleasure.

What Is the Duty of a Statesman to the Voters?

From Edmund Burke, Speech to the Electors of Bristol

According to this famous statement in 1774 of the legislator's responsibility, it is important not simply to carry out passively the voters' wishes, but to deliberate on their behalf—even if a decision ends up going against their wishes.

Certainly, gentlemen, it ought to be the happiness and glory of a representative to live in the strictest union, the closest correspondence, and the most unreserved communication with his constituents. Their wishes ought to have great weight with him; their opinion, high respect; their business, unremitted attention. It is his duty to sacrifice his repose, his pleasures, his satisfactions, to theirs; and above all, ever, and in all cases, to prefer their interest to his own. But his unbiased opinion, his mature judgment, his enlightened conscience, he ought not to sacrifice to you, to any man, or to any set of men living. These he does not derive from your pleasure no, nor from the law and the constitution. They are a trust from Providence, for the abuse of which he is deeply answerable. Your representative owes you, not his industry only, but his judgment; and he betrays, instead of serving you, if he sacrifices it to your opinion.

My worthy colleague says, his will ought to be subservient to yours. If that be all, the thing is innocent. If government were a matter of will upon any side, yours, without question, ought to be superior. But government and legislation are matters of reason and judgment, and not of inclination; and what sort of reason is that, in which the determination precedes the discussion; in which one set of men deliberate, and another decide; and where those who form the conclusion are perhaps three hundred miles distant from those who hear the arguments?

To deliver an opinion, is the right of all men; that of constituents is a weighty and respectable opinion, which a representative ought always to rejoice to hear; and which he ought always most seriously to consider. But *authoritative* instructions, *mandates* issued, which the member is bound blindly and implicitly to obey, to vote, and to argue for, though contrary to the clearest conviction of his judgment and conscience, these are things utterly unknown to the laws of this land, and which arise from a fundamental mistake of the whole order and tenor of our constitution.

Parliament is not a *congress* of ambassadors from different and hostile interests; which interests each must maintain, as an agent and advocate, against other agents and advocates; but parliament is a *deliberative* assembly of *one* nation, with *one* interest, that of the whole; where, not local purposes, not local prejudices, ought to guide, but the general good, resulting from the general reason of the whole. You choose a member indeed; but when you have chosen him, he is not member of Bristol, but he is a member of *parliament*. If the local constituent should have an interest, or should form an hasty opinion, evidently opposite to the real good of the rest of the community, the member for that place ought to be as far, as any other, from any endeavor to give it effect. I beg pardon for saying so much on this subject. I have been unwillingly drawn into it but I shall ever use a respectful frankness of communication with you. Your faithful friend, your devoted servant, I shall be to the end of my life: a flatterer you do not wish for. On this point of instructions, however, I think it scarcely possible we ever can have any sort of difference. Perhaps I may give you too much, rather than too little, trouble.

From the first hour I was encouraged to court your favor, to this happy day of obtaining it, I have never promised you anything but humble and persevering endeavors to do my duty. The weight of that duty, I confess, makes me tremble; and whoever well considers what it is, of all things in the world, will fly from what has the least likeness to a positive and precipitate engagement. To be a good member of parliament is, let me tell you, no easy task; especially at this time, when there is so strong a disposition to run into the perilous extremes of servile compliance or wild popularity. To unite circumspection with vigor, is absolutely necessary; but it is extremely difficult. We are now members for a rich commercial *city*; this city, however, is but a part of a rich commercial *nation*, the interests of which are various, multiform, and intricate. We are members for that great nation, which however is itself but part of a great *empire*, extended by our virtue and our fortune to the farthest limits of the east and of the west. All these wide-spread interests must be considered; must be compared; must be reconciled, if possible. We are members for a *free* country; and surely we all know, that the machine of a free constitution is no simple thing; but as intricate and as delicate as it is valuable. We are members in a great and ancient *monarchy*; and we must preserve religiously the true legal rights of the sovereign, which form the key-stone that binds together the noble and well-constructed arch of our empire and our constitution. A constitution made up of balanced powers must ever be a critical thing. As such I mean to touch that part of it which comes within my reach. I know my inability, and I wish for support from every quarter. In particular I shall aim at the friendship, and shall cultivate the best correspondence, of the worthy colleague you have given me.

I trouble you no further than once more to thank you all; you, gentlemen, for your favors; the candidates, for their temperate and polite behavior; and the sheriffs, for a conduct which may give a model for all who are in public stations.

At Last I Had the Authority. I Slept Soundly.

From Winston S. Churchill, The Gathering Storm

Winston Spencer Churchill was Britain's Prime Minister during World War II and chief architect of the Allied defeat of the Third Reich. He was also a prodigiously talented historian, biographer, and essayist, exemplifying the balance of active and contemplative virtues that recurs throughout this anthology as the key to manliness. An early and persistent critic of Adolf Hitler, in his history of the World War II, Churchill describes the fall of the Chamberlain government after Hitler flagrantly violated the peace agreement he had concluded with Chamberlain at Munich. His warnings about the Nazis finally vindicated, Churchill recounts how he became Prime Minister.

I do not remember exactly how things happened during the morning of May 9, but the following occurred. Sir Kingsley Wood, Secretary of State for Air, was very close to the Prime Minister as a colleague and a friend. They had long worked together in complete confidence. From him I learned that Mr. Chamberlain was resolved upon the formation of a National Government and, if he could not be the head, he would give way to anyone commanding his confidence who could. Thus, by the afternoon, I became aware that I might well be called upon to take the lead. The prospect neither excited nor alarmed me. I thought it would be by far the best plan. I was content to let events unfold. In the afternoon, the Prime Minister summoned me to Downing Street, where I found Lord Halifax, and after a talk about the situation in general, we were told that Mr. Attlee and Mr. Greenwood would visit us in a few minutes for a consultation.

When they arrived, we three Ministers sat on one side of the table and the Opposition leaders on the other. Mr. Chamberlain declared the paramount need of a National Government, and sought to ascertain whether the Labour Party would serve under him. The conference of their party was in session at Bournemouth. The conversation was most polite, but it was clear that the Labour leaders would not commit themselves without consulting their people, and they hinted, not obscurely, that they thought the response would be unfavorable. They then withdrew. It was a bright, sunny afternoon, and Lord Halifax and I sat for a while on a seat in the garden of Number 10 and talked about nothing in particular. I then returned to the Admiralty and was occupied during the evening and a large part of the night in heavy business.

The morning of the tenth of May dawned, and with it came tremendous news. Boxes with telegrams poured in from the Admiralty, the War Office, and the Foreign Office. The Germans had struck their long-awaited blow. Holland and Belgium were both invaded. Their frontiers had been crossed at numerous points. The whole movement of the German Army upon the invasion of the Low Countries and of France had begun.

At about ten o'clock, Sir Kingsley Wood came to see me, having just been with the Prime Minister. He told me that Mr. Chamberlain was inclined to feel that the great battle which had broken upon us made it necessary for him to remain at his post. Kingsley Wood had told him that, on the contrary, the new crisis made it all the more necessary to have a National Government, which alone could confront it, and he added that Mr. Chamberlain had accepted this view. At eleven o'clock, I was again summoned to Downing Street by the Prime Minister. There once more I found Lord Halifax. We took our seats at the table opposite Mr. Chamberlain. He told us that he was satisfied that it was beyond his power to form a National Government. The response he had received from the Labour leaders left him in no doubt of this. The question, therefore, was whom he should advise the King to send for after his own resignation had been accepted. His demeanor was cool, unruffled, and seemingly quite detached from the personal aspect of the affair. He looked at us both across the table.

I have had many important interviews in my public life, and this was certainly the most important. Usually I talk a great deal, but on this occasion I was silent. Mr. Chamberlain evidently had in his mind the stormy scene in the House of Commons two nights before, when I had seemed to be in such heated controversy with the Labour Party. Although this had been in his support and defense, he nevertheless felt that it might be an obstacle to my obtaining their adherence at this juncture. I do not recall the actual words he used, but this was the implication. His biographer, Mr.

Feiling, states definitely that he preferred Lord Halifax. As I remained silent, a very long pause ensued. It certainly seemed longer than the two minutes which one observes in the commemorations of Armistice Day. Then at length Halifax spoke. He said that he felt that his position as a peer, out of the House of Commons, would make it very difficult for him to discharge the duties of Prime Minister in a war like this. He would be held responsible for everything, but would not have the power to guide the assembly upon whose confidence the life of every Government depended. He spoke for some minutes in this sense, and by the time he had finished, it was clear that the duty would fall upon me—had in fact fallen upon me. Then, for the first time, I spoke. I said I would have no communication with either of the Opposition Parties until I had the King's commission to form a Government. On this the momentous conversation came to an end, and we reverted to our ordinary easy and familiar manners of men who had worked for years together and whose lives in and out of office had been spent in all the friendliness of British politics. I then went back to the Admiralty, where, as may well be imagined, much awaited me.

The Dutch Ministers were in my room. Haggard and worn, with horror in their eyes, they had just flown over from Amsterdam. Their country had been attacked without the slightest pretext or warning. The avalanche of fire and steel had rolled across the frontiers, and when resistance broke out and the Dutch frontier guards fired, an overwhelming onslaught was made from the air. The whole country was in a state of wild confusion; the long-prepared defense scheme had been put into operation; the dykes were opened; the waters spread far and wide. But the Germans had already crossed the outer lines, and were now streaming across the causeway which enclosed the Zuyder Zee. Could we do anything to prevent this? Luckily, we had a flotilla not far away, and this was immediately ordered to sweep the causeway with fire, and take the heaviest toll possible of the swarming invaders. The Queen was still in Holland, but it did not seem she could remain there long.

As a consequence of these discussions, a large number of orders were dispatched by the Admiralty to all our ships in the neighborhood, and close relations were established with the Royal Dutch Navy. Even with the recent overrunning of Norway and Denmark in their minds, the Dutch Ministers seemed unable to understand how the great German nation, which, up to the night before, had professed nothing but friendship, and was bound by treaty to respect the neutrality of Holland, so strictly maintained, should suddenly have made this frightful and brutal onslaught. Upon these proceedings and other affairs, an hour or two passed. A spate of telegrams pressed in from all the frontiers affected by the forward heave of the German armies. It seemed that the old Schlieffen Plan, brought up to date with its Dutch extension, was already in full operation. In 1914, the swinging right arm of the German invasion had swept through Belgium, but had stopped short of Holland. It was well known then that had that war been delayed for three or four years, the extra army group would have been ready, and the railway terminals and communications adapted, for a movement through Holland. Now the famous movement had been launched with all these facilities and with every circumstance of surprise and treachery. But other developments lay ahead. The decisive stroke of the enemy was not to be a turning movement on the flank, but a break through the main front. This none of us or the French, who were in responsible command, foresaw. Earlier in the year I had, in a published interview, warned these neutral countries of the fate which was impending upon them and which was evident from the troop dispositions and road and rail development, as well as from the captured German plans. My words had been resented.

In the splintering crash of this vast battle, the quiet conversations we had had in Downing Street faded or fell back in one's mind. However, I remember being told that Mr. Chamberlain had gone, or was going, to see the King, and this was naturally to be expected. Presently a message arrived summoning me to the Palace at six o'clock. It only takes two minutes to drive there from the Admiralty along the Mall. Although I suppose the evening newspapers must have been full of the terrific news from the Continent, nothing had been mentioned about the Cabinet crisis. The public had not had time to take in what was happening either abroad or at home, and there was no crowd about the Palace gates.

I was taken immediately to the King. His Majesty received me most graciously and bade me sit down. He looked at me searchingly and quizzically of some moments, and then said: "I suppose you don't know why I have sent for you?" Adopting his mood, I replied: "Sir, I simply couldn't imagine why." He laughed and said: "I want to ask you to form a government." I said I would certainly do so.

The King had made no stipulation about the Government being national in character, and I felt that my commission was in no formal way dependent upon this point. But in view of what had happened, and the conditions which had led to Mr. Chamberlain's resignation, a Government of national character was obviously inherent in the situation. If I had found it impossible to come to terms with the Opposition Parties, I should not have been constitutionally debarred from trying to form the strongest Government possible of all who would stand by the country in the hour of peril, provided that such a Government could command a majority in the House of Commons. I told the King that I would immediately send for the leaders of the Labour and Liberal Parties, that I proposed to form a War Cabinet of five or six Ministers, and that I hoped to let him have at least five names before midnight. On this I took my leave and returned to the Admiralty.

Between seven and eight, at my request, Mr. Attlee called upon me. He brought with him Mr. Greenwood. I told him of the authority I had to form a Government and asked if the Labour Party would join. He said they would. I proposed that they should take rather more than a third of the places, having two seats in the War Cabinet of five, or it might be six, and I asked Mr. Attlee to let me have a list of men so that we could discuss particular offices. I mentioned Mr. Bevin, Mr. Alexander, Mr. Morrison, and Mr. Dalton as men whose services in high office were immediately required. I had, of course, known both Attlee and Greenwood for a long time in the House of Commons. During the eleven years before the outbreak of war, I had in my more or less independent position come far more often into collision with the Conservative and National Governments than with the Labour and Liberal Oppositions. We had a pleasant talk for a little while, and they went off to report by telephone to their friends and followers at Bournemouth, with whom, of course, they had been in the closest contact during the previous forty-eight hours.

I invited Mr. Chamberlain to lead the House of Commons as Lord President of the Council, and he replied by telephone that he accepted and had arranged to broadcast at nine that night, stating that he had resigned, and urging everyone to support and aid his successor. This he did in magnanimous terms. I asked Lord Halifax to join the War Cabinet while remaining Foreign Secretary. At about ten, I sent the King a list of five names, as I had promised. The appointment of the three Service Ministers was vitally urgent. I had already made up my mind who they should be. Mr. Eden should go to the War Office; Mr. Alexander should come to the Admiralty; and Sir Archibald Sinclair, leader of the Liberal Party, should take the Air Ministry. At the same time I assumed the office of Minister of Defence, without, however, attempting to define its scope and powers.

Thus, then, on the night of the tenth of May, at the outset of this mighty battle, I acquired the chief power in the State, which henceforth I wielded in ever-growing measure for five years and three months of world war, at the end of which time, all our enemies having surrendered unconditionally or being about to do so, I was immediately dismissed by the British electorate from all further conduct of their affairs.

During these last crowded days of the political crises, my pulse had not quickened at any moment. I took it all as it came. But I cannot conceal from the reader of this truthful account that as I went to bed at about three o'clock in the morning, I was conscious of a profound sense of relief. At last I had the authority to give directions over the whole scene. I felt as if I were walking with Destiny, and that all my past life had been but a preparation for this hour and for this trial. Eleven years in the political wilderness had freed me from ordinary party antagonisms. My warnings over the last six years had been so numerous, so detailed, and were now so terribly vindicated, that no one could gainsay me. I could not be reproached either for making the war or with want of preparation for it. I thought I knew a good deal about it all, and I was sure I should not fail. Therefore, although impatient for the morning, I slept soundly and had no need for cheering dreams. Facts are better than dreams.

Pericles's Funeral Oration and Thucydides's Assessment of His Statesmanship

From Thucydides, History of the Peloponnesian War

One of the greatest examples of political oratory in Western history, as recounted by the historian Thucydides. Pericles (495–429 B.C.) encourages his fellow citizens to serve their city loyally because it combines the advantages of a powerful democratic empire with a respect for learning, tolerance, and civilization.

In the course of this winter the Athenians, in accordance with the custom of their forefathers, buried at the public expense those who had first fallen in this war, after the following manner. Having erected a tent, they lay out the bones of the dead three days before, and each one brings to his own relative whatever [funeral offering] he pleases. When the funeral procession takes place, cars convey coffins of cypress wood, one for each tribe; in which are laid the bones of every man, according to the tribe to which he belonged; and one empty bier is carried, spread in the honor of the missing, whose bodies could not be found to be taken up. Whoever wishes, both of citizens and strangers, joins in the procession; and their female relatives attend at the burial to make the wailings. They lay them in the public sepulcher, which is the fairest suburb of the city, and in which they always bury those who have fallen in the wars (except, at least, those who fell at Marathon; but to them, as they considered their valor distinguished above that of all others, they gave a burial on the very spot). After they have laid them in the ground, a man chosen by the state—one who in point of intellect is considered talented, and in dignity is preeminent—speaks over them such a panegyric as may be appropriate; after which they all retire. In this way they bury them: and through the whole of the war, whenever they had occasion, they observed the established custom. Over these who were first buried at any rate, Pericles son of Xanthippus was chosen to speak. And when the time for doing so came, advancing from the sepulcher on to a platform, which had been raised to some height, that he might be heard over as great a part of the crowd as possible, he spoke to the following effect:

"The greater part of those who ere now have spoken in this place, have been accustomed to praise the man who introduced this oration into the law; considering it a right thing that it should be delivered over those who are buried after falling in battle. To me, however, it would have appeared sufficient, that when men had shown themselves brave by deeds, their honors also should be displayed by deeds—as you now see in the case of this burial, prepared at the public expense—and not that the virtues of many should be periled in one individual, for credit to be given him according as he expresses himself well or ill. For it is difficult to speak with propriety on a subject on which even the impression of one's truthfulness is with difficulty established. For the hearer who is acquainted [with the facts], and kindly disposed [toward those who performed them], might perhaps think them somewhat imperfectly set forth, compared with what he both wishes and knows; while he who is unacquainted with them might think that some points were even exaggerated, being led to this conclusion by envy, should he hear anything surpassing his own natural powers. For praises spoken of others are only endured so far as each one thinks that he is himself also capable of doing any of the things he hears; but that which exceeds their own capacity men at once envy and disbelieve. Since, however, our ancestors judged this to be a right custom, I too, in obedience to the law, must endeavor to meet the wishes and views of every one, as far as possible.

"I will begin then with our ancestors first: for it is just and becoming too at the same time, that on such an occasion the honor of being thus mentioned should be paid them. For always inhabiting the country without change, through a long succession of posterity, by their valor they transmitted it free to this very time. Justly then may they claim to be commended; and more justly still may our own fathers. For in addition to what they inherited, they acquired the great empire which we possess, and by painful exertions bequeathed it to us of the present day: though to most part of it have additions been made by ourselves here, who are still, generally speaking, in the vigor of life; and we have furnished our city with everything, so as to be most self-sufficient both for peace and for war. Now with regard to our military achievements, by which each possession was gained, whether in any case it were ourselves, or our fathers, that repelled with spirit hostilities brought against us by barbarian or Greek; as I do not wish to enlarge on the subject before you who are well acquainted with it, I will pass them over. But by what a mode of life we attained to our power, and by what form of government and owing to what habits it became so great, I will explain these points first, and then proceed to the eulogy of these men; as I consider that on the present occasion they will not be inappropriately mentioned, and that it is profitable for the whole assembly, both citizens and strangers, to listen to them.

"For we enjoy a form of government which does not copy the laws of our neighbors; but we are ourselves rather a pattern to others than imitators of them. In name, from its not being administered for the benefit of the few, but of the many, it is called a democracy; but with regard to its laws, all enjoy equality, as concerns their private differences; while with regard to public rank, according as each man has reputation for anything, he is preferred for public honors, not so much from consideration of party, as of merit; nor, again, on the ground of poverty, while he is able to do the state any good service, is he prevented by the obscurity of his position. We are liberal then in our public administration; and with regard to mutual jealousy of our daily pursuits, we are not angry with our neighbor, if he does anything to please himself; nor wear on our countenance offensive looks, which though harmless, are yet unpleasant. While, however, in private matters we live together agreeably, in public matters, under the influence of fear, we most carefully abstain from transgression, through our obedience to those who are from time to time in office, and to the laws; especially such of them as are enacted for the benefit of the injured, and such as, though unwritten, bring acknowledged disgrace [on those who break them].

"Moreover, we have provided for our spirits the most numerous recreations from labors, by celebrating games and sacrifices through the whole year, and by maintaining elegant private establishments, of which the daily gratification drives away sadness. Owing to the greatness too of our city, every thing from every land is imported into it; and it is our lot to reap with no more peculiar enjoyment the good things which are produced here, than those of the rest of the world likewise.

"In the studies of war also we differ from our enemies in the following respects. We throw our city open to all, and never, by the expulsion of strangers, exclude anyone from either learning or observing things, by seeing which unconcealed any of our enemies might gain an advantage; for we trust not so much to preparations and stratagems, as to our own valor for daring deeds. Again, as to our modes of education *they* aim at the acquisition of a manly character, by laborious training from their very youth; while *we*, though living at our ease, no less boldly advance to meet equal dangers. As a proof of this, the Lacedaemonians never march against our country singly, but with all [their confederates] together: while we, generally speaking, have no difficulty in conquering in battle upon hostile ground those who are standing up in defense of their own. And no enemy ever yet encountered our whole united force, through our attending at the same time to our navy, and sending our troops by land on so many different services: but wherever they have engaged with any part of it, if they conquer only some of us, they boast that we were all routed by them; and if they are conquered, they say it was by all that they were beaten. And yet if with careless ease rather than with laborious practice, and with a courage which is the result not so much of laws as of natural disposition, we are willing to face danger, we have the advantage of not suffering beforehand from coming troubles, and of proving ourselves, when we are involved in them, no less bold than those who are always toiling; so that our country is worthy of admiration in these respects, and in others besides.

"For we study taste with economy, and philosophy without effeminacy; and employ wealth rather for opportunity of action than for boastfulness of talking; while poverty is nothing disgraceful for a man to confess, but not to escape it by exertion is more disgraceful. Again, the same men can attend at the same time to domestic as well as to public affairs; and others, who are engaged with business, can still form a sufficient judgment on political questions. For we are the only people that consider the man who takes no part in these things, not as unofficious, but as useless; and we ourselves judge rightly of measures, at any rate, if we do not originate them; while we do not regard words as any hindrance to deeds, but rather [consider it a hindrance] not to have been previously instructed by word, before undertaking in deed what we have to do. For we have this characteristic also in a remarkable degree, that we are at the same time most daring and most calculating in what we take in hand; whereas to other men it is ignorance that brings daring, while calculation brings fear. Those, however, would deservedly be deemed most courageous, who know most fully what is terrible and what is pleasant, and yet do not on this account shrink from dangers. As regards beneficence also we differ from the generality of men; for we make friends, not by receiving, but by conferring kindness. Now he who has conferred the favor is the firmer friend, in order that he may keep alive the obligation by good will toward the man on whom he has conferred it; whereas he who owes it in return feels less keenly, knowing that it is not as a favor, but as a debt, that he will repay the kindness. Nay, we are the only men who fearlessly benefit anyone, not so much from calculations of expediency, as with the confidence of liberality.

"In short, I say that both the whole city is a school for Greece, and that, in my opinion, the same individual would amongst us prove himself qualified for the most varied kinds of action, and with the most graceful versatility. And that this is not mere vaunting language for the occasion, so much as actual truth, the very power of the state, which we have won by such habits, affords a proof. For it is the only country at the present time that, when brought to the test, proves superior to its fame; and the only one that neither gives to the enemy who has attacked us any cause for indignation at being worsted by such opponents, nor to him who is subject to us room for finding fault, as not being ruled by men who are worthy of empire. But we shall be admired both by present and future generations as having exhibited our power with great proofs, and by no means without evidence; and as having no further need, either of Homer to praise us, or anyone else who might charm for the moment by his verses, while the truth of the facts would mar the idea formed of them; but as having compelled every sea and land to become accessible to our daring, and everywhere established everlasting records, whether of evil or of good. It was for such a country then that these men, nobly resolving not to have it taken from them, fell fighting; and every one of their survivors may well be willing to suffer in its behalf.

"For this reason, indeed, it is that I have enlarged on the characteristics of the state; both to prove that the struggle is not for the same object in our case as in that of men who have none of these advantages in an equal degree; and at the same time clearly to establish by proofs [the truth of] the eulogy of those men over whom I am now speaking. And now the chief points of it have been mentioned; for with regard to the things for which I have commended the city, it was the virtues of these men, and such as these, that adorned her with them; and few of the Greeks are there whose fame, like these men's, would appear but the just counterpoise of their deeds. Again, the closing scene of these men appears to me to supply an illustration of human worth, whether as affording us the first information respecting it, or its final confirmation. For even in the case of men who have been in other respects of an inferior character, it is but fair for them to hold forth as a screen their military courage in their country's behalf; for, having wiped out their evil by their good, they did more service collectively, than harm by their individual offenses. But of these men there was none that either was made a coward by his wealth, from preferring the continued enjoyment of it; or shrank from danger through a hope suggested by poverty, namely, that he might yet escape it, and grow rich; but conceiving that vengeance on their foes was more to be desired than these objects, and at the same time regarding this as the most glorious of hazards, they wished by risking it to be avenged on their enemies, and so to aim at procuring those advantages; committing to hope the uncertainty of success, but resolving to trust to action, with regard to what was visible to themselves; and in that action, being minded rather to resist and die, than by surrendering to escape, they fled from the shame of [a discreditable] report, while they endured the brunt of the battle with their bod-

ies; and after the shortest crisis, when at the very height of their fortune, were taken away from their glory rather than their fear.

"Such did these men prove themselves, as became the character of their country. For you that remain, you must pray that you
may have a more successful resolution, but must determine not to
have one less bold against your enemies; not in word alone considering the benefit [of such a spirit], (on which one might descant to
you at great length—though you know it yourselves quite as well—
telling you how many advantages are contained in repelling your
foes;) but rather day by day beholding the power of the city as it
appears in fact, and growing enamored of it, and reflecting, when
you think it great, that it was by being bold, and knowing their duty,
and being alive to shame in action, that men acquired these things;
and because, if they ever failed in their attempt at any thing, they
did not on that account think it right to deprive their country also
of their valor, but conferred upon her a most glorious joint-offer-
ing. For while collectively they gave her their lives, individually they
received that renown which never grows old, and the most distinguished tomb they could have; not so much that in which they are
laid, as that in which their glory is left behind them, to be everlastingly recorded on every occasion for doing so, either by word or
deed, that may from time to time present itself. For of illustrious
men the whole earth is the sepulcher; and not only does the
inscription upon columns in their own land point it out, but in that
also which is not their own there dwells with everyone an unwritten
memorial of the heart, rather than of a material monument. Vieing
then with these men in your turn, and deeming happiness to consist in freedom, and freedom in valor, do not think lightly of the
hazards of war. For it is not the unfortunate, [and those] who have
no hope of any good, that would with most reason be unsparing of
their lives; but those who, while they live, still incur the risk of a
change to the opposite condition, and to whom the difference
would be the greatest, should they meet with any reverse. For more
grievous, to a man of high spirit at least, is the misery which accom-
panies cowardice, than the unfelt death which comes upon him at
once, in the time of this strength and of his hope for the common
welfare.

"Wherefore to the parents of the dead—as many of them as
are here among you—I will not offer condolence, so much as consolation. For they know that they have been brought up subject to
manifold misfortunes; but that happy is *their* lot who have gained

the most glorious—death, as these have—sorrow, as you have; and to whom life has been so exactly measured, that they were both happy in it, and died in [that happiness]. Difficult, indeed, I know it is to persuade you of this, with regard to those of whom you will often be reminded by the good fortune of others, in which you yourselves also once rejoiced; and sorrow is felt, not for the blessings of which one is bereft without full experience of them, but of that which one loses after becoming accustomed to it. But you must bear up in the hope of other children, those of you whose age yet allows you to have them. For to yourselves individually those who are subsequently born will be a reason for your forgetting those who are no more; and to the state it will be beneficial in two ways, by its not being depopulated, and by the enjoyment of security; for it is not possible that those should offer any fair and just advice, who do not incur equal risk with their neighbors by having children at stake. Those of you, however, who are past that age, must consider that the longer period of your life during which you have been prosperous is so much gain, and that what remains will be but a short one; and you must cheer yourselves with the fair fame of these [your lost ones]. For the love of honor is the only feeling that never grows old; and in the helplessness of age it is not the acquisition of gain, as some assert, that gives greatest pleasure, but the enjoyment of honor.

"For those of you, on the other hand, who are sons or brothers of the dead, great, I see, will be the struggle of competition. For every one is accustomed to praise the man who is no more; and scarcely, though even for an excess of worth, would you be esteemed, I do not say equal to them, but only slightly inferior. For the living are exposed to envy in their rivalry; but those who are in no one's way are honored with a goodwill free from all opposition. If, again, I must say anything on the subject of woman's excellence also, with reference to those of you who will now be in widowhood, I will express it all in a brief exhortation. Great will be your glory in not falling short of the natural character that belongs to you; and great is hers, who is least talked of amongst the men, either for good or evil.

"I have now expressed *in word*, as the law required, what I had to say befitting the occasion; and, *in deed* those who are here interred, have already received part of their honors; while, for the remaining part, the state will bring up their sons at the public expense, from this time to their manhood; thus offering both to these and to their posterity a beneficial reward for such contests;

for where the greatest prizes for virtue are given, there also the most virtuous men are found amongst the citizens. And now, having finished your lamentations for your several relatives, depart."

Thucydides' assessment of Pericles:

For as long as Pericles was at the head of the state in time of peace, he governed it with moderation, and kept it in safety, and it was at its height of greatness in his time: and when the war broke out, he appears to have foreknown its power in this respect also. He survived its commencement two years and six months; and when he was dead, his foresight with regard to its course was appreciated to a still greater degree. For he said that if they kept quiet, and attended to their navy, and did not gain additional dominion during the war, nor expose the city to hazard, they would have the advantage in the struggle. But they did the very contrary of all this, and in other things which seemed to have nothing to do with the war, through their private ambition and private gain, they adopted evil measures both toward themselves and their allies; which, if successful, conduced to the honor and benefit of individuals; but if they failed, proved detrimental to the state with regard to the war. And the reason was, that he, being powerful by means of his high rank and talents, and manifestly proof against bribery, controlled the multitude with an independent spirit, and was not led by them so much as he himself led them; for he did not say anything to humor them, for the acquisition of power by improper means; but was able on the strength of his character to contradict them even at the risk of their displeasure. Whenever, for instance, he perceived them unseasonably and insolently confident, by his language he would dash them down to alarm; and, on the other hand, when they were unreasonably alarmed, he would raise them again to confidence. And so, though in name it was a democracy, in fact it was a government administered by the first man. Whereas those who came after, being more on a level with each other, and each grasping to become first, had recourse to devoting [not only their speeches, but] even their *measures*, to the humors of the people. In consequence of this both many other blunders were committed, as was likely in a great and sovereign state, and especially the expedition to Sicily; which was not so much an error of judgment with respect to the people they went against, as that those who had sent them out, by not afterward voting supplies required by the armament, but proceeding with their private criminations, to gain the leadership of the commons, both blunted the spirit of measures in the camp, and for the first time were embroiled with one another in the affairs of the city. But even when they had suffered in Sicily the loss of other forces, and of the greater part of their fleet, and were now involved in sedition at home, they nevertheless held out three years, both against their former enemies, and those from Sicily with them, and moreover against the greater part of their allies who had revolted, and Cyrus, the king's son, who afterward joined them, and who supplied the Peloponnesians with money for their fleet: nor did they succumb, before they were overthrown and ruined by themselves, through their private quarrels. Such a super-abundance of means had Pericles at that time, by which he himself foresaw that with the greatest ease he could gain the advantage in the war over the Peloponnesians by themselves.

The Wolves to the Sheep Dogs: Give Peace a Chance

Aesop

The Wolves thus addressed the Sheep-dogs: "Why should you, who are like us in so many things, not be entirely of one mind with us, and live with us as brothers should? We differ from you in one point only. We live in freedom, but you bow down to, and slave for, men; who, in return for your services, flog you with whips, and put collars on your necks. They make you also guard their sheep, and while they eat the mutton throw only the bones to you. If you will be persuaded by us, you will give us the sheep, and we will enjoy them in common, till we all are surfeited." The Dogs listened favorably to these proposals, and, entering the den of the Wolves, they were set upon and torn to pieces.

6

THE NOBLE MAN

"LET A MAN NOBLY LIVE OR NOBLY DIE," WROTE THE TRAGIC POET Sophocles in the fifth century B.C. But what is nobility? It is an elusive concept, although many writers, artists, and thinkers have tried, in varying and often sublimely beautiful ways, to express it or give it form. "Virtue is the only true nobility," one eighteenth-century essayist advised, and should never be confused with mere conventional social status. Nobility is not a function of birth or inherited privilege, but of character and ability. "There is a natural aristocracy among men," Thomas Jefferson wrote. "The grounds of this are virtue and talents." The Victorians raised their contemplation of nobility to a high art: Alfred, Lord Tennyson wrote that it is "better not to be at all than not be noble," while the Romantic poet William Wordsworth contended that "there is one great society alone on earth, the noble Living and the noble Dead."

Nobility is often praised in war and combat, especially when the situation is dangerous or perhaps even hopeless. "What's brave, what's noble," Shakespeare has Cleopatra say after Mark Antony kills himself and she prepares to take her own life. "Let's do it after the high Roman fashion, and make death proud to take us." An ability to bear up with dignity and fortitude under the blows of fortune, whether delivered in the guise of war, natural disaster, disease, or betrayal, is one of the keys to a noble character. But nobility is just as often ascribed to qualities of mind, to large and inspiring thoughts, to subtle, capacious, and bold-minded insights into life and human nature. "What is poetry?" asks the Victorian art historian and critic John Ruskin. "The suggestion, by the imagination, of noble grounds for noble emotions." Sir Arthur Conan Doyle once observed that "of all ruins, that of a noble mind is the most deplorable."

Nobility is often associated, as well, with a virtuous character. Indeed, for some writers, nobility is the basis for all the moral virtues. Solon, the great law giver of ancient Athens, advises us to "put trust in nobility of character" rather than in the swearing of oaths. According to Cicero, "The nobler a man, the harder it is for

him to suspect inferiority in others." As with gentlemanliness, true
nobility has less to do with class origins than character: In the
words of an old English proverb, "The more noble, the more humble." A noble man will not allow himself or others to be treated like
slaves. Indeed, as Edmund Burke remarks, a truly noble nature
prefers the respect of free citizens to domination over those who
are debased: "He is noble who has priority among free men, not he
who has a sort of wild liberty among slaves." And, of course, nobility is associated with a disdain for shameful, cowardly, deceitful, or
manipulative acts—habits unworthy of a manly and honorable
character. According to many traditional authorities, it is sometimes better to be prepared for death than to go on living in a
degraded or humiliating condition—especially if the price of staying alive is to commit some act of betrayal or treachery against
another. For the most part, unfortunately, argues the Roman
philosopher Seneca, "Men do not care how nobly they live, but
only how long, although it is within the reach of every man to live
nobly, but within no man's power to live long." Since we all have to
die eventually, why not concentrate on living with dignity and
decency for whatever time is allotted to us?

The readings in this section concentrate on several important
dimensions of what it means to be a noble man—valor, integrity,
and honor. Valor in war is not a topic much in fashion today. It is
sometimes implied that even to discuss the possibility that certain
admirable human qualities might arise in situations of combat is
somehow indecent, if not a promotion of war-mongering and violence. But, as readers will discover in this section, few thoughtful
observers of combat have ever praised it unequivocally, or been
blind to the corrupting influence that the savagery of war can have
on a young man's heart and soul. Indeed, what makes these stories
and reflections about military valor so compelling is their sensitivity to war's power either to ennoble or to debase the human character, sometimes in the same man. In the end, however, there is something enduringly inspiring about the idea of being willing to die for
one's country, or for a just cause, whether it be Thermopylae, the
Battle of the Bulge, or struggling to abolish slavery and discrimination. It is worth recalling that the larger meaning of valor is sometimes described as moral courage. Sometimes the bravest men are
not those who are courageous in battle, but those who are steadfast
in the defense of goodness, in aiding the oppressed and helpless,
or—perhaps the hardest battle of all—triumphing over their own
worst impulses.

The ancient Greek word for "noble" was also used to mean "beautiful" or "fine," especially when applied to the soul and its virtues, and this inner beauty of character, feeling, and temper is surely what we are sensing when a man's conduct strikes us as noble. Nobility is an ideal that comprises nearly everything that is most admirable in a man. It includes the virtues of honor, justice, compassion, generosity, and honesty. But to these other virtues, nobility adds something more: a level of extraordinary, even sublime self-sacrifice and steadfastness in the face of peril or oppression, rising at times to almost superhuman heights. A man can be just by refraining from hurting others, obeying the law, and fulfilling his everyday responsibilities as a citizen, friend, or spouse—but nobility is rare. The noble man possesses what the Romans called *integritas*. Integrity is, as the word suggests, an integration of the virtues within a temperament of fortitude, compassion, and patience, and an ability to *remain oneself,* however severely tested by battle, persecution, sickness, bereavement, disappointment and the other challenges to which man must constantly rise.

THE MAN OF VALOR

A Fair Fight

From Thomas Bulfinch, Bulfinch's Mythology

Ten against one isn't fair. Sir Tristram confronts a gang of bullies and deals with a problem of mistaken identity.

Sir Tristram rode through a forest, and saw ten men fighting, and one man did battle against nine. So he rode to the knights and cried to them, bidding them cease their battle, for they did themselves great shame, so many knights to fight against one. Then answered the master of the knights (his name was Sir Breuse without Pity, who was at that time the most villainous knight living): "Sir knight, what have you to do to meddle with us? If you be wise,

depart on your way as you came, for this knight shall not escape."
"It would be a pity," said Sir Tristram, "if so good a knight should be
slain so cowardly; therefore I warn you I will help him with all my
strength."

Then Sir Tristram alighted off his horse, because they were on
foot, that they should not slay his horse. And he smote on the right
hand and on the left so vigorously, that well-nigh at every stroke he
struck down a knight. At last they fled, with Breuse without Pity,
into the tower, and shut Sir Tristram without the gate. Then Sir
Tristram returned back to the rescued knight, and found him sitting under a tree, sore wounded. "Fair knight," said he, "how is it
with you?" "Sir knight," said Sir Palamedes, for he it was, "I thank
you for your great goodness, for ye have rescued me from death."
"What is your name?" said Sir Tristram. He said, "My name is Sir
Palamedes." "Say you so?" said Sir Tristram; "now know that thou
art the man in the world that I most hate; therefore make thee
ready, for I will do battle with thee." "What is your name?" said Sir
Palamedes. "My name is Sir Tristram, your mortal enemy." "It may
be so," said Sir Palamedes; "but you have done overmuch for me
this day, that I should fight with you. Moreover, it will be no honor
for you to have to do with me, for you are fresh and I am wounded.
Therefore, if you must fight me, assign me a day, and I shall meet
you without fail." "You say well," said Sir Tristram; "now I assign you
to meet me in the meadow by the river of Camelot, where Merlin
set the monument." So they were agreed. Then they departed, and
took different ways. Sir Tristram passed through a great forest into
a plain, till he came to a priory, and there he rested with a good
man for six days.

Then Sir Tristram departed, and rode straight into Camelot to
the monument of Merlin, and there he looked about him for Sir
Palamedes. And he perceived a seemly knight, who came riding
against him all in white, with a covered shield. When he came nigh,
Sir Tristram said aloud, "Welcome, sir knight, and well and truly
have you kept your promise." Then they made ready their shields
and spears, and came together with all the might of their horses, so
fiercely, that both the horses and the knights fell to the earth. And
as soon as they might, they quitted their horses, and struck together with bright swords as men of might, and each wounded the
other wonderfully sore, so that the blood ran out upon the grass.
Thus they fought for the space of four hours, and never one would
speak to the other one word. Then at last the white knight spoke,
and said, "Sir, you fight wonderful well, as ever I saw a knight;

therefore if it please you, tell me your name." "Why do you ask my name?" said Sir Tristram; "are you not Sir Palamedes?" "No, fair knight," said he, "I am Sir Launcelot of the Lake." "Alas!" said Sir Tristram, "what have I done? For you are the man of the world that I love best." "Fair knight," said Sir Launcelot, "tell me your name." "Truly," said he, "my name is Sir Tristram de Lyonesse." "Alas! alas!" said Sir Launcelot, "what adventure has befallen me!" And therewith Sir Launcelot kneeled down, and yielded him up his sword; and Sir Tristram kneeled down, and yielded him up his sword; and so either gave other the degree. And then they both went to the stone, and sat them down upon it, and took off their helms, and each kissed the other a hundred times. And then anon they rode toward Camelot, and on the way they met with Sir Gawain and Sir Gaheris, that had promised Arthur never to come again to the court till they had brought Sir Tristram with them.

The Virtues of the Soldier

From Charles de Gaulle, The Edge of the Sword

Can we imagine life without force? No, de Gaulle argues, not only because human nature cannot change, but because ambition and passion are as necessary to noble projects as to base ones. The "virtues of the soldier are an integral part of man's inheritance." A great commander combines intelligence with instinct. War brings out men's basest instincts, but also their finest virtues. While war often serves greed and tyranny, it can also defend the oppressed and spread the ideals of civilization and religion.

Hope though we may, what reason have we for thinking that passion and self-interest, the root cause of armed conflict in men and in nations, will cease to operate; that anyone will willingly surrender what he has or not try to get what he wants; in short, that human nature will ever become something other than it is? Is it really likely that the present balance of power will remain unchanged so long as the small want to become great, the strong to dominate the weak, the old to live on? How are frontiers to be stabilized, how is power to be controlled if evolution continues along the same lines as hitherto? Even supposing that nations should agree, for a time, to conduct their mutual relations in accordance with a sovereign code, how effective could such a code be even if enforced? "Laws unsupported by force soon fall into contempt," said Cardinal de Retz. International agreements will be of little value unless there are troops to prevent their infringement. In whatever direction the world may move, it will never be able to do without the final arbitrament of arms.

Is it possible to conceive of life without force? Only if children cease to be born, only if minds are sterilized, feelings frozen, men's needs anaesthetized, only if the world is reduced to immobility, can it be banished. Otherwise, in some form or another, it will remain indispensable, for, without it, thought would have no driving power, action no strength. It is the prerequisite of movement and the midwife of progress. Whether as the bulwark of authority, the defender of thrones, the motive power of revolution, we owe to it, turn and turn about, both order and liberty. Force has watched over civilization in the cradle; force has ruled empires, and dug the grave of decadence; force gives laws to the peoples and controls their destinies.

It is true to say that the fighting spirit, the art of war, the virtues of the soldier are an integral part of man's inheritance. They have been part and parcel of history in all its phases, the medium through which it has expressed itself. How can we understand Greece without Salamis, Rome without the legions, Christianity without the sword, Islam without the scimitar, our own Revolution without Valmy, the League of Nations without the victory of France? The self-sacrifice of individuals for the sake of the community, suffering made glorious—those two things which are the basic elements of the profession of arms—respond to both our moral and aesthetic concepts. The noblest teachings of philosophy and religion have found no higher ideals.

Should, then, those who control the accumulated strength of France fall into discouragement, the result would be not only peril for the country but a complete rupture of civilization. Into what mad or irresponsible hands might force not fall if its control were relinquished by a wise and highly trained directorate? The time has come for a military elite once more to become conscious of the preeminent role it has to play, and to concentrate anew upon its one and only duty, which is to prepare itself for war. It must lift its head again and fix its eyes upon the heights. Only if the philosophy proper to the soldier is restored will an edge be given to the sword. In that philosophy he will find nobility of outlook, pride in his vocation, and a chance to influence the world outside himself. In it, till the day of glory dawns, he will find the sole reward worth considering.

Great war leaders have always been aware of the importance of instinct. Was not what Alexander called his "hope," Caesar his "luck," and Napoleon his "star" simply the fact that they knew they had a particular gift of making contact with realities sufficiently closely to dominate them? For those who are greatly gifted, this faculty often shines through their personalities. There may be nothing in itself exceptional about what they say or their way of saying it, but other men in their presence have the impression of a natural force destined to master events. Flaubert expresses this feeling when he describes the still adolescent Hannibal as already clothed "in the undefinable splendor of those who are destined for great enterprises."

However, while no work or action can be conceived without the promptings of instinct, these promptings are not sufficient to give the conception a precise form. The very fact that they are "gifts of nature" means that they are simple, crude, and sometimes confused. Now, a leader commands a unit, that is to say a system of complex forces with its own properties and disciplines, which can develop its power only by following a certain pattern. It is here that the intelligence comes into its own. Taking possession of the raw material of instinct, it elaborates it, gives it a specific shape, and makes of it a clearly defined and coherent whole. This done, a due application of method, by establishing the different values of this whole in their order of importance, and by apportioning to its various parts the execution of the plan in time and in space, by linking the different operations, and the phases of those operations, in such a way that they shall be carried out concurrently, will put into the hands of the commander an effective and well-tempered tool. It is essential that some such method, whether good or bad, be employed if the action is not to result in confusion. A bad method is better than no method at all.

If a commander is to grasp the essentials and reject the inessentials; if he is to split his general operation into a number of complementary actions in such a way that all shall combine to achieve the purpose common to every one of them, he must be able to see the situation as a whole, attribute to each object its relative importance, grasp the connections between each factor in the situation, and recognize its limits. All this implies a gift of synthesis which, in itself, demands a high degree of intellectual capacity. The general who has to free the essentials of his problem from the confused mass of their attendant details resembles the user of a stereo-scope who has to concentrate his eyes upon the image before he can see it in relief. That is why great men of action have always been of the meditative type. They have, without exception, possessed to a very high degree the faculty of withdrawing into themselves. As Napoleon said: "The military leader must be capable of giving intense, extended, and indefatigable consideration to a single group of objects."

If the conceiving of an action is to be valid, which means adapted to the circumstances of the case, it calls for a combined effort of intelligence and instinct. Critics of action in warfare, have, however, rarely been willing to admit that these two faculties have each a necessary part to play though no one of them is able to do without the other.

A spirit of enterprise in a commander is never a danger in itself.

It is, on the contrary, an essential element in leadership. A commander has to work, not with a piece of clockwork which "goes" when it is wound up, but with "tool-using men." These men are afraid of death, and suffer from hunger, thirst, lack of sleep, and bad weather. Some are brave, some are not. Some are slow in the uptake, others mentally alert. Some are trusting and loyal, others jealous and insubordinate. In short, they carry within themselves a thousand and one seeds of diversity. To make them act as one it is not enough for a commander to decide in his own mind what should be done, nor even limit himself to issuing orders for the carrying out of his intentions. He must be able to create a spirit of confidence in those under him. He must be able to assert his authority.

This necessary attribute is assisted by a permanent element in all armies, discipline. This is the product of human experience and is independent of the character of this or that individual commander. Force of circumstance, legal enactments, and habit impose it, more or less firmly, on every soldier as such, though its form may differ in different countries, and is shaped by the conditions and moral climate of the times. It is the basic constituent of all armies. By virtue of discipline something resembling a contract comes into being between the leader and his subordinates. It is an understood thing that the latter owe obedience to the former, and that each single component of an organized body must, to the best of his ability, carry out the orders transmitted to him by a higher authority. In this way, a fundamental attitude of goodwill is created which guarantees a minimum degree of cohesion. But it is not enough for a chief to bind his men into a whole through the medium of impersonal obedience. It is on their inner selves that he must leave the imprint of his personality. If he is to have a genuine and effective hold on his men, he must know how to make their wills part and parcel of his own, and so to inspire them that they will look upon the task assigned to them as something of their own choosing. He must increase and multiply the effects of mere discipline and implant in those under him a sort of moral suggestion which goes far beyond all reasoning, and crystallizes round his own person all their potentialities of faith, hope, and devotion.

And so it is that intelligence, instinct, and the leader's authority combine to make the conduct of war what it is. But what are these faculties if not the expression of a powerful and resourceful personality? Other things being equal, it is safe to say that the value of the fighting man is in exact proportion to the value, in terms of personality of those under whose command he serves. Training for war is, first and foremost, training in leadership, and it is literally true, for armies as well as for nations, that where the leadership is good, the rest shall be added unto them.

This selective process, of which everyone approves in principle, comes up, in practice, against many difficulties.

In the first place it is more than usually difficult to attract men of outstanding ability into the army in prolonged periods of peace. What, fundamentally, tempts such men to adopt the profession of arms, is the prospect of power. There can be little doubt that no power is comparable to that of the war leader. So long, therefore, as the probability exists of someday being able to win distinction in the field, men of high quality and distinction will never be lacking worthily to fill the higher posts in the fighting services of countries with a strong military tradition. But a generation which is convinced that it will never again be called upon to fight is unlikely to contain many individuals of first-class quality who will feel any inclination to become regular soldiers, the more so since in a pacifist period soldiers are considered of small use and have little to look forward to in terms either of reputation or money. The strong-minded, therefore, the enterprising, and those of marked personality, are not unnaturally inclined to embark on careers which will give them power and the consideration of their fellows.

Once men, who are capable of leadership, have been absorbed into the army, it is necessary to choose the best from among them, and so to arrange matters that they shall occupy the highest posts.

No task could well be more difficult, for though, time and peace permitting, it is not impossible to judge of the intelligence, and even of the authority, of those in positions of command, there is no opportunity to find out to what extent they possess the true instincts of the fighter. No doubt maneuvers and field exercises provide useful training in appreciation and in reaching quick decisions, but only in an academic and conventional fashion. Such training is fed on theories rather than on facts, for the facts of war cannot be convincingly simulated in a field day's mimic combat. It lacks the great test—that of events—and, more often than not, makes it impossible to distinguish real aptitude from superficial cleverness. It follows that more value is attached to a candidate's ability to learn than to his possible possession of the creative instinct; the art of grasping the immediate features of a situation more than the power to see its essentials; flexibility of mind more than genuine understanding. As Scharnhorst said: "Most which have been trained mechanically triumph in peacetime over those possessing true insight and genius." Furthermore, powerful personalities equipped with the qualities needed in the fighting soldier, and capable of standing up to the tests of great events, frequently lack that surface charm which wins popularity in ordinary life. Strong characters are, as a rule, rough, disagreeable, and aggressive. The man in the street may, somewhat shyly, admit their superiority and pay them lip service, but they are not often liked and, therefore, seldom favored. When it comes to choosing men for high positions, the lot usually falls on the pleasing and docile rather than the meritorious.

The times through which we are living are ill-suited to the choice and formation of military leaders. The very intensity of our recent ordeal has had the effect of letting the spring of determination run down too quickly. There has been a lowering of pressure where strong character is concerned, and we are now in a period of moral lassitude which has brought the profession of arms into disrepute, so that even those whose vocation is strong and determined are afflicted with doubts. What soldier has not been tempted to apply to himself the words once uttered by a famous woman: "Why am I here? I do not know! All the hopes of the century have already been devoured. . . . " In these skeptical days, the chain of French military strength must not be allowed to sag, nor the ardor and high quality of those born to command, to weaken.

War stirs in men's hearts the mud of their worst instincts. It puts a premium on violence, nourishes hatred, and gives free rein to cupidity. It crushes the weak, exalts the unworthy, bolsters tyranny. Because of its blind fury many of the noblest schemes have come to nothing and the most generous instincts have more than once been checked. Time and time again it has destroyed all ordered living, devastated hope, and put the prophets to death. But, though Lucifer has used it for his purposes, so, sometimes, has the Archangel. With what virtues has it not enriched the moral capital of mankind! Because of it, courage, devotion, and nobility have scaled the peaks. It has conferred greatness of spirit on the poor, brought pardon to the guilty, revealed the possibilities of self-sacrifice to the commonplace, restored honor to the rogue, and given dignity to the slave. It has carried ideas in the baggage wagons of its armies, and reforms in the knapsacks of its soldiers. It has blazed a trail for religion and spread across the world influences which have brought renewal to mankind, consoled it, and made it better. Had not innumerable soldiers shed their blood there would have been no Hellenism, no Roman civilization, no Christianity, no Rights of Man, and no modern developments.

Not One Step Back Unless Ordered! The Battle of Stalingrad

From M. S. Shumilov, Colonel-General,
Hero of the Soviet Union
Two Hundred Days of Fire

The Battle of Stalingrad took a ghastly toll in lives, but it was the beginning of the end for the German invasion of Russia in World War II. This account by a participant is vivid, despite the occasional undertone of propaganda.

Supported by artillery and mortars, the enemy deployed over one infantry company against a dozen marines. Potapov was wounded, but he stayed on the battlefield to direct the fire. With every new attack the Marines' strength dwindled. Only two were left to repulse the fourth attack. When the German fire subsided, the wounded Potapov crawled up unnoticed to an enemy machine-

gun nest and pelted it with grenades. Here again he was hit by a
German bullet. After eight hours of bitter fighting, during which
70 Germans were killed, two Marines withdrew to the Don carrying
their wounded fellows on their shoulders. These men could be
counted on.

We resorted to the help of Marines at the first critical situation. In late July the army's left flank came under the direct threat
of being enveloped by the enemy. A large tank group had broken
through from the Tsimlyanskaya area. The 154th Marine Infantry
Brigade was taken from the Don line to cover the army's left flank,
and successfully discharged its mission.

Fierce fighting in the steppeland persisted day and night. The
army's men were acutely aware of the danger, and stubbornly
defended every inch of ground. The extent of their gallantry can be
judged from enemy casualties. Between July 21 and August 1, 1942,
the Nazis lost over 16,000 killed and wounded. The enemy had been
bled white, but this did not mean he was abandoning his intentions.
On the contrary, his advance became all the more frenzied.

The army's main danger was now Hoth's 4th Panzer Army
which had been withdrawn from the Caucasus area. The Nazi command also mounted its satellites against us. The attack was
launched along the Kotelnikovo-Stalingrad railway. Our predicament was critical. Depleted 51st Army units were defending on our
left.

I decided to form a detached group of troops from the 29th
Infantry Division and the 154th Marine Infantry Brigade. The
group fought bravely and inflicted heavy casualties on the enemy.

The news of the exploit of Captain Muratov, a Battalion Commander of the 706th Regiment (204th Infantry Division which had
just arrived from the Soviet Far East), swept the army that same
August. This man was already getting on in years but an energetic
and brave commander and Communist infinitely devoted to his
country. He was admired in the battalion for his warmth and honest severity. The men knew that at a moment of crisis their commander would not fail them, and his courage confirmed their
belief. Muratov's battalion was positioned in the center of the regiment's battle array. It had been cruelly harried and numbered not
more than 20 effective bayonets. Although small, these forces had
to check an enemy that was pressing hard. In such cases, it is not
enough to be merely willing. You have to have skill to hold your
positions with sparse forces. You have to be prepared to fight to the
last gasp. On the eve of the battle, Muratov had given each soldier

his mission, had checked their combat readiness and manned a heavy mounted machine-gun himself.

The minute the early autumn dawn lightened the horizon, the enemy started raining a hurricane of artillery and mortar fire on the battalion's positions. Then a group of Ju–88 bombers dropped their loads on Muratov's men. Clouds of black smoke drifted along the steppe and under their cover tanks rumbled on at high speeds. These were followed by submachine-gunners who fired as they ran. None of Muratov's men wavered. By holding their posts, they drove the infantry off from the armor with gunfire. Battalion commander brought the German submachine-gunners under round after round of flanking fire, knowing that the tanks would lose their efficacy without their infantry. So it turned out. Attack followed attack, and it became more and more difficult to beat them off. The survivors gathered round their commander. "Maxim" was getting bogged down from unslackened fire and water was gurgling in its jacket. Toward nightfall only two men and the wounded Muratov were left alive in the battalion. His wound was bleeding, but he ran from one entrenchment to the other and fired from a rifle to create the illusion that the line was still alive and there was someone to resist.

Dusk had fallen. Battalion commander wrote the following note on a strip of paper: "Six attacks have been repulsed. Several dozen enemy and officers have been killed. There are two of us left. I am keeping up the fire. Muratov." The man who delivered this dispatch described the details of the fighting to regimental commander. The valiant captain had died in an uneven fight without retiring one step from his line.

"Not a step back unless ordered." This stern formula became organically engrained in the flesh and blood of the men and their commanders and inspired discipline of the highest quality which reached the heights of utter selflessness and, as can be seen from the example of Battalion Commander Muratov, self-sacrifice. "Stand and conquer!" was the iron law of discipline on the battlefield.

Muratov, the Communist, wanted to live. His courageous heart loved life, but his passionate patriotic heart was willing to accept death in battle as the situation demanded. It was our fortune that each one of us despised death enough to conquer this insidious and powerful enemy.

Mass heroism in battle in the Volga region's open expanses was the criterion of good behavior.

In this connection I should like to describe the gallant exploit of the men and commanders of the 126th Infantry Division led by Colonel Vladimir Sorokin until the fateful day of August 29. In those dangerous days it was frequently said: A commander is the father of victory, the soul of iron defense. But we did not associate this truth with any definite person. Today I should have no doubt in associating it with Colonel Sorokin. If a divisional commander possesses calm confidence, courage and resolution to perform his duty to the end, then the whole body of commanders and every soldier feels more sure of his strength and is more willing to sacrifice anything for the sake of fulfilling orders.

I saw Colonel Sorokin in action when on August 6 the Nazis, striving to press through to the Volga, delivered a powerful tank attack at rear organizations of the 126th Division which was defending near Abganerovo. It was then that I noticed how demanding Sorokin was of every commander. With a special kind of scrupulousness he would check the readiness of every defender and fire net organization, took an interest in junction security and fixed the directions for counter-attack. In other words he scrutinized all details, and sometimes would even man a machine-gun in order to locate the fire-sector or any possible dead ground where the enemy could accumulate. All this multiplied the men's strength and their staunchness. When the enemy tried to ram the division's battle formations with armor, he failed. Fear of tanks among the men was conspicuously absent. The commanders and political workers had been able to explain to the infantrymen, and in certain cases show, that a tank was not all-powerful and only fearful to those who did not know its weaknesses. It was important to keep one's head during the first attack and even let tanks pass over one's entrenchment—the artillery would take care of them—and then get on with the business of driving off the infantry. Combat experience had shown that without it the German tankmen would return to their initial positions. The division had been tested in the heat of fire and I had complete faith in its combat potential.

Toward late August we realized that the enemy had brought up fresh forces and would make another attempt to advance on Stalingrad along the railway. It was also clear that our units, fairly battered by days on end of intense fighting, would be unable to hold the outer fortified perimeter. The bulk of the army's forces were therefore withdrawn to a new line by a Front order. This shortening of the front secured our defense. But to retreat when the enemy is preparing to lunge is a risky business. Army Command needed a tough unit to cover the retreat of the army's main forces. The 126th Division was chosen. Realizing what a difficult task I was setting Colonel Sorokin I said:

"We are relying on you. Get us out of trouble!"

"If it comes to it," he said, "we'll stand till the end."

On the night of August 28/29 the army began to withdraw, and at daybreak the first group of Nazi bombers loomed up over the the 126th Division battle formations. They swooped down almost vertically and began softening up the main defense line and the artillery positions. Preparatory bombardment lasted 45 minutes and, the moment the German guns and mortars had quietened, enemy infantry and over 200 tanks drove into the attack. This was how Hoth's army launched its new offensive at Stalingrad. I could distinctly see this sinister scene from my observation post. I was tortured by doubt whether they would hold out. The division was spread out in a thin line over a 12-kilometer-long frontage. Its strength had been drained in previous battles and in fact one could hardly call it a division. Nevertheless, the enemy encountered organized rifle, machine-gun and artillery fire. Despite powerful bombardment, defense survived as the men were securely entrenched; it was as if they had grown into the earth and fused with it. The infantry did not flinch, and the tanks did not pass their positions.

Three hours later the same scene was reenacted. Bombers reappeared, followed by preliminary bombardment and armor. The enemy's fire had become more destructive. This was understandable: our defense had exposed itself, the enemy had spotted many weapon emplacements and was firing at them point-blank. Fifteen tanks swept forward to the division's artillery positions. Gun crews engaged tank crews in desperate duels and both sides suffered losses. Here and there only one or two men remained at their guns. It was then that the regiment's Commissar, Senior Political Leader Akimov, trained his gun point blank and kept firing until an enemy shell silenced it. German submachine-gunners were making desperate attempts to penetrate to their tanks, thereby secure the breach and widen it. But again our infantrymen were up to the mark. They severed the submachine-gunners from their armor and pinned them down. The tank group that had broken through retreated with nothing to show but losses.

I had great difficulty in getting in touch with Sorokin who reported on the serious predicament and heavy casualties among both men and commanders. A regimental commander and several battalion commanders had been killed. I sensed a faint note of alarm in divisional commander's voice but he asked no favors. He had a clear idea of his mission. I ordered him to hold out.

Two hours later the Germans mounted another attack. Sorokin was wounded and divisional Chief of Staff was killed. All regimental commanders had been disabled. Reports got more and more grim, but no help could be given. The retreat of the army's main forces was being covered. Everyone who had come under the full weight of this hammer-like blow realized this. No matter how grueling it was, the division did not waver; it did its job. The remains of the division subsequently withdrew to a new line.

This was the army's most trying day.

Years have passed but that day is still fresh in my mind. We left our observation post knowing that the bulk of the army's forces were clear of the enemy and that any day now they would dig their heels into the city's inner fortified perimeter and confront the enemy in an organized manner. We owed this to the heroic 126th Division whose feat to this day remains unknown in its details. Thousands of heroes must be resurrected from obscurity, and this is the duty of the survivors of that unparalleled battle on August 29, 1942.

The fighting maintained its intensity despite the withdrawal of troops to the inner Stalingrad perimeter. The city itself was now in immediate danger. A special order explained to the army's officers and men that this line was the boundary beyond which the enemy was on no account to pass. The order read:

"There is nowhere to retreat to. The Volga is behind us. Not a step back! A glorious death is preferable to the disgrace of retreat."

The disgrace of retreat . . . We were not going to allow it to repeat itself, and it did not repeat itself! The army restrained another furious thrust when the enemy had felt out the junction with the 62nd Army along Kuporosnaya Gully and pressed through to the Volga. He made many more endeavors to hurl us back beneath the Volga's waves but every attempt failed. We did everything in our power to organize a defense, taking our combat experience into account.

As soon as the army reached the inner defensive perimeter, meetings of commanders, their deputies, Communists and Young Communist League members were held in all units and formations. Leaflets were issued, all permeated with one and the same idea: "We shall build a secure defense and turn the approaches to

Stalingrad into a fortress which the enemy shall not penetrate. Not a step back, stand to the last man!"

We succeeded in building a strong defense capable of withstanding massed aircraft, armor, artillery and mortar attacks. Until the end of the Battle of Stalingrad the army did not relinquish an inch of ground although there were countless attempts by the enemy to break through in various sectors.

Iron staunchness forged in the fire of battles for Stalingrad helped us subsequently to withstand crushing blows in the Kursk Bulge, while contending the Dnieper bridgeheads, and to repulse German counter-attacks in all subsequent operations.

The Stalingrads, as we dubbed the veterans of the battle, were the pride and joy of the Guards units. "Where a Stalingrad stands, the enemy shall not pass!" "Where the Stalingrad strikes, the enemy shall not hold his ground." We had good ground for coining these rules of battle.

There were many villages, towns and European capitals along our army's path from the Volga to Prague. But Stalingrad won a permanent place in the hearts of its defenders as the scene of an unforgettable event in the history of the Great Patriotic war. The further we went from Stalingrad the more we thought about it, returning again and again to memorable battles from which we drew the strength for new engagements.

The soldier-liberator realized that sacred and just battles are fought not for the sake of glory but for the sake of life on earth. Stalingrad had risen out of the ash and shone in our souls like a beacon leading on and on to victory itself.

The Lion in Love

Aesop

A Lion demanded the daughter of a woodcutter in marriage. The Father, unwilling to grant, and yet afraid to refuse his request, hit upon this expedient to rid himself of his importunities. He expressed his willingness to accept him as the suitor of his daughter on one condition; that he should allow him to extract his teeth, and cut off his claws, as his daughter was fearfully afraid of both.

The Lion cheerfully assented to the proposal: when however he next repeated his request, the woodman, no longer afraid, set upon him with his club, and drove him away into the forest.

The Meaning of Courage

From John Fitzgerald Kennedy,
Profiles in Courage

Decorated war hero and future President John Fitzgerald Kennedy sums up the importance of courage for democratic leadership in this book from 1956.

This has been a book about courage and politics. Politics furnished the situations, courage provided the theme. Courage, the universal virtue, is comprehended by us all—but these portraits of courage do not dispel the mysteries of politics.

For not a single one of the men whose stories appear in the preceding pages offers a simple, clear-cut picture of motivation and accomplishment. In each of them complexities, inconsistencies and doubts arise to plague us. However detailed may have been our study of life, each man remains something of an enigma. However clear the effect of his courage, the cause is shadowed by a veil which cannot be torn away. We may confidently state the reasons why—yet something always seems to elude us. We think we hold the answer in our hands—yet somehow it slips through our fingers.

Motivation, as any psychiatrist will tell us, is always difficult to assess. It is particularly difficult to trace in the murky sea of politics. Those who abandoned their state and section for the national interest—men like Daniel Webster and Sam Houston, whose ambitions for higher office could not be hidden—laid themselves open to the charge that they sought only to satisfy their ambition for the Presidency. Those who broke with their party to fight for broader principles—men like John Quincy Adams and Edmund Ross—faced the accusation that they accepted office under one banner and yet deserted it in a moment of crisis for another.

But in the particular events set forth in the preceding chapter, I am persuaded after long study of the record that the national interest, rather than a private or political gain, furnished the basic motivation for the actions of those whose deeds are therein described. This does not mean that many of them did not seek, though rarely with success, to wring advantage out of the difficult course they had adopted. For as politicians—and it is surely no disparagement to term all of them politicians—they were clearly justified in doing so.

Of course, the acts of courage described in this book would be more inspiring and would shine more with the traditional luster of hero-worship if we assumed that each man forgot wholly about himself in his dedication to higher principles. But it may be that President John Adams, surely as disinterested as well as wise a public servant as we ever had, came much nearer to the truth when he wrote in his *Defense of the Constitutions of the United States*: "It is not true, in fact, that any people ever existed who love the public better than themselves."

If this be true, what then caused the statesmen mentioned in the preceding pages to act as they did? It was not because they "loved the public better than themselves." On the contrary it was precisely because they did *love themselves*—because each one's need to maintain his own respect for himself was more important to him than his popularity with others—because his desire to win or maintain a reputation for integrity and courage was stronger than his desire to maintain his office—because his conscience, his personal standard of ethics, his integrity or morality, call it what you will— was stronger than the pressure of public disapproval—because his faith that *his* course was the best one, and would ultimately be vindicated, outweighed his fear of public reprisal.

Although the public good was the indirect beneficiary of his sacrifice, it was not that vague and general concept, but one or a combination of these pressures of self-love that pushed him along the course of action that resulted in the slings and arrows previously described. It is when the politician loves neither the public good nor himself, or when his love for himself is limited and is satisfied by the trappings of office, that the public interest is badly served. And it is when his regard for himself is so high that his own self-respect demands he follow the path of courage and conscience that all benefit. It is then that his belief in the rightness of his own course enables him to say with John C. Calhoun: "I never know what South Carolina thinks of a measure. I never consult her. I act to the best of my judgment and according to my conscience. If she approves, well and good. If she does not and wishes anyone to take my place, I am ready to vacate. We are even."

This is not to say that courageous politicians and the principles for which they speak out are always right. John Quincy Adams,
it is said, should have realized that the embargo would ruin New
England but hardly irritate the British. Daniel Webster, according
to his critics, fruitlessly appeased the slavery forces; Thomas Hart
Benton was an unyielding and pompous egocentric; Sam Houston
was cunning, changeable and unreliable. Edmund Ross, in the eyes
of some, voted to uphold a man who had defied the Constitution
and defied the Congress. Lucius Lamar failed to understand why
the evils of planned inflation are sometimes preferable to the
tragedies of uncontrolled depression. Norris and Taft, it is argued,
were motivated more by blind isolationism than Constitutional
principles.

All of this has been said, and more. Each of us can decide for
himself the merits of the courses for which these men fought.

But is it necessary to decide this question in order to admire
their courage? Must men conscientiously risk their careers only for
principles which hindsight declares to be correct, in order for posterity to honor them for their valor? I think not. Surely in the United States of America, where brother once fought against brother,
we did not judge a man's bravery under fire by examining the banner under which he fought.

I make no claim that all of those who staked their careers to
speak their minds were right. Indeed, it is clear that Webster, Benton and Houston could not all have been right on the Compromise
of 1850, for each of them, in pursuit of the same objective of preserving the Union, held wholly different views on that one omnibus
measure. Lucius Lamar, in refusing to resign his seat when he had
violated the instructions of his Legislature, demonstrated courage
in totally opposite fashion from John Tyler, who ended his career in
the Senate because he believed such instructions binding. Tyler, on
the other hand, despised Adams; and Adams was disgusted with
"the envious temper, the ravenous ambition and the rotten heart of
Daniel Webster." Republicans Norris and Taft could not see eye to
eye; and neither could Democrats Calhoun and Benton.

These men were not all on one side. They were not all right or
all conservatives or all liberals. Some of them may have been representing the actual sentiments of the silent majority of their constituents in opposition to the screams of a vocal minority; but most
of them were not. Some of them may have been actually advancing
the long range interests of their states in opposition to the short-

sighted and narrow prejudices of their constituents; but some of them were not. Some of them may have been pure and generous and kind and noble throughout their careers, in the best traditions of the American hero; but most of them were not. Norris, the unyielding bitter-ender; Adams, the irritating upstart; Webster, the businessmen's beneficiary; Benton, the bombastic bully—of such stuff are our real-life political heroes made.

Some demonstrated courage through their unyielding devotion to absolute principle. Others demonstrated courage through their acceptance of compromise, through their advocacy of conciliation, through their willingness to replace conflict with cooperation. Surely their courage was of equal quality, though of different caliber. For the American system of Government could not function if every man in a position of responsibility approached each problem, as John Quincy Adams did, as a problem in higher mathematics, with but a limited regard for sectional needs and human shortcomings.

Most of them, despite their differences, held much in common—the breath-taking talents of the orator, the brilliance of the scholar, the breadth of the man above party and section, and, above all, a deep-seated belief in themselves, their integrity and the rightness of their cause.

The meaning of courage, like political motivations, is frequently misunderstood. Some enjoy the excitement of its battles but fail to note the implications of its consequences. Some admire its virtues in other men and other times, but fail to comprehend its current potentialities. Perhaps, to make clearer the significance of these stories of political courage, it would be well to say what this book is not.

It is not intended to justify independence for the sake of independence, obstinacy to all compromise or excessively proud and stubborn adherence to one's own personal convictions. It is not intended to suggest that there is, on every issue, one right side and one wrong side, and that all Senators except those who are knaves or fools will find the right side and stick to it. On the contrary, I share the feelings expressed by Prime Minister Melbourne, who when irritated by the criticism of the then youthful historian T. B. Macaulay, remarked that he would like to be as sure of anything as Macaulay seemed to be of everything. And nine years in Congress have taught me the wisdom of Lincoln's words: "There are few things wholly evil or wholly good. Almost everything, especially of

Government policy, is an inseparable compound of the two, so that our best judgment of the preponderance between them is continually demanded."

This book is not intended to suggest that party regularity and party responsibility are necessary evils which should at no time influence our decision. It is not intended to suggest that the local interests of one's state or region have no legitimate right to consideration at any time. On the contrary, the loyalties of every Senator are distributed among his party, his state and section, his country and his conscience. On party issues, his party loyalties are normally controlling. In regional disputes, his regional responsibilities will likely guide his course. It is on national issues, on matters of conscience which challenge party and regional loyalties, that the test of courage is presented.

It may take courage to battle one's President, one's party or the overwhelming sentiment of one's nation; but these do not compare, it seems to me, to the courage required of the Senator defying the angry power of the very constituents who control his future. It is for this reason that I have not included in this work the stories of this nation's most famous "insurgents"—John Randolph, Thaddeus Stevens, Robert La Follette and all the rest—men of courage and integrity, but men whose battles were fought with the knowledge that they enjoyed the support of the voters back home.

Finally, this book is not intended to disparage democratic government and popular rule. The examples of constituent passions unfairly condemning a man of principle are not unanswerable arguments against permitting the widest participation in the electoral process. The stories of men who accomplished good in the face of cruel calumnies from the public are not final proof that we should at all times ignore the feelings of the voters on national issues. For, as Winston Churchill has said, "Democracy is the worst form of government—except all those other forms that have been tried from time to time." We can improve our democratic processes, we can enlighten our understanding of its problems, and we can increase our respect for those men of integrity who find it necessary, from time to time, to act contrary to public opinion. But we cannot solve the problems of legislative independence and responsibility by abolishing or curtailing democracy.

For democracy means much more than popular government and majority rule, much more than a system of political techniques to flatter or deceive powerful blocs of voters. A democracy that has no George Norris to point to—no monument of individual conscience in a sea of popular rule—is not worthy to bear the name. The true democracy, living and growing and inspiring, puts its faith in the people—faith that the people will not simply elect men who will represent their views ably and faithfully, but also elect men who will exercise their conscientious judgment—faith that the people will not condemn those whose devotion to principle leads them to unpopular courses, but will reward courage, respect honor and ultimately recognize right.

These stories are the stories of such a democracy. Indeed, there would be no such stories had this nation not maintained its heritage of free speech and dissent, had it not fostered honest conflicts of opinion, had it not encouraged tolerance for unpopular views. Cynics may point to our inability to provide a happy ending for each chapter. But I am certain that these stories will not be looked upon as warnings to beware of being courageous. For the continued political success of many of those who withstood the pressures of public opinion, and the ultimate vindication of the rest, enables us to maintain our faith in the long-run judgment of the people.

And thus neither the demonstrations of past courage nor the need for future courage are confined to the Senate alone. Not only do the problems of courage and conscience concern every office-holder in our land, however humble or mighty, and to whomever he may be responsible—voters, a legislature, a political machine or a party organization. They concern as well every voter in our land—and they concern those who do not vote, those who take no interest in Government, those who have only disdain for the politician and his profession. They concern everyone who has ever complained about corruption in high places, and everyone who has ever insisted that his representative abide by his wishes. For, in a democracy, every citizen, regardless of his interest in politics, "holds office"; every one of us is in a position of responsibility; and, in the final analysis, the kind of government we get depends upon how we fulfill those responsibilities. We, the people, are the boss, and we will get the kind of political leadership, be it good or bad, that we demand and deserve.

These problems do not even concern politics alone—for the same basic choice of courage or compliance continually faces us all, whether we fear the anger of constituents, friends, a board of directors or our union, whenever we stand against the flow of opinion on strongly contested issues. For without belittling the courage with which men have died, we should not forget those acts of courage with which men—such as the subjects of this book—have *lived*. The courage of life is often a less dramatic spectacle than the courage of a final moment; but it is no less a magnificent mixture of triumph and tragedy. A man does what he must—in spite of personal consequences, in spite of obstacles and dangers and pressures—and that is the basis of all human morality.

To be courageous, these stories make clear, requires no exceptional qualifications, no magic formula, no special combination of time, place and circumstance. It is an opportunity that sooner or later is presented to us all. Politics merely furnishes one arena which imposes special tests of courage. In whatever arena of life one may meet the challenge of courage, whatever may be the sacrifices he faces if he follows his conscience—the loss of his friends, his fortune, his contentment, even the esteem of his fellow men—each man must decide for himself the course he will follow. The stories of past courage can define that ingredient—they can teach, they can offer hope, they can provide inspiration. But they cannot supply courage itself. For this each man must look into his own soul.

A Young Man's First Battle

From Leo Tolstoy, War and Peace

Tolstoy's novel unforgettably portrays the attractions and drawbacks of, on the one hand, a life devoted to martial valor and patriotic service, and, on the other, the more retiring inner life of a family man, husband, and father. In this scene, young Nicholas Rostof experiences the confusion, terror, and joy of his first battle.

The squadron in which Rostof served had barely time to mount their horses, before they found themselves face to face with the enemy. Again, as at the bridge over the Enns, there was no one between the squadron and the line of the enemy, and between them lay that terrible gap of the unknown and the dreadful, like the line that divides the living from the dead. All the men felt conscious of that line, and were occupied by the question whether they should pass beyond it or not, and how they should cross it.

The colonel came galloping along the front; and angrily

replied to the questions of his officers, and like a man who in despair insists on his own way, thundered out some command. No one said anything definite, but something had given the squadron an idea that there was to be a charge. The command to fall in was given, then sabres were drawn with a clash. But as yet no one stirred. The army of the left wing and the infantry and the hussars felt that their leaders did not know what to do, and the indecision of the commanders communicated itself to the soldiers.

"If they would only hurry, hurry," thought Rostof, feeling that at last the time was at hand for participating in the intoxication of a charge of which he had heard so much from his comrades, the hussars.

"Forward, with God, children," rang out Denisof's voice, "at a trot!"

In the front rank, the haunches of the horses began to rise and fall. Grachik began to pull on the reins, and dashed ahead. At the right, Rostof could see the forward ranks of his hussars, but farther in front there was a dark streak, which he could not make out distinctly but supposed to be the enemy. Reports were heard, but in the distance.

"Charge!" rang the command, and Rostof felt how his Grachik broke into a gallop and seemed to strain every nerve. He realized that his division was dashing forward and it became more and more exciting to him. He noticed a solitary tree just abreast of him. At first this tree had been in front of him, in the very centre of that line which seemed so terrible. But now he had passed beyond it and there was not only nothing terrible about it, but it seemed ever more and more jolly and lively.

"Oh! how I will slash at them!" thought Rostof, as he grasped the handle of his sabre. "Hurrah-ah-ah-ah!" rang the cheers in the distance. "Now let us be at them if ever," thought Rostof, striking the spurs into Grachik, and overtaking the others, he urged him to the top of his speed. The enemy were already in sight before him. Suddenly, something like an enormous lash cracked all along the squadron. Rostof raised his sabre, in readiness to strike, but just at that instant Nikitenko, a hussar galloping in front of him, swerved aside from him, and Rostof felt, as in a dream, that he was being carried with unnatural swiftness forward, and yet was not moving from the spot. A hussar whom he recognized as Bondarchuk was galloping behind him and looked at him gravely. Bondarchuk's horse shied and he dashed by him.

"What does it mean? Am I not moving? Have I fallen? Am I

dead?" these questions Rostof asked and answered in a breath. He was alone in the middle of the field. In place of the galloping horses and backs of the hussars, he saw all around him the solid earth and stubble. Warm blood was under him. "No, I am wounded and my horse is killed."

Grachik raised himself on his fore legs, but fell back, pinning down his rider's foot. From the horse's head a stream of blood was flowing. The horse struggled but could not rise. Rostof tried to get to his feet, but likewise fell back. His sabre-tasche had caught on the saddle. Where our men were, where the French were, he could not tell. There was no one around him.

Freeing his leg, he got up.

"Where, in which direction, is now that line which so clearly separated the two armies?" he asked himself, and could find no answer. "Has something bad happened to me? Is this the way things take place, and what must be done in such circumstances?" he asked himself again, as he got to his feet; and at this time he began to feel as though something extra were hanging to his benumbed left arm. His wrist seemed to belong to another person. He looked at his hand, but could find no trace of blood on it. "There now, here are our fellows," he exclaimed mentally, with joy, perceiving a few running toward him. "They will help me."

In front of these men ran one in a foreign-looking shako and in a blue capote. He was dark and sunburnt, and had a hooked nose. Two or three others were running at his heels.

One of them said something in a language that was strange and un-Russian. Surrounded by a similar set of men, in the same sort of shakos, stood a Russian hussar. His hands were held; just behind him, they were holding his horse.

"Is our man really taken prisoner? Yes! And will they take me too? Who are these men?" Rostof kept asking himself, not crediting his own eyes. "Can they be the French?"

He gazed at the on-coming strangers, and in spite of the fact that only a second before he had been dashing forward solely for the purpose of overtaking and hacking down these same Frenchmen, their proximity now seemed to him so terrible that he could not trust his own eyes!

"Who are they? Why are they running? Are they running at me? And why? Is it to kill me? *Me*, whom every one loves so?"

He recollected how he was beloved by his mother, his family, his friends, and the purpose of his enemies to kill him seemed incredible.

"But perhaps—they may." For more than ten seconds he stood, not moving from the spot and not realizing his situation.

The foremost Frenchman, with the hooked nose, had now come up so close to him, that he could see the expression on his face. And the heated foreign-looking features of this man, who was coming so swiftly down upon him with fixed bayonet and bated breath, filled Rostof with horror. He grasped his pistol, but instead of discharging it, flung it at the Frenchmen, and fled into the thicket with all his might. He ran not with any of that feeling of doubt and struggle which had possessed him on the bridge at Enns, but rather with the impulse of a hare trying to escape from the dogs. One single fear of losing his happy young life took possession of his whole being. Swiftly gliding among the heather, with all the intensity with which he had ever run when playing tag, he flew across the field, occasionally turning round his pale, kindly young face, while a chill of horror ran down his back.

"No, I'd better not look round," he said to himself, but as he reached the shelter of the bushes, he glanced round once more. The Frenchmen had slackened their pace, and at the very minute that he glanced round, the foremost runner had just come to a stop and was starting to walk back, shouting something in a loud voice to his comrade behind him. Rostof paused. "It cannot be so," he said to himself. "It cannot be that they wish to kill me." But meantime his left arm became as heavy as though a hundredweight were suspended to it. He could not run another step. The Frenchman also paused, and aimed. Rostof shut his eyes and ducked his head. One bullet, then another, flew humming by him. He collected his last remaining energies, took his left arm in his right hand, and hurried into the thicket. Here in the bushes were the Russian rangers.

Make War, Not Love

From William Shakespeare,
All's Well That Ends Well

To th' wars, my boy, to th' wars!
He wears his honor in a box unseen
That hugs his kicky-wicky here at home,
Spending his manly marrow in her arms,
Which should sustain the bound and high curvet
Of Mars's fiery steed. To other regions!

He Had Dreamed of
Battles All His Life

From Stephen Crane,
The Red Badge of Courage

The classic American story of a young man coming of age on the battlefield, first published in 1895. In these opening pages the protagonist, Henry Fleming, thinks back to his initial enlistment in the Union Army. He remembers his mother's advice, his early enthusiasm about the war, and the flattering attentions of civilians as his regiment marched south to face the Confederates. He also remembers when the question that frames the book first came to him: When confronted with real battle, will I run?

The youth was in a little trance of astonishment. So they were at last going to fight. On the morrow, perhaps, there would be a battle, and he would be in it. For a time he was obliged to labor to make himself believe. He could not accept with assurance an omen that he was about to mingle in one of these great affairs of the earth.

He had, of course, dreamed of battles all his life—of vague and bloody conflicts that had thrilled him with their sweep and fire. In visions he had seen himself in many struggles. He had imagined peoples secure in the shadow of his eagle-eyed prowess. But awake he had regarded battles as crimson blotches on the pages of the past. He had put them as things of the bygone with his thought-images of heavy crowns and high castles. There was a portion of the world's history which he had regarded as the time of wars, but it, he thought, had been long gone over the horizon and had disappeared forever.

From his home his youthful eyes had looked upon the war in his own country with distrust. It must be some sort of a play affair. He had long despaired of witnessing a Greek-like struggle. Such would be no more, he had said. Men were better, or more timid. Secular and religious education had effaced the throat-grappling instinct, or else firm finance held in check the passions.

He had burned several times to enlist. Tales of great movements shook the land. They might not be distinctly Homeric, but there seemed to be much glory in them. He had read of marches, sieges, conflicts, and he had longed to see it all. His busy mind had drawn for him large pictures extravagant in color, lurid, with breathless deeds.

But his mother had discouraged him. She had affected to look with some contempt upon the quality of his war ardor and patriotism. She could calmly seat herself and with no apparent difficulty give him many hundreds of reasons why he was of vastly more importance on the farm than on the field of battle. She had had certain ways of expression that told him that her statements on the subject came from a deep conviction. Moreover, on her side, was his belief that her ethical motive in the argument was impregnable.

At last, however, he had made firm rebellion against this yellow light thrown upon the color of his ambitions. The newspapers, the gossip of the village, his own picturings, had aroused him to an uncheckable degree. They were in truth fighting finely down there. Almost every day the newspapers printed accounts of a decisive victory.

One night, as he lay in bed, the winds had carried to him the clangoring of the church bell as some enthusiast jerked the rope frantically to tell the twisted news of a great battle. This voice of the people rejoicing in the night had made him shiver in a prolonged ecstasy of excitement. Later, he had gone down to his mother's room and had spoken thus: "Ma, I'm going to enlist."

"Henry, don't you be a fool," his mother had replied. She had then covered her face with the quilt. There was an end to the matter for that night.

Nevertheless, the next morning he had gone to a town that was near his mother's farm and had enlisted in a company that was forming there. When he had returned home his mother was milking the brindle cow. Four others stood waiting. "Ma, I've enlisted," he had said to her diffidently. There was a short silence. "The Lord's will be done, Henry," she had finally replied, and had then continued to milk the brindle cow.

When he had stood in the doorway with his soldier's clothes on his back, and with the light of excitement and expectancy in his eyes almost defeating the glow of regret for the home bonds, he had seen two tears leaving their trails on his mother's scarred cheeks.

Still, she had disappointed him by saying nothing whatever about returning with his shield or on it. He had privately primed himself for a beautiful scene. He had prepared certain sentences which he thought could be used with touching effect. But her words destroyed his plans. She had doggedly peeled potatoes and addressed him as follows: "You watch out, Henry, an' take good care of yerself. Don't go a thinkin' you can lick the hull rebel army at the start, because yeh can't. Yer jest one little feller amongst a hull lot of others, and yeh've got to keep quiet an' do what they tell yeh. I know how are you, Henry.

"I've knet yeh eight pair of socks, Henry, and I've put in all yer best shirts, because I want my boy to be jest as warm and com'able as anybody in the army. Whenever they get holes, in 'em, I want yeh to send 'em rightaway back to me, so's I kin dern 'em.

"An' allus be careful an' choose yer comp'ny. There's lots of bad men in the army, Henry. The army makes 'em wild, and they like nothing better than the job of leading off a young feller like you, as ain't never been away from home much and has allus had a mother, an' a-learning 'em to drink and swear. Keep clear of them folks, Henry. I don't want yeh to ever do anything, Henry, that yeh would be 'shamed to let me know about. Jest think as if I was a watchin' yeh. If yeh keep that in yer mind allus, I guess yeh'll come out about right.

"Yeh must allus remember yer father, too, child, an' remember he never drunk a drop of licker in his life, and seldom swore a cross oath.

"I don't know what else to tell yeh, Henry, excepting that yeh must never do no shirking, child, on my account. If so be a time comes when yeh have to be kilt or do a mean thing, why, Henry, don't think of anything 'cept what's right, because there's many a woman has to bear up 'ginst sech things these times, and the Lord'll take keer of us all.

"Don't forget about the socks and the shirts, child; and I've put a cup of blackberry jam with yer bundle, because I know yeh like it above all things. Good-by, Henry. Watch out, and be a good boy."

He had, of course, been impatient under the ordeal of this speech. It had not been quite what he expected, and he had borne it with an air of irritation. He departed feeling vague relief.

Still, when he had looked back from the gate, he had seen his mother kneeling among the potato parings. Her brown face, upraised, was stained with tears, and her spare form was quivering. He bowed his head and went on, feeling suddenly ashamed of his purposes.

From his home he had gone to the seminary to bid adieu to many schoolmates. They had thronged about him with wonder and admiration. He had felt the gulf now between them and had swelled with calm pride. He and some of his fellows who had donned blue were quite overwhelmed with privileges for all of one afternoon, and it had been a very delicious thing. They had strutted.

A certain light-haired girl had made vivacious fun at his martial spirit, but there was another and darker girl whom he had gazed at steadfastly, and he thought she grew demure and sad at sight of his blue and brass. As he had walked down the path between the rows of oaks, he had turned his head and detected her at a window watching his departure. As he perceived her, she immediately began to stare up through the high tree branches at the sky. He had seen a good deal of flurry and haste in her movement as she changed her attitude. He often thought of it.

On the way to Washington his spirit had soared. The regiment was fed and caressed at station after station until the youth had believed that he must be a hero. There was a lavish expenditure of bread and cold meats, coffee, and pickles and cheese. As he basked in the smiles of the girls and was patted and complimented by the old men, he had felt growing within him the strength to do mighty deeds of arms.

After complicated journeyings with many pauses, there had come months of monotonous life in a camp. He had had the belief that real war was a series of death struggles with small time in between for sleep and meals; but since his regiment had come to the field the army had done little but sit still and try to keep warm.

He was brought then gradually back to this old ideas. Greek-like struggles would be no more. Men were better, or more timid. Secular and religious education had effaced the throat-grappling instinct, or else firm finance held in check the passions.

He had grown to regard himself merely as a part of a vast blue demonstration. His province was to look out, as far as he could, for his personal comfort. For recreation he could twiddle his thumbs and speculate on the thoughts which must agitate the minds of the generals. Also, he was drilled and drilled and reviewed, and drilled and drilled and reviewed.

The only foes he had seen were some pickets along the river bank. They were a sun-tanned, philosophical lot, who sometimes shot reflectively at the blue pickets. When reproached for this after-ward, they usually expressed sorrow, and swore by their gods that the guns had exploded without their permission. The youth, on guard duty one night, conversed across the stream with one of them. He was a slightly ragged man, who spat skillfully between his shoes and possessed a great fund of bland and infantile assurance. The youth liked him personally.

"Yank," the other had informed him, "yer a right dum good feller." This sentiment, floating to him upon the still air, had made him temporarily regret war.

Various veterans had told him tales. Some talked of gray, bewhiskered hordes who were advancing with relentless curses and chewing tobacco with unspeakable valor; tremendous bodies of fierce soldiery who were sweeping along like the Huns. Others spoke of tattered and eternally hungry men who fired despondent powders. "They'll charge through hell's fire an' brimstone t' git a holt on a haversack, an' sech stomachs ain't a-lastin' long," he was told. From the stories, the youth imagined the red, live bones, sticking out through slits in the faded uniforms.

Still, he could not put a whole faith in veterans' tales, for recruits were their prey. They talked much of smoke, fire, and blood, but he could not tell how much might be lies. They persisently yelled, "Fresh fish!" at him, and were in no wise to be trusted.

However, he perceived now that it did not greatly matter what kind of soldiers he was going to fight, so long as they fought, which fact no one disputed. There was a more serious problem. He lay in his bunk pondering upon it. He tried to mathematically prove to himself that he would not run from a battle.

Previously he had never felt obliged to wrestle too seriously with this question. In his life he had taken certain things for granted, never challenging his belief in ultimate success, and bothering little about means and roads. But here he was confronted with a thing of moment. It had suddenly appeared to him that perhaps in a battle he might run. He was forced to admit that as far as war was concerned he knew nothing of himself.

A sufficient time before he would have allowed the problem to kick its heels at the outer portals of his mind, but now he felt compelled to give serious attention to it.

A little panic-fear grew in his mind. As his imagination went forward to a fight, he saw hideous possibilities. He contemplated the lurking menaces of the future, and failed in an effort to see himself standing stoutly in the midst of them. He recalled his visions of broken-bladed glory, but in the shadow of the impending tumult he suspected them to be impossible pictures.

He sprang from the bunk and began to pace nervously to and fro. "Good Lord, what's th' matter with me?" he said aloud.

He felt that in this crisis his laws of life were useless. Whatever he had learned of himself was here of no avail. He was an unknown quantity. He saw that he would again be obliged to experiment as he had in early youth. He must accumulate information of himself, and meanwhile he resolved to remain close upon his guard lest those qualities of which he knew nothing should everlastingly disgrace him. "Good Lord!" he repeated in dismay.

In this section Henry Fleming faces the enemy after faltering at first, and in this encounter becomes a "war-devil." He had earlier fled, but now Henry stands his ground and, in Crane's words, "he had slept and, awakening, found himself a knight."

This advance of the enemy had seemed to the youth like a ruthless hunting. He began to fume with rage and exasperation. He beat his foot upon the ground, and scowled with hate at the swirling smoke that was approaching like a phantom flood. There was a maddening quality in this seeming resolution of the foe to give him no rest, to give him no time to sit down and think. Yesterday he had fought and had fled rapidly. There had been many adventures. For to-day he felt that he had earned opportunities for contemplative repose. He could have enjoyed portraying to uninitiated listeners various scenes at which he had been a witness or ably discussing the processes of war with other proved men. Too it was important that he should have time for physical recuperation.

He was sore and stiff from his experiences. He had received his fill of all exertions, and he wished to rest.

But those other men seemed never to grow weary; they were fighting with their old speed. He had a wild hate for the relentless foe. Yesterday, when he had imagined the universe to be against him, he had hated it, little gods and big gods; to-day he hated the army of the foe with the same great hatred. He was not going to be badgered of his life, like a kitten chased by boys, he said. It was not well to drive men into final corners; at those moments they could all develop teeth and claws.

He leaned and spoke into his friend's ear. He menaced the woods with a gesture. "If they keep on chasing us, by Gawd, they'd better watch out. Can't stand *too* much."

The friend twisted his head and made a calm reply. "If they keep on a-chasin' us they'll drive us all inteh th' river."

The youth cried out savagely at this statement. He crouched behind a little tree, with his eyes burning hatefully and his teeth set in a curlike snarl. The awkward bandage was still about his head, and upon it, over his wound, there was a spot of dry blood. His hair was wondrously tousled, and some straggling, moving locks hung over the cloth of the bandage down toward his forehead. His jacket and shirt were open at the throat, and exposed his young bronzed neck. There could be seen spasmodic gulpings at his throat.

His fingers twined nervously about his rifle. He wished that it was an engine of annihilating power. He felt that he and his companions were being taunted and derided from sincere convictions that they were poor and puny. His knowledge of his inability to take vengeance for it made his rage into a dark and stormy specter, that possessed him and made him dream of abominable cruelties. The tormentors were flies sucking insolently at his blood, and he thought that he would have given his life for a revenge of seeing their faces in pitiful plights.

The winds of battle had swept all about the regiment, until the one rifle, instantly followed by others, flashed in its front. A moment later the regiment roared forth its sudden and valiant retort. A dense wall of smoke settled slowly down. It was furiously slit and slashed by the knifelike fire from the rifles.

To the youth the fighters resembled animals tossed for a death struggle into a dark pit. There was a sensation that he and his fellows, at bay, were pushing back, always pushing fierce onslaughts of creatures who were slippery. Their beams of crimson seemed to get no purchase upon the bodies of their foes; the latter seemed to evade them with ease, and come through, between, around, and about with unopposed skill.

When, in a dream, it occurred to the youth that his rifle was a impotent stick, he lost sense of everything but his hate, his desire to smash into the pulp the glittering smile of victory which he could feel upon the faces of his enemies.

The blue smoke-swallowed line curled and writhed like a snake stepped upon. It swung its ends to and fro in an agony of fear and rage.

The youth was not conscious that he was erect upon his feet. He did not know the direction of the ground. Indeed, once he even lost the habit of balance and fell heavily. He was up again immediately. One thought went through the chaos of his brain at the time. He wondered if he had fallen because he had been shot. But the suspicion flew away at once. He did not think more of it.

He had taken up a first position behind the little tree, with a direct determination to hold it against the world. He had not deemed it possible that his army could that day succeed, and from this he felt the ability to fight harder. But the throng had surged in all ways, until he lost directions and locations, save that he knew where lay the enemy.

The flames bit him, and the hot smoke broiled his skin. His rifle barrel grew so hot that ordinarily he could not have borne it upon his palms; but he kept on stuffing cartridges into it, and pounding them with his clanking, bending ramrod. If he aimed at some changing form through the smoke, he pulled his trigger with a fierce grunt, as if he were dealing a blow of the fist with all his strength.

When the enemy seemed falling back before him and his fellows, he went instantly forward, like a dog, who, seeing his foes lagging, turns and insists upon being pursued. And when he was compelled to retire again, he did it slowly, sullenly, taking steps of wrathful despair.

Once he, in his intent hate, was almost alone, and was firing, when all those near him had ceased. He was so engrossed in his occupation that he was not aware of a lull.

He was recalled by a hoarse laugh and a sentence that came to his ears in a voice of contempt and amazement. "Yeah infernal fool, don't yeh know enough t' quit when there ain't anything t' shoot at? Good Gawd!"

He turned then and, pausing with his rifle thrown half into position, looked at the blue line of his comrades. During this moment of leisure they seemed all to be engaged in staring with astonishment at him. They had become spectators. Turning to the front again he saw, under the lifted smoke, a deserted ground.

He looked bewildered for a moment. Then there appeared upon the glazed vacancy of his eyes a diamond point of intelligence. "Oh," he said, comprehending.

He returned to his comrades and threw himself upon the ground. He sprawled like a man who had been thrashed. His flesh seemed strangely on fire, and the sounds of the battle continued in his ears. He groped blindly for his canteen.

The lieutenant was crowing. He seemed drunk with fighting. He called out to the youth: "By heavens, if I had ten thousand wild cats like you I could tear th' stomach outa this war in less'n a week!" He puffed out his chest with large dignity as he said it.

Some of the men muttered and looked at the youth in awe-struck ways. It was plain that as he had gone on loading and firing and cursing without the proper intermission, they had found time to regard him. And they looked upon him as a war devil.

The friend came staggering to him. There was some fright and dismay in his voice. "Are yeh all right, Fleming? Do yeh feel all right? There ain't nothin' th' matter with yeh, Henry, is there?"

"No," said the youth with difficulty. His throat seemed full of knobs and burrs.

These incidents made the youth ponder. It was revealed to him that he had been a barbarian, a beast. He had fought like a pagan who defends his religion. Regarding it, he saw that it was fine, wild, and, in some ways, easy. He had been a tremendous figure, no doubt. By this struggle he had overcome obstacles which he had admitted to be mountains. They had fallen like paper peaks, and he was now what he called a hero. And he had not been aware of the process. He had slept and, awakening, found himself a knight.

Henry's regiment has been assigned to fight a well-entrenched Confederate force. On the brink of despair, they endure and their courage returns.

When the two youths turned with the flag they saw that much of the regiment had crumbled away, and the dejected remnant was coming back. The men, having hurled themselves in projectile fashion, had presently expended their forces. They slowly retreat-ed, with their faces still toward the spluttering woods, and their hot rifles, still replying to the din. Several officers were giving orders, their voices keyed to screams.

"Where in hell yeh goin'?" the lieutenant was asking in a sarcastic howl. And a red-bearded officer, whose voice of triple brass
could plainly be heard, was commanding: "Shoot into 'em! Shoot
into 'em, Gawd damn their souls!" There was a *melee* of screetches,
in which the men were ordered to do conflicting and impossible
things.

The youth and his friend had a small scuffle over the flag.
"Give it t'me!" "No, let me keep it!" Each felt satisfied with the
other's possession of it, but each felt bound to declare, by an offer
to carry the emblem, his willingness to further risk himself. The
youth roughly pushed his friend away.

The regiment fell back to the stolid trees. There it halted for a
moment to blaze at some dark forms that had begun to steal upon
its track. Presently it resumed its march again, curving among the
tree trunks. By the time the depleted regiment had again reached
the first open space they were receiving a fast and merciless fire.
There seemed to be mobs all about them.

The greater part of the men, discouraged, their spirits worn by
the turmoil, acted as if stunned. They accepted the pelting of the
bullets with bowed and weary heads. It was of no purpose to strive
against walls. It was of no use to batter themselves against granite.
And from this consciousness that they had attempted to conquer
an unconquerable thing there seemed to arise a feeling that they
had been betrayed. They glowered with bent brows, but dangerously, upon some of the officers, more particularly upon the red-
bearded one with the voice of triple brass.

However, the rear of the regiment was fringed with men, who
continued to shoot irritably at the advancing foes. They seemed
resolved to make every trouble. The youthful lieutenant was perhaps the last man in the disordered mass. His forgotten back was
toward the enemy. He had been shot in the arm. It hung straight
and rigid. Occasionally he would cease to remember it, and be
about to emphasize an oath with a sweeping gesture. The multiplied pain caused him to swear with incredible power.

The youth went along with slipping, uncertain feet. He kept
watchful eyes rearward. A scowl of mortification and rage was upon
his face. He had thought of a fine revenge upon the officer who
had referred to him and his fellows as mule drivers. But he saw that
it could not come to pass. His dreams had collapsed when the mule
drivers, dwindling rapidly, had wavered and hesitated on the little
clearing, and then had recoiled. And now the retreat of the mule
drivers was a march of shame to him.

A dagger-pointed gaze from without his blackened face was held toward the enemy, but his greater hatred was rivetted upon the man, who, not knowing him, had called him a mule driver.

When he knew that he and his comrades had failed to do anything in successful ways that might bring the little pangs of a kind of remorse upon the officer, the youth allowed the rage of the baffled to possess him. This cold officer upon a monument, who dropped epithets unconcernedly down, would be finer as a dead man, he thought. So grievous did he think it that he could never possess the secret right to taunt truly in answer.

He had pictured red letters of curious revenge. "We *are* mule drivers, are we?" And now he was compelled to throw them away.

He presently wrapped his head in the cloak of his pride and kept the flag erect. He harangued his fellows, pushing against their chests with his free hand. To those he knew well he made frantic appeals, beseeching them by name. Between him and the lieutenant, scolding and near to losing his mind with rage, there felt a subtle fellowship and equality. They supported each other in all manner of hoarse, howling protests.

But the regiment was a machine run down. The two men babbled at a forceless thing. The soldiers who had heart to go slowly were continually shaken in their resolves by a knowledge that comrades were slipping with speed back to the lines. It was difficult to think of reputation when others were thinking of skins. Wounded men were left crying on this black journey.

The smoke fringes and flames blustered always. The youth, peering once through a sudden rift in a cloud, saw a brown mass of troops, interwoven and magnified until they appeared to be thousands. A fierce-hued flag flashed before his vision.

Immediately, as if the uplifting of the smoke had been prearranged, the discovered troops burst into a rasping yell, and a hundred flames jetted toward the retreating band. A rolling gray cloud again interposed as the regiment doggedly replied. The youth had to depend again upon his misused ears, which were trembling and buzzing from the melee of musketry and yells.

The way seemed eternal. In the clouded haze men became panic-stricken with the thought that the regiment had lost its path, and was proceeding in a perilous direction. Once the men who headed the procession turned and came pushing back against their comrades, screaming that they were being fired upon from points which they had considered to be toward their own lines. At this cry a hysterical fear and dismay beset the troops. A soldier, who heretofore had been ambitious to make the regiment into a wise little band that would proceed calmly amid the huge-appearing difficulties, suddenly sank down and buried his face in his arms with an air of bowing to a doom. From another a shrill lamentation rang out filled with profane allusions to a general. Men ran hither and thither, seeking with their eyes road of escape. With serene regularity, as if controlled by a schedule, bullets buffed into men.

The youth walked stolidly into the midst of the mob, and with his flag in his hands took a stand as if he expected an attempt to push him to the ground. He unconsciously assumed the attitude of the color bearer in the fight of the preceding day. He passed over his brow a hand that trembled. His breath did not come freely. He was choking during this small wait for the crisis.

His friend came to him. "Well, Henry, I guess this is good-by-John."

"Oh, shut up, you damned fool!" replied the youth, and he would not look at the other.

The officers labored like politicians to beat the mass into a proper circle to face the menaces. The ground was uneven and torn. The men curled into depressions and fitted themselves snugly behind whatever would frustrate a bullet.

The youth noted with vague surprise that the lieutenant was standing mutely with his legs far apart and his sword held in the manner of a cane. The youth wondered what had happened to his vocal organs that he no more cursed. There was something curious in this little intent pause of the lieutenant. He was like a babe which, having wept its fill, raises its eyes and fixes them upon a distant toy. He was engrossed in this contemplation, and the soft underlip quivered from self-whispered words.

Some lazy and ignorant smoke curled slowly. The men, hiding from the bullets, waited anxiously for it to lift and disclose the plight of the regiment.

The silent ranks were suddenly thrilled by the eager voice of the youthful lieutenant bawling out: "Here they come! Right on to us, b'Gawd!" His further words were lost in a roar of wicked thunder from the men's rifles.

The youth's eyes had instantly turned in the direction indicated by the awakened and agitated lieutenant, and he had seen the haze of treachery disclosing a body of soldiers of the enemy. They were so near that he could see their features. There was a recognition as he looked at the types of faces. Also he perceived with dim amazement that their uniforms were rather gay in effect, being light gray, accented with a brilliant-hued facing. Moreover, the clothes seemed new.

These troops had apparently been going forward with caution, their rifles held in readiness, when the youthful lieutenant had discovered them and their movement had been interrupted by the volley from the blue regiment. From the moment's glimpse, it was derived that they had been unaware of the proximity of their dark-suited foes or had mistaken the direction. Almost instantly they were shut utterly from the youth's sight by the smoke from the energetic rifles of his companions. He strained his vision to learn the accomplishment of the volley, but the smoke hung before him.

The two bodies of troops exchanged blows in the manner of a pair of boxers. The fast angry firings went back and forth. The men in blue were intent with the despair of their circumstances and they seized upon the revenge to be had at close range. Their thunder swelled loud and valiant. Their curving front bristled with flashes and the place resounded with the clangor of their ramrods. The youth ducked and dodged for a time and achieved a few unsatisfactory views of the enemy. There appeared to be many of them and they were replying swiftly. They seemed moving toward the blue regiment, step by step. He seated himself gloomily on the ground with his flag between his knees.

As he noted the vicious, wolflike temper of his comrades he had a sweet thought that if the enemy was about to swallow the regimental broom as a large prisoner, it could at least have the consolation of going down with bristles forward.

But the blows of the antagonist began to grow more weak. Fewer bullets ripped the air, and finally, when the men slackened to learn of the fight, they could see only dark, floating smoke. The regiment lay still and gazed. Presently some chance whim came to the pestering blur, and it began to coil heavily away. The men saw a ground vacant of fighters. It would have been an empty stage if it were not for a few corpses that lay thrown and twisted into fantastic shapes upon the sward.

At sight of this tableau, many of the men in blue sprang from behind their covers and made an ungainly dance of joy. Their eyes burned and a hoarse cheer of elation broke from their dry lips.

It had begun to seem to them that events were trying to prove that they were impotent. These little battles had evidently endeavored to demonstrate that the men could not fight well. When on the verge of submission to these opinions, the small duel had showed them that the proportions were not impossible, and by it they had revenged themselves upon their misgivings and upon the foe.

The impetus of enthusiasm was theirs again. They gazed about them with looks of uplifted pride, feeling new trust in the grim, always confident weapons in their hands. And they were men.

On Courage

From Aristotle,
The Nicomachean Ethics

The same evils which terrify one person are not formidable to another; though there are some of such an irresistible nature, as to shake the firmest minds, and to inspire fear into all possessed of understanding. But those objects of terror which surpass not the strength of human nature, differing from each other in magnitude, as well as do the grounds of confidence, courage will discriminate between real and apparent dangers; and make us meet the former, as brave men ought, unshaken and dauntless, subjecting the instinctive emotions of fear to the dictates of reason and of honour. For we betray our weakness, not only when we fear things really not formidable, but when we are affected in an undue degree, or at an improper time, by objects of real danger. A brave man avoids such errors; and, estimating things by their real worth, prefers the grace and beauty of habitual fortitude to the delusive security of deformed cowardice. Yet he is not less careful to avoid that excess of intrepidity, which, being rarely met with, is like many other vices, without a name; though nothing but madness, or a most stupid insensibility, can make any man preserve, amidst earthquakes and inundations, that unshaken composure, which has been ascribed to the Celts. An overweening estimate of the causes of confidence, and a consequent excess of courage, is called audacity; a boastful species of bravery, and the mere ape of true manhood. What the brave man *is*, the rash and audacious man wishes to *appear*; he courts and provokes unnecessary dangers, but fails in the hour of trial; and is, for the most part, a blustering bully, who, under a semblance of pretended courage, conceals no inconsiderable portion of cowardice. But the complete and genuine coward easily betrays himself, by fearing either things not formidable, or things formidable, in an undue degree; and his failing is the more manifest, because it is accompanied with plain indications of pain; he lives in continual alarm, and is therefore spiritless and dejected; whereas courage warms our breasts, and animates our hopes. Such then is the character of true courage, as opposed to audacity on one hand, and cowardice on the other. It holds the middle place between those vicious extremes; it is calm and sedate; and though it never provokes danger, is always ready to meet even death in an honorable cause.

The Coward

From Theophrastus,
The Characters

Now, cowardice would seem to be a failure of spirit caused by fear. On shipboard the coward is the sort of man who mistakes a rocky headland for a pirate brig, and who asks if there are unbelievers aboard when a big wave hits the side. Or he will show up suddenly alongside the helmsman, trying to find out what the weather means or if they are halfway yet; and he explains to the nearest listener that his fright was caused by a dream. Since he expects the worst, he strips off his coat and hands it to a servant—or he pleads, "Get me safe to shore!"

Suppose, again, that he is on active duty. As the infantry advances into battle, he shouts for his friends from home to come over by him. He wants them to stop for a look round before they go farther, it's a job he says, to tell which is the enemy. And as soon as he starts hearing the shouts and seeing men drop, he explains to those on either side of him that all the excitement made him forget to take his sword. So back he runs to the tent, then he sends his orderly out on reconnaissance, hides the sword under a pillow, and takes his time pretending to hunt for it. Also, in case he looks out and sees a wounded man he knows being brought in, he runs to help carry him and tells him, "Keep your spirits up!" He will nurse the man, clean out his wound, sit by him to keep the flies off: anything to avoid going back and facing the enemy. What's more, when the call to battle stations sounds he stays right where he is. "Oh, go to hell with that damned bugling all the the time" is his response. "Won't you ever let the poor fellow get some sleep?" And with blood from the other man's wound all over him, he explains to troops coming back from the front, "Managed to save at least one of my boys, anyway," just as if he had risked his own neck. He makes the men from his part of town come in to see the patient, too, and he keeps on explaining to everybody, "Brought him here myself—carried him the whole way."

"Oh, to Die, to Die for Him!"

From Leo Tolstoy, War and Peace

The Czar reviews his troops. Young Rostof is brought to a peak of martial and patriotic ecstasy as he imagines dying in battle for the splendid and kindly emperor.

On the day following the meeting of Boris and Rostof, a review was held of the Austrian and Russian troops, including those who had just arrived from Russia, as well as those who had made the campaign with Kutuzof. Both the Emperor of Russia, with the tsarevitch, and the Emperor of Austria, with the archduke, reviewed this allied army of eighty thousand men.

Early in the morning, the soldiers, elegantly spruced and attired, began to move, falling into line in front of the fortress. Here thousands of legs and bayonets moved along with streaming banners, and at the command of their officers, halted or wheeled, or formed into detachments, passing by other similar bodies of infantry, in other uniforms.

There, with measured hoof beats and jingling of trappings came the cavalry gayly dressed in blue, red, and green embroidered uniforms with gayly-dressed musicians ahead, riding coal-black, chestnut, and gray horses.

Yonder, stretching out in a long line, with their polished shining cannon, jolting with a brazen din on their carriages, and with the smell of linstocks, came the artillery between the infantry and cavalry, and drew up in the places assigned them. Not only the generals in full dress uniform, with slender waists or stout waists, tightened in to the last degree, and with red necks tightly clasped by their collars, and wearing their scarfs and all their orders; not only the officers, pomaded and decked with all their glories, but all the soldiers, with shining, clean-washed and freshly shaven faces, and with all their appurtenances polished up to the highest lustre, and all the horses gayly caparisoned and groomed so that their coats were as glossy as satin, and every individual hair in their manes in exactly its proper place, had the consciousness that something grave, significant, and solemn was taking place. Every general and every soldier felt his own insignificance, counting himself as merely a grain of sand in this sea of humanity, and at the same time felt his power, when regarded as a part of this mighty whole.

By means of strenuous efforts and devoted energy, the preparations which had begun early in the morning were completed by ten o'clock, and everything was in proper order. The ranks were drawn up across the broad parade ground. The whole army was arranged in three columns; in front the cavalry, then the artillery, and, in the rear the infantry.

Between each division of the army was a space like a street. The three divisions of this army were sharply contrasted with each other; Kutuzof's war-worn veterans—among whom on the right flank in the front row stood the Pavlogradsky hussars—the troops of the Line that had just arrived from Russia, and the regiments of the Guard and the Austrian army. But all stood in one line under one commander, and in identical order.

Like the wind rustling the leaves, a murmur agitated the lines: "They are coming! They are coming!" Vivacious shouts of command were heard, and throughout the whole army, like a wave, ran the bustle of the final preparations.

Far away in front of them, near Olmutz, appeared a group coming toward them. And at this moment, though the day was calm, a gentle breeze, as it were, stirred the army, and seemed to shake the streamers on the pikes, and the unfurled standards clinging to their staffs. It seemed as though the army itself by this slight tremor expressed its gladness at the approach of the emperors. The word of command was heard uttered by one voice,—eyes front! Then like the answering of cocks at daybreak, many voices repeated this command from point to point, and all grew still.

In the death-like silence, the only sound heard was the trampling of horses' feet. This was the suite of the emperors. The two monarchs rode along the left wing, and the bugles of the First Cavalry Regiment burst forth with the general march. It seemed as if it were not the bugles that played this march, but as if the army itself, in its delight at the approach of the emperors, emitted these sounds. Their echoes had not died away, when the Emperor Alexander's affable young voice was distinctly heard addressing the men. He uttered the usual welcome, and the First Regiment gave forth one huzza so deafening, so long drawn out and expressive of joy, that the men themselves were amazed and awestruck at the magnitude and strength of the mass which they constituted.

Rostof standing in the front rank of Kutuzof's army, which the emperor first approached, shared the feeling experienced by every man in that army, a feeling of self-forgetfulness, a proud consciousness of invincibility and of passionate attachment to him on whose account all this solemn parade was prepared. He felt that only a single word from this man was needed for this mighty mass, including himself as an insignificant grain of sand, to dash through fire and water, to commit crime, to face death or perform the mightiest deeds of heroism, and therefore he could not help trembling, could not help his heart melting within him at the sight of this approaching Word.

"Hurrah! Hurrah! Hurrah!" was roared on all sides, and one regiment after another welcomed the sovereigns with the music of the general march, then renewed huzzas, the general march and huzzas on huzzas, which growing louder and louder, mingled in one overpowering deafening tumult.

Until the sovereign came quite close, every regiment in its silence and rigidity seemed like a lifeless body, but as soon as the sovereign came abreast of it, the regiment woke to life and broke out into acclamations which mingled with the roar extending down the whole line past which the sovereign rode. Amid the tremendous deafening tumult of these thousands of voices, through the midst of the armies, standing in their squares as motionless as though they had been carved out of granite, moved easily, carelessly, but symmetrically, and above all with freedom and grace, the hundreds of riders constituting the suites, and in front of all—two men, the emperors! Upon them, and upon them alone, were concentrated the suppressed but eager attention of all that mass of warriors.

The handsome young Emperor Alexander in his Horse-guards' uniform and three-cornered hat worn point forward, with his pleasant face and clear but not loud voice, was the cynosure of all eyes.

Rostof stood not far from the buglers, and his keen glance recognized the emperor while he was still far off, and followed him as he drew near. When the Sovereign had approached to a distance of twenty paces, and Nikolai could clearly distinguish every feature of his handsome and radiant young face, he experienced a sense of affection and enthusiasm such as he had never before felt. Everything, every feature, every motion seemed to him bewitching in his sovereign.

Pausing in front of the Pavlograd regiment, the monarch said something in French to the Emperor of Austria and smiled.

Seeing this smile, Rostof himself involuntarily smiled also, and felt a still more powerful impulse of love toward his sovereign. He felt a burning desire to display this love in some way. He knew that this was impossible, and he felt like weeping.

The sovereign summoned the regimental commander and said a few words to him.

"My God! what would happen to me, if the sovereign were to address me!" thought Rostof. "I should die of happiness!"

The emperor also addressed the officers,—

"Gentlemen," said he, and Rostof listened as to a voice from heaven. How happy he would have been now if he only could die for his Tsar! "I thank you all from my heart! You have won the standards of St. George, prove yourselves worthy of them!"

"Oh, to die, to die for him!" thought Rostof.

The sovereign said a few words more, which Rostof did not catch, and the soldiers, straining their throats, cried "Hurrah! hurrah!"

Rostof also joined with them, leaning forward in his saddle and shouting with all his might, willing to burst his lungs in his efforts to express the full extent of his enthusiasm for his sovereign.

The emperor stood a few seconds in front of the hussars as though he were undecided.

"How can the sovereign be undecided?" mused Rostof; but immediately even this indecision seemed to him a new proof of majesty and charm, like everything else that the sovereign did.

The emperor's indecision lasted only a moment. His foot, shod in a narrow, sharp-pointed boot, such as were worn at that time, pressed against the flank of the English-groomed bay mare on which he sat. The sovereign's hand, in a white glove, gathered up the reins, and he rode off, accompanied by a disorderly, tossing sea of adjutants.

As he kept riding farther and farther down the line, he kept halting in front of the different regiments, and at last only his white plume could be seen by Rostof, distinguishing him from the suite that accompanied the emperors.

In the number of those who accompanied the emperor, he noticed Bolkonsky, lazily and indifferently bestriding his steed. Yesterday evening's quarrel with him came into his mind, and the question arose whether or not he ought to challenge him. "Of course it is out of the question now," thought Rostof. "Is it worth while to think or to talk about such a thing at such a moment as this? At a time when one feels such impulses of love, enthusiasm, and self-renunciation, what consequence are our petty quarrels and provocations? I love the whole world, I forgive every one now!" said Rostof to himself.

After the sovereign had ridden past almost all the regiments, the troops began to move in front of him in the "ceremonial march," and Rostof, on his Bedouin, which he had recently bought from Denisof, rode at the end of his squadron, that is, alone, and in a most conspicuous position before his sovereign.

Just before he came up to where the emperor was, Rostof, who was an admirable horseman, plunged the spurs in Bedouin's flanks, and urged him into that mad, frenzied gallop which Bedouin always took when he was excited. Pressing his foaming mouth back to his breast, arching his tail, and seeming to fly through the air, and spurning the earth, gracefully tossing and interweaving his legs, Bedouin, also conscious the emperor's eyes were fastened on him, dashed gallantly by.

Rostof himself, keeping his feet back, and sitting straight in his saddle, feeling himself one with his horse, rode by his sovereign with disturbed but beatific face; "a very devil," as Denisof expressed it.

"Bravo!" exclaimed the emperor.

"My God! how happy I should be if he would only bid me to dash instantly into the fire!" thought Rostof.

When the review was ended, the officers who had just come from Russia and those of Kutuzof's division, began to gather in groups and talk about the rewards of the campaign, about the Austrians and their uniforms, about their line of battle, about Bonaparte, and what a desperate position he had got himself into now, especially if Essen's corps should join them, and Prussia should take their side.

But more than all else in each of these circles, the conversation was about the Emperor Alexander, and every word that he had spoken was repeated, and everything that he had done was praised, and all were enthusiastic over him.

All had but one single expectation: under the personal direction of the sovereign, to go with all speed against the enemy. Under the command of the emperor himself, it would be an impossibility not to win the victory over any one in the world: so thought Rostof and the majority of the officers.

After this review, all were more assured of victory than they would have been after the winning of two battles.

The Good War

From Studs Terkel,
The Good War

American World War II veterans recall their experiences in the European and Pacific campaigns.

ROBERT RASMUS

I've lived about thirty-eight years after the war and about twenty years before. For me it's B.W. and A.W.—before the war and after the war. I suspect there are lots of people like me. In business, there'll be times when I say, This really worries the heck out of me, but it's really minor compared to having to do a river crossing under fire. (Laughs.)

I get this strange feeling of living through a world drama. In September of '39 when the Germans invaded Poland, I was fourteen years old. I remember my mother saying, "Bob, you'll be in it." I was hoping she'd be right. At that age, you look forward to the glamour and have no idea of the horrors.

Sure enough, I was not only in the army but in the infantry. Step by logistic step, our division was in combat. You're finally down to one squad, out ahead of the whole thing. You're the point man. What am I doing out here—in this world-cataclysmic drama—out in front of the whole thing? (Laughs.)

You saw those things in the movies, you saw the newsreels. But you were of an age when your country wasn't even in the war. It seemed unreal. All of a sudden, there you were right in the thick of it and people were dying and you were scared out of your wits that you'd have your head blown off. (Laughs.)

I was acutely aware, being a rifleman, the odds were high that I would be killed. At one level, animal fear. I didn't like that at all. On the other hand, I had this great sense of adventure. My gosh, going across the ocean, seeing the armies, the excitement of it. I was there.

You have to understand the culture of our company. Most of our privates were college types. They had been dumped en masse into these infantry divisions. The cadre of noncommissioned officers were old-timers. They were mostly uneducated country types, many of them from the South. There was a rather healthy mutual contempt between the noncoms and the privates. This sergeant was the most hated man. One of the nineteen-year-olds, during maneuvers, was at the point of tears in his hatred of this man who was so unreasonable and so miserable. He'd say, "If we ever get into combat, I'm gonna kill 'im. First thing I'll do." Who's the first one killed? This sergeant. I'm sure it was enemy fire. I would bet my life on it. I'm sure the guys who said they would kill him were horrified that their wish came true.

I'm sure our company was typical. We had x percent of self-inflicted wounds. There's no question that a guy would blow his toe off to get out of combat. People would get lost. These combat situations are so confused that it's very easy to go in the other direction. Say you get lost, get sick, get hurt. By the time you get back to your outfit, a couple of days have gone by.

We remember examples of Caspar Milquetoast: ordinary people showing incredible heroism. But you have to accept the fact that in a cross section of people—in civilian life, too—you've got cowards and quitters. Our radio man shot up his radio: he thought we were going to be captured. Panic. I became a bazooka man because our bazooka man threw his weapon away and I picked it up. He ran off.

Our captain said, "Pick up the bodies. We don't leave our dead to the enemy." We're now cut off and have to join the rest of our battalion. We had to improvise stretchers. I took off my field jacket and turned the arms inside out. We poked rifles through the arms and fashioned a stretcher. We got the sergeant on ours and, jeez half his head was blown off and the brains were coming out on my hands and on my uniform. Here's the mama's boy, Sunday school, and now I'm really in it.

I remember lying in that slit trench that night. It was a nightmare. I'd now seen what dead people look like, the color out of their face. I think each person in my squad went through this dream of mine. Daylight came and we moved out into another town. This is twenty-four hours of experience.

Those who really went through combat, the Normandy landings, the heavy stuff, might laugh at this little action we'd been in, but for me . . . We were passing people who were taking over from us, another company. We had one day of this. Our uniforms were now dirty and bloody and our faces looked like we'd been in there for weeks. Now *we* had the feeling: you poor innocents.

We weren't able to bring those bodies back with us. The mortar fire became too much. The next morning, our squad was assigned to go far back and recover the bodies. It was sunshine and quiet. We were passing the Germans we killed. Looking at the individual German dead, each took on a personality. These were no longer an abstraction. These were no longer the Germans of the brutish faces and the helmets we saw in the newsreels. They were exactly our age. These were boys like us.

Looking back on the war, in spite of the really bad times, it was certainly the most exciting experience of my life. As a character in *Terry and the Pirates* once put it so eloquently, "We shot the last act in the first reel." As I see it, at that young age, we hit the climax. Everything after that is anticlimactic.

E. B. (SLEDGEHAMMER) SLEDGE

There was nothing macho about the war at all. We were a bunch of scared kids who had to do a job. People tell me I don't act like an ex-Marine. How is an ex-Marine supposed to act? They have some Hollywood stereotype in mind. No, I don't look like John Wayne. We were in it to get it over with, so we could go back home and do what we wanted to do with our lives.

I was nineteen, a replacement in June of 1944. Eighty percent of the division in the Guadalcanal campaign was less than twenty-one years of age. We were much younger than the general army units.

To me, there were two different wars. There was the war of the guy on the front lines. You don't come off until you are wounded or killed. Or, if lucky, relieved. Then there was the support personnel. In the Pacific, for every rifleman on the front lines there were nineteen people in the back. Their view of the war was different than mine. The man up front puts his life on the line day after day after day to the point of utter hopelessness.

The only thing that kept you going was your faith in your buddies. It was just a case of friendship. I never heard of self-inflicted wounds out there. Fellows from other services said they saw this in Europe. Oh, there were plenty of times when I wished I had a million-dollar wound. (Laughs softly.) Like maybe shootin' a toe off. What was worse than death was the indignation of your buddies. You couldn't let 'em down. It was stronger than flag and country.

With the Japanese, the battle was all night long. Infiltratin' the lines, slippin' up and throwin' in grenades. Or runnin' in with a bayonet or saber. They were active all night. Your buddy would try to get a little catnap and you'd stay on watch. Then you'd switch off. It went on, day in and day out. A matter of simple survival. The only way you could get it over with was to kill them off before they killed you. The war I knew was totally savage.

The Japanese fought by a code they thought was right: *bushido*. The code of the warrior: no surrender. You don't really comprehend it until you get out there and fight people who are faced with an absolutely hopeless situation and will not give up. If you tried to help one of the Japanese, he'd usually detonate a grenade and kill himself as well as you. To be captured was a disgrace. To us, it was impossible, too, because we knew what happened in Bataan.

PETER BEZICH

People in America do not know what war is. I do, and anybody that was in the service. The Russians know. The Polish know. The Jewish know. But the American people have no idea what all-out war is. We never tasted it. I hope we never do.

My brother, he was the all-American kid, Jack Armstrong. He's being elevated in the military. He's a career man. They're checking out his background and all that bull, the FBI. They came to my dad, to his job, and they said somethin' about Russia and all that. This is just after the war, right? And they said, "What're you? Communists or somethin'? You know Russia's our enemy." The curtain and all that stuff. My dad says, "Hey, weren't they fightin' with us?" The government was sayin' they're our allies, and all of a sudden they turn it around and the Russians are no good.

They wanted to know about my brother. Did he have any leanings to the left? Did he do this? Did he do that? I said, "You couldn't find a more all-American kid than my brother." He was in the Battle of the Bulge, yeah.

Now we come to my two sons and Vietnam. I get mad about that patriotism. If your house is on fire, I'll help you put out the fire. If you argue with your wife, I'm not gonna get in between. It's like we had our revolution here. When they talk about reds and redniks, we did our fighting here. The American Revolution. Look what the French did there. We got sucked in by the French.

My war's over, right? Then they come up with Vietnam. My one son was gettin' outa school and he went to Vietnam for a year and a half. The other son refused to be drafted. It wasn't on religious principles, because we're not church people. He said killing was against his principles. Steve didn't burn no draft cards. He said, "I'll go to Vietnam and build hospitals." He was in construction, with me. They even interviewed the guys at work. Steve was the nicest kid you could know. He's a do-gooder. He donates one day a week to Shedd Aquarium for no pay. He's an all-American kid. It's a shame. It has ruined his life.

What he did took more guts than what I did. These big heroes grab him, put 'im in county jail. The kid never had a ticket in his life. It's like takin' a flower and cuttin' it and just throwin' it in a corner.

In Flanders Fields

Lieutenant-Colonel John McRae, M.D.

In Flanders fields the poppies blow
Between the crosses, row on row,
That mark our place; and in the sky
The larks, still bravely singing, fly
Scarce heard amid the guns below.

We are the Dead. Short days ago
We lived, felt dawn, saw sunset glow,
Loved and were loved, and now we lie,
In Flanders fields.

Take up our quarrel with the foe:
To you from failing hands we throw
The torch; be yours to hold it high.
If ye break faith with us who die
We shall not sleep, though poppies grow
In Flanders fields.

Friends Through Fighting:
Robin Hood, Friar Tuck,
and Little John

From Thomas Bulfinch,
Bulfinch's Mythology

Now Robin Hood had instituted a day of mirth for himself and all his companions, and wagers were laid amongst them who should exceed at this exercise and who at that; some did contend who should jump farthest, some who should throw the bar, some who should be swiftest afoot in a race five miles in length, others there were with which Little John was most delighted, who did strive which of them should draw the strongest bow, and be the best marksman. "Let me see," said Little John, "which of you can kill a buck, and who can kill a doe, and who is he can kill a hart, being distant from it by the space of five hundred feet." With that, Robin Hood going before them, they went directly to the forest, where they found good store of game feeding before them. William Scarlock, that drew the strongest bow of them all, did kill a buck, and Little John made choice of a barren fat doe, and the well-directed arrow did enter in the very heart of it; and Midge, the miller's son, did kill a hart above five hundred feet distant from him. The hart falling, Robin Hood stroked him gently on the shoulder, and said unto him, "God's blessing on thy heart, I will ride five hundred miles to find a match for thee." William Scarlock, hearing him speak these words, smiled and said unto him, "Master, what needs that? Here is a Curtal Friar not far off, that for a hundred pound will shoot at what distance yourself will propound, either with Midge or with yourself. An experienced man he is, and will draw a bow with great strength; he will shoot with yourself, and with all the men you have, one after another."

"Sayest thou so, Scarlock?" replied Robin Hood. "By the grace of God I will neither eat nor drink till I see this Friar thou dost speak of." And having prepared himself for his journey, he took Little John and fifty of his best archers with him, whom he bestowed in a convenient place, as he himself thought fitting. This being done, he ran down into the dale, where he found the Curtal Friar walking by the water side. He no sooner espied him, but put on his broadsword and buckler, and put on his head a steel bonnet. The Friar, not knowing who he was, or for what intent he came, did presently arm himself to encounter with him. Robin Hood, coming near unto him, alighted from his horse, which he tied to a thorn tree that grew hard by, and looking wistfully at the Friar, said unto him, "Carry me over the water, thou Curtal Friar, or else thy life lies at the stake." The Friar made no more ado, but took up Robin Hood and carried him on his back; deep water he did stride; he spake not so much as one word to him, but having carried him over, he gently laid him down on the side of the bank; which being done, the Friar said to Robin Hood, "It is now thy turn; therefore carry me over the water, thou bold fellow, or sure I shall make thee repent it." Robin Hood, to requite the courtesy, took the Friar on his back, and not speaking the least word to him, carried him over the water, and laid him gently down on the side of the bank; and turning to him, he spake unto him as at first, and bade him carry him over the water once more, or he should answer it with the forfeit of his life. The Friar in a smiling manner took him up, and spake not a word till he came in the midst of the stream, when, being up to the middle and higher, he did shake him from off his shoulders, and said unto him, "Now choose thee, bold fellow, whether thou wilt sink or swim."

Robin Hood, being soundly washed, got him up on his feet, and prostrating himself, did swim to a bush of broom on the other side of the bank; and the Friar swam to a willow tree which was not far from it. Then Robin Hood, taking his bow in his hand, and one of his best arrows, did shoot at the Friar, which the Friar received in his buckler of steel, and said unto him, "Shoot on, thou bold fellow, if thou shootest at me a whole summer's day I will stand your mark still." "That will I," said Robin Hood, and shot arrow after arrow at him, until he had not an arrow left in his quiver. He then laid down his bow, and drew out his sword, which but two days before had been the death of three men. Now hand to hand they fought with sword and buckler; the steel buckler defends whatsoever blow is given; sometimes they make at the head, sometimes at the foot, sometimes at the side; sometimes they strike directly down, sometimes they falsify their blows, and come in foot and arm, with a free thrust at the body; and being ashamed that so long they exercise their unprofitable valor and cannot hurt one another, they multiply their blows, they hack, they hew, they slash, they foam. At last Robin Hood desired the Friar to hold his hand, and to give him leave to blow his horn.

"Thou wantest breath to sound it," said the Friar; "take thee a little respite, for we have been five hours at it by the Fountain Abbey clock." Robin Hood took his horn from his side, and having sounded it three times, behold where fifty lusty men, with their bended bows, came to his assistance. The Friar, wondering at it, "Whose men," said he, "be these?" "They are mine," said Robin Hood; "what is that to thee?" "False loon," said the Friar; and making a little pause, he desired Robin Hood to show him the same courtesy which he gave him. "What is that?" said Robin Hood. "Thou soundest thy horn three times," said the Friar; "let me now but whistle three times." "Ay, with all my heart," said Robin Hood; "I were to blame if I should deny thee that courtesy." With that the Friar set his fist to his mouth, and whistled three times so shrilly that the place echoed again with it; and behold three and fifty fair ban-dogs (their hair rising on their back, betokening their rage), were almost on the backs of Robin Hood and his companions. "Here is for every one of thy men a dog," said the Friar, "and two for thee." "That is foul play," said Robin Hood. He had scarce spoken that word but two dogs came upon him at once, one before, another behind him, who, although they could not touch his flesh (his sword had made so swift a despatch of them), yet they tore his coat into two pieces. By this time the men had so laid about them that the dogs began to fly back, and their fury to languish into barking. Little John did so bestir himself, that the Curtal Friar, admiring at his courage and his nimbleness, did ask him who he was. He made him answer, "I will tell the truth, and not lie. I am he who is called Little John, and do belong to Robin Hood, who hath fought with thee this day, five hours together; and if thou wilt not submit unto him, this arrow shall make thee." The Friar, perceiving how much he was overpowered, and that it was impossible for him to deal with so many at once, did come to terms with Robin Hood. And the articles of agreement were these: That the Friar should abandon Fountain Dale and Fountain Abbey, and should live with Robin Hood, at his place not far from Nottingham, where for saying mass, he should receive a noble for every Sunday throughout the year, and for saying mass on every holy day, a new change of garment. The Friar, contented with these conditions, did seal the agreement. And thus by the courage of Robin Hood and his yeomen, he was enforced at the last to submit, having for seven long years kept Fountain Dale, not all the power thereabouts being able to bring him on his knees.

The lieutenant of Robin Hood's band was named Little John, not so much from his smallness in stature (for he was seven feet high and more), as for a reason which I shall tell later. And the manner in which Robin Hood, to whom he was very dear, met him was this.

Robin Hood on one occasion being hunting with his men and finding the sport to be poor, said: "We have had no sport now for some time. So I go abroad alone. And if I should fall into any peril whence I cannot escape I will blow my horn that ye may know of it and bear me aid." And with that he bade them adieu and departed alone, having with him his bow and the arrows in his quiver. And passing shortly over a brook by a long bridge he met at the middle a stranger. And neither of the two would give way to the other. And Robin Hood being angry fitted an arrow to his bow and made ready to fire. "Truly," said the stranger at this, "thou art a fine fellow that you must draw your long bow on me who have but a staff by me." "That is just truly," said Robin; "and so I will lay by my bow and get me a staff to try if your deeds be as good as your words." And with that he went into a thicket and chose him a small ground oak for a staff and returned to the stranger.

"Now," said he, "I am a match for you, so let us play upon this bridge, and if one should fall in the stream the other will have the victory." "With all my heart," said the stranger; "I shall not be the first to give out." And with that they began to make great play with their staves. And Robin Hood first struck the stranger such a blow as warmed all his blood, and from that they rattled their sticks as though they had been threshing corn. And finally the stranger gave Robin such a crack on his crown that he broke his head and the blood flowed. But this only urged him the more, so that he attacked the stranger with such vigor that he had like to have made an end of him. But he growing into a fury finally fetched him such a blow that he tumbled him from the bridge into the brook. Whereat the stranger laughed loudly and long, and cried out to him, "Where art thou now, I pry thee, my good fellow?" And Robin replied, "Thou art truly a brave soul, and I will have no more to do with thee to-day; so our battle is at an end, and I must allow that thou hast won the day." And then wading to the bank he pulled out his horn and blew a blast on it so that the echoes flew throughout the valley. And at that came fifty bold bowmen out of the wood, all clad in green, and they made for Robin Hood, and William Stukely said, "What is the matter, my master? you are wet to the skin?" "Truly, nothing is the matter," said Robin, "but that the lad on the bridge has tumbled me into the stream." And on that the archers would have seized the stranger to duck him as well, but Robin Hood forbade them. "No one shall harm thee, friend," said he. "These are all my bowmen, threescore and nine, and if you will be one of us you shall straightway have livery and accountrements, fit for a man. What say you?" "With all my heart," said the stranger; "here is my hand on it. My name is John Little, and I will be a good man and true to you." His name shall be changed," said William Stukely on this. "We will call him Little John, and I will be his godfather."

So they fetched a pair of fat does and some humming strong ale, and there they christened their babe Little John, for he was seven feet high and an ell round at his waist.

THE MAN OF INTEGRITY
AND HONOR

The Great-Souled Man

From Aristotle, The Nicomachean Ethics

Can a man be proud without being arrogant and overbearing? In modern times, we tend to think not. But the ancients believed that a justified pride in one's accomplishments was an important part of manly self-respect. More- over, it could be the basis for good behavior toward others. For Aristotle, a man who possesses "greatness of soul" will not stoop to treat others unjustly or unkindly because it would reveal his need for others as objects of exploita- tion. He is generous and decent toward others precisely because he doesn't need anything from them. In the Ethics, *Aristotle tells us that pride is the crown of all the moral virtues, including courage, self-control and generosi- ty. The proud man is the source of his own self-esteem, amply confirmed by the honor he receives from his fellow citizens.*

Magnanimity, or greatness of soul, as the name imports, is con- versant about great things; what these are let us first consider; con- templating not the quality itself, but the person actuated by it, which will bring us to precisely the same conclusions. A magnanimous man is he, whose character being of great worth, is estimated by himself at its full value. He who forms a grossly false estimate of himself is a fool; and none of the virtues are consistent with folly: while the man who, conscious of his defects, appreciates his small merits by a fair and just standard, may be praised for his good sense and modesty, but cannot pass for magnanimous; which epithet always implies dignity and excel- lence; this beauty of the mind requiring, like that of the body, eleva- tion and magnitude; for persons of a diminutive stature are not called beautiful, but neat and elegant. A mean-spirited man underrates his own merits; and the vainglorious boaster arrogates to himself merits, of which he is by no means possessed; but the more solid merit he pos- sesses, his vainglory is the less; whereas mean-spiritedness is the greater in proportion to the excellence of the worth which is so improperly appreciated by its possessor; for how contemptible would he be, even to himself, were his real character of little or no value! The magnanimous man estimates himself at the highest rate, yet no higher than he ought; and conscious of his inward worth, thinks himself entitled to whatever is held most precious; to what the most exalted of men claim as the highest of all rewards and to what all men confer on the gods as their acknowledged due; in a word, to honor, the greatest and most invaluable of external goods.

Magnanimity, therefore, is peculiarly conversant about honour, and its contrary, ignominy; holding the middle place between vainglory that unfairly courts undue honors, and meanspiritedness that improperly rejects even those that are due. But though, in point of propriety, magnanimity holds the middle place, yet, in excellence and dignity, it rises to the summit; for it heightens and enlarges every virtue; and the most boastful vainglory never proudly arrogated more than true magnanimity has fairly claimed. This illustrious habit of the mind cannot bear an alliance with any kind of vice. It is most opposite to cowardice or injustice; for, from what motive can he, who thinks of nothing so highly as of his own character, exhibit himself under such deformities? And if we apply to particular instances, or survey individual characters, we shall find that those who affect magnanimity without real worth, infallibly expose themselves to ridicule. For, honour, which is the meed of virtue, cannot belong to the worthless; and magnanimity forms, as it were, the ornament of the virtues, since it cannot subsist without them, yet heightens, extends, and magnifies them, wherever they are found.

True magnanimity then is a thing most difficult, since it implies the perfection of moral rectitude. It delights, moderately, in great honors bestowed by the deserving, as meeting with its due, or less: for with perfect virtue no honor can be fully commensurate. It accepts, however, such honors, because nothing better can be bestowed; but of vulgar honors, or from vulgar men, it is altogether disdainful; and is as insensible to their reproach, as careless of their applause. Wealth, power, good or bad fortune, it will meet and sustain with the same dignified composure, neither elated with prosperity nor dejected by adversity; for to a magnanimous man those things are desirable chiefly as the signs of honor; and, if he bears honor itself with moderation, much more must he thus bear those things which are only its signs, and desired merely on its account, since to him who thinks not too highly of honor, nothing besides can possibly appear great. Magnanimity, therefore, sometimes passes for superciliousness; especially since great external prosperity seems to heighten and increase it; for nobility is honored; and men of wealth or power, being distinguished by great superiority of advantages, will always find persons ready to do them honor: and though honor belongs properly to virtue alone, yet virtue, adorned with great external prosperity, will seem doubly entitled to pre-eminence. But, in reality, the most prosperous fortune, when destitute of virtue, does not give any just ground for self-applause; it gives to us neither a high opinion of ourselves, nor a fair claim to be highly thought of by others; and as it is incapable of inspiring true magnanimity, it too frequently begets insolence and superciliousness; since worthless men cannot bear gracefully the gifts of fortune, but abuse their fancied superiority by treating others contemptuously and unjustly; whereas the contempt shown by the truly magnanimous, is just; their opinions being formed on reflection, as those of the multitude are taken up at random.

A man of magnanimity neither courts dangers, nor willingly encounters them on slight occasions. But when a worthy occasion requires it, he is unsparing of his life, thinking that to live is not, under all conditions, desirable. He is eager to confer favors, and ashamed of receiving them: because the former is a mask of superiority, the latter the reverse; he therefore repays every kindness with interest, that the person who first obliged him may become his debtor. He hears with more pleasure a recital of the good offices he has performed, than that of the favors which he has received. Wherefore Thetis does not expatiate on her benefits to Jupiter, nor the Lacedaemonians on those which they had conferred on the Athenians; but rather on the kindness they themselves had received at their hands; for magnanimity, having few wants, seldom needs that assistance which it is always disposed to give; it is lofty towards the great and prosperous, but behaves modestly towards men in moderate circumstances: to rise above the former, has difficulty and dignity; but to magnify ourselves in company with the latter betrays a lowness and littleness of mind, not less ungenerous and vulgar, than making a parade of our strength or courage amidst weakness and cowardice. Magnanimity condemns trivial honors; and disdains, even in great things, to act a secondary role. It is slow in action, and averse to exertion, except when great honor may be obtained, or great actions are to be performed: not busied about many things, but confined to those which are great and splendid. A magnanimous man is as open in his hatred as in his friendship; for concealment is the part of fear; he regards truth more than opinion, and shows himself manifestly in his words and actions, declaring his mind with full freedom; which indicates both his own love of truth and his contempt for the opinions of others: but this openness of character is liable to one exception, for he is much given to *irony*, dissembling his merits before the vulgar, who are unworthy to appreciate them. He can show undue complaisance for no one's humors, except those of his friends; for flattery is a low and servile vice. He is not prone to admire, for he deems nothing great. He is not mindful of injuries, which his magnanimity teaches him to despise. He is no man's panegyrist or slanderer; he talks not of himself, nor does he blame others; not speaking ill even of his enemies, except when their insolence excites his indignation. As to things of small import, or even daily use, he is no petitioner or complainer: for that would show too much concern about them. His possessions are distinguished for their beauty and elegance rather than for their fruitfulness and utility; because the former qualities are more nearly allied to that independence and all-sufficiency to which he aspires. The gait of a magnanimous man is slow; his tone of voice grave, his pronunciation firm. Haste and rapidity betoken too much solicitude. *He* therefore is seldom in haste who deems few things worthy of his pursuit; nor is he often eager who thinks few things of importance: quickness and sharpness of voice proceed from earnestness and eagerness. Such then are the characteristics of magnanimity.

A Counterfeit Man

From William Shakespeare, As You Like It

Rosalind: Were it not better,
Because that I am more than common tall,
That I did suit me all points like a man?
A gallant curtle-axe upon my thigh,
A boar-spear in my hand; and, in my heart
Lie there what hidden woman's fear there will,
We'll have a swashing and a martial outside,
As many other mannish cowards have
That do outface it with their semblances.

Achilles Fights a River
and Learns a Lesson

From Homer, The Iliad

Achilles kills so many Trojans that the River Skamandros runs red with blood. An early environmentalist, the river itself objects to being polluted, and Achilles jumps in the stream to fight the river for its impertinence. The river tries to suck him in and chases him when he scrambles ashore, washing the soil from beneath his feet. It's a comical scene, but it prefigures Achilles's death at an early age for aiming too high for a mortal. Through it, Homer shows that there are cosmic limitations on manly prowess. We cannot achieve everything we want to, no matter how brave and strong-willed we may be. At bottom, human life is tragic because our powers are limited by necessity and chance, and ultimately we all die. This tragic insight should chasten our arrogance and give our ambitions a sense of proportion.

Now swift Achilleus would have killed even more Paionians except that the deep-whirling river spoke to him in anger and in mortal likeness, and the voice rose from the depth of the eddies:

"O Achilleus, your strength is greater, your acts more violent than all men's; since always the very gods are guarding you. If the son of Kronos has given all Trojans to your destruction, drive them at least out of me to the plain, and there work your havoc. For the loveliness of my waters is crammed with corpses, I cannot find a channel to cast my waters into the bright sea since I am congested with the dead men you kill so brutally. Let me alone, then; lord of the people, I am confounded."

Then in answer to him spoke Achilleus of the swift feet:

"All this, illustrious Skamandros, shall be as you order. But I will not leave off my killing of the proud Trojans until I have penned them inside their city, and attempted Hektor strength against strength, until he has killed me or I have killed him." He spoke, and like something more than mortal swept down on the Trojans.

And now the deep-whirling river called aloud to Apollo:

"Shame, lord of the silver bow, Zeus's son; you have not kept the counsels of Kronion, who very strongly ordered you to stand by the Trojans and defend them, until the sun setting at last goes down and darkens all the generous ploughland." He spoke: and spear-famed Achilleus leapt into the middle water with a spring from the bluff, but the river in a boiling surge was upon him and rose making turbulent all his waters, and pushed off the many dead men whom Achilleus had killed piled in abundance in the stream; these, bellowing like a bull, he shoved out on the dry land, but saved the living in the sweet waters hiding them under the huge depths of the whirling current. And about Achilleus in his confusion a dangerous wave rose up, and beat against his shield and pushed it. He could not brace himself with his feet, but caught with his hands at an elm tree tall and strong grown, but this untorn by the roots and tumbling ripped away the whole cliff and with its dense tangle of roots stopped the run of the lovely current and fallen full length in the water dammed the very stream. Achilleus uprising out of the whirlpool made a dash to get the plain in the speed of his quick feet in fear, but the great god would not let him be, but rose on him in a darkening edge of water, minded to stop the labor of brilliant Achilleus and fend destruction away from the Trojans. The son of Peleus sprang away the length of a spearcast running with the speed of the black eagle, the marauder who is at once the strongest of flying things and the swiftest. In the likeness of this he sped away, on his chest the bronze armor clashed terribly, and bending away to escape from the river he fled, but the river came streaming after him in huge noise. And as a man running a channel from a spring of dark water guides the run of the water among his plants and his gardens with a mattock in his hand and knocks down the blocks in the channel; in the rush of the water all the pebbles beneath are torn loose from place, and the water that has been dripping suddenly jets on in a steep place and goes too fast even for the man who guides it; so always the crest of the river was overtaking Achilleus for all his speed of foot, since gods are stronger than mortals. And every time swift-footed brilliant Achilleus would begin to turn and stand and fight the river, and try to discover if all the gods who hold the wide heaven were after him, every time again the enormous wave of the sky-fed river would strike his shoulders from above. He tried, in his desperation, to keep a high spring with his feet, but the river was wearing his knees out as it ran fiercely beneath him and cut the ground from under his feet. Peleides groaned aloud, gazing into the wide sky:

"Father Zeus, no god could endure to save me from the river who am so pitiful. And what then shall become of me? It is not so much any other Uranian god who has done this but my own mother who beguiled me with falsehoods, who told that underneath the battlements of the armored Trojans I should be destroyed by the flying shafts of Apollo. I wish now Hektor had killed me, the greatest man grown in this place. A brave man would have been the slayer, as the slain was a brave man. But now this is a dismal death I am doomed to be caught in, trapped in a big river as if I were a boy and swineherd swept away by a torrent when he tries to cross in a rainstorm."

Moral Courage

From Charles Dickens,
A Tale of Two Cities

Not all bravery is on the battlefield. In one of Dickens' best-known novels, Sidney Carton exchanges his life for another falsely convicted.

They said of him, about the city that night, that it was the peacefullest man's face ever beheld there. Many added that he looked sublime and prophetic.

One of the most remarkable sufferers by the same axe—a woman—had asked at the foot of the same scaffold, not long before, to be allowed to write down the thoughts that were inspiring her. If he had given an utterance to his, and they were prophetic, they would have been these:

"I see Barsad, and Cly, Defarge, the Vengeance, the Juryman, the Judge, long ranks of the new oppressors who have risen on the destruction of the old, perishing by this retributive instrument, before it shall cease out of its present use. I see a beautiful city and a brilliant people rising from this abyss, and, in their struggles to be truly free, in their triumphs and defeats, through long years to come, I see the evil of this time and of the previous time of which this is the natural birth, gradually making expiation for itself and wearing out.

"I see the lives for which I lay down my life, peaceful, useful, prosperous and happy, in that England which I shall see no more. I see Her with a child upon her bosom, who bears my name. I see her father, aged and bent, but otherwise restored, and faithful to all men in his healing office, and at peace. I see the good old man, so long their friend, in ten years' time enriching them with all he has, and passing tranquillity to his reward.

"I see that I hold a sanctuary in their hearts, and in the hearts of their descendants, generations hence. I see her, an old woman, weeping for me on the anniversary of this day. I see her and her husband, their course done, lying side by side in their last earthly bed, and I know that each was not more honored and held sacred in the other's soul, than I was in the souls of both.

"I see that child who lay upon her bosom and who bore my name, a man winning his way up in that path of life which once was mine. I see him winning it so well, that my name is made illustrious there by the light of his. I see the blots I threw upon it, faded away. I see him, foremost of just judges and honored men, bringing a boy of my name, with a forehead that I know and golden hair, to this place—then fair to look upon, with not a trace of this day's disfigurement—and I hear him tell the child my story, with a tender and a faltering voice.

"It is a far, far better thing that I do, than I have ever done; it is a far, far better rest that I go to than I have ever known."

Conquer Fortune
with Patience

From Leon Battista Alberti,
On the Duties and Education of Children

If a young man cultivates the virtues of courage, intelligence, and modesty, he will triumph over adversity by mastering his own inner impulses.

I am one of those who would rather bequeath their children virtue than all the wealth in the world; but this is not up to me, my dear children. What I deemed proper for me to do, I have done. I have always striven to give you those principles, aid, and means by which you might gain praise, favor, and great honors. It is up to you to use the intellect nature gave you, which, I believe, is neither weak nor inferior, and improve it with good studies and habits and by learning arts and letters. You must use the wealth I leave you in such a way as to endear yourselves not only to your family but to others as well. And yet it seems to me that there will be times when you will suffer because of my absence, my dear children. Perhaps you will experience adversity and affliction which, if I were there, would harm you less; for I well know what power Fortune has against young men of tender years and inexperienced minds, with no one to counsel and help them. I have the example of our house which abounds in prudence, wisdom, experience, strength, and firm courage, yet in our present adversity it has learned what power, Fortune, with her fury and iniquity, has against anyone's firm determination and prudent judgment. Be brave and courageous, for adversity is the proving ground of virtue. Is there any man who can gain as much praise and fame for his brave spirit, firm will, great intellect, zeal, and skill in favorable and peaceful circumstances, as he can in difficult times and adversity? So conquer Fortune, with patience. Overcome men's iniquity by persevering in virtue. Adapt yourselves to the times and to necessity with wisdom and prudence. Conform to the usages and customs of men of modesty, good breeding, and discretion. Above all, strive with all your intelligence, skill, zeal, and deeds first to be virtuous, then to appear so. Let nothing be dearer to you, do not desire anything before virtue. You shall first determine that wisdom and knowledge are to be preferred to everything else, and then you will see that the favors of Fortune are of little value. Only honor and fame will have first place in your desires, and you will never prefer wealth to praise. To gain honor and esteem, you will never think of avoiding any undertaking, no matter how arduous and strenuous, and you will persevere in it. You will be satisfied to expect from your labors nothing more than gratitude and renown. Do not doubt, however, that the virtuous will enjoy the fruits of their labors sooner or later. Do not lose confidence and fail to persevere assiduously in the study of excellent arts and rare and praiseworthy matters. Do not fail to learn and retain good doctrines and disciplines, for late payments often include a large interest.

I am not displeased that from a tender age you have had a good opportunity to practice and learn how to oppose and sustain the onslaughts of adversity. I leave you in exile and fatherless, far from your country and your home. It will be to your praise, my dear children, to spend a part, if not all, of your tender years among the harshness and difficulties of necessity and to conquer them. When you reach manhood, you will have achieved victory over your own selves, as it were, if at every age you have had little fear of the malignity of Fortune and have been able to resist her blows.

The Generous Majesty
of His Nature:
Lawrence of Arabia

From Winston S. Churchill,
Great Contemporaries

Despite great changes in the ideals of manliness over the centuries, until roughly World War II, there is an impressive consistency in the way in which the higher kind of manliness is understood and extolled by European and American writers. Consider this brief, eloquent essay on T. E. Lawrence, "Lawrence of Arabia," by Winston Churchill. In form and content, Churchill's praise of Lawrence could almost have been written by Aristotle or Cicero, so closely and naturally does it adhere to the tradition of masculine refinement and honor that reaches back to antiquity. Lawrence, according to Churchill, embodied that same hierarchy of active and contemplative virtues we find stretching through the European tradition back to the ancients. He was a great general, statesman, and leader. But, even more admirable from Churchill's viewpoint, he was an outstanding scholar and author. Admirable as the life of active virtue may be, we are told once again, the life of the mind is even more to be admired. "An epic, a prodigy, a tale of torment, and in the heart of it—a Man."

I did not meet Lawrence till after the war was over. It was the spring of 1919, when the Peace-makers, or at any rate the Treaty-makers, were gathered in Paris and all England was in the ferment of the aftermath. So great had been the pressure in the War, so vast its scale, so dominating the great battles in France, that I had only been dimly conscious of the part played in Allenby's campaigns by the Arab revolt in the desert. But now someone said to me: "You ought to meet this wonderful young man. His exploits are an epic." So Lawrence came to luncheon. Usually at this time in London or Paris he wore his Arab dress in order to identify himself with the interests of the Emir Feisal and with the Arabian claims then under harsh debate. On this occasion, however, he wore plain clothes, and looked at first sight like one of the many clean-cut young officers who had gained high rank and distinction in the struggle.

I did not see Lawrence again for some weeks. It was, if my memory serves me right, in Paris. He wore his Arab robes, and the full magnificence of his countenance revealed itself. The gravity of his demeanor, the precision of his opinions; the range and quality of his conversation; all seemed enhanced to a remarkable degree by the splendid Arab head-dress and garb. From amid the flowing draperies his noble features, his perfectly chiseled lips and flashing eyes loaded with fire and comprehension shone forth. He looked what he was, one of Nature's greatest princes. We got on much better this time, and I began to form that impression of his strength and quality which since has never left me. Whether he wore the prosaic clothes of English daily life or afterward in the uniform of an Air Force mechanic, I always saw him henceforward as he appears in Augustus John's brilliant pencil sketch.

I began to hear much more about him from friends who had fought under his command, and indeed there was endless talk about him in every circle, military, diplomatic and academic. It appeared that he was a savant as well as a soldier: an archaeologist as well as a man of action: a brilliant scholar as well as an Arab partisan.

An important post was offered to Lawrence, and to the surprise of most people, though not altogether to mine, he accepted at once. This is not the place to enter upon the details of the tangled and thorny problems we had to settle. The barest outline will suffice. It was necessary to handle the matter on the spot. I therefore convened a conference at Cairo to which practically all the experts and authorities of the Middle East were summoned. Accompanied by Lawrence, Hubert Young, and Trenchard from the Air Ministry, I set out for Cairo. We stayed there and in Palestine for about a month. We submitted the following main proposals to the Cabinet: First, we would repair the injury done to the Arabs and to the House of the Sherifs of Mecca by placing the Emir Feisal upon the throne of Iraq as King, and by entrusting the Emir-Abdulla with the government of Trans-Jordania. Secondly, we would remove practically all the troops from Iraq and entrust its defense to the Royal Air Force. Thirdly, we suggested an adjustment of the immediate difficulties between the Jews and Arabs in Palestine which would serve as a foundation for the future.

Tremendous opposition was aroused against the first two proposals. The French Government deeply resented the favor shown to the Emir Feisal, whom they regarded as a defeated rebel. The British War Office was shocked at the removal of the troops, and predicted carnage and ruin. I had, however, already noticed that when Trenchard undertook to do anything particular, he usually carried it through. Our proposals were accepted, but it required a year of most difficult and anxious administration to give effect to what had been so speedily decided.

Lawrence's term as a Civil Servant was a unique phase in his life. Everyone was astonished by his calm and tactful demeanor. His patience and readiness to work with others amazed those who knew him best. Tremendous confabulations must have taken place among these experts, and tension at times must have been extreme. But so far as I was concerned, I received always united advice from two or three of the very best men it has ever been my fortune to work with. It would not be just to assign the whole credit for the great success which the new policy secured to Lawrence alone. The wonder was that he was able to sink his personality, to bend his imperious will and pool his knowledge in the common stock. Here is one of the proofs of the greatness of his character and the versatility of his genius. He saw the hope of redeeming in a large measure the promises he had made to the Arab chiefs and of reestablishing a tolerable measure of peace in those wide regions. In that cause he was capable of becoming—I hazard the word—a humdrum official. The effort was not in vain. His purposes prevailed.

The next episode was the writing, the printing, the binding and the publication of his book, *Seven Pillars of Wisdom.* This is perhaps the point at which to deal with this treasure of English literature. As a narrative of war and adventure, as a portrayal of all that the Arabs mean to the world, it is unsurpassed. It ranks with the greatest books ever written in the English language. If Lawrence had never done anything except write this book as a mere work of the imagination his fame would last—to quote Macaulay's hackneyed phrase—"as long as the English language is spoken in any quarter of the globe." *The Pilgrim's Progress, Robinson Crusoe, Gulliver's Travels* are dear to British homes. Here is a tale originally their equal in interest and charm. But it is fact, not fiction. The author was also the commander. Caesar's *Commentaries* deal with larger numbers, but in Lawrence's story nothing that has ever happened in the sphere of war and empire is lacking. When most of the vast literature of the Great War has been sifted and superseded by the epitomes, commentaries and histories of future generations, when the complicated and infinitely costly operations of its ponderous armies are the concern only of the military student, when our struggles are viewed in a fading perspective and a truer proportion, Lawrence's tale of the revolt in the desert will gleam with immortal fire.

We read of grim camel-rides through sun-scorched, blasted lands, where the extreme desolation of nature appalls the traveler. With a motor-car or airplane we may now inspect these forbidding solitudes, their endless sands, the hot savage wind-whipped rocks, the mountain gorges of a red-hot moon. Through these with infinite privation men on camels with shattering toil carried dynamite to destroy railway bridges and win the war, and, as we then hoped, free the world.

Here we see Lawrence the soldier. Not only the soldier but the statesman: rousing the fierce peoples of the desert, penetrating the mysteries of their thought, leading them to the selected points of action and as often as not firing the mine himself. Detailed accounts are given of ferocious battles with thousands of men and little quarter fought under his command on these lava landscapes of hell. There are no mass-effects. All is intense, individual, sentient—and yet cast in conditions which seemed to forbid human existence. Through all, one mind, one soul, one willpower. An epic, a prodigy, a tale of torment, and in the heart of it—a Man.

The impression of the personality of Lawrence remains living and vivid upon the minds of his friends, and the sense of his loss is in no way dimmed among his countrymen. All feel the poorer that he has gone from us. In these days dangers and difficulties gather upon Britain and her Empire, and we are also conscious of a lack of outstanding figures with which to overcome them. Here was a man in whom there existed not only an immense capacity for service, but that touch of genius which everyone recognizes and no one can define. Alike in his great period of adventure and command or in these later years of self-suppression and self-imposed eclipse, he always reigned over those with whom he came in contact. They felt themselves in the presence of an extraordinary being. They felt that his latent reserves of force and willpower were beyond measurement. If he roused himself to action, who should say what crisis he could not surmount or quell? If things were going very badly, how glad one would be to see him come round the corner.

Part of the secret of this stimulating ascendancy lay of course in his disdain for most of the prizes, the pleasures and comforts of life. The world naturally looks with some awe upon a man who appears unconcernedly indifferent to home, money, comfort, rank, or even power and fame. The world feels, not without a certain apprehension, that here is someone outside its jurisdiction; someone before whom its allurements may be spread in vain; someone strangely enfranchised, untamed, untrammeled by convention, moving inde-

pendently of the ordinary currents of human action; a being readily capable of violent revolt or supreme sacrifice, a man solitary, austere to whom existence is no more than a duty, yet a duty to be faithfully discharged. He was indeed a dweller upon the mountain tops
where the air is cold, crisp and rarefied, and where the view on clear
days commands all the Kingdoms of the world and the glory of
them.

Lawrence was one of those beings whose pace of life was faster
and more intense than the ordinary. Just as an airplane only flies by
its speed and pressure against the air, so he flew best and easiest in
the hurricane. He was not in complete harmony with the normal.
The fury of the Great War raised the pitch of life to the Lawrence
standard. The multitudes were swept forward till their pace was the
same as his. In this heroic period he found himself in perfect relation both to men and events.

Lawrence has a full measure of the versatility of genius. He
held one of those master keys which unlock the doors of many kinds
of treasure-houses. He was a savant as well as a soldier. He was an
archaeologist as well as a man of action. He was an accomplished
scholar as well as an Arab partisan. He was a mechanic as well as a
philosopher. His background of somber experience and reflection
only seemed to set forth more brightly the charm and gaiety of his
companionship, and the generous majesty of his nature.

Toussaint L'Ouverture:
Soldier, Statesman, Martyr

From Wendell Phillips, Select Orations

*A tribute to the leader of the Haitian independence movement, Toussaint
L'Ouverture (1743–1803), by the American abolitionist crusader Wendell
Phillips (1811–1844).*

If I stood here to tell you the story of Napoleon, I should take it
from the lips of Frenchmen, who find no language rich enough to
paint the great captain of the nineteenth century. Were I to tell you
the story of Washington, I should take it from your hearts—you, who

think no marble white enough on which to carve the name of the Father of his country. But I am to tell you the story of a negro who has left hardly one written line. I am to glean it from the reluctant testimony of Britons, Frenchmen, Spaniards—men who despised him as a negro and a slave, and hated him because he had beaten them in battle. All the materials for his biography are from the lips of his enemies. Let us pause a moment, and find some things to measure him by. You remember Macaulay says, comparing Cromwell with Napoleon, that Cromwell showed the greater military genius, if we consider that he never saw an army until he was forty; while Napoleon was educated from a boy in the best military schools in Europe. Cromwell manufactured his own army; Napoleon at the age of twenty-seven was placed at the head of the best Europe ever saw. They were both successful; but, says Macaulay, with such disadvantages, the Englishmen showed the greater genius. Whether you allow the inference or not, you will at least grant that it is a fair mode of measurement. Apply it to this negro. Cromwell never saw an army till he was forty; this man never saw a soldier till he was fifty. Cromwell manufactured his own army—out of what? Englishmen—the best blood in Europe. Out of the middle class of Englishmen—the best blood of the island. And with it he conquered what? Englishmen—their equals. This man manufactured his army out of what? Out of what you call the despicable race of negroes, debased, demoralized by two hundred years of slavery, one hundred thousand of them imported into the island within four years, unable to speak a dialect intelligible even to each other. Yet out of this mixed, and as you say, despicable mass he forged a thunderbolt and hurled it at what? At the proudest blood in Europe, the Spaniard, and sent him home conquered; at the most warlike blood in Europe, the French, and put them under his feet, at the pluckiest blood in Europe, the English, and they skulked home to Jamaica. Now, if Cromwell was a general, at least this man was a soldier.

Now, blue-eyed Saxon proud of your race, go back with me to the commencement of the century, and select what statesman you please. Let him be either American or European; let him have a brain the result of six generations of culture; let him have the ripest training of university routine; let him add to it the better education of practical life; crown his temples with the silver locks of seventy years, and show me the man of Saxon lineage for whom his most sanguine admirer will wreathe a laurel, rich as embittered foes have placed on the brow of this negro—rare military skill, profound knowledge of human nature, content to blot out all party distinctions, and trust a state to the blood of its sons—anticipating Sir Robert Peel fifty years, and taking his station by the side of Roger Williams, before any Englishman or American had won the right; and yet this is the record which the history of rival states makes up for this inspired black of St. Domingo.

Some doubt the courage of the negro. Go to Hayti, and stand on those fifty thousand graves of the best soldiers France ever had, and ask them what they think of the negro's sword.

I would call him Napoleon, but Napoleon made his way to empire over broken oaths and through a sea of blood. This man never broke his word. I would call him Cromwell, but Cromwell was only a soldier, and the state he founded went down with him into his grave. I would call him Washington, but the great Virginian held slaves. This man risked his empire rather than permit the slave-trade in the humblest village of his dominions.

You think me a fanatic, for you read history, not with your eyes but with your prejudices. But fifty years hence, when Truth gets a hearing, the Muse of history will put Phocion for the Greek, Brutus for the Roman, Hampden for England, Fayette for France, choose Washington as the bright consummate flower of our earlier civilization, then, dipping her pen in the sunlight, will write in the clear blue, above them all, the name of the soldier, the statesman, the martyr, Toussaint L'Ouverture.

If

Rudyard Kipling

If you can keep your head when all about you
Are losing theirs and blaming it on you;
If you can trust yourself when all men doubt you,
But make allowance for their doubting too;
If you can wait and not be tired by waiting,
Or, being lied about, don't deal in lies,
Or, being hated, don't give way to hating,
And yet don't look too good, nor talk too wise;

If you can dream—and not make dreams your master;
If you can think—and not make thoughts your aim;
If you can meet with triumph and disaster
And treat those two imposters just the same;
If you can bear to hear the truth you've spoken
Twisted by knaves to make a trap for fools,
Or watch the things you gave your life to broken,
And stoop and build 'em up with wornout tools;

If you can make one heap of all your winnings
And risk it on one turn of pitch-and-toss,
And lose, and start again at your beginnings
And never breathe a word about your loss;
If you can force your heart and nerve and sinew
To serve your turn long after they are gone,
And so hold on when there is nothing in you
Except the Will which says to them: "Hold on";

If you can talk with crowds and keep your virtue,
Or walk with kings—nor lose the common touch;
If neither foes nor loving friends can hurt you;
If all men count with you, but none too much;
If you can fill the unforgiving minute
With sixty seconds' worth of distance run—
Yours is the Earth and everything that's in it,
And—which is more—you'll be a Man my son!

Warriors Don't Always Make the Best Husbands

From William Shakespeare,
Henry IV, Part One

Hotspur, as his name suggests, has trouble restraining his lust for a brave warrior's exploits. His uncle tries to get the young man to calm down and think more prudently—but to no avail. Hotspur's wife wishes he had more time for her and less for his horse.

Hotspur.   If he fall in, good night, or sink, or swim!
Send danger from the east unto the west,
So honor cross it from the north to south,
And let them grapple. O, the blood more stirs
To rouse a lion than to start a hare!
Northumberland.   Imagination of some great exploit
Drives him beyond the bounds of patience.
Hotspur.   By heaven, methinks it were an easy leap
To pluck bright honor from the pale-faced moon,
Or dive into the bottom of the deep,
Where fathom line could never touch the ground,
And pluck up drowned honor by the locks,
So he that doth redeem her thence might wear
Without corrival all her dignities;
But out upon this half-faced fellowship!
Worcester.   He apprehends a world of figures here,
But not the form of what he should attend.
Good cousin, give me audience for a while.
Hotspur.   I cry you mercy.
Worcester.   Those same noble Scots that are your prisoners—
Hotspur.   I'll keep them all.
By God, he shall not have a Scot of them!
No, if a Scot would save his soul, he shall not.
I'll keep them, by his hand!

Worcester.   You start away
And lend no ear unto my purposes.
Those prisoners you shall keep.
Hotspur.   Nay, I will! That's flat!
He said he would not ransom Mortimer,
Forbade my tongue to speak of Mortimer,
But I will find him when he lies asleep,
And in his ear I'll hollo "Mortimer."
Nay, I'll have a starling shall be taught to speak
Nothing but "Mortimer," and give it him
To keep his anger still in motion.
Worcester.   Hear you, cousin, a word.
Hotspur.   All studies here I solemnly defy
Save how to gall and pinch this Bolingbroke;
And that same sword-and-buckler Prince of Wales,
But that I think his father loves him not
And would be glad he met with some mischance,
I would have him poisoned with a pot of ale.
Worcester.   Farewell, kinsman: I'll talk to you
When you are better tempered to attend.

Hotspur.   How now, Kate? I must leave you within these two
hours.
Lady.   O my good lord, why are you thus alone?
For what offense have I this fortnight been
A banished woman from my Harry's bed?
Tell me, sweet lord, what is't that takes from thee
Thy stomach, pleasure, and thy golden sleep?
Why dost thou bend thine eyes upon the earth,
And start so often when thou sit'st alone?
Why hast thou lost the fresh blood in thy cheeks
And given my treasures and my rights of thee
To thick-eyed musing and cursed melancholy?
In thy faint slumbers I by thee have watched,
And heard thee murmur tales of iron wars,
Speak terms of manage to thy bounding steed,
Cry "Courage! To the field!" And thou has talked
Of sallies and retires, of trenches, tents,
Of palisadoes, frontiers, parapets,
Of basilisks, of cannon, culverin,
Of prisoners ransom, and of soldiers slain,

And all the currents of a heady fight.
Thy spirit within thee hath been so at war,
And thus hath so bestirred thee in thy sleep,
That beads of sweat have stood upon thy brow
Like bubbles in a late-disturbed stream,
And in thy face strange motions have appeared,
Such as we see when men restrain their breath
On some great sudden hest. O, what portents are these?
Some heavy business hath my lord in hand,
And I must know it, else he loves me not.
Hotspur.   What, ho!

Lady.   What is it carries you away?
Hotspur.   Why, my horse, my love—my horse!
Lady.   Out, you mad-headed ape! A weasel hath not
such a deal of spleen as you are tossed with. In
faith, I'll know your business, Harry, that I will! I
fear my brother Mortimer doth stir about his title
and hath sent for you to line his enterprise; but if
        you go—
Come, come, you paraquito, answer me directly
unto this question that I ask. In faith, I'll break thy
little finger, Harry, and if thou wilt not tell me all
things true.
Hotspur.   Away, away, you trifler! Love? I love thee not;
I care not for thee, Kate. This is no world
To play with mammets and to tilt with lips.
We must have bloody noses and cracked crowns,
And pass them current too. Gods me, my horse!
What say'st thou, Kate? What wouldst thou have with me?
Lady.   Do you not love me? Do you not indeed?
Well, do not then; for since you love me not,
I will not love myself. Do you not love me?
Nay, tell me if you speak in jest or no.
Hotspur.   Come, wilt thou see me ride?
And when I am a horseback, I will swear
I love thee infinitely. But hark you, Kate:
I must not have you henceforth question me
Whither I go, nor reason whereabout.
Whither I must, I must, and—to conclude,
This evening must I leave you, gentle Kate.

I know you wise—but yet no farther wise
Than Harry Percy's wife; constant you are—
But yet a woman; and for secrecy,
No lady closer—for I well believe
Thou wilt not utter what thou dost not know,
And so far will I trust thee, gentle Kate—
Lady.   How? So far?
Hotspur.   Not an inch further. But hark you, Kate:
Whither I go, thither shall you go too;
Today will I set forth, tomorrow you.
Will this content you, Kate?
Lady.   It must of force.

The Happy Warrior

William Wordsworth

Who is the happy Warrior? Who is he
That every man in arms should wish to be?
—It is the generous Spirit, who, when brought
Among the tasks of real life, hath wrought
Upon the plan that pleased his boyish thought:
Whose high endeavors are an inward light
That makes the path before him always bright:
Who, with a natural instinct to discern
What knowledge can perform, is diligent to learn;
Abides by this resolve, and stops not there,
But makes his moral being his prime care;
Who, doomed to go in company with Pain,
And Fear, and Bloodshed, miserable train!
Turns his necessity to glorious gain;
In face of these doth exercise a power
Which is our human nature's highest dower;
Controls them and subdues, transmutes, bereaves
Of their bad influence, and their good receives:
By objects, which might force the soul to abate
Her feeling, rendered more compassionate;
Is placable—because occasions rise

So often that demand such sacrifice;
More skillful in self-knowledge, even more pure,
As tempted more; more able to endure,
As more exposed to suffering and distress;
Thence also, more alive to tenderness.
—'Tis he whose law is reason; who depends
Upon that law as on the best of friends;
Whence, in a state where men are tempted still
To evil for a guard against worse ill,
And what in quality or act is best
Doth seldom on a right foundation rest,
He labors good on good to fix, and owes
To virtue every triumph that he knows:
—Who, if he rise to station of command,
Rises by open means; and there will stand
On honorable terms, or else retire
And in himself possess his own desire;
Who comprehends his trust, and to the same
Keeps faithful with a singleness of aim;
And therefore does not stoop, nor lie in wait
For wealth, or honors, or for worldly state;
Whom they must follow; on whose head must fall,
Like showers of manna, if they come at all:
Whose powers shed round him in the common strife,
Or mild concerns of ordinary life,
A constant influence, a peculiar grace;
But who, if he be called upon to face
Some awful moment to which Heaven has joined
Great issues, good or bad for human kind,
Is happy as a Lover; and attired
With sudden brightness, like a Man inspired;
And, through the heat of conflict, keeps the law
In calmness made, and sees what he foresaw;
Or if an unexpected call succeed,
Come when it will, is equal to the need:
—He who, though thus endued as with a sense
And faculty for storm and turbulence,
Is yet a Soul whose master-bias leans
To homefelt pleasures and to gentle scenes;
Sweet images! which, wheresoe'er he be,
Are at his heart; and such fidelity
It is his darling passion to approve;

More brave for this, that he hath much to love:—
'Tis, finally, the Man who lifted high,
Conspicuous object in a Nation's eye,
Or left unthought-of in obscurity,—
Who, with a toward or untoward lot,
Prosperous or adverse, to his wish or not—
Plays, in the many games of life, that one
Where what the most doth value must be won:
Whom neither shape of danger can dismay
Nor thought of tender happiness betray;
Who, not content that former worth stand fast,
Looks forward, persevering to the last,
From well to better, daily self-surpast:
Who, whether praise of him must walk the earth
Forever, and to noble deeds give birth,
Or he must fall, to sleep without his fame,
And leave a dead unprofitable name—
Finds comfort in himself and his cause;
And, while the mortal mist is gathering, draws
His breath in confidence of Heaven's applause:
This is the happy Warrior; this is He
That every Man in arms should wish to be.

The Value of Adversity
to a Great Man

From Seneca, On Providence

Lucius Annaeus Seneca (5 B.C.–65 A.D.) was a Roman author of philosophical and literary works.

Success comes to the common man, and even to the commonplace ability; but to triumph over the calamities and terrors of mortal life is the part of a great man only. Truly, to be always happy and to pass through life without a mental pang is to be ignorant of one half of nature. You are a great man; but how do I know it if Fortune gives you no opportunity of showing your worth? You have entered as a contestant at the Olympic games, but none other besides you; you gain the crown, the victory you do not gain. You have my congratulations—not as a brave man, but as if you had obtained the consulship or proctorship; you have enhanced your prestige. In like manner, also, I may say to a good man, if no harder circumstance has given him the opportunity whereby alone he might show the strength of his mind, "I judge you unfortunate; you have passed through life without an antagonist; no one will know what you can do—not even yourself." For if a man is to know himself, he must be tested; no one finds out what he can do except by trying. And so some men have presented themselves voluntarily to laggard misfortune, and have sought an opportunity to blazon forth their worth when it was about to pass into obscurity. Great men, I say, rejoice oft-times in adversity, as do brave soldiers in warfare. I once heard Triumphus, a gladiator in the time of Tiberius Caesar, complaining of the scarcity of shows: "How fair an age," he said, "has passed away!"

True worth is eager for danger and thinks rather of its goal than of what it may have to suffer, since even what it will have to suffer is a part of its glory. Warriors glory in their wounds and rejoice to display the blood spilled with luckier fortune. Those who return from the battle unhurt may have fought as well, but the man who returns with a wound wins the greater regard. God, I say, is showing favor to those whom he desires to achieve the highest possible virtue whenever he gives them the means of doing a courageous and brave deed, and to this end they must encounter some difficulty in life. You learn to know a pilot in a storm, a soldier in the battle-line. How can I know with what spirit you will face poverty, if you wallow in wealth? How can I know with what firmness you will face disgrace, ill fame, and public hatred, if you attain to old age amidst rounds of applause—if a popularity attends you that is irresistible, and flows to you from a certain leaning of men's minds? How do I know with what equanimity you would bear the loss of children, if you see around you all that you have fathered? I have heard you offering consolation to others. If you had been offering it to yourself, if you had been telling yourself not to grieve, then I might have seen your true character. Do not, I beg of you, shrink in fear from those things which the immortal gods apply like spurs, as it were, to our souls. Disaster is Virtue's opportunity. Justly may those be termed unhappy who are dulled by an excess of good fortune, who rest, as it were, in dead calm upon a quiet sea; whatever happens will come to them as a change. Cruel fortune bears hardest upon the inexperienced; to the tender neck the yoke is heavy. The raw recruit turns pale at the thought of a wound, but the veteran looks undaunted upon his own gore, knowing that blood has often been the price of his victory. In like manner God hardens, reviews, and disciplines those whom he approves, whom he loves. Those, however, whom he seems to favor, whom he seems to spare, he is really keeping soft against ills to come. For you are wrong if you suppose that any one is exempt from ill. Even the man who has prospered long will have his share some day; whoever seems to have been released has only been reprieved. Why is it that God afflicts the best men with ill health, or sorrow, or some other misfortune? For the same reason that in the army the bravest men are assigned to the hazardous tasks; it is the picked soldier that a general sends to surprise the enemy by a night attack, or to reconnoitre the road, or to dislodge a garrison. Not a man of these will say as he goes, "My commander has done me an ill turn," but instead, "He has paid me a compliment." In like manner, all those who are called to suffer what would make cowards and poltroons weep may say, "God has deemed us worthy instruments of his purpose to discover how much human nature can endure."

Flee luxury, flee enfeebling good fortune, from which men's minds grow sodden, and if nothing intervenes to remind them of the common lot, they sink, as it were, into the stupor of unending drunkenness. The man who has always had glazed windows to shield him from a draught, whose feet have been kept warm by hot applications renewed from time to time, whose dining-halls have been tempered by hot air passing beneath the floor and circulating round the walls—this man will run great risk if he is brushed by a gentle breeze. While all excesses are hurtful, the most dangerous is unlimited good fortune. It excites the brain, it evokes vain fancies in the mind, and clouds in deep fog the boundary between falsehood and truth. Would it not be better, summoning virtue's help, to endure everlasting ill fortune than to be bursting with unlimited and immoderate blessings? Death from starvation comes very gently, but from gorging men explode.

And so, in the case of good men the gods follow the same rule that teachers follow with their pupils; they require most effort from those of whom they have the surest hopes. Do you imagine that the Lacedaemonians hate their children when they test their mettle by lashing them in public? Their own fathers call upon them to endure bravely the blows of the whip, and ask them, though mangled and half-dead, to keep offering their wounded bodies to further wounds. Why, then, is it strange if God tries noble spirits with severity? No proof of virtue is ever mild. If we are lashed and torn by Fortune, let us bear it; it is not cruelty but a struggle, and the oftener we engage in it, the stronger we shall be. The staunchest member of the body is the one that is kept in constant use. We should offer ourselves to Fortune in order that, struggling with her, we may be hardened by her. Gradually she will make us a match for herself.

Triumphing over Adversity

From Frederick Douglass,
Narrative of the Life of Frederick Douglass

Despite the horrors of his life as a slave in the American South, Frederick Douglass (1818–1895) educates himself. Resisting an oppressive overseer gives the young man a sense of manhood and a resolve to be free.

I lived in Master Hugh's family about seven years. During this time, I succeeded in learning to read and write. In accomplishing this, I was compelled to resort to various stratagems. I had no regular teacher. My mistress, who had kindly commenced to instruct me, had, in compliance with the advice and direction of her husband, not only ceased to instruct, but had set her face against my being instructed by anyone else. It is due, however, to my mistress to say of her, that she did not adopt this course of treatment immediately. She at first lacked the depravity indispensable to shutting me up in mental darkness. It was at least necessary for her to have some training in the exercise of irresponsible power, to make her equal to the task of treating me as though I were a brute.

My mistress was, as I have said, a kind and tender-hearted woman; and in the simplicity of her soul she commenced, when I first went to live with her, to treat me as she supposed one human being ought to treat another. In entering upon the duties of a slaveholder, she did not seem to perceive that I sustained to her the relation of a mere chattel, and that for her to treat me as a human being was not only wrong, but dangerously so. Slavery proved as injurious to her as it did to me. When I went there, she was a pious, warm, and tender-hearted woman. There was no sorrow or suffering for which she had not a tear. She had bread for the hungry, clothes for the naked, and comfort for every mourner that came within her reach. Slavery soon proved its ability to divest her of these heavenly qualities. Under its influence, the tender heart became stone, and the lamblike disposition gave way to one of tigerlike fierceness. The first step in her downward course was in her ceasing to instruct me. She now commenced to practice her husband's precepts. She finally became even more violent in her opposition than her husband himself. She was not satisfied with simply doing as well as he had commanded; she seemed anxious to do better. Nothing seemed to make her more angry than to see me with a newspaper. She seemed to think that here lay the danger. I have had her rush at me with a face made all up of fury, and snatch from me a newspaper, in a manner that fully revealed her apprehension. She was an apt woman; and a little experience soon demonstrated, to her satisfaction, that education and slavery were incompatible with each other.

From this time I was most narrowly watched. If I was in a separate room any considerable length of time, I was sure to be suspected of having a book, and was at once called to give an account of myself. All this, however, was too late. The first step had been taken. Mistress, in teaching me the alphabet, had given me the *inch*, and no precaution could prevent me from taking the *ell.*

The plan which I adopted, and the one by which I was most successful, was that of making friends of all the little white boys whom I met in the street. As many of these as I could, I converted into teachers. With their kindly aid, obtained at different times and in different places, I finally succeeded in learning to read. When I was sent on errands, I always took my book with me, and by going one part of my errand quickly, I found time to get a lesson before my return. I used also to carry bread with me, enough of which was always in the house, and to which I was always welcome; for I was much better off in this regard than many of the poor white children in our neighborhood. This bread I used to bestow upon the hungry little urchins, who, in return, would give me that more valuable bread of knowledge. I am strongly tempted to give the names of two or three of those little boys, as a testimonial of the gratitude and affection I bear them; but prudence forbids—not that it would injure me, but it might embarrass them; for it is almost an unpardonable offense to teach slaves to read in this Christian country. It is enough to say of the dear little fellows, that they lived on Philpot Street, very near Durgin and Bailey's ship-yard. I used to talk this matter of slavery over with them. I would sometimes say to them, I wished I could be as free as they would be when they got to be men. "You will be free as soon as you are twenty-one, *but I am a slave for life!* Have not I as good a right to be free as you have?" These words used to trouble them; they would express for me the liveliest sympathy, and console me with the hope that something would occur by which I might be free.

I was now about twelve years old, and the thought of being *a slave for life* began to bear heavily upon my heart. Just about this time, I got hold of a book entitled "The Columbian Orator." Every opportunity I got, I used to read this book. Among much of other interesting matter, I found in it a dialogue between a master and his slave. The slave was represented as having run away from his master three times. The dialogue represented the conversation which took place between them, when the slave was retaken the third time. In this dialogue, the whole argument in behalf of slavery was brought forward by the master, all of which was disposed of by the slave. The slave was made to say some very smart as well as impressive things in reply to his master—things which had the desired though unexpected effect; for the conversation resulted in the voluntary emancipation of the slave on the part of the master.

In the same book, I met with one of Sheridan's mighty speeches on and in behalf of Catholic emancipation. These were choice documents to me. I read them over and over again with unabated interest. They gave tongue to interesting thoughts of my own soul, which had frequently flashed through my mind, and died away for want of utterance. The moral which I gained from the dialogue was the power of truth over the conscience of even a slaveholder. What I got from Sheridan was a bold denunciation of slavery, and a powerful vindication of human rights. The reading of these documents enabled me to utter my thoughts, and to meet the arguments brought forward to sustain slavery; but while they relieved me of one difficulty, they brought on another even more painful than the one of which I was relieved. The more I read, the more I was led to abhor and detest my enslavers. I could regard them in no other light than a band of successful robbers, who had left their homes, and gone to Africa, and stolen us from our homes, and in a strange land reduced us to slavery. I loathed them as being the meanest as well as the most wicked of men. As I read and contemplated the subject, behold! that very discontentment which Master Hugh had predicted would follow my learning to read had already come, to torment and sting my soul to unutterable anguish. As I writhed under it, I would at times feel that learning to read had been a curse rather than a blessing. It had given me a view of my wretched condition, without the remedy. It opened my eyes to the horrible pit, but to no ladder upon which to get out. In moments of agony, I envied my fellow-slaves for their stupidity. I have often wished myself a beast. I preferred the condition of the meanest reptile to my own. Any thing, no matter what, to get rid of thinking! It was this everlasting thinking of my condition that tormented me. There was no getting rid of it. It was pressed upon me by every object within sight or hearing, animate or inanimate. The silver trump of freedom had roused my soul to eternal wakefulness. Freedom now appeared, to disappear no more forever. It was heard in every sound, and seen in every thing. It was ever present to torment me with a sense of my wretched condition. I saw nothing without seeing it, I heard nothing without hearing it, and felt nothing without feeling it. It looked from every star, it smiled in every calm, breathed in every wind, and moved in every storm.

I often found myself regretting my own existence, and wishing myself dead; and but for the hope of being free, I have no doubt but that I should have killed myself, or done something for which I should have been killed. While in this state of mind, I was eager to hear anyone speak of slavery. I was a ready listener. Every little while, I could hear something about the abolitionists. It was some time before I found what the word meant. It was always used in such connections as to make it an interesting word to me. If a slave ran away and succeeded in getting clear, or if a slave killed his master, set fire to a barn, or did anything very wrong in the mind of a slaveholder, it was spoken of as the fruit of *abolition*. Hearing the word in this connection very often, I set about learning what it meant. The dictionary afforded me little or no help. I found it was "the act of abolishing," but then I did not know what was to be abolished. Here I was perplexed. I did not dare to ask anyone about its meaning, for I was satisfied that it was something they wanted me to know very little about. After a patient waiting, I got one of our city papers, containing an account of the number of petitions from the north, praying for the abolition of slavery in the District of Colombia, and of the slave trade between the States. From this time I understood the words *abolition* and *abolitionist*, and always drew near when that word was spoken, expecting to hear something of importance to myself and fellow-slaves. The light broke in upon me by degrees. I went one day down on the wharf of Mr. Waters; and seeing two Irishmen unloading a scow of stone, I went, unasked, and helped them. When we had finished, one of them came to me and asked me if I were a slave. I told him I was. He asked, "Are ye a slave for life?" I told him that I was. The good Irishman seemed to be deeply affected by the statement. He said to the other that it was a pity so fine a little fellow as myself should be a slave for life. He said it was a shame to hold me. They both advised me to run away to the north; that I should find friends there, and that I should be free. I pretended not to be interested in what they said, and treated them as if I did not understand them; for I feared they might be treacherous. White men have been known to encourage slaves to escape, and then, to get the reward, catch them and return them to their master. I was afraid that these seemingly good men might use me so; but I nevertheless remembered their advice, and from that time I resolved to run away. I looked forward to a time at which it would be safe for me to escape. I was too young to think of doing so immediately; besides, I wished to learn how to write, as I might have occasion to write my own pass. I consoled myself with the hope that I should one day find a good chance. Meanwhile, I would learn to write.

The idea as to how I might learn to write was suggested to me by being in Durgin and Bailey's shipyard, and frequently seeing the ship carpenters, after hewing, and getting a piece of timber ready for use, write on the timber the name of that part of the ship for which it was intended. When a piece of timber was intended for the larboard side, it would be marked thus—"L." When a piece was for the starboard side, it would be marked thus—"S." A piece for the larboard side forward, would be marked thus—"L.F." When a piece was for starboard side forward, it would be marked thus—"S.F." For larboard aft, it would be marked "L.A" For starboard aft, it would be marked thus—"S.A." I soon learned the names of these letters, and for what they were intended when placed upon a piece of timber in the shipyard. I immediately commenced copying them, and in a short time was able to make the four letters named. After that, when I met with any boy who I knew could write, I would tell him I could write as well as he. The next word would be, "I don't believe you. Let me see you try it." I would then make the letters which I had been so fortunate as to learn, and ask him to beat that. In this way I got a good many lessons in writing, which it is quite possible I should never have gotten in any other way. During this time, my copy-book was the board fence, brick wall, and pavement; my pen and ink was a lump of chalk. With these, I learned mainly how to write. I then commenced and continued copying the Italics in Webster's Spelling Book, until I could make them all without looking on the book. By this time, my little Master Thomas had gone to school, and learned how to write, and had written over a number of copy-books. These had been brought home, and shown to some of our near neighbors, and then laid aside. My mistress used to go to class meeting at the Wilk Street meeting-house every Monday afternoon, and leave me to take care of the house. When left thus, I used to spend the time in writing in the spaces left in master Thomas's copy-book, copying what he had written. I continued to do this until I could write a hand very similar to that of Master Thomas. Thus, after a long, tedious effort for years, I finally succeeded in learning how to write.

In a very short time after I went to live at Baltimore, my old master's youngest son Richard died; and in about three years and six months after his death, my old master, Captain Anthony died, leaving only his son, Andrew, and daughter, Lucretia, to share his estate. He died while on a visit to see his daughter at Hillsborough. Cut off thus unexpectedly, he left no will as to the disposal of his property. It was therefore necessary to have a valuation of the property, that it might be equally divided between Mrs. Lucretia and Master Andrew. I was immediately sent for, to be valued with the other property. Here again my feelings rose up in detestation of slavery. I had now a new conception of my degraded condition. Prior to this, I had become, if not insensible to my lot, at least partly so. I left Baltimore with a young heart overborne with sadness, and a soul full of apprehension. I took passage with Captain Rowe, in the schooner Wild Cat, and, after a sail of about twenty-four hours, I found myself near the place of my birth. I had now been absent from it almost, if not quite, five years. I, however, remembered the place very well. I was only about five years old when I left, to go and live with my old master on Colonel Lloyd's plantation; so that I was now between ten and eleven years old.

We were all ranked together at the valuation. Men and women, old and young, married and single, were ranked with horses, sheep and swine. There were horses and men, cattle and women, pigs and children, all holding the same rank in the scale of being, and were all subjected to the same narrow examination. Silvery-headed age and sprightly youth, maids and matrons, had to undergo the same indelicate inspection. At this moment, I saw more clearly than ever the brutalizing effects of slavery upon both slave and slaveholder.

After the valuation, then came the division. I have no language to express the high excitement and deep anxiety which were felt among us poor slaves during this time. Our fate for life was now to be decided. We had no more voice in that decision than the brutes among whom we were ranked. A single word from the white men was enough—against all our wishes, prayers, and entreaties—to sunder forever the dearest friends, dearest kindred, and strongest ties known to human beings. In addition to the pain of separation, there was the horrid dread of falling into the hands of Master Andrew. He was known to us all as being a most cruel wretch—a common drunkard, who had, by his reckless mismanagement and profligate dissipation, already wasted a large portion of his father's property. We all felt that we might as well be sold at once to the Georgia traders, as to pass into his hands; for we knew that that would be our inevitable condition—a condition held by us all in the utmost horror and dread.

Master Thomas ridiculed the idea that there was any danger of Mr. Covey's killing me, and said that he knew Mr. Covey; that he was a good man, and that he could not think of taking me from him; that should he do so, he would lose the whole year's wages; that I belonged to Mr. Covey for one year, and that I must go back to him, come what might; and that I must not trouble him with any more stories, or that he would himself *get hold of me,* which meant that he would whip me. I remained all night, and, according to his orders, I started off to Covey's about nine o'clock; and just as I was getting over the fence that divided Mrs. Kemp's fields from ours, out ran Covey with his cowskin, to give me another whipping. Before he could reach me, I succeeded in getting to the cornfield; and as the corn was very high, it afforded me the means of hiding. He seemed very angry, and searched for me a long time. My behavior was altogether unaccountable. He finally gave up the chase, thinking, I suppose, that I must come home for something to eat; he would give himself no further trouble in looking for me. I spent that day mostly in the woods, having the alternative before me—to go home and be whipped to death, or stay in the woods and be starved to death. That night, I fell in with Sandy Jenkins, a slave with whom I was somewhat acquainted. Sandy had a free wife who lived about four miles from Mr. Covey's; and it being Saturday, he was on his way to see her. I told him my circumstances, and he very kindly invited me to go home with him. I went home with him, and talked this whole matter over, and got his advice as to what course it was best for me to pursue. I found Sandy an old advisor. He told me, with solemnity, I must go back to Covey; but that before I went, I must go with him into another part of the woods, where there was a certain *root*, which if I would take some of it with me, carrying it *always on my right side,* would render it impossible for Mr. Covey, or any other white man, to whip me. He said he had carried it for years, and since he had done so, he had never received a blow, and never expected to while he carried it. I at first rejected the idea, that the simple carrying of a root in my pocket would have any such effect as he had said, and was not disposed to take it; but Sandy impressed the necessity with much earnestness, telling me it could do no harm, if it did no good. To please him, I at length took the root, and, according to his direction, carried it upon my right side. This was Sunday morning. I immediately started for home; and upon entering the yard gate, out came Mr. Covey on his way to meeting. He spoke to me very kindly, bade me drive the pigs from a lot near by, and passed on toward the church. Now, this singular conduct of Mr. Covey really made me begin to think that there was something in the *root* which Sandy had given me; and had it been on any other day than Sunday, I could have attributed the conduct to no other cause than the influence of that root; and as it was, I was half inclined to think the *root* to be something more than I at first had taken it to be. All went well till Monday morning. On this morning, the virtue of the *root* was fully tested. Long before daylight, I was called to go and rub, curry, and feed the horses. I obeyed, and was glad to obey. But whilst thus engaged, whilst in the act of throwing down some blades from the loft, Mr. Covey entered the stable with a long rope; and just as I was half out of the loft, he caught hold of my legs, and was about tying me. As soon as I found what he was up to, I gave a sudden spring, and as I did so, he holding to my legs, I was brought sprawling on the stable floor. Mr. Covey seemed now to think he had me, and could do what he pleased; but at this moment—from whence came the spirit I don't know—I resolved to fight; and, suiting my action to the resolution, I seized Covey hard by the throat; and as I did so, I rose. He held on to me, and I to him. My resistance was so entirely unexpected, that Covey seemed taken all aback. He trembled like a leaf. This gave me assurance, and I held him uneasy, causing the blood to run where I touched him with the ends of my fingers. Mr. Covey soon called out to Hughes for help. Hughes came, and while Covey held me, attempted to tie my right hand. While he was in the act of doing so, I watched my chance, and gave him a heavy kick close under the ribs. This kick fairly sickened Hughes, so that he left me in the hands of Mr. Covey. This kick had the effect of not only weakening Hughes, but Covey also. When he saw Hughes bending over with pain, his courage quailed. He asked me if I meant to persist in my resistance. I told him I did, come what might, that he had used me like a brute for six months, and that I was determined to be used so no longer. With that, he strove to drag me to a stick that was lying just out of the stable door. He meant to knock me down. But just as he was leaning over to get the stick, I seized him with both hands by his collar, and brought him by a sudden snatch to the ground. By this time, Bill came. Covey called upon him for assistance. Bill wanted to know what he could do. Covey said, "Take hold of him, take hold of him!" Bill said his master hired him out to work, and not to help to whip me; so he left Covey and myself to fight our own battle out. We were at it for nearly two hours. Covey at length let me go, puffing and blowing at a great rate, saying that if I had not resisted, he would not have whipped me half so much. The truth was, that he had not whipped me at all. I considered him as getting entirely the worst end of the bargain; for he had drawn no blood from me, but I had from him. The whole six months afterwards, that I spent with Mr. Covey, he never laid the weight of his finger upon me in anger. He would occasionally say, he didn't want to get hold of me again. "No," thought I, "you need not; for you will come off worse than you did before."

This battle with Mr. Covey was the turning-point in my career as a slave. It rekindled the few expiring embers of freedom, and revived within me a sense of my own manhood. It recalled the departed self-confidence, and inspired me again with a determination to be free. The gratification afforded by the triumph was a full compensation for whatever else might follow, even death itself. He only can understand the deep satisfaction which I experienced, who has himself repelled by force the bloody arm of slavery. I felt as I never felt before. It was a glorious resurrection, from the tomb of slavery, to the heaven of freedom. My long-crushed spirit rose, cowardice departed, bold defiance took its place; and I now resolved that, however long I might remain a slave in form, the day had passed forever when I could be a slave in fact. I did not hesitate to let it be known of me, that the white man who expected to succeed in whipping must also succeed in killing me.

What Is a Man?

From William Shakespeare,
Hamlet

Can too much thinking undermine a man's resolve?

How all occasions do inform against me
And spur my dull revenge. What is a man,
If his chief good and market of his time
Be but to sleep and feed? A beast, no more.
Sure he that made us with such large discourse,
Looking before and after, gave us not
That capability and godlike reason
To fust in us unused. Now, whether it be
Bestial oblivion, or some craven scruple
Of thinking too precisely on th' event—
A thought which, quartered, hath but one part wisdom
And ever three parts coward—I do not know
Why yet I live to say, "This thing's to do,"
Sith I have cause, and will, and strength, and means
To do't. Examples gross as earth exhort me.
Witness this army of such mass and charge,
Led by a delicate and tender prince,
Whose spirit, with divine ambition puffed,
Makes mouths at the invisible event,
Exposing what is mortal and unsure
To all that fortune, death, and danger dare,
Even for an eggshell. Rightly to be great
Is not to stir without great argument,
But greatly to find quarrel in a straw
When honor's at the stake. How stand I then,
That have a father killed, a mother stained,
Excitements of my reason and my blood,
And let all sleep, while to my shame I see
The imminent death of twenty thousand men
That for a fantasy and trick of fame
Go to their graves like beds, fight for a plot

Whereon the numbers cannot try the cause,
Which is not tomb enough and continent
To hide the slain? O, from this time forth,
My thoughts be bloody, or be nothing worth!

There Was a Time When
Our Forefathers Owned
This Great Island

Red Jacket,
On the Religion of the White Man and the Red

A leader defends the nobility and integrity of his people. In 1805, the Native American leader Red Jacket spoke to a council of the Six Nations after a Christian missionary had proposed that he work among them.

Friend and Brother: It was the will of the Great Spirit that we should meet together this day. He orders all things; and has given us a fine day for our council. He has taken his garment from before the sun, and caused it to shine with brightness upon us. Our eyes are opened that we see clearly, our ears are unstopped that we have been able to hear distinctly the words you have spoken. For all these favors we thank the Great Spirit, and Him only.

Brother, listen to what we say. There was a time when our forefathers owned this great island. Their seats extended from the rising to the setting sun. The Great Spirit had made it for the use of Indians. He had created the buffalo, the deer, and other animals for food. He had made the bear and the beaver. Their skins served us for clothing. He had scattered them over the country and taught us how to take them. He had caused the earth to produce corn for bread. All this He had done for His red children because He loved them. If we had some disputes about our hunting-ground, they were generally settled without the shedding of much blood.

But an evil day came upon us. Your forefathers crossed the great water and landed on this island. Their numbers were small. They found friends and not enemies. They told us they had fled from their own country for fear of wicked men and had come here to enjoy their religion. They asked for a small seat. We took pity on them, granted their request, and they sat down among us. We gave them corn and meat; they gave us poison in return.

The white people, brother, had now found our country. Tidings were carried back, and more came among us. Yet we did not fear them. We took them to be friends. They called us brothers. We believed them and gave them a larger seat. At length their numbers had greatly increased. They wanted more land; they wanted our country. Our eyes were opened, and our minds became uneasy. Wars took place. Indians were hired to fight against Indians, and many of our people were destroyed. They also brought strong liquor among us. It was strong and powerful, and has slain thousands.

Brother, our seats were once large and yours were small. You have now become a great people, and we have scarcely a place left to spread our blankets. You have got our country, but are not satisfied; you want to force your religion upon us.

Brother, continue to listen. You say that you are sent to instruct us how to worship the Great Spirit agreeably to His mind; and, if we do not take hold of the religion which you white people teach, we shall be unhappy hereafter. You say that you are right and we are lost. How do we know this to be true? We understand that your religion is written in a book. If it was intended for us, as well as you, why has not the Great Spirit given to us, and not only to us, but why did He not give to our forefathers the knowledge of that book, with the means of rightly understanding it? We only know what you tell us about it, and, having been so often deceived by the white people, how shall we believe what they say?

Brother, you say there is but one way to worship and serve the Great Spirit. If there is but one religion, why do you white people differ so much about it? Why not all agree, as you can all read the book?

Brother, we do not understand these things: we are told that your religion was given to your forefathers, and has been handed down from father to son. We also have a religion which was given to *our* forefathers, and has been handed down to us: it teaches us *to be thankful for all favors received, to love each other, and to be united: we never quarrel about religion.*

Brother, the Great Spirit made us all: but He has made a great difference between His white and His red children: He has given us different complexions and different customs. To you He has given the arts: to these He has not opened our eyes. Since He has made so great a difference between us in other things, why may He not have given us a different religion? The Great Spirit does right: He knows what is best for His children.

Brother, we do not want to destroy your religion, or take it from you. We only want to enjoy our own.

Brother, we are told that you have been preaching to the white people in this place. These people are our neighbors. We will wait a little, and see what effect your preaching has had upon them. If we find it makes them honest, and less disposed to cheat Indians, we will then consider again of what you have said.

Brother, you have now heard our answer, and this is all we have to say at present. As we are about to part, we will come and take you by the hand: and we hope the Great Spirit will protect you on your journey, and return you safe to your friends.

My Forefathers Were Warriors

Tecumseh to Governor Harrison, 1810

The great Shawnee chief Tecumseh (1768–1813) tried to organize a tribal confederacy to check the relentless westward advance of the white settlers.

It is true I am a Shawnee. My forefathers were warriors. Their son is a warrior. From them I take only my existence; from my tribe I take nothing. I am the maker of my own fortune; and oh! that I could make that of my red people, and of my country, as great as the conceptions of my mind, when I think of the Spirit that rules the universe. I would not then come to Governor Harrison to ask him to tear the treaty and to obliterate the landmark; but I would say to him, "Sir, you have liberty to return to your own country."

The being within, communing with past ages, tells me that once, nor until lately there was no white man on this continent; that it then all belonged to red men, children of the same parents, placed on it by the Great Spirit that made them, to keep it, to traverse it, to enjoy its productions, and to fill it with the same race, once a happy race, since made miserable by the white people, who are never contented but always encroaching. The way, and the only way, to check and to stop this evil, is for all the red men to unite in claiming a common and equal right in the land, as it was at first, and should be yet; for it never was divided, but belongs to all for the use of each. For no part has a right to sell, even to each other, much less to strangers—those who want all, and will not do with less.

The white people have no right to take the land from the Indians, because they had it first; it is theirs. They may sell, but all must join. Any sale not made by all is not valid. The late sale is bad. It was made by a part only. Part do not know how to sell. It requires all to make a bargain for all. All red men have equal rights to the unoccupied land. The right of occupancy is as good in one place as in another. There cannot be two occupations in the same place. The first excludes all others. It is not so in hunting or traveling; for there the same ground will serve many, as they may follow each other all day; but the camp is stationary, and that is occupancy. It belongs to the first who sits down on his blanket or skins which he has thrown upon the ground; and till he leaves it, no other has a right.

The Hero Deepened

From Homer, The Iliad

Achilles kills Hektor and is still so furious that he refuses to return the fallen Trojan's body for a decent burial. Instead, he violates Hektor's body by dragging it around the walls of Troy behind his chariot. Achilles' mother warns him that the gods are angry at his disrespect for such a worthy adversary. The gods admire manly pride, but demand that worthy men honor one another even in enmity; Achilles is exercising a vengeance proper only to the gods themselves.

In his weakness Hektor of the shining helm spoke to him:

"I entreat you, by your wife, by your knees, by your parents, do not let the dogs feed on me by the ships of the Achaians, but take yourself the bronze and gold that are there in abundance, those gifts that my father and the lady my mother will give you, and give my body to be taken home again, so that the Trojans and the wives of the Trojans may give me in death my rite of burning."

But looking darkly at him swift-footed Achilleus answered:

"No more entreating of me, you dog, by knees or parents, I wish only that my spirit and fury would drive me to hack your meat away and eat it raw for the things that you have done to me. So there is no one who can hold the dogs off from your head, not if they bring here and set before me ten times and twenty times the ransom, and promise more in addition, not if Priam son of Dardanos should offer to weigh out your bulk in gold; not even so shall the lady your mother who herself bore you lay you on the death-bed and mourn you: no, but the dogs and the birds will have you all for their feasting."

Then dying, Hektor of the shining helmet spoke to him:

"I know you well as I look upon you, I know that I could not persuade you, since indeed in your breast is a heart of iron. Be careful now; for I might be made into the gods' curse upon you, on that day when Paris and Phoibos Apollo destroy you in the Skaian gates, for all your valor."

He spoke, and as he spoke the end of death closed in upon him, and the soul fluttering free of the limbs went down into Death's house mourning her destiny, leaving youth and manhood behind her. Now though he was a dead man brilliant Achilleus spoke to him:

"Die: and I will take my own death at whatever time Zeus and the rest of the immortals choose to accomplish."

His honored mother came close to him and sat down beside him, and stroked him with her hand and called him by name and spoke to him:

"My child, how long will you go on eating your heart out in sorrow and lamentation, and remember neither your food nor going to bed? It is a good thing even to lie with a woman in love. For you will not be with me for long, but already death and power-ful destiny stand closely above you. But listen hard to me, for I come from Zeus with a message. He says that the gods frown upon you, that beyond all other immortals he himself is angered that in your heart's madness you hold Hektor beside the curved ships and did not redeem him. Come, then, give him up and accept ransom for the body."

Priam, the King of Troy, comes to the Greek camp to beg for his son's body to be returned. As the old man clings like a supplicant to the young man's knees,

Achilles' heart melts as he thinks of his own father far away. Hektor gets his burial rites. At the end of the poem, Achilles is deepened and humanized by his ability to enter into the suffering of someone besides himself. Mourning transcends the divisions of war, and Achilles is a full man at last.

Tall Priam came in unseen by the other men and stood close beside him and caught the knees of Achilleus in his arms, and kissed the hands that were dangerous and manslaughtering and had killed so many of his sons. As when dense disaster closes on one who has murdered a man in his own land, and he comes to the country of others, to a man of substance, and wonder seizes on those who behold him, so Achilleus wondered as he looked on Priam, a godlike man, and the rest of them wondered also, and looked at each other. But now Priam spoke to him in the words of a suppliant:

"Achilleus like the gods, remember your father, one who is of years like mine, and on the door-sill of sorrowful old age. And they who dwell nearby encompass him and afflict him, nor is there any to defend him against the wrath, the destruction. Yet surely he, when he hears of you and that you are still living, is gladdened within his heart and all his days he is hopeful that he will see his beloved son come home from the Troad. But for me, my destiny was evil. I have the noblest of sons in Troy, but I say not one of them is left to me. Fifty were my sons, when the sons of the Achaians came here. Nineteen were born to me from the womb of a single mother, and other women bore the rest in my palace; and of these violent Ares broke the strength in the knees of most of them, but one was left me who guarded my city and people, that one you killed a few days since he fought in defense of his country. Hektor; for whose sake I come now to the ships of the Achaians to win him back from you, and I bring you gifts beyond number. Honor then the gods, Achilleus, and take pity upon me remembering your father, yet I am still more pitiful; I have gone through what no other mortal on earth has gone through; I put my lips to the hands of the man who has killed my children."

So he spoke, and stirred in the other a passion of grieving for his own father. He took the old man's hand and pushed him gently away, and the two remembered, as Priam sat huddled at the feet of Achilleus and wept close for manslaughtering Hektor and Achilleus wept now for his own father, now again for Patroklos. The sound of their mourning moved in the house. Then when great

Achilleus had taken full satisfaction in sorrow and the passion for it had gone from his mind and body, thereafter he rose from his chair, and took the old man by the hand, and set him on his feet again, in pity for the gray head and the gray beard, and spoke to him and addressed him in winged words:

"Ah, unlucky, surely you have had much evil to endure in your spirit. How could you dare to come alone to the ships of the Achaians and before my eyes, when I am one who has killed in such numbers such brave sons of yours? The heart in you is iron. But bear up, nor mourn endlessly in your heart, for there is not anything to be gained from grief for your son; you will never bring him back; sooner you must go through yet another sorrow."

In answer to him again spoke the aged Priam the godlike:

"Do not, beloved of Zeus, make me sit on a chair while Hektor lies yet forlorn among the shelters; rather with all speed give him back, so my eyes may behold him, and accept the ransom we bring you, which is great. You may have joy of it, and go back to the land of your own fathers, since once you have permitted me to go on living myself and continue to look on the sunlight."

Then looking darkly at him spoke swift-footed Achilleus:

"No longer stir me up, old sir. I myself am minded to give Hektor back to you."

The Ascent

From Aleksandr Solzhenitsyn,
The Gulag Archipelago

Marcus Aurelius believed that if a man's soul is free, he is free in the highest sense whether he is an emperor or a slave. Sometimes men experience tyranny of such an overwhelmingly terrifying and degrading kind that their very souls are transmuted. Though at first they may be passive victims, their torment and suffering gradually purify them of their earthly attachments and vanity, liberating the soul from the body and from ambitions for worldly prestige and power. Losing everything most people could not live without, such men achieve an extraordinary spiritual strength that their oppressors cannot touch. In one of our century's most moving affirmations of the power

of the human spirit to survive the worst humiliations and pain inflicted by
tyranny, Aleksandr Solzhenitsyn reflects on how his long years of imprison-
ment in the Gulag miraculously improved him and made him a better man.

And the years go by . . .

Not in swift staccato, as they joke in camp—"winter-summer,
winter-summer"—but a long drawn-out autumn, an endless winter,
an unwilling spring, and only a summer that is short. In the Archipelago . . . summer is short.

Even one mere year, whew, how long it lasts! Even in one year
how much time is left for you to think! For 330 days you stomp out
to line-up in a drizzling, slushy rain, and in a piercing blizzard, and
in a biting and subzero cold. For 330 days you work away at hateful,
alien work with your mind unoccupied. For 330 evenings you
squinch up, wet, chilled, in the end-of-work line-up, waiting for the
convoy to assemble from the distant watchtowers. And then there is
the march out. And the march back. And bending down over 730
bowls of gruel, over 730 portions of grits. Yes, and waking up and
going to sleep on your multiple bunk. And neither radio nor books
to distract you. There are none, and thank God.

And that is only one year. And there are ten. There are twenty-
five . . .

And then, too, when you are lying in the hospital with dystro-
phy—that, too, is a good time—*to think.*

Think! Draw some conclusions from misfortune.

And all that endless time, after all, the prisoners' brains and
souls are not inactive?! In the mass and from a distance they seem
like swarming lice, but they are the crown of creation, right? After
all, once upon a time a weak little spark of God was breathed into
them too—is it not true? So what has become of it now?

For centuries it was considered that a criminal was given a *sentence* for precisely this purpose, to think about his crime for the
whole period of his sentence, be conscience-stricken, repent, and
gradually reform.

But the Gulag Archipelago knows no pangs of conscience! Out of one
hundred natives—five are thieves, and their transgressions are no
reproach in their own eyes, but a mark of valor. They dream of carrying out such feats in the future even more brazenly and cleverly.
They have nothing to repent. Another five . . . *stole* on a big scale,
but not from people; in our times, the only place where one can
steal on a big scale is from the state, which itself squanders the people's money without pity or sense—so what was there for such types

to repent of? Maybe that they had not stolen more and divvied up—and thus remained free? And, so far as another 85 percent of the natives were concerned—they had never committed any crimes whatever. What were they supposed to repent of? That they had thought what they thought? (Nonetheless, they managed to pound and muddle some of them to such an extent that they did repent—of being so depraved . . . Let us remember the desperation of Nina Peregud because she was unworthy of Zoya Kosmodemyanskaya.) Or that a man had surrendered and become a POW in a hopeless situation? Or that he had taken employment under the Germans instead of dying of starvation? (Nonetheless, they managed so to confuse what was permitted and what was forbidden that there were some such who were tormented greatly: I would have done better to die than to have earned that bread.) Or that while working for nothing in the collective-farm fields, he had taken a mite to feed his children? Or that he had taken something from a factory for the same reason?

No, not only do you not repent, but your clean conscience, like a clear mountain lake, shines in your eyes. (And your eyes, purified by suffering, infallibly perceive the least haze in other eyes; for example, they infallibly pick out stool pigeons. And the Cheka-GB is not aware of this capacity of ours to see with the eyes of truth—it is our "secret weapon" against that institution. And State Security slips up here with us.)

It was in this nearly unanimous consciousness of our innocence that the main distinction arose between us and the hard labor prisoners of Dostoyevsky, the hard-labor prisoners of P. Yakubovich. There they were conscious of being doomed renegades, whereas we were confidently aware that they could haul in any free person at all in just the same way they had hauled us in; that barbed wire was only a nominal dividing line between us. In earlier times there had been among the majority . . . the unconditional consciousness of personal guilt, and among us . . . the consciousness of disaster on a mammoth scale.

Just not to perish from the disaster! It had to be survived.

Wasn't this the root cause of the astounding rarity of camp suicides? Yes, rarity, although every ex-prisoner could in all probability recall a case of suicide. But he could recall even more escapes. There were certainly more escapes than suicides! (Admirers of socialist realism can praise me: I am pursuing an optimistic line.) And there were far more self-inflicted injuries, too, than there were suicides! But this, too, is an act indicating love of life—a straightforward calculation of sacrificing a portion to save the whole. I even imagine that, statistically speaking, there were fewer suicides per thousand of the population in camp than in freedom. I have no way of verifying this, of course.

But Skripnikova recalls how a man thirty years old hanged himself in 1931 in the women's toilet in Medvezhyegorsk—and hanged himself on the very day he was to be released! So maybe it was out of a feeling of disgust for the *freedom* of that time? (Two years earlier his wife had abandoned him, but he had not hanged himself then.) Well, the designer Voronov hanged himself in the club of the main camp center of Burepolom. The Communist Party official Aramovich, a second-termer, hanged himself in 1947 in the garret of the machinery-repair factory in Knyazh-Pogost. In Kraslag during the war years Lithuanians who had been reduced to a state of total despair—mainly because nothing in their former lives had prepared them for our cruelties—marched on infantrymen so as to get themselves shot down. In 1949, in the interrogation cell in Vladimir-Volynsk, a young fellow stunned by his interrogation tried to hang himself, but Boronyuk pulled him down in time. At the Kaluga Gates a former Latvian officer who was hospitalized in the camp infirmary began to creep stealthily up some stairs—they led to the incomplete, empty upper stories. The "zechka" nurse saw him and went in pursuit. She caught up with him on the open balcony of the sixth floor. She caught him by the bathrobe, but the suicide slipped off the robe and stepped off into nothingness dressed in his underwear—and flashed past like a white streak of lightning in plain sight of busy Bolshaya Kaluzhskaya Street on a sunny summer day. When Emmi, a German Communist, learned about her husband's death, she left the barracks in subzero weather undressed so as to catch cold. The Englishman Kelly, in the Vladimir Special Purpose Prison, very skillfully cut his veins with the door wide open and the jailer right there on the threshold.

I repeat: There are many others who can recount similar cases—but nonetheless, out of tens of millions who have served time, their total number will be small. Even among these examples, it is clear that a much greater proportion of suicides is accounted for by foreigners, Westerners; for them the transition to the Archipelago . . . was a more shattering blow than for us, so they put an end to it. And suicides were frequent among the loyalists too (but not among the hard-heads). And one can understand why—after all, their heads must have got thoroughly mixed up and filled with incessant buzzing.

How could they stand it? (Zosia Zaleska, a Polish noblewoman who had devoted her entire life to the "cause of Communsim" by serving in the Soviet intelligence service, tried to commit suicide three times during her interrogation: she tried to hang herself—they pulled her down; she cut her veins—but they stopped her; she jumped onto the window sill on the seventh floor—but the drowsy interrogator managed to grab hold of her by her dress. They saved her life three times—so they could shoot her.)

But what if one has nothing to repent of—what then, what then does the prisoner think about all the time? "Poverty and prison . . . give wisdom." They do. But—where is it to be directed?

Here is how it was with many others, not just with me. Our initial, first prison sky consisted of black swirling storm clouds and black pillars of volcanic eruptions—this was the heaven of Pompeii, the heaven of the Day of Judgment, because it was not just anyone who had been arrested, but I—the center of this world.

Our last prison sky was infinitely high, infinitely clear, even paler than sky-blue.

We all (except religious believers) began from one point: we tried to tear our hair from our head, but our hair had been clipped close! . . . How could we? How could we not have seen those who informed against us?! How could we not have seen our enemies? (And how we hated them! How could we avenge ourselves on them?) And what recklessness! What blindness! How many errors! How can they be corrected? They must be corrected all the more swiftly! We must write . . . We must speak out . . . We must communicate . . .

But—there is nothing that we can do. And nothing is going to save us! At the appropriate time we will sign Form 200. At the appropriate time the tribunal will read us our sentence in our presence, or we will learn it in absentia from the OSO.

Then there begins the period of transit prisons. Interspersed with our thoughts about the future camp, we now love to recall our past: How many unused opportunities there were! How many flowers we left uncrumpled! . . . When will we now make up for it? If I only manage to survive—oh, how differently, how wisely, I am going to live! The day of our future *release*? It shines like a rising sun!

And the conclusion is: Survive to reach it! Survive! At any price!

This is simply a turn of phrase, a sort of habit of speech: "at any price."

But then the words swell up with their full meaning, and an awesome vow takes shape: to survive *at any price.*

And as soon as you have renounced that aim of "surviving at any price," and gone where the calm and simple people go—then imprisonment begins to transform your former character in an astonishing way. To transform it in a direction most unexpected to you.

And it would seem that in this situation feelings of malice, the disturbance of being oppressed, aimless hate, irritability, and nervousness ought to multiply. But you yourself do not notice how, with the impalpable flow of time, slavery nurtures in you the shoots of contradictory feelings.

Once upon a time you were sharply intolerant. You were constantly in a rush. And you were constantly short of time. And now you have time with interest. You are surfeited with it, with its months and its years, behind you and ahead of you—and a beneficial calming fluid pours through your blood vessels—patience.

You are ascending . . .

Formerly you never forgave anyone. You judged people without mercy. And you praised people with equal lack of moderation. And now an understanding mildness has become the basis of your uncategorical judgments. You have come to realize your own weakness—and you can therefore understand the weakness of others. And be astonished at another's strength. And wish to possess it yourself.

The stones rustle beneath our feet. We are ascending . . .

With the years, armor-plated restraint covers your heart and all your skin. You do not hasten to question and you do not hasten to answer. Your tongue has lost its flexible capacity for easy oscillation. Your eyes do not flash with gladness over good tidings nor do they darken with grief.

For you still have to verify whether that's how it is going to be. And you also have to work out—what is gladness and what is grief.

And now the rule of your life is this: Do not rejoice when you have found, do not weep when you have lost.

Your soul, which formerly was dry, now ripens from suffering. And even if you haven't come to love your neighbors in the Christian sense, you are at least learning to love those close to you.

Those close to you in spirit who surround you in slavery. And how many of us come to realize: It is particularly in slavery that for the first time we have learned to recognize genuine friendship!

And also those close to you in blood, who surrounded you in

your former life, who loved you—while you played the tyrant over them . . .

Here is a rewarding and inexhaustible direction for your thoughts: Reconsider all your previous life. Remember everything you did that was bad and shameful and take thought—can't you possibly correct it now?

Yes, you have been imprisoned for nothing. You have nothing to repent of before the state and its laws

But . . . before your own conscience? But . . . in relation to other individuals?

Looking back, I saw that for my whole conscious life I had not understood either myself or my strivings. What had seemed for so long to be beneficial now turned out in actuality to be fatal, and I had been striving to go in the opposite direction to that which was truly necessary to me. But just as the waves of the sea knock the inexperienced swimmer off his feet and keep tossing him back onto the shore, so also was I painfully tossed back on dry land by the blows of misfortune. And it was only because of this that I was able to travel the path which I had always really wanted to travel.

It was granted me to carry from my prison years on my bent back, which nearly broke beneath its load, this essential experience: *how* a human being becomes evil and *how* good. In the intoxication of youthful successes I had felt myself to be infallible, and I was therefore cruel. In the surfeit of power I was a murderer, and an oppressor. In my most evil moments I was convinced that I was doing good, and I was well supplied with systematic arguments. And it was only when I lay there on rotting prison straw that I sensed within myself the first stirrings of good. Gradually it was disclosed to me that the line separating good and evil passes not through states, nor between classes, nor between political parties either—but right through every human heart—and through all human hearts. This line shifts. Inside us, it oscillates with the years. And even within hearts, overwhelmed by evil, one small bridgehead of good is retained. And even in the best of all hearts, there remains . . . an unuprooted small corner of evil.

Since then I have come to understand the truth of all the religions of the world: They struggle with the *evil inside a human being* (inside every human being). It is impossible to expel evil from the world in its entirety, but it is possible to constrict it within each person.

And since that time I have come to understand the falsehood of all the revolutions in history: They destroy only *those carriers* of evil contemporary with them (and also fail, out of haste, to dis-

criminate the carriers of good as well). And they then take to themselves as their heritage the actual evil itself, magnified still more.

The Nuremberg Trials have to be regarded as one of the special
achievements of the twentieth century: they killed the very idea of
evil, though they killed very few of the people who had been infected
with it. (Of course, Stalin deserves no credit here. He would have preferred to explain less and shoot more.) And if by the twenty-first century humanity has not yet blown itself up and has not suffocated
itself—perhaps it is this direction that will triumph?

Yes, and if it does not triumph—then all humanity's history
will have turned out to be an empty exercise in marking time, without the tiniest mite of meaning! Whither and to what end will we
otherwise be moving? To beat the enemy over the head with a
club—even cavemen knew that.

"Know thyself!" There is nothing that so aids and assists the
awakening of omniscience within us as insistent thoughts about
one's own transgressions, errors, mistakes. After the difficult cycles
of such ponderings over many years, whenever I mentioned the
heartlessness of our highest-ranking bureaucrats, the cruelty of our
executioners, I remember myself in my captain's shoulder boards
and the forward march of my battery through East Prussia,
enshrouded in fire, and I say: "So were *we* any better?"

When people express vexation, in my presence, over the
West's tendency to crumble, its political short-sightedness, its divi-
siveness, its confusion—I recall too: "Were we, before passing
through Archipelago, more steadfast? Firmer in our thoughts?"

And that is why I turn back to the years of my imprisonment
and say, sometimes to the astonishment of those about me: *"Bless
you, prison!"*

Lev Tolstoi was right when he *dreamed* of being in prison. At a
certain moment that giant began to dry up. He actually needed
prison as a drought needs a shower of rain!

All the writers who wrote about prison but who did not themselves serve time there considered it their duty to express sympathy
for prisoners and to curse prison I . . . have served enough time
there. I nourished my soul there, and I say without hesitation:

"Bless you, prison, for having been in my life!"

(And from beyond the grave come replies: It is very well for
you to say that—when you came out of it alive!)

7

THE AMERICAN MAN

Manhood in America has been a complicated matter, from its earliest days forward. European traditions about the meaning of manliness, including relationships between husbands and wives and fathers and children, migrated to the New World along with the settlers—and yet many early Americans left Europe precisely because they found those older feudal and theocratic patterns of authority oppressive. From the beginning, Americans have prized individual freedom. For the early colonists, this meant above all freedom of conscience to worship as they saw fit. As the new American people grew and put down deeper roots in the soil of the continent, this belief in individual liberty was extended to business, political debate and personal life.

The American founding was thus a kind of experiment in encouraging individual freedom to flourish without impediment or competition from earlier European models of virtue and the common good. But it would be misleading to say that American individualism had no connection at all with those earlier traditions of manliness, fatherhood, and statesmanship. The influence of John Locke and Adam Smith on the principles of the American founding is widely noted, and neither of those philosophers endorsed unbridled selfishness or spontaneous impulse. On the contrary, they argued that an education in moral character was necessary if individual liberty was not to degenerate into licence and anarchy.

Adam Smith is best known for his formulation of the "hidden hand" argument in favor of capitalist free enterprise, on the grounds that markets generally correct their own errors and distribute the rewards of hard work to the meritorious. But Smith based this endorsement of the work ethic on the education of what he called "the inner man" in the moral and intellectual virtues that prevent us from becoming totally absorbed in moneymaking. For Smith firmly believed that men will not treat each other honestly in their business dealings unless those commercial relationships are guided by a wider moral training based on reason and sympathy.

Locke, whose portrait Jefferson hung in a prominent place at Monticello, is perhaps best known for his defense of the individual's right to acquire property. But Locke never maintained that property rights were the basis for all other rights. According to Locke, the first law of nature is the individual's right to freedom from tyranny and other forms of criminal violence and oppression. The practice of this fundamental natural right includes the right to acquire property, worship, move about, and engage in public debate. The right to property is only one among a number of liberties that flow from and demonstrate our more fundamental right to freedom from tyranny.

Locke and his American disciples did not view liberal democracy as a product of the free enterprise economic system. On the contrary, it is liberal democracy that creates and sustains a market economy, and justifies it only to the extent that it facilitates the freedom and dignity of every member of society. Accordingly, like Adam Smith, Locke was also keenly interested in educating young men in the virtues of character, compassion and tolerance necessary for exercising one's rights responsibly. His advice in favor of more flexible and open-minded approaches to child-rearing would become a kind of ideal for American education:

"The business of education . . . is not, as I think, to make [students] perfect in any one of the sciences, but so to open and dispose their minds as may best make them capable of any, when they shall come to apply themselves to it. If men are for a long time accustomed only to one sort or method of thoughts, their minds grow stiff in it, and do not readily turn to another. It is therefore to give them this freedom, that I think they should be made to look into all sorts of knowledge, and exercise their understandings in so wide a variety and stock of knowledge." Free your mind, in other words, and success will follow.

By the time the young French aristocrat Alexis de Tocqueville toured America in the 1830s, eager to acquaint Europeans with this strange, boisterous new society, Americans bore the stamp of this Enlightenment philosophy of individualism on their national character. As Tocqueville remarked, Americans were from the start natural Cartesians—followers of the French rationalist Rene Descartes—even though most may never have read the philosopher's work. Descartes had argued that individuals should take nothing on faith, but subject every belief and observation to their own autonomous powers of reasoning. Doubt everything! was his motto, and although Americans had little taste for philosophy, Tocqueville observed, they practiced this skepticism every day. To this day, indeed, Americans are self-reliant and deeply suspicious of any kind of inherited collective authority. Historically, they have resisted outdated European notions of duty to family, clan, class, and church. Believing democracy and equality to be the only legitimate principles of government, they show no trace of the European deference to aristocracy, and little patience for European traditions of reserve, delicacy, or decorum.

Tocqueville believed there was a clear-cut and unavoidable choice between the American and European ways of life. Both had their merits and shortcomings, but they could not be combined. As the readings in this section suggest, however, there may have been more overlap in the long run than the French aristocrat thought possible. Whether one examines the American brand of heroism in statesmanship and battle, or the evolution of the American character in personal life and family affairs, some themes are uniquely American while others have roots in the older traditions of classical antiquity, feudal Europe and the Renaissance. Age-old aspects of the manly virtues—valor, statesmanship, chivalry and family life— were subjected to unprecedented new challenges as Americans extended their creed of democratic individualism across the mysterious and sometimes dangerous continent. What evolved was a uniquely American hybrid of these ancient aspirations to virtuous manhood.

THE AMERICAN HERO

Freedom in All Just Pursuits

From Thomas Jefferson,
Notes on the State of Virginia

American democracy and civilization brought new complexities to the meaning of manliness. In some ways, Americans drew upon the older classical ideals to provide a model for democratic virtue. In his Notes on the State *of Virginia, Jefferson says the greatest happiness comes from the freedom that a liberal education bestows to develop our highest capacities for just pursuits. Echoing the classical ideal stretching back to Plato and Aristotle, Jefferson maintains that an educated citizenry is essential to good government. True manliness is impossible without learning. Through the study of ancient history and the Greek and Roman classics, young Americans will learn about the high points of moral and intellectual excellence from the past.*

Their memories may here be stored with the most useful facts from Grecian, Roman, European and American history. The first elements of morality too may be instilled into their minds such as, when further developed as their judgments advance in strength, may teach them how to work out their own greatest happiness, by showing them that it does not depend on the condition of life in which chance has placed them, but is always the result of a good conscience, good health, occupation, and freedom in all just pursuits. Those whom either the wealth of their parents or the adoption of the State shall destine to higher degrees of learning, will go on to the grammar schools, which constitute the next stage, there to be instructed in the languages. The learning Greek and Latin, I am told, is going into disuse in Europe. I know not what their manners and occupations may call for; but it would be very ill-judged in us to follow their example in this instance. There is a certain period of life, say from eight to fifteen or sixteen years of age, when the mind like the body is not yet firm enough for laborious and close operations. If applied to such, it falls an early victim to premature exertion; exhibiting, indeed, at first, in these young and tender subjects, the flattering appearance of their being men while they are yet children, but ending in reducing them to be children when they should be men. The memory is then most susceptible and tenacious of impressions; and the learning of languages being chiefly a work of memory, it seems precisely fitted to the powers of this period, which is long enough too for acquiring the most useful languages, ancient and modern. I do not pretend that language is science. It is only an instrument for the attainment of science. But that time is not lost which is employed in providing tools for future operation; more especially as in this case the books put into the hands of the youth for this purpose may be such as will at the same time impress their minds with useful facts and good principles. If this period be suffered to pass in idleness, the mind becomes lethargic and impotent, as would the body it inhabits if unexercised during the same time. The sympathy between body and mind during their rise, progress and decline, is too strict and obvious to endanger our being missed while we reason from the one to the other. As soon as they are of sufficient age, it is supposed they will be sent on from the grammar schools to the university, which constitutes our third and last stage, there to study those sciences which may be adapted to their views. By that part of our plan which prescribes the selection of the youths of genius from among the classes of the poor, we hope to avail the State of those talents which nature has sewn as liberally among the poor as the rich, but which perish without use, if not sought for and cultivated. But of the views of this law none is more important, none more legitimate, than that of rendering the people the safe, as they are the ultimate, guardians of their own liberty. For this purpose the reading in the first stage, where *they* will receive their whole education, is proposed, as has been said, to be chiefly historical. History, by apprising them of the past, will enable them to judge of the future; it will avail them of the experience of other times and other nations; it will qualify them as judges of the actions and designs of men; it will enable them to know ambition under every disguise it may assume; and knowing it, to defeat its views. In every government on earth is some trace of human weakness, some germ of corruption and degeneracy, which cunning will discover, and wickedness insensibly open, cultivate and improve. Every government degenerates when trusted to the rulers of the people alone. The people themselves therefore are its only safe depositories. And to render even them safe, their minds must be improved to a certain degree. This indeed is not all that is necessary, though it be essentially necessary.

The Call to Arms

Patrick Henry, Select Orations

The immortal summons to revolution delivered in 1775 by the brilliant orator and statesman (1736–1799).

No man thinks more highly than I do of the patriotism, as well as abilities, of the very worthy gentlemen who have just addressed the House. But different men often see the same subject in different lights; and, therefore, I hope it will not be thought disrespectful to those gentlemen, if entertaining as I do all opinions of a character very opposite to theirs, I shall speak forth my sentiments freely and without reserve. There is no time for ceremony.

The question before the House is one of awful moment to this country. For my own part, I consider it as nothing less than a question of freedom or slavery; and in proportion to the magnitude of the subject ought to be the freedom of the debate. It is only in this way that we can hope to arrive at truth, and fulfill the great responsibility which we hold to God and our country. Should I keep back my opinions at such a time, through fear of giving offense, I should consider myself as guilty of treason toward my country, and of an act of disloyalty toward the Majesty of Heaven, which I revere above all earthly kings.

Mr. President, it is natural to man to indulge in the illusions of hope. We are apt to shut our eyes against a painful truth, and listen to the song of that siren, till she transforms us into beasts. Is this the part of wise men, engaged in a great and arduous struggle for liberty? Are we disposed to be of the number of those, who, having eyes, see not, and having ears, hear not, the things which so nearly concern their temporal salvation? For my part, whatever anguish of spirit it may cost, I am willing to know the worst, and to provide for it.

I have but one lamp by which my feet are guided; and that is the lamp of experience. I know of no way of judging of the future but by the past. And judging by the past, I wish to know what there has been in the conduct of the British ministry, for the last ten years, to justify those hopes with which gentlemen have been pleased to solace themselves and the House? Is it that insidious smile with which our petition has been lately received? Trust it not, sir; it will prove a snare to your feet. Suffer not yourself to be betrayed with a kiss. Ask yourselves how this gracious reception of our petition comports with those warlike preparations which cover our waters and darken our land. Are fleets and armies necessary to a work of love and reconciliation? Have we shown ourselves so unwilling to be reconciled, that force must be called in to win back our love? Let us not deceive ourselves, sir. These are the implements of war and subjugation; the last arguments to which kings resort.

I ask gentlemen, sir, what means this martial array, if its purpose be not to force us to submission? Can gentlemen assign any other possible motive for it? Has Great Britain any enemy in this quarter of the world to call for all this accumulation of navies and armies? No, sir, she has none. They are sent over to bind and rivet upon us those chains, which the British ministry have been so long forging. And what have we to oppose to them? Shall we try argument? Sir, we have been trying that for the last ten years. Have we anything new to offer upon the subject? Nothing. We have held the subject up in every light of which it is capable; but it has been all in vain. Shall we resort to entreaty and humble supplication? What terms shall we find, which have not been already exhausted? Let us not, I beseech you, sir, deceive ourselves longer. Sir, we have done everything that could be done, to avert the storm which is now coming on. We have petitioned; we have remonstrated; we have supplicated; we have prostrated ourselves before the throne, and have implored its interposition to arrest the tyrannical hands of the ministry and Parliament. Our petitions have been slighted; our remonstrances have produced additional violence and insult; our supplications have been disregarded; and we have been spurned, with contempt, from the foot of the throne! In vain, after these things, may we indulge the fond hope of peace and reconciliation. There is no longer any room for hope. If we wish to be free—if we mean to preserve inviolate those inestimable privileges for which we have been so long contending—if we mean not basely to abandon the noble struggle in which we have been so long engaged, and which we have pledged ourselves never to abandon, until the glorious object of our contest shall be obtained—we must fight! I repeat it, sir, we must fight! An appeal to arms and to the God of Hosts is all that is left us!

They tell us, sir, that we are weak—unable to cope with so formidable an adversary. But when shall we be stronger? Will it be the next week, or the next year? Will it be when we are totally disarmed, and when a British guard shall be stationed in every house? Shall we gather strength by irresolution and inaction? Shall we acquire the means of effectual resistance by lying supinely on our backs and hugging the delusive phantom of hope, until our enemies shall have bound us hand and foot?

Sir, we are not weak if we make a proper use of those means which the God of nature has placed in our power. Three millions of people armed in the holy cause of liberty, and in such a country as that which we possess, are invincible by any force which our enemy can send against us. Besides, sir, we shall not fight our battles alone. There is a just God who presides over the destinies of nations, and who will raise up friends to fight our battles for us. The battle, sir, is not to the strong alone; it is to the vigilant, the active, the brave. Besides, sir, we have no election. If we were base enough to desire it, it is now too late to retire from the contest. There is no retreat but in submission and slavery! Our chains are forged! Their clanking may be heard on the plains of Boston! The war is inevitable—and let it come! I repeat it, sir, let it come!

It is in vain, sir, to extenuate the matter. Gentlemen may cry, Peace, Peace—but there is no peace. The war is actually begun! The next gale that sweeps from the north will bring to our ears the clash of resounding arms! Our brethren are already in the field! Why stand we here idle? What is it that gentlemen wish? What would they have? Is life so dear, or peace so sweet, as to be purchased at the price of chains and slavery? Forbid it, Almighty God! I know not what course others may take; but as for me, give me liberty or give me death!

It Is Natural to Believe
in Great Men

From Ralph Waldo Emerson,
Representative Men

It is natural to believe in great men. If the companions of our childhood should turn out to be heroes, and their condition regal it would not surprise us. All mythology opens with demigods, and the circumstance is high and poetic; that is, their genius is paramount. In the legends of the Gautama, the first men ate the earth and found it deliciously sweet.

Nature seems to exist for the excellent. The world is upheld by the veracity of good men: they make the earth wholesome. They who lived with them found life glad and nutritious. Life is sweet and tolerable only in our belief in such society; and, actually or ideally, we manage to live with superiors. We call our children and our lands by their names. Their names are wrought into the verbs of language, their works and effigies are in our houses, and every circumstance of the day recalls an anecdote of them.

The search after the great man is the dream of youth and the most serious occupation of manhood. We travel into foreign parts to find his works—if possible, to get a glimpse of him. But we are put off with fortune instead. You say, the English are practical; the Germans are hospitable; in Valencia the climate is delicious; and in the hills of the Sacramento there is gold for the gathering. Yes, but I do not travel to find comfortable, rich and hospitable people, or clear sky, or ingots that cost too much. But if there were any magnet that would point to the countries and houses where are the persons who are intrinsically rich and powerful, I would sell all and buy it, and put myself on the road today.

The race goes with us on their credit. The knowledge that in the city is a man who invented the railroad, raises the credit of all the citizens. But enormous populations, if they be beggars, are disgusting, like moving cheese, like hills of ants or of fleas—the more, the worse.

Our religion is the love and cherishing of these patrons. The gods of fable are the shining moments of great men. We run all our vessels into one mold. Our colossal theologies of Judaism, Christianism, Buddhism, Mahometism, are the necessary and structural action of the human mind. The student of history is like a man going into a warehouse to buy cloths or carpets. He fancies he has a new article. If he goes to the factory, he shall find that his new stuff still repeats the scrolls and rosettes which are found on the interior walls of the pyramids of Thebes. Our theism is the purification of the human mind. Man can paint, or make, or think, nothing but man. He believes that the great material elements had their origin from his thought. And our philosophy finds one essence collected or distributed.

If now we proceed to inquire into the kinds of service we derive from others, let us be warned of the danger of modern studies, and begin low enough. We must not contend against love, or deny the substantial existence of other people. I know not what would happen to us. We have social strengths. Our affection toward others creates a sort of vantage or purchase which nothing will supply. I can do that by another which I cannot do alone. I can say to you what I cannot first say to myself. Other men are lenses through which we read our own minds. Each man seeks those of different quality from his own, and such as are good of their kind; that is, he seeks other men, and the *otherest*. The stronger the nature, the more it is reactive. Let us have the quality pure. A little genius let us leave alone.

But *great men*: —the word is injurious. Is there caste? Is there fate? What becomes of the promise to virtue? The thoughtful youth laments the superfoetation of nature. "Generous and handsome," he says, "is your hero; but look at yonder poor Paddy, whose country is his wheelbarrow; look at his whole nation of Paddies." Why are the masses, from the dawn of history down, food for knives and powder? The idea dignifies a few leaders, who have sentiment, opinion, love, self-devotion; and they make war and death sacred; —but what for the wretches whom they hire and kill? The cheapness of man is every day's tragedy. It is as real a loss that others should be low as that we should be low; for we must have society.

Is it a reply to these suggestions to say, Society is a Pestalozzian school: all are teachers and pupils in turn. We are equally served by receiving and by imparting. Men who know the same things are not long the best company for each other. But bring to each an intelligent person of another experience, and it is as if you let off water from a lake by cutting a lower basin. It seems a mechanical advantage, and great benefit it is to each speaker, as he can now paint out his thought to himself. We pass very fast, in our personal moods, from dignity to dependence. And if any appear never to assume the chair, but always to stand and serve, it is because we do not see the company in a sufficiently long period for the whole rotation of parts to come about. As to what we call the masses, and common men—there are no common men. All men are at last of a size; and true art is only possible on the conviction that every talent has its apotheosis somewhere. Fair play and an open field and freshest laurels to all who have won them! But heaven reserves an equal scope for every creature. Each is uneasy until he has produced his private ray unto the concave sphere and beheld his talent also in its last nobility and exaltation.

The heroes of the hour are relatively great; of a faster growth; or they are such in whom, at the moment of success, a quality is ripe which is then in request. Other days will demand other qualities. Some rays escape the common observer, and want a finely adapted eye. Ask the great man if there be none greater. His companions are; and not the less great but the more that society cannot see them. Nature never sends a great man into the planet without confiding the secret to another soul.

One gracious fact emerges from these studies—that there is true ascension in our love. The reputations of the nineteenth century will one day be quoted to prove its barbarism. The genius of humanity is the real subject whose biography is written in our annals. We must infer much, and supply many chasms in the record. The history of the universe is symptomatic, and life is mnemonical. No man, in all the procession of famous men, is reason or illumination or that essence we were looking for; but is an exhibition, in some quarter, of new possibilities. Could we one day complete the immense figure which these flagrant points compose! The study of many individuals leads us to an elemental region wherein the individual is lost, or wherein all touch by their summits. Thought and feeling that break out there cannot be impounded by any fence of personality. This is the key to the power of the greatest men—their spirit diffuses itself. A new quality of mind travels by night and by day, in concentric circles from its origin, and publishes itself by unknown methods: the union of all minds appears intimate; what gets admission to one, cannot be kept out of any other; the smallest acquisition of truth or of energy, in any quarter, is so much good to the commonwealth of souls. If the disparities of talent and position vanish when the individuals are seen in the duration which is necessary to complete the career of each, even more swiftly the seeming injustice disappears when we ascend to the central identity of all the individuals, and know that they are made of the substance which ordaineth and doeth.

The genius of humanity is the right point of view of history.

The Glory of Our Fathers

From Josiah Quincy,
July 4th Oration on the American Revolution

When we speak of the glory of our fathers, we mean not that vulgar renown to be attained by physical strength, nor yet that higher fame to be acquired by intellectual power. Both often exist without lofty thought, or pure intent, or generous purpose. The glory which we celebrate was strictly of a moral and religious character; righteous as to its ends; just as to its means. The American Revolution had its origin neither in ambition, nor avarice, nor envy, nor in any gross passion; but in the nature and relation of things, and in the thence resulting necessity of separation from the parent state. Its progress was limited by that necessity. During the struggle, our fathers displayed great strength and great moderation of purpose. In difficult times, they conducted with wisdom; in doubtful times, with firmness; in perilous, with courage; under oppressive trials, erect; amid great temptations, unseduced; in the dark hour of danger, fearless; in the bright hour of prosperity, faithful.

It was not the instant feeling and pressure of the arm of despotism that roused them to resist, but the *principle* on which that arm was extended. They could have paid the *stamp-tax*, and the *tea-tax*, and other impositions of the British government, had they been increased a thousandfold. But *payment* acknowledged the *right;* and they spurned the consequences of that acknowledgment. In spite of those acts they could have lived, and happily; and bought, and sold, and got gain, and been at ease. But they would have held those blessings, on the tenure of dependence on a foreign and distant power; at the mercy of a king, or his minions; or of councils, in which they had no voice, and where their interests could not be represented, and were little likely to be heard. They saw that their prosperity in such case would be precarious, their possessions uncertain, their ease inglorious.

But, above all, they realized that these burdens, though light to them, would, to the coming age, to us, their posterity, be heavy, and probably insupportable.

Democracy and the Great Man

From Alexis de Tocqueville,
Democracy in America

Based on a nine month visit to the United States during 1831 and 1832, a young French nobleman, Alexis de Tocqueville, produced Democracy in America, *regarded ever since as the single most powerful and prescient diagnosis of democratic civilization in the New World. Here, Tocqueville wonders whether there is a place for great men in the democratic interpretation of history.*

Historians who write in aristocratic ages generally attribute everything that happens to the will and character of particular men, and they will unhesitatingly suppose slight accidents to be the cause of the greatest revolutions. With great sagacity they trace the smallest causes and often leave the greatest unnoticed.

Historians who live in democratic ages show contrary tendencies.

Most of them attribute hardly any influence over the destinies of mankind to individuals, or over the fate of a people to the citizens.

Thus historians who live in democratic times do not only refuse to admit that some citizens may influence the destiny of a people, but also take away from the peoples themselves the faculty of modifying their own lot and make them depend either on an inflexible providence or on a kind of blind fatality. According to them each nation is inexorably bound by its position, origin, antecedents, and nature to a fixed destiny which no efforts can change. Generation is firmly bound to generation, and so going back from age to age, from necessity to necessity, they reach the origin of the world, forging a tight, enormous chain which girds and binds the human race.

Not content to show how events have occurred, they pride themselves on proving that they could not have happened differently. They see a nation which has reached a certain point in its history, and they assert that it was bound to have followed the path that led it there. That is easier than demonstrating how it might have taken a better road.

In reading historians of aristocratic ages, those of antiquity in particular, it would seem that in order to be master of his fate and to govern his fellows a man need only be master of himself. Perusing the histories written nowadays, one would suppose that man had no power, neither over himself nor over his surroundings. Classical historians taught how to command; those of our own time teach next to nothing but how to obey. In their writings the author often figures large, but humanity is always tiny.

If this doctrine of fatality, so attractive to those who write history in democratic periods, passes from authors to readers, infects the whole mass of the community, and takes possession of the public mind, it will soon paralyze the activities of modern society and bring Christians down to the level of Turks.

I would add that such a doctrine is particularly dangerous at the present moment. Our contemporaries are all too much inclined to doubts about free will, since each of them feels himself confined on every side by his own weakness. But they will freely admit the strength and independence of men united in a body social. It is important not to let this idea grow dim, for we need to raise men's souls, not to complete their prostration.

The Sword of Washington!
The Staff of Franklin!

From John Quincy Adams,
Select Orations

Adams, who became President of the United States in 1825, pays tribute to two of the founding fathers.

The *Sword of Washington*! The *Staff of Franklin*! O, sir, what associations are linked in adamant with these names! Washington, whose sword was never drawn but in the cause of his country, and never sheathed when wielded in his country's cause! Franklin, the philosopher of the thunderbolt, the printing-press, and the ploughshare! What names are these in the scanty dialogue of the benefactors of human kind! *Washington* and *Franklin*! What *other* two men whose lives belong to the eighteenth century of Christendom have left a deeper impression of themselves upon the age in which they lived, and upon all after time?

Washington, the warrior and the legislator! In war, contending, by the wager of the battle, for the independence of his country, and for the freedom of the human race—ever manifesting, amid its horrors, by precept and by example, his reverence for the laws of peace, and for the tenderest sympathies of humanity; —in peace, soothing the ferocious spirit of discord, among his own countrymen, into harmony and union, and giving to that very sword, now presented to his county, a charm more potent than that attributed, in ancient times, to the lyre of Orpheus.

Franklin! The mechanic of his own fortune; teaching, in early youth, under the shackles of indigence, the way to wealth, and, in the shade of obscurity, the path to greatness; in the maturity of manhood, disarming the thunder of its terrors, the lightning of its

fatal blast; and wresting from the tyrant's hand the still more afflic-
tive scepter of oppression: while descending into the vale of years,
traversing the Atlantic Ocean, braving, in the dead of winter, the
battle and the breeze, bearing in his hand the Charter of Independence, which he had contributed to form, and tendering, from the
self-created nation to the mightiest monarchs of Europe, the olive-
branch of peace, the mercurial wand of commerce, and the amulet
of protection and safety to the man of peace, on the pathless
ocean, from the inexorable cruelty and merciless rapacity of war.

And, finally, in the last stage of life, with fourscore winters
upon his head, under the torture of an incurable disease, returning to his native land, closing his days as the chief magistrate of his
adopted commonwealth, after contributing by his counsels, under
the Presidency of Washington, and recording his name, under the
sanction of devout prayer, invoked by him to God, to that Constitution under the authority of which we are here assembled, as the
representatives of the North American people, to receive, in their
name and for them, these venerable relics of the wise, the valiant,
and the good founders of our great confederated republic—these
sacred symbols of our golden age. May they be deposited among
the archives of our Government! And may every American who
shall hereafter behold them, ejaculate a mingled offering of praise
to that Supreme Ruler of the Universe, by whose tender mercies
our Union had been hitherto preserved, through all the vicissitudes and revolutions of this turbulent world; and of prayer for the
continuance of these blessings, by the dispensations of Providence,
to our beloved country, from age to age, till time shall be no more!

Illustrious Man!

From Charles James Fox,
Select Orations

The English politician pays tribute to the foreign policy of George Washington.

How infinitely superior must appear the spirit and principles of
General Washington in his late address to Congress compared with
the policy of modern European courts! Illustrious man! Deriving

honor less from the splendor of his situation than for the dignity of his mind. Grateful to France for the assistance received from her in that great contest which secured the independence of America, he did not choose to give up the system of neutrality in her favor; having once laid down the line of conduct most proper to be pursued, not all the insults and provocations of the French minister, Genêt, could at all put him out of his way and bend him from his purpose.

It must, indeed, create astonishment, that, placed in circumstances so critical, and filling a station so conspicuous, the character of Washington should never once have been called in question—that he should, in no one instance, have been accused either of improper insolence, or of mean submission, in his transactions with foreign nations. It has been reserved for him to run the race of glory without experiencing the smallest interruption to the brilliancy of his career. The breath of censure has not dared to impeach the purity of his conduct, nor the eye of envy to raise its malignant glance to the elevation of his virtues. Such has been the transcendent merit and the unparalleled fate of this illustrious man!

How did he act when insulted by Genêt? Did he consider it as necessary to avenge himself for the misconduct or madness of an individual, by involving a whole continent in the horrors of war? No; he contented himself with procuring satisfaction for the insult, by causing Genêt to be recalled, and thus at once consulted his own dignity and the interest of his country. Happy Americans! While the whirlwind flies over one quarter of the globe, and spreads everywhere desolation, you remain protected from its baneful effects by your own virtues, and the wisdom of your government.

Separated from Europe by an immense ocean, you feel not the effect of those prejudices and passions which convert the boasted seats of civilization into scenes of horror and bloodshed. You profit by the folly and madness of the contending nations, and afford, in your more congenial clime, an asylum to those blessings and virtues which they wantonly contemn or wickedly exclude from their bosom! Cultivating the arts of peace, under the influence of freedom, you advance, by rapid strides, to opulence and distinction; and if, by any accident, you should be compelled to take part in the present unhappy contest—if you should find it necessary to avenge insult, or repel injury—the world will bear witness to the equity of your sentiments and the moderation of your views; and the success of your arms will, no doubt, be proportioned to the justice of your cause!

Such Men Cannot Die

From Edward Everett, Select Orations

A tribute to two American heroes from the eminent orator and statesman, Edward Everett (1794–1865).

No, fellow-citizens, we dismiss not Adams and Jefferson to the chambers of forgetfulness and death. What we admired, and prized, and venerated in them, can *never* die, nor, dying, be forgotten. I had almost said that they are now beginning to live—to live that life of unimpaired influence, of unclouded fame, of unmingled happiness, for which their talents and services were destined. They were of the select few, the least portion of whose life dwells in their physical existence; whose hearts have watched while their senses slept; whose souls have grown up into a higher being; whose pleasure is to be useful; whose wealth is an unblemished reputation; who respire the breath of honorable fame; who have deliberately and consciously put what is called life to hazard, that they may live in the hearts of those who come after. Such men do not, *can not die.*

To be cold, and motionless, and breathless, to feel not and speak not: this is not the end of existence to the men who have breathed their spirits into the institutions of their country, who have stamped their characters on the pillars of the age, who have poured their hearts' blood into the channels of the public prosperity. Tell me, ye who tread the sods of yon sacred height, is Warren dead? Can you not still see him, not pale and prostrate, the blood of his gallant heart pouring out of his ghastly wound, but moving resplendent over the field of honor, with the rose of heaven upon his cheek, and the fire of liberty in his eye?

Tell me, ye who make your pious pilgrimage to the shades of Vernon, is Washington indeed shut up in that cold and narrow house? That which made these men, and men like these, cannot die. The hand that traced the charter of independence is, indeed, motionless, the eloquent lips that sustained it are hushed; but the lofty spirits that conceived, resolved, matured, maintained it, and which alone, to such men, "make it life to live," *these* cannot expire:

"These shall resist the empire of decay,
When time is o'er, and worlds have passed away:
Cold in the dust the perished heart may lie,
But that which warmed it once, can never die."

Manly Honor in Democracy and Aristocracy

From Alexis de Tocqueville, Democracy in America

The feudal aristocracy was born of war and for war; it won its power by force of arms and maintained it thereby. So nothing was more important to it than military courage. It was therefore natural to glorify courage above all other virtues. Every manifestation thereof, even at the expense of common sense and humanity, was therefore approved and often even ordained by the manners of the time. The fantastic notions of individuals could affect only the details of such a system.

That a man should regard a tap on the cheek as an unbearable insult and feel bound to kill the man who struck him thus in single combat is an arbitrary rule; but that a noble should not tranquilly suffer an insult, and was dishonored if he let himself be struck without fighting—that was a result of the basic principles and needs of a military aristocracy.

Among opinions current among Americans one still finds some scattered notions detached from the old European aristocratic conception of honor, but they have no deep roots or strong influence. It is like a religion whose temples are allowed to remain but in which one no longer believes.

Amid these half-effaced notions of an exotic honor some new opinions have made their appearance, and these constitute what one might call the contemporary American conception of honor.

I have shown how the Americans are continually driven into trade and industry. The origin, social conditions, political institutions, and even the very land they live in irresistibly impel them in

this direction. Hence they now form an almost exclusively industrial and trading community placed in the midst of a huge new country whose exploitation is their principal interest. That is the characteristic trait which now distinguishes the Americans most
particularly from all other nations.

But all those turbulent virtues which sometimes bring glory
but more often trouble to society will rank lower in the public opinion of this same people. One could disregard them without forfeit-
ing the esteem of one's fellow citizens, and perhaps by acquiring
them one might run a risk of losing it.

American and European medieval conceptions of honor
agree on one point: both rank courage first of virtues and count it
the greatest moral necessity for a man. But the two conceptions
envisage courage in a different light.

In the United States martial valor is little esteemed; the type of
courage best known and best appreciated is that which makes a
man brave the fury of the ocean to reach port more quickly, and
face without complaint the privations of life in the wilds and that
solitude which is harder to bear than any privations, the courage
which makes a man almost insensible to the loss of a fortune labo-
riously acquired and prompts him instantly to fresh exertions to
gain another. It is chiefly courage of this sort which is needed to
maintain the American community and make it prosper, and it is
held by them in particular esteem and honor. To betray a lack of it
brings certain shame.

In America I have sometimes met rich young men temperamentally opposed to any uncomfortable effort and yet forced to
enter a profession. Their characters and their wealth would have
allowed them to stay idle, but public opinion imperiously forbade
that and had to be obeyed. But among European nations where an
aristocracy is still struggling against the current that carries it away,
I have often met men whose needs and inclinations constantly
goaded them to action, who yet remained idle so as not to lose the
esteem of their equals, and who found boredom and discomfort
easier to face than work.

"Towering Genius Disdains a Beaten Path."

From Abraham Lincoln,
Address to the Young Men's Lyceum
in Springfield, Illinois (1838)

Can a democracy find room for "an Alexander, a Caesar or a Napoleon? Never!" A surprising viewpoint from the future president, twenty-two years before his inauguration.

As a subject of the remarks of the evening, *the perpetuation of our political institutions,* is selected.

In the great journal of things happening under the sun, we, the American People, find our account running, under date of the nineteenth century of the Christian era. We find ourselves in the peaceful possession, of the fairest portion of the earth, as regards extent of territory, fertility of soil, and salubrity of climate. We find ourselves under the government of a system of political institutions, conducing more essentially to the ends of civil and religious liberty, than any of which the history of former times tells us. We, when mounting the stage of existence, found ourselves the legal inheritors of these fundamental blessings. We toiled not in the acquirement or establishment of them—they are a legacy bequeathed us, by a *once* hardy, brave, and patriotic, but *now* lamented and departed race of ancestors. Theirs was the task (and nobly they performed it) to possess themselves, and through themselves, us, of this goodly land; and to uprear upon its hills and its valleys, a political edifice of liberty and equal rights; 'tis ours only, to transmit these, the former, unprofaned by the foot of an invader; the latter, undecayed by the lapse of time, and untorn by [usurpation—to the latest generation that fate shall permit the world to know. This task of gratitude to our fathers, justice to] ourselves, duty to posterity, and love for our species in general, all imperatively require us faithfully to perform.

How, then, shall we perform it? At what point shall we expect the approach of danger? By what means shall we fortify against it?

Shall we expect some transatlantic military giant, to step the Ocean, and crush us at a blow? Never! All the armies of Europe, Asia and Africa combined, with all the treasure of the earth (our own excepted) in their military chest; with a Buonaparte for a commander, could not by force, take a drink from the Ohio, or make a track on the Blue Ridge, in a trial of a thousand years.

At what point then is the approach of danger to be expected? I answer, if it ever reach us, it must spring up amongst us. It cannot come from abroad. If destruction be our lot, we must ourselves be its author and finisher. As a nation of freemen, we must live through all time, or die by suicide.

I hope I am over wary; but if I am not, there is, even now, something of ill-omen amongst us. I mean the increasing disregard for the law which pervades the country; the growing disposition to substitute the wild and furious passions, in lieu of the sober judgment of Courts; and the worse than savage mobs, for the executive ministers of justice. This disposition is awfully fearful in any community; and that it now exists in ours, though grating to our feelings to admit, it would be a violation of truth, and an insult to our intelligence, to deny. Accounts of outrages committed by mobs, form the everyday news of the times. They have pervaded the country, from New England to Louisiana; —they are neither peculiar to the eternal snows of the former, nor the burning suns of the latter; —they are not the creature of climate—neither are they confined to the slaveholding, or the non-slaveholding States. Alike, they spring up among the pleasure hunting masters of Southern slaves, and the order loving citizens of the land of steady habits. Whatever, then, their cause may be, it is common to the whole country.

I know the American People are *much* attached to their Government; —I know they would suffer *much* for its sake; —I know they would endure evils long and patiently, before they would ever think of exchanging it for another. Yet, notwithstanding all this, if the laws be continually despised and disregarded, if their rights to be secure in their persons and property, are held by no better tenure than the caprice of a mob, the alienation of their affections from the Government is the natural consequence; and to that, sooner or later, it must come.

Here then, is one point at which danger may be expected.

The question recurs "how shall we fortify against it?" The answer is simple. Let every American, every lover of liberty, every well wisher to his posterity, swear by the blood of the Revolution, never to violate in the least particular, the laws of the country; and never to tolerate their violation by others. As the patriots of seventy-six did to the support of the Constitution and Laws, let every American pledge his life, his property, and his sacred honor; —let every man remember that to violate the law, is to trample on the blood of his father, and to tear the [charter?] of his own, and his children's liberty. Let reverence for the laws, be breathed by every American mother, to the lisping babe, that prattles on her lap—let it be taught in schools, in seminaries, and in colleges; —let it be written in Primmers, spelling books, and in Almanacs; —let it be preached from the pulpit, proclaimed in legislative halls, and enforced in courts of justice. And, in short, let it become the *political religion* of the nation; and let the old and the young, the rich and the poor, the grave and the gay, of all sexes and tongues, and colors and conditions, sacrifice unceasingly upon its altars.

But, it may be asked, why suppose danger to our political institutions? Have we not preserved them for more than fifty years? And why may we not for fifty times as long?

The experiment is successful; and thousands have won their deathless names in making it so. But the game is caught; and I believe it is true, that with the catching, end the pleasures of the chase. This field of glory is harvested, and the crop is already appropriated. But new reapers will arise, and *they*, too, will seek a field. It is to deny, what the history of the world tells us is true, to suppose that men of ambition and talents will not continue to spring up against us. And, when they do, they will as naturally seek the gratification of their ruling passion, as others have so done before them. The question then, is, can that gratification be found in supporting and maintaining an edifice that has been erected by others? Most certainly it cannot. Many great and good men sufficiently qualified of any task they should undertake, may ever be found, whose ambition would aspire to nothing beyond a seat in Congress, a gubernatorial or a presidential chair; *but such belong not to the family of the lion, or the tribe of the eagle,* [.] What! Think you these places would satisfy an Alexander, a Caesar, or a Napoleon? Never! Towering genius disdains a beaten path. It seeks regions hitherto unexplored. It sees *no distinction* in adding story to story, upon the monuments of fame, erected to the memory of others. It *denies* that it is glory enough to serve under any chief. It *scorns* to tread in the footsteps of *any* predecessor, however illustrious. It thirsts and burns for distinction; and, if possible, it will have it, whether at the expense of emancipating slaves, or enslaving freemen. Is it unreasonable then to expect, that some man possessed of the loftiest genius, coupled with ambition sufficient to push it to its utmost stretch, will at some time, spring up among us? And when such a one does, it will require the people to be united with each other, attached to the government and laws, and generally intelligent, to successfully frustrate his designs.

Distinction will be his paramount object; and although he would as willingly, perhaps more so, acquire it by doing good as harm; yet, that opportunity being past, and nothing left to be done in the way of building up, he would set boldly to the task of pulling down.

Here, then, is a probable case, highly dangerous, and such a one as could not have well existed heretofore.

Another reason which *once was*; but which, to the same extent, is *now no more*, has done much in maintaining our institutions thus far. I mean the powerful influence which the interesting scenes of the revolution had upon the *passions* of the people as distinguished from their judgment. By this influence, the jealousy, envy, and avarice, incident to our nature, and so common to a state of peace, prosperity, and conscious strength, were, for the time, in a great measure smothered and rendered inactive while the deep rooted principles of *hate*, and the powerful motive of *revenge*, instead of being turned against each other, were directed exclusively against the British nation. And thus, from the force of circumstances, the bases principles of our nature, were either made to lie dormant, or to become the active agents in the advancement of the noblest of cause[s?]—that of establishing and maintaining civil and religious liberty.

But this state of feeling *must fade, is fading, has faded,* with the circumstances that produced it.

I do not mean to say, that the scenes of the revolution *are now* or *ever will be* entirely forgotten; but that like everything else, they must fade upon the memory of the world, and grow more and more dim by the lapse of time. In history, we hope, they will be read of, and recounted, so long as the Bible shall be read; —but even granting that they will, their influence *cannot be* so universally known, nor so vividly felt, as they were by the generation just gone to rest. At the close of that struggle, nearly every adult male had been a participator in some of its scenes. The consequence was, that of those scenes, in the form of a husband, a father, a son or a brother, a *living history was* to be found in every family—a history bearing the indubitable testimonies of its own authenticity, in the limbs mangled, in the scars of wounds received, in the midst of the very scenes related—a history, too, that could be read and understood alike by all, the wise and the ignorant, the learned and the unlearned. But *those* histories are gone. They *can* be read no more forever. They *were* a fortress of strength; but, what invading foe-men could *never do*, the silent artillery of our time *has done*; the leveling of its walls. They are gone. They *were* a forest of giant oaks; but the all-restless hurricane has swept over them, and left only, here and there, a lonely trunk, despoiled of its verdure, shorn of its foliage; unshading and unshaded, to murmur in a few more gentle breezes, and to combat with its mutilated limbs, a few more ruder storms, then to sink, and be no more.

They *were* the pillars of the temple of liberty; and now, that they have crumbled away, that temple must fall, unless we, their descendants, supply their places with other pillars, hewn from the solid quarry of sober reason. Passion has helped us; but can do so no more. It will in future be our enemy. Reason, cold, calculating, unimpassioned reason, must furnish all the materials for our future support and defence. Let those [materials] be moulded into *general intelligence*, [*sound*] *morality* and, in particular, *a reverence for the constitution and laws*; and, that we improved to the last; that we remained free to the last; that we revered his name to the last; [tha]t, during his long sleep, we permitted no hostile foot to pass over or desecrate [his] resting place; shall be that which to le[arn the last] trump shall awaken our Wash[ington.

Upon these] let the proud fabric of freedom r[est, as the] rock of its basis; and as truly as has been said of the only greater institution, "*the gates of hell shall not prevail against it.*"

Why There Are So Many Men of Ambition in the United States but So Few Lofty Ambitions

From Alexis de Tocqueville,
Democracy in America

The first thing that strikes one in the United States is the innumerable crowd of those striving to escape from their original social condition; and the second is the rarity, in a land where all are actively ambitious, of any lofty ambition. Every American is eaten up with longing to rise, but hardly any of them seem to entertain very great hopes or to aim very high. All are constantly bent on gaining property, reputation, and power, but few conceive such things on a grand scale. That, at first sight, is surprising, since there is no obvious impediment in the mores or laws of America to put a limit to ambition or to prevent its taking wing in every direction.

Equality of conditions hardly seems a sufficient explanation of this strange state of affairs. For when this same equality was first established in France, it gave birth at once to almost unlimited ambitions. Nevertheless, I think that we may find the chief reason for this in the social conditions and democratic manners of the Americans.

Every revolution increases men's ambition, and that is particularly true of a revolution which overthrows an aristocracy.

When the barriers that formerly kept the multitude from fame and power are suddenly thrown down, there is an impetuous universal movement toward those long-envied heights of power which can at last be enjoyed. In this first triumphant exaltation nothing seems impossible to anybody. Not only is there no limit to desires, but the power to satisfy them also seems almost unlimited. Amid this general and sudden change of customs and of laws, when all men and all rules share one vast confusion, when citizens rise and fall at such an unthought-of rate, and when power passes so quickly from hand to hand, no one need despair of snatching it in his turn.

It is also important to remember that those who destroy an aristocracy once lived under its laws; they have seen its splendors and have unconsciously imbibed the feelings and ideas which it conceived. At the moment, therefore, of the dissolution of an aristocracy, its spirit still hovers over the masses, and its instincts are preserved long after it has been conquered.

Thus ambitions are on the grand scale while the democratic revolution lasts; that will no longer be true some considerable time after it has finished.

Men do not in one day forget the memory of extraordinary events which they have witnessed; and the passions roused by revolution by no means vanish at its close. A sense of instability is perpetuated amid order. The hope of easy success lives on after the strange turns of fortune which gave it birth. Longings on a vast scale remain, though the means to satisfy them become daily less. The taste for huge fortunes persists, though such fortunes in fact become rare, and on all sides there are those who eat out their hearts in secret, consumed by inordinate and frustrated ambition.

But little by little the last traces of the battle are wiped out and the relics of aristocracy finally vanish. The great events which accompanied its fall are forgotten. Peace follows war, and order again prevails in a new world. Longings once more become proportionate to the available means. Wants, ideas, and feelings again learn their limits. Men find their level, and democratic society is finally firmly established.

When we come to take stock of a democratic people which has reached this enduring and normal state, it appears very different from the scene we have been contemplating. And we easily come to the conclusion that although high ambitions swell while conditions are in process of equalization, that characteristic is lost when equality is a fact.

When great fortunes have been divided up and education has spread, no one is absolutely deprived of either education or property. When both the privileges and the disqualifications of class have been abolished and men have shattered the bonds which once held them immobile, the idea of progress comes naturally into each man's mind; the desire to rise swells in every heart at once, and all men want to quit their former social position. Ambition becomes a universal feeling.

But equality, though it gives every citizen some resources, prevents any from enjoying resources of great extent, and for this reason desires must of necessity be confined within fairly narrow limits. Hence in democracies ambition is both eager and constant, but in general it does not look very high. For the most part life is spent in eagerly coveting small prizes within reach.

It is not so much the small scale of their wealth as the constant and strenuous efforts requisite to increase it which chiefly diverts men in democracies from high ambitions. They strain their faculties to the utmost to achieve paltry results, and this quickly and inevitably limits their range of vision and circumscribes their powers. They could well be much poorer and yet be more magnanimous.

The few opulent citizens of a democracy constitute no exception to this rule. A man who raises himself gradually to wealth and power contracts in the course of this patient ascent habits of prudence and restraint which he cannot afterward shake off. A mind cannot be gradually enlarged, like a house.

Much the same applies to the sons of such a man. They may, it is true, have been born into a high position, but their parents were humble. They have grown up among feelings and ideas from which it is difficult later to escape. One may suppose that they inherit their father's instincts together with his property.

On the other hand, one may find some poor offshoot of a powerful aristocracy whose ambition is vast, for the opinions traditional to his race and the whole spirit of his caste for some time yet buoy him up above his actual fortune.

Another impediment making it far from easy for men of democratic ages to launch on great ambitions is the length of time that must elapse before they are in a position to undertake any such matter. "It is a great advantage," says Pascal, "to be a man of quality, for it brings one man forward at eighteen or twenty, whereas another must wait till he is fifty, which is a clear gain of thirty years." Ambitious men in democracies generally have to do without those thirty years. Equality, while it allows any man to reach any height, prevents his doing so fast.

In a democratic society, as elsewhere, there are only a few great fortunes to be made. As the careers leading thereto are open without discrimination to every citizen, each man's progress is bound to be slow. When all candidates seem more or less alike and it is difficult to make any choice between them without violating the principle of equality which is the supreme law of democratic societies, the first idea which comes to mind is to make them all go forward at the same rate and submit to the same tests.

Therefore, as men become more alike and the principle of

equality has quietly penetrated deep into the institutions and manners of the country, the rules of advancement become more inflexible and advancement itself slower. It becomes ever more difficult to reach a position of some importance quickly.

From hatred of privilege and embarrassment in choosing, all men, whatever their capacities, are finally forced through the same sieve, and all without discrimination are made to pass a host of petty preliminary tests, wasting their youth and suffocating their imagination. So they come to despair of ever fully enjoying the good things proffered, and when at last they reach a position in which they could do something out of the ordinary, the taste for it has left them.

In China, where equality has for a very long time been carried to great lengths, no man graduates from one public office to another without passing an examination. He has to face this test at every stage of his career, and the idea is now so deeply rooted in the manners of the people that I remember reading a Chinese novel in which the hero, after many ups and downs, succeeds at last in touching his mistress's heart by passing an examination well. Lofty ambition can hardly breathe in such an atmosphere.

What has been said about politics applies to everything else. Equality produces the same results everywhere. Even where no law regulates and holds back advancement, competition has this effect.

Hence great and rapid promotion is rare in a well-established democracy. Such events are exceptions to the general rule. Their very singularity makes men forget how seldom they occur.

The inhabitants of democracies do in the end get a glimpse of all these truths. They do at length appreciate that while the law opens an unlimited field before them, and while all can make some easy progress there, no one can flatter himself that his advance is swift. They see a multitude of little intermediate obstacles, all of which have to be negotiated slowly, between them and the great object of their ultimate desires. The very anticipation of this prospect tires ambition and discourages it. They therefore discard such distant and doubtful hopes, preferring to seek delights less lofty but easier to reach. No law limits their horizon, but they do so for themselves.

I have said that high ambitions were rarer in democratic ages than under aristocracies. I must add that when, despite all natural obstacles, they do appear, they wear another face.

Under aristocracies the career open to ambition is often wide, but it does have fixed limits. In democratic countries its field of action is usually very narrow, but once those narrow bounds are passed, there is nothing left to stop it. As men are weak, isolated, and changeable, and as precedents have little force and laws do not last long, resistance to innovation is half-hearted, and the fabric of society never stands up quite straight or firm. As a result, when ambitious men have once seized power, they think they can dare to do anything. When power slips from their grasp, their thoughts at once turn to overturning the state in order to get it again.

This gives a violent and revolutionary character to great political ambitions, a thing which is seldom seen, to the same extent, in aristocratic societies.

A multitude of petty, very reasonable desires from which occasionally a few higher and ill-controlled ambitions will break out—such is the usual state of affairs in democratic nations. In them one hardly ever finds ambition which is proportionate, moderate, and yet vast.

I have shown elsewhere by what secret means equality makes the passion for physical pleasures and an exclusive interest in immediate delights predominate in the human heart. These instincts of different origin mingle with ambition, and it takes its color from them.

I think that ambitious men in democracies are less concerned than those in any other lands for the interests and judgment of posterity. The actual moment completely occupies and absorbs them. They carry through great undertakings quickly in preference to erecting long-lasting monuments. They are much more in love with success than with glory. What they especially ask from men is obedience. What they most desire is power. Their manners almost always lag behind the rise in their social position. As a result, very vulgar tastes often go with their enjoyment of extraordinary prosperity, and it would seem that their only object in rising to supreme power was to gratify trivial and coarse appetites more easily.

I think that nowadays it is necessary to purge ambition, to control it and keep it in proportion, but that it would be very dangerous if we tried to starve it or confine it beyond reason. The task should be to put, in advance, limits beyond which it would not be allowed to break. But we should be very careful not to hamper its free energy within the permitted limits.

I confess that I believe democratic society to have much less to fear from boldness than from paltriness of aim. What frightens me most is the danger that, amid all the constant trivial preoccupations of private life, ambition may lose both its force and its greatness, that human passions may grow gentler and at the same time baser, with the result that the progress of the body social may become daily quieter and less aspiring.

I therefore think that the leaders of the new societies would do wrong if they tried to send the citizens to sleep in a state of happiness too uniform and peaceful, but that they should sometimes give them difficult and dangerous problems to face, to rouse ambition and give it a field of action.

Moralists are constantly complaining that the pet vice of our age is pride.

There is a sense in which that is true; everyone thinks himself better than his neighbor and dislikes obeying a superior. But there is another sense in which it is very far from the truth, for the same man who is unable to put up with either subordination or equality has nonetheless so poor an opinion of himself that he thinks he is born for nothing but the enjoyment of vulgar pleasures. Of his own free will he limits himself to paltry desires and dares not face any lofty enterprise; indeed, he can scarcely imagine such a possibility.

Thus, far from thinking that we should council humility to our contemporaries, I wish men would try to give them a higher idea of themselves and of humanity; humility is far from healthy for them; what they most lack, in my view, is pride. I would gladly surrender several of our petty virtues for that one vice.

It Was Reserved for Him to Have Command

From Henry Watterson, Select Orations

The courageous life and death by assassination of Abraham Lincoln inspired the eloquence of public speakers for years to come, as in this address from 1895.

From Caesar to Bismarck and Gladstone the world has had its statesmen and its soldiers—men who rose to eminence and power step by step, through a series of geometric progression, as it were, each advancement following in regular order one after the other, the whole obedient to well-established and well-understood laws of cause and effect. They were not what we call "men of destiny." They were "men of the time." They were men whose careers had a beginning, a middle, and an end, rounding off lives with histories, full it may be of interesting and exciting events, but comprehensive and comprehensible, simple, clear, complete.

The inspired ones are fewer. Whence their emanation, where and how they got their power, by what rule they lived, moved, and had their being, we know not. There is no explication to their lives. They rose from shadow and they went in mist. We see them, feel them, but we know them not. They came, God's word upon their lips; they did their office, God's mantle about them; and they vanished, God's holy light between the world and them, leaving behind a memory, half mortal and half myth. From first to last, they were the creations of some special Providence, baffling the wit of man to fathom, defeating the machinations of the world, the flesh, and the devil, until their work was done, then passing from the scene as mysteriously as they had come upon it.

Tried by this standard, where shall we find an example so impressive as Abraham Lincoln, whose career might be chanted by a Greek chorus as at once the prelude and the epilogue of the most imperial theme of modern times?

Born as lowly as the Son of God, in a hovel; reared in penury, squalor, with no gleam of light or fair surrounding; without graces, actual or acquired; without name or fame or official training, it was reserved for him to have command at a supreme moment of a nation's fate.

His Life Now Is Grafted
Upon the Infinite

From Henry Ward Beecher,
Select Orations

A tribute to Lincoln in 1865 from the influential Congregational minister, abolitionist, and orator.

There is no historic figure more noble than that of Moses the Jewish lawgiver. There is scarcely another event in history more touching than his death. He had borne the great burdens of state for forty years, shaped the Jews to a nation, filled out their civil and religious polity, administered their laws, guided their steps, or dwelt with them in all their journeyings in the wilderness; had mourned in their punishment, kept step with their march, and led them in wars, until the end of their labors drew nigh. The last stage was reached. Jordan only lay between them and the promised land. Then came the word of the Lord unto him, "Thou mayest not go over. Get thee up into the mountain, look upon it, and die."

From that silent summit, the hoary leader gazed to the north, to the south, to the west, with hungry eyes. The dim outlines rose up. The hazy recesses spoke of quiet valleys between the hills. With eager longing, with sad resignation, he looked upon the promised land. It was now to him a forbidden land. It was a moment's anguish. He forgot all his personal wants, and drank in the vision of his people's home. His work was done. There lay God's promise fulfilled.

Again a great leader of the people has passed through toil, sorrow, battle, and war, and come near to the promised land of peace, into which he might not pass over. Who shall recount our martyr's sufferings for this people? Since the November of 1860, his horizon has been black with storms. By day and by night he trod a way of danger and darkness. On his shoulders rested a government dearer to him than his own life. At its integrity millions of men were striking at home. Upon this government foreign eyes lowered. It stood like a lone island in a sea full of storms; and every tide and wave seemed eager to devour it. Upon thousands of hearts great sorrows and anxieties have rested, but not on one such, and in such measure, as upon that simple, truthful, noble soul, our faithful and sainted Lincoln. He wrestled ceaselessly, through four black and dreadful purgatorial years, wherein God was cleansing the sin of his people as by fire.

At last the watcher beheld the gray dawn for the country. The mountains began to give forth their forms from out the darkness; and the East came rushing toward us with arms full of joy for all our sorrows. Then it was for him to be glad exceedingly, that had sorrowed immeasurably. Peace could bring to no other heart such joy, such rest, such honor, such trust, such gratitude. But he looked upon it as Moses looked upon the promised land. Then the wail of a nation proclaimed that he had gone from among us. Not thine the sorrow, but ours, sainted soul.

Never did two such orbs of experience meet in one hemisphere, as the joy and the sorrow of the same week in this land. The joy was as sudden as if no man had expected it, and as entrancing as if it had fallen a sphere from heaven. In one hour it lay without a pulse, without a gleam, or breath. A sorrow came that swept through the land as huge storms sweep through the forest and field, rolling thunder along the sky, dishevelling the flowers, daunting every singer in thicket or forest, and pouring blackness and darkness across the land and up the mountains. Did ever so many hearts, in so brief a time, touch two such boundless feelings? It was the uttermost of joy; it was the uttermost of sorrow—noon and midnight, without a space between.

The blow brought not a sharp pang. It was so terrible that at first it stunned sensibility. Citizens were like men awakened at midnight by an earthquake, and bewildered to find everything that they were accustomed to trust wavering and falling. The very earth was no longer solid. The first feeling was the least. Men waited to get straight to feel. They wandered in the streets as if groping after some impending dread, or undeveloped sorrow, or some one to tell them what ailed them. They met each other as if each would ask the other, "Am I awake or do I dream?" There was a piteous helplessness. Strong men bowed down and wept. Other and common griefs belonged to some one in chief: this belonged to all. It was each and every man's. Every virtuous household in the land felt as if its first-born were gone. Rear to his name monuments, found charitable institutions, and write his name above their lintels; but no monument will ever equal the universal, spontaneous, and sublime sorrow that in a moment swept down lines and parties, and covered up animosities, and in an hour brought a divided people into unity of grief and indivisible fellowship of anguish.

And now the martyr is moving in triumphal march, mightier than when alive. The nation rises up at every stage of his coming. Cities and states are his pall-bearers, and the cannon beats the hours with solemn progression. Dead, dead, dead, he yet speaketh! Is Washington dead? Is Hampden dead? Is David dead? Is any man that ever was fit to live dead? Disenthralled of flesh, and risen in the unobstructed sphere where passion never comes, he begins his illimitable work. His life now is grafted upon the infinite, and will be fruitful as no earthly life can be. Pass on, thou that hast overcome! Your sorrows, oh people, are his peace! Your bells, and bands, and muffled drums, sound triumph in his ear. Wail and weep here; God makes it echo joy and triumph there. Pass on!

Four years ago, oh Illinois, we took from your midst an untried man, and from among the people. We return him to you a mighty conqueror. Not thine anymore, but the nation's; not ours, but the world's. Give him place, oh ye prairies! In the midst of this great continent his dust shall rest, a sacred treasure to myriads who shall pilgrim to that shrine to kindle anew their zeal and patriotism. Ye winds that move over the mighty places of the West, chant requiem! Ye people, behold a martyr whose blood, as so many articulate words, pleads for fidelity, for law, for liberty!

I Have a Dream

Martin Luther King Jr.

Delivered before the Lincoln Memorial on August 28, 1963, this is the best-known speech of the illustrious and heroic civil rights leader. In keeping with his deeply held theological convictions, Dr. King believed that a man's inner spiritual strength to do good came through renouncing violence, and that no Americans could be free so long as any Americans were oppressed.

I am happy to join with you today in what will go down in history as the greatest demonstration for freedom in the history of our nation.

Fivescore years ago, a great American, in whose symbolic shadow we stand today, signed the Emancipation Proclamation. This momentous decree came as a great beacon light of hope to millions of Negro slaves who had been seared in the flames of withering injustice. It came as a joyous daybreak to end the long night of their captivity.

But one hundred years later, the Negro still is not free; one hundred years later, the life of the Negro is still sadly crippled by the manacles of segregation and the chains of discrimination; one hundred years later, the Negro lives on a lonely island of poverty in the midst of a vast ocean of material prosperity; one hundred years later, the Negro is still languished in the corners of American society and finds himself in exile in his own land.

So we've come here today to dramatize a shameful condition.

In a sense we've come to our nation's capital to cash a check. When the architects of our republic wrote the magnificent words of the Constitution and the Declaration of Independence, they were signing a promissory note to which every American was to fall heir. This note was the promise that all men, yes, black men as well as white men, would be guaranteed the unalienable rights to life, liberty, and the pursuit of happiness.

It is obvious today that America has defaulted on this promissory note in so far as her citizens of color are concerned. Instead of honoring this sacred obligation, America has given the Negro people a bad check; a check which has come back marked "insufficient funds." We refuse to believe that there are insufficient funds in the great vaults of opportunity of this nation. And so we've come to cash this check, a check that will give us upon demand the riches of freedom and security of justice.

We have also come to this hallowed spot to remind America of the fierce urgency of now. This is no time to engage in the luxury of cooling off or to take the tranquilizing drug of gradualism. Now is the time to make real the promises of democracy; now is the time to rise from the dark and desolate valley of segregation to the sun-lit path of racial justice; now is the time to lift our nation from the quicksands of racial injustice to the solid rock of brotherhood; now is the time to make justice a reality for all God's children. It would be fatal for the nation to overlook the urgency of the moment. This sweltering summer of the Negro's legitimate discontent will not pass until there is an invigorating autumn of freedom and equality.

Nineteen sixty-three is not an end, but a beginning. And those who hope that the Negro needed to blow off steam and will now be content, will have a rude awakening if the nation returns to business as usual.

There will be neither rest nor tranquillity in America until the Negro is granted his citizenship rights. There whirlwinds of revolt will continue to shake the foundations of our nation until the bright day of justice emerges.

But there is something that I must say to my people who stand on the warm threshold which leads into the palace of justice. In the process of gaining our rightful place we must not be guilty of wrongful deeds.

Let us not seek to satisfy our thirst for freedom by drinking from the cup of bitterness and hatred. We must forever conduct our struggle on the high plane of dignity and discipline. We must not allow our creative protest to degenerate into physical violence. Again and again we must rise to the majestic heights of meeting physical force with soul force.

The marvelous new militancy which has engulfed the Negro community must not lead us to a distrust of all white people, for many of our white brothers, as evidenced by their presence here today, have come to realize that their destiny is tied up with our destiny and they have come to realize that their freedom is inextricably bound to our freedom. This offensive we share, mounted to storm the battlements of injustice, must be carried forth by a biracial army. We cannot walk alone.

And as we walk, we must make the pledge that we shall always march ahead. We cannot turn back. There are those who are asking the devotees of civil rights, "When will you be satisfied?" We can never be satisfied as long as the Negro is the victim of the unspeakable horrors of police brutality.

We can never be satisfied as long as our bodies, heavy with fatigue of travel, cannot gain lodging in the motels of the highways and the hotels of the cities. We cannot be satisfied as long as the Negro's basic mobility is from a smaller ghetto to a larger one.

We can never be satisfied as long as our children are stripped of their selfhood and robbed of their dignity by signs saying "for whites only." We cannot be satisfied as long as a Negro in Mississippi cannot vote and a Negro in New York believes he has nothing for which to vote. No, we are not satisfied, and we will not be satisfied until justice rolls down like waters and righteousness like a mighty stream.

I am not unmindful that some of you have come here out of excessive trials and tribulations. Some of you have come fresh from narrow jail cells. Some of you have come from areas where your quest for freedom left you battered by the storms of persecution and staggered by the winds of police brutality. You have been the veterans of creative suffering. Continue to work with the faith that unearned suffering is redemptive.

Go back to Mississippi; go back to Alabama; go back to South Carolina; go back to Georgia; go back to Louisiana; go back to the slums and ghettos of the northern cities, knowing that somehow this situation can, and will be changed. Let us not wallow in the valley of despair.

So I say to you, my friends, that even though we must face the difficulties of today and tomorrow, I still have a dream. It is a dream deeply rooted in the American dream that one day this nation will rise up and live out the true meaning of its creed—we hold these truths to be self-evident, that all men are created equal.

I have a dream that one day on the red hills of Georgia, sons of former slaves and sons of former slave-owners will be able to sit down together at the table of brotherhood.

I have a dream that one day, even the state of Mississippi, a state sweltering with the heat of injustice, sweltering with the heat of oppression, will be transformed into an oasis of freedom and justice.

I have a dream my four little children will one day live in a nation where they will not be judged by the color of their skin but by the content of their character. I have a dream today!

I have a dream that one day, down in Alabama, with its vicious racists, with its governor having his lips dripping with the words of interposition and nullification, that one day, right there in Alabama, little black boys and black girls will be able to join hands with little white boys and white girls as sisters and brothers. I have a dream today!

I have a dream that one day every valley shall be exalted, every hill and mountain shall be made low, the rough places shall be made plain, and the crooked places shall be made straight and the glory of the Lord will be revealed and all flesh shall see it together.

This is our hope. This is the faith that I go back to the South with.

With this faith we will be able to hew out of the mountain of despair a stone of hope. With this faith we will be able to transform the jangling discords of our nation into a beautiful symphony of brotherhood.

With this faith we will be able to work together, to pray together, to struggle together, to go to jail together, to stand up for freedom together, knowing that we will be free one day. This will be the day when all of God's children will be able to sing with new meaning—"my country 'tis of thee; sweet land of liberty; of thee I sing; land where my fathers died, land of the pilgrim's pride; from every mountain side, let freedom ring"—and if America is to be a great nation, this must become true.

So let freedom ring from the prodigious hilltops of New Hampshire.

Let freedom ring from the mighty mountains of New York.

Let freedom ring from the heightening Alleghenies of Pennsylvania.

Let freedom ring from the snow-capped Rockies of Colorado.

Let freedom ring from the curvaceous slopes of California.

But not only that.

Let freedom ring from Stone Mountain of Georgia.

Let freedom ring from Lookout Mountain of Tennessee.

Let freedom ring from every hill and molehill of Mississippi, from every mountainside, let freedom ring.

And when we allow freedom to ring, when we let it ring from every village and hamlet, from every state and city, we will be able to speed up that day when all of God's children—black men and white men, Jews and Gentiles, Catholics and Protestants—will be able to join hands and to sing in the words of the old Negro spiritual, "Free at last, free at last; thank God Almighty, we are free at last."

A Man Among Men

From Theodore Roosevelt,
The Americanism of Theodore Roosevelt

An address by TR on service and citizenship at the Harvard Union in 1907.

Unless democracy is based on the principle of service by everybody who claims the enjoyment of any right, it is not true democracy at all. The man who refuses to render, or is ashamed to render, the necessary service is not fit to live in a democracy. And the man who demands from another a service which he himself would esteem it dishonorable or unbecoming to render is to that extent not a true democrat. No man has a right to demand a service which he does not regard as honorable to render; nor has he a right to demand it unless he pays for it in some way, *the payment to include respect of the man who renders it.* Democracy must mean mutuality of service rendered, and of respect for the service rendered.

The educated man who seeks to console himself for his own lack of the robust qualities necessary to bring success in American politics by moaning over the degeneracy of the times instead of trying to better them, by railing at the men who do the actual work of political life instead of trying himself to do the work, is a poor creature, and, so far as his feeble powers avail, is a damage and not a help to the country.

You may come far short of this disagreeable standard and still be a rather useless member of society. Your education, your cultivation, will not help you if you make the mistake of thinking that it is a substitute for instead of an addition to those qualities which in the struggle of life bring success to the ordinary man without your advantages. Your college training confers no privilege upon you save as tested by the use you make of it. It puts upon you the obligation to show yourselves better able to do certain things than your fellows who have not had your advantages. If it has served merely to make you believe that you are to be excused from contact with the actual world of men and events, then it will prove a curse and not a blessing. If on the other hand you treat your education as a weapon the more in your hands, a weapon to fit you to do better in the hard struggle of effort, and not as excusing you in any way from taking part in practical fashion in that struggle, then it will be a benefit to you.

Let each of you college men remember in after life that in the fundamentals he is very much like his fellows who have not been to college, and that if he is to achieve results, instead of confining himself exclusively to disparagement of other men who have achieved them, he must manage to come to some kind of working agreement with these fellows of his. There are times, of course, when it may be the highest duty of a citizen to stand alone, or practically alone. But if this is a man's normal attitude—if normally he is unable to work in combination with a considerable body of his fellows—it is safe to set him down as unfit for useful service in a democracy. In popular government results worth having can only be achieved by men who combine worthy ideals with practical good sense; who are resolute to accomplish good purposes, but who can accommodate themselves to the give and take necessary where work has to be done, by combination. Moreover, remember that normally the prime object of political life should be to achieve results and not merely to issue manifestoes—save, of course, where the issuance of such manifestoes helps to achieve the results. It is a very bad thing to be morally callous, for moral callousness is disease. But inflammation of the conscience may be just as unhealthy so far as the public is concerned; and if a man's conscience is always telling him to do something foolish he will do well to mistrust its workings. The religious man who is most useful is not he whose sole care is to save his own soul, but the man whose religion bids him strive to advance decency and clean living and to make the world a better place for his fellows to live in; and all this is just as true of the ordinary citizen in the performance of the ordinary duties of political life. . . .

The last ten years have been years of great achievement for this Nation. During that period we have dealt and are dealing with many different matters of great moment. In all these matters there have been some men in public life and some men in private life whose action has been at every point one of barren criticism or fruitless obstruction. These men have had no part or lot in the great record of achievement and success; the record of good work worthily done. Some of these men have been college graduates but all of them have been poor servants of the people, useless where they were not harmful. All the credit of the good thus accomplished in the public life of this decade belongs to those who have done affirmative work in such matters as those I have enumerated above, and not to those who, with more or less futility, have sought to hamper and obstruct the work that has thus been done.

In short, you college men, be doers rather than critics of the deeds that others do. Stand stoutly for your ideals; but keep in mind that they can only be realized, even partially, by practical methods of achievement. Remember always that this Republic of ours is a very real democracy, and that you can only win success by showing that you have the right stuff in you. The college man, the men of intellect and training, should take the lead in every fight for civic and social righteousness. He can take that lead only if in a spirit of thoroughgoing democracy he takes his place among his fellows, not standing aloof from them, but mixing with them, so that he may know, may feel, may sympathize with their hopes, their ambitions, their principles—and even their prejudices—as an American among Americans, as a man among men.

Were We Truly Men?

John Fitzgerald Kennedy

What defines a man? In his 1952 inaugural speech as a Senator-elect from Massachusetts, John F. Kennedy gave an eloquent answer.

For of those to whom much is given, much is required. And when at some future date the high court of history sits in judgment on each of us, recording whether in our brief span of service we fulfilled our responsibilities to the state, our success or failure, in whatever office we hold, will be measured by the answers to four questions:

First, were we truly men of courage, with the courage to stand up to one's enemies, and the courage to stand up, when necessary, to one's associates, the courage to resist public pressure as well as private greed?

Second, were we truly men of judgment, with perceptive judgment of the future as well as the past, of our own mistakes as well as the mistakes of others, with enough wisdom to know what we did not know, and enough candor to admit it?

Third, were we truly men of integrity, men who never ran out on either the principles in which we believed or the people who believed in us, men whom neither financial gain nor political ambition could ever divert from the fulfillment of our sacred trust?

Finally, were we truly men of dedication, with an honor mortgaged to no single individual or group, and compromised by no private obligation or aim, but devoted solely to serving the public good and the national interest?

Courage, judgment, integrity, dedication—these are the historic qualities of the Bay Colony and the Bay State, the qualities which this state has consistently sent to Beacon Hill here in Boston and to Capitol Hill back in Washington. And these are the qualities which, with God's help, this son of Massachusetts hopes will characterize our government's conduct in the four stormy years that lie ahead. Humbly I ask His help in this undertaking; but aware that on earth His will is worked by men, I ask for your help and your prayers as I embark on this new and solemn journey.

Robin Hood or
the White House?

From Mark Twain,
The Adventures of Tom Sawyer

In Tom Sawyer, *Mark Twain evokes the heroism of boyhood on the frontier. Young men are still attracted to their damsels, and the life of Robin Hood seems much more alluring than that of high political office.*

He wandered far from the accustomed haunts of boys, and sought desolate places that were in harmony with his spirit. A log raft in the river invited him, and he seated himself on its outer edge and contemplated the dreary vastness of the stream, wishing, the while, that he could only be drowned, all at once and unconsciously, without undergoing the uncomfortable routine devised by nature. Then he thought of his flower. He got it out, rumpled and wilted, and it mightily increased his dismal felicity. He wondered if *she* would pity him if she knew? Would she cry, and wish that she had a right to put her arms around his neck and comfort him? Or would she turn coldly away like all the hollow world? This picture brought such an agony of pleasurable suffering that he worked it over and over again in his mind and set it up in new and varied lights, till he wore it threadbare. At last he rose up sighing and departed in the darkness.

About half past nine or ten o'clock he came along the deserted street to where the Adored Unknown lived; he paused a moment; no sound fell upon his listening ear; a candle was casting a dull glow upon the curtain of a second-story window. Was the sacred presence there? He climbed the fence, threaded his stealthy way through the plants, till he stood under that window; he looked up at it long, and with emotion; then he laid him down on the ground under it, disposing himself upon his back, with his hands clasped upon his breast and holding his poor wilted flower. And thus he would die—out in the cold world, with no shelter over his homeless head, no friendly hand to wipe the deathdamps from his brow, no loving face to bend pityingly over him when the great agony came. And thus *she* would see him when she looked out upon the glad morning, and oh! Would she drop one little tear upon his poor, lifeless form, would she heave one little sigh to see a bright young life so rudely blighted, so untimely cut down?

Now as to this girl. What had he done? Nothing. He had meant the best in the world, and been treated like a dog—like a very dog. She would be sorry some day—maybe when it was too late. Ah, if he could only die *temporarily*!

But the elastic heart of youth cannot be compressed into one constrained shape long at a time. Tom presently began to drift insensibly back into the concerns of this life again. What if he turned his back, now, and disappeared mysteriously? What if he went away—ever so far away, into the unknown countries beyond the seas—and never came back any more! How would she feel then! The idea of being a clown recurred to him now, only to fill him with disgust. For frivolity and jokes and spotted tights were an offense, when they intruded themselves upon a spirit that was exalted into the vague August realm of the romantic. No, he would be a soldier, and return after long years, all war-worn and illustrious. No—better still, he would join the Indians, and hunt buffaloes and go on the warpath in the mountain ranges and the trackless great plains of the Far West, and away in the future come back a great chief, bristling with feathers, hideous with paint, and prance into Sunday-school, some drowsy summer morning, with a blood-curdling war-whoop, and sear the eyeballs of all his companions with unappeasable envy. But no, there was something gaudier even than this. He would be a pirate! That was it! *Now* his future lay plain before him, and glowing with unimaginable splendor. How his name would fill the world, and make people shudder! How gloriously he would go plowing the dancing seas, in his long, low, black-hulled racer, the *Spirit of the Storm*, with his grisly flag flying at the fore! And at the zenith of his fame, how he would suddenly appear at the old village and stalk into church, brown and weather-beaten, in his black velvet doublet and trunks, his great jack-boots, his crimson sash, his belt bristling with horse-pistols, his crime-rusted cutlass at his side, his slouch hat with waving plumes, his black flag unfurled, with the skull and cross-bones on it, and hear with swelling ecstasy the whisperings, "It's Tom Sawyer the Pirate!—The Black Avenger of the Spanish Main!"

Then Tom became Robin Hood again, and was allowed by the treacherous nun to bleed his strength away through his neglected wound. And at last Joe, representing a whole tribe of weeping outlaws, dragged him sadly forth, gave his bow into his feeble hands, and Tom said, "Where this arrow falls, there bury poor Robin Hood under the greenwood tree." Then he shot the arrow and fell back and would have died, but he lit on a nettle and sprang up too gaily for a corpse.

The boys dressed themselves, hid their accoutrements, and went off grieving that there were no outlaws any more, and wondering what modern civilization could claim to have done to compensate for their loss. They said they would rather be outlaws a year in Sherwood Forest than President of the United States forever.

MANHOOD IN AMERICA

The Democratic Dad

From Alexis de Tocqueville,
Democracy in America

Although in some ways American civilization drew upon and developed European ideals of manliness from the ancient, medieval and Renaissance eras, life in the new world was so different from anything in the European heritage that new experiences of manliness and fatherhood were bound to emerge. Alexis de Tocqueville, in Democracy in America, *registers a European aristocrat's impression of how the meaning of family life has changed in America because of democratic equality. There are no Catos in Ohio. The old paterfamilias of Roman fame—the father who rules like a benevolent but absolute king over his family—cannot survive transplanting to the new world. As Tocqueville sees it, democracy weakens the father's authority over his children, but increases the open display of affection between them. Your children don't think you're a king. But you can shoot hoops with them or have a pillow fight. This would not have gone down well in ancient Rome.*

In America the family, if one takes the word in its Roman and aristocratic sense, no longer exists. One only finds scattered traces thereof in the first years following the birth of children. The father then does, without opposition, exercise the domestic dictatorship which his sons' weakness makes necessary and which is justified by both their weakness and his unquestionable superiority.

But as soon as the young American begins to approach man's estate, the reins of filial obedience are daily slackened. Master of his thoughts, he soon becomes responsible for his own behavior. In America there is in truth no adolescence. At the close of boyhood he is a man and begins to trace out his own path.

It would be wrong to suppose that this results from some sort of domestic struggle, in which, by some kind of moral violence, the son had won the freedom which his father refused. The same habits and principles which lead the former to grasp at independence dispose the latter to consider its enjoyment as an incontestable right.

So in the former one sees none of those hateful, disorderly passions which disturb men long after they have shaken off an established yoke. The latter feels none of those bitter, angry regrets which usually accompany fallen power. The father has long anticipated the moment when his authority must come to an end, and when that time does come near, he abdicates without fuss. The son has known in advance exactly when he will be his own master and wins his liberty without haste or effort, as a possession which is his due and which no one seeks to snatch from him.

In countries organized on the basis of an aristocratic hierarchy, authority never addresses the whole of the governed directly. Men are linked one to the other and confine themselves to controlling those next on the chain. The rest follows. This applies to the family as well as to all associations with a leader. In aristocracies society is, in truth, only concerned with the father. It only controls the sons through the father; it rules him, and he rules them. Hence the father has not only his natural right. He is given a political right to command. He is the author and support of the family; he is also its magistrate.

In democracies, where the long arm of the government reaches each particular man among the crowd separately to bend him to obedience to the common laws, there is no need for such an intermediary. In the eyes of the law the father is only a citizen older and richer than his sons.

When conditions generally are very unequal and this inequality is permanent, the conception of superiority works on the imagination of men. Even if the law gave no parental prerogatives, custom and public opinion would supply them. But when men are little different from one another and such differences are not permanent, the general conception of superiority becomes weaker and less defined. It would be useless for a legislator to put the man who obeys in a position of great inferiority compared to him who gives the orders; mores bring these two men close to one another and daily put them more on a level.

So, then, if I do not see any particular privileges accorded to the head of a family in the legislation of an aristocratic people, I can nonetheless rest assured that his power is much respected there and of wider extent than in a democracy, for I know that, whatever the laws may be, the superior will always seem higher and the inferior lower in aristocracies than in democracies.

When men are more concerned with memories of what has been than with what is, and when they are much more anxious to know what their ancestors thought than to think for themselves, the father is the natural and necessary link between the past and the present, the link where these two chains meet and join. In aristocracies, therefore, the father is not only the political head of the family but also the instrument of tradition, the interpreter of custom, and the arbiter of mores. He is heard with deference, he is addressed always with respect, and the affection felt for him is ever mingled with fear.

When the state of society turns to democracy and men adopt the general principle that it is good and right to judge everything for oneself, taking former beliefs as providing information but not rules, paternal opinions come to have less power over the sons, just as his legal power is less too.

A perusal of the family correspondence surviving from aristocratic ages is enough to illustrate the difference between the two social states in this respect. The style is always correct, ceremonious, rigid, and cold, so that natural warmth of heart can hardly be felt through the words.

But among democratic nations every word a son addresses to his father has a tang of freedom, familiarity, and tenderness all at once, which gives an immediate impression of the new relationship prevailing in the family.

An analogous revolution changes the relations between the children.

As in aristocratic society, so in the aristocratic family, all positions are defined. Not only the father holds a rank apart and enjoys immense privileges; the children too are by no means equal among one another; age and sex irrevocably fix the rank for each and ensure certain prerogatives. Democracy overthrows or lowers all these barriers.

In the aristocratic family the eldest son, who will inherit most of the property and almost all the rights, becomes the chief and to a certain extent the master of his brothers. Greatness and power are his; for them there is mediocrity and dependence. But yet it would be a mistake to suppose that in aristocracies the privileges of the eldest are profitable to him alone and that they excite nothing but jealousy and hatred around him.

The eldest usually takes trouble to procure wealth and power for his brothers, the general reputation of the house reflecting credit on its head. And the younger sons try to help the eldest in all his undertakings, for the greatness of power of the head of the family increase his ability to promote all the branches of the family. So the various members of the aristocratic family are closely linked together; their interests are connected and their minds are in accord, but their hearts are seldom in harmony.

Democracy too draws brothers together, but in a different way.

Under democratic laws the children are perfectly equal, and consequently independent; nothing forcibly brings them together, but also nothing drives them apart. Having a common origin, brought up under the same roof, and treated with the same care, as no peculiar privilege distinguishes or divides them, the affectionate and frank intimacy of childhood easily takes root among them. Scarcely anything can occur to break the bond thus formed at the start of life, for brotherhood daily draws them together, and there is no cause for friction.

Not interest, then, but common memories and the unhampered sympathy of thoughts and tastes draw brothers, in a democracy, to one another. Their inheritance is divided, but their hearts are free to unite.

This gentleness of democratic manners is such that even the partisans of aristocracy are attracted by it, and when they have tasted it for some time, they are not at all tempted to return to the old and respectful formalities of the aristocratic family. They gladly keep the family habits of democracy, provided they can reject its social state and laws. But these things hold together, and one cannot enjoy the one without putting up with the others.

What I have said about filial love and fraternal affection applies to all the spontaneous feelings rooted in nature itself.

If a certain way of thinking or feeling is the result of particular conditions of life, when the conditions change, nothing is left. Thus law may make a very close link between two citizens; if the law is repealed, they separate. Nothing could have been tighter than the bond uniting lord and vassal in the feudal world. Now those two men no longer know each other. The fear, gratitude, and affection which once joined them have vanished. One cannot find a trace of them.

But it is not like that with feelings natural to man. Whenever a law attempts to shape such feelings in any particular way, it almost always weakens them. By trying to add something, it almost always takes something away, and they are always stronger if left to themselves.

Democracy, which destroys or obscures almost all social conventions and which makes it harder for men to establish new ones, leads to the complete disappearance of almost all the feelings originating in such conventions. But it only modifies those of the other sort and often affords them an energy and gentleness which they had not before.

I think that I may be able to sum up in one phrase the whole sense of this chapter and of several others that preceded it. Democracy loosens social ties, but it tightens natural ones. At the same time as it separates citizens, it brings kindred closer together.

An American Father:
Robert E. Lee

From Captain Robert E. Lee,
Recollections and Letters of General Robert E. Lee

The two representative men of the North and South, Lincoln and Lee, present a fascinating study in contrasts. Lincoln, who dedicated his public life to a just cause, was a troubled husband and a distracted father, pursuing

*his duties to his family against an undertow of melancholy. Lee, who in his
public life defended the Confederacy, and therefore the evil of slavery, was by
contrast a model gentleman, father, and leader of youth in his private and
post-war life. Idolized by his children, he was firm and set high standards for
them, and they dreaded his bad opinion. And yet he was also a warm and
loving father who rough-housed with them and took an interest in everything that concerned their happiness, including their love lives. He took
pleasure in his duty to his family, softening his demanding standards with
gentleness and wry humor. Famed as a warrior, Lee nevertheless took a keen
interest in the family household, including its economy and aesthetic comforts—not only because his disabled wife needed his help, but because Lee
liked living graciously and didn't think it was beneath a man to enjoy beautiful and orderly surroundings. Perhaps most impressively, his fatherly care
extended from his own children to the young men at Washington College,
where he ended his life as a much loved president. Despite his extraordinary
feats on the battlefield, Lee always prized liberal education and learning
above martial fame and tried to instill the same conviction in his students.
This memoir was written by his son, Captain Robert E. Lee.*

The first vivid recollection I have of my father is his arrival at
Arlington, after his return from the Mexican War. I can remember
some events of which he seemed a part, when we lived at Fort
Hamilton, New York, about 1846, but they are more like dreams,
very indistinct and disconnected—naturally so, for I was at that time
about three years old. But the day of his return to Arlington, after
an absence of more than two years, I have always remembered. I
had a frock or blouse of some light wash material, probably cotton,
a blue ground dotted over with white diamond figures. Of this I was
very proud, and wanted to wear it on this important occasion.

From that early time I began to be impressed with my father's
character, as compared with other men. Every member of the
household respected, revered and loved him as a matter of course,
but it began to dawn on me that every one else with whom I was
thrown held him high in their regard. At forty-five years of age he
was active, strong, and as handsome as he had ever been. I never
remember his being ill. I presume he was indisposed at times; but
no impressions of that kind remain. He was always bright and gay
with us little folk, romping, playing, and joking with us. With the
older children, he was just as companionable, and I have seen him
join my elder brothers and their friends when they would try their
powers at a high jump put up in our yard. The two younger children he petted a great deal, and our greatest treat was to get into

his bed in the morning and lie close to him, listening while he talked to us in his bright, entertaining way. This custom we kept up with until I was ten years and over. Although he was so joyous and familiar with us, he was very firm on all proper occasions, never indulged us in anything that was not good for us, and exacted the most implicit obedience. I always knew that it was impossible to disobey my father. I felt it in me, I never thought why, but was perfectly sure when he gave an order that it had to be obeyed. My mother I could sometimes circumvent, and at times took liberties with her orders, construing them to suit myself; but exact obedience to every mandate of my father was a part of my life and being at that time. He was very fond of having his hands tickled, and, what was still more curious, it pleased and delighted him to take off his slippers and place his feet in our laps in order to have them tickled. Often, as little things, after romping all day, the enforced sitting would be too much for us, and our drowsiness would soon show itself in continued nods. Then, to arouse us, he had a way of stirring us up with his foot—laughing heartily at and with us. He would often tell us the most delightful stories, and then there was no nodding. Sometimes, however, our interest in his wonderful tales became so engrossing that we would forget to do our duty— when he would declare, "No tickling, no story!" When we were a little older, our elder sister told us one winter the ever-delightful "Lady of the Lake." Of course, she told it in prose and arranged it to suit our mental capacity. Our father was generally in his corner by the fire, most probably with a foot in either the lap of myself or youngest sister—the tickling going on briskly—and would come in at different points of the tale and repeat line after line of the poem—much to our disapproval—but to his great enjoyment.

My father was the most punctual man I ever knew. He was always ready for family prayers, for meals, and met every engagement, social or business, at the moment. He expected all of us to be the same, and taught us the use and necessity of forming such habits for the convenience of all concerned. I never knew him late for Sunday service at the Post Chapel. He used to appear some minutes before the rest of us, in uniform, jokingly rallying my mother for being late, and for forgetting something at the last moment. When he could wait no longer for her, he would say that he was off and would march along to church by himself, or with any of the children who were ready. There he sat very straight—well up the middle aisle—and, as I remember, always became very sleepy, and sometimes even took a little nap during the sermon. At that time, this drowsiness of my father's was something awful to me, inexplicable. I know it was very hard for me to keep awake, and frequently I did not; but why he, who to my mind could do everything that was right, without any effort, should sometimes be overcome, I could not understand, and did not try to do so.

It was against the rules that the cadets should go beyond certain limits without permission. Of course they did go sometimes, and when caught were given quite a number of "demerits." My father was riding out one afternoon with me, and, while rounding a turn in the mountain road with a deep woody ravine on one side, we came suddenly upon three cadets far beyond the limits. They immediately leaped over a low wall on the side of the road and disappeared from our view. We rode on for a minute in silence; then my father said: "Did you know those young men? But no; if you did, don't say so. I wish boys would do what is right, it would be so much easier for all parties!"

Lee writes to his wife:

"You do not know how much I have missed you and the children, my dear Mary. To be alone in a crowd is very solitary. In the woods, I feel sympathy with the trees and birds, in whose company I take delight, but experience no pleasure in a strange crowd. I hope you are all well and will continue so, and, therefore, must again urge you to be very prudent and careful of those dear children. If I could only get a squeeze at that little fellow, turning up his sweet mouth to 'keese baba!' You must not let him run wild in my absence, and will have to exercise firm authority over all of them. This will not require severity or even strictness, but constant attention and an unwavering course. Mildness and forbearance will strengthen their affection for you, while it will maintain your control over them."

In a letter to one of his sons he writes as follows:

"I cannot go to bed, my dear son, without writing you a few lines, to thank you for your letter, which gave me great pleasure. . . . You and Custis must take great care of your kind mother and dear sisters when your father is dead. To do that you must learn to be good. Be true, kind and generous, and pray earnestly to God to enable you to keep His Commandments 'and walk in the same ways all the days of your life.' I hope to come on soon to see that little baby you have got to show me. You must give her a kiss for me, and one to all the children, to your mother, and grandmother."

The expression of such sentiments as these was common to my father all through his life, and to show that it was all children, and not his own little folk alone that charmed and fascinated him, I quote from a letter to my mother:

". . . I saw a number of little girls all dressed up in their white frocks and pantalets, their hair plaited and tied up with ribbons, running and chasing each other in all directions. I counted twenty-three nearly the same size. As I drew up my horse to admire the spectacle, a man appeared at the door with the twenty-fourth in his arms.

"'My friend,' said I, 'are all these your children?'

"'Yes,' he said, 'and there are nine more in the house, and this is the youngest.'

"Upon further inquiry, however, I found that they were only temporarily his, and that they were invited to a party at his house. He said, however, he had been admiring them before I came up, and just wished that he had a million of dollars, and that they were all his in reality. I do not think the eldest exceeded seven or eight years old. It was the prettiest sight I have seen in the west, and, perhaps, in my life. . . ."

My father had had nearly four years' experience in charge of the young men at West Point. The conditions at that place, to be sure, were very different from those at the one to which he was now going, but the work in the main was the same—to train, improve and elevate. I think he was influenced, in making up his mind to accept this position, by the great need of education in his State and in the South, and by the opportunity that he saw at Washington College for starting almost from the beginning, and for helping, by his experience and example, the youth of his country to become good and useful citizens.

In addition to his duties as a college president, my father had to make all the arrangements for his new home. The house assigned him by the college was occupied by Dr. Madison, who was to move out as soon as he could. Carpenters, painters and glaziers had to be put to work to get it into condition; furniture, carpets, bedding to be provided, a cook procured, servants and provisions supplied.

My mother was an invalid and absent, and as my sisters were with her, everything down to the minutest detail was done by my father's directions and under his superintendence. He had always been noted for his care and attention to little things, and that trait, apparent in him when a mere lad, practiced all through his busy and eventful life, stood him in good stead now. The difficulties to be overcome were made greater by the scarcity and inaccessibility of supplies and workmen and the smallness of his means. In addition, he conducted a large correspondence, always answering every letter. To every member of his family he wrote continually, and was interested in all our pursuits, advising and helping us as no one else could have done.

His letters to his daughters tell, in a playful way, much of his life, and are full of the quiet humor in which he so often indulged. We were still at "Derwent," awaiting the time when the house in Lexington should be ready. It had been decided that I should remain and accompany my mother and sisters to Lexington, and that some of us, or all, should go up the river to "Bremo," the beautiful seat of Dr. Charles Cocke, and pay a visit there before proceeding to Lexington. Here is a letter from my father to his daughter Mildred:

"Lexington, October 29, 1865.

"*My Precious Life*: Your nice letter gave me much pleasure and made me the more anxious to see you. I think you girls, after your mother is comfortable at 'Bremo,' will have to come up and arrange the house for her reception. You know I am a poor hand and can do nothing without your advice. Your brother, too, is wild for the want of admonition. Col. Blair is now his 'fidus Achates,' and as he is almost as gray as your papa, and wears the same uniform, all gray, he is sometimes taken for him by the young girls, who consider your brother the most attentive of sons, and giving good promise of making a desirable husband. He will find himself married some of these days before he knows it. You had better be near him. I hope you give attention to Robert. Miss Sallie will thaw some of the ice from his heart. Tell her she must come up here, as I want to see her badly. I do not know what you will do with your chickens, unless you take them to 'Bremo,' and thus bring them here. I suppose Robert would not eat 'Laura Chilton' and 'Don Ella McKay.' I have scarcely gotten acquainted with the young ladies. They look very nice in the walks, but I rarely get near them. Traveller is my only companion; I may also say my pleasure. He and I, whenever practicable, wander out in the mountains and enjoy sweet confidence. The boys are plucking out his tail, and he is presenting the appearance of a plucked chicken. Two of the belles of the neighborhood have recently been married—Miss Mattie Jordan to Dr. Cameron, and Miss Rose Cameron to Dr. Sherod. The former couple go to Louisburg, West Virginia, and start tomorrow on horseback, the bride's trousseau in a baggage wagon; the latter to Winchester. Miss Sherod, one of the bridesmaids, said she knew you there. I did not attend the weddings, but have seen the pairs of doves. Both of the brides are remarkable in this county of equestrianism for their good riding and beauty. With true affection, Your fond father,

"R. E. Lee."

My father was always greatly interested in the love affairs of his relatives, friends, and acquaintances. His letters during the war show this in very many ways. One would suppose that the general commanding an army in active operations could not find the time even to think of such trifles, much less to write about them; but he knew of very many such affairs among his officers and even his men, and would on occasion refer to them before the parties themselves, very much to their surprise and discomfiture.

My father was much interested in all the arrangements of the house, even to the least thing. He would laugh merrily over the difficulties that appalled the rest of us. Our servants were few and unskilled, but his patience and self-control never failed. The silver of the family had been sent to Lexington for safe-keeping early in the war. When General Hunter raided the Valley of Virginia and advanced upon Lexington, to remove temptation out of his way, this silver, in two large chests, had been intrusted to the care of the old and faithful sergeant at the Virginia Military Institute, and he had buried it in some safe place known only to himself. I was sent out with him to dig it up and bring it in. We found it safe and sound, but black with mold and damp, useless for the time being, so my father opened his camp chest and we used his forks, spoons, plates, etc., while his campstools supplied the deficiency in seats. He often teased my sisters about their experiments in cookery and household arts, encouraging them to renewed efforts after lamentable failures. When they succeeded in a dish for the table, or completed any garment with their own hands, he was lavish with his praise. He would say:

"You are all very helpless; I don't know what you will do when I am gone," and "If you want to be missed by your friends—be useful."

He at once set to work to improve all around him, laid out a vegetable garden, planted roses and shrubs, set out fruit and yard trees, made new walks and repaired the stables, so that in a short time we were quite comfortable and very happy. He at last had a home of his own, with his wife and daughters around him, and though it was not the little farm in the quiet country for which he had so longed, it was very near to it, and it gave rest to himself and those he loved most dearly.

His duties as president of Washington College were far from light. His time was fully occupied, and his new position did not relieve him from responsibility, care and anxiety. He took pains to become acquainted with each student personally, to be really his guide and friend. Their success gratified and pleased him, and their failures, in any degree, pained and grieved him. He felt that he was responsible for their well-doing and progress, and he worked very hard to make them good students and useful men.

The grounds and buildings of the college soon began to show his care, attention, and good taste. In all his life, wherever he happened to be, he immediately set to work to better his surroundings.

The professors and students of the two institutions of learning were constant visitors, especially in the evenings, when young men came to see the girls. If his daughters had guests, my father usually sat with my mother in the dining-room adjoining the drawing-room. When the clock struck ten he would rise and close the shutters carefully and slowly, and, if that hint was not taken, he would simply say "Good night, young gentlemen." The effect was immediate and lasting, and his wishes in that matter, finally becoming generally known, were always respected. Captain W., who had very soon found out the General's views as to the time of leaving, was told on one occasion that General Lee had praised him very much.

"Do you know why?" said the Captain. "It is because I have never been caught in the parlor at ten o'clock. I came very near it last night, but got out into the porch before the General shut the first blind. That's the reason he called me a 'fine young man.'"

The loss of his brother was a great sorrow to him. They were devoted to each other, having always kept warm their boyish love. Smith's admiration for and trust in my father were unbounded, and it was delightful to see them together and listen to the stories of the happy long ago they would tell about each other. No one could be near my Uncle Smith without feeling his joyful influence. My sister Mary, who knew him long and well, and who was much attached to him, thus writes:

"No one who ever saw him can forget his beautiful face, charming personality, and grace of manner which, joined to a nobility of character and goodness of heart, attracted all who came in contact with him, and made him the most generally beloved and popular of men. This was especially so with women, to whom his conduct was that of a *preux chevalier*, the most chivalric and courteous; and, having no daughters of his own, he turned with the tenderest affection to the daughters of his brother Robert."

After all the arrangements connected with this sad event had been completed, my father went up to "Ravensworth" to see "Aunt Maria," who had always been a second mother to his brother. There, amid the cool shades of this lovely old home, he rested for a day or two from the fatigues of travel and the intense heat. During this visit, as he passed the room in which his mother had died, he lingered near the door and said to one present:

"Forty years ago, I stood in this room by my mother's death-bed! It seems now but yesterday!"

In March, 1870, General Lee, yielding to the solicitations of friends and medical advisers, made a six-weeks' visit to Georgia and Florida. He returned greatly benefited by the influence of the genial climate, the society of friends in those States, and the demonstrations of respect and affection of the people of the South; his physical condition, however, was not greatly improved. During this winter and spring he had said to his son, General Custis Lee, that his attack was mortal; and had virtually expressed the same belief to other trusted friends. And now, with that delicacy that pervaded all his actions, he seriously considered the question of resigning the presidency of Washington College, "fearful that he might not be equal to his duties." After listening, however, to the affectionate remonstrances of the faculty and board of trustees, who well knew the value of his wisdom in the supervision of the college and the power of his mere presence, and example upon the students, he resumed his labors with the resolution to remain at his post and carry forward the great work he had so auspiciously begun.

Wednesday, September 28, 1870, found General Lee at the post of duty. In the morning he was fully occupied with the correspondence and other tasks incident to his office of president of Washington College, and he declined offers of assistance from members of the faculty, of whose services he sometimes availed himself. After dinner, at four o'clock, he attended a vestry-meeting of Grace (Episcopal) church. The afternoon was chilly and wet, and a steady rain had set in, which did not cease until it resulted in a great flood, the most memorable and destructive in this region for a hundred years. The church was rather cold and damp, and General Lee, during the meeting, sat in a pew with his military cape cast loosely about him. In a conversation that occupied the brief space preceding the call to order, he took part, and told with marked cheerfulness of manner and kindliness of tone some pleasant anecdotes of Bishop Meade and Chief-Justice Marshall. The meeting was protracted until after seven o'clock by a discussion touching the rebuilding of the church edifice and the increase of the rector's salary. General Lee acted as chairman, and, after hearing all that was said, gave his own opinion, as was his wont, briefly and without argument. He closed the meeting with a characteristic act. The amount required for the minister's salary still lacked a sum much greater than General Lee's proportion of the subscription, in view of his frequent and generous contributions to the church and other charities, but just before the adjournment, when the treasurer announced the amount of the deficit still remaining, General Lee said in a low tone, "I will give that sum."

"General Lee's closing hours were consonant with his noble and disciplined life. Never was more beautifully displayed how long and severe education of mind and character enables the soul to pass with equal step through this supreme ordeal; never did the habits and qualities of a lifetime, solemnly gathered into a few last sad hours, more grandly maintain themselves amid the gloom and shadow of approaching death. The reticence, the self-contained composure, the obedience to proper authority, the magnanimity, and the Christian meekness, that marked all his actions, still preserved their sway, in spite of the inroads of disease and the creeping lethargy that weighed down his faculties."

A letter from my mother to a dear friend tells the same sad story:

". . . My husband came in. We had been waiting tea for him, and I remarked: 'You have kept us waiting a long time. Where have you been?' He did not reply, but stood up as if to say grace. Yet no word proceeded from his lips, and he sat down in his chair perfectly upright and with a sublime air of resignation on his countenance, and did not attempt to a reply to our inquiries. That look was never to be forgotten, and I have no doubt he felt that his hour had come; for though he submitted to the doctors, who were immediately summoned, and who had not even reached their homes from the same vestry meeting, yet his whole demeanor during his illness showed one who had taken leave of earth. He never smiled, and rarely attempted to speak, except in his dreams, and then he wandered to those dreadful battle-fields. Once when Agnes urged him to take some medicine, which he always did with reluctance, he looked at her and said, 'It is no use.' But afterward took it. When he became so much better the doctor said 'You must soon get out and ride your favorite gray!' He shook his head most emphatically and looked upward. He slept a great deal, but knew us all, greeted us with a kindly pressure of the hand, and loved to have us around him. For the last forty-eight hours he seemed quite insensible of our presence. He breathed more heavily, and at last sank to rest with one deep-drawn sigh. And oh, what a glorious rest was in store for him!"

"A Natural Made Gentleman"

From William H. Herndon,
Letters and Papers

Sometimes a man's virtues are tested by an unhappy marriage and shine through in spite of it. Lincoln's marriage was bleak, but his remorse over his inability to love his wife as she would have liked seemed to intensify his resolve to fulfill his duties to the family conscientiously. Lincoln's gentleness and love of justice persevered through the sadness of his marital life and a life-long streak of melancholy. He is a great exemplar of Aristotle's maxim that virtue begins as habit and ends up as one's true disposition. As his memoirist Herndon concludes, despite his humble origins, Lincoln was a "natural made gentleman."

Mr. Lincoln was the best man, the kindest, tenderest, noblest, loveliest, *since Christ.* He was better and purer than Washington; and in mind he stands incomparable, grandly looming up. He is now the great central figure of American History. God bless Abraham Lincoln!

Again—did you know that Mr. Lincoln was "*as crazy as a loon*" *in this city in 1841*; that he did not sit, did not attend to the Legislature, but in part, if any (special session of 1841); that he was then deranged? Did you know that he was forcibly arrested by his special friends here at that time; that they had to remove all razors, knives, pistols, etc., from his room and presence, that he might not commit suicide? Did you know that his crazy bout was partly caused by *that old original love* coming in conflict with *new relations about to be assumed?* His fidelity *was sublime.* Did you know that all Lincoln's struggles, difficulties, etc., between himself and wife were partly, if not wholly, caused by Mrs. L's cognition that Lincoln did not love her, and *did love another?* Lincoln told his wife that he did not love her, did so before he was married to her; she was cognizant of the fact that Lincoln loved another. Did you know that the *Hell* through which Lincoln passed was caused by these things? Mrs. Lincoln's knowledge that Lincoln did not love her and did love another caused much trouble between them. I say, Lincoln told her *he did not love her.* The world does not know her, Mrs. L.'s sufferings, her trials, and the causes of things. Sympathize with her. I shall never rob Mrs. Lincoln of her justice—justice due her. Poor woman! She will yet have her rewards.

Mrs. Lincoln will scold me, poor woman, without knowing I am her friend, determined to put her right before the world for all time. She too had borne her cross, and she shall have justice if I live. Would that I could but talk to you one hour. Mr. and Mrs. Lincoln's marriage was an unfortunate one, and I say to you that what I know and shall tell only ennobles both—that is to say, it will show that Mrs. L. has had cause to suffer, and be almost crazed, while Lincoln self-sacrificed himself rather than to be charged with dishonor. Such a man the world never saw—and never will see again. God bless him—so pure, so tender, so good, so honorable, so noble, so lovely, the very noblest and loveliest man since this orb began to spin. Mr. Lincoln was shoved through her furnace, but, poor woman, she rebelled! Lincoln suffered as it were by crucifixion for forty-five or fifty years; and that process caused his glory, and yet the world doesn't, it seems, want to know it. You have perceived that I am not a very orthodox Christian and yet I believe that Lincoln was God's chosen one.

I cannot frame a genealogical tree of the Lincoln family for three generations, other than you find in your records.

What I stated to Arnold was and is true. Mr. Lincoln loved Ann

Rutledge to his death, no mistake. He next courted Miss Owens, and next Mary Todd, and while so doing he lit on Miss Edwards's face. Lincoln never loved, i.e., dearly loved, his "Mary"—he was engaged to her when Miss Edwards ran across his path. His vow to Ann Rutledge's love and death, his promise to Mary and their engagement, and Miss Edwards flitting across the path, etc., made Lincoln crazy the *second time*—see Judge Logan's (in a little book I last sent you), see Stuart's, Miss Edwards's, and other testimony in your records. *You must read over and over again the records.* If anything is proved, what I say to Arnold is proved. I know many if not all the facts myself. Lincoln, Speed, and I slept together for two or three years, i.e., slept in the same home, I being Speed's clerk; and Lincoln sleeping with Speed. I have heard Lincoln talk about the matter, and from what I know and from what I have been told by others in whom I have implicit confidence and trust, I say, if what I told Arnold is not proved, *nothing can be proved.* You may reduce the elements of causation this way: say that Lincoln's honor was pledged to Miss Todd, that he saw and loved another woman, Miss Edwards, and that he desired to break away from Miss Todd and to join Miss Edwards, and that the struggle caused the second crazed spells, and yet—I know that the Ann Rutledge element entered as strong as any element. His vow to her or her memory, etc., was as strong as his honor at any other time. Do you see? Read over your records again and again. It will save you much trouble and me too. The two suppositions of which you speak are not [undeciphered]. Co-existing, do co-exist nevertheless. The second insanity springs from his old love of Ann Rutledge. His engagements with his "sweet Mary," and his determination to break that engagement off, and to marry Miss Edwards if he could, I repeat, was the cause of his second insanity. These facts do co-exist and were the sole cause of his second insanity. I hate to differ from you, but I can't avoid it, nor see the difficulty you do. Excuse me. Read your records closely again and again.

It happened that sometimes Lincoln would come down to our office of a Sunday with one or two of his little children, hauling them in the same little wagon, and in our office, then and there, write declarations, pleas, and other legal papers. The children—spoilt ones to be sure—would tear up the office, scatter the books, smash up pens, spill the ink, and p–s all over the floor. I have felt many and many a time that I wanted to wring their little necks, and yet out of respect for Lincoln I kept my mouth shut. Lincoln did not note what his children were doing or had done. When Lincoln finished his business, he would haul his children back home and meet the same old scolding or a new and intensified one. He bore all quite philosophically. Jesus, what a home Lincoln's was! What a wife!

You wish to know more about Lincoln's domestic life. The history of it is a sad, sad one, I assure you. Many and many a time I have known Lincoln to come down to our office, say at 7 a.m., sometimes bringing with him his then young son Bob. Our office was on the west side of the public square and upstairs. The door that entered our office was, the up half, of glass, with a curtain on the inside made of calico. When we did not wish anyone to see inside, we let down the curtain on the inside. Well, I say, many and many a time have I known Lincoln to come down to our office, sometimes Bob with him, with a small lot of cheese, crackers, and "bologna" sausages under his arm; he would not speak to me, for he was full of sadness, melancholy, and I suppose of the devil; he would draw out the sofa, sit down upon it, open his breakfast, and divide between Bob and himself. I would as a matter of course know that Lincoln was driven from home, by a club, knife, or tongue, and so I would let down the curtain on the inside, go out, and lock the door behind me, taking the key out and with me. I would stay away, say an hour, and then I would go into the office on one pretense or another, and if Lincoln did not then speak, I did as before, go away, etc. In the course of another hour I would go back, and if Lincoln spoke, I knew it was all over, i.e., his fit of sadness, etc. Probably he would say something or I would, and then he would say: "Billy, that puts me in mind of a story," he would tell it, walk up and down the room, laughing the while, and now the dark clouds would pass off his withered and wrinkled face and the God-blessed sunshine of happiness would light up *those* organs o'er which the emotions of that good soul played their gentle dance and chase. Friend, I can see all this now acting before me and am sad.

I wish to state some facts abut Lincoln's domestic relations which I do not want to be forgotten. About the year 1857 a man by the name of Barrett was passing along Eighth Street near Lincoln's house; he saw a long, tall man running and saw a little low, squatty woman with a butcher knife in her hand in hot pursuit; he looked and saw that Lincoln was the man and Mrs. Lincoln was the woman. Lincoln's house on Eighth Street fronts westward. He ran eastward down the walk in his own lot. Stephen Whitehurst lived in the same block. His house fronted east, the house being east of Lincoln's. The consequence is that the back doors looked into each other. Whitehurst was on that day—Sunday if I recollect the time, the day—standing in the back door of his own house and saw what happened. Lincoln ran down the walk in his own lot but, seeing the people coming from church or going to it, he stopped short and quick and wheeled around, caught Mrs. Lincoln by the back of the neck and at the seat of her drawers, carried or pushed her squealing along the walk back to the house—Lincoln's house—got her to the door of the kitchen, opened it, pushed her in, at the same time, to use Whitehurst's expression, gave her a hell of a slap on her seat, saying to her: "There now, stay in the house and don't be a d—d fool before the people."

Again in the winter of 1857 the Supreme Court was in session and Lincoln had an important suit to argue. He came in the clerk's office, the law library room too; his nose was plastered up, fixed up with court plaster. Now for the facts. Lincoln had on the day before become somewhat abstracted, thoughtful, and let the fire in Mr. and Mrs. Lincoln's sitting room nearly die out. Mrs. Lincoln came to the door of the sitting room from the kitchen and said: "Mr. Lincoln, put some wood on the fire." Lincoln did not hear her and neglected the repair of the fire. Mrs. Lincoln came to the sitting room again and said, "Mr. Lincoln, mend up the fire," it having got low down. Lincoln did not hear Mrs. Lincoln; she came in again and picked up a stick of wood and said: "Mr. Lincoln, I have told you now there three times to mend the fire and you have pretended that you did not hear me. I'll make you hear me this time," and she blazed away at Lincoln with a stick of stovewood and hit him on the nose and thus banged it up. Someone in the courtroom asked Lincoln what was the matter; he made an evasive reply in part to the question. Lincoln's girl stated this, if others did not know it. From what I know of the facts, it is more probable that it is true than untrue. I believe it; it went around among the members of the bar as true. Many such quarrels did take place between Lincoln and his wife. Lincoln's domestic life was a home hell on this globe.

Mr. Lincoln was a kind of fatalist in some aspects of his philosophy, and skeptical in his religion. He was a sad man, a terribly gloomy one—a man of sorrow, if not of agony. This, his state, may have arisen from a defective physical organization, or it may have arisen from some fatalistic idea, that he was to die a sudden and a terrible death. Some unknown power seemed to buzz about his consciousness, his being, his mind, that whispered in his ear: "Look out for danger ahead!" This peculiarity in Mr. Lincoln I had noticed for years, and it is no secret in this city. He has said to me more than once: "Billy, I feel as if I shall meet with some terrible end." He did not know what would strike him, nor when, nor where, nor how hard; he was a blind intellectual Samson, struggling and fighting in the dark against the fates. I say on my own personal observation that he felt this for years. Often and often I have resolved to make or get him to reveal the causes of his misery, but I had not the courage nor the impertinence to do it.

When you are in some imminent danger or suppose you are, when you are suffering terribly, do you not call on some power to come to your assistance and give you relief? I do, and all men do. Mr. Lincoln was in great danger, or thought he was, and did as you and I have done; he sincerely invoked and fiercely interrogated all intelligences to give him a true solution of his state—the mysteries and his destiny. He had great, too great, confidence in the common judgment of an uneducated people. He believed that the common people had truths that philosophers never dreamed of; and often appealed to that common judgment of the common people over the shoulders of scientists. I am not saying that he did right. I am only stating what I know to be facts, to be truths.

Mr. Lincoln was in some phases of his nature very, very superstitious; and it may be—it is quite probable that he, in his gloom, sadness, fear, and despair, invoked the spirits of the dead to reveal to him the cause of his states of gloom, sadness, fear, and despair. He craved light from all intelligences to flash his way to the unknown future of his life.

May I say to you that I have many, many times thoroughly sympathized with Mr. Lincoln in his intense sufferings; but I dared not obtrude into the sacred ground of his thoughts that are so sad, so gloomy, and so terrible.

To sum up, let us say that here is a very sensitive, diffident, unobtrusive, natural-made gentleman; his mind was strong and deep, sincere and honest, patient and enduring, with a good heart filled with the love of mercy and with a conscience that loved justice, having no vices, only negative defects with many positive virtues; he is strong, self-reliant, honest, full of practical sagacities, manly, noble; he stands high in the foremost [ranks] of man in all ages, their equal, if not their superior, one of the very best types of free institutions and this Christian civilization; and if I were to deliver a eulogy freed from all rhetoric of extravagant eulogy, I say here was a man in his general life [who?] thought strongly, willed firmly, and acted nobly, and in whose life and death the world is lifted to a higher plane of existence.

Men and Women in America

From Alexis de Tocqueville,
Democracy in America

Among aristocratic peoples birth and fortune often make a man and a woman such different creatures that they would never be able to unite with one another. Their passions draw them together, but social conditions and the thoughts that spring from them prevent them from uniting in a permanent and open way. The necessary result of that is a great number of ephemeral and clandestine connections. Nature secretly gets her own back for the restraint imposed by laws.

Things do not happen in the same way when equality of conditions has swept down all the real or imaginary barriers separating man and woman. No girl then feels that she cannot become the wife of the man who likes her best, and that makes irregular morals before marriage very difficult. For however credulous passion may make us, there is hardly a way of persuading a girl that you love her when you are perfectly free to marry her but will not do so.

The same cause is at work, though in a more indirect way, after marriage.

Nothing does more to make illegitimate love seem legitimate in the eyes both of those who experience it and of the watching crowd than forced marriages or ones entered into by chance.

In a country where the woman can always choose freely and where education has taught her to choose well, public opinion is inexorable against her faults.

The severity of the Americans is in part due to this cause. They regard marriage as a contract which is often burdensome but every condition of which the parties are strictly bound to fulfill, because they knew them all beforehand and were at liberty not to bind themselves to anything at all.

The same cause which renders fidelity more obligatory also renders it easier.

The object of marriage in aristocratic lands is more to unite property than persons, so it can happen sometimes that the husband is chosen while at school and the wife at the breast. It is not surprising that the conjugal tie which unites the fortunes of the married couple leaves their hearts to rove at large. That is the natural result of the spirit of the contract.

But when each chooses his companion for himself without any external interference or even prompting, it is usually nothing but similar tastes and thoughts that bring a man and a woman together, and these similarities hold and keep them by each other's side.

I would say that while democratic peoples allow women the right to choose their husbands freely, they have been careful to educate their understanding beforehand and to give their wills the strength necessary for such a choice; but the girls who in an aristocracy secretly escape from paternal authority to throw themselves into the arms of a man whom they have had neither time nor capacity to judge lack all these guarantees. One should not be surprised that they make ill use of their free choice the first time they avail themselves of it, nor that they make such cruel mistakes when, without receiving a democratic education, they wish, in marriage, to follow democratic customs.

But there is more to it than that.

When a man and a woman wish to come together in spite of the inequalities of an aristocratic social system, they have immense obstacles to overcome. After they have broken down or eloped from the ties of filial obedience, they must by a further effort escape the sway of custom and the tyranny of opinion; and then, when they have finally reached the end of this rough passage, they find themselves strangers among their natural friends and relations; the prejudice which they have defied separates them. This situation soon wears down their courage and embitters their hearts.

If, then, it happens that spouses united in this way are first unhappy and then guilty, one ought not to suppose that this is because they chose freely, but rather because they live in a society which does not allow such a choice.

One should also not forget that the same energy which makes a man break through a common error almost always drives him on beyond what is reasonable, that to enable him to dare to declare war, even legitimately, on the ideas of his country and age means that he must have something of violence and adventure in his character, and people of this type, whatever direction they take, seldom achieve happiness or virtue. That, one may say in passing, is the reason why, even in the case of the most necessary and hallowed revolution, one seldom finds revolutionaries who are moderate and honest.

There is therefore no just ground for surprise if, in an age of aristocracy, a man who chooses to consult nothing but his taste and inclination in selecting a wife soon finds that irregular morals and wretchedness break into his home life. But when such behavior is part of the natural and usual order of things, when the social system makes it easy, when paternal authority supports it and public opinion recognizes it, one should not doubt that the internal peace of families will be increased thereby and conjugal faith better protected.

Almost all the men in a democracy either enter politics or practice some calling, whereas limited incomes oblige the wives to stay at home and watch in person very closely over the details of domestic economy.

All these separate and necessary occupations form as many natural barriers which, by keeping the sexes apart, make the solicitations of the one less frequent and less ardent and the resistance of the other easier.

Not that equality of conditions could ever make man chaste, but it gives the irregularity of his morals a less dangerous character. As no man any longer has leisure or opportunity to attack the virtue of those who wish to defend themselves, there are at the same time a great number of courtesans and a great many honest women.

Such a state of affairs leads to deplorable individual wretchedness, but it does not prevent the body social from being strong and alert; it does not break up families and does not weaken national morality. Society is endangered not by the great profligacy of a few but by the laxity of all. A lawgiver must fear prostitution much less than intrigues.

The disturbed and constantly harassed life which equality makes men lead not only diverts their attention from lovemaking by depriving them of leisure for its pursuit but also turns them away by a more secret but more certain path.

Everyone living in democratic times contracts, more or less, the mental habits of the industrial and trading classes; their thoughts take a serious turn, calculating and realistic; they gladly turn away from the ideal to pursue some visible and approachable aim which seems the natural and necessary object of their desires. Equality does not by this destroy the imagination, but clips its wings and only lets it fly touching the ground.

No men are less dreamers than the citizens of democracy; one hardly finds any who care to let themselves indulge in such leisurely and solitary moods of contemplation as generally precede and produce the great agitations of the heart.

They do, it is true, set great store on obtaining that type of deep, regular, and peaceful affection which makes life happy and secure. But they would not willingly chase violent and capricious emotions which disturb life and cut it short.

What do you expect from society and its government? We must be clear about that.

Do you wish to raise mankind to an elevated and generous view of the things of this world? Do you want to inspire men with a certain scorn of material goods? Do you hope to engender deep convictions and prepare the way for acts of profound devotion?

Are you concerned with refining mores, elevating manners, and causing the arts to blossom? Do you desire poetry, renown, and glory?

Do you set out to organize a nation so that it will have a powerful influence over all others? Do you expect it to attempt great enterprises and, whatever be the result of its efforts, to leave a great mark on history?

If in your view that should be the main object of men in society, do not support democratic government; it surely will not lead you to that goal.

Men Who Greatly Dared

From Theodore Roosevelt,
The Americanism of Theodore Roosevelt

There was scant room for the coward and the weakling in the ranks of the adventurous frontiersmen—the pioneer settlers who first broke up the wild prairie soil, who first hewed their way into the primeval forest, who guided their white-topped wagons across the endless leagues of Indian-haunted desolation, and explored every remote mountain-chain in the restless quest for metal wealth. Behind them came the men who completed the work they had roughly begun: who drove the great railroad system over plain and desert and mountain pass; who stocked the teeming ranches, and under irrigation saw the bright green of the alfalfa and the yellow of the golden stubble supplant the gray of the sagebrush desert; who have built great populous cities—cities in which every art and science of civilization are carried to the highest point—on tracts which, when the nineteenth century had passed its meridian, were still known only to the grim trappers and hunters and the red lords of the wilderness with whom they waged eternal war.

Such is the record of which we are so proud. It is a record of men who greatly dared and greatly did; a record of wanderings wider and more dangerous than those of the Vikings; a record of endless feats of arms, of victory after victory in the ceaseless strife waged against wild man and wild nature. The winning of the West was the great epic feat in the history of our race.

We have then a right to meet today in a spirit of just pride in the past. But when we pay homage to the hardy, grim, resolute men who, with incredible toil and risk, laid deep the foundations of the civilization that we inherit, let us steadily remember that the only homage that counts is the homage of deeds—not merely of words. It is well to gather here to show that we remember what has been done in the past by the Western pioneers of our people, and that we glory in the greatness for which they prepared the way. But lip-loyalty by itself avails very little, whether it is expressed concerning a nation or an ideal. It would be a sad and evil thing for this country if ever the day came when we considered the great deeds of our forefathers as an excuse for our resting slothfully satisfied with what has been already done. On the contrary, they should be an inspiration and appeal, summoning us to show that we too have courage and strength; that we too are ready to dare greatly if the need arises; and, above all, that we are firmly bent upon that steady performance of everyday duty which, in the long run, is of such incredible worth in the formation of national character.

We hold work not as a curse but as a blessing, and we regard the idler with scornful pity. It would be in the highest degree undesirable that we should work in the same way or at the same things, and for the sake of the real greatness of the nation we should in the fullest and most cordial way recognize the fact that some of the most needed work must, from its very nature, be unremunerative in a material sense. Each man must choose so far as the conditions allow him the path to which he is bidden by his own peculiar powers and inclinations. But if he is a man he must in some way or shape do a man's work. If, after making all the effort that his strength of body and of mind permits, he yet honorably fails, why, he is still entitled to a certain share of respect because he has made the effort.

It is character that counts in a nation as in a man. It is a good thing to have a keen, fine intellectual development in a nation, to produce orators, artists, successful business men; but it is an infinitely greater thing to have those solid qualities which we group together under the name of character—sobriety, steadfastness, the sense of obligation toward one's neighbor and one's God, hard common sense, and, combined with it, the lift of generous enthusiasm toward whatever is right. These are the qualities which go to make up true national greatness.

I recollect saying to a young friend who was about to enter college, "My friend, I know that you feel that you ought to be a good man; now, be willing to fight for your principles whenever it is necessary; if you're willing enough to fight, nobody will complain about your being too virtuous."

If you accept only the weak man, who cannot hold his own, as the type of virtuous man, you will inevitably create an atmosphere among ordinary, vigorous young men in which they will translate their contempt of weakness into contempt of virtue. My plea is that the virtuous man, the decent man, shall be a strong man, able to hold his own in any way, just because I wish him to be an agent in eradicating the misconception that being decent somehow means being weak; I want this to apply to every form of decency, public as well as private.

The worst development that we could see in civic life in this country would be a division of citizens into two camps, one camp containing nice, well-behaved, well-meaning little men, with receding chins and small feet, men who mean well and who if they are insulted feel shocked and want to go home; and the other camp containing robust and efficient creatures who do not mean well at all. I wish to see our side—the side of decency—include men who have not the slightest fear of the people on the other side. I wish to see the decent man in any relation of life, including politics, when hustled by the man who is not decent, able so to hold his own that the other gentleman shall feel no desire to hustle him again. My plea is for the virtue that shall be strong and that shall also have a good time.

Remember always that the securing of substantial education, whether by the individual or by a people, is attained only by a process, not by an act. You can no more make a man really educated by giving him a certain curriculum of studies than you can make a people fit for self-government by giving it a paper constitution. The training of an individual so as to fit him to do good work in the world is a matter of years; just as the training of a nation to fit it successfully to fulfill the duties of self-government is a matter, not of a decade or two, but of generations. There are foolish empiricists who believe that the granting of a paper constitution, prefaced by some high-sounding declaration, of itself confers the power of self-government upon a people. This is never so. Nobody can "give" a people "self-government," any more than it is possible to "give" an individual "self-help." You know that the Arab proverb runs, "God helps those who help themselves." In the long run, the only permanent way by which an individual can be helped is to help him help himself, and this is one of the things your University should inculcate. But it must be his own slow growth in character that is the final and determining factor in the problem.

In this long and even tedious but absolutely essential process, I believe your University will take an important part. When I was recently in the Sudan I heard a vernacular proverb, based on a text in the Koran, which is so apt that, although not an Arabic scholar, I shall attempt to repeat it in Arabic: "Allah ma el saberin, izza sabaru"—God is with the patient, *if they know how to wait.*

Young Husbands

From Albert J. Beveridge,
The Young Man and the World

Albert J. Beveridge's The Young Man and the World *(1906) was a collection of essays that had originally appeared in* The Saturday Evening Post. *His book reflects a taste for popular moralizing and uplift widespread at the turn of the century. It's a characteristic exhortation to Victorian virtue in an American context.*

Your father made the old home. Prove yourself worthy of him by making the new home. He built the roof-tree which sheltered you. Build you a roof-tree that may in its turn shelter others. What abnormal egotism the attitude of him who says, "This planet, and all the uncounted centuries of the past, were made for *me* and nobody else, and I will live accordingly. I will go it alone."

"I wish John had not married so young," said a woman of wealth, fashion, and brilliant talents in speaking of her son.

"Why, how old was he?" asked her friend. "Twenty-five,"said she; "he ought to have waited ten years longer." "I think not," was the response of the world-wise man with whom she was conversing. "If he got a good wife he was in great luck that he did not wait longer."

"No," persisted the mother, "he ought to have taken more time 'to look around.' These early marriages interfere with a young man's career."

This fragment of a real conversation, which is typical of numberless others like it, reveals the false and shallow philosophy which, if it becomes our code of national living, will make the lives of our young people abnormal and our twentieth-century civilization artificial and neurotic. Even now too many people are thinking about a "career." Mothers are talking about "careers" for their sons. Young men are dreaming of their "careers."

It is assumed that a young man can "carve out his career" if his attention is not distracted and his powers are not diminished by a wife and children whom he must feed, clothe, and consider. The icy selfishness of this hypothesis of life ought to be enough to reject it without argument. Who is any man, that he should have a "career"? And what does a "career" amount to, anyway?

I am assuming that you are man enough to be a man—not a mere machine of selfishness on the one hand, or an anemic imitation of masculinity on the other hand. I am assuming that you think—and, what is more important, feel—that Nature knows what she is about; that "God is not mocked"; and that therefore you propose to live in harmony with universal law.

Therefore, I am assuming that you have established, or will establish, the new home in place of the old home. I am assuming that you will do this before there is a gray hair in your head or a wrinkle under your eye.

Of course nobody means that young men should hurl themselves into matrimony. The fact that it is advisable for you to learn to swim does not mean that you should jump into the first stream you come to, with your clothes and shoes on. Undoubtedly you ought first to get "settled"; that is, you ought to prepare for what you are going to do in life and begin the doing of it. Don't take this step while you are in college. If you mean to be a lawyer, you ought to get your legal education and open your office; if a business man, you should "get started"; if an artisan, you should acquire your trade, etc. But it is inadvisable to wait longer.

It is not necessary for you to "build up a practice" in the profession, or make a lot of money in business, or secure unusual wages as a skilled laborer. Begin at the beginning, and live your lives together, share your hardships together, and let your fortune, good or ill, be of your joint making.

Of course you will spend all of your extra time at home. That is what home is for. Live in your home; do not merely eat and sleep there. It is not a boarding-house, remember that. Books are there, and music and a human sympathy and a marvelous care for you, under whose influence alone the soul of a young man grows into real grandeur, power, and beauty. And be sure that you let each day have its play-hour.

Speaking of politics, I have always thought men, young and old, ought to consult their wives and families about how they cast their ballot. What right has any man to vote as he individually thinks best? He is the head of the family, after all. This Republic is not made up of individuals; it is made up of families. Its unit is not the boarding-house, but the home.

Of course, being an American and a gentleman, you will have the American gentleman's conception of all womanhood, and his adoring reverence for the one woman who has blessed him with her life's companionship. You will cherish her, therefore, in that way which none but the American gentleman quite understands. You will be gentle with her, and watchful of her health and happiness.

You will be ever brave and kind, wise and strong, deserving that respect which she is so anxious to accord you; earning that devotion which by the very nature of her being she must bestow on you; winning that admiration which it is the crowning pride of her life to yield to you; and, finally, receiving that care which only her hands can give, and a life-long joy which, increasing with the years, is fullest and most perfect when both your heads are white and your mutual steps no longer wander from the threshold of that "new home" which you built in the beginning of your lives, and which is now the "old home" to your children, who beneath its roof "rise up and call you blessed."

Moral Force Gives a Man Both Fearlessness and Tranquillity

From Ralph Waldo Emerson,
Sermons

It is quite important to observe that more is required of you than to say and do what is agreed on all hands to be right. I have said, every man is an original mind. It follows, that there is some peculiar merit which it is yours to seek and find. You must work after your own fashion, and not after that of anybody else. You must be virtuous and wise in your own way, as much as you must speak in your own tone, and not mimic other people's. The first resolute efforts at a virtuous life, are often embarrassed by vain attempts to cooperate in those good works which are most in vogue. There are, perhaps, many benevolent projects—certain plans of instruction, or of charity, or of public reform, which interest the community, but which fail to affect you. Let them alone. If you have given them a fair examination, and doubt their efficacy, or are satisfied that you have not power to forward them, do not praise them because they are popular and because other people think they ought to have your support. Do not use a stronger expression in commending the best cause than your own feeling will justify. Do not put at risk the integrity of your own character, and neutralize the force of your own talents by giving a half support to any thing which, however good it may be, is not good for you—is not the place appointed for you. There is something—be assured, there is something—which does seem to you good and wise. Praise that; aid that; give yourself to that; and not the less because you find yourself in the minority, no, nor even if you should find yourself alone.

It is wonderful the amount of moral force which strict consistency of character—the habit of regarding not only what is true in words, but what is true for himself, a fit object for his advocacy—bestows upon the words of a single-minded person. You feel that it is not he who speaks, so much as truth and reason which speak through him.

One more mark of the man we describe is his fearlessness and habitual tranquillity. God rewards those who obey him with peace. The person who implicitly follows the leading of his own mind casts off from himself the responsibility of his words and actions and throws that responsibility upon God. Whilst a man rests upon the simple perception of the rectitude of his action, he has nothing to do with consequences. He is above them. He has nothing to do with the effect of his example. God will take care of his example. He is following God's finger and cannot go astray. Whilst I walk according to my conscience, I know I shall never be ashamed. When I have adhered to it, I know my conduct is capable of explanation though I may have wholly forgotten the circumstances.

I have enumerated some of the traits of this desirable character. I wish it was in my power to show the striking contrast to the tameness and slavishness of our ordinary habits that is presented by a life thus springing ever fresh from an active mind; to show the grace and the power of a man not hampered by little fears nor mean ambition but walking in the world with the free step of Adam in the Garden, which was all his own by the highest right; a man who when known is found to unite every endearing sportive grace to a sublime self-subsistency.

I see fragments of this character everywhere; they make the sweetness and virtue of society, but the individual in high or in humble life who holds this purpose steadily before him—how rarely is he found.

Finally, in answer to any, if such there be, who shall say, "This quality of genuineness or truth of character is good, but is there not something better?" I will add the remark that the conviction must be produced in our minds that this *truth of character is identical with a religious life*; that they are one and the same thing; that this voice of your own mind is the voice of God, that the reason why you are bound to reverence it is because it is the direct revelation of your Maker's will, not written in books many ages since nor attested by distant miracles but writ in the flesh and blood, in the faculties and emotions of your constitution.

Family Life and the
Average Man's Duty

From Theodore Roosevelt,
The Americanism of Theodore Roosevelt

The Nation is in a bad way if there is no real home, if the family is not of the right kind; if the man is not a good husband and father, if he is brutal or cowardly or selfish, if the woman has lost her sense of duty, if she is sunk in vapid self-indulgence or has let her nature be twisted so that she prefers sterile pseudo-intellectuality to that great and beautiful development of character which comes only to those whose lives know the fullness of duty done, or effort made and self-sacrifice undergone.

In the last analysis the welfare of the State depends absolutely upon whether or not the average family, the average man and woman and their children, represent the kind of citizenship fit for the foundation of a great nation; and if we fail to appreciate this we fail to appreciate the root morality upon which all healthy civilization is based.

There are certain old truths which will be true as long as this world endures, and which no amount of progress can alter. One of these is the truth that the primary duty of the husband is to be the homemaker, the breadwinner for his wife and children, and that the primary duty of the woman is to be the helpmeet, the housewife, and mother. The woman should have ample educational advantages; but save in exceptional cases the man must be, and she need not be, and generally ought not to be, trained for a lifelong career as the family breadwinner.

Of course there is now and then a man who in some given crises plays the hero although on other occasions he plays the brute—there are such cases; but it is a mighty unsafe thing to proceed upon the assumption that because a man is ordinarily a brute he will therefore be a hero in a crisis. Disregarding the exceptions, and speaking normally, no man can be of any service to the State, no man can amount to anything from the standpoint of usefulness to the community at large, unless first and foremost he is a decent man in the close relations of life. No community can afford to think for one moment that great public service, that great material achievement, that ability shown in no matter how many different directions, will atone for the lack of a sound family life.

Multiplication of divorces means that there is something rotten in the community, that there is some principle of evil at work which must be counteracted and overcome or widespread disaster will follow. In the same way, if the man preaches and practices a different code of morality for himself than that which he demands that his wife shall practice, then no profession on his part of devotion to civic ideals will in the least avail to alter the fact that he is fundamentally a bad citizen. I do not believe in weakness. I believe in a man's being a man; and for that very reason I abhor the creature who uses the expression that "a man must be a man" in order to excuse his being a vile and vicious man.

The Whistle

From Benjamin Franklin,
Essays Humorous, Moral and Literary

Franklin wrote this story for his nephew.

When I was a child, at seven years old, my friends on a holiday, filled my pockets with coppers. I went directly to a shop where they sold toys for children; and, being charmed with the sound of a *whistle,* that I met by the way in the hands of another boy, I voluntarily offered him all my money for one. I then came home, and when whistling all over the house, much pleased with my *whistle,* but disturbing all the family. My brothers and sisters and cousins, understanding the bargain I had made, told me I had given four times as much for it as it was worth. This put me in mind what good things I might have bought with the rest of the money; and they laughed at me so much for my folly that I cried with vexation; and the reflection gave me more chagrin than the *whistle* gave me pleasure.

This, however, was afterward of use to me, the impression continuing on my mind; so that often, when I was tempted to buy some unnecessary thing, I said to myself, *Don't give too much for the whistle,* and so I saved my money.

As I grew up, came into the world, and observed the actions of men, I thought I met with many, very many, who *gave too much for the whistle.*

When I saw any one too ambitious of court favor, sacrificing his time in attendance on levees, his repose, his liberty, his virtue, and perhaps his friends, to attain it, I have said to myself, *This man gave too much for his whistle.*

When I saw another fond of popularity, constantly employing himself in political bustles, neglecting his own affairs, and ruining them by that neglect; *He pays indeed,* says I, *too much for this whistle.*

If I knew a miser, who gave up every kind of comfortable living, all the pleasure of doing good to others, all the esteem of his fellow-citizens, and the joys of benevolent friendship, for the sake of accumulating wealth; *Poor man,* says I, *you do indeed pay too much for your whistle.*

When I meet a man of pleasure, sacrificing every laudable improvement of the mind, or of his fortune, to mere corporeal sensations; *Mistaken man,* says I, *you are providing pain for yourself instead of pleasure: you give too much for your whistle.*

If I see one fond of fine clothes, fine furniture, fine equipages, all above his fortune, for which he contracts debts, and ends his career in prison; *Alas,* says I, *he has paid dear, very dear, for his whistle.*

When I see a beautiful, sweet-tempered girl, married to an ill-natured brute of a husband; *What a pity it is,* says I, *that she has paid so much for a whistle.*

In short, I conceived that great part of the miseries of mankind were brought upon them by the false estimates they had made of the value of things, and by their giving too much for their *whistles.*

The College Man

From Albert J. Beveridge,
The Young Man and the World

Watch out for tobacco, alcohol, and those Eastern colleges.

You can succeed—I repeat it—college or no college; all you have to do in the latter case is to put on a little more steam. And remember that some of the world's sages of the practical have closed their life's wisdom with the deliberate opinion that a college education is a waste of time, and an over-refinement of body and of mind.

Still, with all this in mind, my advice is this: Go to college. Go to the best possible college for *you.* Patiently hold on through the sternest discipline you can stand, until the course is completed. It will not be fatal to your success if you do not go; but you will be better prepared to meet the world if you do go. I do not mean that your mind will be stored with much more knowledge that will be useful to you if you go through college than if you do not go through college.

Probably the man who keeps at work at the business he is going to follow through life, during the years when other men are studying in college, acquires more information that will be "useful" to him in his practical career. But the college man who has not thrown away his college life comes from the training of his alma mater with a mind as highly disciplined as are the wrist and eye of the skilled swordsman.

Nobody contends that a college adds an ounce of brain power. But if college opportunities are not wasted, such mind as the student does have is developed up to the highest possible point of efficiency. The college man who has not scorned his work will understand any given situation a great deal quicker than his brother who, with equal ability, has not had the training of the university.

The spirit with which you enter college is just as important as going to college at all. It is more important. For if a man has the spirit that will get for him all that a college education has to give, it will also make him triumph in a contest with the world, even if he does not get his college education. It will only be a little harder for him, that is all.

But if a man has not that mingled will and wish for a college education flaming through his young veins that makes him capable of any sacrifice to get through college, I do not see what good a college education will do him—no, nor any other kind of an education. The quicker such a man is compelled to make his own living without help from any source, the better for him.

This one word of definite helpfulness on this subject: Do not choose any particular college because you want to be known as a Yale man, a Harvard man, a Princeton man, or any other kind of man. Remember that the world cares less than the snap of its fingers what particular *college* man you are.

What the world cares about is that you should *be* a man—a real *man.*

Nobody cares what college you went to. Nobody cares whether you went to college at all.

But everybody cares whether you are a real force among men; and everybody cares more and more as it becomes clearer and clearer that you are not only a force, but a trained, disciplined force. That is why you ought to go to college—to be a trained, disciplined force. But how and where you got your power—the world of men and women is far too interested in itself to be interested in that.

When you do finally go to college, take care of yourself like a man. I am told that there are men in college who have valets to attend them, their rooms, and their clothes. Think of that!

While I am on this subject I might as well say another thing: Do not think that you have got to smoke in order to be or look like a college man. A pipe in the mouth of a youth does not make him look like a college man, or any other kind of man. It merely makes him look absurd, that is all. And if there is ever a time on earth when you do not need the stimulus of tobacco, it is while you are in college.

Tobacco is a wonderful vegetable. It is, I believe, the only substance in the world which at the same time is a stimulant and a narcotic, a heart excitant and a nerve sedative. Very well. You are too young yet to need a heart stimulant, too young to need anything to quiet your nerves.

If at your tender age your nerves are so inflamed that they must be soothed, and if at the very sunrise of your life your heart is so feeble that it must be forced with any stimulant, you had better quit college. College is no place for you if you are such a decadent; yes, and you will find the world a good deal harder place than college.

Cut out tobacco, therefore. For a young fellow in college it is a ridiculous affectation—nothing more. Why? Because you do not need tobacco; that is why. At least you do not need it yet. The time may come when you will find tobacco helpful, but it will not be until you have been a long while out of college. As to whether tobacco is good for a man at any stage of life the doctors disagree, and "where doctors disagree, who shall decide?"

Ruskin says that no really immortal work has been done in the world since tobacco was introduced; but we know that this is not true. I would not be understood as having a prejudice for or against the weed. Whether a full-grown man shall use it or not is something for himself to decide. Personally I liked it so well that I made up my mind a long time ago to give it up altogether.

But there is absolutely no excuse for a man young enough to still be in college to use it at all. And it does not look right. For a boy to use tobacco has something contemptible about it. I will not argue whether this is justified or not. That is the way most people feel about it. Whether their feeling is a prejudice or not, there is no use of your needlessly offending their prejudice and this is to be taken into account. For you want to succeed, do you not? Very well. You cannot mount a ladder of air; you must rise on the solid stepping-stones of the people's deserved regard.

And, of course, you will not disgrace yourself by drinking. There is absolutely nothing in it. If you have your fling at it you will learn how surely Intoxication's apples of gold turn to the bitterest ashes in eating. But when you do find how fruitless of everything but regrets dissipation is, be honest with yourself and quit it. Be honest with the mother who is at home praying for you, and quit it. But this is weak advice. Be honest with that mother who is at home praying for you, and *never begin it.* That's the thing—*never begin it!*

In a word, be a man; and you will be very little of a man, very little indeed, if you have got to resort to tobacco and liquor to add to your blood and conduct that touch of devilishness which you may think is a necessary part of manliness. Indeed, between fifteen and thirty years of age your veins will be quite full enough of the untamed and desperate. I do not object in the least to this wild mustang period in a man's life.

Is a fellow to have no fun? you will say. Of course, have all the fun you want; the more the better. But if you need stimulants and tobacco to key you up to the capacity for fun, you are a solemn person indeed.

One thing I must warn you against, and warn you supremely: the critical habit of mind which somehow or other a college education does seem to produce. This is especially true of the great universities of our East.

A Man Must Be a Nonconformist

From Ralph Waldo Emerson, Sermons

There is a time in every man's education when he arrives at the conviction that envy is ignorance; that imitation is suicide; that he must take himself for better or worse as his portion; that though the wide universe is full of good, no kernel of nourishing corn can come to him but through his toil bestowed on that plot of ground which is given to him to till. The power which resides in him is new in nature, and none but he knows what that is which he can do, nor does he know until he has tried. Not for nothing one face, one character, one fact, makes much impression on him, and another none. It is not without preestablished harmony, this sculpture in the memory. The eye was placed where one ray should fall, that it might testify of that particular ray. Bravely let him speak the utmost syllable of his confession. We but half express ourselves, and are ashamed of that divine idea which each of us represents. It may be safely trusted as proportionate and of good issues, so it be faithfully imparted, but God will not have his work made manifest by cowards. It needs a divine man to exhibit anything divine. A man is relieved and gay when he has put his heart into his work and done his best; but what he has said or done otherwise shall give him no peace. It is a deliverance which does not deliver. In the attempt his genius deserts him; no muse befriends; no invention, no hope.

Trust thyself: every heart vibrates to that iron string. Accept the place that divine providence has found for you, the society of your contemporaries, the connexion of events. Great men have always done so, and confided themselves childlike to the genius of their age, betraying their perception that the Eternal was stirring at their heart, working through their hands, predominating in all their being. And we are now men, and must accept in the highest mind the same transcendent destiny; and not inched in a corner, not cowards fleeing before a revolution, but redeemers and benefactors, pious aspirants to be noble clay under the Almighty effort let us advance on Chaos and the Dark.

What pretty oracles nature yields us on this text in the face and behavior of children, babes, and even brutes. That divided and rebel mind, that distrust of a sentiment because our arithmetic has computed the strength and means opposed to our purpose, these have not. Their mind being whole, their eye is as yet unconquered, and when we look in their faces, we are disconcerted. Infancy conforms to nobody: all conform to it; so that one babe commonly makes four or five out of the adults who prattle and play to it. So God has armed youth and puberty and manhood no less with its own piquancy and charm, and made it enviable and gracious and its claims not to be put by, if it will stand by itself. Do not think the youth has no force, because he cannot speak to you and me. Hark! In the next room who spoke so clear and emphatic? It seems he knows how to speak to his contemporaries. Good Heaven! It is he! It is that very lump of bashfulness and phlegm which for weeks has done nothing but eat when you were by, and now rolls out these words like bell-strokes. It seems he knows how to speak to his contemporaries. Bashful or bold then, he will know how to make us seniors very unnecessary.

The nonchalance of boys who are sure of a dinner, and would disdain as much as a lord to do or say aught to conciliate one, is the healthy attitude of human nature. How is a boy the master of society; independent, irresponsible, looking out from his corner on such people and facts as pass by, he tries and sentences them on their merits, in the swift, summary way of boys, as good, bad, interesting, silly, eloquent, troublesome. He cumbers himself never about consequences, about interest; he gives an independent, genuine verdict. You must court him; he does not court you. But the man is as it were clapped into jail by his consciousness. As soon as he has once acted or spoken with eclat he is a committed person, watched by the sympathy or the hatred of hundreds, whose affections must now enter into his account. There is no Lethe for this. Ah, that he could pass again into his neutral, godlike independence! Who can thus lose all pledge and, having observed, observe again from the same unaffected, unbiased, unbribable, unaffrighted innocence, must always be formidable, must always engage the poet's and the man's regards. Of such an immortal youth the force would be felt. He would utter opinions on all passing affairs, which being seen to be not private but necessary, would sink like darts into the ear of men and put them in fear.

These are the voices which we hear in solitude, but they grow faint and inaudible as we enter into the world. Society everywhere is in conspiracy against the manhood of every one of its members. Society is a joint-stock company, in which the members agree, for the better securing of his bread to each shareholder, to surrender the liberty and culture of the eater. The virtue in most request is conformity. Self-reliance is its aversion. It loves not realities and creators, but names and customs.

Whoso would be a man, must be a nonconformist.

A foolish consistency is the hobgoblin of little minds, adored by little statesmen and philosophers and divines. With consistency a great soul has simply nothing to do. He may as well concern himself with his shadow on the wall. Out upon your guarded lips! Sew them up with packthread, do. Else if you would be a man speak what you think today in words as hard as cannon balls, and tomorrow speak what tomorrow thinks in hard words again, though it contradict every thing you said today. Ah, then, exclaim the aged ladies, you shall be sure to be misunderstood! Misunderstood! It is a right fool's word. Is it so bad then to be misunderstood? Pythagoras was misunderstood, and Socrates, and Jesus, and Luther, and Copernicus, and Galileo, and Newton, and every pure and wise spirit that ever took flesh. To be great is to be misunderstood.

A Successful Man

From Theodore Roosevelt,
The Americanism of Theodore Roosevelt

Imagine speaking like this to students today. A speech delivered by TR at the Prize Day Exercises at Groton School, May 24, 1904.

If you leave Groton, and the college to which you afterward go, if you go to any—if you leave simply with the feeling that you have had ten delightful years; that you have just barely got through your examinations; that you have graduated; that you are not positively disgraced; that you have met decent people, and that life has been easy and it won't be your fault if it does not continue as easy— if that is the feeling with which you have left school and college, then you are poor creatures, and there is small good that will ever come out of you.

Of course, the worst of all lives is the vicious life; the life of a man who becomes a positive addition to the forces of evil in a community. Next to that—and when I am speaking to people who, by birth and training and standing, ought to amount to a great deal, I have a right to say only second to it in criminality—comes the life of mere vapid ease. Of all the miserable people that I know I should put high in the top rank those who reach middle age having steadfastly striven only to amuse themselves as they went through life. If there ever was a pursuit which stultified itself by its very condition, it is the pursuit of pleasure as the all-sufficing end of life.

Happiness cannot come to any man capable of enjoying true happiness unless it comes as the sequel to duty well and honestly done. To do that duty you need to have more than one trait. You will meet plenty of well-meaning people who speak to you as if one trait were enough. That is not so. You might just as well in any rough sport in any game, think that a man could win by mere strength if he was clumsy; or by mere agility and precision of movement without strength; or by strength and agility if he had no heart. You need a great many qualities to make a successful man on a nine or an eleven; and just so you need a great many different qualities to make a good citizen. In the first place, of course, it is almost tautological to say that to make a good citizen the prime need is to be decent in thought, clean in mind, clean in action; to have an ideal and not to keep that ideal purely for the study—to have an ideal which you will in good faith strive to live up to when you are out in life. If you have an ideal only good while you sit at home, an ideal that nobody can live up to in outside life, then I advise you strongly to take that ideal, examine it closely, and then cast it away. It is not a good one. The ideal that it is impossible for a man to strive after in practical life is not the type of ideal that you wish to hold up and follow. Be practical as well as generous in your ideals. Keep your eyes on the stars, but remember to keep your feet on the ground.

Be truthful; a lie implies fear, vanity or malevolence; and be frank; furtiveness and insincerity are faults incompatible with true manliness. Be honest, and remember that honesty counts for nothing unless back of it lie courage and efficiency. If in this country we ever have to face a state of things in which on one side stand the men of high ideals who are honest, good, well-meaning, pleasant people, utterly unable to put those ideals into shape in the rough field of practical life, while on the other side are grouped the strong, powerful, efficient men with no ideals, then the end of the Republic will be near. The salvation of the Republic depends—the salvation of our whole social system depends—upon the production year by year of a sufficient number of citizens who possess high ideals combined with the practical power to realize them in actual life.

You often hear people speaking as if life was like striving upward toward a mountain peak. That is not so. Life is as if you were traveling a ridge crest. You have the gulf of inefficiency on one side and the gulf of wickedness on the other, and it helps not to have avoided one gulf if you fall into the other. It shall profit us nothing if our people are decent and ineffective. It shall profit us nothing if they are efficient and wicked. In every walk of life, in business, politics; if the need comes, in war; in literature, science, art, in everything, what we need is a sufficient number of men who can work well and who will work with a high ideal. The work can be done in a thousand different ways. Our public life depends primarily not upon the men who occupy public positions for the moment, because they are but an infinitesimal fraction of the whole. Our public life depends upon men who take an active interest in that public life; who are bound to see public affairs honestly and competently managed; but who have the good sense to know what honesty and competency actually mean. And any such man, if he is both sane and high-minded, can be a greater help and strength to any one in public life than you can easily imagine without having had yourselves the experience. It is an immense strength to a public man to know a certain number of people to whom he can appeal for advice and for backing; whose character is so high that baseness would shrink ashamed before them; and who have such good sense that any decent public servant is entirely willing to lay before them every detail of his actions, asking only that they know the facts before they pass final judgment.

Success does not lie entirely in the hands of any one of us. From the day the tower of Siloam fell, misfortune has fallen sometimes upon the just as well as the unjust. We sometimes see the good man, the honest man, the strong man, broken down by forces over which he had no control. If the hand of the Lord is heavy upon us the strength and wisdom of man shall avail nothing. But as a rule in the long run each of us comes pretty near to getting what he deserves. Each of us can, as a rule—there are, of course, exceptions—finally achieve the success best worth having, the success of having played his part honestly and manfully; of having lived so as to feel at the end he has done his duty; of having been a good husband, a good father; of having tried to make the world a little better off rather than worse off because he has lived; of having been a doer of the word and not a hearer only—still less a mere critic of the doers. Every man has it in him, unless fate is indeed hard upon him, to win out that measure of success if he will honestly try.

The Young Man's Second Wind: On Facing the World at Fifty

From Albert J. Beveridge,
The Young Man and the World

Baby Boomers, there's hope for you yet.

Life has three tragedies: loss of honor, loss of health, and the black conclusion of men past middle life who think they have failed—played the game and lost. The young man starting out in life has my heart; but the man past fifty who feels that he has failed has my heart absolutely and with emphasis. Apparently he has so much to contend against—the onsweep of the world, the pitying attitude of those of his own age who have succeeded, and, over all, his secret feeling of despair. But the last is the only fatal element in his problem.

As a matter of fact, the man past middle life who has not achieved distinct success very possibly has only been "finding himself," to use Mr. Kipling's expression. Perhaps he has only been growing. Certainly he has been accumulating experience, knowledge, and the effective wisdom which only these can give.

And if his failure has not been because he is a fraud, and because people found it out—if he has been, and is, genuine—it may be that he has been unconsciously preparing for continuous, enduring, and possibly great success, if he only will.

I should say that the very first thing for this man to do is to see that he does not get soured. That attitude of character is an acid which will destroy all success. Keep yourself sweet, no matter how snail-like your progress has been, no matter how paltry your apparent achievements. If you are already soured on men and the world, change that condition by a persistent habit of optimism. All death shows an acid reaction. Hopefulness is the alkaline in character.

Make "looking on the bright side" a habit. It can be done. Mingle with people as much as possible—especially with the young and buoyant and beautifully hopeful. Be a part of passing events. Read the daily newspapers. Form the habit of picking out the brighter aspects of occurrences. There is an astonishing tonic in the daily newspaper. When you read it, the blood of the world's great vitality is pouring through you.

I know a man who is now a millionaire, but who at the age of forty was without a dollar. He is now not over fifty-five. He had spent all those forty years watching for his opportunity—aye, getting ready for it. When it came, his beak was sharpened, his talons keen as needles and strong as steel, and he swooped down upon that opportunity like a bird of prey.

"No," said he, "I did not get discouraged. I was living, and my wife and children were living; and Vanderbilt was not doing any more than that, after all. I felt all the time that I was getting ready. I worked a good deal harder than I have since I achieved my fortune. Somehow, up to the time it came I had not felt equal to my chance; for I knew that my opportunity would be a large one when it came, and I knew that it would come. It did come."

Business men said for the first two or three years, "What a change of luck Mr.— has had! But he is not equal to it. He has never accomplished anything heretofore."

Yes, but he had been getting ready. He had been saving vitality, building up character, indexing and pigeonholing experiences, accumulating and systematizing a long-continued series of observations and all the potentialities of intellect and personality out of which, when applied to proper conditions, success alone is forged.

And so he gathered to himself great riches, and the poor man of a few years ago is now—of course, of course, and alas! If you like—a member of one of the most powerful trusts in the country.

Get yourself into the current of Circumstance—"in the swim," as the colloquialism has it. A man of large experience and important achievement said to me not long ago: "I am afraid I am getting to be a back number." That was a distinct note of degeneration. If he thought so that thought was the best evidence of the fact.

Do not get it into your head that you are out of step with the times. That in itself will paralyze both intellect and will. It is an admission of permanent failure. No matter whether you think the changed conditions and methods of business, society, and affairs, which almost each day brings, are inferior or superior to the old conditions and methods or not, you must keep abreast of them; take in the spirit of them.

An attitude of protest against the progressive order of things may be heroic, but it is not practical or effective. These conditions and methods which make you feel like a "back number" may not be the best; if they are not, try to make them the best, if you will, but do not attempt to perfect them backward by returning to yesterday. The world is very impatient of *apparent retrogression*; it hurts its egotism.

"What! Go back to old conditions?" says the World. "Never! Never! Progress, alone, for me!"

But sometimes it means motion, not progress; for true progress might possibly be a return to old and superior methods. No matter, I am speaking of *your* practical, personal, and material success now. I am not speaking to you as a reformer or as a teacher of the elemental truths. *You* are a searcher past fifty years of age, after the flesh-pots. Very well, then. Do not run amuck of the world. Join in its progress, even if that progress seems to you to be unreal.

At the risk of iteration, I again urge constant mingling with people. It is from them that you must draw your success, after all. A man over fifty who feels that his life is a failure is apt to emphasize the outward manners and inward habits of thought of his earlier days, as he would, if he could, stick to the old styles and fashions of apparel of the days of his youth. To do the latter would be to call attention at once to his antiquity; but to retain his old mental attitude is antiquity indeed.

People are quick to see, feel, and know that you are in deed and in truth not of the present day. When they think that, you are discredited and at an unnecessary disadvantage. Therefore mingle with men. Don't withdraw into yourself. Don't be a turtle. Be an active and present part of society, not only that your whole mind and whole conscious being may be kept fresh and growing, but that people may not perceive the contrary. Growing! Growth! It is only a question of that, after all. No man can ultimately fail who has kept himself alive, and therefore kept himself growing. If you find that you have ceased to grow, start up the process again. Make yourself take an interest in large and constructive things of the present moment in your city, county, state, and country, and in the world.

The mind and character of man are the two great exceptions to the entire constitution of the universe. Decay is the law that controls everything else except these; but thought and character need never decay. They may be kept growing as long as life endures. Who shall deny that the philosophers of India are right, and that mind and character may continue to grow throughout illimitable series of existences?

Only two classes of men are hopeless: those who think to prevail by fraud and the contrivances of indirection, and those whose minds and characters have begun to disintegrate, or degenerate, if you like the latter word better. There is every reason why character should each day get a truer bearing, why the mind each day should become more luminous, elevated, and accurate.

The Stoics said that even temperament might be given steadiness and poise by an exercise of philosophy and will, and the lives of many of them seemed to prove it. And if all this is true, your fifty years have given you an arsenal of power that is a considerable advantage over younger men, if you will but use it; and it is to point out some of the methods for its use, and some of the mistakes which I have observed men in your condition make, that this paper is written.

The details of his early catastrophes are not worthwhile here. The point is that they did not affect him except to make him stronger. They were the Thor-like blows with which Fate forged the unconquerableness of this man. For unconquerable he has become.

He has carried through daring plans; he has brought great financial institutions that opposed him to their knees; from the throne of his audacity he has dictated terms to boards of trade, and made the princes of the houses of commercial royalty his servants.

But if you look at his brow of power, at the merciless and yet delicate and sensitive lips, you will become conscious of why he succeeded—why he must eventually have succeeded anywhere. But such a man is no example for you unless you are such a man yourself—and in that case, you need no examples of any kind. You are your own example.

I read with keen interest, the other day, a feature article in one of our great daily newspapers, giving incidents in the careers of fifteen American millionaires who made their fortunes after they were fifty. But all these had the luck of the never-say-die men. They were all of the class that Emerson describes as having an excess of arterial circulation.

Every failure to them was simply an access of information. They regarded each loss as another piece of instruction in the game. Fortune always gives the winnings to such as these at last. Fortune loves a daring player; and while she may rebuff him for a while, it is only to gild the refined gold of his ultimate achievings.

Another thing. Go you to church. Use clean linen. Wear good and well-fitting clothing. Take care of your shoes. Look after all the details of your personal grooming. In short, observe all the methods which human experience has devised to keep men from degenerating. There is an unalterable connection between the physical and mental and moral.

The old saying that "cleanliness is next to godliness" has beneath it all the philosophy of civilization.

It is an easy process that produces tramps. A few days' growth of beard, the tolerance of certain personal habits of indolence, and your tramp begins, vaguely, but none the less surely, to appear. This is accompanied by a falling off in clear-cut thought [and] a blurring of the moralities.

The historic instances of great success past fifty are numerous and inspiring. They begin with Moses, who was forty years of age when "he slew the Egyptian," and they come down to our present day; to Bismarck, who, while so brilliant as a young man that he attracted the attention of Europe, was not great till he was past forty-five; to Disraeli, who, though so dazzling in his youth and early prime that he astounded Parliament and filled the press with comment, was not constructive or permanent in his success till comparatively late in life.

Think, too, of those historic successes of which there was not the faintest sign until far past middle life—they are not many, to be sure, but they are inspiring. Some of the great headlands that shoulder out into the history—Washington, Lincoln, and the like—became visible to the world after forty-five.

Of course, it is true that the immense majority of the world's great achievers—generals, statesmen, poets, philosophers, inventors, builders—have been young men. But the noble exceptions contain sufficient encouragement for you if you still have the heart of purpose.

I like to think of a man fighting his best fight just at the end of life. There has always been something attractive to me about the expression of Western hardihood, "Dying with his boots on," and the attitude of character that it describes.

No Man Is Happy If
He Does Not Work

From Theodore Roosevelt,
The Americanism of Theodore Roosevelt

I wish to preach, not the doctrine of ignoble ease, but the doctrine of the strenuous life, the life of toil and effort, of labor and strife; to preach that highest form of success which comes, not to the man who desires mere easy peace, but to the man who does not shrink from danger, from hardship, or from bitter toil, and who out of these wins the splendid ultimate triumph.

A life of slothful ease, a life of that peace which springs merely from lack either of desire or of power to strive after great things, is as little worthy of a nation as of an individual. I ask only that what every self-respecting American demands from himself and from his sons shall be demanded of the American Nation as a whole. Who among you would teach your boys that ease, that peace, is to be the first consideration in their eyes—to be the ultimate goal after which they strive? You men of Chicago have made this city great, you men of Illinois have done your share, and more than your share, in making America great, because you neither preach nor practice such a doctrine. You work yourselves, and you bring up your sons to work. If you are rich and are worth your salt, you will teach your sons that though they may have leisure, it is not to be spent in idleness; for wisely used leisure merely means that those who possess it, being free from the necessity of working for their livelihood, are all the more bound to carry on some kind of non-remunerative work in science, in letters, in art, in exploration, in historical research—work of the type we most need in this country, the successful carrying out of which reflects most honor upon the

Nation. We do not admire the man of timid peace. We admire the man who embodies victorious effort; the man who never wrongs his neighbor, who is prompt to help a friend, but who has those virile qualities necessary to win in the stern strife of actual life. It is hard to fail, but it is worse never to have tried to succeed.

In the last analysis a healthy state can exist only when the men and women who make it up lead clean, vigorous, healthy lives; when the children are so trained that they shall endeavor, not to shirk difficulties, but to overcome them; not to seek ease, but to know how to wrest triumph from toil and risk. The man must be glad to do a man's work, to dare and endure and to labor; to keep himself, and to keep those dependent upon him.

As it is with the individual, so it is with the nation. It is a base untruth to say that happy is the nation that has no history. Thrice happy is the nation that has a glorious history. Far better it is to dare mighty things, to win glorious triumphs, even though check-ered by failure, than to take rank with those poor spirits who nei-ther enjoy much nor suffer much, because they live in the gray twi-light that knows not victory nor defeat. If in 1861 the men who loved the Union had believed that peace was the end of all things, and war and strife the worst of all things, and had acted up to their belief, we would have saved hundreds of thousands of lives, we would have saved hundreds of millions of dollars. Moreover, besides saving all the blood and treasure we then lavished, we would have prevented the heartbreak of many women, the dissolu-tion of many homes, and we would have spared the country those months of gloom and shame when it seemed as if our armies marched only to defeat. We could have avoided all this suffering simply by shrinking from strife. And if we had thus avoided it, we would have shown that we were weaklings, and that we were unfit to stand among the great nations of the earth. Thank God for the iron in the blood of our fathers, the men who upheld the wisdom of Lincoln, and bore sword or rifle in the armies of Grant!

I preach to you, then, my countrymen, that our country calls not for the life of ease but for the life of strenuous endeavor. The twentieth century looms before us big with the fate of many nations. If we stand idly by, if we seek merely swollen, slothful ease and ignoble peace, if we shrink from the hard contests where men must win at hazard of their lives and at the risk of all they hold dear, then the bolder and stronger peoples will pass us by, and will win for themselves the domination of the world. Let us therefore bold-ly face the life of strife, resolute to do our duty well and manfully;

resolute to uphold righteousness by deed and by word; resolute to be both honest and brave, to serve high ideals, yet to use practical methods. Above all, let us shrink from no strife, moral or physical, within or without the nation, provided we are certain that the strife is justified, for it is only through strife, through hard and dangerous endeavor, that we shall ultimately win the goal of true national greatness.

Your work is hard. Do you suppose I mention that because I pity you? No; not a bit. I don't pity any man who does hard work worth doing. I admire him. I pity the creature who doesn't work, at whichever end of the social scale he may regard himself as being. The law of worthy work well done is the law of successful American life.

Work and love, using each in its broadest sense—work, the quality which makes a man ashamed not to be able to pull his own weight, not to be able to do for himself as well as for others without being beholden to any one for what he is doing. No man is happy if he does not work. Of all miserable creatures the idler, in whatever rank of society, is in the long run the most miserable. If a man is utterly selfish, if utterly disregardful of the rights of others, if he has no ideals, if he works simply for the sake of ministering to his own base passions, if he works simply to gratify himself, small is his good in the community. I think even then he is probably better off than if he is an idler, but he is of no real use unless together with the quality which enables him to work he has the quality which enables him to love his fellows, to work with them and for them for the common good of all.

8

THE INVISIBLE MAN

As WE ENTER THE NEW MILLENNIUM, THE MEANING OF MANLIness is increasingly unclear and fragmented. The Rolling Stones' paean to alienation, "Shattered," might serve as an anthem for our disaffection with traditional ideals. Up until at least World War II, a more or less continuous tradition from Plato to Theodore Roosevelt had codified a subtle, complex, and yet common vision of manhood. In the last few generations, by contrast, the meaning of manliness seems to have exploded into a million shards of shrapnel. What follows is a sampling of those fragments, from a statement by rebel icon James Dean to a sketch of teenage Goth culture, as conveyed by fiction, lyrics, poetry, and journalism.

Some of these fragments are bleak indeed. They speak of homelessness both physical and spiritual, of aimlessness and despair; of young men who have forgotten what it is to feel, or who cannot put those feelings into words because no one has taught them the vocabulary of love and honor. Hence, while they have strong passions, and strong loves, those passions often remain mute, baffled, and stifling because they can find no release and relief in the expression of honest and delicate sentiments.

But the panorama isn't all bleak. Contemporary man may be an invisible man, but you can still see his shadow as he walks those lonely streets. As often as these fragments are depressing and nihilistic, just as often they are full of naive wonder, generous feeling, a longing for heroism and adventure, and a burning desire to be decent toward others and be treated decently in return. Through the shadows there are occasional flares of brilliance, honest and authentic intimations of what men have lost, and of what it still could mean to be a good man, husband, parent, and citizen. No one who knows many young people today is likely to capitulate entirely to despair. Young men still want heroes, and they still want to be heroes. They still want to fall in love and prove themselves worthy of their beloved's affection. The young man who may be invisible today will soon reemerge into the sunlight.

R E B E L L I O N   A N D   D E S P A I R

The End of Something

From Ernest Hemingway,
In Our Time

The twentieth century brought a new kind of brutality to both love and war. Heroism and chivalry seemed outmoded in both spheres. Ernest Hemingway's characters embody this shift from the traditional vocabulary of romance to baffled inarticulateness: "Love isn't fun anymore."

We were in a garden at Mons. Young Buckley came in with his patrol from across the river. The first German I saw climbed up over the garden wall. We waited till he got one leg over and then potted him. He had so much equipment on and looked awfully surprised and fell down into the garden. Then three more came over further down the wall. We shot them. They all came just like that.

In the old days Hortans Bay was a lumbering town. No one who lived in it was out of sound of the big saws in the mill by the lake. Then one year there were no more logs to make lumber. The lumber schooners came into the bay and were loaded with the cut of the mill that stood stacked in the yard. All the piles of lumber were carried away. The big mill building had all its machinery that was removable taken out and hoisted on board one of the schooners by the men who had worked on the mill. The schooner moved out of the bay toward the open lake carrying the two great saws, the traveling carriage that hurled the logs against the revolving, circular saws and all the rollers, wheels, belts and iron piled on a hull-deep load of lumber. Its open hold covered with canvas and lashed tight, the sails of the schooner filled and it moved out into the open lake, carrying with it everything that had made the mill a mill and Hortons Bay a town.

The one-story bunk houses, the eating-house, the company

store, the mill offices, and the big mill itself stood deserted in the acres of sawdust that covered the swampy meadow by the shore of the bay.

Ten years later there was nothing of the mill left except the broken white limestone of its foundations showing through the swampy second growth as Nick and Marjorie rowed along the shore. They were trolling along the edge of the channel-bank where the bottom dropped off suddenly from sandy shallows to twelve feet of dark water. They were trolling on their way to the point to set night lines for rainbow trout.

"There's our old ruin, Nick," Marjorie said.

Nick, rowing, looked at the white stone in the green trees.

"There it is," he said.

"Can you remember when it was a mill?" Marjorie asked.

"I can just remember," Nick said.

"It seems more like a castle," Marjorie said

Nick said nothing. They rowed on out of sight of the mill, following the shore line. Then Nick cut across the bay.

"They aren't striking," he said.

"No," Marjorie said. She was intent on the rod all the time they trolled, even when she talked. She loved to fish. She loved to fish with Nick.

Close beside the boat a big trout broke the surface of the water. Nick pulled hard on one oar so the boat would turn and the bait spinning far behind would pass where the trout was feeding. As the trout's back came up out of the water the minnows jumped wildly. They sprinkled the surface like a handful of shot thrown into the water. Another trout broke water, feeding on the other side of the boat.

"They're feeding," Marjorie said.

"But they won't strike," Nick said.

He rowed the boat around to troll past both the feeding fish, then headed it for the point. Marjorie did not reel in until the boat touched the shore. They pulled the boat up the beach and Nick lifted out a pail of live perch. The perch swam in the water in the pail. Nick caught three of them with his hands and cut their heads off and skinned them while Marjorie chased with her hands in the bucket, finally caught a perch, cut its head off and skinned it. Nick looked at her fish.

"You don't want to take the ventral fin out," he said. "It'll be all right for bait but it's better with the ventral fin in."

He hooked each of the skinned perch through the tail. There

were two hooks attached to a leader on each rod. Then Marjorie rowed the boat out over the channel-bank, holding the line in her teeth, and looking toward Nick, who stood on the shore holding the rod and letting the line run out from the reel.

"That's about right," he called.

"Should I let it drop?" Marjorie called back, holding the line in her hand.

"Sure. Let it go." Marjorie dropped the line overboard and watched the baits go down through the water.

She came in with the boat and ran the second line out the same way. Each time Nick set a heavy slab of driftwood across the butt of the rod to hold it solid and propped it up at an angle with a small slab. He reeled in the slack line so the line ran taut out to where the bait rested on the sandy floor of the channel and set the click on the reel. When a trout, feeding on the bottom, took the bait it would run with it, taking line out of the reel in a rush and making the reel sing with the click on.

Marjorie rowed up the point a little so she would not disturb the line. She pulled hard on the oars and the boat went way up the beach. Little waves came in with it. Marjorie stepped out of the boat and Nick pulled the boat high up the beach.

"What's the matter, Nick?" Marjorie asked.

"I don't know," Nick said, getting wood for a fire.

They made a fire with driftwood. Marjorie went to the boat and brought a blanket. The evening breeze blew the smoke toward the point, so Marjorie spread the blanket out between the fire and the lake.

Marjorie sat on the blanket with her back to the fire and waited for Nick. He came over and sat down beside her on the blanket. In back of them was the close second-growth timber of the point and in front was the bay with the mouth of Hortons Creek. It was not quite dark. The fire-light went as far as the water. They could both see the two steel rods at an angle over the dark water. The fire glinted on the reels.

Marjorie unpacked the basket of supper.

"I don't feel like eating," said Nick.

"Come on and eat, Nick."

"All right."

They ate without talking, and watched the two rods and the fire-light in the water.

"There's going to be a moon tonight," said Nick. He looked across the bay to the hills that were beginning to sharpen against the sky. Beyond the hills he knew the moon was coming up.

"I know it," Marjorie said happily.

"You know everything," Nick said.

"Oh, Nick, please, cut it out! Please, please, don't be that way!"

"I can't help it," Nick said. "You do. You know everything. That's the trouble. You know you do."

Marjorie did not say anything.

"I've taught you everything. You know you do. What don't you know, anyway?"

"Oh, shut up," Marjorie said. "There comes the moon."

They sat on the blanket without touching each other and watched the moon rise.

"You don't have to talk silly," Marjorie said. "What's really the matter?"

"I don't know."

"Of course you know."

"No I don't."

"Go on and say it."

Nick looked on at the moon, coming up over the hills.

"It isn't fun anymore."

He was afraid to look at Marjorie. Then he looked at her. She sat there with her back toward him. He looked at her back. "It isn't fun anymore. Not any of it."

She didn't say anything. He went on. "I feel as though everything was gone to hell inside of me. I don't know, Marge. I don't know what to say."

He looked on at her back.

"Isn't love any fun?" Marjorie said.

"No," Nick said. Marjorie stood up. Nick sat there, his head in his hands.

"I'm going to take the boat," Marjorie called to him. "You can walk back around the point."

"All right," Nick said. "I'll push the boat off for you."

"You don't need to," she said. She was afloat in the boat on the water with the moonlight on it. Nick went back and lay down with his face in the blanket in the fire. He could hear Marjorie rowing on the water.

He lay there for a long time. He lay there while he heard Bill come into the clearing walking around through the woods. He felt Bill coming up to the fire. Bill didn't touch him, either.

"Did she go all right?" Bill said.

"Yes," Nick said, lying, his face on the blanket.

"Have a scene?"

"No, there wasn't any scene."

"How do you feel?"

"Oh, go away, Bill! Go away for a while."

Bill selected a sandwich from the lunch basket and walked over to have a look at the rods.

Oh Damn Them All, Thought the Adolescent

From John Cheever, Bullet Park *(1966)*

John Cheever chronicled the spiritual emptiness behind the affluence of suburbia in the 1950s and '60s. For an adolescent, the suburbs are a plush prison of frustration and artificiality.

The lights of Powder Hill twinkled, its chimneys smoked and a pink plush toilet-seat cover flew from a clothesline. Seen at an improbable distance by some zealous adolescent, ranging over the golf links, the piece of plush would seem to be the imprimatur, the guerdon, the accolade and banner of Powder Hill behind which marched, in tight English shoes, the legions of wife swapping, Jew-baiting, booze-fighting spiritual bankrupts. Oh damn them all, thought the adolescent. Damn the bright lights by which no one reads, damn the continuous music which no one hears, damn the grand pianos that no one can play, damn the white houses mortgaged up to their rain gutters, damn them for plundering the ocean for fish to feed the mink whose skins they wear and damn their shelves on which there rests a single book—a copy of the telephone directory, bound in pink brocade. Damn their hypocrisy, damn their cant, damn their credit cards, damn their discounting the wilderness of the human spirit, damn their immaculateness, damn their lechery and damn them above all for having leached from life that strength, malodorousness, color and zeal that give it meaning. Howl, howl, howl.

"Most Young Men Do Not Stand Like Ramrods or Talk Like Demosthenes."

James Dean's defense of
Rebel Without a Cause *(1955)*

At the age of twenty-four, James Dean was an avatar of moody confusion and yearning to an entire generation of young men.

Since I'm only 24 years old, I guess I have as good an insight into this rising generation as any other young man my age. And I've discovered that most young men do not stand like ramrods or talk like Demosthenes. Therefore, when I do play a youth, such as in Warner Bros. *Rebel Without a Cause*, I try to imitate life. The picture deals with the problems of modern youth. It is the romanticized conception of the juvenile that causes much of our trouble with misguided youth nowadays. I think the one thing this picture shows that's new is the psychological disproportion of the kids' demands on the parents. Parents are often at fault, but the kids have some work to do, too. But you can't show some far-off idyllic conception of behavior if you want the kids to come and see the picture. You've got to show what it's really like, and try to reach them on their own grounds. You know, a lot of times an older boy, one of the fellows the young ones idolize, can go back to the high school kids and tell them, "Look what happened to me! Why be a punk and get in trouble with the law? Why do these senseless things just for a thrill?" I hope *Rebel Without a Cause* will do something like that. I hope it will remind them that other people have feelings. Perhaps they will say, "What do we need all that for?" If a picture is psychologically motivated, if there is truth in the relationship in it, then I think that picture will do good. I firmly believe *Rebel Without a Cause* is such a picture.

The Dark Side:
Why Teenaged Boys Are Drawn
to Insanity, Death and War

Finbarr O'Reilly,
The Globe and Mail *[Toronto] (1998)*

In the wake of the shooting rampages in Jonesboro and at Columbine High, a national debate unfolded over the causes of violence in young males. Does rock music contribute to destructive fantasies of death and madness? Or do young people need to learn about the dark side of life? The questions emerge from a discussion of the twenty-five-year legacy of Pink Floyd, whose albums are being passed from Baby Boomer parent to '90s teens.

There are eight Pink Floyd posters covering virtually every centimeter of the door and walls of Brad Bertrand's pocket-sized bedroom in the student residence at Ryerson University. But the posters are only the beginning of his shrine to the musical gods known as Pink Floyd.

A half-dozen postcards are stuck to the remaining space on the walls and several Pink Floyd–related books and magazines are stacked on a little white TV. Almost 50 CDs featuring Pink Floyd or the solo efforts of its members and seven Floyd concert videos and films are stuffed in a cubbyhole. There's even an entire shelf devoted to Pink Floyd vinyl, much of which would have been made well before Bertrand, a slight-figured, 19-year-old first-year computer science student with a mop of blond hair, was even born. The only dissenting decor is a Maple Leafs pillow and a Blue Jays towel.

"My room always looks like this," said Bertrand, who started listening to Pink Floyd about four years ago, "except messier."

At the foot of his bed is a stereo accompanied by waist-high speakers that pump out, you guessed it, Pink Floyd anthems day and night. One album that has been getting more than its usual share of play in recent weeks is *Dark Side of the Moon*, which turns 25 on Monday. Since its release on March 23, 1973, the album with nothing but a prism and rainbow shaft of light against black background on its cover has sold more than 29 million copies—the biggest album ever by a British band—and it continues to sell more than a million copies every year. Despite never reaching No. 1 in Britain and only briefly hitting No. 1 in North America, *Dark Side* was on the Billboard Top 200 for a record 740 weeks. That translates into 14 years on the charts.

Released during the era of concept albums—flowing musical creations rather than a collection of individual tracks—*Dark Side* was the result of a collaborative effort among musicians Dave Gilmour, Roger Waters, Nick Mason, Rick Wright and engineer Alan Parsons, who was employed by Abbey Road studios where *Dark Side* was recorded. Songwriter Syd Barrett, one of the group's founders, had left in 1968 because of drug problems, but his decline was the inspiration for *Dark Side's* theme of insanity.

While *Dark Side's* original listeners may have moved on to Frank Sinatra, many of their children have latched on to it for similar reasons.

"It was a stoner album then and it's a stoner album now," said Daniel Richler, the host of CBC Newsworld's pop-culture show *Big Life*.

But apart from the album's obvious use as a soundtrack for experiments with mind-altering chemicals, the songs' lyrics dealing with insanity, death, time and war, among other themes, also appeal to a newer generation who use the album as a guide through youthful growing pains.

"I know a number of teen-agers—all boys—who listen to it obsessively," Richler said. "I was 16 in 1973 and I remember as a teen-ager I felt split, like I was a square peg in the round hole of life and *Dark Side* was a glorious endorsement of this disassociation."

Twenty-five years later, Bertrand hears the same message. *Dark Side* helps him break away from the world of his parents. "I used to go to church for many years, but now I question that and question many other things that were constants in my life," he said. "It's a battle of emotions between what you've been told and what you believe in your heart."

And while *Dark Side* may appeal strongly to teen-aged men, young women don't want to be left out of the loop of youthful disassociation.

"The song 'Time' really speaks to me," said Giselle Culver, a 22-year-old journalism student who was introduced to *Dark Side* by a boyfriend when she was 18. "It makes me question and reacquaint myself with what's important in life. I think what the album is really about is feeling outside the conventions of the life with a white picket fence, family and a dog. It's about transcending the conventional ideas of success and making money and collecting things.

"But most of all it's about being honest about the fact that you're confused and that life doesn't fit into neat little boxes."

Fans endure, and so does *Dark Side*'s influence on contemporary music, such as *OK Computer*, last year's critically acclaimed album by British band Radiohead that covers much of the same musical and lyrical territory as *Dark Side*.

"[*Dark Side*] is one of those mammoth albums that has aged very well," said broadcaster and author Alan Cross, who hosts *The Ongoing History of New Music*, a weekly radio documentary. "If you put it on 25 years later it doesn't sound as dated as something by Jethro Tull or Yes. *Dark Side* is like *Sgt. Pepper's* or the Sex Pistols' *Never Mind the Bollocks*—all were watershed albums that changed everything that followed.

"Those universal themes of death, money, insanity and time have that transgenerational appeal. It's not just the kind of record that could be handed from older brother to younger brother, but now from father to son."

That's exactly how 20-year-old Dennis Nikitenko was introduced to Pink Floyd while growing up in Ukraine. His father had a cassette of *The Wall* and his uncle owned a copy of *Momentary Lapse of Reason*. After listening to those tapes, he bought cassettes of all the other pink Floyd albums. But it wasn't until he moved to Canada about two years ago that he really discovered *Dark Side*.

"I only got into it about a month ago," said Nikitenko, his Ukranian accent still hugging his words. "Before that I had only old cassette. I was amazed how different it is when sound recording is good. This changed my perspective of the album. But for me, sound is more important than lyrics because I didn't understand them before. Now I get best of both worlds."

Nikitenko and Bertrand are pals, linked by the love of Pink Floyd. Both are members of Echoes, an online Pink Floyd mailing list with almost 1,000 subscribers around the globe. At Ryerson's orientation week last September, the two bonded when Nikitenko arrived in an Echoes T-shirt.

"It turned out Dennis was in first-year computer science as well and we had common classes together," said Bertrand. "Now we help each other with school work, drink together and talk about Floyd. It's amazing getting to know somebody from a totally different country and atmosphere with a different story of getting into Floyd."

Pink Floyd, and *Dark Side* in particular, has the ability to span culture as well as age, said Cross. "*Dark Side* is the musical equivalent of a Chicago Bulls T-shirt. It's revered, enjoyed and almost worshiped everywhere. It's become part of a common language."

And while Floyd disciples don't have a label such as the Grateful Dead's Deadheads, *Dark Side* takes fandom to another level. Fans insist that playing *Dark Side* in sync with the 1939 film *The Wizard of Oz* showed some uncanny coincidences in the timing of the music and the film: the song *Brain Damage* is sung as Scarecrow sings "If I Only Had a Brain," and the heartbeat at the end of the album coincides with Dorothy listening to the Tin Man's lack of a heart. Some disciples are currently lobbying to have Pink Floyd perform *Dark Side* at the pyramids in Egypt to mark the turn of the millennium, and Ottawa resident Gary Aube has created a website (http://infoweb.magi.com/~gaube/) devoted to marking the millennium with a Pink Floyd laser moonshot that would reflect a laser beam from a darkened new moon back down to Earth.

Aube is one of those parents, like Nikitenko's father, who passed *Dark Side* on to his 16-year-old daughter Natalie.

"I guess it's a matter of wanting your children to appreciate music that was part of your generation," said the 48-year-old who has worked as a programming director and a general manager of rock music stations in Ottawa and Toronto. "*Dark Side* is such an iconic album, it's a good one to choose. Kids need to be exposed to darker elements as well as to happy little pop songs."

What Then Shall We Choose? Weight or Lightness?

From Milan Kundera,
The Unbearable Lightness of Being

If every second of our lives recurs an infinite number of times, we are nailed to eternity as Jesus Christ was nailed to the cross. It is a terrifying prospect. In the world of eternal return the weight of unbearable responsibility lies heavy on every move we make. That is why Nietzsche called the idea of eternal return the heaviest of burdens (*das schwertze Gewicht*).

If eternal return is the heaviest of burdens, then our lives can stand out against it in all their splendid lightness.

But if heaviness of burdens crushes us, we sink beneath it, it pins us to the ground. But in the love poetry of every age, the woman longs to be weighed down by the man's body. The heaviest of burdens is therefore simultaneously an image of our life's most intense fulfillment. The heavier the burden, the closer our lives come to the earth, the more real and truthful they become.

Conversely, the absolute absence of a burden causes man to be lighter than air, to soar into the heights, take leave of the earth and his earthly being, and become only half real, his movements as free as they are insignificant.

What then shall we choose? Weight or lightness?

Video Games Get Very Very Ugly: Masochism, Mutilation, Prostitution

Charles Mandel,
The Globe and Mail *[Toronto] (1998)*

What role if any do video games play in the disturbing spate of violent acts recently committed by young males? This essay provides a disturbing look at what your son may actually be doing at his computer.

Duke Nukem runs forward, grabs the shotgun and pumps a round into the chamber. "Groovy," intones the video-game hero in his gravelly voice, just before he starts blasting alien scum into a gory pulp.

Sound violent? Not to some video-game developers, apparently. Major U.S. software companies are about to make such infamous "splatter" games as Duke Nukem and Doom seem like child's play as they prepare to release a new wave of titles this fall that enable players to manipulate photorealistic images of humans into acts of torture, mutilation and even—if you can believe it—prostitution.

Interplay Productions proudly promotes its Wild 9 as the first-ever action game that encourages players to torture enemies. Shiny Entertainment, a subsidiary of Interplay, is completing work on Messiah, a game in which a cherub tries to cleanse the world of corruption. "Ever seen a body with 10,000 volts run through it?" the game's advertising slogan teases. "Want to?"

Not to be outdone, Virgin Interactive is set to release Thrill Kill, a series of gladiator-style battles between demented characters that bite and tear at each other in a torture-chamber setting.

And Max Payne, a vigilante-style game (whose hero is not-so-subtly named after the "maximum pain" he likes to inflict on his victims), is coming soon from 3D Realms and Remedy Entertainment. The game recently inspired editors of *PC Gamer Magazine* to exclaim: "While Duke Nukem raised a few eyebrows with his testosterone-charged quips, alienbashing violence and girl-happy lifestyle, Max Payne's vendetta-fueled exploits and shocking amount of violence are likely to have the senators squealing."

Other pain-packing titles due out in the next year include Deathtrap Dungeon and Dungeon Keeper II (which, according to Computer Gaming World Magazine, "offers improved graphics, more creatures and better ways to torture").

What is also striking about such games is that they are being released by large, well-established companies. Interplay, for example, is one of the largest U.S.–based entertainment-software publishers, with sales in the past six months of $81-million. And Virgin Interactive is the software arm of Richard Branson's multibillion-dollar British media conglomerate.

But then, the stakes are high. Since video-gaming giant GT Interactive Software acquired Duke Nukem from creator Formgen in 1996, the company has sold more than four million copies globally. Those sales have helped solidify GT Interactive's position as the second largest entertainment-software publisher in the United States, after Electronic Arts, with annual revenue of $531 million. In total, the U.S. gaming market was worth $1.3 billion in 1997, according to market-research firm PC Data. Globally, the figure is $17 billion.

While game developers say the violence is aimed purely at adults, others point out there are few safeguards to prevent the software from falling into the hands of children. Stephen Kline, a professor of communications at Simon Fraser University in Burnaby, British Columbia, who has taught courses on video-gaming culture, recently released a study that concludes parents tend to pay no attention to what their kids play. And, according to Kline's survey of 650 youth, video games—whether computer-based CD-ROM's or Nintendo, Sony or Sega console games—help shape children's outlook on the world.

"Heavy gamers show different kinds of judgments than light gamers," Kline said in an interview. "Female gamers especially—and there are some—show the classic desensitization effect. They rate things like blood and guts, rape and sexual aggression as less offensive, as less violent, than the light and moderate gamers."

Kline's study states that roughly one in four children is addicted to gaming (specifically, 24 per cent play between seven and 30 hours a week).

That's not all. In this new world of gaming, where there's violence there often is sex. Fallout 2, a soon-to-be released game set in a postnuclear holocaust era, features the chance to "fall in love, get married and pimp your spouse for a little extra chump change. Hey, it's a dark and dangerous world." Prostitution also features prominently in the aforementioned Messiah, whose characters include several scantily clad hookers.

MAYHEM MILESTONES

While not all of the following games made a killing at the cash register, they rank as classic carnage moments. Chris Charla, editor of the gaming magazine *Next Generation*, walked us through some psycho highlights of the past 22 years:

Death Race 2000: This arcade-style game from 1976 was the first of the very violent titles. A forerunner to today's graphically vivid Carmageddon, the object is to run over people who on contact would turn into little white crosses.

Splatterhouse: A sort of cross between the Halloween movie series and the *Texas Chainsaw Massacre.* You are a man in a hockey mask armed with a chainsaw running through a house killing monsters.

Mortal Kombat: Released in the late eighties, it was among the first to explore the martial-arts theme. The key action is to rip your opponent's heart out.

Wolfenstein 3D: In 1992, graphics technology had progressed to the point where the player could move through three-dimensional space and thus get close, personal and very gory. The revolutionary Wolfenstein 3D fired the opening salvo in the 3D revolution.

Night Trap: With its full-motion video sequence of a woman in a scanty night dress being pursued by monsters, this game caused U.S. senators in 1993 to raise a hue and cry and call for a rating system.

Carmaggedon: The British Board of Film and Video Classification refused a rating certificate to Carmaggedon in 1997, when the British press were still fussing over the recent release of David Cronenberg's controversial film *Crash*.

Postal: A 1997 game consisting of an armed man shooting unarmed bystanders in settings such as fast-food restaurants. It nearly triggered a U.S. postal strike in protest.

Sin: Shooting took on a new level of realism in this 1997 release. A shot in the arm, for example, causes the victim to collapse in a way that is different from, say, a blow to the head.

On the horizon: Thrill Kill, a viciously violent fight game, promises to be among the more shocking titles this fall.

Television's Virus of Violence and the Jonesboro Schoolyard Shootings

Lieutenant-Colonel Dave Grossman,
The Virginian-Pilot *[Hampton Roads, VA] (1998)*

In this hard-hitting essay, a retired infantry officer and expert on the psychology of violence lays the blame for Jonesboro and other shooting sprees by young males squarely at the doorstep of the television networks. There is a direct link, Colonel Grossman argues, between television's glamorization of violence and alienated boys' search for recognition through violent acts.

Folks here noticed something interesting about the network television crews that swarmed in like the second of some series of biblical plagues two months ago. What we noticed about the TV folks was this: They have blood on their hands, and they know it, yet they dare not admit it.

The U.S. television networks will stick their lenses anywhere and courageously expose anything. Like flies crawling on open wounds, they find nothing too private or too shameful for their probing—except themselves, and their share of guilt in the terrible crime that happened here.

That crime, as the world now knows, was the March 24 school-yard shooting deaths of four schoolgirls and a teacher. Ten others were wounded and two boys, 11 and 13, are in jail, charged with the murders.

And it happened in Jonesboro, my home. Before retiring here, I spent almost a quarter of a century as an army infantry officer and a psychologist, learning how to enable people to kill. Believe me, we are very good at it. And just as the army enables killing, we are doing the same thing to our kids—but without the military's safeguards.

The TV networks are responsible for traumatizing and brutalizing our children as they watch violent acts—a thousand a month, according to the latest research financed by the cable industry itself—at a young, vulnerable age when they cannot tell the difference between reality and fantasy. Children really only know what they have been taught, and we have taught them, ever so cleverly, to laugh and cheer at violence. In Jonesboro, we saw an indication of just how good a job we have done.

I spent the first three days after the shooting at Westside Middle School, counseling teachers, students and parents. One high-school teacher told me about the reaction she got when she informed her students that someone was shooting at their little brothers, sisters and cousins in the middle school.

"They laughed," she told me in amazement. "They laughed."

We have raised a generation of barbarians who have learned to associate violence with pleasure, like the Romans who cheered and snacked as the Christians were slaughtered in the Colosseum.

A TV commentator told me not long after the shootings, "Well, we only have one real violent show on our network, *NYPD Blue*. I'll admit that it's bad, but it's only one night a week."

I wondered how she would feel if someone said, "Well, I only beat my wife in front of the kids one night a week." The effect is the same. According to *USA Weekend*, *NYPD Blue* star Kim Delaney was shocked to discover that under-age viewers watch her show, which is rated TV–14 for gruesome crimes, raw language and explicit sex. "You're not supposed to know who I am!" she told a group of young children who recognized her.

The copycat aspect of the Jonesboro murders is another twist to juvenile crime that the TV networks would rather not talk about.

Research in the 1970s demonstrated the effect of "cluster suicides," in which the local TV reporting of teen suicides was directly responsible for causing numerous copycat suicides of young, impressionable teen-agers. Somewhere in every population there are potentially suicidal kids who will say to themselves, "Well, I'll show all those people who have been mean to me. I know how to get my picture on TV, too."

Today, TV stations generally do not "do" suicides. But when pictures of teen-age *killers* appear on TV, the effect is the same: Somewhere there is a potentially violent little boy who says to himself, "Well, I'll show all those people who have been mean to me. I know how to get my picture on TV, too."

And thus we get clusters of copycat murders that work their way across the United States like a virus spread by the six o'clock news. In the latest outbreak, in Springfield, Oregon, on Thursday, a 15-year-old high-school student who'd been suspended a day earlier for bringing a gun to school returned with his .22-caliber rifle and two handguns and opened fire in a packed cafeteria. When the rampage was over, two students were dead and 22 injured. The bodies of his parents were found later at his home.

The lineage of the Jonesboro shootings can first be picked up less than six months before, at Pearl, Mississippi. A 16-year-old boy was accused of killing his mother and then going to his school and shooting nine students, two of whom—one his ex-girlfriend—died.

Two months later, it spread to Paducah, Kentucky, where a 14-year-old boy was arrested for killing three students and wounding five others.

A very important step occurred in Stamps, Arkansas, 15 days after Pearl and just a little over 90 days before Jonesboro. A 14-year-old boy, angry at his schoolmates, hid in the woods and fired at children as they came out of school. Sound familiar? Only two children were injured in this crime, so most of the world didn't hear about it. But it got great regional TV coverage, and two little boys across the state in Jonesboro couldn't have helped but hear about it.

This is not to say that TV violence is the only reason for these terrible murders. The easy availability of guns, the prevalence of family breakdown, the violence kids absorb from Hollywood movies and video games—all of these are topics that the TV industry would much rather tell us about. But while they focus on the mote in the eye of their neighbors, we are obliged to point out the huge, bleeding splinter in their electronic eye.

The data linking TV violence and violent crime is more scientifically sound than that linking tobacco and cancer. More than 200 studies have identified a clear cause-and-effect relationship. Thus, we are probably very close to a time when the TV networks will be treated like the tobacco industry and brought to their knees by lawsuits.

The American Medical Association, the American Academy of Pediatrics and the American Psychiatric Association, as well as their equivalents in other nations, have made definitive, unequivocal statements about the link between violence in the media and violent crime. The APA, in its 1992 report "Big World, Small Screen," said flatly that the "scientific debate is over." With few exceptions, every nation that has fed violent images to its children as entertainment is paying the same tragic price.

You may ask: But what about the responsibility of parents to "just turn it off"? Every single one of the parents of the 15 shooting victims in Jonesboro could have protected their children from TV violence in this way, and it wouldn't have done a bit of good, because, somewhere, there were two little boys whose parents didn't "just turn it off."

On the night of the shootings, clergy and counselors were working in small groups in the hospital waiting room, comforting relatives and friends of the shooting victims. Then they noticed one woman who had been sitting silently, alone.

A counselor went up to the woman and discovered that she was the mother of one of the girls who had been killed. She had no friends, no husband, no family with her as she sat in the hospital, stunned by her loss. "I just came to find out how to get my little girl's body back," she said. But the body had been taken to Little Rock, 160 kilometers away, for an autopsy. In her dazed state of mind, her very next concern was, "I just don't know how we're going to pay for the funeral. I don't know how we can afford it."

That little girl was truly all she had in all the world. Come to Jonesboro, my friend, hunt up this mother, and tell her how she should "just turn it off."

Every parent desperately needs to be warned of the impact of TV on children, just as we would warn parents of a rampant carcinogen. But our key means of public education in America is the national TV networks—using the public airwaves we have licensed to them. And they are stonewalling.

The hard-hitting investigative reporters of shows such as *60 Minutes* have always been our heroes. They are the ones we counted on to swoop down like Superman and rescue us from corporate oppressors. But now it is the networks that are the irresponsible, heartless corporate killers who put profits ahead of lives. Our heroes are nothing more than hypocrites.

In the days after the Jonesboro shootings, I was interviewed for Canadian national TV, the BBC, and many U.S. and international radio stations and newspapers. But the U.S. television networks simply would not touch this aspect of the story. Never, in my experience as a historian and a psychologist, have I seen any institution in America so clearly abusing their publicly licensed authority and power to cover up their guilt.

Time after time, idealistic young network producers contacted me, fascinated by the irony that an expert in the field of violence and aggression was living right here in Jonesboro and was at the school almost from the beginning. But unlike the stories in all the other media, these network items always died a sudden, silent death when the powers-that-be said, "Yeah, we need this story like we need a hole in the head."

Many times since the shooting, I have been asked, "Why weren't you on TV talking about the stuff in your book?"—meaning *On Killing: The Psychological Cost of Learning to Kill in War and Society* (Little Brown, 1996). And every time my answer had to be, "The TV networks are burying this story. They know they are guilty and they want to delay the inevitable retribution as long as they can."

I accuse. I accuse the U.S. TV networks of inciting the violent deaths of thousands of innocent Americans across many decades, and I accuse them of abusing the public airwaves in a conspiracy to cover up their guilt.

I've been there, and I am angry. I've seen the horror and the blood and the death of the innocents, and I personally have heard some of the world's foremost experts lay the blame squarely on the doorstep of TV. And I personally have seen the networks kill this story.

I'm mad as hell at the hypocrisy of the U.S. TV networks. And, in the name of the people of Jonesboro, Arkansas, and in the name of all innocent lives sacrificed on this alter of glass, I hereby publicly challenge the networks to honestly discuss and examine their guilt.

NBC, ABC, CBS, Fox and all you others, turn the cameras on yourselves and see: You have the blood of innocents on your hands.

Why the U.S. Won't
Go to War

Michael Kelly,
The Times *of London (1997)*

The rise of nihilistic violence at home (Jonesboro, Littleton, and a string of less-well-publicized incidents) is ironically paralleled by a strong aversion for military combat abroad. The U.S. is willing to use massive force (Iraq, Kosovo), but apparently only if its ground troops are spared direct contact with the enemy. Thus, as Michael Kelly observes, Americans are spared the painful lesson known to other peoples: that there are things worth fighting and dying for.

In the summer and autumn of 1995, as the war in Bosnia was winding down, I spent a couple of months in Bihac, a small, handsome mountain city in the northwest corner of the country then entering its last days under Serbian siege. Bihac was defended by the Bosnian Army's V Corps, which had built itself up from a few platoons of local volunteers armed with Kalashnikovs and hunting rifles into a great, if unconventional, fighting force. For more than two years the V Corps held off a vastly better-armed encircling force, and the war they fought was more like 1917 than 1995.

The soldiers at the front lived for months at a time in slit trenches and scant bunkers of sandbags and tree branches, dug in along wooded ridges and hills. They had, for most of the war, so little ammunition that it was common for troops to go into battle with 20 rounds apiece. They fought in short, furious, bursts, emerging from their holes in the mud to charge the enemy line in shooting, stabbing, shrieking onslaughts that usually ended with everyone on one side or the other wounded or dead.

These soldiers were mostly young and mostly untrained, but they had become greatly familiar with war and familiarity had bred its usual contempt. While they still feared death, they no longer respected it. This had some unhappy consequences. There was a lot of mental depression in Bihac. But the devaluation of life had also served its great purpose. It had freed the people from their normal inhibitions about killing and being killed, and this in turn had kept them from being killed. Accepting death, it turned out, was indispensable to defeating death.

This is a troubling idea to contemplate as the United States worries, again, about what to do about Baghdad. Saddam Hussein's ability to agitate America rests on his understanding that America has developed a phobia of military death. While the Americans have become weirdly numb to the horror of death in the civilian sphere (on the streets, in the movies), they have evolved what amounts to a zero tolerance policy for death on the battlefield, and not just American death, any death. In Bosnia, America watched the Serbs conduct a genocidal campaign, and did nothing of practical import for three years, because they didn't want to be— responsible for anyone being killed—not even the perpetrators of genocide.

The Gulf conflict was, per capita, probably the most death-free war ever waged. In all the war, there was only one scene of really troubling mass slaughter, the savaging by air and by tank of the Iraqi forces fleeing home from their rout in Kuwait. And this scene ended the war.

Looking at the burned, exploded bodies a few days after the attack, it seemed obvious to me that the war must instantly end; there could be no justification for continuing unilateral slaughter. This seemed obvious to a lot of other people too, some of them professional military men and some of them advisers to the President. So the war ended, abruptly and disastrously, with Saddam Hussein in power and protected by the well-paid, heavily armed Republican Guard, which American forces could have destroyed in a few days then.

It seems obvious to me now that what seemed obvious to me then was the usual result of a little knowledge intruding suddenly on total ignorance. I had never seen the results of war, and the results horrified me out of my wits. In this, I was of course typical of my generation of reporters. The result is, in matters military, a press corps that is forever suffering a collective case of the vapors. At the least exposure to the most unremarkable facts of military life—soldiers can be brutes and pigs, generals can be stupid, bullets can be fatal—we are forever shocked, forever reaching for the sal volatile.

The media's generational horror at war's truths reflects the larger society's views, and this larger society includes the military itself. Not since Vietnam has America faced a serious war, involving a serious level of death (and Vietnam's 58,000 American coffins were a fraction of the butcher's bills paid in the great wars), and that conflict ended a quarter of a century ago. We are a nation in which there are fewer and fewer people, and they are older and older people, who accept what every 12-year-old in Bihac knows: that there are things worth dying for, and killing for.

So, Americans will let Saddam Hussein stall them until he has hidden what weapons of mass deaths he needs to hide, and then he will let the UN inspectors back in, and the Americans will live with that. Or they will inflict some suffering on Iraq, and kill some people, but not too many, because the people—the American people, that is—will not be able to stand the pictures. And the Americans can live with that too. But one of these days, somebody—the North Koreans come to mind—is going to start a real war. And then we will find out what we can really live with.

Gender Traits Tie
T.V. Execs in Knots

Brian Lowry,
Los Angeles Times *(1998)*

Some may deny that men and women are different, but in the business world, understanding those differences is connected to big profits. For instance, men and women watch television in very different ways; the viewing habits of men are harder to pin down because they have shorter attention spans. Women are loyal to their shows, prefer dramas, and pay attention to the story line. Men prefer action scenes, military hardware, sports, and incessant channel surfing. What a surprise!

When the CBS series *JAG* is screened for test audiences, producers have noticed that while the more emotional scenes resonate with women, it's the military drama's "hardware" that causes the dials to rise among men.

"When you come to an action scene, the women will drop off, and the men will peak incredibly," says executive producer Donald P. Bellisario. The consistency of that dynamic underscores how men and women watch television differently, as well as changes in a wired-for-cable world that contribute to such a rift, prompting many couples to adjourn to separate rooms to watch TV on their own.

The major networks find attracting men especially difficult, which helps explain a dizzying series of sports TV deals as programmers seek showcases to reel in that audience at least temporarily. The frenzy peaked in January, when Disney (through ABC and ESPN), CBS and Fox agreed to pay a mind-boggling $17.6 billion for broadcast rights to National Football League games.

Beyond being drawn to different genres, research indicates that men are generally less willing to commit time to an ongoing TV series and more apt to flip around during commercial breaks.

"Men have fewer appointment shows," says Kelly Kahl, CBS' vice president of scheduling, adding that with the exception of sports events—such as the recent National Collegiate Athletic Association basketball championship—"our ability to get men in front of the set is minimal."

The gender disparity begins with simple math: Women outnumber men and generally watch more television. According to estimates by Nielsen Media Research, the average woman 18 and older—a population estimated at 100.6 million in the United States—tunes in 4 1/2 hours daily, about 40 minutes more than average for the country's 92.3 million adult males.

"It's much easier to reach women any place on television. There's more of us and we spend more time watching," says Jean Pool, executive vice president of North American media-buying services at J. Walter Thompson. "It's just a fact and always has been that men are harder to reach on television than women."

The data become more significant when coupled with an anecdotal observation that hasn't eluded women or stand-up comics—namely, men are more likely to channel-surf, flipping idly from station to station.

"(A woman) will watch a two-hour movie, and the guy will watch 15 things during the same time," says Tim Brooks, senior vice president of research at USA Networks.

A *Los Angeles Times* poll conducted in September concluded that four out of 10 men said they always or frequently change channels when a commercial comes on, compared to 28 percent of women; by contrast, 7 percent of men said they never flip around during a program, as opposed to 17 percent of women.

"Men are masters of the remote control, and they will surf more easily than women do. That's clearly a challenge," says Artie

Bulgrin, vice president of research and sales development at cable sports network ESPN. "Sports, out of all the TV genres, is certainly the most vulnerable to switching."

In descending order, men polled by the *Times* cited network news, network sports, cable sports, movies, comedies and cable news as the programming they watched most. Women also led their list with network news but followed with comedies, dramas, soap operas and movies.

Women were more than twice as likely to mention dramas among their favorite forms of programming, while four times as many men chose sports. Based on a breakdown of prime-time networks series, the current television season's No. 1 show among men, *Monday Night Football,* doesn't crack the Top 20 with women.

Other programs exclusive to the men's roster include Fox's Sunday lineup of *The X-Files, King of the Hill* and *The Simpsons,* as well as NBC's *Law & Order.* Shows unique to women were *Diagnosis Murder, Cosby, Mad About You, Promised Land* and *Everybody Loves Raymond.*

"In the broader strokes, women tend to be more story-oriented, men more action- and comedy-oriented," Smith says.

Many popular programs cross gender lines, especially *Seinfeld,* which is second on both lists. Other shows preferred by both men and women include *Friends, Touched by an Angel, 60 Minutes, Home Improvement, Frasier* and *The Drew Carey Show.*

In shows common to both, however, the percentage of the female population that tunes in is invariably higher.

"Choice" is the operative word in television. Based on Nielsen data, roughly three-quarters of all households have two or more TV sets and, with increasing frequency, men, women and children scatter to watch the programs they want separately.

Cable, of course, has exacerbated the problem of getting families to watch together, by providing channels catering to a wide variety of highly specific interests.

Women appear to be more willing to watch programs that traditionally appeal to men than the other way around, including those that contain violence.

Networks have experienced some success tinkering with shows that possess a stronger male following in order to make them more attractive to women. NBC's *Law & Order* replaced two members of the originally all-male cast with women, for example, in a conscious effort to make the long-running show more accessible to them.

One of the casualties gradually inflicted by such advances as multiple televisions and VCRs is family viewing, and the days when everyone crowded around one TV together to watch *Bonanza* or *The Cosby Show*. With digital technology that promises to expand the number of channels further, the day may be coming, in fact, where Bruce Springsteen won't sing about "57 channels and nothing on" but rather a channel with something on—viewed alone— for every one of us.

Roll Back the Red Carpet for Boys

Donna Laframboise,
The Globe and Mail *[Toronto] (1998)*

Are boys the main victim group in today's society? Feminism may be blinding us to the dimensions of their problems.

Every now and again, in random bits and pieces, we run up against the fact that being male isn't the red-carpet experience much of recent feminism would have us believe.

Young males are more likely to be physically abused by their parents, to drop out of school and to face unemployment than their female counterparts. Between the ages of 15 and 24, they take their own lives five times as often. As adults, males are more likely to be homeless, more prone to alcohol and gambling addictions, twice as likely to be robbed or murdered, nine times more likely to be killed in an occupational accident and go to their graves six years earlier (on average) than their sisters.

Yet so attached are we to the view that the patriarchy has designed the world for the benefit of males that these truths fail to sink in. Although headlines would scream and alarm bells would ring if the opposite were the case, inequality isn't an important social issue when males are being shortchanged.

Talk about youth suicide, for instance, and you'll be informed that what really deserves attention is not the appalling number of dead male bodies, but the fact that girls say they *attempt* suicide more often than do boys.

The latest examples of this "who cares, they're only guys" mentality are reports that girls are outperforming boys in school. In 1996, six out of 10 high-school honors graduates in Ontario and British Columbia were female.

Even though girls were besting boys a decade earlier (in 1986, 53 per cent of Ontario honors grads and 57 per cent of those in B.C. were girls), the 1990s have been replete with media commentary telling us it's girls who merit our concern. In 1994, Myra and David Sadker's book *Failing at Fairness: How Our Schools Cheat Girls* appeared. A year later, Michele Landsberg wrote a column in the *Toronto Star* titled "School Sexism So Routine It's Almost Invisible." A news story, also in the *Star*, about the higher-than-average Montreal dropout rate implied we should be concerned about this phenomenon partly because "45 per cent of dropouts are young women." Despite being in the majority, the boys weren't worth mentioning.

When girls do worse in math and science, when they don't sign up for skilled trades or engineering, it's the system's fault. Their parents aren't encouraging them, the schools are male-oriented and unwelcoming, the boys are harassing them and society is sending them traditional-role-model messages.

But when boys do poorly, it's their own fault. Even though they're children, the responsibility gets loaded directly onto their meager shoulders. In a recent *Globe* article ("Where the Boys Aren't: At the Top of the Class, Feb. 26), educators tell the media that "too many boys don't seem to be even trying," and blame "a boy culture that celebrates bravado, lassitude and stupidity." Rather than ask boys for their input, the reporter interviewed girls who criticized the boys' study habits.

The fact that masculinity and intellectualism have always been an uneasy fit (football players get dates, bookworms don't) doesn't even make it into the conversation.

The idea that boys may be confused about whether or not they should excel, since feminism has drawn a straight line between female oppression and male achievement, isn't discussed.

The fact that elementary schools are dominated by female teachers who scold and punish boys more frequently than they do girls, and that boys suffer from more learning disabilities, isn't mentioned.

The notion that educators, parents and governments have spent the past 15 years ignoring boys, so it's little wonder that they themselves have become complacent about their performance, isn't considered.

Girls are victims of circumstance and boys are masters of their own fate. Girls are molded and manipulated by social pressures; boys make conscious choices. Girls get to blame everyone but themselves; everyone gets to blame boys.

Wasn't feminism supposed to be about abolishing double standards?

Marginal Men

From Barbara Ehrenreich,
Essays, Thought and Style *(1996)*

Two vicious murders of teenage girls on Long Island are the occasion for Barbara Ehrenreich's reflections on the sources of violence in young males. When a young man's pride has no honorable outlet (like a decent job), it will degenerate into violence and "the politics of gesture."

Crime seems to change character when it crosses a bridge or a tunnel. In the city, crime is taken as emblematic of the vast injustices of class and race. In the suburbs, though, it's intimate and psychological—resistant to generalization, a mystery of the individual soul. Recall the roar of commentary that followed the murderous assault on a twenty-eight-year-old woman jogging in Central Park. Every detail of the assailants' lives was sifted for sociological significance: Were they poor? How poor? Students or dropouts? From families with two parents or one? And so on, until the awful singularity of the event was lost behind the impersonal grid of Class, Race, and Sex.

Now take the Midtown Tunnel east to the Long Island Expressway, out past the clutter of Queens to deepest suburbia, where almost every neighborhood is "good" and "social pathology" is something you learn about in school. Weeks before the East Harlem youths attacked a jogger, Long Islanders were shaken by two murders which were, if anything, even more inexplicably vicious than the assault in Central Park. In early March, the body of thirteen-year-old Kelly Tinyes was found in the basement of a house just down the block from her own. She had been stabbed, strangled, and hit with a blunt instrument before being mutilated with a bayonet. A few weeks later, fourteen-year-old Jessica Manners was discovered along the side of a road in East Setauket, strangled to death, apparently with her own bra, and raped.

Suspects have been apprehended. Their high-school friends, parents, and relatives have been interviewed. Their homes and cars have been searched; their photos published. We know who they hung out with and what they did in their spare time. But on the scale of large social meanings, these crimes don't rate. No one is demanding that we understand—or condemn—the white communities that nourished the killers. No one is debating the roots of violence in the land of malls and tract homes. Only in the city, apparently, is crime construed as something "socioeconomic." Out here it's merely "sick."

But East Setauket is not really all that far from East Harlem. If something is festering in the ghetto, something very similar is gnawing away at Levittown and East Meadow. A "way of life," as the cliché goes, is coming to an end, and in its place a mean streak is opening up and swallowing everything in its path. Economists talk about "deindustrialization" and "class polarization." I think of it as the problem of *marginal men:* they are black and white, Catholic and Pentecostal, rap fans and admirers of technopop. What they have in common is that they are going nowhere—nowhere legal, that is.

Consider the suspects in the Long Island murders. Twenty-one-year-old Robert Golub, in whose basement Kelly Tinyes was killed, is described in *Newsday* as an "unemployed bodybuilder." When his high-school friends went off to college, he stayed behind in his parents' home in Valley Stream. For a while, he drove a truck for a cosmetics firm, but he lost that job, in part because of his driving record: his license has been suspended twelve times since 1985. At the time of the murder, he had been out of work for several months, constructing a life around his weight-lifting routine and his dream of becoming an entrepreneur.

Christopher Loliscio, the suspect in the Manners case, is nineteen, and, like Golub, lives with his parents. He had been in trouble before, and is charged with third-degree assault and "menacing" in an altercation that took place on the campus of the State University at Stony Brook last December. Loliscio does not attend college himself. He is employed as a landscaper.

The suburbs are full of young white men like Golub and Loliscio. If they had been born twenty years earlier, they might have found steady work in decent-paying union jobs, married early, joined the volunteer fire department, and devoted their leisure to lawn maintenance. But the good blue-collar jobs are getting sparser, thanks to "deindustrialization"—which takes the form, in Long Island, of cutbacks in the defense and aerospace industries. Much of what's left is likely to be marginal, low-paid work. Nationwide, the earnings of young white men dropped 18 percent between 1973 and 1986, according to the Census Bureau, and the earnings of male high-school dropouts plunged 42 percent.

Landscaping, for example—a glamorous term for raking and mowing—pays four to five dollars an hour; truck driving for a small firm is in the same range: not enough to pay for a house, a college education, or even a mid-size wedding reception at the VFW hall.

And even those modest perquisites of life in the subyuppie class have become, in some sense, "not enough." On Long Island, the culture that once sustained men in blue-collar occupations is crumbling as more affluent settlers move in, filling the vacant lots with their new, schooner-shaped, $750,000 homes. In my town, for example, the last five years saw the bowling alley close and the blue-collar bar turn into a pricey dining spot. Even the volunteer fire department is having trouble recruiting. The prestigious thing to join is a $500-a-year racquetball club; there's just not much respect anymore for putting out fires.

So the marginal man lives between two worlds—one that he aspires to and one that is dying, and neither of which he can afford. Take "Rick," the twenty-two-year-old son of family friends. His father is a machinist in an aerospace plant which hasn't been hiring anyone above the floor-sweeping level for years now. Not that Rick has ever shown any interest in his father's trade. For one thing, he takes too much pride in his appearance to put on the dark green company-supplied work clothes his father has worn for the past twenty years. Rick has his kind of uniform: pleated slacks, high-tops, Italian knit cardigans, and a $300 leather jacket, accessorized with a gold chain and earring stud.

To his parents, Rick is a hard-working boy for whom things just don't seem to work out. For almost a year after high school, he worked behind a counter at Crazy Eddie's, where the pay is low but at least you can listen to rock and roll all day. Now he has a gig doing valet parking at a country club. The tips are good and he loves racing around the lot in the Porsches and Lamborghinis of the stockbroker class. But the linchpin of his economic strategy is living at home, with his parents and sisters, in the same room he's occupied since third grade. Rick is a long way from being able to afford even a cramped, three-bedroom house like his family home; and, given the choice, he'd rather have a new Camaro anyway.

If this were the seventies, Rick might have taken up marijuana, the Grateful Dead, and vague visions of a better world. But like so many of his contemporaries in the eighties, Rick has no problem with "the system," which, in his mind, embraces every conceivable hustle, legal or illegal. Two years ago, he made a tidy bundle dealing coke in a local dance club, bought a $20,000 car, and smashed it up. Now he spends his evenings as a bouncer in an illegal gambling joint—his parents still think he's out "dancing"—and is proud of the handgun he's got stowed in his glove compartment.

Someday Rick will use that gun, and I'll probably be the first to say—like Robert Golub's friends—"but he isn't the kind of person who would hurt *anyone.*" Except that even now I can sense the danger in him. He's smart enough to know he's only a cut-rate copy of the upscale young men in GQ ads and MTV commercials. Viewed from Wall Street or Southampton, he's a peon, a member of the invisible underclass that parks cars, waits on tables, and is satisfied with a five-dollar tip and a remark about the weather.

He's also proud. And there's nowhere for him to put that pride except into the politics of gesture; the macho stance, the seventy-five-mile-per-hour takeoff down the expressway, and eventually maybe, the drawn gun. Jobs are the liberal solution; conservatives would throw in "traditional values." But what the marginal men—from Valley Stream to Bedford-Stuyvesant—need most of all is *respect.* If they can't find that in work, or in a working-class lifestyle that is no longer honored, they'll extract it from someone weaker—a girlfriend, a random jogger, a neighbor, perhaps just any girl. They'll find a victim.

THE CONFUSIONS OF LOVE

The Dangerous Game
of Dating

Jonathan Foreman,
The Women's Quarterly

What constitutes a "date"? An English observer of American women is puzzled by its many meanings.

People back in my homeland of England often ask me if American women are as sexually aggressive as they have heard. British males who don't really know this country are convinced that American women are all fierce, perpetually complaining feminists who throw themselves at men with startling force and frequency. "Is it true they just come up to you in bars and ask you to sleep with them?" one fellow asked.

The truthful answer is, "Uh, not usually." American women are no more likely to be sexually hyperactive than their British counterparts; in fact, British women are a far better bet if you meet them at a bar. (Surveys have shown that the Brits are the most promiscuous people in Western Europe—far more so than the French.)

Despite this society's openness about sex, American women often have remarkably frustrating sex lives. This is not because American women are in any way prudish. On the contrary. It is mainly because the rules of "dating" wreak such havoc on relations between the sexes.

I have lived in this country for a decade, my father was American, I spent all my school vacations in California, and I still don't really understand what Americans mean by "dating." It is hard to believe, I know, but we simply don't have "dating" in England. This is not as strange as it sounds. We still have sex lives; we still marry and have children. Indeed, we have successfully done all these things for centuries. So far as I know, "dating" scarcely exists outside the United States.

For example, I once heard one of my American female colleagues say, "I'm dating three guys right now, nothing serious." I was stunned. Could she really be sleeping with three men simultaneously? A lawyer friend explained she was not sleeping with them, she was merely "dating" them—in other words, going out to dinner with them. I asked this friend if that meant that any time a man has dinner with a woman they are on a date. Not at all, she explained. For a dinner to be a date, there has to be romantic intent.

At this point, I thought I understood dating. It was a kind of reconnaissance made in a restaurant before two people embarked on a relationship; no carnal activity was involved except eating.

But there are many times when the context is less clear. If I meet an unmarried woman and she tells me she has been dating someone for three weeks, or three years, what does that mean? Is she single? (As a European, I would be happy to treat all women as potential lovers—I was brought up to look at a woman's eyes, not her ring finger—but as I live here I prefer to avoid misunderstandings.)

There are a host of ancillary questions, all of which depend on correct interpretation of this mysterious concept. How do I know if a lunch, dinner, or drink with a woman constitutes a "date"? Many American women feel they should not sleep with you, or in extreme cases, even kiss you, until the second or third "date." Yet some women don't count a dinner date if she has invited the man out, or if neither person has used the actual phrase, "It's a date."

More quaintly, others require the man to pay for the woman if the occasion is to count as a "date." (Presumably such women see dating as a transaction that is partly financial: Each of the three dates is an installment paid in advance. The man's return takes the form of what lawyers call consortium: a combination of company, domestic work, and sexual favors.)

What I want to know is how many dates have to take place before you can say you are "dating" someone? Why should "dating" someone imply exclusivity? And can you sleep with a woman without "dating" her?

This last goes to the root of what is wrong with the idea of "dating." For the foreigner, the whole weird system with its vagueness and simultaneous rigidity speaks to a linguistic shortage. Americans simply don't have enough words to describe all the variations of sexual relationships. And they are uncomfortable in relationships that are not easily defined by phrases like "engaged to," "one-night stand," or "going out with." This is especially true of American women who are well known to enjoy long, late-night conversations during which they and their consorts endeavor to define and describe their "relationship."

The confused notion of the "date" stems in large part from its origins in a 1950s suburban mating ritual. The original date was essentially a way of formalizing fraternization in an era when arranged marriages were old-fashioned, chaperones were impractical, and automobiles let teenagers escape parental discipline.

In an era when people married young, you were only supposed to date someone if the relationship had a chance of "going somewhere." A date was presumed to be the first step on the road to marriage. Hence, parental disapproval if their child dated somebody from the wrong race or class.

We never developed the dating system in England because we couldn't afford cars in the 1950s, or suburbs for that matter. And English cars, for all their elegance, were either too small and uncomfortable for sex, or driven only by the chauffeur. So we developed a system so fluid and practical it is barely a system at all.

I really came to understand it as a student at Cambridge in the early 1980s. First, everyone drank a great deal (but not beer) and flirted all the time. I would have dinner (or lunch, tea, or drinks) with female friends. Sometimes we would sleep together afterward. With some girls this became a regular event. With other girls you would sleep with them only once, but continue to see them as friends.

With still others, the friendship would always be platonic. It was only when you started to have sex with someone regularly that the nomenclature of your relationship became important. And the questions were: Was this an affair, should you try to keep it secret, or would you start "going out"? It was simple, and great fun.

And it continued when we all moved to London and started jobs, except that about a quarter of the people I knew married within three years of graduation. Three years later another quarter were hitched. After a decade, three quarters if not more of my contemporaries have tied the knot, proving that the English model makes for both happy single people and coupling off at a reasonably young age. It is New York, and not London, that is prowled by thousands of anxious thirty-something men and women, all nervously watching their mirrors for signs of decreasing value.

The dating system may have worked well in 1950s suburbia, but it doesn't work in big cities today. Politically correct puritanism is one reason. Human mating rituals conducted without benefit of drinking, smoking, and dancing are either joylessly crude or excessively calculated. Without flirtation, they become very dreary indeed. And these days flirting is a dying art. Badly executed flirtation can cost you your career and may land you in court.

Also, in the golden age of the 1950s people who "dated" usually knew each other from their high school or by parental introduction. Questions of suitability were thus settled long before the actual "date," the main point of which seems to have been to test sexual chemistry. Today, "dating" frequently involves asking someone very boring, bureaucratic questions about their career, their family, and interests.

Blind dates are the worst of all, essentially a job interview with your sexual self-esteem at stake. And they can wreck your relationships with the people who set you up. Not only might your date reject you, but when you see her you instantly know what league your friends think you are in.

The answer, of course, is not to "date." Ask people out to dinner. Go out for coffee in the afternoon. Don't only ask people who are suitable, and don't think of it as "step one" in some kind of scientific experiment. Your oldest and best friend could be the one for you, or your boss. That is what romance is all about: spontaneity, adventure—all things incompatible with "dating."

Collecting Broken Glass

From Nino Ricci, In a Glass House

Ricci's trilogy of novels follows Vittorio Innocente, a boy transplanted from Italy to the New World in the 1950s, as he struggles to learn from a father rendered weak and embittered by financial burdens, cultural dislocation, and the betrayal of his wife—Vittorio's mother, who died giving birth to another man's child while en route to join her husband in Canada. Broken in spirit, Mario Innocente makes gestures toward raising his son, and yet the example he sets leaves the boy sullen and confused.

For several weeks after the planting, my father and I were alone on the farm. Gelsomina came by on Saturdays to do laundry and cook up soup and sauce for the following week; the baby remained at Tsi' Alfredo's. But though we were together more often now, my father seemed still merely a kind of element I had to move through, my body tensing against him like a single hard muscle when he was near, taking in only his animal scent and then the shape he cut like black space in a landscape.

For a week or so he had me clean out an old chicken coop in a barn. The coop was crammed with all manner of refuse, busted packing crates, hoops of thick wire, old farm implements with decayed leather harnesses; every morning a swallow would swoop out in a swift arc from a nest there when my father and I came in, slashing a quick hieroglyph in the air like a secret signal before disappearing in the branches of a mulberry tree across the lane. My father would give me a few terse instructions before he went off on his own chores; but then as soon as he'd gone everything he said became a haze. When he came back to check on me he'd see my mistakes at once.

"I told you to pile those crates against the other wall, where they'd be out of the way." And in fifteen minutes of swift, precise work he'd redo what I'd spent a whole morning on.

After the barn, he set me to work collecting broken glass in the alleys between the greenhouses. But now it was exactly the mistakes he warned me about in advance that I invariably fell into.

"Don't fill the wheelbarrow too full," he said, "or you'll spill it."

But I did pile it too full; and even feeling its weight begin to lean as I lifted its handles, already seeing in my mind how it would spill, watching the image unfurl there like a premonition, still I tried to push it forward. There was a tremendous crash when it tilted, the glass splintering through the wall of one of the greenhouses. In a moment my father was standing over me, his face flushed.

"*Per la madonna*—" It was the first time I had seen his anger so plain and uncurbed, so ice-hard. "Is it possible you can't do anything the way I tell you?"

I had steeled myself instinctively against a blow. But the blow didn't come, and afterwards, when my father bent quick and silent to pick up the glass I had spilled, he appeared chastened by his outburst as if he had been the one who had suffered some humiliation.

He left me less on my own from then on, often keeping me beside him to be his helper. He'd make comments sometimes while he worked, or curse some problem in a way that was oddly intimate and frank, as if he'd forgotten I was merely a child. But usually he was silent, the work taking him over, bringing out in him a hard-edged concentration that seemed to free me from him even though it was exactly then that I was most aware of him, the tawny muscles of his arms and neck, the patches of sweat on his clothes, his ghostly familiarity like a mirror I looked into.

At noon, he'd send me home ahead of him to put soup on the stove or set the water heating for pasta for our lunch. If we ran out of the food Gelsomina had left, he'd fry up onion and eggs, scraping the eggs onto our plates with a casual violence, a mash of grease and broken yolks and scorched whites, though I preferred them to the porcelain-smooth ones Gelsomina used to prepare. He listened to the radio while we ate, odd music at first and then a voice, the same one every day, my father turning the volume up when it came on.

"*Mbeh*," he'd say afterwards, "maybe we'll get a little more sun after all, if you can believe all the stupidities they say on that thing."

Once when we were all hoeing beans in the front field, someone came to visit us, a gray-haired man in a checked suit and dark glasses. He pulled up in the courtyard in a large blue car and came toward us smiling broadly, his hand outstretched.

"Mario," he said. "Mario, Mario, *como stai, paesano?*"

After his greeting, he and my father began to speak in what must have been English. They talked for a long time, and I had the sense from the way my father was laughing and smiling that speaking in English brought out some different person in him, one more relaxed and good-humored. But when the man had gone, my father grew canny.

"That was the guy I bought the farm from," he said. "Those Germans—*paesano* this, *paesano* that, everyone's a *paesano*. But the old bastard just wanted to make sure I don't forget to pay him."

And yet he was smiling, the old man's visit apparently having heartened him.

He took me into town with him that night to a sort of bar, a long dim room with a counter on one side and a row of rickety tables on the other. There were several men talking around one of the tables at the back, a few wearing the striped gray-and-white uniform that my father had worn when he'd worked at the factory. My father nodded in greeting toward them, but his good mood appeared to pass from him suddenly. He ordered an ice cream for me and a coffee for himself from the man behind the counter; but one of the men at the table had turned to him.

"*Dai*, Mario, let's get a game going. We need a fourth, these others here are too afraid to put a little money on the table."

My father stared into his coffee.

"Maybe they're the smart ones," he said. "Nobody gives you something for nothing."

"What are you saying, for the fifty cents we play for you couldn't even buy a whore in Detroit."

The other men laughed.

"*Sì*, fifty cents," my father said, still talking into his cup though his energy was clearly drawn toward the men now. "It took half a day to make that when I came here—"

"Oh, always the same story! *Dai*, sit down, you'll be a rich man soon, when the checks start coming in from the farm."

"The farm—at least what I made before, I could put in my pocket. Now I'm just working for the bank. And then that damned German, still worried about the four cents I owe him—"

"What does he have to do with it? Didn't he get his money from the Farm Credit?"

My father had turned to face them. With the mention of the German his good humor began to return.

"*Mbeh*, we kept a little back because of all the work that had to be done, he'd left the place to rot like that. So today he comes around, in his suit and new car, still thinking about those few pennies, though the contract says he doesn't see another cent until October—"

"*Che scostumat'*. What did you tell him?"

"Don't think he was stupid enough to say a word about the money. You know how they are, always smiling, *amico, paesano*. But the whole time he was looking around, checking to see how things were, asking about the crop, about the prices. So I smiled too. I told him if he wanted to see how the crop was, he could come back in July and I'd give him a bushel of beans."

The other men laughed.

"And he'll be back for those beans, too," one of them said.

My father stayed to play cards.

"You can be my banker," he said, pulling up a chair for me beside him.

"That means every time he wins," one of the others said, "you take five percent."

"And if he loses he gives you the farm."

They played until late, making laconic conversation at first but then becoming more and more involved in the game. At the end my father gave me some change from the money he'd won.

"What are you doing, Mario," one of the men said, "you want to spoil him? That's half a day's wages."

The Sinking of Mature Romance

Michael Medved,
The Ottawa Citizen *(1998)*

From the Duke and Duchess of Windsor to the movie Titanic, *Michael Medved laments, modern pop culture undermines the idea of love as a mature partnership by exalting florid romanticism, sexual flamboyance, and narcissism.*

In February, Sotheby's in New York staged a gala auction honoring one of the most celebrated couples of the 20th century—and inadvertently emphasized the emptiness and destructiveness of the most common contemporary concepts of romance.

This royal garage sale brought in some $23 million U.S. by selling off 40,000 possessions of the late Duke and Duchess of Windsor. The items purchased ranged from monogrammed china toothbrush cups and an elaborately painted porcelain commode to the Duchess's mink garters and a boxed slice of their 1937 wedding cake. The Windsors accumulated their tacky treasures during 35 years of marriage, most of which they spent as rulers of a "15-acre kingdom" outside of Paris following his abdication from the British throne for the sake of "the woman he loved."

This dramatic gesture, in which England's handsome young monarch (he spent only 11 months as Edward VIII) gave up his kingdom to marry a twice-divorced American commoner, captured the imagination of most of the world. A look back on Edward's decision some 60 years later, however, suggests the dangers of allowing passion and sentiment to rule our lives and the lives of our children.

Edward and his wife, the former Wallis Warfield Simpson, bore no offspring and remained painfully irrelevant—and vaguely sympathetic to Hitler—during his country's hour of maximum trial (and maximum heroism) in the Second World War. They hosted many glittering dinner parties, accumulated a great deal of fashionable jewelry, but ultimately struck most acquaintances and observers as hopelessly shallow and even pathetic.

Edward gave up a kingdom but what, precisely, had he gained? He began his affair with Mrs. Simpson while she was still living with her second husband, allowing his sexual obsession to overrule all sense of morality and duty.

Unfortunately, popular culture regularly exalts precisely this sort of decision—celebrating couples who defy convention and rationality in the name of some higher "love." This is by no means a new theme in Western civilization, but with its amplification by movies, TV and pop music it has become an especially destructive one for our children. Even cartoons for six-year-olds (*The Little Mermaid, Pocahontas*) glorify the idea of barely pubescent young people disregarding their parents' expectations and displaying deeper wisdom by following their hearts—and hormones

On a more substantive level, we all thrill to the emotions evoked by Romeo and Juliet (and by the deathless poetry Shakespeare provides for them), but as the popular recent movie version with Leonardo DiCaprio and Claire Danes forcefully reminds us, the relationship of the world's most famous romantics culminated in the double suicide of two teenagers. In the abstract, we may view their fate as noble and grand, but would any sane parents welcome the notion of their own children following the path of these two "star cross'd lovers"?

Nor should parents accept the handsome lead characters in the smash hit *Titanic* as a suitable standard for romance. This motion picture, with all its cinematic grandeur, can sweep away the resistance of even the most skeptical viewers and obscure the crucial context of its central relationship. After all, 17-year-old Rose (Kate Winslet) meets earnest but penniless Jack (Leonardo DiCaprio) on board the great ship and then less than five days later, despite the fact that she's engaged to another man, makes love to him in the back seat of a car being transported in the ship's hold. This fleeting but overwhelming experience transforms her entire life, and continues to haunt her more than 80 years later.

This florid romanticism hardly classifies as the "loveless sex" so regularly (and appropriately) condemned in recent entertainment, but in a sense it may be even more dangerous for our kids. Though conventional wisdom suggests that the irresponsible behavior of unattached males accounts for most of the destructive sexual activity among today's youth, the changed values of females have resulted in even deeper damage.

Many, if not most, boys have always sought to take advantage of available girls, pushing sexuality just as far as those girls would let them; social order has always depended on the young woman's ability (and determination) to draw a line and say no. Most of the females who now say yes, endangering their own futures and the institution of marriage itself, do not do so out of commitment to the "Playboy philosophy"; they do so for the sake of what they view as grand, timeless, life-changing passions. For these young women, notions of pre-marital surrender in the cause of lofty, irrational love will prove far more seductive than the allure of recreational sex.

As an alternative, responsible adults should stress a more wholesome sense of romanticism—emphasizing joyous fulfillment rather than tragic doom, offering a warming hearth rather than a consuming bonfire, bringing young people closer to their parents rather than dividing them, honoring life rather than death. Despite tortured romantic conventions that have been rattling around our culture since medieval times, common sense and lasting love are anything but incompatible; they are, in fact, indispensably connected.

Rather than accepting the ardent young lovers on board *Titanic* (or in hundreds of lesser films) as appropriate examples of romantic commitment, consider some of the older couples, with dozens of grandchildren and decades of unflagging friendship and devotion, who seem to turn up in nearly all American families. Mature love involves a productive life together, shared values, common commitment to faith and the future, rather than indulging in flamboyant but empty gestures like those perpetrated by the Duke and Duchess of Windsor. If we can teach our children that romance at its best involves embracing, rather than abdicating responsibility, then their love lives may leave behind more substantive contributions than mink garters and moldy wedding cake.

Enchanting and Repulsive:
What Is Gothic?

From Michelle Wauchope,
What is Gothic? An Exploration of Youth Culture

The shootings at Columbine High School drew attention to the "Goth" sub-culture, since the accused were dressed in that fashion. Is Goth some dark cel-ebration of Satanism and evil? Or is it an update of late-nineteenth-century Decadence with a few Vampiric touches added? Goth is a worldwide phe-nomenon, as this essay posted on the Net by a first-year Australian university student testifies. In its stylistic and erotic flamboyance, she observes, "Romanticism and beauty become juxtaposed with the shock value of punk."

The Gothic subculture has been in existence for around six-teen years, making it one of the most enduring of youth cultures. However, what Gothic really is about is rarely known outside "the scene."

This is due in part to the non-confrontational nature of the subculture, as well as mainstream media's omission to report on things and events pertaining to the Gothic subculture.

As with any youth culture, music and fashion are major con-tributors to the Gothic identity and is what attracts most people to the scene. Unlike many youth cultures, Gothic also has a strong lit-erature base.

Behind the music and fashion, is a specific fascination with the darker side of life. The people in the scene share a familiar outlook on life, as well as often having similar past histories.

While the subculture started in England, there are now people all over the world who consider themselves Gothics. In Australia there is a particularly active scene.

While the phenomena of youth cultures has often been explored, both in the media and in various cultural and psychologi-cal studies, little research has been conducted on the Gothic subcul-ture. As a result, very little is known about what constitutes Gothic.

The Gothic subculture is one of the most misunderstood of youth cultures, often referred to as a "cult" and blamed for youth suicides. While it does celebrate horror, the darker side of life and often Gothics have a blatant disregard for organized religion, this is a matter of personal choice and not a form of "cult" or peer pressure.

There are rules and modes of behavior within the scene, however what they are is hard to define. There is frequent discussion about "what constitutes Gothic" by the Gothics themselves, but no one has come up with any concrete answers.

The Gothic movement can be linked to a single London nightclub called the Batcave, which opened in 1981. It sprang up from what remained of the punk scene and as such, many bands now synonymous with Gothic were first known as Punk. The Batcave fostered these bands as well as their audience. This first wave of Goths took the elements of punk that they liked; the spirit of rebellion, the shocking edge of fashion and music, a high pleasure principle and a penchant for all things black.

These original "Gothics" were reputedly so named by *NME* and *Sounds*. These music magazines took the term from Siouxsie Sioux (of the Banshees) who used it to describe the new direction her punk band was taking. The pop journalists used it as a pigeonhole for many bands around at the time, actually covering three separate styles of music with the label, as they were only occupied with the look of the Gothics.

The fans of these bands used elements of punk as a statement, adopting bondage and fetish wear as well as aspects of German expressionism, but along the way adopted various regalia from the Victorian era, blending the term "Gothic" with Gothic Literature. Now the two are synonymous. Romanticism and beauty became juxtaposed with the shock value of punk.

The Batcave was the crucial meeting point, the place to dress up and be seen. It encouraged the narcissistic and elitist attitude carried by most Gothics over the rest of society, but it must also be seen that this attitude is a feature of most youth cultures.

In the second wave, the connection with Gothic literature became the driving force. The original idea of fun was replaced with intelligent introspection. The Gothic subculture became a refuge for the freaks of society, the people who valued escapism and angst more than reality and anger. These new pale-faced, black-swatched, hair-sprayed night dwellers used the look to scare and repel, to avoid acceptability. It was this new breed of Gothics that elicited the most derision and they were painted as morbid and maudlin. This image set up links between suicide and "other evils" with the subculture in the minds of "normal" people.

Recently there has been another wave of ideas, this time called "Dark Wave." It has taken the separate genres of Industrial and Techno music and fused it with the dark elements of Gothic.

"Dark Wave" has also been adopted by many as an alternative label to "Gothic," avoiding the negative connotations the word has come to represent.

Literature has also received new lifeblood with many techno-culture books being popular reading, as well as the propagation of "net.goths" (Goths on the Internet). Goth debates thrive on the Internet, as it is one of the few mediums [where] such debate can flourish. In the real world, debate on Gothic is taboo. The unwritten rule is if you don't know if something is Gothic or not, then you can't be Gothic. Also there is a reluctance for Gothics to proclaim themselves as such, or to talk about the subculture, creating a paradox.

While other subcultures that emerged at the same time as Gothic, such as New Romantic and New Wave, have come and gone, the movement continues to replenish itself with fresh blood of new bands and fans.

The Gothic subculture is small in comparison to other more mainstream youth cultures, such as rave and hip-hop. The resulting lack of media coverage, coupled with the unusual dress and behavioral standards of the Gothics, has created many misconceptions about the subculture.

"Supposedly" Gothic guys are all gay because they wear make-up and nail polish. While the scene encourages androgyny and makes no distinction between gay and straight, mainstream society is not as open-minded. Consequently, male Gothics are often the targets of homophobic attacks, both verbal and physical.

Gothics are apparently all Satanists. This misconception can be attributed to the wearing and idolizing of religious and pagan symbols and imagery, as well as the rejection of organized religion. What the "normal" people fail to understand is that Satanism is also an organized religion, and thus just as likely to be rejected by the Gothic community. More importance is placed on individual strength; structured religion is looked down upon as an emotional crutch for the weak. The rejection of organized religion is usually made through disillusionment with hypocritical religious people.

The Gothic love of introspective music, penchant for dark imagery and romanticizing of death, is often blamed for teenage suicide. This is a reactionary response and a fallacy. It ignores many other important factors involved in suicides, pushing the blame on a perceived "influence" rather than the problems within the victim's life. It also ignores the fact that many people gain stability and friends from the Gothic culture, and are out to have fun rather than withdrawing into themselves.

Gothics allegedly lead a promiscuous lifestyle. Many "normals" go to Gothic nightclubs believing that "Goths are easy." Monogamy is preferred by most Goths, although other relationship types are more accepted within the subculture than elsewhere. This presumption of sexual promiscuity is based more on the body worshiping style of dress many Goths adopt. Bondage and fetish wear, while often worn for their shock value and "kinky-ness," are certainly not seen as obscene or inappropriate clothing.

Vampirism is another trait attributed to Gothics. While some may involve themselves in drinking blood, either their own or a partner's, most Gothics are merely interested in the erotic romance embodied by the vampires in Gothic literature. Within the Gothic scene, people who claim to be Vampires are treated as fools and jokes.

There are many "looks" in the Gothic subculture, but black is by far the dominant color in the Gothic wardrobe. While it is a color symbolising death and mourning as well as "evil," it also has the practical side of being easy to coordinate. Other colors make an appearance more as an accessory. These are usually jewel colors or plain white.

Fabric plays an important role in clothes. Rich fabrics—silk, satin, velvet, embroidery borrowed from Victorian or Medieval imagery—as well as P.V.C. and leather from the Punks are just as important as the color or cut of the clothes.

Gothic makeup is often similar to that of the German expressionists, with heavy eyeliner and a white pancake base. The need to be pale leads many Gothics to shun sunlight, this in turn adds fuel to the perceptions of vampirism and of general mystique.

Accessories play an important role. Boots, collars, studs and chains tend to be favorites. Lots of silver jewelry is a must, bracelets, earrings, necklaces and rings, either of a religious or pagan nature.

Although the "look" plays an important role both as a form of identification and as a personal statement, many Goths also denounce them as superficial trappings and not a true indicator of a "real" Gothic. This concept is in direct opposition to the "old Goth" way of thinking.

Gothic literature is not tied down to a particular time period. While it proliferated throughout the Victorian era, the devices and imagery used in that time period are still being used in "Modern

Gothic." Many works considered as being Gothic literature also existed long before the Romantic age.

Authors such as Edgar Allan Poe, Bram Stoker, Mary Shelley, Kafka and H. P. Lovecraft are still widely read, as are poets and philosophers such as Baudelaire, Byron, Shelley and Nietzsche.

There is no concrete rule as to behavior or philosophy. The Gothic subculture is a dynamic structure, fusing the best bits from many past cultures with current ideas. It is for this reason that Gothic is just as relevant today as it was sixteen years ago.

A few general concepts can be stated with some reasonable authority. Open mindedness is prized above all else. Gothics consider themselves "above" normal society and pride themselves on tolerance, intelligence and understanding. Whether or not they maintain this standard is debatable. Often Gothics become disdainful and intolerant of outsiders and petty-minded as to the "standards of Gothic."

A celebration of the mind is also often encountered. Education is considered important, and even those who haven't undertaken tertiary studies are often verbose on the topic of literature. Perhaps because of this, there is less drug use than in other youth cultures. This is not to say it doesn't exist, just that the people who take them and the quantities involved tend to be less when compared with current youth cultures such as "Rave" or "Indy-kids."

Dad? I Wish I'd Known You When You Were Little

From Raymond Carver,
Bicycles, Muscles, Cigarettes *(1988)*

A quiet story of a father recalling his father for his son.

"I'm sorry," Hamilton said. "I'm sorry you had to see something like that," Hamilton said to his son.

They kept walking and when they reached their block, Hamilton took his arm away.

"What if he'd held up a knife, Dad? Or a club?"

"He wouldn't have done anything like that," Hamilton said.

"But what if he had?" his son said.

"It's hard to say what people will do when they're angry," Hamilton said.

They started up the walk to their door. His heart moved when Hamilton saw the lighted windows.

"Let me feel your muscle," his son said.

"Not now," Hamilton said. "You just go in now and have your dinner and hurry up to bed. Tell your mother I'm all right and I'm going to sit on the porch for a few minutes."

The boy rocked from one foot to the other and looked at his father, and then he dashed into the house and began calling, "Mom, Mom!"

He sat on the porch and leaned against the garage wall and stretched his legs. The sweat had dried on his forehead. He felt clammy under his clothes.

He had once seen his father—a pale, slow-talking man with slumped shoulders—in something like this. It was a bad one, and both men had been hurt. It had happened in a cafe. The other man was a farmhand. Hamilton had loved his father and could recall many things about him. But now he recalled his father's one fistfight as if it were all there was to the man.

He was still sitting on the porch when his wife came out.

"Dear God," she said and took his head in her hands. "Come in and shower and then have something to eat and tell me about it. Everything is still warm and Roger has gone to bed."

But he heard his son calling him.

"He's still awake," she said.

"I'll be down in a minute," Hamilton said. "Then maybe we should have a drink."

She shook her head. "I really don't believe this yet."

He went into the boy's room and sat down at the foot of the bed.

"It's pretty late and you're still up, so I'll say goodnight," Hamilton said.

"Goodnight," the boy said, hands behind his neck, elbows jutting.

He was in his pajamas and had a warm fresh smell about him that Hamilton breathed deeply. He patted his son through the covers.

"You take it easy from now on. Stay away from that part of the neighborhood, and don't let me ever hear of you damaging a bicycle or any other personal property. Is that clear?" Hamilton said.

The boy nodded. He took his hands from behind his neck and

began picking at something on the bedspread.

"Okay, then," Hamilton said, "I'll say goodnight."

He moved to kiss his son, but the boy began talking.

"Dad, was Grandfather strong like you? When he was your age, I mean, you know, and you—"

"And I was nine years old? Is that what you mean? Yes I guess he was," Hamilton said.

"Sometimes I can hardly remember him," the boy said. "I don't want to forget him or anything, you know? You know what I mean, Dad?"

When Hamilton did not answer at once the boy went on. "When you were young, was it like it is with you and me? Did you love him more than me? Or was it just the same?" the boy said abruptly. He moved his feet under the covers and looked away. When Hamilton still did not answer, the boy said, "Did he smoke? I think I remember a pipe or something."

"He started smoking a pipe before he died, that's true," Hamilton said. "He used to smoke cigarettes a long time ago and then he'd get depressed or something or other and quit, but later he'd change brands and start again. Let me show you something," Hamilton said. "Smell the back of my hand."

The boy took the hand in his, sniffed it, and said, "I guess I don't smell anything, Dad, what is it?"

Hamilton sniffed the hand and then the fingers. "Now I can't smell anything either," he said. "It was there before, but now it's gone." Maybe it was scared out of me he thought. "I wanted to show you something. All right, it's late now. You better go to sleep," Hamilton said.

The boy rolled onto his side and watched his father walk to the door and watched him put his hand to the switch. And then the boy said, "Dad? You'll think I'm pretty crazy, but I wish I'd known you when you were little. I mean, about as old as I am right now. I don't know how to say it, but I'm lonesome about it. It's like—it's like I miss you already if I think about it now. That's pretty crazy, isn't it? Anyway, please leave the door open." Hamilton left the door open, and then he thought better of it and closed it halfway.

Born to Lose in 1962

Social Distortion,
Somewhere Between Heaven and Hell *(1992)*

I was brought in this world 1962
I didn't have much choice you see
But by the time I was eight I could tell it was too late.
I was already barking up the wrong tree.
When I was in school you thought I was a fool, in trouble breaking
    all the rules.
I was absent from class, my daddy spanked my bare ass, but I sure
    tried hard to be cool.
Born to lose was what they said,
You know I was better off dead.
Born to lose, you're just bad news,
You don't get no second chance.
It was a hot summer night in mid July,
A hangover and a black eye.
Your momma said I was a loser, a dead end cruiser, and deep
    inside
I knew that she was right. . . .

Sex and That
Postmodernist Girl

From David Foster Wallace,
Brief Interviews with Hideous Men *(1998)*

If you're not confused about love in the nineties already, read this one.

K—: "What does today's woman want. That's the big one."

E—: "I agree. It's the big one all right. It's the what-do-you-call . . . "

K—: "Or put another way, what do today's women *think* they want versus what do they really deep down *want*."

E—: "Or what do they think they're supposed to want."

Q.

K—: "From a male."

E—: "From a guy."

K—: "Sexually."

E—: "In terms of the old mating dance."

K—: "Whether it sounds Neanderthal or not, I'm still going to argue it's the big one. Because now the whole question today's become such a mess."

E—: "You can say that again."

K—: "Because now the modern woman has an unprecedented amount of contradictory stuff laid on her about what it is she's supposed to want and how she's expected to conduct herself sexually."

E—: "The modern woman's a mess of contradictions that they lay on themselves that drives them nuts."

K—: "It's what makes it so difficult to know what they want. Difficult but not impossible."

E—: "Like take your classic Madonna-versus-whore contradiction. Good girl versus slut. The girl you respect and take home to meet Mom versus the girl you just fuck."

K—: "Yet let's not forget that overlaid atop this is the new feminist-slash-postfeminist expectation that women are sexual agents, too, just as men are. That it's okay to be sexual, that it's okay to whistle at a man's ass and be aggressive and go after what you want. That it's okay to fuck around. That for today's woman it's almost mandatory to fuck around."

E—: "With still, underneath, the old respectable-girl-versus-slut thing. It's okay to fuck around if you're a feminist but it's also not okay to fuck around because most guys aren't feminists and won't respect you and won't call you again if you fuck around."

K—: "Do but don't. A double bind."

E—: "A paradox. Damned either way. The media perpetuates it."

K—: "You can imagine the load of internal stress all this dumps on their psyches."

E—: "Come a long way baby, my ass."

K—: "That's why so many of them are nuts."

E—: "Out of their minds with internal stress."

K—: "It's not even really their fault."

E—: "Who wouldn't be nuts with that kind of mess of contradictions laid on them all the time in today's media culture?"

K—: "The point being that this is what makes it so difficult, when for example you're sexually interested in one, to figure out what she really wants from a male."

E—: "It's a total mess. You can go nuts trying to figure out what tack to take. She might go for it, she might not. Today's woman's a total crapshoot. It's like trying to figure out a Zen koan. Where what they want's concerned, you pretty much have to just shut your eyes and leap."

K—: "I disagree."

E—: "I meant metaphorically."

K—: "I disagree that it's impossible to deduce what it is they really want."

E—: "I don't think I said *impossible*."

K—: "Though I do agree that in today's postfeminist era it's unprecedentedly difficult and takes some serious deductive firepower and imagination."

E—: "I mean if it were really literally *impossible* then where would we be as a species?"

K—: "And I do agree that you can't necessarily go just by what they *say* they want."

E—: "Because are they only saying it because they think they're supposed to?"

K—: "My position is that actually most of the time you *can* figure what they want, I mean almost logically deduce it, if you're willing to make the effort to understand them and to understand the impossible situation they're in."

E—: "But you can't just go by what they say, is the big thing."

K—: "There I'd have to agree. What modern feminists-slash- post-feminists will *say* they want is mutuality and respect of their individual autonomy. If sex is going to happen, they'll say, it has to be by mutual consensus and desire between two autonomous equals who are each equally responsible for their own sexuality and its expression."

E—: "That's almost word for word what I've heard them say."

K—: "And it's total horseshit."

E—: "They all sure have the empowerment-lingo down pat, that's for sure."

K—: "You can easily see what horseshit it is if you start by recognizing the impossible double bind we've already discussed."

E—: "It's not all that hard to see."

Q.

K—: "That she's expected to be both sexually liberated and autonomous and assertive, and yet at the same time she's still conscious of the old respectable-girl-versus-slut dichotomy, and know that some girls still let themselves be used sexually out of a basic lack of self-respect, and she still recoils at the idea of ever being seen as this kind of pathetic roundheel sort of woman."

E—: "Plus remember the postfeminist girl now knows that the male sexual paradigm and the female's are fundamentally different—"

K—: "*Mars and Venus.*"

E—: "Right, exactly, and she knows that as a woman she's naturally programmed to be more high-minded and long-term about sex and to be thinking more in relationships terms than just fucking terms, so if she just immediately breaks down and fucks you she's on some level still getting taken advantage of, she thinks."

K—: "This, of course, is because today's postfeminist era is also today's postmodern era, in which supposedly everybody now knows everything about what's really going on underneath all the semiotic codes and cultural conventions, and everybody supposedly knows what paradigms everybody is operating out of, and so we're all as individuals held to be far more responsible for our sexuality, since everything we do is now unprecedentedly conscious and informed."

E—: "While at the same time she's still under this incredible biological pressure to find a mate and settle down and nest and breed; for instance, go read this thing *The Rules* and try to explain its popularity any other way."

K——: "The point being that women today are now expected to be responsible both to modernity and to history."

E——: "Not to mention sheer biology."

K——: "Biology's already included in the range of what I mean by *history*."

E——: "So you're using *history* more in a Foucaultian sense."

K——: "I'm talking about history being a set of conscious intentional human responses to a whole range of forces of which biology and evolution are a part."

E——: "The point is it's an intolerable burden on women."

K——: "The real point is that in fact they're just logically incompatible, these two responsibilities."

E——: "Even if modernity *itself* is a historical phenomenon, Foucault would say."

K——: "I'm just pointing out that nobody can honor two logically incompatible sets of perceived responsibilities. This has nothing to do with history, this is pure logic."

E——: "Personally, I blame the media."

K——: "So what's the solution."

E——: "Schizophrenic media discourse exemplified by, like, for example *Cosmo*—on one hand be liberated, on the other make sure you get a husband."

K——: "The solution is to realize that today's women are in an impossible situation in terms of what their perceived sexual responsibilities are."

E——: "I can bring home the bacon mm *mm* mm *mm* fry it up in a pan mm *mm* mm *mm*."

K——: "And that, as such, they're naturally going to want what any human being faced with two irresolvably conflicting sets of responsibilities is going to want. Meaning that what they're *really* going to want is some way *out* of these responsibilities."

E——: "An escape hatch."

K——: "Psychologically speaking."

E——: "A back door."

K——: "Hence the timeless importance of: *passion*."

E——: "They want to be both responsible and passionate."

K——: "No, what they want is to experience a passion so huge, overwhelming, powerful, and irresistible that it obliterates any guilt or tension or culpability they might feel about betraying their perceived responsibilities."

E—: "In other words what they want from a guy is *passion*."

K—: "They want to be swept off their feet. Blown away. Carried off on the wings of. The logical conflict between their responsibilities can't be resolved, but their postmodern *awareness* of this conflict can be."

E—: "Escaped. Denied."

K—: "Meaning that, deep down, they want a man who's going to be so overwhelmingly passionate and powerful that they'll feel that they have no choice, that this thing is bigger than both of them, that they can forget there's even such a *thing* as postfeminist responsibilities."

E—: "Deep down, they want to be irresponsible."

K—: "I suppose in a way. I agree, though I don't think they can really be faulted for it, because I don't think it's conscious."

E—: "It dwells as a Lacanian cry in the infantile unconscious, the lingo would say."

K—: "I mean it's understandable, isn't it? The more these logically incompatible responsibilities are forced on today's females, the stronger their unconscious desire for an overwhelmingly powerful, passionate male who can render the whole double bind irrelevant by so totally overwhelming them with passion that they can allow themselves to believe they couldn't help it, that the sex wasn't a matter of conscious choice, that they can be held responsible for, that ultimately if *anyone* was responsible it was the *male.*"

E—: "Which explains why the bigger the so-called feminist, the more she'll hang on you and follow you around after you sleep with her."

K—: "I'm not sure I'd go along with that."

E—: "But it follows that the bigger the feminist, the more grateful and dependent she's going to be after you've ridden in on your white charger and relieved her of responsibility."

K—: "What I disagree with is E—'s scornful use of *so-called.* I just don't think that today's feminists are being consciously insincere in all their talk about autonomy. Just as I don't think they're strict-ly to blame for the terrible bind they've found themselves in. Though deep down I do have to agree that women are historically ill-equipped for taking genuine responsibility for themselves."

Q.

E—: "I don't suppose either of you saw where the Little Wranglers' room was in this place."

K—: "I don't mean that in any kind of just-another-Neanderthal-male-grad-student-putting-down-women-because-he's-too-insecure-

to-countenance-their-sexual-subjectivity way. And I'd go to the wall
to defend them against scorn or culpability for a situation that is
clearly not their fault."

E—: "Because it's getting to be time to answer nature's page, if you
know what I mean."

K—: "I mean, even looking at the evolutionary aspect, you have to
agree that a certain lack of autonomy-slash-responsibility was an
obvious genetic advantage as far as primitive human females went,
since a weak sense of autonomy would drive a primitive female
toward a primitive male to provide food and protection."

E—: "While your more autonomous, butch-type female would be
out hunting on her own, actually competing with the males for
food."

K—: "But the point is that it was the less self-sufficient less
autonomous females who found mates and bred."

E—: "And raised offspring."

K—: "And thus perpetuated the species."

E—: "Natural selection favored the ones who found mates instead
of going out hunting. I mean, how many cave paintings of female
hunters do you ever see?"

K—: "Historically, we should probably note that once the quote-
unquote *weak* female has mated and bred, she shows an often
spectacular sense of responsibility where her offspring are concerned. It's not that females have no capacity for responsibility.
That's not what I'm talking about."

E—: "They do make great moms."

K—: "What we're talking about here is single adult preprimipara
females, their genetic-slash-historical capacity for autonomy, for as
it were *self*-responsibility, in their dealings with males."

E—: "Evolution has bred it out of them. Look at the magazines.
Look at romance novels."

K—: "What today's woman wants, in short, is a male with both the
passionate sensitivity and the logical firepower to discern that all
her pronouncements about autonomy are actually desperate cries
in the wilderness of the double bind."

E—: "They all want it. They just can't *say* it."

K—: "Putting you, today's interested male, in the paradoxical role
of almost their therapist or priest."

E—: "They want absolution."

K—: "When they say, 'I am my own person,' 'I do not need a man,'
'I am responsible for my own sexuality,' they are actually telling
you precisely what they want you to make them forget."

E—: "They want to be rescued."

K—: "They want you on one level wholeheartedly to agree and respect what they're saying and on another, deeper level to recognize that it's all complete horseshit and to gallop in on your white charger and overwhelm them with passion, just as males have been doing since time immemorial."

E—: "That's why you can't take what they say at face value or it'll drive you nuts."

K—: "Basically it's all still an elaborate semiotic code, with the new postmodern semions of autonomy and responsibility replacing the old premodern semions of chivalry and courtship."

E—: "I really do have to see a man about a prancing pony."

K—: "The only way not to get lost in the code is to approach the whole issue logically. What is she really saying."

E—: "No doesn't mean yes, but it doesn't mean no, either."

K—: "I mean, the capacity for logic is what distinguished us from animals to begin with."

E—: "Which, no offense, but logic's not exactly a woman's strong suit."

K—: "Although if the whole sexual *situation* is illogical, it hardly makes sense to blame today's woman for being weak on logic or for giving off a constant barrage of paradoxical signals."

E—: "In other words, they're not responsible for not being responsible, K—'s saying."

K—: "I'm saying it's tricky and difficult but that if you use your head it's not impossible."

E—: "Because think about it: if it was really *impossible,* where would the species be?"

K—: "Life always finds a way."

Each Other

Patrick Buckley

A college application, later published in the New York Post, *expresses a teenager's vision of the importance of male role models—within the family or without.*

April 25, 1992, was a day that forever changed my life. A month earlier the friendly UPS man had delivered a box that contained some plans and many pieces of wood. The plans were for a complicated radio-controlled sailboat that I had ordered as a birthday present from a model company. I had been building model cars since I was nine but when I opened this box I was blown away. It was just wood. There were no plastic parts nicely designed to fit together or any photo instructions. The only direction given was one large blueprint.

For one or two weeks I struggled, trying to figure out where to begin. There was no one in my house who could help. My mother was certifiably *mechanically impaired* and I rarely saw my father, who lived in Florida. So on that hot April day, I decided to do something that most cynical New Yorkers would regard as a waste of time. I decided to go to the model-boat basin in Central Park in search of someone who would help to build my boat. As I trekked across the park with my mom, she told me not to be disappointed if we couldn't find anyone who could help.

"People in New York are very busy," she warned, trying to soften the blow of any potential rejection. "But maybe someone can refer us to a class or a book that will help." My mother was always very protective of me and I knew, even at that early age, how it pained her that I didn't have a father in my life. She was pessimistic, but my resolve increased as we neared the boat pond. I had been there many times just to look at the boats and to climb on the nearby bronze *Alice in Wonderland* sculpture.

As we neared the basin, my enthusiasm grew as the masts of model sailboats bobbing on the water appeared through the trees. The boats were on average four or five feet long and had six- to eight-foot-tall masts. They were very large models that inspired awe in children, including me. In front of the boathouse were a number of men walking around with radio controls. As I was a shy 11-year-old, my mom started doing most of the talking. Then I noticed an older gentleman with a small number of people around him. He didn't have a radio control, but he was answering questions and handing out sheets of information about model suppliers.

My mom and I started asking him questions. His name was Hal and he had been building models since he was 9 years old. He was now 72. A well-mannered gentleman, he'd grown up in Brooklyn, served in the Navy during WWII, and had worked as a top engineer for the Bell Laboratories. I told him about the model sailboat kit I'd received for my birthday and that I didn't know where to begin. I'm not sure what I expected him to do. Maybe, I innocently thought, he has a sheet that will explain the art of wooden model building. What happened was something I could never imagine.

"Well, if you like, I could help get you organized and maybe give you a hand with the first step," Hal said, to my surprise. We made an appointment to meet after school the next day and that "first step" turned into over three hundred hours. Three hundred hours of after-school work that included first finishing my homework and then intense, complicated, fascinating, and detailed instruction on the fine art of boat building. For hours each day, designs were drawn with precision, plans were carefully studied, and materials and tools were meticulously handled. We logged our hours, created a budget that we honored, turned our beautiful living room into a wood shop replete with sawdust, paint fumes, tools, and stains, and patiently and painstakingly crafted our boat.

Every day, rain, shine, or snow, Hal arrived on time and ready for work. For years my father, and then my stepfather, had broken many promises to me. My dad would say he'd come, and time and time again he wouldn't show up. I remember my stepfather turning to me and saying "I don't have time for this sh—!" when I came to him as a 5-year-old with my hand-drawn invitation to an important school event. Missed school plays, missed graduations, missed birthdays, missed athletic events . . . camping trips that never happened: that was what I was used to. Hal never broke a single promise to me. Not once. Even when he was sick (he'd had several heart attacks and suffered from heart disease), he would show up on time, ready to go to work.

Hal and I worked diligently for a year on that boat. At times, it was a real struggle for me to stay on course because, as an 11-year-old, my attention often wandered and the work was not always exciting. But Hal's dedication profoundly influenced me. By his own example, he taught me important lessons about how to be organized, how to set priorities, and how to be responsible. He also, through working with me on the design of the electronics for the boat, played a pivotal role in developing my passion for science.

In May 1993, we launched the *Marilu,* named after my godmother. I'm proud to say that she is the most photographed boat in the park. She has a 6-foot mast, a 4-foot cherry-red hull, and a varnished mahogany deck that you can see your reflection in. The following September, we started work on a second boat. The *Sequin,* a model tugboat from Maine, took over 500 hours to build and was complete with radio-controlled steam, a detailed interior of the captain's cabin, and double-planked hull—all built from scratch.

When I was 11, Hal explained to me that he had always wanted to give back for all the opportunities he's been given, but he'd never found a way to do it. At the time I did not fully understand what he meant. Now, as a 17-year-old, when I reflect on the experience of building boats with him, I understand that through being his student and friend, he had not only helped me but I helped him, by filling that missing part of his life.

My friendship with Hal has taught me so many great lessons about patience, loyalty, endurance, education, and commitment. It has also affirmed my optimism about life and helped me to understand that despite the heartache and losses we may have, we also have, if we look and if we believe, the most important and powerful gift of all: *each other.*

"I Don't Want to Sacrifice Myself or My Family."

Interview with Kurt Cobain by Robert Hilburn,
Los Angeles Times *(1992)*

Kurt Cobain and Courtney Love were one of those iconic couples of the adversarial culture, a grunge Antony and Cleopatra. Cobain's suicide note was an extraordinary farewell from an unhappy man full of love for his family and "the guilt and empathy I have for everyone." This interview with Cobain a few weeks after the birth of his daughter reveals the complicated man behind the icon.

"I don't want my daughter to grow up and someday be hassled by kids at school. . . . I don't want people telling her that her parents were junkies."

Kurt Cobain, the 25-year-old leader of the acclaimed and hugely successful rock group Nirvana, is sitting in the living room of his Hollywood Hills apartment, holding Frances, his and Courtney Love's 4-week-old baby.

It's Cobain's first formal interview in almost a year, and it takes time to open up.

A shy, sensitive man, he speaks easily about his daughter, but there's one thing he's uncomfortable talking about even though he knows he has to.

Nirvana is the hottest new band to come along in years, and several of the articles on the group have speculated about Cobain's alleged drug use.

He now admits that he's used drugs, including heroin, but never as much as has been rumored or reported in the rock press. He also says in a quiet, but forceful, way that he is now drug-free.

"There's nothing better than having a baby," says Cobain disarmingly.

"I've always loved children. I used to work summers at the YMCA and be in charge of like 30 preschool kids.

"I knew that when I had a child, I'd be overwhelmed and it's true. I can't tell you how much my attitude has changed since we've got Frances. Holding my baby is the best drug in the world."

Yet Cobain, whose music speaks eloquently about the anger and alienation of youth, worries that the persistent rumors are threatening to turn him into a stereotype of a wasted rock 'n' roller. He also doesn't want to be a bad role model for the group's teen-age fans.

He knows some people won't believe him when he says drugs are no longer part of his life, but he still feels compelled to speak out.

"I would say I tried to set the record straight," he says, when asked how he'd respond to someone who questions his sincerity. "That's all I can do. We have a lot of young fans and I don't want to have anything to do with inciting drug use. People who promote drug use are [expletive]. I chose to do drugs. I don't feel sorry for myself at all, but have nothing good to say about them. They are a total waste of time."

While it was Cobain's songwriting skills that enabled the band to achieve mainstream success, it was his link to the underground/punk world that made him uneasy in the mainstream spotlight. Not only did the mainstream represent compromise and superficiality to him, but he also felt overwhelmed by the pressures that were thrust upon him.

"I guess I must have quit the band about 10 different times in the last year," he says, handing the baby to his wife, who has joined him in the living room.

"I'd tell my manager or the band, but most of the time I would just stand up and say to Courtney, 'OK, this is it.' But it would be over in a day or two. . . . The music is usually what brings me back."

"The biggest thing that affected me was all the insane rumors, the heroin rumors . . . all this speculation going on. I felt totally violated. I never realized that my private life would be such an issue."

Danny Goldberg, an Atlantic Records executive who remains one of the managers of the band, confirmed in a separate interview that he's seen a dramatic change in Cobain since last spring.

"Kurt is someone who had a hard time dealing with the unexpected intensity of the success," Goldberg said. "He came from a very difficult background, literally didn't have his own apartment when I first started managing him. Then, in a matter of a few months, he became an international celebrity. He got confused for a while, but seems to have bounced back. He has a healthy baby and is functioning the best I've ever seen him."

Goldberg says he thinks becoming a father has helped Cobain get a perspective on his career and life.

"I believe the day (last spring) I saw a change was when he had these ultrasound (pictures) of the baby. They are like little black-and-white Polaroid photos and you see the baby's hands and things in the womb. He put it up on his wall at home.

"I think that took him out of thinking about himself and made him start thinking about the next phase of his life, where no matter what happens, this person was going to be in his life. He came out of the 'Oh, man, I was a punk rocker and now I'm a rock star and I never wanted to be a rock star' attitude. He was so thrilled about having a baby."

Back in his apartment, Cobain takes his daughter from his wife and reflects on the future. He is looking forward to what he thought only a few months ago might be impossible: recording another album.

"We've been wanting to record a really raw album for almost a year and it looks like we are finally ready to do it," he says. "I have been prescribed some stomach medicine that has helped ease the pain and I've been going to a pain management clinic. I also meditate. We'd like to put the album out before we go on tour again early next year."

He pauses after the mention of touring. The band followed the MTV Awards with concerts in Seattle and Portland, but they were the group's only U.S. dates this year.

"We might not go on any more long tours," he says, hesitantly. "The only way we could tour is if I could find some way to keep my stomach from acting up. We could record and play shows once in a while, but to put myself in the physical strain of seven months of touring is too much for me. I would rather be healthy and alive. I don't want to sacrifice myself or my family."

9

CONCLUSION: A RETURN TO MANLINESS?

Is it too soon to speak of a return to manliness at the end of the twentieth century? In the last section of this anthology, readers can sample what might be taken as a series of distress calls from the Zeitgeist. It would take another book as long as this one to chronicle exactly how—let alone why—a nobly inspiring tradition of manliness that stretches more or less continuously from classical Athens to the lifetimes of our parents and grandparents should, in the last thirty years, have come close to perishing. Doubtless it has something to do with what I call the Myth of the '60s. People of my generation who came of age during that decade entertained the fantastic notion that human beings could invent themselves literally out of nothing, free of any inherited religious or historical traditions, motivated by a desire for the pure, uninhibited freedom to do exactly as one pleased. Like all utopian projects, it was a fantasy that few, if any, of us actually achieved (or, in our heart of hearts, even seriously wanted). But we did manage to establish it as a cultural orthodoxy, passing on to the next generation much of our disastrous presumption in believing that nothing just, good, or true had happened in human history before our time. Most of those of my generation who pioneered this ill-fated revolution had themselves received a traditional liberal education in the humanities and sciences. They battened off the very tradition they worked assiduously to undermine. It was their children who became the true children of the revolution, victims of the myth that humans can "construct" their "identities" out of nothing. The disappearance of the positive tradition of manliness through relentless simplification and caricature, to the point where it bears no resemblance to its actual teachings, is one by-product of that vast shipwreck of culture.

And yet it would be a great mistake to see in these distress calls from the Zeitgeist grounds for only despair or pessimism. In fact, as a baby boomer, I take great encouragement in many ways from the sensibilities and tastes of young people in their twenties and thirties today. Students today are often criticized by their elders for their lack of political commitment, but I find them mercifully free of the ideological fixations of my own generation. Depending on the specific issue, most of them are capable of holding views from every shade in the political spectrum, defying the old left-wing/right-wing labels. Even aesthetically, the minimalist ethos of the '90s has been vastly more appealing than the bloated hippie establishmentarianism of the seventies, with its aging, paunchy Woodstock legends and drug-dealers-turned-moguls. That pale, hollow-cheeked, emaciated kid who frightens you with his shaved head and Doc Martens might well own his own business—and be a lover of the Great Books. You needn't assume the gay men you know are necessarily left wing—they could be cultural conservatives, while liberal on other issues.

As far as the problem of manliness is concerned, the excerpts in the last section are, on balance, at least as encouraging as they are discouraging. It's easy to be dismayed by the foul language, the hardened attitude to casual loveless sex, the worship of mindless violence, the cheap attitudinizing and wish to scandalize the grown-ups. Yes, it's all there. But, as the readings in the earlier sections demonstrate, to some extent young men have always been this way at their worst—cocky, libidinous, disdainful of their elders based on nothing, prone to violence. And, let's not forget, sometimes they're right to be angry. Sometimes their parents *are* utterly contemptible, their teachers boring, their jobs mindless and exploitive.

The difference between today's young man and his predecessors is the lack of a framing tradition for guidance, an orderly, challenging and intelligent process by which a young man can grow out of that immaturity by channeling those rambunctious energies into learning and duty. But, given the languishing of that framing tradition in recent decades, what is perhaps more remarkable than the nihilism so easily observable in youth culture is how many sound and justified frustrations, and dignified if unclarified longings, still shine through to us from these contemporary fragments. Not only is the passion still instinctual, but so is the search for an intelligible and satisfying outlet. Crude and raw though they may sometimes be, the lyrics, poems, stories, music, and styles of young people in the '90s still evoke a longing for heroism, adventure, self-overcoming, spiritual testing, romantic love, family life, and service to a noble calling. In the spirit of that cautious optimism about the return of manliness, I offer some concluding observations.

I began this book by remarking that the last three decades had witnessed one of the most remarkable efforts at social engineering in human history—a state-sponsored campaign, organized throughout the education system and in all major public institutions, to eradicate the psychological and emotional differences between men and women. Two generations have been brought up as the products of this vast experiment. From the moment they enter kindergarten to their final courses in university, they are required to subscribe to a new doctrine of human relations without precedent in known experience: that there are no inherent differences in character between men and women.

This doctrine now influences everything in contemporary society from how children and young adults are schooled, to pension plans, gender quotas for hiring, the enforcement of laws relating to domestic violence, and admission to military academies. And yet, as everyone with eyes to see and ears to listen realizes, this pervasive public orthodoxy bears little resemblance to the actual world of boys and girls and men and women in which we all live, and has had virtually no long-acting effect on the behavior of either sex. Everywhere you look, you will see the pronounced differences between male and female psychology, motivation, interests, and sentiments. These differences should not, and for the most part now do not, have any bearing on the equal opportunity of women to compete on an equal basis as individuals for the earned rewards of hard work and talent. But they are, and for the most part should be respected as important dimensions of the quality of our personal lives, and how our personal lives lead us in distinct ways to responsible interactions with our friends, loved ones, and fellow citizens. The psychological and emotional differences between men and women are not barriers to their friendship and mutual respect. On the contrary, they are the only sure basis for them, because they are rooted in human nature, providing men and women with different paths to the same goals. Instead of men and women fencing themselves off from those emotional differences, we should each be learning from the other about the plenitude and richness of our shared human destiny. As Socrates tells Callicles in Plato's dialogue the *Gorgias*, until you can be sure that a single other human being has benefited from intimacy with you, you are not fit to go into a wider forum and presume to tell others their duties or how they should live.

One of the most encouraging signs about contemporary youth culture is that it is precisely here, on the margins of respectable society where the energies of young people in their teens and twenties can find release, that a sensitivity to the emotional and aesthetic differences between men and women remains and may even be increasing, and in a way that is completely compatible with the equality of women and men. One of my favorite films is Fellini's *Satyricon*, because of the way it takes you beneath the marble facade of the Roman Empire's splendid civic hypocrisy—a military autocracy tricked out as the Stoic defender of republican dignity—into the underworld of Epicurean license, a kaleidoscope of polymorphous sexuality in which senators frolic with slaves. There is a broad, if hardly precise, analogy with our world in the closing years of the twentieth century. Beneath our arid public orthodoxy about men and women—the world of the right-thinking upper middle classes with their Birkenstocks and pasta machines, where the men are sensitive and the women empowered, and both work at interchangeable jobs as lawyers, academics, and civil servants—there lies the fecund subterranean realm of youth culture, which utterly repudiates this upper realm even as it confusedly tries to profess its values. Every decade or so, one of these beautiful young gods gives up his life, like Osiris or Dionysus, so that his dismemberment might reinvigorate the festivals of the bacchantes. In the '90s, the beautiful young death couple Kurt Cobain and Courtney Love reign, as different from each other as could be: he the fallen warrior, she the punk queen of hearts tending the ashes of her fallen hero like a postmodernist Isis. Both are a touch androgynous, not because they lack male or female sexuality but because, on the contrary, they have it in abundance. Like aristocratic nonconformists of the past such as Alcibiades, they cultivate androgyny as a sign of their excess of feeling and will, and their unity of style. A real man and a real woman, equal in their differences, both exceedingly strong antinomian personalities who exude love, ambition, and longing.

The prevailing public orthodoxy forbids us to entertain the thought that men and women, while equal in their intellectual and moral capacities for a successful and fulfilling life, might be different in their temperaments, emotional rhythms and sensitivity to others, and that each sex might be, in some cases, better suited for certain kinds of activity than the other. But, given the tension between the daylight realm of orthodoxy and the subterranean realm of youth culture, it is plain that many people, especially young men and women, find the idea of a genderless society unbelievable, restrictive, and boring. Moreover, the sheer unreality of this model, its naive and arrogant expectation, perennially doomed to failure by human nature, that some kind of gender-neutral new human personality will emerge from decades of relentless social engineering and propaganda, is arguably increasing tension and hostility between men and women. Precisely because young people, in particular, are too passionate to make themselves over into junior yuppies dedicated to careers and to orderly, respectable relationships bereft of stress and adventure (which is what the orthodoxy requires of them), they try superficially to accommodate themselves to the upper realm of Birkenstocks and Laura Ashley, while banishing their less manageable impulses to the Dionysian underworld of dance clubs, raves, booze cans, body piercing, recreational drugs, and our whole plethora of aesthetic and erotic subcultures.

I know that some of my readers must be wondering by this point how a writer who worked for the first Reagan administration transition team could have taken leave of his senses so fully as to speak in anything but horrified tones of the after-hours pursuits of young people today. But I was also a student and friend for many years of Allan Bloom, and while I cannot say what he would think of my specific observations, I can say that I write from a position very much in sympathy with his own understanding of, and insight into, the longings of the young. I hasten to add that my sympathies toward this Dionysian realm are strictly qualified, and I will get to that qualification in a moment. But I am sympathetic, because this fecund underworld is the only place left where young people can express their intimations of erotic release. Erotic obsession can lead down a dark alleyway toward every imaginable depth of degradation. But it can also stir in us a longing for transcendence, through our absorption in someone or something higher and better than ourselves. No matter how jaded a young man is, no matter how much premature and bad experience he has had with drugs and exploitive sex, the simple but profound moment of dawning need will prompt in him the words men's hearts have always spoken: I love you, I admire you, I need you. When we love others for their bodily beauty, it is possible to stay there and sample only the limited and repetitive pleasures of physical lust. But most people, even in their enthrallment with the beloved's bodily beauty, glimpse through that shell a beauty of soul and spirit that draws them upward, because they need those virtues to achieve some sort of repose in their own hearts and minds. The sheen of the hair, the flush in the face, the curve of the lips—none of these is merely physical. They are embodiments of the soul's capacity for nobility,

shining through the fleshly carapace like fire shining through
ivory.

And yet, and yet—here is where the qualification must come.
Taken on its own terms, the Dionysian world of youth culture is ultimately just as much a distortion of human psychology, character,
and satisfied longing as the daylight realm of nine-to-five productivity and middle-class feminist orthodoxy that it repudiates. Why?
Because to experience the passions there, one must by and large
sacrifice any sense of reason or balance. The heart may still prompt
us to find those natural words of love. But it is hard for a young
man to hear that inner voice in the din of the surrounding subcultures, all of which urge him to gratify his spontaneous impulses
without regard for the accompanying excesses of vulgarity, coarseness, and self-absorption. Indeed, there is an insidious connection
between the daylight and nighttime realms, because many of the
nine-to-fivers are engaged in converting the nighttime images of
the Dionysian realm into commodities for our daytime amusement. What starts as criminal lust seeps up into the pederastic flir-
tations of underwear ads or movies about snuff films to titillate suburban moviegoers at Cinema 1–2–3–4–5–6–7–8 off the interstate.

Socrates was initiated into the mysteries of the god Eros by a
wise and majestic woman, the mysterious prophetess Diotima. As
she tells him, there is a logic peculiar to love. Diotima's Ladder
ranks the objects of erotic longing in a hierarchy, ascending from
bodily love upward through family life, the civic virtues, and, on the
highest rung, philosophical contemplation. Properly explored and
articulated, our erotic attachment to another leads us in and of
itself to cultivate the virtues of character—moderation, honesty,
gratitude, compassion, and honor—that make us worthy of love in
the eyes of the beloved. We try to be virtuous because we want to be
worthy of being loved. But, in today's world, the orderly side of the
human soul has been sucked into the desert of contemporary legal
proceduralism and the redesigning of the human personality to rid
it of precisely these same erotic longings and their potential for
bringing our virtues of character to fruition. As a consequence of
this artificial and agonizing split between an arid public rationality
and uncontrolled private impulse, the passion experienced in the
subcultures of music and entertainment rarely advance beyond the
first rung of Diotima's Ladder—sheer carnal desire. Raves, dance
clubs, casual drugs, piercing, being in a band, cheating, swapping,
experimenting with bondage and sadomasochism—here, one can
experience that side of Eros that sweeps us away in the sheer pas-

sion and excitement of love, the release from the boundaries of the body through mortification, the thrill of losing oneself in a crowd all excited by the same primal rhythms. But it can't get you any further. You never advance further up the rungs of Diotima's Ladder toward transcendence. Eros remains on the level of ecstasy (the name of this popular party drug is very revealing). But young people are hard pressed to find the quiet place where their passion for another acts as a mirror in which to see themselves through the eyes of the one they love, and so find an erotic motive to perfect their virtues. If the wisdom of the West about manliness contained in this anthology could be summed up in two words, they would be: Love perfects. It is this very idea that is at the heart of the traditions that have shaped our civilization—and that has well-nigh been lost in the changes our society has seen in the last half century. If contemporary man is to regain his sense of purpose, of nobility, of his place in the world, he cannot do better than to look to the past, and to take to heart its lessons about virtue, manliness, and—above all—love.